ON THE DOGMA OF THE CHURCH

An Historical Overview of the Sources of Ecclesiology

СВ· ИЛАРИѠНЪ

БЕЗ ЦЕРК ВИ НѢСТЬ СПА СЕ́ НЇА

New Hieromartyr Saint Hilarion Troitsky (1886-1929)
Scroll reads: "Without the Church there is no salvation."

ON THE DOGMA
OF THE CHURCH

An Historical Overview of
the Sources of Ecclesiology

St. Hilarion (Troitsky) the Hieromartyr

Translated by Fr. Nathan Williams

Uncut Mountain Press

ON THE DOGMA OF THE CHURCH
An Historical Overview of the Sources of Ecclesiology
© 2022
Uncut Mountain Press

uncutmountainpress.com

Cover Artwork by George Weis.

Scriptural quotations are primarily taken from the King James Version. The translator has emended some quotations to better reflect the original Greek text. Citations from the Psalms are primarily taken from *The Psalter According to the Seventy*, translated from the Septuagint Version of the Old Testament by the Holy Transfiguration Monastery, Brookline, MA.

Library of Congress Cataloging-in-Publication Data

On the Dogma of the Church: An Historical Overview of the Sources of Ecclesiology—1st ed.
St. Hilarion Troitsky, Hieromartyr, 1886–1929.
Translated by Fr. Nathan Williams.

ISBN: 978-1-63941-006-4

I. Orthodox Christian Ecclesiology
II. Orthodox Christian History

To my dear Nikolai Petrovich Sapozhnik on his nameday, with my sincere wishes that he will serve the Church under another name, from the author. 1912, XII, 6.

CONTENTS

FOREWORD

Printed from the publication *Essays on the History of the Dogma Concerning the Church* ["Очерки из истории догмата о Церкви"] (Sergiev Posad: 1912), authored by Vladimir Troitsky, acting senior lecturer at the Moscow Theological Academy. . . . The text is printed with slight stylistic corrections; words added for clarity are in square brackets. Citations from Holy Scripture are placed in double quotes. Words stressed by the author are in boldface type.

English edition: Translated from the book *Hieromartyr Hilarion (Troitsky): Works in Three Volumes* ["Священномученик Иларион (Троицкий). Творения в трех томах"] (Moscow: Sretensky Monastery, 2004). Words added by the translator to better reflect the Russian source, including when quoting English translations of works cited, are in square brackets. Except where otherwise noted, scriptural quotes are taken from the King James Version of the Bible. Excerpts from the book of Psalms are taken from *The Psalter According to the Seventy* (© 1974, Holy Transfiguration Monastery, Brookline, MA; all rights reserved).

ABOUT THE AUTHOR

St. Hilarion (Troitsky) the Hieromartyr

Upon graduating from the theological academy in 1910 with a Ph.D. in theology, Vladimir Troitsky stayed on as a professorial fellow. A year later he was appointed to the post of senior lecturer of the department of the Holy Scripture of the New Testament. It may be presumed that it was about this time when work began on his master's dissertation, "Essays on the History of the Dogma Concerning the Church"—a topic to which the author would repeatedly return and which became one of the most important in the theological and literary legacy of the hieromartyr.

Individual chapters of the future dissertation were published in *Bogoslovsky Vestnik* in May–October of 1912 as separate articles: "The Concept of the Church in Anti-Jewish Polemics with Donatism," "The Question of the Church in Dogmatic Polemics with Donatism: Optatus of Milevis," and "The Question of the Church in the Polemics of the Blessed Augustine against the Donatists" (unfinished). The chief theses of the future dissertation were examined in the work "The New Testament Doctrine Concerning the Church," published in *Golos Tserkvi* in the March, May, and June editions for 1912. Written when the author was still a very young man (26 years of age), this work astounds by its author's scholarly and theological maturity and profound knowledge of the source material, especially the works of the holy fathers and literature of the early Church.

Work on the master's dissertation lasted two years. In the spring of 1912 it was completed and presented for the approval of the reviewers: S.S. Glagolev, professor of the department of apologetics at the Moscow Theological Academy, and M.D. Muretov, professor of the department of the Holy Scripture of the New Testament. On September 25 of the same year, on the feast day of the venerable Sergius of Radonezh, Vladimir Troitsky wrote a foreword to his dissertation and submitted it to the synodal printshop in Sergiev Posad. In late November the appointed reviewers gave their responses. In his review S.S. Glagolev in particular stated, "Books such as that of Mr. Troitsky rarely appear in Rus. Its advent marks a red-letter day for theological scholarship." Prof. M.D. Muretov noted that the work by Mr. Troitsky "not only supplements, but wholly surpasses the works of his Russian predecessors," and concluded his review with words of high praise: "If it were up to me, without the slightest hesitation I would declare Troitsky's dissertation fully worthy not only of a master's degree, but of a Ph.D." See the minutes of the assemblies of the board of the Moscow Theological Academy for 1912, *Bogoslovsky Vestnik* [1913], № 7–8, 584, 589; M.D. Muretov, critical bibliographical note on the book by Vl[adimir] Troitsky, "Essays on the History of the Dogma Concerning the Church" [Sergiev Posad: 1912], *Bogoslovsky Vestnik* (1913), February, March. For additional reviews see "There is No Christianity without the Church" ["Без Церкви нет христианства"], *Donskoy Pravoslavny Vestnik* (1915), № 3; A. Pologov, *Dushepoleznaya Chtenie* (1913), № 4; concerning the defense of the dissertation on December 11, 1912, see *Tserkovnye Vedomosti*, addendae (1912) № 50. For responses concerning the awarding of the degree, see "A Red-Letter Day for Theological Scholarhip," *Russkoe Slovo* (1913), № 12.

The defense of the dissertation took place on December 11, 1912, at the assembly of the Board of the Moscow Theological Academy in the presence of its rector, Fyodor (Poldeyevsky), bishop of Volokolamsk, and the entire academic body. In keeping with tradition, the defense took place in the form of a debate. On January 16, 1913, the Holy Synod confirmed Vladimir Troitsky's master's degree in theology and his post as senior lecturer. In March of the same year his master's thesis received the Macarius Award.

PREFACE

The dogma concerning the Church may be termed the self-identification of the Church. It is this dogma that determines what the Church is and what distinguishes it from all that is not the Church. The Church is not a phenomenon of the natural earthly order: the mysterious depths of church life, in accordance with the unfailing promise of Christ the Savior, are always and invariably enveloped by the grace-filled power of the Holy Spirit. The full depth of this mystical life of the Church is not of course subject to logical definitions and scholarly research: it is given directly to him who participates in it, as Hilary of Poitiers expressed in the words: "Hoc ecclesiae proprium est, ut tunc intellegatur, cum arguitur" (*On the Trinity* 7.4).[1] For this reason we may say that the self-identification of the Church is experienced specifically by one who dwells in the Church and is a living member of her living body.

Nevertheless, since the inception of the Church the theological thought of church writers has undertaken, among other things, to define the essence of the Church and its properties in concepts comprehensible to the human mind. The brief definition of the Church presented in its Symbol of Faith could not be sufficient, since inevitable questions arose regarding the understanding of the credal definition itself, and the very life of the Church insistently demanded that these questions be answered. The life of each person and his outward actions is intimately linked to his self-identification. Likewise, the outward life of the Church in many of its manifesta-

---

1 "This is the peculiar property of the Church, that when she makes herself known, then she is understood."

tions is determined by the Church's understanding of itself—that is, by the dogma concerning the Church. The questions that arose throughout history concerning church practice roused church theological thought to a more detailed clarification of the very concept of the Church. The same was required by the distortion of the true understanding of the Church wrought by heretics and schismatics. The first centuries of Christianity are peculiar in that throughout them the Church frequently had to contend with errors that deviated from the truth specifically in the doctrine concerning the Church. In the first centuries of church life we see several fairly complex movements founded on ideas linked in one way or another to the dogma concerning the Church. This is why, more than at any other time, ecclesiastical theological thought in the first centuries focused its attention on clarifying the concept of the Church. The heresies and schisms that appeared in the Church merely spurred the fathers and teachers of the Church, "having received wisdom from God, to set forth dogmas, which of old the fishermen set down in simple words, through the power of the Spirit in understanding; for thus was it fitting to acquire a simple exposition of our Faith" (sessional hymn, January 30).

The *Essays on the History of the Dogma Concerning the Church* here presented are therefore devoted to a study of the pivotal points in the efforts of early church theological thought toward expounding and elucidating church doctrine concerning the Church. These pivotal points are determined by the most prominent anti-Church movements, founded on a distorted understanding of the Church, with which the theologians of the early Church did literary battle. These movements are Judaistic Christianity, Gnosticism, Montanism, Novatianism, and Donatism. We therefore preface this study of the church writers' dogmatic struggle against these anti-Church phenomena with a brief overview of the New Testament teaching concerning the Church.

Each of the above phenomena in its own right could be the subject of a whole series of scholarly studies. Hence, in our essays we will not be pursuing monographic exhaustiveness. Rather, we will primarily focus on studying those dogmatic outcomes on the

question of the Church that resulted from dogmatic polemics motivated by one or another of the above phenomena. In our essays
the ends in view will be not those of church history, but rather of
the history of dogma. Only by thus limiting the task will it become
possible to unite all the essays here presented into a single study,
since the most prominent anti-Church movements of old which we
have noted may only be combined from the standpoint of dogmatic
history—from the standpoint of the Christian teaching concerning
the Church that unfolded in the struggle to combat them.

It is the author's view that a study of various questions from
the history of the dogma concerning the Church is of vital importance to church life and the duty of church theological scholarship.
The question of the Church is always an interesting and important question. One ought always to proceed from the concept of
the Church when resolving questions of church life, and frequently
these questions essentially comprise a repetition or modification of
old ones. The gates of hell, arrayed against the Church in the up-
rising of heresies and errors, to this day give rise to numerous anti-Church phenomena. Combating these phenomena is the task of
the ecclesiastical figures of the day, but this fight must be grounded
in the ancient Church and linked to the treasury of the theological knowledge of the catholic Church. One cannot help but notice how in our time questions arise and are discussed that have
long been quite sufficiently resolved by the writers of the ancient
Church. Who is not aware that the question of the Church is the
chief, principle question in modern polemics with sectarianism in
various forms? And of course, in conducting these polemics one
must always bear in mind the dogmatic conclusions reached by the
theological thought of the ancient Church. This is why a study on
the history of the dogma concerning the Church is able to meet the
modern needs of church life.

Western scholars have long and extensively been engaged in
scholarly research of the history of the dogma concerning the
Church—Catholics and predominantly Protestants, people who
are strangers to the Church; for Alexei Khomyakov quite justifiably
called Catholicism and Protestantism "heresies against the dogma

of the essence of the Church, against its faith in its own self." The
conclusions drawn by scholarship outside the Church in studying
the history of the dogma concerning the Church are what oblige
theological scholars within the Church to take up this important
subject themselves. We people of the Church believe and confess
that we belong to that Church which Christ and His holy apostles
established. In the Symbol of Faith we call our church "apostolic."
The history of the dogma concerning the Church is for us nothing
less than the history of the academic and theological elucidation
of the ever unified and unchanging concept of the Church. The
Church and her self-identification have remained unified and unchanged from the time of Christ and the apostles to our own. Only
scholarly and theological elucidation of the dogma concerning
the Church has altered in its breadth and depth. But scholarship
outside the Church takes an entirely different stance. *Die Entstehung der altkatholischen Kirche* [*The Rise of the Old Catholic Church*] is the
title of a work by Albrecht Ritschl, which more than half a century hence laid the groundwork for that resolution of questions of
church history and dogmatic history which—with certain amend-
ments—is advanced to this day by adherents of the Ritschl school,
predominantly in Protestant scholarship. The very title of the work
is highly typical. To the question, "What is the origin of the ecumenical Church?" one who is within the Church may answer concisely and definitively: "The Church was founded by our Lord Jesus
Christ, the Son of God, and His holy apostles." If however entire exhaustive studies can be written on the origin of the Church,
it is apparent that the authors of these studies take a completely
different view of the Catholic Church. Similarly titled Protestant
works chronologically span over two hundred years; clearly, in the
opinion of their authors, the Church "originated" over the course
of entire centuries. Christ and the apostles did not establish the
catholic Church; if indeed they did establish any Church at all, it
was certainly not the one that later became known as the catholic
Church. The latter Church originated on its own out of various elements, influenced by numerous conditions, and in the final analysis
actually contradicts Christ and the apostles. It was not heretics and

schismatics who distorted the concept of the Church, but rather the Church itself gradually altered its essence, retreating from its former self-identification. For many Protestant scholars, the ancient anti-Church heretical movements we mentioned before are vestiges of the ancient concept of the Church, as surmised based on scant and ambiguous information. Thus, it was not heretics who distorted the ancient doctrine concerning the Church, but the Church itself which, in condemning Montanism, for example, condemned and declared as heresy something that was formerly ecclesial—its own doctrine concerning the Church. The Church as Christ and His apostles envisioned it lasted for a very short time: by the second century the catholic Church that had "originated" declared it a heresy, destroyed it, and usurped its place. What was formed was not the apostolic Church, but a Church hostile to that of the apostles. Along with historical events in the life of the Church, changes of the most radical kind were also taking place in the very concept of the Church. For example, in the third century a doctrine of the sanctity of the Church was developed in total contradiction to what had been said on the subject in the second century.

It seems it would not be an overstatement to say that this kind of idea of the history of the dogma concerning the Church kills and undermines all faith in the Church. If we agree with the Protestant exposition of the history of the dogma concerning the Church, we must discard the ninth article of the Symbol of Faith, which combines the catholic Church with the apostolic Church. It is therefore the duty of theological scholarship within the Church to give its own exposition of the history of the dogma concerning the Church, which may be used to counter how that history is framed outside the Church. To this day, we might observe, this duty remains almost entirely undischarged. There have been works devoted to the history of the dogma concerning the Church, but these have long become obsolete and do not at all consider the new questions that have arisen in this arena of scholarly knowledge over the last several decades.

It is this circumstance that determines the nature of the present work. On various questions pertaining to the history of the dogma concerning the Church we are preceded by scholars outside the Church with whom we have a significant and fundamental difference of opinion. By the same token, there are a great many works dealing in one way or another with the history of the dogma concerning the Church, since the history of the dogma concerning the Church is intimately linked to the history of various aspects of church life, and the teaching of various church writers concerning the Church has its explanation in the historical circumstances of their lives and their ecclesiastical and literary work. For this reason nearly every scholarly book on the history of the Church or patristic theology has proven to have some bearing on certain questions, often minute and highly particular, in our own study. Such an abundance of scholarly literature renders us completely unable to systematically review all the opinions expressed on each of the multitudinous and very nearly innumerable questions in our study. If we were to undertake not to leave a single stated opinion without exposition and analysis, we would have to write an entire study on each separate question. Only by adopting a different approach can we combine an entire series of complex, intertwined questions of the greatest importance in a single study. We therefore choose the approach of historical criticism of the primary sources. Our attention will be concentrated primarily on remnants of early church literature—on essays by the writers of the ancient Church who undertook to elucidate the teaching of the Church. The multitudinous scholarly works we have studied served merely as our aids in achieving this stated goal. Nevertheless, we hold it impossible to completely pass over in silence all the variety and richness of content of these frequently monumental, informative, and interesting works, and at times we will not be sparing with quotes and citations therefrom. We merely do not undertake their complete and systematic usage; else we would constantly be obliged to stray far from the topic at hand. We will concentrate only on the most general ideas, most frequently encountered among modern scholars of church history and dogmatic history, and, holding the majority of these ideas inadmissible for theological scholarship within the Church, in our study of the primary sources along with a positive exposition and explanation of their substance we will point out facts within them that disprove or at least shake the foundations of Protestant scholarship's prevailing representation of the history of the dogma concerning the Church.

In our desire to discern the development of ecclesial self-identification in the writings and theological literature of the ancient Church in the course of our study, we may at times have erred from the truth by incorrectly conveying the thinking of the ancient Church and passing off our own folly as church doctrine. We can therefore do no better than to say in the words of the blessed Augustine: "Quod vera esse perspexeris, tene, et Ecclesiae catholicae tribue; quae falsa, respue et mihi qui homo sum ignosce" (*On True Religion* 10:20).[2] The author holds all doubt as to the perfect truth of the one Orthodox Church of Christ to be unacceptable; such doubt may result either from ignorance or from sinfulness. Laboring on the question of the Church has taught the author to read the prayer for the Church from the daily commemorations with particular love and trepidation of heart:

"Among the first remember, O Lord, Thy Holy, Catholic, and Apostolic Church, which Thou hast preserved by Thy precious Blood, and establish, strengthen, and expand, increase, pacify, and keep Her unconquerable by the gates of hades; calm the dissensions of the churches, quench the raging of the nations, and quickly destroy and uproot the rising of heresy, and bring them to naught by the power of Thy Holy Spirit."

September 25, 1912
Commemoration of the Venerable Sergius

---

2 "As many things as you will have ascertained to be true, keep, and bestow them to the catholic Church; those that you will have perceived to be false, spit them out, and forgive me who am a man."

FIRST ESSAY

The New Testament Doctrine Concerning the Church

Introductory Note: The New Testament doctrine concerning the Church could be the subject of a separate study. Even in Russian theological literature there are special works devoted to it, such as Ivan Mansvetov's *The New Testament Doctrine Concerning the Church* ["Новозаветное учение о Церкви"] (Moscow: 1879) and the work by E. Akvilonov, *Scholarly Definitions of the Church and the Apostolic Doctrine Concerning It as the Body of Christ* ["Научные определения Церкви и апостольское учение о ней как о Теле Христовом"] (Saint Petersburg: 1894). In this study, the subject of which is the history of the dogma concerning the Church, we naturally can provide only a very general outline of the doctrine of the New Testament, which, having no independent and absolute scholarly value, can only serve as a kind of introduction to the history of **dogma** proper concerning the Church. Nevertheless, in the chapters of our study that follow we will sometimes have to turn to the sacred books of the New Testament. In addition, the very history of the dogma concerning the Church is, in a sense, a commentary on the doctrine of the New Testament.

It was a great and solemn moment in the history of mankind when the Lord Jesus Christ exclaimed in His prayer as high priest: "Holy Father, keep through thine own name those whom thou hast given me, that they may be one, as we are. ... Neither pray I for these alone, but for them also which shall believe on me through their word; that they all may be one; as thou, Father, art in me, and I in thee, that they also may be one in us" (Jn. 17:11, 20–21).

These words of Christ's prayer already give a clear definition of the essence of the Church. Christ came to earth to save the world;[3] hence, Christianity likewise is not merely a teaching received by the intellect and maintained differently by each. No, Christianity is life, in which individual persons are so greatly united among themselves that their union may be likened to the essential unity of the Persons of the Holy Trinity. It was for this, that men might be made a unity, the Church, that the Lord Jesus Christ prayed to His Heavenly Father. Christ places love as the foundation for men's unification in the Church. Pointing to the unanimity of the Persons of the Holy Trinity as the ideal of the Church, in the same prayer He said: "[Let] the love wherewith thou hast loved me be in them, and I in them" (cf. Jn. 17:26).[4] It was this incomparable mutual love of the Persons of the Holy Trinity that the Lord Jesus Christ exhorted His disciples to emulate in His parting conversation with them: "A new commandment I give unto you, That ye love one another; as I have loved you, that ye also love one another. By this shall all men know that ye are my disciples, if ye have love one to another" (Jn. 13:34–35; cf. 15:2).

But that men might enter this union of love, that they might be united into the Church, **human nature itself had to be recreated**, as it had become contaminated by sin which always opposes any human unity. In His conversation with Nicodemus the Lord Jesus Christ talks about how a man must be born anew.[5] It is for this very rebirth of human nature, for this recreation thereof, that the incarnation of the Son of God and His death on the cross were needed.[6] In the person of Christ mankind became participant in the divine nature; for without the incarnation of the Son of God the unification of men in the Church would have been impossible. **The Church has as its foundation the incarnation of the Son of God,** Christ the God-man. When the apostle Peter confessed Jesus Christ to be the Son of the Living God, Jesus answered

---

3 See Jn. 3:17.

4 See Jn. 15:10: "Ye shall abide in my love; even as I abide in his love."

5 See Jn. 3:3, 5, 7.

6 See Jn. 3:13–17.

him: "Upon this rock I will build my church" (Mt. 16:18). Only
through the incarnate Only-begotten Son of God do people receive
true life, the life that is eternal, and hence "he that believeth not" in
the Only-begotten Son of God "is condemned already" (Jn. 3:18):
for him true life is impossible.[7] In order to be a living member of
reborn mankind, one must have a real connection with Christ the
God-man. For this reason Christ said: "Abide in me, and I in you.
As the branch cannot bear fruit of itself, except it abide in the vine;
no more can ye, except ye abide in me. I am the vine, ye are the
branches: He that abideth in me, and I in him, the same bringeth
forth much fruit: for without me ye can do nothing. If a man abide
not in me, he is cast forth as a branch, and is withered; and men
gather them, and cast them into the fire, and they are burned" (Jn.
15:4–6). Lest the latter occur, Christ promised to abide with His
Church "even unto the end of the world" (Mt. 28:20).

The life of reborn mankind, the life of the Church, is sustained
by its constant connection with God. The life of the Church is a
supernatural life. In order to enter the Church, one must be born
from on high, born of water and the Spirit (cf. Jn. 3:3, 5); he must
be begotten of the Spirit.[8] For the natural man this rebirth is so incomprehensible that it seems as impossible as it would be to "enter
the second time into his mother's womb, and be born" (Jn. 3:4).
While Jesus was not yet glorified, His followers did not have the
Spirit, but even then He spoke in veiled language, citing the Old
Testament prophecies, speaking "of the Spirit, which they that
believe on him should receive ("περὶ τοῦ πνεύματος, οὗ ἔμελλον
λαμβάνειν οἱ πιστεύοντες εἰς αὐτόν," Jn. 7:39). But the Lord Jesus
Christ especially spoke of the Holy Spirit and of being reborn of
Him throughout His entire parting conversation. Here the Lord's
speech is perfectly clear and distinct: "I will pray the Father, and he
shall give you another Comforter, that he may abide with you for
ever. … But the Comforter, which is the Holy Ghost, whom the Father will send in my name, he shall teach you all things, and bring all
things to your remembrance, whatsoever I have said unto you" (Jn.

---

7 See 1 Jn. 5:12.

8 See Jn. 3:6.

14:16, 26). "He, the Spirit of truth ... will guide you into all truth (ὑμᾶς εἰς πᾶσαν τὴν ἀλήθειαν," Jn. 16:13). Consequently, the Holy Spirit will guide (ὁδηγήσει) all Christians and the entire Church on the path of the fullness of the truth—that is, not only theoretical truth, but also moral truth. Πᾶσα ἡ ἀλήθεια [all truth]—this is the whole life of the born-again man,[9] and this life is of the Holy Spirit. Before His ascension Christ also said to His disciples that in a few days they would be "baptized with the Holy Ghost" (Acts 1:5), Who would endue them with "power from on high" (Lk. 24:49).[10]

Thus, according to the teaching of Jesus Christ Himself, His **Church is the supernatural grace-filled joining of men reborn by the God-man into a union of love.**

In its historical manifestation this grace-filled community naturally must differ significantly from all other, natural human coalitions into communities. This is the Kingdom of Heaven; it is "not of this world" (Jn. 18:36);[11] it is not worldly in nature; it is not like political kingdoms, founded upon power and coercion. When certain of Christ's disciples, not understanding the nature of the new unification of men which He preached, asked for themselves ordinary earthly power in His kingdom, He answered them: "Ye know not what ye ask. ... Ye know that the princes of the Gentiles exercise dominion over them, and they that are great exercise authority upon them. But it shall not be so among you: but whosoever will be ... chief among you, let him be your servant" (Mt. 20:22, 25–27; cf. Mk. 10:38, 42–44; Lk. 22:25–26). In Christ was fulfilled the prophecy concerning the meek king: He entered into Jerusalem not upon a horse, but upon an ass,[12] and He entered to suffer for men. In the desert Christ rejected the devil's temptation to convert all men by force.[13] The Lord sent His apostles not as fearsome conquerors,

---

9 Vgl.: Paul Wolff, *Die Entwickelung der einen christlichen Kirche durch Athanasius, Augustin, Luther. Eine kirchen-und dogmengeschichtliche Studie* (Berlin: 1889), 2–6.

10 See Acts 1:8: "Λήψεσθε δύναμιν ἐπελθόντος τοῦ ἁγίου Πνεύματος ἐφ' ὑμᾶς" ("ye shall receive power, after that the Holy Ghost is come upon you").

11 See Jn. 14:27; 15:19; 17:14, 16.

12 See Mt. 21:5–7; Mk. 11:2, 7; Lk. 19:30, 35.

13 See Lk. 4:6; Mt. 4:6, 9.

but simply as humble preachers who possessed nothing but their preaching, who could only conquer the hearts of men. The Church is joined only by one who responds to the word of preaching with uncoerced faith;[14] hence, to call down fire from heaven upon the unbelievers would have been infidelity to the new spirit of Christ.[15] In the Church itself there can be no external authority.[16] But the new source and the new grace-filled basis for unification establish a community in which the members are far more closely linked than in any natural community. Jesus Christ Himself envisioned this community as a tree;[17] that is, He spoke of the organic unity of all believers, so that even the very life of the reborn man is unthinkable outside this organic unity. This contrast of the Church to worldly kingdoms causes its members to be as though set apart from the world and no longer to belong to it. For this the world hates them and persecutes them in diverse ways,[18] but the Church vanquishes the world only by a "spirit of meekness" (1 Cor. 4:21).[19]

This being its nature, the Church can only be one. Two separately growing trees are not connected in any way: only the branches of a single tree are organically connected to each other. The existence of two separate Churches would contradict the very essence of church unity. Even Christ Himself spoke of one fold and one Shepherd.[20] Upon the rock of Peter's confession Christ built the Church (τὴν ἐκκλησίαν), not the Churches. All believers are "brethren" (Mt. 23:8). The Lord spoke of this same unity in His high priestly prayer, asking "that they all may be one" (Jn. 17:21).

Being one, the Church of Christ encompasses the entire world: it knows no territorial or national bounds. The Old Testament, which was limited to the Jewish nation alone, has come to an end. After

---

14 See Mk. 16:16.

15 See Lk. 9:54–56.

16 See Mt. 23:8–10.

17 See Jn. 15:4–6.

18 See Jn. 15:16, 18–21; 16:2–4, 20, 33; 17:14, 16.

19 See Mt. 5:5; Lk. 12:32.

20 See Jn. 10:16.

the Lord's parable of the vineyard, members of the Jewish people themselves said that the Lord ought to give the vineyard to other husbandmen, and thereby they pronounced just judgment upon themselves.[21] In place of the limited Old Testament Church, Christ built His Church, into which "many shall come from the east and west, and shall sit down [in it] with Abraham, and Isaac, and Jacob" (Mt. 8:11). Christ was sent into the world, not to the Hebrew nation alone. He came for the salvation of the whole world and was the light of the world (cf. Jn. 8:12). Hence, worship of God the Father is not tied to a particular place, for "true worshippers shall worship the Father in spirit and in truth" (Jn. 4:23). Elucidating the parable of the good sower, Christ said: "The field is the world," and "He that soweth the good seed is the Son of man" (Mt. 13:38, 37). When first sending the apostles forth to preach, the Lord Jesus Christ limited the place of their preaching to the borders of Palestine: they were to preach only to the lost sheep of the house of Israel (cf. Mt. 10:6). In another instance He said the same concerning Himself.[22] But this does not mean that before His sufferings Christ actually limited His work solely to the national borders of Israel. There are other passages that speak with perfect clarity of the universalism of the Gospel. To His disciples Christ foretold that they would be "hated of all nations (ὑπὸ πάντων τῶν ἐθνῶν)" (Mt. 24:9). In His eschatological talk He said that "this gospel of the kingdom shall be preached in all the world for a witness unto all nations" (ἐν ὅλῃ τῇ οἰκουμενῃ εἰς μαρτύριον πᾶσι τοῖς ἔθνεσι)" (Mt. 24:14). Before the end "the gospel must ... be published among all nations (εἰς πάντα τὰ ἔθνη)" (Mk. 13:10). When in Bethany, in the house of Simon the leper, the woman anointed His head with precious ointment, the Lord said: "Wheresoever this gospel shall be preached throughout the whole world (εἰς ὅλον τὸν κόσμον), this also that she hath done shall be spoken of for a memorial of her" (Mk. 14:9).[23] Finally, when He appeared to His disciples after His resurrection from the dead, in sending them forth to preach the Lord Jesus Christ said to

21 See Mt. 21:33–43.

22 See Mt. 15:24.

23 See Mt. 26:13: "ἐν ὅλῳ τῷ κόσμῳ" ("in the whole world").

them with absolute clarity and without ambiguity: "Go ye ... and teach all nations (πάντα τὰ ἔθνη)" (Mt. 28:19); "Go ye into all the world (εἰς τὸν κόσμον ἅπαντα) ... preach the gospel to every creature (πάσῃ τῇ κτίσει)" (Mk. 16:15). "Ye shall be witnesses unto me both in Jerusalem, and in all Judaea, and in Samaria, and unto the uttermost part of the earth (ἕως ἐσχάτου τῆς γῆς)" (Acts 1:8).

Thus, the extraordinary unification of all mankind in love to the point of oneness must take place in the Church of Christ. It must also be added that this unification—that is, the Church itself—is not presented as a thing desirable or merely anticipated. The Church is not just a conceivable entity: it is a real, historically palpable phenomenon. Christ said that His followers are "in the world," although "not of the world." "I pray not that thou shouldest take them out of the world," He said to God the Father, "but that thou shouldest keep them from the evil" (Jn. 17:11, 14–15). Consequently, by its nature the Church is not a worldly phenomenon, not an ordinary one in the usual order of things, but its members are in the world, and in the world they must carry out the teaching of Christ. In the natural world Christ has laid the foundation for a special, supernatural community, one that will exist alongside natural phenomena.[24]

Finally, those who enter the Church are not magically transformed into higher beings of a superterrestrial order. In their earthly lives, with the help of the Holy Spirit the members of the Church must overcome in themselves their sinful nature. The Holy Spirit "will guide" believers "into all truth" (Jn. 16:13). Hence, in the Gospel there is no trace of the idea that the Church is a community of morally perfect, conclusively saved individuals: no, it is a **community of those working out their salvation**, a community which the Holy Spirit is **guiding** to perfection (ὁδηγήσει εἰς πᾶσαν τὴν

---

24 See Ivan Mansvetov, *The New Testament Teaching Concerning the Church* ["Новозаветное учение о Церкви"], 74–75. In general, see chapter 1, "The Life of the Church on Earth, As Viewed From Without" ["Жизнь Церкви на земле, рассматриваемая с внешней стороны"], 74–124. Cf. Alfred Loisy, *L'Évangile et L'Église.* 4-me éd. (Ceffonds: 1908), 153: "On a vue que l'Évangile de Jésus avait déjà un rudiment d'organisation sociale, et que le royaume aussi devait avoir forme de société."

ἀλήθειαν, "into all truth").[25] The seeds of new spiritual life gradually sprout forth in the members of the Church, influenced by the full
diversity of various individuals: the same seed produces different
yields.[26] This is why tares are also found among the pure wheat, and
they are left to grow together until they can be destroyed without
harming the wheat.[27] At the end of the world, in the kingdom of the
Son of Man there will be "things that offend, and them which do
iniquity" (Mt. 13:41). The Lord Jesus Christ likened His kingdom
to a feast to which all the paupers, the halt, the lame, and the blind
were brought, to which both the good and the evil were gathered.[28]
For each individual member of the Church there is an ultimate
authority and a supreme judge. One who disobeys the Church falls
away from it and becomes estranged from it, like a heathen and a
publican, and consequently is deprived of the grace-filled aid that
is essential for true life.

    We have briefly noted the chief traits of the Church, defined
by the words of the Lord Jesus Christ Himself. As may be seen, the
Gospel contains no teaching concerning the Church that is devel-
oped to any degree of detail,[29] and based on the clear witness of the
Gospel we can give only a very general definition of the Church.
**The Church is a community of believers in the Lord Jesus
Christ, the Son of God—people reborn by Him and the
Holy Spirit, united in love and attaining perfection under
the incessant action of the Holy Spirit.**

    If we turn to the earliest events in Christian history, we will see
clearly how believers assimilated the concept of the Church from
the very beginning.

---

25 Vgl. Wolff. op. cit., 3–4.

26 See Mt. 13:19–23.

27 See Mt. 13:29–30.

28 See Lk. 14:21, Mt. 22:10.

29 "In the question of the Church it is important to bear in mind with all
possible clarity both what the Gospel teaches and what it does not teach." Prof.
M.M. Tareyev, *Fundamentals of Christianity* ["Основы христианства"], Vol. 2
(Sergiev Posad: 1908), 345n.

In accordance with Christ's command, the little flock of His followers tarried in Jerusalem.[30] The new human community was not begun as every natural human community is supposed to begin. Within a few days Christ's followers were baptized by the Holy Spirit: all were filled with the Holy Spirit, and at the time the holy apostle Peter saw in this the fulfillment of the prophecy of Joel.[31] Upon receiving the Holy Spirit, the believers formed the Church, and **Christianity never existed without the Church.** In the earliest pages of history believers appear before us as a like-minded and concordant community,[32] which took upon itself the name *Church* (ἐκκλησία).[33] It matters not that the word ἐκκλησία is used only twice in the Gospel; the Church existed long before the Gospels themselves were written. Only a few years had passed after the

---

30 See Lk. 24:49, Acts 1:8, 12

31 See Acts 2:4, 6

32 See Acts 2:42, etc.

33 The very name ἐκκλησία [*ecclesia*] also defines certain properties of the society so designated. Not every "society" and not every "assembly" may be called an ἐκκλησία, but rather only an assembly of people who are united by something. In the classic use of the word, ἐκκλησία signified an assembly of citizens: ἐκκλησία = οἱ ἔκκλητοι [those called forth], which was convened by a special κῆρυξ [herald]. The ἐκκλησία was an assembly constituted by law. Hence, an ἐκκλησία has two attributes: structured unity and convention (κλῆσις, ἐκκαλεῖν). A philological analysis of the word ἐκκλησία is given by Dr. Hermann Cremer (*Biblisch-theologisches Wörterbuch der Neutestamentlichen Gräcität*, 9-te Auflage [Gotha: 1902], 548–551), and also by S.K. Smirnov (*Philological Notes on a Comparison of New Testament and Classical Language in Reading the Epistle of the Apostle Paul to the Ephesians* ["Филологические замечания о языке новозаветном в сличении с классическим при чтении Послания апостола Павла к Ефесеям"] [Moscow: 1873], 83–85) and Rudolph Sohm (*Church Structure in the First Centuries of Christianity* ["Церковный строй в первые века христианства"], A. Petrovsky and P. Florensky, trans. [Moscow: 1906], 33–38). It is quite noteworthy that in Latin the word ἐκκλησία was not translated, but merely transcribed as *ecclesia*, although there are several Latin words for denoting a community. Clearly, not one Latin word was found to fully and precisely convey the meaning of the Greek ἐκκλησία, which expresses the idea that God set a portion of mankind apart and **called** them into a special community. See Prof. Adolf Deissmann, *Licht vom Osten: Das Neue Testament und die Neuentdeckten Texte der Hellenistisch-Römischen Welt.* 2-te und 3-te Aufl. (Tübingen: 1909), 79–80.

Lord's ascension when Saul, a zealot of the Jewish law, as he himself later repeatedly recalls, "persecuted the church of God" (Gal.
1:13).[34] Consequently, the Church existed even for one who was
himself outside the Church.

Without a connection to this community there were no Christians: to believe in Christ meant **to join the Church**, as is repeatedly expressed in the book of the Acts of the Apostles, which
states that "the Lord added to the church daily such as should be
saved" (Acts 2:47). According to the apostles, every believer was like
a branch grafted onto the tree of church life. The need for every
person who believed specifically to join the church community is
seen with particular clarity in the story of Saul's conversion. On the
road to Damascus, Saul was miraculously changed from a persecu-
tor into a follower of Christ. In Damascus, however, the Lord sent
Ananias to him: Ananias baptized him, after which Saul was in Damascus for several days with the disciples; and after Barnabas told
the apostles of him he spent time with them.[35] Thus, even one who
later became a great apostle, whom in Ananias's vision the Lord
called a chosen vessel,[36] immediately after his conversion **joins the
Church** as a visible and distinct community.

The degree to which the initial Church was defined as a community is beautifully expressed in the book of the Acts of the Apostles: "Of the rest (λοιπῶν) durst no man join himself (κολλᾶσθαι)
to them" (Acts 5:13). This statement need only be combined with
that cited above—"The Lord added to the church ... such as should
be saved" (Acts 2:47)—and we will clearly see what a definite and
sharply delimited entity the Church comprised in the very first days
of its existence.

---

34 Vgl. Prof. Dr. Schanz, "Der Begriff der Kirche," *Theologische Quartalschrift*
(1893), 535; Carl Weizsäcker, *Das apostolische Zeitalter der christlichen Kirche*, 3-te Aufl.
(Tübingen und Leipzig: 1902), 597; Pierre Batiffol, *L'église naissante et le catholicisme*,
3-me éd. (Paris: 1909), 90–91.

35 See Acts 9:1–28.

36 See Acts 9:15.

The community of Christ's followers grew ever larger.[37] After the persecution of believers in Jerusalem, the Christians that "were scattered abroad went every where preaching the word" (Acts 8:4). The idea of a supernational Church was clearly acknowledged by all, and hence at the very outset Samaritans were received into the Church,[38] and Phillip baptized the Ethiopian.[39] In a special vision the Lord revealed to the apostle Peter that he was not to consider any man defiled and unclean, and Peter opened his mouth and said: "Of a truth I perceive that God is no respecter of persons: but in every nation he that feareth him, and worketh righteousness, is accepted with him" (Acts 10:34–35). To be sure, soon certain of the Jewish Christians would have reneged on this idea, "and when Peter was come up to Jerusalem, they that were of the circumcision contended with him, saying, Thou wentest in to men uncircumcised, and didst eat with them" (Acts 11:2–3). But this misconception was quickly put to rest. When the apostle Peter relayed to them all that had happened, and "when they heard these things, they held their peace, and glorified God, saying, Then hath God also to the Gentiles granted repentance unto life" (Acts 11:18). The ministry of the great "apostle to the gentiles" was begun, and the supernationality of the Church of Christ is clearly, definitively, and obligatorily expressed in the decree of the Apostolic Council that declared the Mosaic law to be non-binding for Christians from among the gentiles.[40] After this the apostles of Christ spread the faith in every place, even to the uttermost parts of the earth, and it was the Church that the apostles spread, establishing an organized religious community.[41]

At this same time, in the apostolic epistles we also encounter theoretical reflections on the Church. First and foremost we must

---

37 See Acts 6:7.

38 See Acts 8:14.

39 See Acts 8:26–39.

40 See Acts 15:23–29.

41 Vgl. Loisy, *L'Évangile et L'Église*, 134–138.

note that the apostles employed **Old Testament terminology** to express the idea of the Church.

The very term ἐκκλησία may be closely linked to the fully corresponding Hebrew term לָהָק (*qāhāl –Ed.*) The Hebrew word לָהָק is a solemn designation for a religious assembly: לָהָק is a community in its relation to God, and for this reason this name is primarily applied to the Hebrew nation as a whole לְהָקַה־לָכ (*kal-ha qahal*—literally, "all of the assembly" –*Ed.*).

The Seventy translate לָהָק primarily using the word ἐκκλησία.[42] In the Gospel, as noted above, the word ἐκκλησία is encountered only twice, and both times in the Gospel of Matthew, which was written for the Jews and hence clearly reflects the Old Testament worldview. The Gospel says only that Christ will build **His** Church—not just any Church. When speaking of excommunication of the disobedient from the Church, the expressions used are of an expressly Old Testament or even Jewish nature: "Let him be unto thee as an heathen man and a publican" (Mt. 18:17).[43] The expressions ἡ ἐκκλησία τοῦ Θεοῦ ["the church of God"] or ἐκκλησία τοῦ Χριστοῦ ["church of Christ"], frequently encountered in the New Testament,[44] likewise fully correspond to the Old Testament קָהָל תְדַע (*qehal adath "congregated assembly" YHWH –Ed.*).[45] The fact that from the very beginning the term adopted to signify the Chris-

---

42 Sometimes לָהָק is also translated as συναγωγή ["congregation," "synagogue"], but rarely. The word συναγωγή is usually conveyed by the Hebrew word עדה ("congregation"), which signifies an ordinary assembly.

43 Cf. Jn. 9:2. See Prof. M.M. Tareyev, *Fundamentals of Christianity*, Vol. 2, 346–347. Friedrich Loofs, *Leitfaden zum Studium der Dogmengeschichte*, 4-te Aufl. (Halle: 1906), §6.2b., 38. Gustav Hoenicke, *Das Judenchristentum im ersten und zweiten Jahrhundert* (Berlin: 1908), 346–347, 248–249. Incidentally, in addition to the link with Old Testament terminology, Cremer notes a contrast to the Jewish synagogue. See *Biblisch-theologisches Wörterbuch*, 549.

44 Acts 20:28; Rom. 16:16; 1 Cor. 1:2, 10:32, 11:16, 22, 15:9; Gal. 1:22; 1 Thess. 2:14; 1 Tim. 3:5, 15, etc.

45 Num. 16:3, 20:4; Deut. 23:2–4, 9; 1 Chron. 28:2; Mic. 2:5. Cf. לחק םיחלְאָח 13, 1. Vgl.: J. Meritan, "L'Ecclésiologie de l'épître aux Éphésiens," *Revue biblique internationale* (1898), vol. 7, 346–347. Ioseph Knabenbaur, *Cursus Scripturae Sacrae 1, 2. Evangelium secundum s. Matthaeum, pars altera* (Parisiis: 1893), 54.

tian Church was ἐκκλησία, a term closely linked to Old Testament terminology, speaks to the establishment of the **oneness** that permeated the initial Church. In the Old Testament there was one תֵדַע לְהָק, and in the New Testament likewise ἡ ἐκκλησία τοῦ Θεοῦ ["the church of God"] was one—all the more so given that in synagogal literature the corresponding אֱלֹהָק is used primarily to signify *all* Israel.[46] The Old Testament basis of the term ἐκκλησία, first and foremost, gives it universal significance: ἐκκλησία signifies the **whole united visible earthly Church**, and only then is this name applied to the individual community.[47]

To be sure, of the 110 instances where ἐκκλησία is used in the New Testament, 90 times it signifies not the universal Church, but a local Christian community, usually of a particular city.[48] But

---

46 Cremer, *Biblisch-theologisches Wörterbuch*,[4] 550.

47 "That Christ gave the name ἐκκλησία to the community which He founded is of particular polemic significance against the Protestants. The Protestants carry on about their 'invisible' Church. But in the concept of the ἐκκλησία there is a strong visible aspect. For this reason the expression 'invisible Church' contains a *contradictio in adjecto*. There can be no invisible Church. In the invisible one can participate only spiritually, but in the ἐκκλησία this is only possible in the body." –Prof. V.V. Bolotov, *Lectures on the History of the Early Church* ["Лекции по истории древней Церкви"], 1st ed. (Saint Petersburg: 1907), 13.

48 In the singular and with the article, ἐκκλησία ordinarily signifies: (1) the initial Church of Jerusalem and Judea, when there were no other Churches— Acts 5 and 8, 1, 3; Gal. 1:13; 1 Cor. 15:9; Phil. 3:6; (2) all the Churches in Judea, Samaria, and Galilee—Acts 9:31; (3) the local Church in Jerusalem—Acts 11:22, 12:1, 5, 15:4. In Thessalonica—1 Col. 1:1, 2 Col. 1:1. In Corinth—1 Cor. 1:2, 6:4, 14:12, 23; 2 Cor. 1:1; Rom. 16:23. In Kechries—Rom. 16. In Laodicea— Col. 4:16. In Antioch—Acts 13:1, 15:2. The seven Churches in Asia—Rev. 2 and 3. In Ephesus—Acts 11:21, 14:27, 20:17. 1 Tim. 5:16. In Caesarea—Acts 18:22, and in a similar sense Jas. 5:14, 3 Jn. 9:10. (4) The assembly of the local Church—Acts 15:22, 1 Cor. 14:33. 5) The house church in Ephesus—1 Cor. 16:19. In Rome—Rom. 16:9. In Collosae—Col. 4:15, Philem. 2.

The word ἐκκλησία in the singular without the article means: (1) each local Church in a given region—Acts 12:23; (2) every local Church in general—1 Cor. 14:4, 4:17, Phil. 4:15; (3) the assembly of a local Church—1 Cor. 14:29, 36, 11:18, Jn. 1:3, 6, 9.

Ἐκκλησία in the plural means: (1) the totality of all the local Churches of a particular district with specified or presumed names: in Judea—1 Thess. 2:14, Gal. 1:22. In Galatia—1 Cor. 16:1, Gal. 1:2. In Syria and Cilicia—Acts 15:41.

this is easily explained by the fact that the authors of the sacred books wrote them either to individual Christian communities or concerning individual Christian communities. For this reason the term ἐκκλησία, encountered comparatively often in the sense of a local Church, cannot contradict the fact that the chief and original meaning of the word ἐκκλησία is that of the Christian Church in totality.[49]

In Derbe and Lystra—Acts 16:5. In Macedonia—2 Cor. 8:1, 19. In Asia—1 Cor. 16:19, Rev. 1:4, 11, 20, 2:7, 11, 17, 29, 3:6, 13, 22, 22:16; (2) an indeterminate number of local Churches—2 Cor. 11:8, 28, 8:23–24, Rom. 16:4, 10; (3) the totality of all the local Churches—2 Thess. 1:4, 2 Cor. 7:17, 11:16, 14:32, 2 Cor. 12:13; (4) the assembly of all the local Churches—1 Cor. 15:24.

Ἐκκλησία in the singular signifies: (1) the one universal Church, which the local individual Church comprises—1 Cor. 10:32, 11:22, and, probably, 12:28; Acts 20:28, 1 Tim. 3:5, 15; (2) the one universal Church in the absolute—Col. 1:18, 24, Eph. 1:22, 3:10, 21, 5:23–25, 27, 29, 42, Mk. 16:18.

–V.N. Myshtsyn, *Organization of the Christian Church in the First Two Centuries* ["Устройство христианской Церкви в первые два века"] (Sergiev Posad: 1909), 432n. Vgl. *A Concordance of the Greek Testament*, Rev. W.F. Moulton and Rev. A.S. Geden, eds., 2nd ed. (Edinburgh: 1899), 316–317.

49 Worthy of particular note in this instance is the opinion of Cremer, which we think appropriate to cite here. "That ἐκκλησία initially meant the whole commonwealth (*die Gesammtgemeinde*) and only secondarily the individual community is clearly seen from the Old Testament basis, as well as from the founding words of Christ (Mt. 16:18), which are grounded in the basis of the Old Testament concept of תִדָעְ לָהָק. There is a conflicting opinion that ἐκκλησία initially signified a separate community, and that this alone gave rise to the later significance of the whole commonwealth, by which token the words of Christ (Mt. 16:18) would have to be declared inauthentic. This opinion is based on an ignorance of or disregard for the Old Testament basis of the word's usage, and is characteristic of the value of this operation of 'critical history'" (*Biblisch-theologisches Wörterbuch*[9], 550). Rudolph Sohm maintains that in the New Testament ἐκκλησία means only the universal Church, while the individual community is called ἐκκλησία only as a reflection of the one universal community. "There is only the one *ecclesia*, the assembly of **all Christianity as a whole**, but this one *ecclesia* manifests itself in innumerable forms. ... The local assembly or house community as such does not exist. That we can actually refer to the general assembly of the Christians of a given city as the assembly of a local community is not that it is as this assembly of the local community, but as a manifestation of the *ecclesia*, the assembly of the whole Christian nation. The assembly of the Christians of one locality bears the name *ecclesia* because it comprises the assembly not of this local community,

The term ἅγιοι ["holy," "saints"], by which Christians are frequently called in the New Testament apostolic epistles, is another
word that has its basis in the Old Testament,[50] corresponding to
the Hebrew שׁוֹדָק (qadosh "**holy**"). In the Old Testament, שׁוֹדק
is ordinarily applied to God, and it is applied to objects or people
only when they are intimately linked or dedicated to God. Hence,
the idea of sanctity in the Old Testament is explicitly linked with
the idea of the Hebrew nation being divinely chosen.[51] It is in this
sense of being chosen by God that the Hebrew nation is called
holy,[52] and sometimes the Jews themselves are called "holy ones,"
or saints—שׁוֹדים.[53] It is worthy of note that in the New Testament
likewise ἅγιοι is sometimes joined to κλητοί ["called"], ἐκλεκτοί
["elect"], and ἠγαπημένοι ["beloved"].[54]

---

but of all Christianity" (*Church Structure in the First Centuries of Christianity*, 40–41).
But naturally in this instance Sohm is proceeding from his own dogmatically
prejudiced views. In Sohm's opinion, the word ἐκκλησία in the New Testament
signifies not a phenomenon, but only an abstract concept.

50 The term ἅγιοι is used to signify Christians in Acts 9:13, 32, 1 Pet. 2:1,
Rom. 1:7, 15:25–27, 1 Cor. 6:2, 7:14, 2 Cor. 1:1–2, 13:12, 8:4, 9:1, 16:15, Col.
1:2, 4, 26, 3:12, Eph. 1:1, 4, 15, 2:29, 3:18, 5:3, Philem. 4:21–22, 1 Thess. 5:27,
1 Tim. 5:10, Tit. 2:3, Philem. 5, Heb. 3:1, 6:10.

51 Cremer, *Biblisch-theologisches Wörterbuch*[9], 44 ff., esp. 54.

52 Deut. 7:6, 14:2, 21, Ex. 19:6, Deut. 26:19, 28:9, etc.

53 שׁוֹדים (*qedoshim*) Deut. 33:3, Ps. 15:3, 33:10, Jer. 2:3, etc.

54 Col. 3:12, Rom. 1:7, 2 Cor. 1:2, 1 Pet. 1:1. "Inasmuch as believers are taken
out of the sinful world and received into communion with God the Redeemer
through the Holy Spirit, to them also the epithet ἅγιοι is applied" (S.M. Zarin, *Asceticism in Orthodox Christian Doctrine* ["Аскетизм по православно-христианскому
учению"], vol. 1, book 2 [Saint Petersburg: 1907], 19n). "The apostle Paul ascribes the initial significance of one 'initiated' and apportioned to the words ἅγιοι
and κλητοί ἅγιοι ["called saints"], without perfection of life being in complete
harmony with the loftiness of the calling. This is the meaning in which the majority of Old Testament writers use the Hebrew שׁוֹדק" (J. Meritan, *Revue biblique*
[1897], vol. 7, 348). Cf. also: Schanz, "Der Begriff der Kirche," *Theologische Quartalschrift* (1893), 547–548. Incidentally, Cremer denies any sense of chosenness in
the Hebrew שׁוֹדק. The idea of chosenness, he holds, is primarily highlighted by
the Old Testament term םידיסח (*hasidim* "faithful/loyal ones"–Ed.), which the
Seventy usually render as **ὅσιοι**, but this translation did not carry over into the
New Testament, and for this reason the New Testament *ἅγιοι*, in replacing שׁוֹדק

In this instance the expression of the apostle Peter stands out particularly: "Ye are a chosen generation, a royal priesthood, an holy nation, a peculiar people (γένος ἐκλεκτόν, βασίλειον ἱεράτευμα, ἔθνος ἅγιον, λαὸς εἰς περιποίησιν," 1 Pet. 2:9).[55] Here the Christian community is characterized by terms wholly taken from the Old Testament,[56] of which the latter expression—"a peculiar people"[57]—is particularly characteristic. In the books of the Old Testament the Hebrew nation is called the portion of Jehovah חֵלֶק הֹוָהי (heleq YHVH "portion of YHVH"–Ed.),[58] and the very term לֶבֶח (portion) conveys the idea of strict distinction and apartness.[59]

All these Old Testament designations of Christians tell us that in its early days the Church understood itself to be every bit as much a definite and actual entity as the Hebrew nation of the Old Testament had been. The New Testament writers, being Jews themselves, found it possible to call a new community, the Church, by Hebrew terms with which they were familiar. For this reason we may say that the Old Testament terminology as applied to the New Testament Church testifies to the prevailing clear **awareness of the unity of the Church** not only in a dogmatic sense, but in an actual one. The Church, so to speak, is the sole cord-measured **portion of God**.

Now that we have indicated the Old Testament basis for the terms by which the Church has called itself since the earliest days

---

and םידיסח, preserves in its meaning the idea of election. See Cremer, *Biblisch-the-ologisches Wörterbuch*[9], 57.

55 See 2 Pet. 1:10: "Ὑμῶν τὴν κλῆσιν καὶ ἐκλογὴν" ("your calling and election").

56 Is. 43:20–21, Ex. 19:5.

57 Other translations read "a purchased people" (DRB), "a people for God's own possession" (ESV), "a people belonging specially to God" (WNT). –*Trans.*

58 This is the rendering of Deuteronomy 32:9. The text as it was written was לֶבֶח םָדְהַ meaning "measuring line" (see footnote 59), not *hebel YHVH*. Deut. 32:9, Ex. 19:5, Deut. 4:20, 9:26, 29.

59 The Hebrew word לֶבֶח means a cord (Jos. 2:15)—in particular, a cord for measuring land (לֶבֶח םָדְהַ—Mic. 2:5, Zech. 2:5). Hence the meaning of a measured portion of land, or land bounded by specific borders (Jos. 19:9, Deut. 3:4, Jos. 18:5, Num. 18:20, 24, 32:19, Ruth 4:6, Wisd. 2:5, and many others).

of its existence, we will proceed to expound on the teaching of the apostle Paul concerning the Church. Other New Testament writers say very little of the Church, and for this reason we will not treat them separately, but will mention them concurrently as we expound on the teaching of the apostle Paul.[60]

The apostle Paul speaks of the Church in many of his epistles, sometimes in considerable detail. The apostle seems to have the idea of the Church ever before him, and as necessary, so far as circumstances require, expresses it in his epistles. At times the actual words of the apostle are not entirely plain, but his general idea of the Church is always clear. It is vain to seek a gradual development of the idea of the Church in the apostle's own words: in all his epistles that make any reference to the Church this idea is so permeated with wholeness and oneness as to preclude any discussion of there being a gradual development of the idea of the Church in the apostle's own writings. Only the external form of speech changes depending on the circumstances and the various needs of the readers of the apostolic epistles. The teaching concerning the Church remains constant.[61]

Most frequently the apostle Paul calls the Church the **Body** (σῶμα).[62]

From this alone, that the Church is called the Body, its two chief properties may be inferred. First of all, a body is an organism. All members of a body are inseparably united into one. One blood flows throughout the whole body; all the members of the body are united to each other by their very existence. An individual member of the body lives and develops not by itself, but only in an organic connection with the whole body. A body is not a random mechanical collection of members, each isolated in its own life, but rather it is explicitly a single organism with a single, indivisible life.

---

60 Certain expressions of the apostle Paul require further explanation in order to be correctly understood. For this reason we will accompany our elucidation of the apostle Paul's teaching concerning the Church with certain exegetical notes.

61 Cf. reasoning of J. Meritan, *Revue biblique* (1898), vol. 7, 343–344, 353.

62 Rom. 12:4–5, 1 Cor. 6:15, 10:17, 12:13, 27, Eph. 1:23, 4:4, 12, 16, 25, 5:23, 30, Col. 1:18, 21, 2:19, 3:15.

On the other hand, a body is not something self-sufficient. Organic life is inherent in the body, but this is by no means sufficient for the body to live. There must be a spirit that enlivens the body. In Holy Scripture the body is in fact perceived as an organ of the spirit. The human spirit lives "in this tabernacle," and also departs from it.

Both these features—the organic link between the individual members and the need for an enlivening Spirit—the apostle Paul expounds with application to the Church.

In his epistle to the Ephesians the apostle Paul determines who becomes a member of the Church. To the gentiles he writes: "Wherefore remember, that ye being in time past Gentiles in the flesh, who are called Uncircumcision by that which is called the Circumcision in the flesh made by hands; that at that time ye were without Christ, being aliens from the commonwealth of Israel, and strangers from the covenants of promise, having no hope, and without God in the world: but now in Christ Jesus ye who sometimes were far off are made nigh by the blood of Christ. For he is our peace, who hath made both one, and hath broken down the middle wall of partition between us; having abolished in his flesh the enmity, even the law of commandments contained in ordinances; for to make in himself of twain one new man, so making peace; and that he might reconcile both unto God in one body by the cross, having slain the enmity thereby: and came and preached peace to you which were afar off, and to them that were nigh. For through him we both have access by one Spirit unto the Father" (Eph. 2:11–18).

In these words of the apostle Paul we perceive the following ideas. Before Christ came into the world, the Jews were the chosen people—πολιτεία τοῦ Ἰσραήλ ["commonwealth of Israel"]. The Jews enjoyed great advantages[63] that the gentiles lacked, from which the latter were estranged.[64] The promises were contracted in

---

63 See Rom. 9:4–5.

64 "Χωρὶς Χριστοῦ ["without Christ"]. Χωρίς indicates the loss of something by removal from that object. The apostle is referring not to the Gentile readers of the epistle, but to the Gentiles in general as a whole." (Prof. D.I. Bogdashevsky, *The Epistle of the Holy Apostle Paul to the Ephesians* ["Послание св. ап. Павла к

the Hebrew nation, which came to be theocratically structured,[65] while the gentiles were godless people who served creation (cf. Rom. 1:25).[66] The law was given to the Jews alone (νόμος τῶν ἐντολῶν [law of commandments]), and this law was the subject of enmity between them and the gentiles: it stood like a wall between gentiles and Jews (τὸ μεσότοιχον τοῦ φραγμοῦ [the middle wall of partition]).[67] And so it was until the coming of Christ. But Christ by His dogmas and ideals abolishes the Old Testament νόμος ἐντολῶν [law of commandments], the law that determines all things and that punished for all things, which only served to reveal human weakness and merely brought the Old Testament people to a realization of the need for another means of justification. In place of the law, with its commandments inscribed on tablets of stone, a law is given which is written on "tables of the heart" (2 Cor. 3:3), a law "of faith ... the law of the Spirit of life" (Rom. 3:27, 8:2). Christ's death on the cross opened a new path of salvation.[68] It is on this path that the distinction between Jews and gentiles is destroyed, both Jews and gentiles becoming **one**—τὰ ἀμφότερα ἕν. Of Jews and gentiles a **new man** is made (τοὺς δύο. . . εἰς ἕνα καινὸν ἄνθρωπον), so that the gentiles are made fellow heirs with the Jews, participants in the promises, and together with them they comprise **one Body.**[69]

Ефесянам"] [Kiev: 1904], 383.)

65 See Bogdashevsky, op. cit., 385.

66 Bogdashevsky, *The Epistle of the Holy Apostle Paul to the Ephesians* (Kiev: 1904), 383–389.

67 See the explanation of Eph. 2:14–15 by Prof. Bogdashevsky, op. cit., 391–404. See Bishop Theophan, *Explanation of the Epistle of the Holy Apostle Paul to the Ephesians* ["Толкование Послания св. апостола Павла к Ефесеям"], 2nd ed. (Moscow: 1893), 173: "The wall of God's people was the law by which they served God and pleased Him, and by which they were justified before Him of their sins and drew near to Him. But this same law served as a wall that partitioned God's people off from other nations, so that neither the former nor the latter could join together in any way."

68 See Rom. 10:4, Col. 2:14; Prof. Bogdashevsky, op. cit., 402–407; Bp. Theophan, op. cit., 173–174, 178.

69 Cf. Rom. 9:21–26. Eph. 2:16 contains this expression: "That he might reconcile both ... in one body" ("καὶ ἀποκαταλλάξῃ τοὺς ἀμφοτέρους ἐν ἑνὶ

In the writings of St. John Chrysostom we find a profound and quite exhaustive explanation of these last words of the apostle. "What is this, 'both one?' He does not mean this, that He hath raised us to that high descent of theirs, but that he hath raised both us and them to a yet higher. ... The promise indeed He gave to the Israelites, but they were unworthy; to us He gave no promise, nay,

---

σώματι"). Certain exegetes understand ἐν σῶμα [one body] to mean the Church, thereby combining ἐν σῶμα in verse 16 with εἰς καινὸς ἄνθρωπος [one new man] in verse 15. Concerning this see Prof. Bogdashevsky, op. cit., 407. But in New Testament word usage, nouns with the preposition ἐν [in] are quite frequently inserted to denote *dativus instrumentalis* (cf. Friedrich Blass, *Grammatik des Neutestamentliche Griechisch* [Göttingen: 1896], §38.1 t.g. 41.1, 114–115, 127). By comparison with Col. 1:20–22 and 1 Pet. 2:24, ἐν σῶμα [one body] should be understood to mean the Body of Christ, which served to reconcile gentiles and Jews. The ancient commentators of the Church understood the expression to mean exactly this. (See for example St. John Chrysostom, *Homilies on Ephesians* 5.3: "'In one body,' saith he, and that His own, 'unto God.' How is this effected? By Himself, he means, suffering the due penalty." [The Russian source adds the words "on the Cross. –*Trans.*] [NPNF[1] 13:73.] St. Ephraim the Syrian: "And He reconciled both in one body, which is slain for both" (*Works*, part 7 [MTA: 1895], 184–185 [Rus. ed.]). St. John of Damascus, *On the Epistle to the Ephesians* (PG 95:833a). But naturally the idea that Jews and gentiles were united in one Body, in the sense of one Church, is by no means foreign to the apostle. In Eph. 3:6 the apostle calls the gentiles σύσσωμα [of the same body]. "Insomuch as he called the faithful one Body," writes the blessed Theodoret, "he says that the gentiles were made of one body with them" (*Works*, part 7 [Moscow: 1861], 430 [Rus. ed.]). See also Prof. Bogdashevsky, op. cit., 441–442. In interpreting Eph. 2:16, Bl. Theodoret likewise combines the two ideas: "He reconciled both, that is, those who believed from among the gentiles and the Jews, in one Body, offered for all, so that they might comprise one Body. And the apostle called all believers one man because all have one Head—the Master Christ—and the Body is comprised of those who have been vouchsafed salvation" (*Works*, part 7, 427–428 [Rus. ed.]). Ecumenius asserts the same: "ἐν τῇ σαρκί · τουτέστι, διὰ τῆς σαρκὸς αὐτοῦ" ["in the flesh, that is, through his flesh"] (PG 118:1197a). "ἐν ἑνὶ σώματι τῷ Θεῷ. Οἶον γινομένους ἐν σῶμα, οὗ αὐτός ἐστι κεφαλή" ["in one body, God; that is to say, them becoming one body, of which He is the head"] (PG 118:1197c). Mansvetov likewise combines both these ideas (*The New Testament Teaching on the Church*, 70–71), although the author offers no exegesis. Bl. Theophylact follows Chrysostom, but cites the opinion of several [other commentators]: "Both, who had become as though one Body, of which He is the Head, He reconciled with God" (*Explanation of the Epistle to the Galatians, Ephesians, and Philippians* ["Толкование на послания к Галатам, Ефесеям и Филиппийцам"] [Kazan: 1884], 107).

we were even strangers, we had nothing in common with them; yet
hath He made us one, not by knitting us to them, but by knitting
both them and us together into one."[70] "It is not that the Gentile
is become a Jew, but that both the one and the other are entered
into another condition. ... Laying hold on the one hand of the Jew,
and on the other of the Gentile, and Himself being in the midst,
[Christ] blended them together, made all the estrangement which
existed between them to disappear, and fashioned them anew from
above by fire and by water; no longer with water and earth, but with
water and fire. ... He became a Jew by circumcision, He became
accursed, He became a Gentile without the law, and was over both
Gentiles and Jews. 'One new man,' saith he, 'so making peace.'
Peace for them both towards God, and towards each other.[71] For
so long as they continued still Jews and Gentiles, they could not
have been reconciled. And had they not been delivered each from
his own peculiar condition, they would not have arrived at another
and a higher one. For the Jew is then united to the Gentile when
he becomes a believer. It is like persons being in a house, with two
chambers below, and one large and grand one above: they would
not be able to see each other, till they had got above."[72]

---

70 John Chrysostom, *Homilies on Ephesians* 5.2 (NPNF[1] 13:71). And further: "I
will give you an illustration. Let us suppose there to be two statues, the one of
silver, the other of lead, and then that both shall be melted down, and that the
two shall come out gold. Behold, thus hath He made the two one. Or put the case
again in another way. Let the two be, one a slave, the other an adopted son: and
let both offend Him, the one as a disinherited child, the other as a fugitive, and
one who never knew a father. Then let both be made heirs, both trueborn sons.
Behold, they are exalted to one and the same dignity, the two are become one,
the one coming from a longer, the other from a nearer distance, and the slave
becoming more noble than he was before he offended." [In the Russian source,
the text reads: "the only difference being that ... the one who was nearer reached
the Father first." –*Trans.*].

71 In the Russian source the meaning of the last three sentences differs significantly: "He transfigured both the Jew, who who was circumcised and under the
curse, and the Greek, who was outside the law, **into one new man** more exalted
than both the Jew and the Greek." –*Trans.*

72 Chrysostom, *Homilies on Ephesians* 5.3 (NPNF[1] 13:72–73).

The apostle Paul briefly reiterates the same idea as in the epistle to the Ephesians in other passages as well, when he says that "if any man be in Christ, he is a new creature (καινὴ κτίσις)" (2 Cor. 5:17), and that "in Christ Jesus neither circumcision availeth any thing, nor uncircumcision, but a new creature (καινὴ κτίσις)" (Gal. 6:15). "There is neither Jew nor Greek, there is neither bond nor free, there is neither male nor female: for ye are **all one** in Christ Jesus" (Gal. 3:28). The new man lacks both the national and the social distinctions of the old man.[73] For the apostle, the Church of God is one new community, outside of which the Jews and the Greeks stand in their isolation.[74]

Finally, in this same new existence—that is, in the Church—the apostle Paul also includes the triumphant synaxis of the "church of the firstborn, which are written in heaven, and to God the Judge of all, and to the spirits of just men made perfect" (Heb. 12:23). Christ is master of both the living and the dead,[75] and by His Cross He reconciled "things in earth [and] things in heaven" (Col. 1:20).[76]

It is this **new existence of mankind that the apostle calls the Church and characterizes as a Body**.[77] This comparison

---

73 See Col. 3:9–11. Regarding the catholicity of the Church as taught by the apostle Paul, J. Meritan notes: "It is apparent that Paul does not view catholicity as a mere quality among Jews and gentiles converted to the bosom of the Christian commonwealth. Perfect equality becomes a reality after the death of Christ, and the promises of old, since they presupposed an inequality of states, have no more reason for existence. In a divine sense the apostle sees all nations as equally called, and only one humanity in Christ and through Christ" (*Revue biblique*, vol. 7 [1893], 357. Cf. 355–356.). But St. John Chrysostom, in speaking of the elevation of all mankind to a new higher state, delves more deeply into the thinking of the apostle.

74 1 Cor. 10:32: "Give none offence, neither to the Jews, nor to the Gentiles, nor to the church of God."

75 See Rom. 14:9.

76 "What is this one body? The faithful throughout the whole world, both which are, and which have been, and which shall be" (Chrysostom, *Homilies on Ephesians* 10 [NPNF¹ 13:99]).

77 See Archpriest Evgeny Akvilonov (*The Church* ["Церковь"], 229–239) for a detailed elucidation of the concept of the Body; however, this elucidation is given here independently of the text of the epistles of the apostle Paul.

of the Church with a body the apostle himself elucidates in greater detail on several occasions.[78] "Many"—that is, all who enter the Church—"are one body in Christ, and every one members one of another" (Rom. 12:5). "The body is one, and hath many members, and all the members of that one body, being many, are one body. ... The body is not one member, but many. If the foot shall say, Because I am not the hand, I am not of the body; is it therefore not of the body? And if the ear shall say, Because I am not the eye, I am not of the body; is it therefore not of the body? ... God [hath] set the members every one of them in the body, as it hath pleased him" (1 Cor. 12:12, 14–16, 18). "We have many members in one body, and all members have not the same office" (Rom. 12:4).[79] "The eye cannot say unto the hand, I have no need of thee: nor again the head to the feet, I have no need of you. ... God hath tempered the body together, having given more abundant honour to that part which lacked. That there should be no schism in the body; but that the members should have the same care one for another. And whether one member suffer, all the members suffer with it; or one member be honoured, all the members rejoice with it. ... And God hath set some in the church, first apostles, secondarily prophets, thirdly teachers, after that miracles, then gifts of healings, helps, governments, diversities of tongues" (1 Cor. 12:21, 24–26, 28).[80]

---

78 In his writings the apostle Paul likewise compares the Church with a tree. See Rom. 11:17–24.

79 "As the members of the body differ in their function, so also the grace-filled gifts of the Spirit are varied and diverse." (St. Ephraim the Syrian, *Works*, part 7, 50 [Rus. ed.]). "By the example of the body and its members he lays low the great haughtiness of pretentiousness" (Bl. Theophylact, *Explanation of the Epistle to the Romans* ["Толкование на Послание к Римлянам"] [Kazan: 1866], 168).

80 Cf. Rom. 12:6: "[We have] gifts differing according to the grace that is given to us ... according to the proportion of faith." "In order to humble those who exalt themselves, he says that this is given by God, and he calls this 'gifts'; and in order to rouse the slothful he shows, conversely, that we also contribute something, and he says: 'whether prophecy ... according to the proportion of faith.' [In the Russian, 'if prophecy, according to the measure of faith.' —*Trans.*] Though grace, it is not simply poured out, but rather He pours it out in the measure to which the vessel of faith presented to receive it is able to hold" (Bl. Theophylact, *Explanation of the Epistle to the Romans*, 169 [Rus. ed.]). Theophylact echoes John

According to the apostle, this bodily union of men in the one Body of the Church is possible because a **new principle for life** has been given. This is not the Jewish law or civil laws, which unite only outwardly. Divine **power,**[81] **the Holy Spirit,** has been bestowed for life and piety. Both gentiles and Jews have "access by one Spirit unto [God] the Father" (Eph. 2:18). In the epistle to the Ephesians, in passing the apostle compares the Church with a building. It is a "building fitly framed together," built up as "an habitation of God through the Spirit" (Eph. 2:21–22)[82]—that is, through the action of the Holy Spirit. Just as the individual members of a body each have their own special meaning and their own special purpose, so also in the body of the Church each member has his own gift. The very name *gift* indicates that it is not of natural origin, that it does not result from man's natural strength and abilities, but that it is something higher. The apostle Paul views all the Christian virtues as a manifestation of the one Holy Spirit. "There are diversities of gifts, but the same Spirit. ... The manifestation of the Spirit is given to every man to profit withal. For to one is given by the Spirit the word of wisdom; to another the word of knowledge by the same Spirit; to another faith by the same Spirit; to another the gifts of healing by the same Spirit; to another the working of miracles; to another prophecy; to another discerning of spirits; to another divers kinds of tongues ... all these worketh that one and the selfsame Spirit, dividing to every man severally as he will" (1 Cor. 12:4, 7–11). In the epistle to the Romans the apostle lists ministering, ruling, and almsgiving as gifts of the Spirit.[83] To the mind of the apostle, in the Church there are no gifts that would serve each person in isolation;

Chrysostom (see Chrysostom, *Homilies on Romans* 21 [NPNF¹ 11:501–506]). Concerning the division of spiritual gifts the apostle Paul writes [in more detail] in 1 Cor. 12:1–11.

81 See 2 Pet. 1:3: "πάντα ἡμῖν τῆς θείας δυνάμεως αὐτοῦ τὰ πρὸς ζωὴν καὶ εὐσέβειαν δεδωρημένης" ("his divine power hath given unto us all things that pertain unto life and godliness").

82 Bogdashevsky, *Epistle of the Holy Apostle Paul to the Ephesians,* 425.

83 See Rom. 12:6–8.

rather, all gifts serve for the common benefit of the whole Church.[84] With regard to the Source they are **gifts**; with regard to the Church they are **ministries**.[85] Each ministry is a "**manifestation of the Spirit** (ἡ φανέρωσις τοῦ πνεύματος)" (1 Cor. 12:7).[86] And herein lies the source of the oneness of all in the Church. "By one Spirit are ... all baptized into one body ... and have been all made to drink into one Spirit (εἰς ἓν πνεῦμα)" (1 Cor. 12:13).[87] The apostle seems especially desirous of drawing attention to the oneness of the Source of all good works performed for the common benefit of the

---

84 "Although we have the grace of diverse gifts, nevertheless they are all given for service to the Church." (St. Ephraim the Syrian, *Works*, part 7, 50 [Rus. ed.]). "Why then one more, and another less? There is nothing to cause this [in the Russian, "this is of no significance" –*Trans.*], he would say, but the matter itself is indifferent; for every one contributes towards 'the building.' And by this too he shows, that it is not of his own intrinsic merit that one has received more and another less, but that it is for the sake of others." (John Chrysostom, *Homilies on Ephesians* 11 [NPNF[1] 13:103].) See Bl. Theodoret, *Works*, part 7, 256 [Rus. ed.].

85 The apostle Peter expressed this idea particularly beautifully: "Ἕκαστος καθὼς ἔλαβε χάρισμα, εἰς ἑαυτοὺς αὐτὸ διακονοῦντες ὡς καλοὶ οἰκονόμοι ποικίλης χάριτος" ("As every man hath received the gift, even so minister the same one to another, as good stewards of the manifold grace," 1 Pet. 4:10). See Rom. 12:7. Here, ministry is taken in the general sense: apostleship is called ministry, and every good spiritual work is also ministry. Naturally, this term is also employed to signify private activity, but here it is used generally (cf. St. John Chrysostom, *Homilies on Romans* 21 [NPNF[1] 11:501]). "He calls them not virtues, but gifts. 'That which you have received,' he says, 'is a gift from God, and not your doing: grace has given it to you. ... By ministry understand every spiritual work in general." (Bl. Theophylact, *Explanation of the Epistle to the Romans*, 169–170 [Rus. ed.]). "He said this of the ministries so as to more greatly console the sorrowing. For on hearing the name *gift* and receiving less, he might sorrow that he was cheated in the giving. But not so on hearing of a *ministry*, for this suggests labor and sweat. Why do you sorrow when He has commanded others to labor more, and has spared you?" (Bl. Theophylact, *Exposition of the Epistle to the Corinthians* ["Толкование на Послание к Коринфянам"], 153 [Rus. ed.]).

86 "Gift, action, and ministry are all the same. The difference is solely one of words, but the things are the same. What is a gift is also a ministry, and what is a ministry is also action" (Saint John of Damascus, *On the Epistle to the Corinthians* 1 [PG 95:664d–665a]).

87 "He instructs as to why all we believers are called one Body" (Bl. Theodoret, *Works*, part 7, 257 [Rus. ed.]).

Church. In listing the spiritual gifts, as we have seen, after each of
them the apostles indicates the Source of the gift—the Holy Spirit.
Each gift is bestowed specifically by the same one Holy Spirit—ἐν
τῷ αὐτῷ πνεύματι. "Everywhere the apostle appends the words:
'**in the same Spirit**,' '**by the same Spirit**,' thereby teaching
that the issues are diverse, but the Source is indubitably one."[88] In
concluding his enumeration of the gifts, the apostle again repeats:
"All these worketh that one and the selfsame Spirit (πάντα δὲ ταῦτα
ἐνεργεῖ τὸ ἓν καὶ τὸ αὐτὸ πνεῦμα)" (1 Cor. 12:11).[89]

In other passages, in defining the Church the apostle Paul says
that it is not only **one Body**, but also **one Spirit**. To the Ephesians
the apostle Paul writes that they strive to preserve oneness of Spirit,
and he calls the Church one Body and one Spirit.[90] Here the holy
fathers see not oneness of mind or oneness of heart and oneness of
religious convictions, as certain Western exegetes would interpret
this,[91] but the **one Spirit of God,** which permeates the Body of
the Church, and this is in keeping with the text.[92] "What is this

---

88 Bl. Theodoret, *Works,* part 7, 256 (Rus. ed.).

89 "He said not merely 'the Spirit,' but: 'one and the same Spirit,' teaching
that some gifts do not come from one spirit, and others from another, but that
both these the others are of one Spirit" (Bl. Theodoret, *Works,* part 7, 256–257
[Rus. ed.]).

90 Cf. Eph. 4:3–4.

91 Prof. D.I. Bogdashevsky, *Epistle of the Holy Apostle Paul to the Ephesians,* 504n5.
Cf. Meritan: "This probably refers not to the soul of each member severally, but
rather to the life spirit of the Church, to the πνεῦμα [spirit], which is the source
of common life. When this spirit is present and acts within a person, he invariably
unites with his brethren, at least in spirit. Ἑν σῶμα καὶ ἓν πνεῦμα [One body and
one spirit], Paul reasons, are two interdependent things. This is because only one
πνεῦμα enlivens all the members, so that the Body might be one" (*Revue biblique,*
vol. 7, 363).

92 Greek text: Σπουδάζοντες τηρεῖν τὴν ἑνότητα τοῦ πνεύματος [Endeavour-
ing to keep the unity of the Spirit]—text. recept. specifically reads Πνεύματος,
with a capital letter. The apostle Paul does not use πνεῦμα to signify likemind-
edness; this he signifies with words derived from ψυχή. Like-minded—σύμψυχοι
(Phil. 2:2), in one spirit—μιᾷ ψυχῇ (Phil. 1:27). Cf. "one soul"—ψυχὴ μία (Acts
4:32). Frequently in the New Testament the word ὁμοθυμαδὸν ["with one accord"] is used: Acts 1:14, 2:46, 4:24, 5:12, 7:57, 8:6, 12:20, 15:25, 18:19; Rom.

'unity of Spirit?' In the human body there is a spirit which holds all together, though in different members. So is it also here; for to this end was the Spirit given, that He might unite those who are separated by race and by different manners."[93] "He is, by this expression, shaming them into unanimity, saying, as it were, 'Ye who have received one Spirit, and have been made to drink at one fountain, ought not to be divided in mind.'"[94] Blessed Theophylact of Bulgaria expresses the same idea in clearer form: "As in the body the spirit is a principle that connects and unites everything, though the members are different, so also in believers there is the Holy Spirit, Who unites all, though we differ from one another by descent, by customs, and by occupations."[95] "All of you have been vouchsafed one grace; one Source pours forth diverse streams. You have received one Spirit, and you comprise one Body."[96] "One body in the sense of the Body of Christ, which is the Church; and one Holy

---

15:6.

93 St. John Chrysostom, *Homilies on Ephesians* 9 (NPNF[1] 13:97). In the Russian translation, "spirit" is replaced with "soul," although in the Greek text πνεῦμα is used. (PG 62:72.)

94 St. John Chrysostom, *Homilies on Ephesians* 11 (NPNF[1] 13:102). As we see, Chrysostom combines both interpretations, but in his own interpretation also like-mindedness has as its basis the one Spirit of God. Patriarch Photius clearly expresses this idea of Chrysostom when he writes: "Σπουδάζοντες ἀλλήλους τηρεῖν καὶ φυλάττειν ἐν σῶμα καὶ ἓν πνεῦμα κατὰ τὴν ἑνότητα τοῦ πνεύματος, καθὼς ἡμᾶς τὸ ἅγιον ἥνωσε πνεῦμα, καθὼς καὶ ἐκκλήθητε [endeavouring to keep one another and to guard one body and one spirit according to the unity of the spirit, just as the Holy Spirit united us, just as ye were also called" (PG 118:1213c). The blessed Jerome makes the same connection between like-mindedness and oneness of the Holy Spirit: "Rightly it is said to the Ephesians, who were already pursuing unity of the Holy Spirit, 'endeavoring to keep the unity of the Spirit in the bond of peace.' For a person who is exhorted to endeavor to preserve something is a person who has something" (*Works*, book 17, 296 [Rus. ed.]). Bishop Theophan likewise combines the two explanations (*Explanation of the Epistle to the Ephesians*, 266–269 [Rus. ed.]). But on page 270 he writes: "Such is the essence of Christianity that those who confess it are one; that all believers comprise **one** living Body of living members, in Which **one** Spirit dwells."

95 Blessed Theophylact, *Explanation of the Epistle to the Ephesians*, 123. We find the same almost verbatim in the writings of Photius (PG 118:1213).

96 Blessed Theodoret, *Works*, part 7, 431 (Rus. ed.).

Spirit—specifically one Distributor and Sanctifier of all."[97] This
reading of the given passage is shared by Prof. D.I. Bogdashevsky:
"Unification of Spirit is a unity that the Spirit creates or produces.
Ἡ ἑνότης τοῦ Πνεύματος [the unity of the Spirit]—this is the unity
from the Spirit of God that abides in the Church."[98]

It is the Spirit of God, permeating the whole Body of the
Church, bestowing various gifts upon all the members of this Body,
Who makes new life possible for mankind. He "worketh [in us] both
to will and to do of his good pleasure" (Phil. 2:13). It is He that
unites all into one Body, and He does so specifically by filling hearts
with love, which in man's natural state cannot be the principle of
his life and his relations with other people. "Love is of God" (1 Jn.
4:7);[99] these words of the apostle John could serve as the theme of a
whole series of apostolic ideas. God "hath bestowed love upon us"
(cf. 1 Jn. 3:1); hence, love is frequently called "God" (ἡ ἀγάπη τοῦ
Θεοῦ [the love of God]).[100] "The love of Christ constraineth" the
members of the Church (2 Cor. 5:14), "and the Lord [directs the]
hearts [of all] into the love of God" (ὁ κύριος κατευθύναι ὑμῶν τὰς
καρδίας εἰς τὴν ἀγάπην τοῦ θεοῦ)" (2 Thess. 3:5). Finally, the apostle Paul says: "The fruit of the Spirit is love" (Gal. 5:22).[101] "The
love of God is shed abroad in our hearts by the Holy Ghost which
is given unto us" (Rom. 5:5).[102] God saved us by renewal of the
Holy Spirit (διὰ ἀνακαινώσεως Πνεύματος Ἁγίου), "which he shed
on us abundantly through Jesus Christ our Saviour" (Tit. 3:5–6).[103]

---

97 Blessed Jerome, *Works*, part 7, 297 (Rus. ed.).

98 Bogdashevsky, *Epistle of the Holy Apostle Paul to the Ephesians*, 505.

99 See 1 Jn. 5:1, 19, 4:4: "Ὑμεῖς ἐκ τοῦ Θεοῦ ἐστε [Ye are of God]." 3 Jn. 11:
"He that doeth good is of God."

100 Jn. 5:42, 1 Jn. 2:5, 3:17, 5:3, Jud. 21, Rom. 5:5. Cf. 2 Cor. 13:13, 2 Thess.
3:5. This refers not to God's love for men, but to men's love for each other, and
this love is called God's.

101 See Rom. 15:30: "Διὰ τῆς ἀγάπης τοῦ Πνεύματος [for the love of the
Spirit]." Col. 1:8: "τὴν ὑμῶν ἀγάπην ἐν Πνεύματι [your love in the Spirit]."

102 "Ἡ ἀγάπη τοῦ Θεοῦ ἐκκέχυται ἐν ταῖς καρδίαις ἡμῶν διὰ Πνεύματος
Ἁγίου τοῦ δοθέντος ἡμῖν." See 1 Thess. 4:8.

103 Cf. 1 Jn. 3:24, 4:13, Rom. 8:11: "Ζωοποιήσει καὶ τὰ θνητὰ σώματα ὑμῶν

"As when a house is in a ruinous state no one places props under it, nor makes any addition to the old building, but pulls it down to its foundations, and rebuilds it anew; so in our case, God has not repaired us, but has made us anew. For this is 'the renewing of the Holy Ghost.' He has made us new men. How? 'By His Spirit.'"[104] In Christians there lives the Spirit of God, which is why they are able to live "not in the flesh, but in the Spirit" (Rom. 8:9):[105] they are led by the Spirit of God (Πνεύματι Θεοῦ ἄγονται).[106] Consequently, **the Holy Spirit dwelling in the Church gives the member of the Church the power to be a new creature, and to be governed by love in his life.**

The teaching of the apostle Paul concerning the Church as an organic unity of persons renewed by the Holy Spirit closely dovetails in this instance with his teaching on love as the basis for the chief principle of Christian life. This dovetailing is rarely observed by modern exegetes, but the holy fathers of the Church refer to it. For example, concerning the comparison of the Church with a body Blessed Theodoret says: "This likening befits the teaching on love."[107] And St. John Chrysostom, explaining the words concerning "one Body," says: "The love Paul requires of us is ... that which cements us together, and makes us cleave inseparably to one another, and effects as great and as perfect a union as though it were between limb and limb. For this is that love which produces great and glorious fruits."[108] Indeed, in reading the epistle of the apostle Paul we observe that in his writings the teaching on love is inseparably linked with the teaching on the Church. All Christian morality, to the apostle's mind, is grounded in the dogmatic doctrine concern-

---

διὰ τοῦ ἐνοικοῦντος αὐτοῦ πνεύματος ἐν ὑμῖν [he... shall also quicken your mortal bodies by his Spirit that dwelleth in you.]."

104 St. John Chrysostom, *Homilies on Titus* 5.3 (NPNF[1] 13:538). See Blessed Theodoret, *Works*, part 7, 742 (Rus. ed.).

105 See 2 Thess. 2:13: "Εἰς σωτηρίαν ἐν ἁγιασμῷ πνεύματος [to salvation through sanctification of the Spirit]."

106 See Rom. 8:14. See Jn. 16:13.

107 Theodoret, *Works*, part 7, 134 (Rus. ed.).

108 Chrysostom, *Homilies on Ephesians* 11.1 (NPNF[1] 13:102).

ing the Church. For example, in the epistle to the Romans the apostle precedes his expansive discourses on Christian morality[109] with a brief teaching on the Church as a Body.[110] In the first epistle to the Corinthians the teaching on the Church[111] is followed by a "New Testament ode to love."[112] In the epistles to the Ephesians and the Colossians the apostle Paul combines three ideas: (1) the gentiles led an impious way of life;[113] (2) in the Church they, together with the Jews, become a new creature; and (3) in the Church they now live according to love.[114]

Thus, the Church is what the apostle Paul calls the new creature, living according to the love of Christ; but this new creature he also places in close relation to Christ Himself. The apostle calls the Church a Body, and this name already suggests a Head. "Christ is the head of the church" (Eph. 5:23). In the epistle to the Ephesians the apostle delivers a solemn discourse depicting the greatness of Christ. God "raised him from the dead, and set him at his own right hand in the heavenly places, far above all principality, and power, and might, and dominion, and every name that is named, not only in this world, but also in that which is to come: and hath put all things under his feet, and gave him to be the head over all things to the church, which is his body" (Eph. 1:20–23).[115]

---

109 See Rom. 12:9–15.

110 See Rom. 12:4–8.

111 See 1 Cor. 12:12–30.

112 See 1 Cor. 13:1–13.

113 See Eph. 4:17–19, 5:8, 11–14, Col. 2:13, 3:5–7. See 1 Pet. 4:3–5.

114 See Eph. 4:20–6:8, Col. 3:1–5, 7–17, esp. 3:14: "Ἐπὶ πᾶσι δὲ τούτοις τὴν ἀγάπην, ἥτις ἐστὶ σύνδεσμος τῆς τελειότητος [And above all these things... charity, which is the bond of perfectness]." Cf. also: 1 Pet. 4:8–11. In the writings of the apostle Peter likewise, Christian life which has love as its basis is contrasted to pagan life, but he offers no connected teaching regarding the Church.

115 For a philological analysis of verse 22 ("καὶ αὐτὸν ἔδωκε κεφαλὴν ὑπὲρ πάντα τῇ ἐκκλησίᾳ"), see Bogdashevsky, Epistle of the Holy Apostle Paul to the Ephesians, 325–326. See Eph. 5:30: "We are members of his body, of his flesh, and of his bones."

Such is the Head that God gave the Church! "Amazing again, whither hath He raised the Church? as though he were lifting it up by some engine, he hath raised it up to a vast height, and set it on yonder throne; for where the Head is, there is the body also."[116] The new existence, comprising as it were a single organism, is headed by Christ. Here in the teaching of the apostle Paul soteriology intersects with ecclesiology. Christ is the New Adam of the saved human race,[117] which comprises the Church, "the Savior of the body (σωτὴρ τοῦ σώματος)" (Eph. 5:23). This new human race, or the Church, is especially closely linked to its Head, which the apostle seems to repeat twice in a row. He says that Christ is the Head of the Church, but then he also adds that the Church is the Body of Christ. In different forms the same idea is expressed concerning the close link between Christ and the Church.[118]

---

116 Chrysostom, *Homilies on Ephesians* 3 (NPNF[1] 13:62). "What is meant by 'over all things?'" Chrysostom goes on to ask. "Either that Christ is above all that is visible and contemplated with the mind, or that the highest of all the benefactions He has rendered is that He made His Son the Head." [This excerpt is missing from the English source; translation by current translator. −*Trans.*] St. Isidore of Pelusium: "In addition to all the other gifts (ὑπὲρ τὰ ἄλλα πάντα χαρίσματα), He also gave to her that Christ is her Head" (PG 78:880d). Bishop Theophan also says: "God exalted mankind in the person of the Savior; but highest of all is that He gave Him to be the Head of the Church" (*Explanation of the Epistle to the Ephesians,* 122). Bishop Theophan also presents a different explanation of the words ὑπὲρ πάντα ["over" or "in addition to all things"]: "By understanding πάντα [all things] to mean all classes of creatures, we may [say] thus: all is subject to Him, but He is the Head of the Church alone. Bypassing all other creatures, God made Him the head of the Church alone, joining Him in a living union only with the Church" (ibid.). But the prefix ὑπέρ, Prof. Bogdashevsky observes, can have no such meaning (op. cit., 326n5).

117 See 1 Cor. 15:22, 45. See Rom. 5:14, 17–19, 21. "But not only in this way hath He honored us, in exalting that which is of ourselves, but also in that He hath prepared the whole race in common to follow Him, to cling to Him, to accompany His train" [The Russian differs somewhat: "to follow Him, to have that which He had, and to inherit His glory" −*Trans.*] (Chrysostom, *Homilies on Ephesians* 3.2 [NPNF[1] 13:62]). Bishop Theophan writes the same: "We had fallen away. God the Word takes on humanity that He might reunite it with God" (op. cit., 123 [Rus. ed.]).

118 In this regard St. John Chrysostom observes: "In order then that when

This closeness of the Church to Christ the apostle likewise depicts in the same epistle to the Ephesians: the apostle not only likens the relationship between the Church and Christ to that between the body and the head, but to the words "which is his body" he also adds "the fullness of him that filleth all in all (τὸ πλήρωμα τοῦ τὰ πάντα ἐν πᾶσι πληρουμένου)" (Eph. 1:23). "For all commentators these words comprise a sort of exegetical *crux*."[119] It is clear that by these words the apostle is lending emphasis to his discourse on the closeness of Christ to the Church, but the question is how to understand πλήρωμα [fullness]. Just prior to these words the apostle mentioned the Church, and so it is natural to see the Church in τὸ πλήρωμα [the fullness]. But in what sense are we to understand the word τὸ πλήρωμα itself? Is its meaning here active or passive? If the word τὸ πλήρωμα is ascribed an active significance, the resulting idea is that **the Church is the fullness of Christ,** or the fulfillment of Christ— τοῦ πάντα ἐν πᾶσι πληρουμένου [of him that filleth all in all].

This explanation of this passage is accepted by St. John Chrysostom, who writes: "'The fullness of Christ is the Church.' And rightly, for the complement of the head is the body, and the complement of the body is the head. ... [The apostle] introduces [Christ, the head] as having need of each single one and not only of all in common and together; for unless we be many, and one be the hand, and another the foot, and another some other member, the whole body is not filled up. It is by all then that His body is filled up. Then is the head filled up, then is the body rendered perfect, when we are all knit together and united."[120] Chrysostom's commentary

---

you hear of the Head you may not conceive the notion of supremacy only, but also of consolidation, and that you may behold Him not as supreme Ruler only, but as [the actual] Head of a body[, the apostle adds:] 'The fullness of Him that filleth all in all.' ... As though this [the name of 'Head'] were not sufficient to show the close connection and relationship [of the Church to Christ]." (St. John Chrysostom, *Homilies on Ephesians* 3 [NPNF¹ 13:62].) Ecumenius likewise repeats this, adding: "σωματικῶς φησίν, ἡμῶν ἐστὶ κεφαλή [bodily, he says, he is our head]" (PG 118:1185c).

119 Bogdashevsky, op. cit., 33.

120 Chrysostom, *Homilies on Ephesians* 3.2 (NPNF¹ 13:62).

is echoed by Ecumenius[121] and Blessed Theophylact, of whom the latter explains Chrysostom's reasoning thus: "Christ is fulfilled and completed, as it were, by all the members in the person of all believers: He is fulfilled, as it were, by the hand in the person of the man who is merciful and who otherwise aids the weak; He is fulfilled, as it were, by the foot in the person of the man who undertakes a journey to preach and who looks after his brethren; and by another member He is fulfilled in another believer."[122] The blessed Jerome expresses this same idea more crudely, understanding it to mean the quantitative increase of the Church, the Body of Christ.[123] The idea of Christ being fulfilled by the Church is also clearly and distinctly expressed by Bishop Theophan: "The Church is the fulfillment of Christ, perhaps similarly to the way a tree is the fulfillment of a seed. That which the seed contains in reduced form, the tree manifests fully matured. ... In and of Himself He is complete and all-perfect, but He has not yet fully drawn mankind to Himself. It is gradually drawn into ever greater communion with Him, and through this it fulfills Him, as it were, through this enabling His work to come to complete fulfillment."[124]

Philologists disagree, however, as to the definition of πλήρωμα [fullness]. Some allow for an active meaning,[125] while others under-

---

121 PG 118:1185c.

122 Bl. Theophylact, *Explanation of the Epistle to the Ephesians*, 93–94.

123 "He did not say, 'Who filleth all in all,' but, 'Who is filled by all in all.' For it is one thing to fill, and another to be filled, since in the first case it signifies one who is acting, while in the second—one who is the object of an action. Indeed, as a general is augmented when his forces increase each day, new regions appear, and the size of the population increases, so also our Lord Jesus Christ Himself is filled in all in the sense that all believe in Him and come to faith in Him each day; but in such a way that He is filled by all in all—that is, that all who believe in Him are filled with all the virtues and, in accordance with the Gospel, enable Him (*faciunt eum*) to be perfected in maturity, wisdom, and grace not only with God, but also with men." (*Works*, part 17, 250 [Rus. ed.].)

124 Bl. Theophylact, *Explanation of the Epistle to the Ephesians*, 126–127. Incidentally, this idea also surfaces in the writings of Mansvetov (op. cit., 245).

125 Garless, Oltramar, et al. See Bogdashevsky, op. cit., 333–334n4. See Dr. S. Ch. Schirlitz, *Griechisch-Deutsches Wörterbuch zum Neuen Testamente*, 5-te Auflage,

stand πλήρωμα exclusively in the passive sense.[126] If the meaning of πλήρωμα is passive, the passage would mean that **the Church is fulfilled by Christ**. "The apostle calls the assembly of the faithful 'the Church': he calls it the Body of Christ and the fulfillment of the Father because the Father has filled it with every kind of gift and in it, as the prophet says, He lives and walks."[127] "All is filled by Him, and He in all."[128] "All believers comprise the Church and, being filled by God, make it to be filled by Him."[129] It is this interpretation, according to Prof. Bogdashevsky, that is the simplest and most natural. The Church is fullness, τὸ πεπληρωμένον, or, in a derivative sense, perfection—absolute perfection. This reference to the Church as πλήρωμα should be understood as an indication of its essence: it is filled—that is, fulfilled or perfected; it is the fullness of the power of Christ.[130]

---

neu bearbeitet von Dr. Th. Eger (Giessen: 1893), 339–340: "1) das, womit etwas erfüllt wird. 2) das, was erfüllt, vol, ganz ist."

126 Cremer, *Biblisch-theologisches Wörterbuch*, 878: "Stets im passiven Zinne, nur verschieden, je nachdem es auf das relative oder auf das absolute πληρουν zurückzuführen ist." Franciscus Zorell, *Novi Testamenti lexicon graecum* (Parisiis: 1911), 464: "πλήρωμα sec. etymologiam significat 'id quod τῷ πληροῦν producitur', i.e. τὸ πληρωμένον." The same is decisively stated by Prof. Bogdashevsky: "Like all words ending in μα and signifying abstract or concrete concepts, it is passive in meaning" (op. cit., 333).

127 Blessed Theodoret, part 7, 422. Thus, Blessed Theodoret understands τὰ τοῦ πάντα πληρωμένου to mean God the Father. Prof. Bogdashevsky refutes a similar interpretation by Erasmus, Vetshtein, and Meir (op. cit., 330 and n3).

128 Saint Ephraim the Syrian, *Works*, part 7, 182 (Rus. ed.).

129 Bishop Theophan, op. cit., 124. Bishop Theophan allows for the possibility of a third interpretation of the word πλήρωμα, applying it not to the Church, but to the Lord. This results in an idea paralleled in Col. 2:9: "In him dwelleth all the fullness (πλήρωμα) of the Godhead bodily." "God gave the Church a Head Who is above all things; for it is itself the fullness of the Godhead, the fullness of Him Who fills all things with Himself" (ibid.). Given τὰ τοῦ πάντα πληρωμένου, here also the subject is God the Father.

130 Op. cit., 336. The passive significance of πλήρωμα—without any analysis of the text—is also accepted by Mansvetov (*The New Testament Teaching Concerning the Church*, 90–91): "The apostle seemingly wishes to amplify his idea of inner intimate fellowship between Christ and the Church, representing this in the figure of the fulfillment (πλήρωμα) of the latter by the former." Here it should be noted

But if even if we accept the second interpretation of the passage in question, nevertheless we may append to it Chrysostom's idea, which contains nothing contradictory to the teaching of the apostle Paul. Professor Bogdashevsky offers a superb and quite grounded line of reasoning on the subject: "The thinking behind this interpretation (of Chrysostom) is quite profound, and it must not be completely ignored as being obviously baseless. With full force it emphasizes the intimate link between Christ and the Church, for the head is not separable from the body, but rather is inseparably connected to it, and the life of the body is not an indifferent matter for the head. It goes without saying that the fulfillment pertains not to the essence of Christ, Who is complete and all-perfect, but to the work of Christ, which is only fully realized through the Church. As the head is conceivable only when there is a body, so also the Savior and Redeemer is conceivable only when there are those who are saved and redeemed."[131]

The apostle Paul likewise depicts the relationship between Christ and the Church in the semblance of the relationship between husband and wife. This image was a familiar and even a kindred one for Paul. The books of the Old Testament quite frequently depicted the relationship between God and the Hebrew nation as the relationship between husband and wife, and the covenant between God and His people was like a marital union.[132] This same image is also adopted in the New Testament.[133] The apostle Paul discusses this image in particular detail when he speaks of marriage.

---

that the concept of the Church being filled with Christ closely dovetails with the apostle's earlier thought concerning the Church being filled with the Holy Spirit, which is expressed with particular clarity in the words of the apostle John: "That we dwell (μένομεν) in him, and he in us, because he hath given us of his Spirit (ὅτι ἐκ τοῦ πνεύματος αὐτοῦ δέδωκεν ἡμῖν)" (1 Jn. 4:13; cf. 3:24).

131 Op. cit., 333. Cf. the above words of His Grace Theophan. The first meaning of Eph. 1:23 is also allowed for by Franz Zorell (*Novi Testamenti lexicon graecum*, 464).

132 Deut. 32:19; Jer. 2:2, 3:20; Ezek. 16:32; Hos. 2:2; Mal. 2:14. Cf. Ex. 20:5, 34:14; Kgs. 10:6, 19:31; Ps. 77:58, 78:5; Is. 9:7, etc.

133 See 2 Cor. 11:2. With particular frequency the image of a bride is applied to the Church in Revelations: Rev. 19:7–8, 21:2, etc.

The marital union, according to the apostle, is holy in the degree to which it reflects the union between Christ and the Church. For this reason the apostle supports his every council regarding marriage with a reference to Christ and the Church. "The husband is the head of the wife, even as Christ is the head of the church: and he is the saviour of the body. Therefore as the church is subject unto Christ, so let the wives be to their own husbands in every thing. Husbands, love your wives, even as Christ also loved the church, and gave himself for it; that he might sanctify and cleanse it with the washing of water by the word, that he might present it to himself a glorious church, not having spot, or wrinkle, or any such thing; but that it should be holy and without blemish. ... For no man ever yet hated his own flesh; but nourisheth and cherisheth it, even as the Lord the church: for we are members of his body, of his flesh, and of his bones. ... This is a great mystery: but I speak concerning Christ and the church" (Eph. 5:23–27, 29–30, 32). Here Christ is presented as the renewer of human life: He founded and cleansed the Church, and He gave Himself for it so that it might be pure and without spot. In interpreting this passage the holy fathers give even more attention to the relationship between Christ and the Church than between husband and wife. In the same place the apostle Paul quotes Gen. 2:24: "For this cause shall a man leave his father and mother, and shall be joined unto his wife, and they two shall be one flesh." Many commentators of old understand these words allegorically in application to the union between Christ and the Church, taking the "mystery" in verse 32 to mean the mystical relationship between Christ and the Church.[134] "For the present ... saith he, I speak regarding Christ, that having left the Father, He came down, and came to the Bride, and became **one Spirit** [with her]."[135]

---

134 This interpretation was especially widespread in places where Holy Scripture was predominantly interpreted using the allegorical method—i.e., primarily in Alexandria. As Anastasius of Sinai testifies (PG 89:860), a great many of the exegetes of old interpreted the entire history of the six days of the creation of the world as applying to Christ and the Church. See the sixth fragment of Papias in *Die apostolischen Väter*, herausgeg. von F.X. Funk, 2-te, verbesserte Aufl. (Tübingen: 1906), 130.

135 Chrysostom, *Homilies on Ephesians* 20.4 (NPNF[1] 13:146). Cf. Ecumenius:

Thus, "man" here means the God-man, and "leaving father and mother" means His incarnation. "Christ Himself, leaving the Father on high, united Himself to the Church. But He left Him only visibly, in the sense of the incarnation."[136] "Just as the Church left the idols and devotion to her former life as to father and mother, so also Christ Himself left His Father in the Heavens and His Mother on earth and died for the Church, that by His death He might enliven the Church which He had loved and, having raised it up, might lead it into His Kingdom."[137] This allegorical interpretation of Gen. 2:24 is expressed with particular clarity by the blessed Jerome, who views these words of Adam as prophetic.[138] Naturally, this interpretation is merely a more or less consistently developed allegory, and lacks sufficient substantiation in the text.

Certain modern exegetes wish to see these same words as indicating a union of Christ and the Church that is merely anticipated at the parousia.[139] But aside from the obvious contrivedness of this interpretation, it is contradicted by the entire teaching of the apostle Paul concerning the Church, since the apostle views the union of Christ and the Church as actual, and not merely anticipated. Besides, in this passage of the epistle to the Ephesians a reference

---

"Τῷ Χριστῷ ἐξὸν μένειν ἐπὶ τῆς ἰδίας δόξης, ἐταπείνωσεν ἑαυτὸν ἐνανθρωπήσας ἵνα προσκολληθῇ τῇ Ἐκκλησίᾳ καὶ ἐγένοντο οἱ δύο εἰς πνεῦμα ἕν [although it was possible for Christ to remain in His own glory, he humbled himself by becoming man so that He might join Himself to the Church, and the two became one spirit {trans. —ED.}]" (PG 118:1245a)

136 Blessed Theodoret, *Works*, part 7, 447 (Rus. ed.).

137 St. Ephraim the Syrian, *Works*, 7, 196 (Rus. ed.).

138 "Contrary to the belief of many, the whole story of Adam and Eve recorded in the book of Genesis cannot be easily applied to Christ and the Church; but only that which is set in this passage. ... Indeed, the first man and first prophet Adam foretold this concerning Christ and the Church—namely, that our Lord and Savior would leave His Father, God, and His mother, the Heavenly Jerusalem, and would come to earth for the sake of His Body, the Church. He created it from His rib and for its sake the Word became flesh." (*Works*, book 17, 360 [Rus. ed.])

139 Concerning this see Bogdashevsky, op. cit., 640–641.

to a future union of Christ with the Church would have carried no conviction with regard to husbands and wives.

Thus, it is more natural to understand the "mystery" mentioned in verse 32 to mean the marriage of a husband and wife, to which the entire foregoing speech of the apostle refers.[140] Nevertheless, the apostle sees the mystery of marriage as grounded in the mystery of the union between Christ and the Church. To the apostle's earlier words concerning Christ's regard for the Church, characterizing it as the regard of the Head for the Body, the apostle here adds a depiction of Christ's constant care for the Church, so that this care may serve as an example for the husband in his relationship with his wife.

Up until now we have set forth the teaching of the apostle Paul concerning the Church as the panhuman organic unity of a redeemed and reborn new creation with Christ as its head. The apostle also explicitly indicates **the purpose of the existence of the Church.**

When the apostle speaks of various gifts and ministries in the Church, he briefly defines the general purpose of the Church's existence. Gifts and ministries, according to the apostle, exist "for the perfecting of the saints ... for the edifying of the body of Christ (πρὸς τὸν καταρτισμὸν τῶν ἁγίων, εἰς οἰκοδομὴν τοῦ σώματος τοῦ Χριστοῦ)" (Eph. 4:12).[141] The edifying of the Body of Christ, that is the Church, is made perfect, and this edification consists of the perfection of the saints.

Here *saints* must be understood to mean all Christians, who are called ἅγιοι in the sense of being set apart or sanctified. And the Church with all its gifts serves for their perfection—πρὸς τὸν καταρτισμόν. The New Testament *hapax legomenon* καταρτισμός can have two meanings: (1) to restore something to

---

140 Ibid., 642.

141 We combine these two expressions as two parallel thoughts, and we join the majority of exegetes in applying the intervening εἰς ἔργον διακονίας ["for the work of the ministry"] to ἔδωκεν ["he gave"] in verse 11. See Cremer, *Biblisch-theologisches Wörterbuch*, 187; Bogdashevsky, op. cit., 541–543.

its inherent state, to correct,[142] and (2) to make perfect in general. The second meaning also corresponds to the most frequently used meaning of the verb καταρτίζω.[143] Consequently, the idea expressed is this: the gifts that exist in the Church and serve to benefit it have as their purpose to make Christians perfect in a moral sense. To this we may also add 2 Cor. 13:9, where the related word κατάρτισις is used. The apostle says that he prays for the perfection of the Corinthians (τὴν ὑμῶν κατάρτισιν). Here, of course, their moral perfection is meant. It is the second sense in which exegetes predominantly understand καταρτισμός.[144] But it seems that both meanings do not preclude each other, if one takes into account the overall theological views of the apostle Paul. Man's advancement in moral perfection is simultaneously the restoration of man's primordial state. In Christ man once again receives that which he had lost in Adam.[145] The primordial state of man is the only one inherent in him, for the sake of which he was created. Salvation is deliverance from sin, which distorted human nature, and hence it may be called the restoration of that state in which human nature was prior to Adam's fall into sin. Hence, the concept of moral perfection (καταρτισμός in the second sense) must coincide with the concept of restoration of the authentic property of human nature (the first meaning of καταρτισμός).

The apostle goes on to characterize καταρτισμὸν τῶν ἁγίων [for the perfecting of the saints] in greater detail: "Till we all come

---

142 See Gal. 6:1, where the verb καταρτίζετε [restore] is used.

143 1 Cor. 1:10, 2 Cor. 13:11. Concerning the meaning of the verb καταρτίζω and related words see Cremer, *Biblisch-theologisches Wörterbuch*, 185–187; Franz Zorell, *Novi Testamenti lexicon graecum*, 293. This verb pertains to the moral sphere, and hence one cannot understand the perfecting of the saints to mean their quantitative increase, as does Mansvetov (see *The New Testament Teaching Concerning the Church*, 102). The concept of the Church's quantitative increase is visible rather in the words "for the edifying of the body of Christ," where we find the word οἰκοδομή [lit. building]. See His Grace Theophan, *Explanation of the Epistle to the Ephesians*, 295–296, which also mentions missionary community.

144 Cremer, *Biblisch-theologisches Wörterbuch*,[9] 187; Bogdashevsky, *Epistle of the Holy Apostle Paul to the Ephesians*, 540.

145 See Rom. 5:12–21.

in the unity of the faith, and of the knowledge of the Son of God, unto a perfect man, unto the measure of the stature of the fullness of Christ: that we … speaking the truth in love, may grow up into him in all things, which is the head, even Christ" (Eph. 4:13, 15).[146] This is said in reference to the Church; hence, "all" should be understood to mean Christians, and not all people in general.[147] All Christians in the Church must achieve unity of faith and the knowledge of the Son of God. This should not be understood as mere theoretical agreement or religious and dogmatic like-mindedness.[148] "Oneness of faith" is an essential condition of belonging to the Church, but here the apostle uses faith and knowledge (ἐπίγνωσις) of the Son of God in a more profound sense, as may be seen from the addendum "unto a perfect man, unto the measure of the stature of the fullness of Christ." Every person must be made ἀνὴρ τέλειος [perfect man], perfect in faith and also in life,[149] which is inseparable from faith.[150] The words εἰς μέτρον ἡλικίας τοῦ πληρώματος τοῦ Χριστοῦ [unto the measure of the stature of the fullness of Christ] allow for a twofold interpretation: ἡλικία may mean (1) height, stature or (2) age (aetas). If we accept the first sense, then the peak of

---

146 We consider it superfluous to conduct a minute philological analysis of the words cited from the apostle's epistle to the Ephesians, as this has been done in the work by Prof. D.I. Bogdashevsky.

147 "But to me it seems that he is speaking of all men" (Blessed Jerome, *Works*, book 17, 307 [Rus. ed.]). "Acquire them more and more, until not a single unbeliever remains. … One faith, so that no non-Christians might remain" (Bishop Theophan, op. cit., 297).

148 "One knowledge of the Son of God, so that among Christians likewise there might be no dissent, but that all alike might understand what is the Son of God and what is the work of salvation accomplished by Him on earth, and how each can and must assimilate it unto himself" (Bishop Theophan, op. cit., 297). In the words of the apostle Paul Mansvetov sees an indication of the Church's goal in the cognitive sphere.

149 Here Cremer translates τέλειος as *ausgewachsen* (*Biblisch-theologisches Wörterbuch*[9], 990).

150 "This is unity of faith, when we all are one, when we shall all alike acknowledge the common bond" (Chrysostom, NPNF[1] 13:105). "That we might be united together in the faith and in the sovereignty of God" (St. Ephraim the Syrian, *Works*, part 7, 191 [Rus. ed.]).

perfection is the stature of the fullness of Christ, while in the second sense it is the age at which the fullness of Christ can be assimilated. In the first instance, τοῦ πληρώματος τοῦ Χριστοῦ is *genetivus possesionis ("genitive of possession"–Ed.);* in the second—*genetivus qualitatis ("genitive of quality"–Ed.).* In context this refers to ages, and so it is better to adopt the second interpretation. In the Church Christians must achieve the age at which they will assimilate the fullness of Christ. Here the idea is the same as in the apostle's words about how Christ must be reflected in Christians,[151] and how every man must be perfect (τέλειος) in "Christ Jesus" (Col. 1:28). In Christ "dwelleth ... the fullness of the Godhead" (Col. 2:9), and whoever loves Christ and keeps His commandments will be loved by the Father, Who will come to him and make His abode with him.[152] Christians can have "the mind of Christ" (1 Cor. 2:16); in them there must be "this mind (τοῦτο φρονείσθω ἐν ὑμῖν) ... which was also in Christ Jesus" (Phil. 2:5).

In this sense, verse 13 is supplemented by verse 15: having true love (ἀληθεύοντες ἐν ἀγάπῃ),[153] we "may grow up into him in all things, which is the head, even Christ." "He commands us to have true love, and by it to cultivate a wealth of virtue in the Master Himself."[154] "Our Lord has become our standard of perfection."[155] He is an ideal type, as it were, of which we must be imitators, and through Him the measure of the stature of our inner man is attained.[156] Without Christ we can do nothing.[157] All aspects of the life of believers (τὰ πάντα) must be permeated with Christ, with His spirit; to Him they must be elevated, so to speak, and by Him they must be inspired.[158] In the Church Christians must progress toward

---

151 See Gal. 4:19; cf. Eph. 3:19.

152 See Jn. 14:23; cf. Rev. 3:20–21.

153 Bogdashevsky, op. cit., 553–556.

154 Bl. Theodoret, *Works,* part 7, 437 (Rus. ed.).

155 St. Ephraim the Syrian, *Works,* part 7, 192 (Rus. ed.).

156 Ibid., 192.

157 See Jn. 15:5.

158 Bogdashevsky, op. cit., 556–557. Here, "may grow up" (αὐξήσωμεν) is understood figuratively.

perfection, until, "having presented themselves to God as a worthy habitation, they might have Him abiding within themselves. For this is the measure of the stature of the fullness of Christ."[159]

The apostle Paul also depicts the process by which renewed mankind becomes like unto Christ. The passages where this process is depicted are very nearly the most incomprehensible in the New Testament, especially in the Slavonic text, and for this reason we will cite them in Greek: Πᾶν τὸ σῶμα συναρμολογούμενον καὶ συμβιβαζόμενον διὰ πάσης ἁφῆς τῆς ἐπιχορηγίας κατ' ἐνέργειαν ἐν μέτρῳ ἑνὸς ἑκάστου μέρους τὴν αὔξησιν τοῦ σώματος ποιεῖται εἰς οἰκοδομὴν ἑαυτοῦ ἐν ἀγάπῃ (Eph. 4:16).[160] Οὐ κρατῶν τὴν κεφαλήν, ἐξ οὗ πᾶν τὸ σῶμα διὰ τῶν ἁφῶν καὶ συνδέσμων ἐπιχορηγούμενον καὶ συμβιβαζόμενον αὔξει τὴν αὔξησιν τοῦ Θεοῦ (Col. 2:19).[161] In the words of St. John Chrysostom, he (the apostle) formulated his thoughts rather unclearly, out of a desire to say everything all at once.[162] First and foremost, in both passages cited the apostle notes the link between Christ and the Church (ἐξ οὗ, οὐ κρατῶν [from whom, not holding]. Christ laid the foundation of church life, and the whole process of this life is governed by Him.[163] The whole

---

159 Bp. Theophan, op. cit., 298.

160 "[From whom] the whole body fitly joined together and compacted by that which every joint supplieth, according to the effectual working in the measure of every part, maketh increase of the body unto the edifying of itself in love." For an explanation of this verse see Mansvetov, op. cit., 143–160, and Bogdashevsky, op. cit., 557–565.

161 "[N]ot holding the Head, from which all the body by joints and bands having nourishment ministered, and knit together, increaseth with the increase of God."

162 Chrysostom, Homilies on Ephesians 11.3. "Only a mind illumined by the gift of wisdom and the revelation of the Holy Spirit, caught up into contemplation of the works of God and man, into spheres beyond this world—only this luminous mind of the apostle could see into the mystery of the wondrous edifice of the Church. But then, when this mind that had soared to the heights wished to give verbal form to its lofty contemplations so as to impart them to the ages, words proved powerless to encompass all the wealth and fullness of their content" (Mansvetov, The New Testament Teaching Concerning the Church, 161).

163 The apostle Paul particularly expresses this idea in his epistle to the Colossians, 2:18.

Body is in a state of process: it is compiled and comingled, and hence the present tense forms are employed—συναρμολογούμενον καὶ συμβιβαζόμενον—indicating a continuous action. The former pertains to ordinary things, the latter—to persons, and here the latter emphasizes the former. Consequently, the Church is a unity of living personalities in the process of perfection.[164]

This unity increases in perfection διὰ πάσης ἁφῆς τῆς ἐπιχορηγίας. Of the numerous interpretations of these words, two are most typical: the first can be linked to the Russian translation of these words,[165] and the second—to the Slavonic.[166] First and foremost we must establish how ἐπιχορηγία is to be understood.[167] In the New Testament this word is encountered in expressions such as these: "through... the supply (διὰ ἐπιχορηγίας) of the Spirit of Jesus Christ" (Phil. 1:19). "He ... that ministereth to you the Spirit, and worketh miracles among you (ὁ ἐπιχορηγῶν ὑμῖν τὸ πνεῦμα, καὶ ἐνεργῶν δυνάμεις ἐν ὑμῖν)" (Gal. 3:5). "He that ministereth (ἐπιχορηγῶν) seed to the sower" (2 Cor. 9:10). This word usage

---

164 Bogdashevsky, op. cit., 560. "By the one (συναρμολογούμενον) the apostle characterizes the actual image of the body as an articulated organism, while by the other (συμβιβάζειν) he expresses that the members that comprise this organism are independent and free individuals." (Mansvetov, op. cit., 145.)

165 "Из Которого все тело, составляемое и совокупляемое посредством всяких взаимно скрепляющих связей, при действии в свою меру каждого члена, получает приращение для созидания самого себя в любви" (Eph. 4:16 RUSV). (*Translator's note:* literally, "From Whom the whole body, joined and brought together *by mutually binding joints*, through the working in measure of every member, receives increase unto the edifying of itself in love." Cf. KJV: "From whom the whole body fitly joined together and compacted *by that which every joint supplieth*, according to the effectual working in the measure of every part, maketh increase of the body unto the edifying of itself in love.")

166 "Из негоже все тело, составляемо и счиневаемо приличне всяцем осязанием подаяния, по действу в мере единыя коеяждо части, возращение тела творит в создание самаго себе любовию" (Eph. 4:16—Church Slavonic translation). (*Translator's note:* literally, "From whom the whole body, fittingly comprised and compiled *by every touch of bestowal*, according to the working in measure of each and every member, works the increase of the body unto the edifying of itself by love.")

167 In classic Greek, the word χορηγεῖν (χορός + ἄγειν) means to appoint a choir for festivities.

gives grounds for understanding ἐπιχορηγία to mean the bestowal of the gifts of the Holy Spirit, as indeed many of the holy fathers[168] and certain exegetes[169] understand this passage. Many translate the preceding words—διὰ πάσης ἁφῆς—as "through all manner of ligaments,"[170] and here the ligament is taken to mean either the actual bestowing of the Holy Spirit, or else the ligament is understood as a condition for this bestowal. But this translation of the words διὰ πάσης ἁφῆς, aside from its philological shortcomings,[171] usually results in a loss of the established meaning of the term ἐπιχορηγία. Thus, the Russian translation—"by means of various mutually binding ligaments"—completely omits the concept expressed by the word ἐπιχορηγία. There is no mention whatsoever of a bestowal of the Spirit. In the book by Ivan Mansvetov, although the established meaning of ἐπιχορηγία is acknowledged in passing, the author also offers an apology for the Russian translation, so that the shade of meaning that ἐπιχορηγία imparts to the whole verse is lost completely.[172]

---

168 "Distribution of gifts"—"ἡ χορηγία τῶν χαρισμάτων" Chrysostom, *Homilies on Ephesians* 11.3 (PG 62:84). "Gifts of the Spirit": St. Ephraim the Syrian, *Works*, vol. 7, 192 (Rus. ed.). "Divides spiritual gifts": Bl. Theodoret, *Works*, vol. 7, 438 (Rus. ed.). Bl. Theophylact: "The words 'by every touch of bestowal' [see the literal translation of the Slavonic in end note 162 –*Trans.*] show that the Spirit, poured out by the Head, perceptibly touches each" (op. cit., 132). "**Bestowal** is the giving of the grace of the Holy Spirit" (Bp. Theophan, op. cit., 308). "Subjugens diversa dona dedisse sanctis suis Filium Dei, scilicet in aedificationem Ecclesiae" ("After subduing he gave different gifts to his saints, the Son of God of course, for the edification of the Church –Ed.)(Magnus Aurelius Cassiodorus, *Complexiones in epistulas apostolorum* [PL 70:1347b]).

169 Bogdashevsky, *The Epistle of the Holy Apostle Paul to the Ephesians*, 560. See 561nn3, 4; Mansvetov, op. cit., 152. This understanding of ἐπιχορηγία excludes the interpretation of some who say that it means mutual aid or support. See Bogdashevsky, op. cit., 560n3. See also the published works of Ephraim the Syrian, part 7, 192n3 (Rus. ed.).

170 See Franz Zorell, *Novi Testamenti lexicon graecum*, 85, 216, sub vv. ἁφή, ἐπιχορηγία.

171 Concerning the philological shortcomings see Bogdashevsky, op. cit., 561–562.

172 Mansvetov, *The New Testament Teaching Concerning the Church*, 152–153. Cf.

Hence, the word ἁφή must be understood in a different sense. Ἁφή is derived from the verb ἅπτω, and hence first and foremost it can mean "contact," "touch," and only then "the senses" in general. Saint John Chrysostom actually uses the word αἴσθησις [sense-perception] in its place.[173] Opponents of this interpretation point to Col. 2:19, where in their opinion ἁφή cannot possibly mean the sensory faculty, but rather indicates a connection, an adhesion.[174] But to our mind in Col. 2:19 likewise ἁφαί may signify the assimilation of the Holy Spirit (ἐπιχορηγούμενον), by means of which, as by the aid of external connections (συνδέσμων), the Body of the Church increases.[175] But what is essential to note is the close link in the apostle's words between the increase of the Church and the grace-filled

150–151, which offers this literal translation: "by means of every ligament of bestowal or imparting." This is then paraphrased: "by means of every ligament of bestowal or imparting of life force, or: by means of every ligament that bestows or imparts life force." The author then reasons as follows: "But since life force is bestowed by means of the nerves, by which all the individual and smallest organs and parts of the body are bound to each other and to the central organ, these nerves may be called ligaments that bind the body both by the means of linkage and at the same time by the bestowal of vital elements to all its parts. Thus we arrive at a new definition of ligaments—as mutual bonds—and hence we can retain this translation of the expression 'διὰ πάσης ἁφῆς τῆς ἐπιχορηγίας': 'by means of all mutually binding ligaments' (or 'that bind each other')." We see clearly how in these fairly inconsistent arguments the word τῆς ἐπιχορηγίας becomes further and further displaced, until the author arrives at the text of the Russian translation, where not the slightest hint of this word is found.

173 Chrysostom, *Homilies on Ephesians* 11.3 (NPNF[1] 13:105; PG 62:84): "But what is the meaning of this, 'by the touch of the supply'? that is to say, by the sensitive faculty (διὰ τῆς αἰσθήσεως)." "'*Touch* is what the apostle called the sensory faculty, because it too is one of the five senses, and by means of a part he named the whole" (Bl. Theodoret, *Works*, part 7, 438 [Rus. ed.]). "Through all perception" (St. Ephraim the Syrian, *Works*, part 7, 192 [Rus. ed.]).

174 Mansvetov, *The New Testament Teaching Concerning the Church*, 147. De Wette calls this interpretation "die einseitige Erklärung," and also refutes it by citing Col. 2:19 (*Kurze Erklärung der Briefe*, 2-te Aufl. [Leipzig: 1847], 144).

175 This is precisely how Bl. Theodoret interprets Col. 2:19: "The body of the Church receives from the Master Christ both the sources of doctrine and the wellspring of salvation. What the joints are to the body, the apostles, prophets, and teachers are to the makeup of the Church" (*Works*, part 7, 503–504 [Rus. ed.]). Cf. Bogdashevsky, op. cit., 563.

actions of the Holy Spirit. The entire verse in question is permeated with this idea. In Eph. 4:16, aside from ἐπιχορηγία, which we
have analyzed, we find the words: κατ᾽ ἐνέργειαν ἐν μέτρῳ, ἑνὸς
ἑκάστου μέρους [according to the working in measure of each and
every member]. These words should be seen as a repetition of the
concept already familiar to us—that of the distribution of the gifts
of the Holy Spirit among believers,[176] especially since the apostle
spoke of the distribution of gifts only a few verses prior: "Unto every one of us is given grace according to the measure of the gift of
Christ" (Eph. 4:7).

The words of the apostle Paul thus far considered depict the life
of the Body of the Church in this form: the entire Body is continually united more and more harmoniously by means of assimilation
of the grace-filled gifts of the Holy Spirit.[177] These grace-filled gifts
of the Holy Spirit act in each member of the Church in one way
or another, in accordance with his strengths and abilities,[178] and

---

176 See Rom. 12:6, 1 Cor. 12:4–11. These same words, in our opinion, confirm the understanding of the word ἐπιχορηγία adopted above, in the sense of
the gifts of the Holy Spirit.

177 Thus, the Slavonic translation of "διὰ πάσης ἁφῆς τῆς ἐπιχορηγίας"—
"всяцем осязанием подаяния" ("by every touch of bestowal" –Trans.)—however difficult it may be to comprehend, more accurately conveys the meaning
of the Greek source. Many Old Slavonic translations render διὰ πάσης ἁφῆς
τῆς ἐπιχορηγίαςas follows: "всем обличением даянья" ("by all manifestation
of bestowal" –Trans.) (Tolstovsky, Alex., Pogodinsky №27, etc.—see Prof. G.A.
Voskresensky, The Old Slavonic Apostol, 5th ed. [Sergiev Posad: 1908], 288–289).
This translation, in our view, very aptly accentuates the idea that assimilation
of the gifts of the Holy Spirit is simultaneously a manifestation of this bestowal in
church ministry. Alexei Khomyakov's translation of Eph. 4:16 is most unfortunate: "from which the whole Body, harmonizing and agreeing in every ligament
that abides, by the action of power commensurate with each member, works the
growth of the body which edifies itself in love." The translation of K.P. Pobedon-
ostsev little corresponds to the Greek text, although it partially reflects the idea it
contains: "And the whole Body, in the makeup and union of the members each
reciprocally working according to its measure, receives from Him the power of
growth, unto the edification of itself in love."

178 The words "κατ᾽ ἐνέργειαν ἐν μέτρῳ, ἑνὸς ἑκάστου μέρους [according to
the working in measure of each and every member]" are most frequently applied
to those that follow: "τὴν αὔξησιν ποιεῖται [maketh increase]." But since assimi-

thus the Body of the Church τὴν αὔξησιν τοῦ σώματος ποιεῖται εἰς οἰκοδομὴν ἑαυτοῦ ἐν ἀγάπῃ.[179] The form of ποιεῖται [maketh] suggests an inner process of growth.[180] Ἐν ἀγάπῃ [in love] should be applied not to εἰς οἰκοδομὴν [unto the edifying], as some apply it,[181] even understanding love as the goal of development, but rather to αὔξησιν ποιεῖται [maketh increase]. Love is the new principle of life for renewed mankind,[182] and all perfection and increase of the church organism is dependent on the participation of the individual members in the law of love. This entire process of increase is the work of the grace of God,[183] but the assimilation of this grace (ἀφῆς τῆς ἐπιχορηγίας) is naturally possible only when there is love. Without love, the gifts received by a given member would prove useless for the life of the whole Body, for that member would be wrapped up in himself, not knowing the other members, and completely isolated.[184] Besides, without love the very assimilation of the gifts of

---

lation of the gifts of the Holy Spirit and moral growth are intimately connected, the meaning will suffer no essential change whatsoever if we apply the words "κατ᾽ ἐνέργειαν ἐν μέτρῳ, ἑνὸς ἑκάστου μέρους" to the foregoing "διὰ πάσης ἀφῆς τῆς ἐπιχορηγίας," as does Bl. Theophylact: "Christ distributes His gifts of grace to our souls, which are His members—not simply, but **according to the measure of each part**—that is, so far as each is able to receive them" (op. cit., 131). Cf. Chrysostom, *Homilies on Ephesians* 11.3.

179 Here τοῦ σώματος [of the body] is used in place of the semantically necessary ἑαυτοῦ [of itself], since the subject πᾶν τὸ σῶμα [the whole body] is significantly removed.

180 Nevertheless, Mansvetov also speaks of outward increase as the constant, ceaseless joining of more and more new members to the Church, and the expansion of her borders from one locality to the next, from country to country, and the acquisition of an ever increasing number of followers (op. cit., 158).

181 Bogdashevsky, *The Epistle of the Holy Apostle Paul to the Ephesians*, 564n2. Cf. De Wette, op. cit., 150. A preference for this understanding is apparently also shared by the blessed Jerome, who writes: "This whole edifice, through which the Body of the Church increases one part at a time, will be filled with mutual love within itself" (*Works*, part 17, 310 [Rus. ed.]).

182 See Eph. 3:17: "rooted and grounded in love."

183 See Eph. 3:16: "to be strengthened with might by his Spirit in the inner man."

184 Bogdashevsky, op. cit., 564.

the Holy Spirit would be impossible. "But wherefore doth he add, 'in love'?" asks St. John Chrysostom. "Because in no other way is it possible for that Spirit to descend. For as, in case a hand should happen to be torn from the body, the spirit which proceeds from the brain seeks the limb, and if it finds it not, does not leap forth from the body, and fly about and go to the hand, but if it finds it not in its place, does not touch it; so also will it be here, if we be not bound together in love."[185]

In assimilating the gifts of the Spirit in common love, unto the common good, the Church in all of its members achieves its edification (εἰς οἰκοδομὴν ἑαυτοῦ), that is, its perfection.[186]

The interpretation of Eph. 4:16 here presented is fully in keeping with the general structure of the views of the apostle Paul,[187] and this is precisely how the holy fathers understand this passage. In explaining the verse in question, St. John Chrysostom writes: "For the souls of men being dependent upon Him [Christ] as members [of the spirit], His provident care, and supply of the spiritual gifts according to a due proportion in the measure of every single mem-

---

185 Chrysostom, *Homilies on Ephesians* 11.3 (NPNF¹ 13:105–106). "Love builds up, and makes men cleave one to another, and be fastened and fitted together. ... If therefore we desire to have the benefit of that Spirit which is from the Head, let us cleave one to another. For there are two kinds of separation from the body of the Church; the one, when we wax cold in love, the other, when we dare commit things unworthy of our belonging to that body; for in either way we cut ourselves off from the 'fullness of Christ'" (ibid., 106.). Cf. Ecumenius: "Ἄνευ γὰρ ταύτης (ἀγάπης) οὐκ ἄν εἴς τινα καταβαίη τὸ πνεῦμα τὸ ἅγιον [for with this {sc. love} the Holy Spirit would not descend on anyone" (PG 118:1224d). St. Ephraim the Syrian expresses this idea: "Mutual need of one another among the members of the Church sows great love among them" (*Works*, part 7, 192 [Rus. ed.]).

186 The blessed Jerome likens the process of the perfection of the Church to the growth of a child's body, in which "gradually all the members grow in parts, but in such a way that they appear to grow not for themselves, but for the body." The blessed Jerome understands perfection to mean that each member will be perfect in its own measure and ministry—for example, a fallen angel will become as he was created, while a man cast out of paradise will once again be restored as a cultivator of paradise (*Works*, part 17, 310–311 [Rus. ed.]).

187 Cf. Prof. N.N. Glubokovsky, *The Preaching of Holy Apostle Paul in its Origin and Substance* ["Благовестие святого апостола Павла по его происхождению и существу"], book 2 (Saint Petersburg: 1910), from 670 on.

ber, effects their increase. … For that spirit which is supplied to the members from the head, 'touches,' each single member, and thus actuates it. As though one should say, 'the body receiving the supply [of the spirit] according to the proportion of its several members, thus maketh the increase'; or, in other words, 'the members receiving the supply [of the spirit] according to the proportion of their proper measure, thus make increase'; or otherwise again thus, 'the spirit flowing plenteously from above, and touching all the members, and supplying them as each is capable of receiving it, thus maketh increase.'"[188] Blessed Theophylact[189] echoes these ideas of Chrysostom. Blessed Theodoret[190] and St. John of Damascus[191] say

---

188 Chrysostom, *Homilies on Ephesians* 11.3 (NPNF[1] 13:105).

189 "The body grows and is edified through the fact that the bestowal of the Spirit touches its members and He acts in them, or that through it He gives the power to act" (*Explanation of the Epistle to the Ephesians*, 132 [Rus. ed.]).

190 "The Master Christ, comprising the Head, divides the spiritual gifts, uniting the members of the Body into a single ordered whole" (*Works*, part 7, 438 [Rus. ed.]).

191 In *On the Epistle to the Ephesians*. "Σῶμα αὐτοῦ ἡ ἐκκλησία κατὰ τὴν μετάληψιν τοῦ ἁγίου Πνεύματος. Ἡ Ἐκκλησία ἐστίν, ἡ δεκτική, φησί, τοῦ διήκοντος, τῶν οὐρανίων μὲν πάλαι, νῦν δὲ καὶ ἐπιγείων [His body is the Church, in proportion to the participation in the Holy Spirit. The Church, he says, is she that receives Him who pervades [all things], the heavenly things formerly and now the earthly ones as well" (PG 95:828d, 829a). "'Ὥσπερ ἐν σώματος αὐξήσει, φθάσωμεν εἰς τοσοῦτον ὕψος ἅπαντες, ὡς πρὸς τὴν κεφαλὴν ἡμῶν συναρμοσθῆναι τὸν Χριστόν. Ὅς ἐφεστὼς ἡμῖν κατὰ τὴν θεϊκὴν ἐξοχήν, μεταδίδωσιν ἡμῖν ἑαυτὸν κατὰ τὴν οἰκονομίας συνάφειαν, ἑαυτῷ συνάπτων ἡμᾶς καὶ ἀλλήλοις, καθ' ἣν ἔχομεν πρὸς ἀλλήλους ὥσπερ ἐν οἰκοδομῇ συναρμογήν, καὶ καθὸ τὴν ἐπιχορηγίαν τοῦ Πνεύματος ἕκαστος δύναται δέχεσθαι, τῆς ἐπὶ τῇ αὐξήσει τελειώσεως εἰς ἀγάπην συνκεφαλαιουμένης [As in the increase of a body, let us reach to so great a height as to be fitted together to our head, Christ. He, standing over us according to the divine prominence, imparts to us Himself according to the union of the economy [of our salvation], joining us to Himself and to each other; according to this [union] we are combined with each other as in a bulding and in so far as each is able to receive the supply {ἐπιχορηγία} of the Spirit, while the various members are being joined together and increasing toward perfection through love]" (PG 95:844a).

the same. Bishop Theophan expresses ideas that are perfectly patristic in nature.[192]

In contemplating the overall picture of this brief exposition of
the teaching of the apostle Paul concerning the Church, one cannot help but note that in all the passages of his epistles analyzed
he has in mind **one Church** of Christ. He depicts the Church in
the form of the Body of Christ. Naturally, it is unthinkable that by
the Church the apostle could have meant the individual Christian
community. Both Jews and gentiles are recreated by Christ into one
body, one new man. In the Church, two worlds are mingled into
one. Clearly, the ecclesiological idea of the apostle encompasses a
broader expanse than an isolated community. This same concept of
a single Church is indicated by the comparison of the marital union
of husband and wife to the union between Christ and the Church.
This image of the bride of Christ can only be understood to mean
the one Church of Christ.[193]

It must be concluded that the apostle always instilled this idea of
the one Church into the consciousness of the numerous Christian
communities that he established in great numbers, spreading God's
good news "from Jerusalem ... unto Illyricum" (Rom. 15:19). In
assimilating the ecclesiological ideas of the apostle to the gentiles,

---

192 St. Theophan the Recluse, *Explanation of the Epistle to the Ephesians*, 307:
"The Christian faith unites the faithful unto Christ and in this way comprises of
them all a single ordered Body. Christ creates this Body, imparting Himself to
each and bestowing grace upon him effectively and palpably, so that this Spirit
of grace, descending upon each, makes him what he ought to be in the Body of
the Church of Christ. The Body of Christ, being united in an orderly fashion by
this bestowal of the Spirit, then grows within itself to the measure in which each
member answers his purpose or acts to the benefit of the Church by the whole
fullness of the gift of grace received."

193 Regarding Eph. 5:32, εἰς Χριστὸν καὶ εἰς τὴν ἐκκλησίαν ["concerning
Christ and the church"], J. Meritan notes: "It is quite difficult to see a local
church in that which the apostle, it seems, applies to the Christian community
viewed in totality" (*Revue biblique internationale*, vol. 7 [1898], 354. Cf. also 356,
357, 361–362, 368). In concluding his analysis of the ecclesiological views of the
apostle Paul in his epistle to the Ephesians, Meritan says: "Catholicity and unity—these are the two great ecclesiological theses of the epistle to the Ephesians"
(ibid., 369).

the Christian must by necessity think of himself as a member of the one Church of Christ.[194] "The eye cannot say unto the hand, I have no need of thee." A member of the Church of Corinth could not have understood these words of the apostle to mean that he could not say, "I do not need you" only to a member of his own local church. A member of the Body of Christ is any believer, wherever he may be: [hence,] in the thinking of the apostle a Corinthian could not say to each Ephesian or Roman, "I do not need you."[195] The idea of the unity of the Church had to have predominated in all Christian communities.[196]

But was this idea of the unity of the Church only an idea, one in which people believed, or was it also somehow manifested outwardly? We could of course concur with those scholarly researchers who say that the idea of a united religious society has never yet been realized in actuality. "If we compare the Church of the mid-third century with the state of Christianity 150–200 years prior," says Harnack, "we will find that now there is indeed a religious society, whereas previously there had only been communities that believed in a Celestial Church whose terrestrial reflection they were, and strove to give it some sort of expression by some sort of means (*mit den einfachsten Mitteln*– *"with the easiest method"* –*Ed.*), and as strangers and sojourners on earth they lived in the future."[197] Neither in

---

194 G. Hoennicke asserts that few people found the theology of Paul understandable. Frequently they simply slavishly accepted the apostles' words, which they did not understand correctly. Hence, in the time that followed the apostle Paul's ideas had an insignificant influence on the religious consciousness of Christian communities (*Das Judenchristentum*, 242). But for ecclesiological views, at any rate, an exception ought to be made: the idea of one all-encompassing Church, at least, could have been quite comprehensible to anyone.

195 St. Isidore of Pelusium interprets 1 Cor. 12:27 [as follows] (καὶ μέλη ἐκ μέρους [members in particular]): "The church you have is a member of (the Church) that is everywhere, and hence it would be right for you to be of one mind not only among yourselves (for there were disagreements among them), but also with all those of your creed throughout the world, uprooting all discord" (PG 89:1169c–d).

196 "The one Church was one of the first and fundamental concepts of Christianity" (Myshtsyn, *The Organization of the Christian Church*, 429).

197 *Lehrbuch der Dogmengeschichte*, 4-te Aufl. 1-er Bd. (Tübingen: 1909), 52. Dr.

the first nor even until the end of the second century were there any forms of Church-wide juridical organization; there were no councils nor any primacy that would have had binding authority for individual churches. All the local churches were independent of each other and comprised units that were completely self-sufficient juridically.[198] However, the opinions cited, especially that of Harnack, may only be adopted with significant caveats. It is of course true that Christianity did not proceed from juridical standards. In founding the new Christian community the apostles did not start by putting forward a plan for organization and bylaws that would regulate relations between the communities. The work of Christ Himself was incomparably more profound: He brought new life for men—the recreation of human nature. For this reason it is difficult to find in His teaching any guidelines for the practical ordering of affairs. In the apostolic epistles, though there are indeed several indications of the day-to-day doings of believers, these indications are random, fragmentary, and do not comprise the chief object of the apostles' concern. The holy apostles likewise were occupied with teaching believers, with the rebirth of the Jews and the Greeks into a new man.[199] But every new life that appears on earth, whatever the principles upon which it is based, invariably takes on certain **outward** forms. In every place and at every time, anarchism has

---

Julius Köstlin says nearly the same: "Each separate community had to understand itself to be spiritually linked with all of Christianity and to strive to present this unity as outwardly expressed" (*Das Wesen der Kirche nach Lehre und Geschichte des Neuen Testamentes mit vornehmlicher Rücksicht auf die Streitfrage zwischen Protestantismus und Katholicismus*, 2-te Aufl. Gotha [1872], 90). "After the death of the apostles, the union linking individual Christian communities to each other was only a union of common faith, the consciousness of a common unity (*des Zusammengefasstseins*) beneath one Head and a free and living interaction between them. There was not yet a well-regulated organization connecting and uniting them outwardly" (D. Thomasius, *Die Dogmengeschichte der Alten Kirche*, 2-te Aufl. [Erlangen: 1886], 28. Vgl. 103).

198 Myshtsyn, op. cit., 430. Harnack, *Entstehung und Entwickelung der Kirchenverfassung und des Kirchenrechts*, 35; Friedrich Loofs, *Leitfaden zum Studium der Dogmengeschichte*, §12.1, 72–80.

199 Cf. Acts 6:2: "It is not reason that we should leave the word of God, and serve tables."

been a mere dream. Christianity is "in the world," and it would be a perfectly incomprehensible miracle if it had promptly brought heaven down to earth.[200] But since Christianity did not begin with form, but with inner content, it is perfectly understandable that little outward organization was in evidence at the initial stages. This statement applies to the whole corpus of the Christian Church. Individual communities, of course, had to have an outward structure from the very outset. But the idea of one Church was also manifested outwardly. External juridical unification was lacking, but there was internal moral unification, and the one Church was not just an idea, but an actual fact. For when the apostle Paul said that he "persecuted the church of God" (Gal. 1:13), he naturally meant the entire Church, and before him he saw this one Church as a living reality, so that he equated it with such realities as the Greeks and the Jews.[201] In certain forms this reality was also manifested outwardly.

The apostles themselves, of course, had no juridical authority, but they had moral authority as apostles of the Lord. They were witnesses of the earthly life of the Lord Jesus Christ,[202] Who Himself "named [them] apostles" (Lk. 6:13). Hence their authority in the Church. One who rejects the apostles rejects Christ; hence, Christians had to abide "in the apostles' doctrine" (Acts 2:42). We see that the apostles sometimes act together,[203] and in general maintain unity among themselves.[204] The twelve apostles (δώδεκα) enjoyed particular authority and were the first agency that united the

---

200 "Extreme Protestants have always wished and continue to wish to see a Christianity estranged from all form. But is there any such Christianity, or could there by? Without a doubt, such will Christianity be in the paradise of heaven." –Prof. A.P. Lebedev, "The 'Essence of Christianity' as depicted by church historian Adolph Harnack" ("«Сущность христианства» по изображению церквоного историка Адольфа Гарнака"), *Bogoslovsky vestnik* (1901), vol. 3, 437. Cfr.: A. Loisy, *L'évangile et l'église*, 136–137, 146.

201 1 Cor. 11:32. Cfr.: Batiffol, *L'église naissante et le catholicisme*,[3] 90–91.

202 Cf. Acts 1:21–22.

203 Cf. Acts 6:2.

204 Cf. Gal. 2:9.

Church.[205] Later on the charismatics, of whom we learn from *The Teachings of the Twelve Apostles*, were also a sort of nerve uniting the individual communities.[206]

The work of the apostle Paul clearly shows that the apostle not only preached the idea of one Church in word and in writing, but also strove to unite the individual communities to each other. All the churches founded by the apostle Paul were already united by virtue of having been established by the same person. The apostle Paul was a sort of linking hub for the different churches: in his epistles he customarily sends greetings on behalf of one church to others, and appends greetings from individual persons.[207] We find similar greetings in the general epistles, as well.[208] The epistles of the apostle Paul also inform us that there was an exchange of apostolic epistles among the communities: in some cases the apostle seems to au-

---

205 "The unification of the individual churches was still more clearly expressed in the absolute submission of all to their common instructors—the apostles. Nor was this the result of coercion or compulsion, but the action of a meek spirit and their unwavering certainty of the divine appointment of their ministry. To what purpose was compulsion, when one who strayed from this union or was cut off in chastisement for his sins punished his own self, making himself unhappy and worthy of pity?" (A.V. Gorsky, *The History of the Gospel and of the Apostolic Church* ["История евангельская и Церкви апостольской"], 2nd ed. [Holy Trinity-Sergius Lavra: 1902], 438).

206 "In the global work of teaching the Christian communities, segmented [and dispersed] over an enormous expanse, had one solitary strong link and basis for union. These were the apostles and prophets, who went from place to place and everywhere were received with great honor—and only they can explain to us why the development of the communities in different provinces, despite the differences in local conditions, nevertheless display a certain degree of homogeneity in its process" (A. Harnack, *Die Mission und Ausbreitung des Christentums in den ersten drei Jahrhunderten*, 2-te Aufl. [Leipzig: 1906], 286). Thomasius likewise sees in the apostles (in the broad sense of the word) the dignity of the whole Church (op. cit., 28). Vgl. Harnack's "Prolegomena" to the edition of the *Didache* [Διδαχή] in the text *Untersuchungen zur Geschichte der altchristlichen Literatur*, herausgegeben von Oscar von Gebhardt und Adolf Harnack, 2.1 (Leipzig: 1884). "The apostles, prophets, and teachers were the link of dispersed Christianity" (103–105, 112).

207 See Rom. 16:16, 21–23, 1 Cor. 16:19–20, 2 Cor. 13:12, Phil. 4:22, Col. 4:10–12, 14–15.

208 See 1 Pet. 5:13, 3 Jn. 15.

thorize this exchange,[209] so that each of his epistles was encyclical, as it were, and known in different churches.[210] This is also attested by the epistle of the apostle Peter written "to the strangers scattered throughout Pontus, Galatia, Cappadocia, Asia, and Bithynia" (1 Pet. 1:1). In the apostle Paul's epistles we encounter expressions such as, "so ordain I in all churches" (1 Cor. 7:17), and, "as in all churches of the saints" (1 Cor. 14:33). He sends Timothy to the Corinthians so that he might remind them "of my ways which be in Christ, as" he (Paul) teaches "every where in every church" (1 Cor. 4:17). The apostle calls the Thessalonians "followers of the churches of God which in Judaea are in Christ Jesus" (1 Thess. 2:14), while of the Romans he writes that their "faith is spoken of throughout the whole world" (Rom. 1:8). The entire history of the apostle Paul shows how persistently he strove to unite the individual churches dispersed throughout the world. He is always inspired by the idea of one Church, which he desires to see accomplished.[211]

The apostle envisions the newly established churches as being closely linked not only with each other, but primarily with the ancient Church of Jerusalem. "If the Gentiles" have united with the Jews in "spiritual things, their duty is also to minister unto them in carnal things" (Rom. 15:27).[212] But particularly noteworthy are those passages of the apostle Paul's epistles that refer even to the practice of material assistance among the Christian communities. This material interaction (κοινωνία) was a sort of institution: the question of κοινωνία arose when the new communities were first established, as may be seen from the epistle to the Galatians (2:9–10): "James, Cephas, and John, who seemed to be pillars ... gave to me

---

209 See Col. 4:16.

210 See 2 Pet. 3:15–16.

211 "Sein Gedanke ist die eine Kirche, welcher gerade die Einteilung der Gemeinden in Provinzen zum Bewusstsein der Einheit und zum gemeinsamen Handeln verhelfen muss" (C. Weizsäcker, *Das apostolische Zeitalter*, 598). Vgl.: G. Hoennicke, *Das Judenchristentum*, 251.

212 The Russian translation of ἐκοινώνησαν—сделались участниками ("have been made participants")—does not entirely accurately convey the meaning of the original.

and Barnabas the right hands of fellowship; that we should go unto the heathen, and they unto the circumcision. Only they would that we should remember the poor; the same which I also was forward to do." And indeed, we repeatedly encounter the practice of alms-giving and aid among the Churches.[213] In the apostle's writings we even find indications of the regulation of charitable collections: in various Churches he institutes the same system of collecting alms.[214] The apostle Paul constantly desires that the Church of Jerusalem acknowledge his missionary activity,[215] and he tries to collect donations for it in the various places where he preached. Furthermore, the apostle even considers it the duty of the Christians from among the gentiles to donate for the benefit of the Jerusalem community (ὀφειλέται αὐτῶν εἰσιν [their debtors they are]).[216] Finally, we must note that at the very outset of Christian life we encounter the so-called Apostolic Council. Paul and Barnabas along with several others go from Antioch to the apostles and presbyters in Jerusalem to resolve the confusion caused by certain of those who had come from Judea. "Then pleased it the apostles and elders with the whole church, to send chosen men of their own company to Antioch with Paul and Barnabas; namely, Judas surnamed Barsabas and Silas, chief men among the brethren: and they wrote letters by them after this manner; The apostles and elders and brethren send greeting unto the brethren which are of the Gentiles in Antioch and Syria and Cilicia" (Acts 15:22–23). How should this circumstance be viewed? Did the Apostolic Council have any judicial authority? Was it convened according to some preestablished charter? Clearly, it was not. Nevertheless, the Council resolved the question that had arisen in Antioch, and it sent an epistle to the Christians of Antioch, Syria, and Cilicia. The relations between the churches were not regulated, but these relations did exist, and they expressed the idea of the conciliar unity of the Church of Christ.

213 See 2 Cor. 8:1–4, 19–21; 9:1–5, 12; Phil. 4:10–12, 18; Rom. 15:25–28; Acts 11:27–30.

214 See 1 Cor. 16:1–4, 2 Cor. 8:11–19.

215 See Acts 21:19 and the verses that follow.

216 See Rom. 15:27.

It is perfectly clear that interaction among the neighboring churches was particularly frequent and even routine, so that groups of Churches of a sort emerged. This is seen even from the salutations of the apostle Paul. In the epistles to the Corinthians he sends a greeting and blessing "with all the saints which are in all Achaia" (2 Cor. 1:1) and from all the Churches of Asia.[217] The apostle speaks of the brethren "in all Macedonia" (1 Thess. 4:10) and of "the churches of Galatia" (1 Cor. 16:1).[218]

Protestant scholarly researchers particularly emphasize the isolation and complete independence of the individual Christian communities, but ought we to speak of independence in a context where no one made this independence the cornerstone of their religious expectations? The religious expectation was the idea of one Catholic Church of Christ, one church Body. When a community was founded, there hardly arose the question of that community's independence, of how it related to the other communities, of its administrative structure, etc. On the contrary, from the very outset each new Christian community entered into the closest of relations with the other communities founded previously. The concern of Paul, the apostle to the gentiles, was not that communities be independent, but that they be inseparably linked to the Church of Jerusalem. The apostle held separation between the Christians from among the gentiles and those from among the Jews to be a tremendous misfortune, one that he made every effort to prevent.[219] It was not an organization that came to life, but a new principle of spiritual life: the principle of love. And this principle caused each person to consider the other as above himself. This is how the mutual relations between the Christian communities should be envisioned. Protestant scholarly researchers, in our opinion, are far more concerned with these Christian communities' independence than the communities were themselves.

---

217 See 1 Cor. 16:19.

218 Cf. the book of Revelation, which was written to the seven churches in Asia (1:4).

219 Vgl.: Weizsäcker, *Das apostolische Zeitalter*, 597–599.

Even in the initial period of the apostolic fathers, interaction between the churches never ceased. Let us note several facts. Clement,
bishop of Rome, wrote on behalf of the whole Church of Rome to
Corinth, where there were certain irregularities. Naturally, he had
no judicial basis for doing so, but Christian life never follows a judicial path. Clement's letter, as Eusebius relates, commanded great
respect not only in Corinth, but in the neighboring churches: it was
even read publicly.[220] Polycarp, bishop of Smyrna, wrote a letter to
Philippi. By oral talks and exhortations Ignatius of Antioch, while
en route from Syria to Rome, strengthened the faith of Christians
in the cities through which he traveled and guarded them against
heretics.[221] We would have to quote a significant portion of the letters of Saint Ignatius if we wished to typify the intercourse of the
Christian communities of the day. In his epistles to the Philadelphians, the Smyrnaeans, and to Polycarp, Saint Ignatius advises
them to send an ambassador to Antioch, for example, regarding
the cessation of persecutions, that they might rejoice together in the
common assembly,[222] that there he might extol unwaning love for
the glory of God[223] and congratulate them with the joy that peace
had settled among them, their greatness had returned, and their
small body had been restored (τὸ ἴδιον σωματεῖον).[224] To Polycarp
Ignatius writes: "Since I ... could not write to all the churches, you
shall write to those churches nearest, as one who knows the will of
God, that they also might do the same. Whoever is able might send
couriers (πεζούς), and others—letters through those sent by you."[225]
The exchange of letters is expressively attested to by the epistle
of Polycarp. "You and Ignatius," says Polycarp, "have written to

---

220 Eusebius, *Church History* 3.16.2 (GrchSch. 9.1:230.1–5).

221 Ibid., 274–280.

222 Ignatius, *Epistle to the Philadelphians* 10.

223 Idem, *To Polycarp* 7.2 (ANF 1:96): "It is fitting, O Polycarp, most blessed
in God, to assemble a very solemn council, and to elect one whom you greatly
love, and know to be a man of activity, who may be designated the messenger
of God." Cf.: *To the Smyrnaeans* 11.2 (ANF 1:91): "Elect some worthy delegate."

224 Idem, *To the Smyrnaeans* 11.2; cf. 11.3 (ANF 1:91).

225 Idem, *To Polycarp* 8.1 (ANF 1:96).

me that, if anyone should go to Syria, he should take your epistles there, which I will do if a convenient time arises, either myself or I will send someone. The letters which Ignatius sent to us and others in our possession we have sent to you as you required: they are appended to this epistle; of them you can derive much benefit, for they contain faith, patience, and every kind of instruction concerning our Lord."[226]

It is quite clear that the existence of all these epistles was occasioned by the moral authority possessed by their authors; but apparently common moral connections were sufficient if the Church had no need of artificial judicial norms to express the idea of its unity. That there was no unity of outward organization was not because this was supposedly contrary to the Christian idea of the Church, as Protestant scholars are inclined to represent the matter,[227] but only because in actuality a more profound and intimate unity existed. Those forms of interaction among the churches noted in the early days of the Church's existence better attest that Christians were suffused with the idea of one Church than do the forms of later, purely formal, documentary interactions. With good reason Tertullian, by whose time a complete church organization existed, said: "The unity of the Church is proven by the fellowship of the world, the name of fraternity, and the rendering (*contessaratio*) of hospitality."[228] Obviously, in his eyes church unity was more proven by the actual unification of the Church than by various organizations.[229] The unity of Christian "fraternity" was not idealistic,[230] but very real

---

226 *Epistle of Polycarp to the Philippians* 13.1–2 (ANF 1:119). "Die apostolischen Väter," herausgeg. von F.X. Funk, 114–115. Here the following addendum is made: "Et de ipso Ignatio et de his qui cum eo sunt, quod certius agnoventis, significate." ("And of Ignatius himself, and of those who are with him, signify what you have certainly recognized" –Ed.)

227 For example, Sohm.

228 Tertullianus, *The Prescription Against Heretics* 20 (PL 2:37b). Cf.: "κοινὸν ὄνομα καὶ ἐλπίς [common name and hope]," Ignatius, *To the Ephesians* 1.2 (ANF 1:49).

229 Vgl.: Harnack, *Prolegomena zu Διδαχή*, TU 2.1, 88–89.

230 Vgl.: Loofs, *Leitfaden der Dogmengeschichte* §14.2, 88–89.

indeed. Common beliefs and common expectations roused Christians to outward unity, as is also expressed in the Didache.[231] The Didache also contains a eucharistic prayer that in poetic form twice entreats the Lord God to gather His Church from all the ends of the world, from the four winds, into His kingdom.[232] This passage of the eucharistic prayer in the Didache is customarily reevaluated. The conclusion drawn is that supposedly Christians at that time understood the essence of the Church to require unity only in the βασιλεία τοῦ Θεοῦ [kingdom of God].[233] But if we consider that at that time Christianity was actually dispersed in little communities from one end of the earth to the other, this form of prayer becomes quite understandable. Christians of that time could not even have imagined that a time could come when the Christian faith would conquer the world and there would be a single outwardly organized Church. This unity was of course highly desirable, and Christians strove for it as much as they were able. But the complete accomplishment of outwardly organized unity seemed a thing very far off. In this same prayer we note that, although it refers to the dispersion of the Church, it refers specifically to *the Church*, and not to Churches. It is apparent that the author envisions all these communities scattered to the ends of the earth as a single Church. Finally, it should be noted that, along with the words cited, the same prayer vividly expresses the typically early Christian expectation of the im-

---

231 "Εἰ γὰρ ἐν τῷ ἀθανάτῳ κοινωνοί ἐστε, πόσῳ μᾶλλον ἐν τοῖς θνητοῖς [for if ye are partakers in that which is immortal, how much more in things which are mortal?]" (4.8).

232 "Ὥσπερ ἦν τοῦτο τὸ κλάσμα διεσκορπισμένον ἐπάνω τῶν ὀρέων καὶ συναχθὲν ἐγένετο ἕν, οὕτω συναχθήτω σου ἡ ἐκκλησία ἀπὸ τῶν περάτων τῆς γῆς εἰς τὴν σὴν βασιλείαν [Even as this broken bread was scattered over the hills, and was gathered together and became one, so let Thy Church be gathered together from the ends of the earth into Thy kingdom]" (9, 4). Μνήσθητι, κύριε, τῆς ἐκκλησίας σου, τοῦ ῥύσασθαι αὐτὴν ἐν τῇ ἀγάπῃ σου, καὶ σύναξον αὐτὴν ἀπὸ τῶν τεσσάρων ἀνέμων, τὴν ἁγιασθεῖσαν, εἰς τὴν σὴν βασιλείαν, ἣν ἡτοίμασας αὐτῇ [Remember, Lord, Thy Church, to deliver it from all evil and to make it perfect in Thy love, and gather it from the four winds, sanctified for Thy kingdom which Thou hast prepared for it]" (9.5).

233 Harnack, *Prolegomena*, TU I2.1, 88.

minent Coming of Christ and the end of the world.[234] If the end of the world was to come so soon, naturally the idea of organizing a single Church must have been of secondary importance in the consciousness of Christians. In general, it is our opinion that this prayer in the *Didache* attests only to the fact that the first-century Christians could not yet imagine the entire global historical mission of Christianity, but that even they believed that the Church, although dispersed, was one.[235]

The unity of the Church as a "fraternity" is also expressed in another historic first-century document—the epistle of Clement of Rome to the Corinthians. This epistle concludes with a prayer not only for the Corinthians, but for all those in every place called by God. Clement asks to be notified of the desired and long-awaited peace and accord, that the Church of Rome might also rejoice in the prosperity of that of Corinth.[236]

For the history of the dogma concerning the Church, it is our opinion that all these testimonies and circumstances of ancient times that we have briefly cited prove the truth that **since the very beginning the idea of the Church as a visible, historically existent community of the followers of Christ has not been foreign to Christians**. Since the very beginning of time, the one Church has been for Christians not something cerebral accepted on faith, but a very real actuality.[237]

---

234 "Ἐλθέτω χάρις καὶ παρελθέτω ὁ κόσμος οὗτος. Ὡσαννὰ τῷ Θεῷ Δαυΐδ. εἴ τις ἅγιός ἐστιν, ἐρχέσθω· εἴ τις οὐκ ἔστι, μετανοείτω· μαρὰν ἀθά· ἀμήν [Let grace come, and let this world pass away. Hosanna to the God of David! If any one is holy, let him come; if any one is not so, let him repent. Maran atha. Amen.]" (10.6).

235 For more detail on the oneness of the Church (or of Christianity) according to the *Didache*, see Harnack in the prolegomena to the edition of the *Didache*, TU 2.1.

236 65.1–2. Vgl. A. Harnack, *Der erste Klemensbrief* (Berlin: 1909), 53.

237 Dr. Schanz, "Der Begriff der Kirche," *Theologische Quartalschrift* (1893), 552: "An eine abstrakte, ideale, unsichtbare Kirche dachte man in Altertum überhaupt nicht." Cf. the contrasting opinion of Loofs, *Leitfaden der Dogmengeschichte*, 3-te Aufl. (Halle: 1893), §12.5.55: "The oneness of the whole Church in which they believed had neither outward signs nor visible guarantees." (In the fourth edition this phrase is absent—cf. 79–80). Vgl. §19.1, 130.

The one, visible Church was preached by the holy apostles: they themselves founded one Church, and that same one Church has existed since the very beginning.

SECOND ESSAY

The Concept of the Church in Anti-Judean Polemics of the First Two Centuries

Christianity began not with a doctrine, not with a formula, but with a renewal of life. Hence, despite a united life, initially a certain variance in doctrine was possible. Love united the hearts of all into one. There was no room for theoretical differences of opinion—or rather, if such theoretical differences of opinion did exist, they had little bearing on life.[238] This is how we must envision the life of the Christian Church in the early days of its existence. At that time there was no precise, unified, detailed formulation of Christian teaching that was obligatory for all. It must be supposed that only the most general, most fundamental truths were taught in precise form, whereas no such unity was present in the formulation of individual particular aspects of Christian teaching.

But the Church could not remain in this state for long. Historical circumstances very quickly prompted the Christian Church to more precisely define various subjects in its teaching. These circumstances were occasioned first and foremost by the historical en-

---

238 Cf. *Epistle of Barnabas* 1.6: "Τρία οὖν δόγματά ἐστιν κυρίου· ζωῆς ἐλπίς, ἀρχὴ καὶ τέλος πίστεως ἡμῶν, καὶ δικαιοσύνη, κρίσεως ἀρχὴ καὶ τέλος, ἀγάπη, εὐφροσύνης καὶ ἀγαλλιάσεως ἔργων ἐν δικαιοσύνῃ μαρτυρία [The doctrines of the Lord, then, are three: the hope of life, the beginning and the completion of our faith; and righteousness, the beginning and the completion of judgement; love, witness of gladness and rejoicing of works in righteousness]".

vironment that Christianity had entered. This historical environment very quickly declared itself to be something separate, a sort of antithesis to Christianity, and one way or another Christianity had to determine its relations with that historical environment. This marked the start of the development of precise definitions of Christian doctrine, and it was this that marked the beginning of the history of all dogma, including particularly the dogma concerning the Church. The dogma concerning the Church may be likened to ecclesiastical self-identification. In its self-identification the personality determines what it *is* and what it *is not*; in self-identification "what I am" is defined as opposed to "what I am not."

In the same way, in the dogma concerning the Church Christianity determines what it is, and it determines this as opposed to foreign phenomena arising from its historical environment. As his self-identification matures, a person defines himself, and a return to his former state of uncertain self-identification becomes no longer possible for him. In the same way, once the Church has dogmatically defined any subject of its doctrine, it can no longer lose that dogmatic formula.

In the history of each dogma one may observe a gradual transition from variety to unity. In particular, the doctrine concerning the Church that the holy apostles delivered to Christians was more of a general *idea* of the Church than an intricately developed *dogma*. From the very beginning, the life of Christian communities put forward a series of varied questions to which no direct answer was to be found in the teaching of the apostles. Guided by the general idea of the apostolic teaching, these questions were answered as well as possible by applying the general teaching of the apostles to individual cases. It is perfectly natural that at first there was no Church-wide doctrine concerning the Church that was definitively formulated in all minutiae. Church thinkers therefore needed to more precisely define the concept of the Church as opposed to the foreign phenomena whose environment the Church had entered.

The historical environment which Christianity had entered was, first and foremost, Judaism. The self-identification of Judaism at the time differed sharply from the Christian doctrine concerning the

Church, and this alone gave sufficient impetus for Christian consciousness to focus on the doctrine concerning the Church. Judaism at the time when Christianity encountered it may be characterized by two features: firstly, the strict nationalism of the Jewish religion, and secondly, the external, ritual nature of that religion. The second feature may actually be treated solely as the development and augmentation of the first: the nationalism of the religion was closely linked with the ritual life of Judaism. Rituals made one a Jew (proselytism), while without rituals a Jew was a renegade to his own tribe. At its very outset Christianity spread among the Jews, and therefore it could not immediately break ties with Judaism. We know that for a long time the Roman authorities did not distinguish between Christians and Jews, and for the Jews themselves Christianity was at first perceived merely as the Nazarite heresy (ἡ τῶν Ναζωραίων αἵρεσις), as we see from the words of the orator Tertullian before Felix.[239] In the early days the Christian community, which consisted of Jews, assembled together with the apostles in the temple in Jerusalem, as the book of Acts relates, and performed all the rituals of the Jewish law. But soon in the Christian Church a question arose with regard to Judaism—a question prompted by the conversion of the gentiles. The question was promptly raised as to whether the law was obligatory for Christians from among the gentiles. The Christians from among the Jews could not soon renounce their inherent nationalistic views on religion, and were inclined to view gentile converts to the faith as proselytes. And so we see at the very beginning of Christian history that "certain men which came down from Judaea [to Antioch] taught the brethren, and said, Except ye be circumcised after the manner of Moses, ye cannot be saved" (Acts 15:1). These words may be viewed as the recurring theme of statements made by Jewish Christians throughout the first two centuries of Christian history. The old Tübingen school headed by Baur envisioned the matter thus: in opposition to Jewish nationalism, the apostle Paul developed the idea of a universal Christian Church. A struggle begins between this thesis and antithesis. The first century of church history is filled with the struggle between

---

239 Acts 24:5.

Petrinism and Paulinism: sometimes one side emerged victorious, sometimes the other. Ultimately both opposites synthesized, producing the catholic Church, with both sides making certain concessions. Consequently, in the view of scholars in this arena, the idea of a universal Church is the product of a struggle between Petrinism and Paulinism. Today, all the ideas of the old Tübingen school may be considered so largely abandoned by scholarly thought that we may bypass them without examination.[240] It should however be noted that to more recent scholarship the Tübingen school bequeathed a confusion of concepts—Judaistic Christianity and gentile Christianity—of which Harnack complained.[241] Harnack himself broke with the aforementioned Tübingen ideas completely, and puts forward arguments that are perfectly logical. Harnack applies the term "Judaistic Christians" to those Christians from among the Jews who considered the Mosaic Law essential to a greater or lesser degree. This Judaistic Christianity should be juxtaposed not to gentile Christianity,[242] but to the Christian religion as a universal and anti-nationalistic religion.[243] Historical research within the catholic Church (*im Katholicismus*) fails to find any element alongside Christianity that could be termed a Judaistic Christian element.[244] From this standpoint it must be acknowledged that the idea of the Christian Church did not develop gradually amid a struggle between two opposites. No, the idea of the Church originated alongside Chris-

---

240 We encounter the ideas of the Tübingen school, albeit in somewhat more moderate form, in Albrecht Ritschl's *Die Entstehung der altkatholischen Kirche*, 2-te Auflage (Bonn: 1857), 248 ff. "The first compromise in favor of Judaism is indicated in the resolution of the Apostolic Council" (Ritschl, 251–252). Vgl. Friedrich Nitsch, *Grundiss der Christlichen Dogmengeschichte*, 1-er Teil (Berlin: 1870), 37–38. But Thomasius reasons quite differently regarding the resolution of the Apostolic Council (*Dogmengeschichte*², 49–50).

241 *Dogmengeschichte*⁴, 310–311.

242 Vgl. Ritschl: "The opposite of Judaistic Christianity in the period from the time of the apostles to the exclusion of Jewish Christians from the Church is gentile Christianity, and not Pauline Christianity" (*Die Entstehung der altkath. Kirche*, 271).

243 *Dogmengeschichte*⁴, 312.

244 Ibid. 1, 315.

tianity. Judaistic Christianity should therefore be viewed not as a factor in the formative process of the concept of the Church, not as one of the elements that contributed to the sum total, but as a heresy—a departure from the already existent Christian Church. But the conflict with this aberration gave ecclesiastical writers numerous occasions to develop the idea of the Christian Church in contrast to Judaism. This is the more true in that from the very beginning the Christian Church appropriated the Old Testament, viewing it as its own early history and thereby liberating it from historical and national conditions. Consequently, from the very beginning the Church had to establish and determine its relations with the Old Testament.

There is a view among scholars that the anti-Jewish polemics of the first centuries emerged from exclusively apologetic objectives, and were not polemics in the narrow sense. Supposedly only the latter polemics were directed against actual Jews, while the objections that the Jew or the Judaistic Christian could have raised are only rarely disproven, or are touched on only when absolutely necessary. These anemic unhistorical and merely theoretical polemics would have been impossible in bitter disputes with an actual opponent. In actuality, the opponent is a mere fiction; he has no perspective distinct from that of the Christian. Hence, he is not the Jew that actually existed, but the Jew whom the Christian feared. Here the seeming polemics are always apologetics, and the concept of the Church was formed specifically in apologetic interests.[245]

It must be acknowledged that this view has considerable validity. From the very beginning, the Church had to juxtapose itself to Judaism, to the false church of the Jews, and this juxtaposition had to have influenced the development of the self-identification of the Church, wholly independently of how it regarded actual representatives of the Jewish worldview. In historic early Christian

---

245   Here we have presented Harnack's view of the anti-Jewish polemics as expressed in his earliest works: "... Über den sogenannten zweiten Brief des Clemens an die Korinther" (*Zeitschrift für Kirchengeschichte* [1876], Bd. 1 [Heft 3], 344–345, Anm. Vgl. 359). But in particular see *Die Altercatio Simonis Iudaei et Theophili Christiani nebst Untersuchungen über die antijüdische Polemik in der alten Kirche*, TU 1.3 (Leipzig: 1883), 63–64.

manuscripts one may observe ideas concerning the Church that
are the fruit of this ideological juxtaposition to Judaism. But the
actual polemics can hardly be ignored completely. It is true that
we know very little concerning the interrelations of the Jews and
the Christians, but from this it hardly follows no polemics between
Jews and Christians actually occurred.[246] The polemical works of
church writers may be considered reverberations of actual reality,
and not of merely imaginary polemics. Judaistic Christianity did in
fact exist. We find references to the Judaistic heretics in the works
of many church writers, and hence this heresy may be presumed to
have been of significant proportions. The existence in the Church
itself of people permeated with Judaistic tendencies, coupled with
the actual polemics against Judaism, were important factors in the
swift development of the self-identification of the Church.

What ideas, then, were expressed by the disseminators of Judaistic tendencies?

In the dialogue between Justin the Philosopher and Trypho the
Jew, the latter poses the question: will a person be saved who acknowledges Christ, believes in and obeys Him, and in addition to
this desires to observe these injunctions also? Justin's response shows
that there were two kinds of Judaizing Christians: some considered
the Mosaic Law obligatory only for Christians from among the Jews,
and even only for themselves; while others, like Trypho at the start
of the dialogue, demanded that former gentiles also observe the

---

246 Harnack asserts that from the time of Domitian the Church's contact with
the synagogue and the Palestinian Ebionites was highly insignificant. Although
the Talmud makes mention of it, it may be asserted that, aside from the small
districts of Syria and Palestine, it marked an exception in the empire (*Die Altercatio
Simonis Iudaei*, TU 1.3, 63). But cf. the arguments of Rudolf Knopf, *Das Nachapostolische Zeitalter* (Tübingen: 1905), 346. See also G. Hoennicke, *Das Judenchristentum*,
241–248, 249–252. The latter considers Justin's *Dialogue with Trypho*, for example,
to be a vivid picture of how in the mid-second century disputes were conducted
between Jews and Christians in Asia Minor (246). Indications of Christianity
in the Talmud are analyzed in a dedicated appendix to Hoennicke's book *Der
Minäismus* (381–400). The author concludes that although in certain passages of
the Talmud polemics against Christianity may be noted, in general rabbinical literature contains little information that could help to answer the question of how
the Jews regarded the Christian movement in the first and second centuries (400).

law, asserting that without observing this law salvation is impossible for all without exception, and they desired no fellowship with those who did not observe the law.[247] Justin himself was favorably inclined toward the first kind of Judaizing Christians,[248] while stating that he did not accept the second kind.[249] But at the same time among the Christians there were those who held that Judaizing Christians of both the first and the second kind were cut off from the Church, and were afraid even to converse or take food with them.[250] These words of Justin attest that in his day there was no difference of opinion regarding strict Judaizers: they were not considered members of the Christian community. But it must be thought that this delimitation of the Church from the Judaizers existed not only in the second century: even before this time, strongly marked Judaistic tendencies always met with resistance in the Christian community. The epistle of the apostle Paul to the Galatians already proclaims Christian freedom from the Mosaic Law. These words of the apostle Paul alone show that even then there were false brethren from among the Jews who wished to enslave all Christians to the law. But no, the apostle writes: "we gave place by subjection ... not for an hour; that the truth of the gospel might continue with" the Christians (Gal. 2:4–5). Even at that time those born of Abraham after the flesh were persecuting those born after the Spirit.[251] And it was not just Paul, the apostle to the gentiles, who rejected the Jewish

247 *Dialogue with Trypho*, 46–47 passim (*Corpus apologetarum christianorum saeculi secundi*, edidit Io. Car. Th. eques de Otto, vol. 1, 2 [Ienae: MDCCCLXXVII], 152–160; ANF 1:217–219.

248 Justin Martyr, *Dialogue with Trypho* 47: "If some, through weak-mindedness (τῆς γνώμης), wish to observe such institutions as were given by Moses, from which they expect some virtue, but which we believe were appointed by reason of the hardness of the people's hearts ... then I hold that we ought to join ourselves to such, and associate with them in all things as kinsmen (ὡς ὁμοσπλάγχνοις) and brethren" (ANF 1:218; CAC 1.2:158).

249 Justin Martyr, *Dialogue with Trypho* 47 (CAC 1.2:158).

250 Justin Martyr, *Dialogue with Trypho* 47 (ANF 1:218–219; CAC 1.2:158). Vgl.: Friedrich Böhringer, *Die Alte Kirche*, 1-er Band, 1-er Teil, 2-te Ausgabe (Stuttgart: 1873), 172.

251 See Gal. 4:29.

law for gentiles. In his epistles the apostle Peter supported Paul's authority, against which the Judaizing Christians were rebelling. The apostle Peter writes: "Account that the longsuffering of our Lord is salvation; even as our beloved brother Paul also according to the wisdom given unto him hath written unto you" (2 Pet. 3:15).[252] The moderate type of Judaistic tendencies were of course constantly supported in the Church of Jerusalem. But the Christian community in Jerusalem, which had initially held an illustrious position, gradually fell into increasing decline, along with the decline of the Hebrew nation.[253] The destruction of Jerusalem shook the position of the Church of Jerusalem to the core. The Christians, as we know, migrated to Pella, and Eusebius notes that from that time the saints completely forsake both the royal city and the whole land of Judea.[254] Epiphanius relates that the Christians did return to Jerusalem,[255] but the Jerusalem community no longer enjoyed its former authority. The date of the final collapse of the Judaistic Christian community and Jerusalem must be set in A.D. 136, when following the Bar Kokhba revolt[256] Hadrian forbade the Jews even to approach the region of Jerusalem, so that in Jerusalem, which was renamed, no Jews were left.[257] According to Justin, before the

252 From Peter's subsequent words it is clear that even at that time the work of the apostle Paul was being distorted by those who were not confirmed, unto [their] own destruction.

253 Concerning the history of the Church of Jerusalem, see Myshtsyn, *The Organization of the Christian Church*, 67–73. See also Ritschl, op. cit., 415–419; Harnack, *Entstehung und Entwickelung der Kirchenverfassung*, 25–30.

254 Eusebius, *Church History* 3.5.3 (GrchSch. 9.1:196.15–20).

255 Concerning evidence of the return of Christians to Jerusalem, see Myshtsyn, *The Organization of the Christian Church*, 69–71.

256 Ritschl likewise considers the insurrection of Bar Kokhba a decisive point in history (*Die Entstehung der altkath. Kirche*, 258–259).

257 Eusebius, op. cit. 4.6.3–4 (GrchSch. 9.1:307.4–11). See Justin Martyr, *First Apology* 47: "Death is decreed against a Jew apprehended entering [Jerusalem]" (ANF 1:178; CAC 1.1:132). According to Tertullian (*Against the Jews* 3 [PL 2:624a]) and secular historians, all who were circumcised were prohibited from entering Jerusalem, and Justin says that circumcision was a sign so that only the Jews might endure the afflictions which justly befell them, and so that none of

end of Jerusalem fanatical Jews considered Christians their enemies and opponents and persecuted them just as the pagans did. Bar Kokhba, the leader of the Jewish revolt, likewise gave Christians over to torture if they did not renounce Jesus Christ.[258] Once those of the circumcision had been driven out of Jerusalem, the Judaizers conclusively lost all significance for the life of the Church. As they became still more isolated in their legalistic tendencies, they eventually degenerated into two sects: the Ebionites and the Nazarenes. From that time on, in Jerusalem also the Church was comprised of gentiles, and Mark became its first bishop after the bishops from among those of the circumcision.[259]

In hereseological literature the Judaizers are characterized by three traits. Firstly, they considered observance of the Old Testament law obligatory for Christianity, as well.[260] Secondly, they rejected the authority of the apostle Paul, calling him an apostate from the law, while avowing that Peter observed all the rites of the law.[261] Thirdly, they denied the seedless birth of Christ the Savior,

---

them might dare to enter Jerusalem (*Dialogue with Trypho* 16 [ANF 1:202; CAC 1.2:58]).

258 Justin Martyr, *First Apology* 31 (CAC 1.1:94).

259 Eusebius, op. cit. 4.6.4 (GrchSch. 9.1:308.11–13).

260 Justin Martyr, *Dialogue with Trypho* 46–47. "They practice circumcision, persevere in the observance of those customs which are enjoined by the law, and are ... Judaic in their style of life" (Irenaeus, *Against Heresies* 1.26.2 [ANF 1:352]). Eusebius, op. cit. 3.27.2 (GrchSch. 9.1:256.5–7), Epiphanius, Haer. 30.2.21, 26, etc. (ἔθεσιν Ἰουδαϊκοῖς ζῶσι, κατὰ νόμον φάσκοντες δικαιοῦσθαι [they live by Jewish customs, saying that they are justified by the law]). Hippolytus, *Refutation of all Heresies* 7.34 (PG 16:3342b).

261 Irenaeus, *Against Heresies* 1.26.2, 3.15.1. "These men, moreover, thought that it was necessary to reject all the epistles of the apostle (Paul), whom they called an apostate from the law; and they used only the so-called Gospel according to the Hebrews and made small account of the rest" (Eusebius, *Church History* 3.27.4 [NPNF² 1:159; GrchSch. 9.1:256.13–16]). Epiphanius relates that the Ebionites not only considered the apostle Paul an apostate from the law, but by saying that he was of Tarsus they suppose him to be of Greek descent. They then state that he is a Greek, the son of a Greek mother and a Greek father: "He came to Jerusalem and spent a fair amount of time there. He desired to take the daughter of a priest to wife and for this purpose became a proselyte and was

Who in their opinion was a Man, Who following His election was anointed and made the Christ for His righteous life, as He had fulfilled the entire law.[262] Of these three points of the Ebionite teaching, the first is of primary importance for the issue at hand. Clearly, the apostle Paul's teaching that the Church was an organism for all mankind, in which there is neither Greek nor Jew, but all comprise "a new creature," was completely repudiated by those who adopted the Judaistic nationalistic tendencies. The essence of the New Testament Church, in the opinion of the Ebionites, was not that in it all mankind is reformed into a new creature, but merely that all nations convert to Judaism through proselytism.[263] It should however

---

circumcised. Then, upon not receiving the maiden, he was angered and began writing against circumcision, against the Sabbath, and against the statutes of the law" (Haer. 30.16 [PG 41:432d–433a; cf. 25]. Concerning what manner of actions was ascribed to the apostle Peter, see Idem 15, 21).

262 Justin Martyr, *Dialogue with Trypho* 48–49 [CAC 1.2:162 sqq]). Irenaeus, *Against Heresies* 3.11.7, 3.21.1, 4.33.4, 5.1.3. "The ancients quite properly called these men Ebionites, because they held poor and mean opinions concerning Christ. For they considered him a plain and common man, who was justified only because of his superior virtue, and who was the fruit of the intercourse of a man with Mary" (Eusebius, *Church History* 3.27.1–2 [NPNF² 1:159; GrchSch. 9.1:256.1–4]). Epiphanius, Haer. 30.2, 3, 27, 29–31: "Truly impoverished in understanding, hope, and works is he who declares Christ to be a mere man" (Ibid. 17 [PG 41:433b]). "They received the name of Ebionites, which signified the poverty of their understanding. For this is the name by which a poor man is called among the Hebrews" (Eusebius, op. cit. 3.27.6 [NPNF² 1:160; GrchSch. 9.1:256.20–22]). Cf. Ignatius, *Epistle to the Philadelphians* 6.1. "...τὸν Ἰησοῦν λέγοντες δεδικαιῶσθαι ποιήσαντα τὸν νόμον διὸ καὶ Χριστὸν αὐτὸν τοῦ Θεοῦ ὠνομάσθαι, καὶ Ἰησοῦν, ἐπεὶ μηδεὶς τῶν ἑταίρων ἐτέλεσε τὸν νόμον· εἰ γὰρ καὶ ἕτερός τις πεποιήκει τὰ ἐν νόμῳ προστεταγμένα ἦν ἂν ἐκεῖνος ὁ Χριστός [... saying that Jesus was justified by fulfilling the law. And therefore it was that he was named Christ of God and Jesus, since not one of the rest had observed completely the law. For if even any other had fulfilled the commandments in the law, he would have been that Christ]" Hippolytus, *Refutation of all Heresies* 7.22 (PG 16:3342b); cf. 9.14 (PG 16:3390b).

263 In the *Dialogue with Trypho* we read: "These words (Is. 42:6, 7), indeed, sirs, refer also to Christ, and concern the enlightened nations; or will you say again, He speaks to them of the law and the proselytes? Then some of those who had come on the second day cried out as if they had been in a theatre, 'But what? does He not refer to the law, and to those illumined by it? Now these are prose-

be noted that the other two points of Ebionite teaching mentioned are closely linked to the first. The apostle Paul, who especially labored in elucidating the Christian concept of the Church, was rejected by the Judaizers specifically on the grounds of their nationalistic views, which they extended even to the Christian Church. We have already noted that the ecclesiology of the apostle Paul is closely related to his christology: the new creature likewise required the New Adam. In the Jewish understanding of the Church, the incarnation of God was unnecessary. For the Jews in the time of Justin, the anticipated Messiah was merely ἄνθρωπος ἐξ ἀνθρώπων [man from men].[264] Thus, we make bold to assert that the Ebionite heresy was based specifically on a distorted understanding of the Christian doctrine concerning the Church. They rejected the apostolic teaching concerning the Church, and they rejected the Church as such, refusing to see anything new in Christianity with respect to Judaism.[265] Hence, the conflict between church writers and the Ebionites has a certain significance in the history of the dogma concerning the Church, whereas the christology of the Ebionites has left no discernible traces in dogmatic history.[266] At the same time, it should be noted that all the Judaistic tendencies were so opposed to the New Testament concept of the Church that it remained only to reject them from the standpoint of the newly formed concept of the Church.[267] Hence, in the history of the dogma concerning the Church, juxtaposition of the Church to Judaism was of no great significance. This juxtaposition left no discernible trace; it barely gave occasion to develop a positive doctrine concerning the Church. Consequently, anti-Jewish polemical literature serves rather to show us how the apostolic teaching was assimilated by the earliest church

---

lytes'" (Justin Martyr, *Dialogue with Trypho* 122 [ANF 1:260; CAC 1.2:438]). What the desires of the Judaizers were is quite clear. Cf. *Epistle of Barnabas* 3.6: "ἵνα μὴ προσρησσώμεθα ὡς ἐπήλυτοι [προσήλυτοι] τῷ ἐκείνων νόμῳ [so that we might not be beaten by their law as proselytes]."

264 Justin Martyr, *Dialogue with Trypho* 49 (CAC 1.2:164).

265 Vgl. Thomasius, *Die Dogmengeschichte*, 58.

266 Harnack, *Dogmengeschichte*[4] 1, 314, 317.

267 Vgl. Ritschel, *Die Entstehung der altkath. Kirche*, 253.

writers and how it was juxtaposed to the Judaistic errors. Simultaneously, this same literature shows us the arguments with which early
church thought justified the fact that the Church appropriated the
Old Testament while rejecting Judaism.

The New Testament Scriptures establish a very definite view of
the Church and how it related to Judaism. Of the sacred books of
the New Testament, the most strikingly anti-Jewish tone is found
in the Gospel of John and the epistle to the Hebrews. Here we
see clearly expressed the idea that the lawful and valid significance
of the Old Testament existed up until the Church of Christ was
established. Once the Church of Christ is established, there is no
more need for the Old Testament with its sacrificial rites and all
its laws in general. The Holy Scripture of the Old Testament is of
value in that it contains prophecies and prefigurations of the New
Testament Church. The prophetic and typological understanding
of the Old Testament Scriptures had to be replaced by a literal understanding of them. Christ Himself said that the Scriptures testi-
fied concerning Him. Not only the prophets, but even Moses wrote
concerning Christ.[268] The bronze serpent prefigured the crucifixion
of Christ upon the Cross,[269] and the manna—the New Testament
"bread of life."[270] The law concerning the Passover lamb, that not
a bone of it be broken, likewise indicated the unbroken legs of the
crucified Christ.[271] The epistle to the Hebrews offers a critique of
the Old Testament law,[272] making it clear that the New Testament
is necessary[273] and that the Old Testament law was merely a shadow of the good things to come, and not the actual image of those
things (οὐκ αὐτὴν τὴν εἰκόνα τῶν πραγμάτων).[274] The apostle no
longer recognizes the Hebrew nation, set apart for a particular, inti-

---

268 See Jn. 5:39, 45–47.

269 See Jn. 3:14.

270 See Jn. 6:32 and the verses that follow.

271 See Jn. 19:32–36.

272 See Heb. 7:11–28, 9:13, 10:1–4.

273 See Heb. 8:7–13.

274 See Heb. 10:1.

mate relationship with God, but rather speaks only of the meaning of the Old Testament institutions. When the Jews say that they are Jews, they lie, because they are not Jews, but a satanic assembly (συναγωγὴ τοῦ σατανᾶ).[275] The Church is the true Israel of God.[276]

This reasoning concerning the Old Testament God and the people of Israel is naturally advanced by New Testament writers because they espouse the idea of the Church of Christ as a new creation, in which there can be no national boundaries. The church writers of the first two centuries who polemicized with the Judaizers preserve and further develop this same idea of the Church, and consequently nearly all of them share this reasoning concerning the Old Testament, as well.

One epistle, written under the name of the apostle Barnabas, does not speak of the Church directly, but nevertheless the concept of the Church found in this epistle is quite clear and definite, although expressed in only a very few remarks. Jesus Christ was destined by His appearance to free from darkness those hearts that were given over to the iniquity of error, and the Father commands Him to prepare a holy people for himself.[277] Christ came to prepare for Himself a new people (αὐτὸς ἑαυτῷ τὸν λαὸν τὸν καινόν ἑτοιμάζων[278]). He offered His flesh for the sins of this new people (ὑπὲρ ἁμαρτιῶν τοῦ λαοῦ τοῦ καινοῦ[279]), so that His wound might restore us to life,[280] and so as to free us from darkness.[281] The words of Scripture, "Let us make man in our image, after our likeness"

275 See Rev. 2:9; cf. 3:9.

276 See Gal. 6:16. For more detail concerning the New Testament doctrine that the Church is the true Israel, see R. Knopf's *Das Nachapostolische Zeitalter,* 346–353. See also Nathanael Bonwetsch, "Der Schriftbeweis für die Kirche aus der Heiden als das wahre Israel bis auf Hippolyt," in *Theologische Studien: Theodor Zahn zum 10. Oktober, 1908 dargebracht* (Leipzig: 1908), 3–6.

277 *Epistle of Barnabas* 14.5–6: "Αὐτῷ ὁ πατὴρ ἐντέλλεται ... ἑτοιμάσαι ἑαυτῷ λαὸν ἅγιον."

278 *Epistle of Barnabas* 5.7.

279 *Epistle of Barnabas* 7.5.

280 *Epistle of Barnabas* 7.2: "ἵνα ἡ πληγὴ αὐτοῦ ζωοποιήσῃ ἡμᾶς."

281 *Epistle of Barnabas* 14.6.

(Gen 1:26), pertain to Christians.[282] The Son of God performed a
second work of creation (δευτέραν πλάσιν) at the end of time,[283] renewed men by the remission of sins, made men different (ἐποίησεν
ἡμᾶς ἄλλον τύπον), and restored them (ὡς ἂν δὴ ἀναπλάσσοντος
αὐτοῦ ἡμᾶς), so that they now have a childlike soul.[284] "The habitation of our heart is a holy temple to the Lord."[285] "Having received
the forgiveness of sins, and placed our trust in the name of the
Lord, we have become new creatures, formed again from the beginning (πάλιν ἐξ ἀρχῆς κτιζόμενοι). Wherefore in our habitation God
truly dwells in us. How? His word of faith; His calling of promise; the wisdom of the statutes (δικαιωμάτων); the commands of
the doctrine; He himself prophesying in us; He himself dwelling in
us."[286] The Spirit is poured out upon Christians from the bountiful
wellspring of the Lord.[287] Christians have been given the right to be
the people of the inheritance (εἰς λαὸν κληρονομίας).[288]

As for how the Church regards the Old Testament, the epistle of Barnabas adopts a view that is quite extraordinary for all of
early church literature. The Old Testament, as it was assimilated
by historical Jewish culture, did not at all fulfill God's design in its
thinking. God promised with an oath to give the law to the Hebrew people. And indeed, Moses received from the Lord two tablets, written with the finger of the hand of the Lord, and brought
them down from the mountain to give them to the people. But the
Jews had cast an idol, and so Moses threw down the tablets, and
the tablets of the Lord's testament were broken. "Their covenant
was broken, in order that the covenant of the beloved Jesus might

282 *Epistle of Barnabas* 6.12.

283 *Epistle of Barnabas* 6.13.

284 *Epistle of Barnabas* 6.11. Cf. 6.14: "ἴδε οὖν ἡμεῖς ἀναπεπλάσμεθα [Behold,
therefore, we have been refashioned]."

285 *Epistle of Barnabas* 6.15 (ANF 1:141): "Ναὸς ἅγιος, ἀδελφοί μου, τῷ κυρίῳ
τὸ κατοικητήριον ἡμῶν τῆς καρδίας []." Cf. 16.10.

286 *Epistle of Barnabas* 16.8–9 (ANF 1:147). Cf. 15.7: "Καινῶν δε γεγονότων
πάντων ὑπὸ κυρίου [all things having been made new by the Lord]."

287 *Epistle of Barnabas* 1.3.

288 *Epistle of Barnabas* 14.1.

be sealed upon our heart, in the hope which flows from believing in Him."[289] We, having been made heirs, received the covenant of our Lord Jesus Christ.[290] In the passages cited we may observe the idea that the New Testament is the very one that was traced upon the tablets broken by Moses.[291] Thus, in actuality, until Christ came into the world there was no covenant between God and the Hebrew people.[292] In the opinion of the epistle's author, the Jews completely failed to understand the law of Moses. They had been deceived by an evil angel (ἄγγελος πονηρὸς ἐσόφιζεν αὐτούς),[293] and for this reason they began understanding the law literally.[294] For this reason we cannot say that the covenant of the Jews (ἐκείνων) is ours as well; for the covenant belongs only to Christians, while the Jews lost the covenant for all time when Moses received it.[295] There is truth hidden in the law, but one must know how to discover it. The purpose of the epistle is that its readers might have perfect knowledge (γνῶσις).[296] This *gnosis*, the epistle states, is nothing less than an alle-

---

289 *Epistle of Barnabas* 4.7–8 (ANF 1:139): "ἵνα ἡ τοῦ ἠγαπημένου Ἰησοῦ ἐγκατασφραγισθῇ εἰς τὴν καρδίαν ἡμῶν ἐν ἐλπίδι τῆς πίστεως αὐτοῦ."

290 *Epistle of Barnabas* 14.5

291 Cf. *Epistle of Barnabas* 14.1: "He did give [the covenant to the Jews]; but they were not worthy to receive it, on account of their sins" (ANF 1:146).

292 Cf. Knopf, *Das nachapostolische Zeitalter*, 356. F. Loofs. *Leitfaden der Dog-mengeschichte*, §14.4a, 90. Paralleling the latter idea, we may cite a passage from "Peter's Preaching": "ἐκεῖνοι μόνοι οἰόμενοι τὸν Θεὸν γινώσκειν οὐκ ἐπίστανται, λατρεύοντες ἀγγέλοις καὶ ἀρχαγγέλοις, μηνὶ καὶ σελήνῃ [thinking that only they know God, they {that is, the Jews} do not understand, worshipping angels and archangels, the month and the moon]" (Clement of Alexandria, *Stromata* 6.5.41.2 [GrchSch. 15:452.8–10]). The same is found in the Apology of Aristides, 14.4: "In their imagination they conceive that it is God they serve; whereas by their mode of observance it is to the angels and not to God that their service is rendered." –J. Geffken, *Zweigriechische Apologeten* (Leipzig and Berlin: 1907). A. Pokrovsky, *Aristides the Philosopher and his Recently Discovered Apology* ["Философ Аристид и его недавно открытая апология"] (Sergiev Posad: 1898).

293 *Epistle of Barnabas* 9:4.

294 *Epistle of Barnabas* 2:9; 4:6; 10:9, 12; 16:1–2.

295 *Epistle of Barnabas* 4:6–7.

296 *Epistle of Barnabas* 1:5.

gorical method of interpreting the books of the Old Testament.[297] Using this method of interpretation, in all the Old Testament statutes of the law the author sees only a moral meaning,[298] and in all events—a prefiguration of New Testament events.[299] The allegorical method of interpreting the books of the Old Testament predominates among all the church writers of the first two centuries,[300] but only the author of the epistle of Barnabas expresses the idea that the Old Testament Hebrews also ought to have understood their law in an exclusively allegorical sense.

Thus, the author of the "epistle of Barnabas" appropriates the Old Testament likewise for the Church, because he speaks only of the Christian Church. The new race of men restored by Christ and united into the Church is the only human community with which God has entered into a covenant.

Other authors, polemicists against the Jews, adhere more closely to the sacred writers of the New Testament in their views of the sig-

---

297 *Epistle of Barnabas* 6.9: "τί δὲ λέγει ἡ γνῶσις; μάθετε [What, then, says Knowledge? Learn]." Cf. 6.10, 13.7, 9.8: "τίς οὖν ἡ δοθεῖσα αὐτῷ γνῶσις [What, then, was the knowledge given to him]." This is followed by an allegorical interpretation of the number 318 (Gen 17.23–27).

298 Concerning sacrifices, *Epistle of Barnabas* 2:4–10; fasts—3:1–6; the meaning of circumcision—9:1–7; the dietary commandments have a moral significance—10:1–11; the meaning of the law concerning the sabbath—15:1–8. The Jewish temple refers to a spiritual temple created for the Lord—16:1–10.

299 The promise of the land of Canaan to Abraham, Isaac, and Jacob signifies the incarnation of the Son of God (*Epistle of Barnabas* 6:8–10). The day of purification signifies the sufferings of Christ down to the details (7:4–11). The sacrifice of the red heifer had the same meaning (8:11–6). The 318 men whom Abraham circumcised indicate the name of Christ and the cross by their number: "No one has been admitted by me to a more excellent piece of knowledge" (9:8–9). The bronze serpent: "Thou hast in this also [an indication of] the glory of Jesus; for in Him and to Him are all things" (12:5–7). Joshua was likewise an indication of Jesus Christ (12:8–10). The story of Rebekah indicates that Christians are the heirs of the covenant (13:1–6). Cf. N. Bonwetsch, *Der Schriftbeweis für die Kirche*, 6–8.

300 Concerning the inevitability of this method given the predominant theory of the divine inspiration of the sacred books, see Dr. Iohannes Leipoldt, *Geschichte des neutestamentlichen Kanons*, 1-er Theil. (Leipzig: 1907), 20–22. (See also Ludwig Diestel. *Geschichte des Alten Testamentes in der christlichen Kirche* (Iena: 1869), 30.

nificance of the Old Testament for the Church. That is to say, they acknowledge that the Old Testament had a temporary significance: it prepared men to enter into the Church through prophecies and prefigurations.[301] The law itself spoke of its own abolition and of the need for the New Testament. The Church is that covenant of God, made now with all of mankind, and not with the Hebrew nation alone.

Christ bestowed a new law, as was foretold in the Old Testament.[302] Jesus Christ, the only Son begotten of God, His Word and First-born and Power, Who by His will became Man, imparted His teaching to Christians for the conversion and restoration of the human race.[303] "Now ... an eternal and final law—namely, Christ — has been given to us, and the covenant is trustworthy, after which there shall be no law, no commandment, no ordinance."[304] This new law must encompass all mankind: all mankind now becomes

---

301 "'And in short, sirs,' said I, 'by enumerating all the other appointments of Moses, I can demonstrate that they were types, and symbols, and declarations of those things which would happen to Christ, of those who it was foreknown were to believe in Him, and of those things which would also be done by Christ Himself.'" –Justin Martyr, *Dialogue with Trypho* 42 (ANF 1:216; CAC 1.2:142). Indeed, employing an allegorical method of interpretation, St. Justin sees the entire Old Testament as nothing but prophecies and prefigurations of the New Testament Church, which encompasses all nations. See N. Bonwetsch, *Der Schriftbeweis für die Kirche*, 8–12. A detailed account of the polemics of St. Justin against the Jews is found in F. Böhringer's *Die alte Kirche*, B. 1. Th. 1, 174–204. Vgl. A. Ritschl, *Die Entstehung der altkath. Kirche*, 312–330.

In addition to Justin the Philosopher, a number of Old Testament prophecies and prefigurations concerning Christ and the Church are cited by St. Irenaeus of Lyons in the fourth book of *Against Heresies* (particularly chapters 7, 9, 10, 11, 12, 15–18, 20, 21, 25, and 31) and in his recently discovered work, *Demonstration of the Apostolic Preaching*, and also by Tertullian in the second half of his treatise *Against the Jews*. See Bonwetsch, *Der Schriftbeweis für die Kirche*, 12–15; cf. notes of Thomasius's *Die Dogmengeschichte*, 123.

302 Justin Martyr, *Dialogue with Trypho* 11, 12, 13 (ANF 1:199–201; CAC 1.2:40). Idem 24: "There is now another covenant, and another law has gone forth from Zion" (ANF 1:206; CAC 1.2:84).

303 Justin Martyr, *Apologies* 1.23 (ANF 1:170–171).

304 Justin Martyr, *Dialogue with Trypho* 11 (ANF 1:200; CAC 1.2:42). Cf. Barn. 2:6.

the new Israel, the new people. "If, therefore, God proclaimed a new covenant which was to be instituted, and this for a light of the nations, we see and are persuaded that men approach God, leaving their idols and other unrighteousness, through the name of Him who was crucified, Jesus Christ, and abide by their confession even unto death, and maintain piety. Moreover, by the works and by the attendant miracles, it is possible for all to understand that He is the new law, and the new covenant, and the expectation of those who out of every people wait for the good things of God. For the true spiritual Israel, and descendants of Judah, Jacob, Isaac, and Abraham (who in uncircumcision was approved of and blessed by God on account of his faith, and called the father of many nations), are we."[305] "This [law] is for all universally."[306] People of all countries, whether slaves or free, if they believe in Christ and acknowledge the truth in His words and in the words of His prophets, know that they will be together with Him in that land and will receive an eternal and incorruptible inheritance.[307] Those nations that enter the Church will be completely changed. In explaining Psalm 44, Justin the Philosopher says: "The word of God speaks to those who believe in Him as being one soul, and one synagogue (συναγωγή), and

---

305 Justin Martyr, *Dialogue with Trypho* 11 (ANF 1:200; CAC 1.2:42–44). God blesses this nation and calls it Israel and His inheritance; you are deceiving yourselves, as though you alone were Israel, and you curse a people that is blessed by God—ibid. 123 (ANF 1:261; CAC 1.2:442). We who keep the commandments of Christ, from Christ who has begotten us for God, are not only called Jacob, Israel, Judah, Joseph, and David, but also true sons of God, and are such in actual fact—ibid. (ANF 1:261). "All who through Him have fled for refuge to the Father, constitute the blessed Israel"—ibid. 125 (ANF 1:262; CAC 1.2:446). People from every nation who submit to His will through Christ ... must be Jacob and Israel—ibid. 130 (ANF 1:265; CAC 1.2:464). We comprise the true generation of Israel—ibid. 135 (ANF 1:267; CAC 1.2:480).

306 Justin Martyr, *Dialogue with Trypho* 11 (ANF 1:200; CAC 1.2:42). Ibid. 29: "Let us glorify God, all nations gathered together" (ANF 1:208; CAC 1.2:96). Ibid. 134: Jacob served Laban for the cattle that were speckled and of every aspect; Christ likewise endured slavery even to the point of the cross for various people of every aspect (πολυειδῶν) from every nation, acquiring them by His blood and the mystery of the cross (ANF 1:267; CAC 1.2:478).

307 Justin Martyr, *Dialogue with Trypho* 139 (ANF 1:269; CAC 1.2:490, 492).

one church, as to a daughter; ... it thus addresses the church which has sprung from His name and partakes of His name (for we are all called Christians) ... [and teaches][308] us also to forget [our] old ancestral customs."[309] In another place Justin describes in detail the renewal of the gentiles that is accomplished in the Church, where they are freed of unclean garments, meaning sins, and "are the true high priestly (ἀρχιερατικόν) race of God."[310] "After that Righteous One was put to death, we flourished as another people, and shot forth as new and prosperous corn. ... We are not a people to be despised, nor a barbarous race, nor such as the Carian and Phrygian nations; but God has even chosen us, and He has become manifest to those who asked not after Him. ... But we are not only a people, but also a holy people (λαὸς ἅγιος). ... This is that nation which God of old promised to Abraham, when He declared that He would make him a father of many nations; not meaning, however, the Arabians, or Egyptians, or Idumæans."[311] In his dialogue with Trypho, Justin calls this people the children of God: this perturbed his readers, and he was obliged to prove this thesis.[312] As proof he cites the words of Psalm 81: "Ye are gods, and all of you the sons of the Most High." "The Holy Ghost," says Justin, "reproaches men because they were made like God, free from suffering and death, provided that they kept His commandments, and were deemed deserving of the name of His sons, and yet they, becoming like Adam and Eve, work out death for themselves. ... Thereby it is demonstrated that all men are deemed worthy of becoming 'gods' (θεοί), and of having power to become sons of the Highest."[313]

---

308 The English translation cited has been altered to align more closely with the Russian translation. –*Trans.*

309 Justin Martyr, *Dialogue with Trypho* 63 (ANF 1:229; CAC 1.2:224).

310 Justin Martyr, *Dialogue with Trypho* 116 (ANF 1:257; CAC 1.2:416).

311 Justin Martyr, *Dialogue with Trypho* 119 (ANF 1:258–259; CAC 1.2:426). Justin substantiates this last thesis in the chapters that follow: 121, 122, 123.

312 Justin Martyr, *Dialogue with Trypho* 124: "I saw that they were perturbed because I said that we are the sons of God" (ANF 1:261; CAC 1.2:446).

313 Justin Martyr, *Dialogue with Trypho* 124 (ANF 1:262; CAC 1.2:446, 448).

The greatest church writer of the second century, St. Irenaeus, bishop of Lyons, in his teaching on the essence of the Christian Church as opposed to Judaism, wholly aligns himself with the theology of the apostle Paul, which he defends against the groundless attacks of the Judaizers. The latter were particularly displeased by the teaching reflected in the epistles of the apostle Paul concerning the universal Christian Church as a new work performed by the incarnate Son of God. Affirming the authority of the apostle Paul, St. Irenaeus shows that the apostle's teaching concerning the Church was alive not only in the profound theological thinking of the bishop of Lyons, but also in church consciousness in general of that time so proximate to that of the apostles. "Those, therefore, who do not accept (*qui non recipiunt*) of [the apostle Paul] ... who was chosen by God for this purpose, that he might boldly bear His name, as being sent to the forementioned nations, do despise the election of God, and separate themselves from the company of the apostles (*ab apostolorum conventu*). For neither can they contend that Paul was no apostle, when he was chosen for this purpose."[314] We must then observe how St. Irenaeus **inseparably links ecclesiology with christology.** The Ebionites did not see the work of Christ as effecting so radical a change in humanity as the apostle Paul taught concerning this, and so they had no need to acknowledge the divinity of Christ. The writers of the Church—both Justin[315] and Irenaeus—insist on the divinity of Christ. This necessity of the divinity of Christ the Savior for the founding of the Christian Church is expressed with particular clarity in the words of St. Irenaeus: "But if a thought of this kind should then suggest itself to you, to say, What then did the Lord bring to us by His advent?—know ye that He brought all [possible] novelty (*omnem novitatem*), by bringing Himself who had been announced. For this very thing was proclaimed beforehand, that a novelty (*novitas*) should come to renew and quicken (*innovatura et*

---

314 Irenaeus of Lyons, *Against Heresies* 3.15.1 (ANF 1:439; PG 7:917b–c). A similar refutation of all the accusations and slander that the Ebionites brought against the apostle Paul is made by Epiphanius, Haer. 30.25.

315 Justin Martyr, *Dialogue with Trypho* 48 (ANF 1:219).

vivificatura) mankind."[316] Consequently, the work of Christ lies not in a new teaching, but in the renewal and quickening of mankind, for which Christ had to be the incarnate Son of God. "Others again reject the coming of the Son of God and the dispensation of His incarnation, which the apostles delivered and the prophets declared beforehand, even such as should be the summing up of mankind, as we have shown you in brief: and such also are reckoned amongst those who are lacking in faith."[317] Through the work of Christ the perfection of our humanity is to be accomplished; consequently, the ecclesiology of St. Irenaeus is wholly placed within his overall soteriological system. We would greatly digress if we were to begin a detailed exposition of the soteriology of St. Irenaeus,[318] and therefore we will make only a brief observation. The soteriology of Irenaeus of Lyons is clearly and concisely expressed in his own words as follows: "The Son of the Most High God ... would become the Son of man for this purpose, that man also might become the son of God."[319] "The Word of God, our Lord Jesus Christ ... through His transcendent love [became] what we are, that He might bring us to be even what He is Himself (*uti nos perficeret esse quod est ipse*)."[320] "Christ Jesus, the Son of God ... because of His surpassing love towards His creation, condescended to be born of the virgin, He Himself uniting (*adunans*) man through Himself to God,"[321] and be-

---

316 Irenaeus of Lyons, *Against Heresies* 4.34.1 (ANF 1:511).

317 Irenaeus of Lyons, *The Demonstration of the Apostolic Preaching*, chapter 99, Armitage Robinson, trans. (London: Society for Promoting Christian Knowledge, and New York: The Macmillan Co., 1920), 150.

318 The soteriology of St. Irenaeus in his own words is presented in great detail in Böhringer's *Die alte Kirche*, 2-ter Band. 2-ter Theil, 2-te Ausgabe (Stuttgart: 1873), 547–567. See also Prof. I.V. Popov, *The Idea of Deification in the Ancient Eastern Church* ("Идея обожения в древневосточной Церкви") (Moscow: 1909), 3–21.

319 Irenaeus of Lyons, *Against Heresies* 3.10.2 (ANF 1:424; PG 7:873b).

320 Irenaeus of Lyons, *Against Heresies* 5, preface (ANF 1:526; PG 7:1120b).

321 Irenaeus of Lyons, *Against Heresies* 3.4.2 (ANF 1:417; PG 7:856a). Cf. 5.16.2: "The Word of God was made man, assimilating Himself to man, and man to Himself, so that by means of his resemblance to the Son, man might become precious to the Father" (ANF 1:544; PG 7:1167b–c). 4.20.4: "Our Lord

stowed the inheritance of incorruption (*incorruptelae*).[322] Creation becomes of one image and one body (*conformatum et concorporatum*) with
the Son of God. Creation receives the Word and ascends to Him,
surpassing the angels and being made after the image and likeness
of God.[323] Thus, salvation lies in the **deification** of mankind. **The
Church itself consists of mankind that has set out on the
path to deification.**[324] "These things ... were accomplished in
the Lord's person; and the same [is still true] with regard to us, the
body following the example of the Head."[325] A new life is created.
"Not by the much speaking of the law, but by the brevity of faith
and love, men were to be saved. ... So then by our faith in Him
He has made our love to God and our neighbour to grow, making
us godly and righteous and good."[326] In saved mankind there can
no longer be any national boundaries: the Old Testament law falls
away on its own when the new law is given. "[Christ] would not
send back the redeemed to the legislation of Moses ... but would
have them live in newness by the Word, through faith in the Son of
God and love."[327] Christ, Irenaeus teaches, also calls to the Church
the gentiles, who have no need of the law. Formerly they were a
wilderness and a waterless place,[328] but now they are freed from the

---

Jesus Christ ... in the last times was made a man among men, that He might join
the end to the beginning, that is, man to God" (ANF 1:488; PG 7:1034b).

322 Irenaeus of Lyons, *Against Heresies* 3.5.3 (ANF 1:418; PG 7:860c).

323 Irenaeus of Lyons, *Against Heresies* 5.36.3 (ANF 1:567; PG 7:1224b–c).

324 Irenaeus of Lyons, *Against Heresies* 4.20.12 (ANF 1:492; PG 7:1042a): "It
will be God's good pleasure to take out a Church which shall be sanctified by
fellowship (*communicatione*) with His Son."

325 Irenaeus of Lyons, *Against Heresies* 4.34.1 (ANF 1:512; PG 7:1086b).

326 Irenaeus of Lyons, *The Demonstration of the Apostolic Preaching* 87, 141. "By
faith in Him we learn to love God with all our heart, and our neighbour as ourselves" (ibid. 95, 147). Through faith in Him we learn to love God with all our
heart, and our neighbor as ourselves (ibid. 95). Irenaeus of Lyons, *Against Heresies*
3.5.2: "Jesus Christ ... redeemed us from apostasy with His own blood, so that we
should also be a sanctified people" (ANF 1:418; PG 7:860a).

327 Irenaeus of Lyons, *The Demonstration of the Apostolic Preaching* 89, 142.

328 Irenaeus of Lyons, *The Demonstration of the Apostolic Preaching* 89, 142. In this
composition the polemical juxtaposition of the essential points of true Christian

law, for they have received the Lord of the law, the Son of God.[329]
"By means of the marriage of Moses, was shown forth the noetic
(νοητός)[330] marriage of the Word (Gr. Ἰησοῦ, Lat. *Verbi*); and by
means of the Ethiopian bride, the Church taken from among the
Gentiles was made manifest; and those who do detract from, accuse, and deride it, shall not be pure (καθαροί). For they shall be full
of leprosy, and expelled from the camp of the righteous."[331] "Various coloured sheep were allotted to this Jacob as his wages; and the
wages (*merces*) of Christ are human beings, who from various and
diverse nations come together into one cohort (*cohortem*) of faith. ...
Christ [raised] up sons of God, both from freemen and from slaves
after the flesh, bestowing upon all, in the same manner, the gift of
the Spirit, who vivifies (*vivificantis*) us. But he (Jacob) did all things for
the sake of the younger, she who had the handsome eyes, Rachel,
who prefigured the Church, for which Christ endured (*sustinuit*) patiently."[332] The New Testament Church is distinguished by absolute
universalism. All nations are admitted to the door of new life and
the revelation of the New Testament.[333] Irenaeus symbolically explains the story of Gideon's fleece. The fleece was an image of the
people. First the dew was upon the fleece, then it was everywhere

---

doctrine to the heretical comprises the basis for all the arguments. Chapters 87–
96 in particular ("wertvollste Abschnitt der ganzeii Schrift," as Harnack notes—
TU. 31.1, *Nachwort*, 63), contain an animated exposition of the teaching on how
converted gentiles are free from the law of Moses. Cf. the observation of Prof.
Sagarda, *Christian Reading* ["Христианское чтение"], vol. 223, 487, 879–880.

329 Irenaeus of Lyons, *The Demonstration of the Apostolic Preaching* 95, 147: "We
need not the Law as a tutor." Cf. Irenaeus of Lyons, *Against Heresies* 3.5.3.

330 Not present in the English source quoted. –*Trans.*

331 Irenaeus of Lyons, *Against Heresies* 4.20.12 (ANF 1:492; PG 7:1042c–1043a).
Cf.: 4.21.2: "The children brought forth by Rebecca were a prediction of the two
nations" (ANF 1:493). 4.21.3: "The latter people has snatched away the blessings
of the former from the Father, just as Jacob took away the blessing of this Esau.
For which cause his brother suffered the plots and persecutions of a brother, just
as the Church suffers this self-same thing from the Jews" (ANF 1:493). Cf. Justin
Martyr, *Dialogue with Trypho* 134.

332 Irenaeus of Lyons, *Against Heresies* 4.21.3 (ANF 1:493; PG 7:1045b, 1046a).

333 Irenaeus of Lyons, *Against Heresies* 3.17.2 (PG 7:929d).

but on the fleece. This shows that the Hebrews will no longer have the Holy Spirit from God, but rather the dew—that is, the Spirit of God that descended upon the Lord—will be upon the whole earth.[334] Christ, "appearing in these last times, the chief corner-stone, has gathered into one, and united those that were far off and those that were near; that is, the circumcision and the uncircumcision, enlarging Japhet, and placing him in the dwelling of Shem."[335] The glorious Church is now everywhere, and in every place has now dug itself a winepress, since in every place there are those who receive the Spirit.[336] Wisdom openly lifts up her voice in the streets, preaches upon the high walls, and continually speaks in the city gates (cf. Prov. 1:20–21).[337] Everywhere the Church preaches the truth.[338] This unification of all mankind in the Church is the result of the incarnation of the Son of God, since this incarnation renewed human nature.[339] "All things had entered upon a new phase, the Word arranging after a new manner the advent in the flesh (*Verbo nove disponente carnalem adventum*), that He might win back (*ascriberet*) to God that human nature (*hominem*) which had departed from God; and therefore men were taught to worship God after a new fashion;"[340] "that by the putting away of the enmity towards God, which is unrighteousness, we should obtain peace with Him, doing that which is pleasing to Him."[341] "By the new calling a change of hearts in the Gentiles came to pass through the Word of God, when He was made flesh and tabernacled with men."[342]

---

334 Irenaeus of Lyons, *Against Heresies* 3.17.3 (PG 7:930b–c).

335 Irenaeus of Lyons, *Against Heresies* 3.5.3 (ANF 1:418; PG 7:860a).

336 Irenaeus of Lyons, *Against Heresies* 4.36.2 (PG 7:1091c–1092a).

337 Irenaeus of Lyons, *Against Heresies* 4.20.1 (PG 7:1177b–c).

338 Irenaeus of Lyons, *Against Heresies* 4.20.1 (PG 7:1177c).

339 Irenaeus of Lyons, *Against Heresies* 4.24.1: "Hominem in hominibus factum, reformasse quidem humanum genus" (ANF 1:495; PG 7:1049c).

340 Irenaeus of Lyons, *Against Heresies* 3.10.2 (ANF 1:424). Here also (see above) it is noteworthy that soteriology transitions directly into ecclesiology.

341 Irenaeus of Lyons, *The Demonstration of the Apostolic Preaching* 86, 140.

342 Irenaeus of Lyons, *The Demonstration of the Apostolic Preaching* 94, 145.

The effectual renewal of mankind redeemed by Christ is accomplished by the Holy Spirit, Who became a moral force creating new life in the Church. "The Holy Spirit ... fashioned the new way of godliness and righteousness."[343] This thesis is expounded in detail in many passages of the writings of St. Irenaeus. "This Spirit ... as Luke says, descended at the day of Pentecost upon the disciples after the Lord's ascension, having power to admit all nations to the entrance of life, and to the opening of the new covenant; from whence also, with one accord in all languages, they uttered praise to God, the Spirit bringing distant tribes to unity, and offering to the Father the first-fruits of all nations. Wherefore also the Lord promised to send the Comforter, who should join (*aptaret*) us to God. For as a compacted lump of dough cannot be formed of dry wheat without fluid matter, nor can a loaf possess unity, so, in like manner, neither could we, being many, be made one in Christ Jesus without the water from heaven. And as dry earth does not bring forth unless it receive moisture, in like manner we also, being originally a dry tree, could never have brought forth fruit unto life without the voluntary rain from above.[344] For our bodies have received unity among themselves (*unitatem*) by means of that laver which leads to incorruption; but our souls, by means of the Spirit."[345] "The Lord [commends] to the Holy Spirit His own man, who had fallen among thieves."[346] Christ recapitulated (*recapitulatus est*) human nature in Himself: "Uniting man to the Spirit, and causing the Spirit to dwell (*collocans*) in man, He is Himself made the head

343 Irenaeus of Lyons, *The Demonstration of the Apostolic Preaching* 89, 143. Cf. 93: "Our hearts being withdrawn and taken away from the stony worship by means of faith behold God, and become sons of Abraham, who was justified by faith" (145).

344 Here the Russian source differs from the English translation, reading literally: "... in like manner we also, being many, could not become one (*unum*) in Christ Jesus without water from heaven." –*Trans.*

345 Irenaeus of Lyons, *Against Heresies* 3.5.3 (ANF 1:418; PG 7:929c–930a). "The Lord, receiving this as a gift from His Father, does Himself also confer it upon those who are partakers of Himself (*qui ex ipso participantur*), sending the Holy Spirit upon all the earth." Ibid.; cf. 3.17.3.

346 Irenaeus of Lyons, *Against Heresies* 3.17.3 (ANF 1:445; PG 7:930c–d).

of the Spirit, and gives the Spirit to be the head of man (*Spiritum dans esse hominis caput*)."[347] He poured out "upon the human race the life-giving seed (*vitale semen*)—that is, the Spirit of the remission of sins, through means of whom we are quickened."[348] "The Lord ... has also poured out the Spirit of the Father for the union and communion of God and man, imparting indeed God to men by means of the Spirit, and, on the other hand, attaching man to God by His own incarnation."[349] This Spirit, then, living on after Christ in His followers, transfigures their whole life, so that they become a holy people. "We do now receive a certain portion of His Spirit, tending towards perfection, and preparing us for incorruption, being little by little accustomed to receive and bear God; which also the apostle terms 'an earnest,' that is, a part of the honour which has been promised us by God, where he says in the Epistle to the Ephesians, 'In which ye also, having heard the word of truth, the Gospel of your salvation, believing in which we have been sealed with the Holy Spirit of promise, which is the earnest of our inheritance.' This earnest, therefore, thus dwelling in us, renders us spiritual even now, and the mortal is swallowed up by immortality. 'For ye,' he declares, 'are not in the flesh, but in the Spirit, if so be that the Spirit of God dwell in you.' This, however, does not take place by a casting away of the flesh, but by the impartation of the Spirit. For those to whom he was writing were not without flesh, but they were those who had received the Spirit of God, 'by which we cry, Abba, Father.' If therefore, at the present time, having the earnest, we do cry, 'Abba, Father,' what shall it be when, on rising again, we behold Him face to face; when all the members shall burst out into a continuous hymn of triumph, glorifying Him who raised them from the dead, and gave the gift of eternal life? For if the earnest, gathering man into itself, does even now cause him to cry, 'Abba, Father,' what

347 Irenaeus of Lyons, *Against Heresies* 5.20.2 (ANF 1:548; PG 7:1178c).

348 Irenaeus of Lyons, *Against Heresies* 4.31.2 (ANF 1:505; PG 7:1009b).

349 Irenaeus of Lyons, *Against Heresies* 5.1.1: "Effundente Spiritum Patris in adunitionem et communionem Doi et hominis, ad homines deponente Deum per Spiritum, ad Deum autem rursus imponente hominem per suam incarnationem" (ANF 1:527; PG 7:1121c). Cf. *Works*, 447 [Rus. ed.].

shall the complete grace of the Spirit effect, which shall be given to men by God? It will render us like unto Him, and accomplish the will of the Father; for it shall make man after the image and likeness of God."[350] The Spirit of God "did also descend upon the Son of God, made the Son of man, becoming accustomed in fellowship with Him to dwell in the human race, to rest with human beings, and to dwell in the workmanship of God, working (orans) the will of the Father in them, and renewing them from their old habits into the newness of Christ (renovans eos a vetustate in novitatem Christi)."[351] In general, people are saved by the name of the Lord Jesus Christ and the Spirit of God.[352] It is this new regenerated people that Irenaeus calls a chosen generation,[353] a holy people. Of stones God raised up children unto Abraham. The prophesy of Hosea was fulfilled: "I will call that which was not (my) people, my people; and her that was not beloved, beloved. It shall come to pass that in the place where it was called not my people, there shall they be called sons of the Living God" (Hos. 2:23, 1:10).[354]

Mankind's moral advancement is only possible in the Church. The Spirit of God, which enlivens New Testament mankind, has been conferred upon the Church,[355] which is the salt of the earth.[356] "Where the Church is, there is the Spirit of God; and where the Spirit of God is, there is the Church, and every kind of grace."[357]

---

350 Irenaeus of Lyons, *Against Heresies* 5.8.1 (ANF 1:533; PG 7:1141b–1142a). Cf. *Fragments* 35: ὡς παιδία νεόγονα (ANF 1:574; PG 7:1248c).

351 Irenaeus of Lyons, *Against Heresies* 3.17.1 (ANF 1:444; PG 7:929c).

352 Irenaeus of Lyons, *Against Heresies* 5.11.1 (ANF 1:537; PG 7:1150c).

353 Irenaeus of Lyons, *Against Heresies* 4.3.14: "The streams of the Holy Spirit in a dry land, to give water to the elect people of God (genus electum Dei)" (ANF 1:511; PG 7:1082c).

354 Irenaeus of Lyons, *The Demonstration of the Apostolic Preaching* 93, 144–145.

355 Irenaeus of Lyons, *Against Heresies* 3.17.3 (ANF 1:445; PG 7:930c). Cf. 3.24.1 (PG 7:966b).

356 Irenaeus of Lyons, *Against Heresies* 4.31.3 (ANF 1:505; PG 7:1070a).

357 Irenaeus of Lyons, *Against Heresies* 3.24.1 (ANF 1:458; PG 7:966c). Cf. idem: "Spiritus requiescens super eam (Ecclesiam) [the Spirit resting on the Church]" (PG 7:1078b).

The Church is the seed of Christ, and through the Lord it receives adoption (*adoptionem*) to God.[358] "The Spirit of God, by whom all things were made—was commingled and united with flesh—that is, with His own workmanship; by which commixture and unity the two synagogues—that is, the two churches (*congregationes*)—produced from their own father living sons to the living God."[359] And the Church, by the action of the Holy Spirit dwelling within it, restores in men the perfection which they had lost, and the image of God that they had distorted. "This gift of God has been entrusted to the Church, as breath was to the first created man (*ad inspirationem plasmationi*), for this purpose, that all the members receiving it may be vivified (*vivificentur*); and the [means of] communion with Christ has been distributed throughout it, that is, the Holy Spirit, the earnest of incorruption, the means of confirming our faith, and the ladder of ascent to God."[360] "The Word ... is Himself the Head of the Church; while the Spirit is in us all, and He is the living water, which the Lord grants (*praestat*) to those who rightly believe in Him."[361] "Those persons who are not bringing forth the fruits of righteousness, and are, as it were, covered over and lost among brambles, if they use diligence, and receive the word of God as a graft, arrive at the pristine nature of man (*in pristinam veniunt hominis naturam*)—that which was created after the image and likeness of God."[362] Thus, "what we had lost in Adam—namely, to be according to the image and likeness of God—[we have recovered] in Christ Jesus."[363]

---

358 Irenaeus of Lyons, *Against Heresies* 5.32.2 (ANF 1:561; PG 7:1211b).

359 Irenaeus of Lyons, *Against Heresies* 4.31.2 (ANF 1:505; PG 7:1070a)—thus St. Irenaeus interprets the story involving Lot (Gen. 19:31–35).

360 Irenaeus of Lyons, *Against Heresies* 3.24.1 (ANF 1:458; PG 7:966b).

361 Irenaeus of Lyons, *Against Heresies* 5.18.2 (ANF 1:546; PG 7:1173a).

362 Irenaeus of Lyons, *Against Heresies* 5.10.1 (ANF 1:536; PG 7:1148b).

363 Irenaeus of Lyons, *Against Heresies* 3.18.1 (ANF 1:446; PG 7:932b). *Against Heresies* 5.32.1: Creation is restored to its primal state (*ipsam conditionem reintegratam in pristinum*) (ANF 1:561; PG 7:1210c). *Against Heresies* 5.33.1: "He will Himself renew the inheritance of the earth, and will re-organize the mystery of the glory of [His] sons" (ANF 1:562; PG 7:1212b).

Thus, in his polemics against the Jews Irenaeus counters the narrow Jewish interpretation of Christianity from a purely national-istic standpoint with the doctrine concerning the Church as **a new kind of people, restored to their original divine image, living according to the law of love and achieving deifica-tion through the action of the Holy Spirit.**

This definition of the Church after Irenaeus may be consid-ered definitively established in ecclesiastical literature. The Jewish tendencies were countered with the doctrine of the Church as a universal, new, perfect nation. Eusebius and Epiphanius said of the Ebionites that they held "poor and mean opinions concerning Christ."[364] But this poor and mean opinion of the Ebionites con-cerning Christ was closely linked to their poor and mean opinion concerning the Church. The church polemicists presented the rich, exalted teaching concerning the Church as mankind restored to its primal state. The Church appropriated the Old Testament, but spe-cifically as an old, temporary testament of prophecies and prefigu-rations of the New Testament, in which all nations are united into a single new nation—that is, into the Church.

The second century bequeathed to the third a firmly established exegetical tradition, according to which the entire Old Testament is a single unbroken prefiguration and proclamation of the New Testament Church. It is upon the soil of this tradition that St. Hip-polytus of Rome stands, as may be seen from his recently discov-ered exegetical works in the Georgian tongue—explanations of the Song of Songs,[365] the blessing of Jacob, the blessing of Moses, and the battle between David and Goliath.[366] The chief idea of all these

364 Eusebius, *The Church History of Eusebius* 3.27.1 (NPNF² 1:159); cf. Epipha-nius, Haer. 30.17.

365 Hippolytus, *Explanation of the Song of Solomon*. Georgian text based on a 10th-century manuscript, researched, translated, and published by N. Marr. See *Texts on and Investigations of Armenian and Georgian Philology* ("Тексты и разыскания по армяно-грузинской филологии"), publishing house of the department of Eastern languages, Imperial University of Saint Petersburg (Saint Petersburg: 1901). *Hippolyts, Kommentar zum Hohelied: auf Grund von N. Marrs Ausgabe des grusini-schen Textes herausgegeben von G. Nathanael Bonwetsch*, TU 23.2 (Leipzig: 1902).

366 *Drei georgisch erhaltene Schriften von Hippolytus herausgegeben von G. Nath. Bon-*

works is specifically that the New Testament Church took the place of the Old Testament Israel.[367] The gentiles were as though in the wilderness, and out of that wilderness came the Church (Song of Sol. 3:6), in order to become the bride of Christ.[368] Jacob in his time prophesied (Gen. 49:13) that all nations would be gathered into the Church as into a sort of harbor.[369] Moses prophesied that the gentiles would be with Christ as in a single ship.[370] Christ came to save all nations.[371] In the Church the gentiles became "fellow citizens of the saints."[372] The Old Testament likewise foretells even details such as the fact that Saul would persecute the Church. This was foretold by Jacob when, in blessing Benjamin, from whose tribe Saul descended, he called him a ravenous wolf (Gen. 49:27).[373]

All that could be said against the Jews had already been said. Tertullian himself, despite his outstanding polemical talents, in polemics with the Jews offers hardly anything new in comparison with Justin, for example. It may be said that the polemical material had been wholly exhausted, and that later writers only repeat what had already been said.[374] Tertullian's treatise *Against the Jews* in particular

---

wetsch, TU 26.1a (Leipzig: 1904).

367 All materials pertaining to this subject have been compiled by Bonwetsch. See TU 23.2, 4, *Der Gedankengang des Kommentars*, 81–87. TU 26.1a, *Einleitung*, IX–XIII. *Der Schriftbeweis für die Kirche*, 16–20.

368 Hippolytus, *Explanation of the Song of Solomon* 26.1, TU 23.2, 71.11–25.

369 Hippolytus, *The Blessing of Jacob* 20.2–3, TU 26.1a, 32. Cf. *On Daniel* 4.37.5 (GrchSch. 1.1:284.10–11). *Explanation of the Song of Solomon* 8.7.27, 12 TU 23.2, 43.17–18; 78.13–16.

370 Hippolytus, *The Blessing of Moses* 17.2, TU 26.1a, 69. Cf. *On Christ and Antichrist* 59.

371 Hippolytus, *The Blessing of Moses* 13.5, TU 26.1a, 64.9–11.

372 Hippolytus, *Explanation of the Song of Solomon* 26.1, TU 23.2, 71.18–22.

373 Hippolytus, *The Blessing of Jacob* 28:2, TU 26.1a, 45–46. Cf. Tertullian, *Against Marcion* 5.1 (CSEL 47:569.22 sqq).

374 See Nikolai Shternov, *Tertullian, Presbyter of Carthage* ("Тертуллиан, пресвитер Карагенский") (Kursk: 1889), 115. I. Turmel, *Tertullien*, 2-me edit. (Paris: 1905), 1.

is likewise devoid of originality.[375] There Tertullian demonstrates that the Old Testament foretells that the ancient rites shall cease so as to give way to the promises of a new law, and so that they "that sit in darkness and the shadow of death" (Ps. 106:10) might be illumined by the Light from above.[376] With the coming of Christ the promised new law is now in force (*legem novam promissam nunc operari*).[377] This law is for all nations. All nations leave the abyss of human error and enter into the knowledge of the Lord, the knowledge of God the Creator and of God His Christ, as was foretold by the prophets.[378] For example, the prophet Isaiah proclaimed that by the will of the Father the incarnate Son of God would establish the Church from among the gentiles also.[379] The Son of God enlightened the whole earth with the rays of His Gospel. The nations that did not know Jesus Christ now acknowledge Him, and the nations which formerly did not know Christ will be converted to Him.[380] The nations are admitted to the law of God.[381] But when the author speaks of the Church, he speaks not of nations, but calls the

---

375 Böhringer, *Die alte Kirche,* 3-ter Theil Stuttgart (1873), 740. A great many scholars considered this treatise by Tertullian surreptitious, and considered it an unsuccessful later compilation. Concerning this, see E. Noeldechen, *Tertullian's Gegen die Iuden auf Einheit, Echtheit, Enstehung geprüft,* TU 12.2 (Leipzig: 1894), 14–24. Noeldechen himself speaks in favor of the authenticity of the treatise (89–91).

376 Tertullian, *Against the Jews* 6 (PL 2:647c–648c). Cf. *Against Marcion* 3.24: *Iacob, qui quidem posterioris et praelatioris populi figura est, id est nostri* (CSEL 47:420.24–25); 4.25: Is. 49:6. *Christum illuminatorem nationum designavit* (CSEL 47:504.23–24); 4.1: Is. 51:4. *Judicaverat atqueverat nationes quoque inluminandas per evangelii legem atque sermonem* (CSEL 47:424.3–4). Tertullian likewise sees prophecies concerning entry into the Church in Ps. 2:7–8:3 (*Against Marcion* 3.20.22; 4.25 [CSEL 47:410.15–22; 415.3 sqq., 505.20 sqq.]), Is. 42:4, 6–7 (3.20; 5. 2. [CSEL 47:410.19 sqq., 573.1 sqq.]), 52:5, 7; 2 (3.22; 5.2 [CSEL 47:414.26–415.3; 572.25–573.3), and others. Cf. N. Bonwetsch, *Der Schriftbeweis für die Kirche,* 14–15.

377 *Against the Jews* 6 (PL 2:648a).

378 *Against the Jews* 12 (PL 2:672c–673a).

379 Is. 49:12, 18, 21. *Deus homo erat natus, aedificaturus ecclesiam ex voluntate patris ex allophylis quoque. –Against Marcion* 4.13 (CSEL 47:458.19–21).

380 *Against the Jews* 14 (PL 2:682a–b).

381 Idem (PL 2:636a).

whole Church a single nation. Our nation has proven the youngest
(*minor*), because it obtained the knowledge of divine mercy at the
end of time.[382] "Our nation," "the Christian nation," "the younger
nation," having forsaken the idols that it formerly served, converted
to that God from Whom Israel had apostatized. Thus, the younger
nation surpassed the elder, having acquired the grace (*gratiam*) of
divine patronage that Israel had lost.[383]

We have presented the doctrine concerning the Church that
formed in the works of church writers in their polemics with the
Jews and with Judaizing Christians, and which was juxtaposed to
the narrow nationalistic concept of the Church as a union of all
nations under the law of Moses. But the idea of the Church as a
universal society of regenerated mankind is expressed not only in
the foregoing works of the church polemicists of old. This idea is
clearly discernible in all the earliest manuscripts of early church
literature, even if their authors did not set themselves the explicit
task of polemicizing against Judaistic tendencies. This shows that it
was not polemics against Judaism that produced the concept of the
Church, but rather these polemics drew their content from church
consciousness. The earliest church writers contrasted the Church
as a **new nation** not only with Judaism, but also with paganism.[384]

One of the most ancient manuscripts of the early Church, *The
Epistle of Clement of Rome to the Corinthians*, was written for the pur-
pose of polemicizing with the Judaizers; yet even in this epistle the
Church is defined just as in much later polemical works.[385] The epis-

---

382 Idem (PL 2:636b).

383 Idem (PL 2:636c–637a). Concerning Isarel's violation of the covenant
with God, see *Against Marcion* 4.31 (CSEL 47:527.10 sqq). See also 4.14.17 (CSEL
47:462.24 sqq., 477.5 sqq.). For a more detailed treatment of Tertullian's polemics with the Jews, see the book by N. Shternov, *Tertullian*, 100–113.

384 Juxtaposition of Christians to the Old Testament people of God is the
chief concept for all manuscripts of this time. As formerly Israel had a special
relationship with God, so now Christians are the true people of the twelve tribes,
living in dispersion amid a world that is foreign to them. This range of concepts
and expressions must be continually kept in mind by anyone reading the writings
of post-apostolic times. R. Knopf, *Das nachapostolische Zeitalter*, 347–348.

385 It is presumed that the author of this epistle was a Jew, hence the numer-

tle repeatedly refers to Christians as chosen or called;[386] God chose them as a peculiar people (εἰς λαὸν περιούσιον)[387] through Christ.[388] Christians are the chosen portion for the Lord,[389] a holy portion (ἁγία μερίς),[390] a nation chosen from among the nations (ἔθνος ἐκ μέσου ἐθνῶν).[391] Christians are the host of God,[392] the flock of Christ,[393] and the members of Christ (τὰ μέλη τοῦ Χριστοῦ).[394] Christians are brought up under the tutelage of the good God,[395] so that they live a particular, praiseworthy way of life.[396] They can have an insatiable desire to do good (ἀκόρεστος πόθος εἰς ἀγαθοποιΐαν),[397] and in love they achieve perfection.[398] It may also be noted that Clement closely links perfection of Christian life to the fullness of the grace of the Holy Spirit.[399] Finally, this grace-endowed and chosen people, Clement teaches, has supplanted the Old Testament Israel

---

ous traces of Old Testament thinking in his epistle. From a philological standpoint, Semitisms in the epistle are also pointed out. Concerning this, see I. B. Lightfoot. *The Apostolic Fathers* 1 (London: 1890), 59; and G. Hoennicke, *Das Judenchristentum,* 279–280.

386   1 Clem 1:1; 2:4; 6:1; 46:4; 49:5; 58:2. 59:2, 3; 64.

387   1 Clem. 64; cf. Tit 2:14.

388   1 Clem 50:7, 64, 65:2.

389   1 Clem 29:1: "ὃς ἐκλογῆς μέρος ἡμᾶς ἐποίησεν ἑαυτῷ." Cf. 8:5: "ἀγαπητοὶ αὐτοῦ [His beloved]."

390   1 Clem 30:1.

391   1 Clem 29:3. Cf. Deut. 4:34, 12:2; Num. 18:27; 2 Chron. 31:14.

392   1 Clem. 37:1, 41:1.

393   1 Clem. 16:1, 44:3, 54:2.

394   1 Clem. 46:7.

395   1 Clem. 56:16: "Πατὴρ γὰρ ἀγαθὸς ὢν παιδεύει εἰς τὸ ἐλεηθῆναι ἡμᾶς διὰ τῆς ὁσίας παιδείας αὐτοῦ [for being a good Father, he chastiseth us that we may receive mercy through His holy chastisement]." Cf. 37:1.

396   1 Clem. 54:4: "Οἱ πολιτευόμενοι τὴν ἀμεταμέλητον πολιτείαν τοῦ Θεοῦ." Cf. 48:1.

397   1 Clem. 2:2; cf. 2:7.

398   1 Clem. 49:5, 50:3.

399   1 Clem. 2:2: "οὕτως εἰρήνη βαθεῖα καὶ λιπαρὰ ἐδέδοτο ... καὶ πλήρης πνεύματος ἁγίου ἔκχυσις ἐπὶ πάντας ἐγίνετο." Cf. 46:6, 50:3.

in relation to God; hence, Abraham and the other Old Testament righteous ones are the fathers of the Christians.[400]

Christianity is also defined as a new life in *The Teaching of the Twelve Apostles*. There the eucharistic prayer offers up thanksgiving for the life and knowledge that have been manifested through Jesus Christ.[401]

In a sermon known as the *Second Epistle of Clement*,[402] the prophecy of Is. 54:1 is applied to the Christian Church: our Church was formerly barren, before children were given her.[403] The preacher also calls the Church a "nation," and this nation takes the place of the Old Testament Hebrew nation. "Our people seemed to be outcast from God, but now, through believing, have become more numerous than those who are reckoned to possess God."[404] In the closing doxology of this same sermon, Christianity is called a heavenly life.[405]

The epistles of Ignatius of Antioch, in which polemics against the Judaizers are clearly in evidence, repeatedly express the teaching concerning the Church as the new life of all mankind, as a new nation that takes the place of the Old Testament nation of the Hebrews.[406] "It is absurd (ἄτοπόν ἐστιν) to profess Christ Jesus, and

---

400   1 Clem. 31:2: "ὁ πατὴρ ἡμῶν Ἀβραάμ [our father Abraham]." Cf. 30:7, 60:4. Cf. also Heb. 2:16: "σπέρματος ʽΑβραάμ ἐπιλαμβάνεται [he taketh hold of the seed of Abraham]."

401   Didache 9:3: "εὐχαριστοῦμέν σοι, πάτερ ἡμῶν, ὑπὲρ τῆς ζωῆς καὶ γνώσεως, ἧς ἐγνώρισας ἡμῖν διὰ Ἰησοῦ τοῦ παιδός σου [we give thanks to Thee, our Father, for the life and knowledge which Thou hast manifested to us through Jesus Thy child]." Cf. Didache 10:2.

402   The composition of this sermon dates back to perhaps the first half of the second century. See F. X. Funk, *Kirchengeschichtliche Abhandlungen und Untersuchungen*, 3-ter Band (Paderborn: 1907), 261. Cf. A. Harnack, *Die Chronologie der altchristlichen Literatur bis Eusebius*, 1-er. Bd. (Leipzig: 1897), 447–449.

403   2 Clem. 2:1.

404   2 Clem. 2:3 (ANF 7:517).

405   2 Clem. 20:5: "Δι᾽ οὗ καὶ ἐφανέρωσεν ἡμῖν τὴν ἀλήθειαν καὶ τὴν ἐπουράνιον ζωήν [through whom He also revealed to us the truth and the heavenly life]."

406   The concept of a new human race lies at the center of Ignatius's overall

to Judaize. For Christianity did not embrace Judaism, but Judaism Christianity, that so every tongue which believeth might be gathered together to God."[407]

Priests are a good thing, but still better is the High Priest to Whom the Holy of Holies is entrusted, and to Whom alone are entrusted the mysteries (τὰ κρυπτά) of God. He is the door to the Father, through whom Abraham, Isaac, and Jacob, the prophets, the apostles, and the Church all enter. All this is for union with God (εἰς ἑνότητα Θεοῦ).[408] In the latter words may be seen the idea of restoration of union with God through Jesus Christ. Christ is our true Life.[409] Before Christ came into the world, the whole world was in the power of the prince of this world (ἄρχων τοῦ αἰῶνος τούτου).[410] Christ has established a new man,[411] who is in constant spiritual and bodily communion with Him.[412] Death is overcome by Christ,[413] and the Church has been given incorruption.[414] Christians are the true "stones of the temple of the Father, prepared for the building of God the Father, and drawn up on high by the instrument (διὰ τῆς μηχανῆς) of Jesus Christ, which is the cross, making use of the Holy Spirit as a rope (σχοινίῳ), while your faith was the means by which you ascended (ἀναγογεὺς ὑμῶν), and your love the way

---

views on Christianity. F. Loofs, *Leitfaden der Dogmengeschichte*, §15.2, 99.

407 Irenaeus of Lyons, *Epistle to the Magnesians* 10:3: "εἰς ὅν πᾶσα γλῶσσα πιστεύσασα εἰς Θεὸν συνήχθη." Cf. 8:1.

408 Irenaeus of Lyons, *Epistle to the Philadelphians* 9:1.

409 Irenaeus of Lyons, *Epistle to the Smyrnaeans* 4:1: "τὸ ἀληθινὸν ἡμῶν ζῆν." Cf. *Epistle to the Magnesians* 1.

410 Irenaeus of Lyons, *Epistle to the Ephesians* 19:1.

411 Irenaeus of Lyons, *Epistle to the Ephesians* 20:1: "οἰκονομία εἰς τὸν καινὸν ἄνθρωπον."

412 Irenaeus of Lyons, *Epistle to the Ephesians* 10:3.

413 Irenaeus of Lyons, *Epistle to the Ephesians* 19:3.

414 Irenaeus of Lyons, *Epistle to the Ephesians* 17:1: "διὰ τοῦτο μύρον ἔλαβεν ἐπὶ τῆς κεφαλῆς αὐτοῦ ὁ κύριος, ἵνα πνέῃ τῇ ἐκκλησίᾳ ἀφθαρσίαν [to this end did the Lord receive myrrh upon His head, that He might breath incorruption for the Church]." Cf. *Epistle to the Magnesians* 6:2: "εἰς τύπον καὶ διδαχὴν ἀφθαρσίας [unto a type and instruction of incorruption]."

which led up to God. Ye, therefore, as well as all your fellow-travellers, are God-bearers, temple-bearers, Christ-bearers, bearers of holiness, adorned in all respects with the commandments of Jesus Christ."[415] Christians are a pious community (τὸ Θεῷ πλῆθος).[416] In the *Martyrdom of Polycarp*, Christians are called a "devout and godly race" and the "race of the righteous."[417] Melito of Sardis wrote to the emperor: "The **race (γένος) of the pious is now suffering persecution**, being driven about."[418]

The *Epistle to Diognetus* also refers to Christians as a new race (καινὸν γένος).[419] The Christian is a new man, as one newly born.[420]

The philosopher Aristeides, in describing Christian teaching and the customs of the Christians, exclaims: "Verily, this is a new people (καινόν ἐστι τὸ ἔθνος), and there is something divine (lit: a divine admixture— θεῖόν τι ἐπιμεμιγμένον αὐτῷ) in the midst of them."[421]

"Assuredly the race of the Christians is more blessed than all the men who are upon the face of the earth. ... Their doctrine is the gateway of light. Wherefore let all who are without the knowledge of God draw near thereto; and they will receive incorruptible words, which are from all time and from eternity. So shall they ap-

---

415 Irenaeus of Lyons, *Epistle to the Ephesians* 9:1–2. Cf. 15:3. *Epistle to the Magnesians* 12.

416 Irenaeus of Lyons, *Epistle to the Trallians* 8:2.

417 *Martyrdom of Polycarp* 3:2 (ANF 1:40): "Πᾶν τὸ πλῆθος, θαυμάσαν τὴν γενναιότητα τοῦ θεοφιλοῦς καὶ θεοσεβοῦς γένους τῶν Χριστιανῶν, ἐπεβόησεν [the entire crowd cried out, admiring the courage of the God-loving and God-fearing race of the Christians]." See also Funk, *Die Apostolischen Vater,* 117. Ibid., 14:1 (ANF 1:42): "ὁ Θεὸς... παντὸς τοῦ γένους τῶν δικαίων, οἳ ζῶσιν ἐνώπιόν σου [O God of all the race of the righteous, who are alive before Thee]." Funk, 121. "Γένος τῶν δικαίων." *The Pastor of Hermas* 9.17.5 (ANF 2:50).

418 Eusebius, *Church History* 4.26.5 (NPNF² 1:205; GrchSch 9.1:384.3–4). For more similar expressions, see A. Harnack, *Die Mission und Ausbreitung des Christentums* I, 209 ff.

419 *Epistle to Diognetus* 1 (ANF 1:25). Funk, cit. ed., 134.

420 *Epistle to Diognetus* 2:1 (ANF 1:25): "Γενόμενος ὥσπερ ἐξ ἀρχῆς καινὸς ἄνθρωπος." Funk, op. cit., 134.

421 *Apology of Aristides* 16.4 (ANF 9:278). Geffcken, 26.17–18.

pear before the awful judgment which through Jesus the Messiah is destined to come upon the whole human race."[422] [423]

The same idea of the Church as a new creation is expressed symbolically in *The Pastor of Hermas.* Hermas saw the building of a tower—the Church. The pastor showed him a large field, around which stood twelve mountains, each of a different appearance (ἄλλην καί ἄλλην ἰδέαν ἔχοντα τὰ ὄρη).[424] Virgins carried stones from these mountains, passed through a door, and gave them to the builders of the tower, who received them and did the building. The tower was built upon a great stone and above a gate.[425] The stones were of various colors (χρόαις ποικίλαις). And when these stones of various form (οἱ λίθοι οἱ ποικίλοι) were placed into the building, they became equally white and changed their varied colors (ὅμοιοι ἐγένοντο λευκοὶ καὶ τὰς χρόας τὰς ποικίλας ἤλλασσον).[426] The vision describes the building of the tower in considerable detail, and at the end an explanation is given. The stone and the gate are the Son of God. The Son of God is more ancient than all creation, insomuch that He was present at the Council of His Father concerning the making of creation. He appeared in latter times, and became a new gate so that by it those who desire to be saved might enter into the Kingdom of God. No one will enter into the kingdom of God unless he receives the name of the Son of God.[427] The kingdom of God, depicted by the tower, is none other than the Church.[428] The twelve mountains signify the twelve tribes that inhabit the whole world: among them the Son of God was preached

---

422 Here the Russian translation differs significantly from the English source cited, which literally reads: "… and they will receive incorruptible and eternal words, in order that, having escaped punishment at the awful judgment to come, they may appear as participants in new life." –*Trans.*

423 *Apology of Aristides* 17.5 (ANF 9:279). Geffcken, 27.

424 *The Pastor of Hermas* 3.9.1.4 (ANF 2:43).

425 *The Pastor of Hermas* 3.9.4.1–2 (ANF 2:44).

426 *The Pastor of Hermas* 3.9.4.5 (ANF 2:44).

427 *The Pastor of Hermas* 3.9.12.1–5 (ANF 2:47–48).

428 *The Pastor of Hermas* 3.9.13.1 (ANF 2:48): "ὁ πύργος ἡ ἐκκλησία ἐστιν."

through the apostles.[429] As the mountains are varied, so is the mind
and inner disposition of the nations (αἱ ποικιλίαι τοῦ νοὸς τῶν ἐθνῶν
καὶ ἡ φρόνησις). But all the nations under heaven, having heard the
preaching, believed and were named with a single name of the Son
of God; hence, having received His seal (that is, the Holy Spirit), all
have received one spirit (φρόνησιν) and one mind (ἕνα νοῦν), and
they now have one faith and one love. For this reason the tower was
made of a single hue (μιᾷ χρόᾳ), shining like the sun. They have
come together as one and become one Body (ἓν σῶμα).[430]

This vision and its explanation precisely and explicitly expresses
that idea of the Church which, as we have seen, the church writers contrasted to the Judaistic tendencies. In *The Pastor of Hermas*
likewise the Church contains all nations within herself, but this unification of nations is not external, like the state of Rome, but internal: their spiritual countenance is changed, and they all become
one Body, one soul, one Church; and this union of nations within
the Church is the fruit of the incarnation of the Son of God and
the gift of the Holy Spirit.[431] Occasionally Hermas's reasoning concerning the Church echoes the ecclesiology of the holy apostle Paul
almost verbatim.

To all the testimonials cited above it should also be added that
that the religious and historical philosophy of Clement of Alexandria is wholly rooted in the concept of two nations—the Greeks
and the Jews, who, trained up by God, are to rise up to unity in a
third nation.[432] Interpreting the words of Christ, "Where two or
three are gathered together in my name, there am I in the midst

---

429 This passage has a parallel: the Law of God is given to the whole world,
and that law is the Son of God, preached in all the ends of the earth (*The Pastor
of Hermas* 3.8.3.2).

430 *The Pastor of Hermas* 3.9.17.1–2, 4–5. Cf. the preceding, 3.9.13.5: "You see
that the tower became of one stone with the rock. So also they who have believed
on the Lord through His Son, and are clothed with these spirits, shall become one
spirit, one body, and the colour of their garments shall be one" (ANF 2:48). For
a detailed explanation of *The Pastor of Hermas* 3.9, see Theodor Zahn, *Der Hirt des
Hermas* (Gotha: 1868), 224 ff.

431 Cf. Th. Zahn, *Der Hirt des Hermas*, 243–244.

432 A. Harnack, *Die Mission und Ausbreitung des Christentum* I, 213.

of them" (Mt. 18:20), Clement says: "The harmony of the many, inferred from the three with whom the Lord is present, might be the one church, the one man, the one race (τὸ γένος τὸ ἕν). … Was not the third [people] created out of the two [that is, the Jews and the Greeks] into one new man, in whom he now moves, and dwells in the church itself?"[433] Those raised on the teachings of the Hellenes and the children of the law of Moses, having come to faith, are conjoined into the single race of a saved people.[434] This people Clement frequently calls new and young, to whom a correspondingly New Testament has been given.[435] Men have become a new

---

433 Clement of Alexandria, *Stromata* 3.70.1–2, from William Rader, *The Church and Racial Hostility* (Tübingen: Mohr, 1978), 16–17. "Εἴη δ᾽ ἂν καὶ ἡ ὁμόνοια τῶν πολλῶν ἀπὸ τῶν τριῶν ἀριθμουμένη, μεθ᾽ ὧν ὁ Κύριος, ἡ μία ἐκκλησία, ὁ εἷς ἄνθρωπος, τὸ γένος τὸ ἕν… τρίτος δὲ ἦν ἐκ τῶν δυεῖν κτιζόμενος εἰς εἰς καινὸν ἄνθρωπον, ᾧ δὴ ἐμπεριπατεῖ τε καὶ κατοικεῖ ἐν αὐτῇ τῇ ἐκκλησίᾳ; [The agreement of many, which is indicated by the number "three," with whom the Lord is present, might also be the one Church, the one man, and the one race… And was not the third the one which is made out of the two into a new man in which he walks and dwells, in the Church itself?]" (GrchSch. 15:227.27–29, 228.1–3).

434 Clement of Alexandria, *Stromata* 6.5.42.2: "Ἐκ γοῦν τῆς Ἑλληνικῆς παιδείας, ἀλλὰ καὶ ἐκ τῆς νομικῆς, εἰς τὸ ἕν γένος τοῦ σῳζομένου συνάγονται λαοῦ οἱ τὴν πίστιν προσιέμενοι [Accordingly, then, from the Hellenic training, and also from that of the law are gathered into the one race of the saved people those who accept the Faith]" (GrchSch. 15:452.24–26).

435 Clement of Alexandria, *The Instructor (Paedagogus)* 1.5.19.4: "ὁ καινὸς ἡμεῖς λαός, τρυφερὸς ὡς παῖς [the new people which we are, is delicate as a child]" (GrchSch. 12:101.30–31). 1.5.20.2: "νήπιαι γὰρ αἱ νέαι φρένες εἰσίν, ἐν παλαιᾷ τῇ ἀφροσύνῃ αἱ νεωστὶ συνεταί, αἱ κατὰ τὴν διαθήκην τὴν καινὴν ἀνατείλασαι [For the new minds, which have newly become wise, which have sprung into being according to the new covenant, are infantile in the old folly]" (GrchSch. 12:101.30–31). 1.5.20.3: "πρὸς νόησιν ἀεὶ ἀκμάζομεν, ἀεὶ νέοι καὶ ἀεὶ ἤπιοι καὶ ἀεὶ καινοί· χρὴ γὰρ εἶναι καινοὺς τοὺς λόγου καινοῦ μετειληφότας [we are always growing to maturity in intelligence, are always young, always mild, always new: for those must necessarily be new, who have become partakers of the new Word]" (GrchSch. 12:102 3–5). Cf. *The Instructor* 1.7.57.1: "τὸ ὄνομα τὸ καινὸν τῷ νέῳ λαῷ τῷ νηπίῳ [the new name for the new people — the babe]" (GrchSch. 12:123.32–33). Cf. 1.7.58.1 (GrchSch. 12:124.14), 1.7.59.1: "καινῷ δὲ καὶ λαῷ καινὴ καὶ νέα διαθήκη δεδώρηται [but to the fresh and new people has also been given a new covenant]" (125.1).

people because they are reborn by Christ. For this reason Clement calls Christians "newborns."[436]

Thus, in direct contrast to the Judaizers, the church writers expounded and developed the teaching concerning the Church as a "new people"—new in the highest sense of the word. The Church is not only a new people, but also a holy one. This self-identification and self-definition of the Church is full of profound significance, as is particularly seen in the system of Irenaeus, and is in full accord with the teaching of the apostle Paul concerning the Church. Passages where this consciousness is expressed in various forms abound throughout all of ancient literature, which attests to the fact that the Church has been the subject of Christian thought since the very beginning of Christianity.[437]

The exalted doctrine concerning the Church as a new and holy nation existed not only in theory, but also in practice. Not only did contemplative thought and the theses of abstract dogmatic teaching speak of the Church as a new and holy nation, but the very life of the Church attested to this truth. Justin the Philosopher once said, "We ... are called and are the true sons of God."[438] There had to have been support in the actual life of the Church in order to say these words.[439] But all the apologists of ancient times unanimously and continually state the same, and in their writings numerous parallels with the words of St. Justin may be found. All depict the moral state of the gentile world in its most frightful aspect, frequent-

---

436 Clement of Alexandria, *The Instructor* 1.7.59.3: "καθὸ εἰς κλῆσιν καὶ σωτηρίαν νεογνοὶ γεγόναμεν [according to which we have become newly-born unto calling and salvation]" (GrchSch. 12:125.14–15.

437 Harnack. *Dogmengeschichte* I, 172. Cf. *Die Mission und Ausbreitung des Christentums* I, 207.

438 Justin Martyr, *Dialogue with Trypho* 123 (ANF 1:261). Cf. Ibid. 119: "a nation ... God-fearing, righteous, and delighting the Father" (ANF 1:259).

439 Cf. Tatian's *Address to the Greeks* 32: "In speaking we do not utter falsehood" (ANF 2:78).

ly repeating the well-known words of the apostle Paul in his epistle
to the Romans (see Rom. 1:24–32). In contrast to the gentile world,
the Christian life of the Church is presented specifically as the life
of a new race of men, the life of a holy nation. The philosopher
Aristides, in describing the state of the gentile and Jewish worlds,
says of the Christians: "They do not commit adultery nor fornication, nor bear false witness, nor embezzle what is held in pledge, nor
covet what is not theirs. They honour father and mother, and show
kindness to those near to them; and whenever they are judges, they
judge uprightly. They do not worship idols [made] in the image of
man; and whatsoever they would not that others should do unto
them, they do not to others; and of the food which is consecrated to
idols they do not eat, for they are pure. And their oppressors they
appease (lit: comfort) and make them their friends (προσφιλεῖς);
they do good to their enemies; and their women, O King, are pure
as virgins, and their daughters are modest; and their men keep
themselves from every unlawful union and from all uncleanness, in
the hope of a recompense to come in the other world. Further, if
one or other of them have bondmen and bondwomen or children,
through love towards them they persuade them to become Christians, and when they have done so, they call them brethren without
distinction. They do not worship strange gods, and they go their
way in all modesty and cheerfulness. Falsehood is not found among
them; and they love one another, and from widows they do not turn
away their esteem; and they deliver the orphan from him who treats
him harshly."[440] One who joined the Christian Church immediately
observed himself becoming a new creature, entering into a peculiar
holy society, as Justin the Philosopher expresses. "We … formerly
delighted in fornication, but now embrace chastity alone; we who
formerly used magical arts, dedicate ourselves to the good and un-
begotten God; we who valued above all things the acquisition of
wealth and possessions, now bring what we have into a common

---

440 *Apology of Aristides* 15.4–7 (ANF 9:277). Geffcken, p. 24. Cf. 16.7–12, 16.1–
2. "Such, O King, is the commandment of the law of the Christians, and such
is their manner of life." 15.2. "The Christians are just and good, and the truth is
set before their eyes, and their spirit is long-suffering." 17.2.

stock, and communicate to every one in need; we who hated and destroyed one another, and on account of their different manners would not live with men of a different tribe, now, since the coming of Christ, live familiarly with them, and pray for our enemies, and endeavour to persuade those who hate us unjustly to live conformably to the good precepts of Christ, to the end that they may become partakers with us of the same joyful hope of a reward from God the ruler of all."[441]

The *Epistle to Diognetus* likewise describes the "wonderful and confessedly striking method of life" of the Christians.[442]

Tatian's speech against the Hellenes is almost entirely devoted to a description of the debauchery in the gentile world, and along with this, albeit as an aside, he notes several times that the life of the Christians is entirely different.[443]

Minucius Felix, in defending Christians from the slander that was being spread concerning Christian assemblies, says that the gentiles were projecting their traits onto the Christians, while the Christians were distinguished by moral purity.[444]

---

441 Justin Martyr, *Apologies* 1.14 (ANF 1:167). Cf. ibid. 1.15: "Many, both men and women, who have been Christ's disciples from childhood, remain pure at the age of sixty or seventy years; and I boast that I could produce such from every race of men. For what shall I say, too, of the countless multitude of those who have reformed intemperate habits, and learned these things?" (ANF 1:167). Similarly, in the *Epistle of Barnabas* 16.7: "Before we believed in God, the habitation of our heart was corrupt and weak (φθαρτὸν καὶ ἀσθενές), as being indeed like a temple made with hands. For it was full of idolatry, and was a habitation of demons, through our doing such things as were opposed to [the will of] God" (ANF 1:147). These words are also cited by Clement of Alexandria in his *Stromata* 2.20.116.4 (ANF 2:372). Justin Martyr, *Dialogue with Trypho* 119: "We have left already the way of living in which we used to spend our days, passing our time in evil after the fashions of the other inhabitants of the earth" (ANF 1:259; GAG 1.2:426). Irenaeus says that for this reason Christians need no law, because they have become infants unto malice (*The Demonstration of the Apostolic Preaching* 96).

442 *Epistle of Mathetes to Diognetus* 5 (ANF 1:27). *Die apost. Väter*, pp. 136–137.

443 Tatian, *Address to the Greeks* 32–33 (ANF 2:78–79).

444 *The Octavius of Minucius Felix* 31: "You continue the story of incest, even although you have no consciousness of your crime. But we maintain our modesty not in appearance, but in our heart we gladly abide by the bond of a single mar-

Athenagoras says exactly the same,[445] as does Tertullian on many occasions.[446] All these testimonies of the apologists may be summarized in the words of the *Epistle to Diognetus:* "To sum up all in one word—what the soul is in the body, that are Christians in the world."[447] Such was the mind of Christianity: it was in full accord with the exalted teaching concerning the Church as a new and holy race of men. Life justified and substantiated dogma.

In polemics against the Jews in the first centuries another idea should be noted. Above we presented the doctrine of the *Epistle of Barnabas,* according to which the Jews did not understand their own law, so that the historical existence of Judaism with its institutions was, essentially, the result of nothing but a misunderstanding. But the majority of early ecclesiastical authors, as we have already stated, did not share this opinion, and considered the Old Testament an authentic divine institution. In the writings of other church authors, however, we likewise encounter the idea that the New Testament is more ancient than the Old. The Church is only called a new nation, but in its essence it is **the most ancient of nations**: for it is none other than primordial nature restored. The norms of this nature existed before the law of Moses; hence, in its essence, the law

---

riage; in the desire of procreating, we know either one wife, or none at all. We practice sharing in banquets, which are not only modest, but also sober: for we do not indulge in entertainments nor prolong our feasts with wine; but we temper our joyousness with gravity (*gravitate hilaritatem temperamus*), with chaste discourse, and with body even more chaste (divers of us unviolated) enjoy rather than make a boast of a perpetual virginity of a body" (ANF 4:192). Cf. *Apology of Aristides* 17.2: "They ... impute their monstrous impurity in turn to the Christians" (ANF 9:279).

445 Athenagoras, *A Plea for the Christians* 32, 33, 31 (ANF 2:145–147); J. Geffcken, *Zwei griechische Apologeten,* 151 f.

446 Tertullian, *The Apology* 2 (ANF 3:18–20). Cf. *Ad Uxorem* 1.6 (PL 1:1284). For more detail see Adhemar d'Ales, *La theologie de Tertullien* (Paris: 1905), 26–33.

447 *Epistle of Mathetes to Diognetus* 6.1 (ANF 1:27). *Die apostolischen Väter,* p. 137. Trypho said to Justin (*Dialogue with Trypho* 10): "You, professing to be pious, and supposing yourselves better than others, are not in any particular separated from them, and do not alter your mode of living from the nations" (ANF 1:199). But Trypho, as we see from the words that follow, wished that Christians might differ from others by observing the law of Moses: "You observe no festivals or sabbaths, and do not have the rite of circumcision."

of Christ is more ancient than the law of Moses which was given on
Sinai.[448] Before the law of Moses a law was given to Adam and Eve.
This law is primeval and universal (*generalis et primordialis Dei lex*),
given to all nations. There was also the unwritten natural law, by
which the patriarchs were saved. The Christian faith was prefigured
in Abraham, and he was the patriarch of that faith and in a sense its
prophet (*patriarcha nostrae fidei, et velut propheta fuit*). For this reason the
apostle Paul (see Gal. 3:5–9) called him not only a prophet of faith,
but also the father of those of the gentiles who believe in Christ.
The Christian faith and the faith of Abraham are one and the same
(*una et eadem illius et nostra fides*).[449]

But along with this historical thinking on the ancientness of the
Christian Church as opposed to Judaism, in certain other historic
literary works we find mystical allegorical and apocalyptic thinking
on the pre-worldly origin of the Church. This idea is most extensively expressed in the homily known as the *Second Epistle of Clement.*
The preacher says: "Brethren, if we do the will of God our father,
we shall be of the first Church, that is, spiritual, that hath been
created before the sun and moon."[450] Some substantiation for this
thesis is also found in an allegorical interpretation of the Old Testament. "I do not, however, suppose ye are ignorant that the living
Church (ἐκκλησία ζῶσα) is the body of Christ; for the scripture
saith, 'God made man, male and female.' The male is Christ, the female is the Church. And the Books and the Apostles plainly declare
that the Church is not of the present, but from the beginning (τὴν
ἐκκλησίαν οὐ νῦν εἶναι, ἀλλὰ ἄνωθεν). For she was spiritual, as our
Jesus also was, but was manifested (ἐφανερώθη) in the last days that
He might save us."[451] Being spiritual, the Church was manifested in

---

448 Tertullian, *Against the Jews* 2 (PL 2:637b–c, 638b, c; 639a).

449 Irenaeus of Lyons, *Against Heresies* 4.21.1 (ANF 1:492).

450 2 Clem. 14:1: "Ὥστε, ἀδέλφοί, ποιοῦντες τὸ θέλημα τοῦ πατρὸς ἡμῶν
Θεοῦ ἐσόμεθα ἐκ τῆς ἐκκλησίας τῆς πρώτης, τῆς πνευματικῆς, τῆς πρὸ ἡλίου καὶ
σελήνης ἐκτισμένης" (ANF 7:521).

451 2 Clem. 14:1 (ANF 7:521). In the latter words we may note a certain
similarity to the words of the apostle Peter, where Christ is called the Lamb fore-
ordained before the foundation of the world (προεγνωσμένου πρὸ καταβολῆς

the Flesh of Christ. The Church is the Body, and Christ is the Spirit.[452] Christ and the Church comprise a kind of gnostic syzygy, and the properties of Christ are projected onto the Church: as Christ existed before the sun and the moon came to be, so also the Church existed; but in confirmation of this the author cites the passage on the creation of man, who naturally appeared after the creation of the sun and the moon. Furthermore, in speaking of the creation of the Church (ἐκτισμένης), is the author not opening the door to the idea that Christ also is created? In general it should be stated that this homily's speculation regarding the Church is highly ambiguous and unclear,[453] but it is apparent that here the Christian Church is juxtaposed to the Church of the Jews,[454] and the precedence of the former is indicated by its antiquity and universality.[455]

The same idea of the preexistence of the Church is found in *The Pastor of Hermas*. Hermas saw an elderly woman, and a youth who appeared to him in a dream told him that this woman was the Church of God. "I said to him, 'Why then is she an old woman?' 'Because,' said he, 'she was created first of all. On this account is she old. And for her sake was the world made.'"[456] Although here the Church is called the first creation, it is not linked to Christ as in the homily of Clement.[457]

κόσμου), but made manifest (φανερωθέντος) in the latter times for us (1 Pet. 1:20).

452 2 Clem. 14:3–4 (ANF 7:521). The idea that the Church existed prior to the coming of Christ may also be seen in 2 Clem. 2.1, 3.

453 R. Knopf, *Das nachapostolische Zeitalter*, 239. Cf. E. M., *Revue internationale de théologie* (1910), 142: "Ces resonnements alambiques qui ne prouvent rien."

454 Cf. A. Harnack, "Ueber den sogenannten zweiten Brief des Clemens an die Korinther," in *Zeitschrift für Kirchengeschichte* (1876), Bd. 1, 343.

455 Cf. Dr. Daniel Völter, *Die apostolischen Väter neu untersucht* 2.1. "Die älteste Predigt aus Rom (Der sogenannte zweite Clemensbrief)" (Leiden: 1908), 32.

456 *The Pastor of Hermas* 1.2.4.1: "ὅτι, φησίν, πάντων πρώτη ἐκτίσθη · διὰ τοῦτο πρεσβυτέρα · καὶ διὰ ταύτην ὁ κόσμος κατηρτίσθη" (ANF 2:12).

457 Concerning the difference between *The Pastor* and the homily regarding the teaching concerning the Church, see Loofs, *Leitfaden der Dogmengeschichte*, §14.5d, 97, Anm. 4–5: "In Clement's homily (14.3) the preexistent Church is equated with πνεῦμα ἅγιον, while in *The Pastor* (3.9.1.1, 24.4; 2.11.8) the Spirit manifested in Christ acts in the Church. For Hermas, πνεῦμα is the Son of God, and the Church is a creation."

Another passage from *The Pastor* may be presumed to contain the idea that the Church was created along with the world. Hermas cites a passage from what was read by the elderly woman who appeared to him, in which a discussion of the creation of the world is immediately followed by these words: "By His own wisdom and providence has [He] created His holy Church, which He has blessed."[458]

Given the predominance of allegorical scriptural interpretation in the early Church, the story of the creation of the world was frequently interpreted as applying to Christ and the Church, as shown by positive although later testimonials. Anastasius of Sinai, in contemplating the six days of creation, attests that the ancient exegetes—Papias of Hierapolis, Clement, Pantaenus, and Ammonius—interpreted the entire six days of creation as applying to Christ and the Church.[459] Concerning Origen, Socrates the Scholastic reports: "He more particularly explains this mystery in the ninth volume of his *Comments upon Genesis*, where he shows that Adam and Eve were types of Christ and the church. That holy man Pamphilus, and Eusebius who was surnamed after him, are trustworthy witnesses on this subject: both these witnesses, in their joint life of Origen and admirable defense of him in answer to such as were prejudiced against him, prove that he was not the first who made this declaration, but that in doing so he was the mere expositor of the mystical (μυστικήν) tradition of the church."[460] But this detailed allegorical explanation of the story of creation is not

---

458 *The Pastor of Hermas* 1.1.3.4 (ANF 2:11).

459 "Λαβόντες τὰς ἀφορμὰς ἐκ Παπίου τοῦ πάνυ, τοῦ Ἱεραπολίτου, τοῦ τῷ ἐπιστηθίῳ φοιτήσαντος, καὶ Κλήμεντος καὶ Πανταίνου τοῦ τῆς Ἀλεξανδρέων ἱερέως· καὶ Ἀμμονίου τοῦ σωφοτάτου, τῶν ἀρχαίων καὶ πρὸ τῶν συνόδων ἐξηγητῶν, εἰς Χριστὸν καὶ τὴν ἐκκλησίαν πᾶσαν τὴν ἐξαήμερον νοησάντων [receiving our starting-point from the great Papias of Hierapolis, who was student of the bosom friend, and Clemet and Pantaenus the priests of Alexandria, and Ammonius the most wise, the ancient exegetes before the councils, who understood the entire six-day creation as signifying Christ and the Church]." –Migne (PG 89:860), Papiasfragm. 6; Funk, *Die apostolischen Väter,* 130.

460 Socrates Scholasticus, *The Ecclesiastical History of Socrates Scholasticus* 3.7 (NPNF[2] 2:81). *Socrates' Ecclesiastical History, with an introduction by William Bright,* 2ed (Oxford: 1893), 145.

inseparably linked to the opinion that the Church was preexistent, and hence it would be groundless to ascribe this opinion to all the above-mentioned early church writers, and there is insufficient data to state that it was widespread in the early Church.[461]

In the history of the dogma concerning the Church, the idea of the preexistence of the Church is coincidental. It was rooted in the realistic mindset of the people of that time,[462] and in a sense it echoes Gnostic ideas.[463] Parallels to this are pointed out in the teaching of the Elcesaites.[464] The teaching of the apostle Paul (see Eph. 5) has nothing in common with this opinion. As it was inseparably linked with the allegorical method of scriptural interpretation,[465] the doctrine of the preexistence of the Church was naturally left with no support when this method of interpretation lost its overwhelming predominance. The conflict with Gnostics taught church writers to use great discretion in employing analogies and allegories, and a correlation between Christ and the Church so reminiscent of gnostic syzygy no longer had a rightful place in church theology.[466] Consequently, the aforementioned idea of the preexistence of the Church could not leave any noticeable trace in the history of the dogma concerning the Church.

---

461 As does R. Knopf in *Das nachapostolische Zeitalter*, 343–344, Anm. 2.

462 Harnack, *Zeitschrift für Kirchengeschichte* (1876), Bd. 1, 343.

463 E. M., *Revue internationale de théologie* (1910), 192. At the same time, in *Excerpts of Theodotus* 42.3 we read: "Τὸ σῶμα τοῦ Ἰησοῦ, ὅπερ ὁμοούσιον ἦν τῇ ἐκκλησίᾳ [the body of Jesus, which was of one essence with the Church]" (GrchSch. 17:120.7). *Excerpts of Theodotus* 13.4: "ἡ σάρξ τὸ σῶμα αὐτοῦ ἐστιν, ὅπερ ἐστὶν ἡ ἐκκλησία, ἄρτος οὐράνιος, συναγωγὴ εὐλογημένη [the flesh is His body, which is the Church, heavenly bread, a blessed synagogue]" (GrchSch. 17:111.11–12. *Excerpts of Theodotus* 41.2: "πρὸ καταβολῆς κόσμου λέγεται ἡ ἐκκλησία ἐκλελέχθαι [the Church is said to have been chosen before the foundation of the world]" (GrchSch. 17:119.22–23).

464 G. Hoennicke, *Das Judenchristentum*, 360.

465 Harnack, *Dogmengeschichte*[4], 413–414, Anm. 4. Cf. Schanz, "Der Begriff der Kirche," *Theologische Quartalschrift* (1893), 564.

466 Harnack, *Zeitsehrift für Kirchengeschichte* (1876), Bd. I, 344–345 Anm.; *Dogmengeschichte*[4] 1, 172.

St. Irenaeos of Lyons

THIRD ESSAY

The Teaching of the Anti-Gnostic Writers Concerning the Church

In the preceding essay we outlined the teaching concerning the Church that was presented in early Christian literature in opposition to Judaistic nationalistic tendencies. But Judaism was not the only environment that Christianity entered at its outset. Very quickly Christianity began to have dealings with the gentile world, and this gentile world met the Christians with persecutions. Between Christianity and paganism there were also no small number of ideological antitheses; hence, here too bitter conflict ensued. The gentile world threw down the gauntlet to Christianity, but it also gave the Church the means and the weapons for the fight. The Christian Church was joined by people with an education, who began to combat paganism with its own weapons. These were the apologists. While retaining their former knowledge and education, the apologists made a complete break with their former pagan worldview. But not all were capable of this change in outlook upon encountering Christianity. Upon acquaintance with Christian teaching, many wished to accept Christianity while retaining their former religious and philosophical views. This produced an amalgamation of Christian and philosophical elements. This was the beginning of Christian **Gnosticism**. It should be noted that in this amalgamation of Christianity and philosophical elements, Christianity suffered. This is naturally because Christanity can only be exclusive, and it in no way allows for eclecticism.

The ideological atmosphere of the second century is filled with gnostic systems of every kind. The early church polemicists say that gnostic systems sprouted up like mushrooms, and they likened Gnosis itself to a many-headed monster such as the Lernaean Hydra.[467] The task of classifying this multitude of different gnostic systems presents considerable difficulty even for trained specialists.[468] No less controversial in academia is the question of where Gnosis originated.[469] It is clear that it is the fruit of a syncretism of Hellenic philosophy and Eastern cults, and many are inclined to see in Gnosticism a predominance of Hellenistic elements that lend particular overtones to all its Eastern constructs.[470] Church writers also point to Greek philosophy as the source of the gnostic systems.[471] Nevertheless, Gnosis was not philosophy alone: it was religious philosophy, which considered itself the most perfect religion and sought its validation in revelation.[472] The Gnostics cannot be contrasted to believers as philosophers: they too wished to be people of religion. But they sought religion primarily in the resolution of global problems: where did man come from? What are his origins? Where did evil come from, and why?[473] It is also characteristic of the Gnostics that

---

467 See Irenaeus, *Against Heresies* 1.29.1, 30.15 (ANF 1:353, 358; PG 7:691b, 704a). Hippolytus, *Refutation of all Heresies* 5.11 (PG 16:3159b). Cf. Epiphanius, Haer. 31.1 (PG 41:473b).

468 Thomasius, *Dogmengeschichte* 1, 77. Vgl. 83: "Wie nebelgebilde, auf welche die Sonne einzelne Strahlen wirft, sehen wir diese mannigfaltigen gnostischen Syteme an."

469 Harnack, *Dogmengeschichte*⁴ 1, 250 ff. Loofs F., *Leitfaden der Dogmengeschichte*, §16.3, 106–108.

470 Ibid., vgl. Nitzsch, op. cit., 54–55.

471 "Heresies are themselves instigated (*subornantur*) by philosophy. From this source came the Æons, and I known not what infinite forms. … From the same source came Marcion's better god, with all his tranquillity (*de tranquillitate*); he came of the Stoics. … The same subject-matter is discussed over and over again by the heretics and the philosophers; the same arguments are involved" (Tertullian, *Prescription Against Heretics* 7 [ANF 3:246; PL 2:22a]).

472 Harnack, *Dogmengeschichte*⁴ 1, 251

473 "Unde malum, et quare? Et unde homo, et quomodo?" (Tertullian, *Prescription Against Heretics* 7 [PL 2:22b].

they wished to enter into fellowship with the higher world by means of thoughts, imaginings, and feelings. They saw Gnosis as religion in its highest form, but Gnosis is not rationalism. The vulgar rationalism of our own time was completely foreign to the Gnostics. The Gnostics were too aristocratic to feel any attraction to ever-democratic rationalism. They made gnosis dependent on "revelation," but this revelation, they taught, was accessible not to everyone, but only to the elect. Only the spiritual man (πνευματικὸς ἄνθρωπος) was capable of possessing gnosis (γνῶσις).[474] In this higher gnosis Christianity can only be one of its composite parts, along with Semitic and Hellenistic elements.[475] The Gnostics assimilated Christian revelation and wished to use it to validate their religious and philosophical constructs. "What are these sheep's clothing's, but the external surface of the Christian profession? Who are the ravening wolves but those deceitful senses and spirits which are lurking within to waste the flock of Christ?"—so says Tertullian.[476] What is more, the Gnostics frequently declared themselves to be true Christians, and protested when they were called heretics. False teachings were preached under the name of Christianity.[477] The tremendous

---

474 Particular emphasis is placed on this nature of Gnosticism by lic. theol. Rudolf Liechtenhan. See *Die Offenbarung im Gnosticismus* (Göttingen: 1901), 84–85, 98–103, 162–164. See V.V. Bolotov, *Lectures on the History of the Ancient Church* ["Лекции по истории древней Церкви"] 2, 174–175.

475 Harnack, *Dogmengeschichte*⁴ 1, 253–254. Thomasius, *Dogmengeschichte*, 85; Knopf, *Das nachapostolsiche Zeitalter*, 336–337.

476 Tertullian, *Prescription Against Heretics* 4 (ANF 3:244; PL 2:18b).

477 Various Gnostic sects wished to remain in the Church while altering its teaching. Concerning the Valentinians Irenaeus reports that they did not wish to separate from the Church (*Against Heresies* 3.15.2), and Tertullian states that Valentine was driven out of the Church (*Prescription Against Heretics* 30). Hippolytus tried to prove that the Marcosians were not Christians, but Pythagorians (*Refutation of All Heresies* 6.52 [ANF 5:97–98; PG 16:3282b]: "Οὐ Χριστοῦ μαθηταί, ἀλλὰ Πυθαγόρου"). The Naassenes considered themselves to be the only true Christians. (Hippolytus, *Refutation of All Heresies* 5.9: "Καὶ ἐσμὲν ἐξ ἁπάντων ἀνθρώπων ἡμεῖς χριστιανοὶ μόνοι ἐν τῇ τρίτῃ πύλῃ ἀπαρτίζοντες τὸ μυστήριον καὶ χριόμενοι ἐκεῖ ἀλάλῳ χρίσματι, ἐκ κέρατος, ὡς Δαβίδ [And out of all men only we are Christians, completing the mystery in the third gate and being there anointed by a speechless chrism, from a horn, as was David]" [PG 16:3159–

danger that Gnosticism presented for the Church is perfectly clear,
especially at a time when faith was waning and the Church, like the
burning bush, was surrounded by a devouring flame.[478] Gnosticism
concerned the Church directly, and it was destined to have a great
influence on how the Church defined its doctrine.[479]

Among the Gnostics there was a unique phenomenon, known
as Marcionism. Although Marcion is ordinarily treated as a gnostic,
his situation is so entirely unique that many have difficulty numbering him with the Gnostics.[480] Marcion was a practical man, not
a speculator. He did not want to found the first school or the first
religious society; rather, he wanted to reform the Church, which

3160]). The Marcionite Megethius, in disputing with Adamantius, insists that
he is a Christian (*Dialogues* 1.8). Dr. C.P. Caspari, *Kirchenhistorische Anecdota nebst
neuen Ausgaben patristischer und kirchlich-mittelalterlicher Schriften* 1 (Christiania: 1883),
12–13 (GrchSch. 4:16 ff): "They appropriated for themselves the name of Christians, and they scandalize the gentile nations," says Epiphanius of the Carpocratians—Haer. 27.3 (PG 41:368a). See also Irenaeus, *Against Heresies* 3.15.2 (ANF
1:439–440; PG 7:918b), and Tertullian, *Against the Valentinians* 27: "Plane et ipsi
imaginarii Christiani [Christians themselves being indeed nothing but imaginary
beings!]" (CSEL 47:204.6).

478 Tertullian, *Scorpiace* 1 (CSEL 20.1:145.6. sqq).

479 Concerning this, see Harnack, *Dogmengeschichte* 1, 359–360; Thomasius.
85–86; Ritschl, *Die Entstehung der altkath. Kirche*, 338–340; Böhringer, *Die alt Kirche*,
2-ter Teil., 282–283; Reinhold Seeberg, *Studien zur Geschichte des Begriffs der Kirche*
(Erlangen: 1885), 16; Nitzsch, op. cit., 55–56; Loofs, *Leitfaden der Dogmengeschichte*,
§§ 16.6, 19.5, 110–111, 136; Knopf, *Das nachap. Zeitalt*, 339; Shternov, *Tertullian*,
127–228; Archimandrite Sylvester, *The Teaching Concerning the Church in the First
Three Centuries of Christianity* ["Учение о Церкви ю первые три века христианства"] (Kiev: 1872), 167–169; "The Dogmatic system of St. Irenaeus of Lyons
in Relation to the Gnostic Teachings of the Second Century" ["Догматическая
система св. Иринея Лионского в связи с гностическими учениями II века"],
Pravoslavny sobesednik (1874), vol. 2, 191–193.

480 Thomasius, op. cit., 81; Harnack, *Dogmengeschichte⁴*, 292 ff; Böhringer, *Die
alte KiSeeburche*, 2 Th., 371; Loofs, *Leitfaden der Dogmengeschichte⁴*, § 17.1, 111–112;
Bolotov, *Lectures* ["Лекции"], 2nd ed., 226–227; Liechtenhan, *Die Offenbarung im
Gnosticismus*, 34; Theodor Zahn, *Geschichte des neutestamentlichen Kanons*, 1-er Bd. 2-te
Hälfte (Erlangen und Leipzip: 1889), 586 ff.

in his opinion misunderstood and distorted the teaching of Christ, introducing elements of Judaism into it. When the Church did not adopt his reforms, Marcion separated from it. Epiphanius says of him that he was the son of a bishop, and was excommunicated from the Church by his father. He went to Rome, and when here too he was not accepted he declared, "I will break your Church apart and introduce schism into it for all time." And indeed he introduced no small schism, but he failed to break the Church apart; rather, he himself broke away along with those who believed him.[481] Tertullian likewise describes the open separation of Marcion from the Church.[482] Marcion founded his own church,[483] which existed for quite some time. Epiphanius writes, "Having deceived a great many people, Marcion assembled a school, which to this day lives on in many forms. Even now this heresy is found in Rome and Italy, in Egypt and Palestine, in Arabia and Syria, on Cyprus and in the Thebaid, and even in Persia and other places. For in these lands this crafty man acquired great power for his deceit."[484] Marcion himself declared himself a church reformer.[485] And yet the teaching of Marcion was absolutely opposed to that of the Church.

But if Gnosis and Marcion in particular[486] were so explicitly hostile toward the Christian Church, it is quite clear that the Church, recognizing the full extent of the danger Gnosticism presented, had to still more clearly and decisively express its own doctrine. Divisions and heresies were still unfamiliar to the Church; church doc-

481 Epiphanius, Haer. 42.1.2 (PG 41:696–697).

482 Tertullian, *Against Marcion* 4.4 (ANF 3:348–349; CSEL 47:429.15–16); *On the Flesh of Christ* 2 (PL 2:801a).

483 Idem. 5: "Habet plane et illud ecclesias, sed suas, tam posteras quam adulteras [It too, of course, has its churches, but specially its own—as late as they are spurious]" (CSEL 47:430.26–27).

484 Epiphanius, Haer. 42.1 (PG 41:696b).

485 Harnack, *Dogmengeschichte* 1, 305. Anm. 2. Vgl. Loofs, *Leitfaden der Dogmengeschichte*, §17.3, 113; Pierre Batiffol, *L'église naissante et le catholicisme*, 277, 281, 282; Th. Zahn, *Geschichte des neutest. Kanons* 1 Bd., 596.

486 Clement of Alexandria calls Marcion a giant of atheism: "ὁ θεομάχος οὗτος γίγας." See *Stromata* 3.4; 25.2 (GrchSch. 15:207.10).

trine had not yet been formulated in detail; there were variations in thinking that reconciled themselves on the basis of a shared life and shared hopes. Gnosticism affected the essence of the Christian faith, distorting it in its chief, fundamental points. This was no longer an insignificant difference of opinion: it was a heresy, and not just a heresy, but a phenomenon that threatened to dissolve into itself the whole substance of Christianity, leaving nothing of it but a few peripheral traits and reinterpreting its whole substance in its own way. Given this situation, the Christian Church had either to perish or to firmly establish its own essence in specific formulas. As we have seen from the foregoing, the Church as yet had no definitive doctrine concerning the Church. A "new people," a "new creation," an "ancient people"—all these definitions were too general. With the advent of Gnosticism there arose a need for norms that would define what was true and what was false, what was of the Church and what was heretical. And indeed, we see that in combating Gnosticism the Church established these very norms. Church writers conducted in-depth polemics with the Gnostics, engaging in a detailed analysis of their systems, but ordinarily they would precede these polemics by defining the fundamental concept of the Church. The doctrine concerning the Church, it may be said, comprises one of the cardinal points of anti-Gnostic polemics, and the works of the anti-Gnostic writers are of exceptional importance in the history of the dogma concerning the Church. Prominent anti-Gnostic writers—St. **Irenaeus of Lyons and Tertullian,** presbyter of Carthage—allot considerable attention in their polemical compositions to the question of the Church. "Irenaeus, in all things adorned by the Holy Spirit, as a courageous ascetics raised up by the Lord (ὡς γενναῖος ἀθλητὴς ὑπὸ τοῦ Κυρίου προβεβλημένος), anointed with the heavenly gifts (ἐπαλειφθεὶς τοῖς ἐπουρανίοις χαρίσμασι) of true faith and knowledge,"[487] maybe called the Athanasius of the second century.[488] The ardent and judicially educated Tertullian devoted the greater part of his literary work to polemics with Gnosis,[489]

---

487 Epiphanius, Haer. 31, 33 (PG 41:537c–d).

488 *Pravoslavny sobesednik* (1874), vol. 2, 181–182.

489 Dr. Karl Adam, *Der Kirchebegriff Tertullians. Forschungen zur Christlichen Litera-*

making the same points against the heretics as did Irenaeus, some-times further developing and uniquely elucidating them.[490] In the polemical works of Irenaeus and Tertullian, the doctrine concern-ing the Church may be said to have been definitively expressed for the first time.

In the systems of the Gnostics one frequently encounters specu-lative comments concerning the Church.[491] But these comments had no significance in the overall system of Gnosticism, and in no way influenced the establishment of the true understanding of the Church.[492] Church writers were motivated to develop the teaching on the Church specifically by the Gnostics' stance on Christian rev-elation. Gnosticism was not an enthusiastic movement like Montan-

---

tur-und Dogmengeschichte, herausgeg. von Dr. Ehrhard und Dr. I. Kirsch, 6. Band, 4 Helft (Paderborn: 1907), 23.

490 Cf. Adhémar d'Alès, *La théologie de Tertullien,* 213, 60. Batiffol, *L'église nais-sante et le catholicisme,*[3] 317.

491 These comments cannot be combined into a single system, as they are varied and conflicting. First and foremost, the Church is one of the aeons, which is usually placed in syzygy with man. Irenaeus, *Against Heresies* 1.1.1.2, 8.5; 11.1, 15.3 (PG 7:448a, 449a, 537a, 561a, 620A, 621b). Tertullian, *Prescription Against Heretics* 33 (PL 2:55a); *Against the Valentinians* 39 (CSEL 47:211.20); Hippolytus, *The Refutation of All Heresies,* 6.30, 43, 46, 51, 53; 10.13 (PG 16:3238c, 3263b, 3270b, 3279b, 3282b, 3287b, 3427b). On the other hand, the Church is the seed of the mother (the Achamoth) and is a figure of the Church On High—"ἀντίτυπον τῆς ἄνω ἐκκλησίας" (Irenaeus, *Against Heresies* 1.5.6; Cf. 1.8.4 [PG 7:501b, 529a]). Tertullian, *Against the Valentinians* 25: "Hoc semen ecclesiam dicunt, ecclesiae su-pernae speculum [To this seed they give the name of Church, the mirror of the church above]" (CSEL 47:202.4–5). "This constitutes the true and holy Church, which has become the appellation, the meeting together, and the union (*conven-tio et adunatio*) of the father of all, of the first man, of the son, of the second man, of Christ their son, and of the woman who has been mentioned"—Ire-naeus, *Against Heresies* 1.30.2 (ANF 1:354; PG 7:695b). Finally these are named: "Τρεῖς ἐκκλησίαι, ἀγγελική, ψυχική, χοϊκή · ὀνόματα δὲ αὐταῖς ἐκλεκτή, κλητή, αἰχμάλωτος [there are three churches — angelic, psychical, earthly; and the names of these are elect, called, captive]"—Hippolytus, *The Refutation of All Her-esies* 5.6, 10.9 (PG 16:3125b–3126b). See also the notes in the *Excerpta ex Theodot.* 13.1, 17.1, 21.3, 26.1, 33.2, 40.2, 41, 42.3, 58.1 (GrchSch. 17:111.4–6; 112.8–9; 113.26–27; 115.15–16; 117.22–24; 119.13–15, 22–23; 120.7; 126.8 ff.

492 Seeburg, *Studien zur Geschichte des Begriffs der Kirche,* 16.

ism; it offered no new revelation in the narrow sense of that word.[493]
The Gnostics cited the same revelation that was in the Church,
the same theological sources that the Church possessed. They too
wished to test their every word against the teaching of the Savior.[494]
"It is not only from the writings of the evangelists and the apostles
that they endeavour to derive proofs for their opinions ... they deal
in the same way with the law and the prophets."[495] "They actually
treat of the Scriptures and recommend (their opinions) out of the
Scriptures! To be sure they do. From what other source could they
derive arguments concerning the things of the faith, except from
the records of the faith?"[496] But two completely different streams
cannot flow from the same source. Gnosis did not originate from
Christ and His Gospel, but only later turned to Christian theological sources, which it read with its prejudiced theories.[497] Quite obviously, not everything in Holy Scripture could favor the gnostic constructs, and so in order to better adapt the Holy Scriptures to their
own religious and philosophical systems the Gnostics were obliged
to make various changes to the sacred books. Distorting the doctrine presupposed corrupting the theological sources, as well.[498] And

---

493 This conclusion was reached by Liechtenhan (*Die Offenbarung im Gnosticismus*, 42) after extensively researching the position of prophecy in various Gnostic
sects (5–42).

494 Ptolemy, *Letter to Flora* 10: "Μετὰ καὶ τοῦ κανονίσαι πάντας τοὺς λόγους τῇ
τοῦ Σωτῆρος διδασκαλίᾳ." Epiphanius, Haer. 33.7 (PG 41:568c).

495 Irenaeus, *Against Heresies* 1.3.6 (ANF 1:320), PG 7:477a.

496 "Sed ipsi de Scripturis agunt, et de Scripturis suadent. Aliunde scilicet
suadere non possent de rebus fidei, nisi ex litteris fidei?" (Tertullian, *The Prescription Against Heretics* 14 [ANF 3:250; PL 2:33a]). Cf. *On the Resurrection of the Flesh* 63:
"Hae (haereses) sine aliquibus occasionibus scripturarum audere non poterant
[these heresies would be unable to put on a bold front without some countenance
from the Scriptures]" (CSEL 47:125, 5–7).

497 Irenaeus, *Against Heresies* 1.9.3 (ANF 1:330; PG 7:544a): "Their whole system ... they falsely dream into existence, and thus inflict injury on the Scriptures,
while they build up their own hypothesis (ἰδίαν ὑπόθεσιν ἀναπλασάμενοι)."

498 Tertullian, *The Prescription Against Heretics* 38: "Quibus fuit propositum
aliter docendi, eos necessitas coegit aliter disponendi instrumenta doctrinae.
Alias enim, non potuissent aliter docere, nisi aliter haberent, per quae docer-
ent [On those whose purpose it was to teach differently, lay the necessity of

indeed, all who wrote against the Gnostics attest that they would begin by distorting the text of the Holy Scriptures.[499] When they would cite Holy Scripture in denouncing the Gnostics, the latter, according to Irenaeus, would begin blaming the Scriptures them-selves, alleging that they were inaccurate and at variance in their rendering (*varie sint dictae*).[500] The Gnostics rejected several books of Holy Scripture, one sect rejecting some books and another reject-ing others.[501] They rejected the writings of the evangelist Luke.[502] They did not accept the Gospel of John.[503] The Ebionites only used the Gospel of Matthew. "Those who separate Jesus from Christ" give preference to the Gospel of Mark. The followers of Valenti-nus predominantly (*plenissime utentes*) use the Gospel of John.[504] The heretics do "not receive certain Scriptures; and whichever of them it does receive, it perverts by means of additions and diminutions, for the accomplishment of it own purpose; and such as it does re-ceive, it receives not in their entirety."[505] Apelles, according to Hip-polytus, took from the Gospels and the apostolic writings only what pleased him (τὰ ἀρέσκοντα).[506] Furthermore, certain Gnostics had additional sacred books. "Those who are from Valentinus, being … altogether reckless, while they put forth their own compositions (*conscriptiones*), boast that they possess more Gospels than there re-ally are. Indeed, they have arrived at such a pitch of audacity, as to entitle their comparatively recent writing 'the Gospel of Truth,'

---

differently arranging the instruments of doctrine. They could not possibly have effected their diversity of teaching in any other way than by having a difference in the means whereby they taught]" (PL 2:62a).

499 For more detail concerning this treatment of the New Testament Scrip-tures by the Valentinians and Basilides, see Th. Zahn, *Geschichte des neutestamentli-chen Kanons*, Bd. 1.2, 718–763, 763–774.

500 Idem. Col. 846a.

501 Idem. Col. 890A.

502 Idem. Col. 915–916.

503 Idem. Col. 890B.

504 Idem. Col. 884b–C.

505 Tertullian, *The Prescription Against Heretics* 17 (PL 2:35a).

506 Hippolytus, *Refutation of all Heresies* 7.38 (PG 16:3346a).

though it agrees in nothing with the Gospels of the Apostles, so
that they have really no Gospel which is not full of blasphemy."[507]
Among the Gnostics there circulated innumerable apocryphal and
spurious (νόθων) writings that they themselves had compiled.[508] Irenaeus further attests that the Gnostics did not use the Scriptures in
their authentic and complete form, but disregarded the order of
and connection between the Scriptures, and "sundered the members of the truth." They would rearrange and modify the words of
Scripture. "Collecting a set of expressions and names scattered here
and there [in Scripture], they twist them, as we have already said,
from a natural to a non-natural sense."[509] "These persons patch together old wives' fables, and then endeavour, by violently drawing
away from their proper connection, words, expressions, and parables whenever found, to adapt the oracles (τὰ λόγια) of God to their
baseless fictions."[510] To the holy father this is as if a person were to
disassemble a mosaic depiction of a king, rearrange the tiles, and
make a depiction of a dog or a fox, and then say, "This is that self-
same royal portrait."[511] In another place, to illustrate the Gnostics'
arbitrary treatment of the text of Holy Scripture, Irenaeus cites the
example of using verses selected from *The Iliad* and *The Odyssey* to
describe Hercules. "He who is acquainted with the Homeric writings will recognise the verses indeed, but not the subject to which
they are applied, as knowing that some of them were spoken of
Ulysses, others of Hercules himself, others still of Priam, and others
again of Menelaus and Agamemnon."[512]

---

507 Irenaeus, *Against Heresies* 3.11.9 (ANF 1:428; PG 7:891a–b).

508 Irenaeus, *Against Heresies* 1.20.1 (PG 7:653a). Concerning the pseudo-epi-
graphical literature of the Gnostics, see Liechtenhan, *Die Offenbarung im Gnosticismus*, 43 ff; "Die pseudepigraphe Litteratur der Gnostiker," in *Zeitschrift für die
neutestamentliche Wissenschaft* (1902), 222–237, 286–299.

509 Irenaeus, *Against Heresies* 1.9.4 (ANF 1:330; PG 7:544a–b).

510 Irenaeus, *Against Heresies* 1.8.1 (ANF 1:326; PG 7:521, 524).

511 Idem. (PG 7:521a–b).

512 *Against Heresies* 1.9.4: "Though he will acknowledge the gems, he will
certainly not receive the fox instead of the likeness of the king" (ANF 1:330;
PG 7:545a, 548a). All these words and examples are also borrowed verbatim

Marcion was unique in his treatment of Holy Scripture. He adopted a more decisive and forthright approach to the tendential criticism of scriptural texts.[513] Based on the idea that the Old and New Testaments were completely opposed to each other,[514] Marcion discarded from the New Testament books all that did not support his own opinion.[515] Church polemicists customarily define Marcion's regard for the books of Holy Scripture with the words *circumcidere*,[516] *caedere*,[517] *delere*,[518] and the like. Tertullian says of Marcion that he openly and directly used the sword, not the pen, committing murder against Scripture in the name of his own

---

by Epiphanius of Cyprus, Haer. 31.24, 29 (PG 41:520–521, 529–532). Tertullian finds that the Gnostics' treatment of Holy Scripture resembles how the poet Hosidius Geta compiled the poem *Medea* from lines by Virgil and homerocentones: "Qui de carminibus Homeri propria opera more centonario ex multis hinc inde compositis in unum sarciunt corpus"—*The Prescription Against Heretics* 39 (PL 2:64–65). Concerning this usage of Holy Scripture by the Gnostics see Liechtenhan (69–70, 79–81).

513 Vgl.: Liechtenhan, op.cit., 81–83.

514 Tertullian, *Against Marcion* 1.19: "Separatio legis et evangelii proprium et principale opus est Marcionis [Marcion's special and principal work is the separation of the law and the gospel]" (CSEL 47:314.22–23. Cf. *The Prescription Against Heretics* 30: "Marcion Novum Testamentum a Vetere separavit [Marcion separated the New Testament from the Old]" (PL 2:50a). See also *Against Marcion* 1.21, 4.1 (CSEL 47:318.10–12, 423.2–3).

515 *Adamantius* 2.18: "Ὅσα οὖν μὴ νοήσαντες κατέλειψαν ἑαυτοῖς ἐναντιούμενα, ταῦτα ὥσπερ ἐπιφυλλίδας ἀναλεξάμενος ἐκ τῶν ἀποστολικῶν καὶ προφητικῶν φωνῶν [Therefore as many things as they, not understanding them, have left behind as being in opposition to themselves, these things like small grapes will I pick up from the apostolic and prophetic utterances]" (GrchSch. 4:96.8–11).

516 "To cut around, to trim; to mutilate". Irenaeus, *Against Heresies* 1.27.4: "Manifeste ansus est circumcidere Scripturas [he dared openly to mutilate the Scriptures]" (PG 7:689b). Cf. 1.27.2; 3.11.7; 3.12.12; 14.4 (PG 7:688b, 884b, 906a, 916c); Epiphanius, Haer. 42.12: "Παρέκοψε πολλὰ τῶν μελῶν [he cut off many of the members]" (PG 41:813a).

517 "To cut to pieces." Tertullian, *Against Marcion* 4.2 (CSEL 47:426.27).

518 "To erase, efface, blot out." Tertullian, *On the Flesh of Christ* 2 (PL 2:800–801).

doctrine;[519] while Irenaeus concisely summarizes the outcome of Marcion's work: Marcion and his followers undertook to truncate (*ad intercidendas*) the Scriptures, refusing to acknowledge some entirely, while abbreviating (*decurtantes*) the Gospel of Luke and the epistles of Paul, and only considering legitimate (*legitima*) that which they had thus abbreviated (*minoraverunt*).[520] Taking from Scripture all that suited him, Marcion compiled his "Gospel" and the so-called "Apostolic Writing" (ἀποστολικόν). These included parts of ten of the epistles of the apostle Paul and part of the "Epistle to the Laodiceans." It is this work of Marcion which Epiphanius analyzes in detail in his *Panarion*.[521]

---

519 Tertullian, *Prescription Against Heretics* 38: "Marcion exerte et palam machaera, non stylo usus est: quoniam ad materiam suam caedem Scripturarum confecit [Marcion expressly and openly used the knife, not the pen, since he made such an excision of the Scriptures as suited his own subject-matter]" (PL 2:62–63). Cf. *Against Marcion* 5.18: "De mania haeretici praecidendi non miror, si syllabas subtrahit, cum paginas totas plerumque subducit [As our heretic is so fond of his pruning-knife, I do not wonder when syllables are expunged by his hand, seeing that entire pages are usually what he draws away]" (CSEL 477:638.5–6).

520 Irenaeus, *Against Heresies* 3.12.12 (PG 7:906a). Cf. 3.11.7, 9; 1.27.2. [Marcion persuaded his disciples that he was more deserving of trust than the apostles who had delivered the Gospel; while he himself delivered to them not the Gospel, but a particle of the Gospel [*particulam Evagelii*]" (PG 7:688b). The distortion of Holy Scripture by Marcion is described in greater detail by Tertullian. See *Against Marcion* 4.2–5 (CSEL 47:426 sqq).

521 Epiphanius, Haer. 42.11–12 (PG 41:709–813). Epiphanius himself characterizes Marcion's view of Scripture as follows: "I shall proceed to what is written by Marcion, or rather what has been falsified. For he accepts only the Gospel of Luke, truncated at its beginning because it relates concerning the conception of the Savior and His coming in the flesh. But not only the beginning was cut off by this person, who harmed himself rather than the Gospel, but also at the end and in the middle he cut out many words of truth, while adding others over what was written. And he employs solely the outline (τῷ χαρακτῆρι) of the Gospel of Luke. Of the epistles of the holy apostle he includes ten; these alone he uses, and even then not all that is written in them, but rather truncating some chapters while altering others" (Haer. 42.9 [PG 41:708b]). A complete study of Marcion's treatment of the New Testament is given by Th. Zahn—see *Geschichte des neutestamentlichen Kanons*, Bd. 1, 585–718.

Such was the Gnostics' treatment of the books of Holy Scripture.[522] In its struggle against Gnosis the Church had to determine its position on the sources of its theology. The earliest ecclesiastical literature did not discuss the topic. Writers would cite the sayings of the apostles and evangelists, calling them "Scripture" (γραφή), but the extent of this "Scripture"—which writings were authoritative and which were not—was distinctly absent. The canon of sacred books varied from one Church to the next. In many Churches, alongside the writings of the evangelists and the apostles, "Scripture" was also held to include the works of later church writers, such as the epistle of Clement to the Corinthians, the epistle of Barnabas, the Pastor of Hermas, and others.[523] The conflict with Gnosis required a definite canon of the books of the Holy Scripture of the New Testament, especially since Marcion had already compiled his own "canon," from which all that did not coincide with his teaching had been eliminated. This made it essential for the Church to precisely define those Scriptures that would substantiate its own teaching. The Church needed to reckon up its apostolic inheritance.[524]

Church writers call the books of Holy Scripture the pillar and confirmation (στῦλος καὶ στήριγμα) of the Church,[525] the foundation and pillar of the Christian faith (fundamentum et columnam fidei nostrae),[526] and so they indignantly reject the unceremonious treatment of them that was typical of the heretics. "All who destroy

---

522 Incidentally, this treatment of the text of Holy Scripture was common to all the heretics of old. Epiphanius relates much the same regarding the Ebionites (Haer 30.13–14 [PG 41:428–429]), as does an unknown author concerning the Monarchians of the second century. See Eusebius, *Church History* 5.28.13, 15 (CrchSch. 9.1:504.11, 25–26).

523 For more detail on this see Th. Zahn, *Geschichte des neutestamentlichen Kanons*, Bd. 1, 326–368.

524 Th. Zahn, *Geschichte des neutest. Kanons*, Bd. 1, 586.

525 Irenaeus, *Against Heresies* 3.11.8 (PG 7:885a).

526 Irenaeus, *Against Heresies* 3.1.1 (PG 7:844a): "We have learned from none others the plan of our salvation, than from those through whom the Gospel has come down to us, which they did at one time proclaim in public, and, at a later period, by the will of God, handed down to us in the Scriptures."

(οἱ ἀθετοῦντες) the form of the Gospel are vain, unlearned, and
also audacious; those, [I mean,] who represent the aspects of the
Gospel as being either more in number than as aforesaid, or, on the
other hand, fewer."[527] "There shall be no light punishment [inflict-
ed] upon him who either adds or subtracts anything from the Scripture."[528] The Scriptures originated from the apostles.[529] Irenaeus attests that each Gospel was written by known persons.[530] Against the
"Gospel of Truth" of the Valentinians Irenaeus says that only the
apostles conveyed the true and sure (vera et firma) Gospel. God created all things in harmony and accord, and for this reason the Gospel
must be harmonious and in good order (bene compositam et bene com-
paginatam esse).[531] St. Irenaeus demonstrates that there are only four
Gospels—no more, no less. His evidence, however, is not historical,
but dogmatic and symbolic. The four corners of the earth, the four
primary winds, the Cherubim have four faces, the four living creatures, the four chief commandments—all this proves that there can
only be four Gospels.[532]

   Tertullian differs in his reasoning. He begins by denying that
the heretics have any right to Scripture at all. Before disputing concerning Scripture one must first examine to whom the Scriptures
belong, so as not to grant men access to whom they by no means belong.[533] The Scriptures are the sole property of the Church, which

---

527 Idem 3.11.9 (ANF 1:429; PG 7:890a).

528 Idem 5.30.1 (ANF 1:559; PG 7:1204b–c).

529 Idem 3.1.1, 3.5.1, 4.34.1, 4.35.2 (PG 7:844, 857b–c, 1083c, 1087c). Cf.
Tertullian, Against Marcion 4.2 (CSEL 47:426.6 sqq).

530 Idem 3.1.1. Irenaeus's testimony is also cited by Eusebius. See Church History 5.8.2–7 (GrchSch. 9.1:442–446).

531 Idem 3.11.9 (PG 7:891–892).

532 Idem 3.11.8 (PG 7:885–899).

533 The Prescription Against Heretics 15 (PL 2:33b–34a). "If in these lie their resources, before they can use them, it ought to be clearly seen to whom belongs the
possession of the Scriptures (cujus sint Scripturae)"—Ibid. 19 (PL 2:36a). It should
be noted that Tertullian ascribes little importance to inquiries into the Scriptures,
as may be seen from his expressions that follow (The Prescription Against Heretics 14):
"Fides, inquit, tua te salvum fecit: non exercitatio Scripturarum. ... Exercitatio
in curiositate consistit, habens gloriam solam de peritiae studio. Cedat curiositas

originated together with them.[534] As for the heretics, they should not be permitted to debate the Scriptures. The heretics are not Christians, and so they have no right to the Christian Scriptures.[535] The Church has every right to inquire: "Who are you? ... As you are none of mine, what have you to do with that which is mine? Indeed, Marcion, by what right do you hew my wood? By whose permission, Valentinus, are you diverting (*transvertis*) the streams of my fountain? By what power, Apelles, are you removing my landmarks? This is my property. Why are you, the rest, sowing and feeding here at your own pleasure? This (I say) is my property. I have long possessed it; I possessed it before you. I hold sure title-deeds from the original owners themselves, to whom the estate[536] belonged (*ab ipsis auctoribus quorum fuit res*). I am the heir of the apostles. ... As for you, they have, it is certain, always held you as disinherited, and rejected you as strangers—as enemies."[537] Such are the arguments that we find in the treatise *The Prescription Against Heretics.* Tertullian provides more detailed proof of the authenticity of the sacred books of the Church in his broadest and most exhaustive polemical work, *Against Marcion.* But here too the fundamental arguments directly dovetail with the ideas already expressed in *The Prescription Against Heretics.* "*Olim possideo* [I have long possessed it]"—in *Against Marcion* Tertullian develops these two words from *The Prescription* into a detailed argument of antiquity. Beginning here with a discussion

---

fidei; cedat gloria saluti ["Your faith," He says, "has saved you," not your skill in the Scriptures... Skill consists in curious art, having for its glory simply the readiness that comes from knack. Let such curious art give place to faith; let such glory yield to salvation]" (PL 2:32a). Cf. 7 (PL 2:24a).

534 Idem (PL 2:62b).

535 Idem 37: "Non esse admittendos haereticos ad ineundam de Scripturis provocationem. ... Ita non Christiani nullum jus capiunt Christianarum litterarum [heretics ought not to be allowed to challenge an appeal to the Scriptures... Thus, not being Christians, they have acquired no right to the Christian Scriptures]" (PL 2:61b). Cf. 45: "Certis, et justis, et necessariis praescriptionibus repellendas a collatione Scripturarum [they must all be refuted on definite, equitable, and necessary rules, without any comparison with the Scriptures]" (PL 2:74a).

536 In the Russian translation, "Scripture." *–Trans.*

537 Tertullian, *The Prescription Against Heretics* 37 (ANF 3:261; PL 2:61b–c).

of the Gospels, Tertullian establishes the following principle: that
which is more ancient is more true; falsehood is the distortion of
truth.[538] In Tertullian's opinion, the argument of ancientness is the
sole means of resolving the question of the authenticity of the Gospels; otherwise opponents will endlessly accuse each other of having
falsified Scriptures. It must be resolved which is more ancient: the
books of the Church or those of Marcion.[539] But the "Gospel" of
Marcion is clearly of a later origin. The Gospels were present in the
Church before Marcion, and Marcion himself when he belonged
to the Church recognized the Gospels of the Church; his own he
composed only after he was cast out of the Church and fell into
heresy.[540] Consequently, Marcion is a distorter of the Gospel that
had been in usage in the Church from the time of Tiberius to the
time of Antonius.[541]

---

538 Tertullian, *Against Marcion* 4.5: "Id verius quod prius [that is truer which
is later]" (CSEL 47:430.11); 4.5: "Veritas falsum praecedat necesse est [it must
needs be that truth therefore precede error]" (432.10–11); 4.4: "In quantum
enim, falsum corruptio est veri, in tantum praecedat necesse est veritas falsum.
Prior erit res passione et materia aemulatione [For, inasmuch as error is falsification of truth, it must needs be that truth therefore precede error. A thing must
exist prior to its suffering any casualty; and an object must precede all rivalry to
itself]" (428.27–429.2). Cf. *The Prescription Against Heretics* 31 (PL 2:51b).

539 Idem 4.4: "Ego meum dico verum. Marcion suum; ego Marcionis adfir-
mo adulteratum, Marcion meum; quis inter nos determinabit, nisi temporis ratio,
ei praescribens auctoritatem, quod antiquius repperietur, et ei praejudicans viti-
ationem, quod posterius revincetur? [I say that my Gospel is the true one; Marcion, that his is. I affirm that Marcion's gospel is adulterated; Marcion, that mine
is. Now what is to settle the point for us, except it be that principle of time, which
rules that the authority lies with that which shall be found to be more ancient;
and assumes as an elemental truth, that corruption belongs to the side which shall
be convicted of comparative lateness in its origin?]" (CSEL 47:428.23–27).

540 Idem 4.4. (CSEL 47:429.10–16).

541 Idem 4.4: "Quod ergo pertinet ad evangelium interim Lucae, quatenus
communio ejus inter nos et Marcionem de veritate disceptat, adeo antiquius
Marcionis est quod est secundum nos, ut et ipse illi Marcion aliquando cred-
iderit, cum et pecuniam in primo calore fidei catholicae ecclesiae contulit, pro-
jectam mox cum ipso, posteaquam in haeresim suam a nostra veritate desciit
[With regard, then, to the pending question, of Luke's Gospel (so far as its being
the common property of ourselves and Marcion enables it to be decisive of the

Thus, in polemics with the Gnostics concerning Holy Scripture, the church theologians of the time established that the books of Holy Scripture belong to the Church. The Church is the custodian of the truth, which is based upon the sacred books that it has included in its canon. Simultaneously, the Church began to more precisely define the canon of New Testament books, although the process of ratifying a Church-wide canon would not be completed for a long time to come. In the history of the dogma concerning the Church it is most important to note that in the period in question the Church expressed its doctrine concerning itself as the custodian of the books of Holy Scripture. "It behoves us ... to flee to the Church, and be brought up in her bosom, and be nourished with the Lord's Scriptures. For the Church has been planted as a garden (*paradisus*) in this world; therefore says the Spirit of God, 'Thou mayest freely eat from every tree of the garden' [see Gen. 2:16], that is, Eat ye from every Scripture of the Lord."[542] In the Church the Scriptures are preserved without falsification, without addition or curtailment; here the Scriptures are read without distortion.[543]

But the polemics could not stop at the question of the authenticity of the books of Holy Scripture. Tertullian and Irenaeus polemicized based on the books of Holy Scripture,[544] but then the Gnostics also continually made use of Scripture, employing the same Scriptures that the Church accepted. Both Gnostics and the Church were shown to draw their doctrine from the same source; hence, how to extract the true doctrine from this source had to be

---

truth,) that portion of it which we alone receive is so much older than Marcion, that Marcion himself once believed it, when in the first warmth of faith he contributed money to the Catholic church, which along with himself was afterwards rejected, when he fell away from our truth into his own heresy]" (CSEL 47:429.26–28, 30–31; 430.1).

542 Irenaeus, *Against Heresies* 5.20.2 (ANF 1:548; PG 7:1178a–b).

543 Idem 4.33.8: "Sine fictione Scripturarum tractatio plenissima, neque additamentum neque ablationem recipiens, et lectio sine falsatione [without any forging of Scriptures, by a very complete system of doctrine, and neither receiving addition nor {suffering} curtailment; and reading without falsification]" (ANF 1:508; PG 7:1077b).

544 Concerning this, see Thomasius, *Dogmengeschichte* 1, 131–135.

determined. Standards for using Holy Scripture had to be established. This gave rise to the question of how to interpret and understand Holy Scripture.

To begin with, the boldest view of the body of books of Holy
Scripture, that maintained by the Valentinians, was rejected. In the
opinion of the Valentinians, various parts of Holy Scripture are of
various merit. The apostles alloyed the words of the Savior with
elements of the law, and not only the apostles but even the Lord
Himself spoke at times as the Demiurge, at times from a middle
place, and at times from the heights (*a medietate, interdum autem a sum-
mitate fecisse sermones*).[545] Nothing is known of the basis on which the
Valentinians separated Scripture by origin.[546] St. Irenaeus decisively
rejects this view of Holy Scripture. He says that perfection and defect, knowledge and ignorance, truth and error, light and darkness
cannot be united into one. The Lord never spoke sometimes under
the influence of the heights, sometimes under that of imperfection
(*nunquam modo quidem de principali, modo vero de subjecta deminoratione*),
and was not at once a Teacher of both knowledge and ignorance.[547]

---

545 Irenaeus, *Against Heresies* 3.2.2 (PG 7:847a). Cf. 1.7.3: "They divide the
prophecies [into different classes], maintaining that one portion was uttered by
the mother (ἀπὸ τῆς μητρός), a second by her seed (ἀπὸ τοῦ σπέρματος), and a
third by the Demiurge. In like manner, they hold that Jesus uttered some things
under the influence of the Saviour, others under that of the mother, and others
still under that of the Demiurge" (ANF 1:326; PG 7:516b–517a). Cf. *The Refutation of all Heresies* 10.9: "Καὶ ὁμοῦ δι' αὐτοῦ λελαληκέναι τὰς τρεῖς οὐσίας τοῖς
τρισὶ γένεσι [and that the three essences had spoken through him to the three
races]" (PG 16:3419b).

546 Liechtenhan conjectures that what Jesus said under the influence of the
Savior was compiled by the Valentinians in the "Εὐαγγέλιον ἀληθείας" [Gos-
pel of truth], so that the division of Jesus' words into the three classes specified
apparently pertained to the canonical Gospels of the Church, and not to the
"Gospel of Truth," which by its very name could not have contained anything
imperfect that originated from the Demiurge. See *Die Offenbarung im Gnosticismus,*
69–70. But Irenaeus calls the "Gospel of Truth" "in nihilo conveniens apostolorum Evangeliis [not at all in harmony with the Gospels of the evangelists]"
(*Against Heresies* 3.11.9, PG 7:891b), and for this reason in all probability we may
join Zahn in deeming this "Gospel" a separate, additional Gospel (*Geschichte des
neutest. Kanons* 1, 750; cf. 748–750).

547 *Against Heresies* 4.35.2 (PG 7:1087–1088).

All of Scripture is from God alone; the prophets said nothing under inspiration from various gods.[548]

But the most widespread Gnostic view of Holy Scriptures was from the standpoint of the so-called theory of accommodation. According to this theory, Jesus Christ and His apostles did not always speak clearly and definitely, but rather adapted to the current state of their hearers.[549]

Christ Himself taught the apostles in images and parables, but sometimes, alone and apart, He clearly and openly taught only those who were able to receive the fullness of the truth in pure form.[550] Christ said, "Seek, and ye shall find" (Mt. 7:7, Lk. 11:9). In these words, the Gnostics saw a commandment: to seek hidden meaning in the allegorical form of the Gospel narrative,[551] and they used these words as grounds for all their allegorical interpretations of Holy Scripture. Not only the parables, but everything in Holy Scripture was subjected to the Gnostics' allegorical interpretations.[552] "To use a common proverb, they strive to weave ropes

---

548 Idem (PG 7:838a).

549 This theory is expounded and analyzed by St. Irenaeus (*Against Heresies* 3.5.1–2, 12.6, 13 [PG 7:858–859, 898c–899b]).

550 Excerpta ex scriptis Theodoti 66. "Ὁ Σωτὴρ τοὺς ἀποστόλους ἐδίδασκεν, τὰ μὲν πρῶτα τυπικῶς καὶ μυστικῶς, τὰ δὲ ὕστερα παραβολικῶς καὶ ἡνιγμένως, τὰ δὲ τρίτα σαφῶς καὶ γυμνῶς κατὰ μόνας [The Saviour taught the disciples, the first things in types and mystically, the second things in parables and riddles, and the third things clearly and nakedly in private]" (GrchSch 17:128.24–26). Cf. Irenaeus, *Against Heresies* 2.27.2: "Et ipsi testantur dicentes in absconso haec eadem Salvatorem docuisse non omnes, sed aliquos discipulorum, qui possunt capere, et per argumenta, et aenigmata, et parabolas ab eo significata intelligentibus [they themselves testify, when they maintain that the Saviour privately taught these same things not to all, but to certain only of His disciples who could comprehend them, and who understood what was intended by Him through means of arguments, enigmas, and parables]" (PG 7:803c). See also 1.3.1 (PG 7:468).

551 Tertullian polemicizes against this application of Christ's words. See *The Prescription Against Heretics* 8–12.

552 Concerning how the Gnostics demonstrated the necessity of allegorically interpreting Holy Scripture, see lic. Carola Barth, *Die Interpretation des Neuen Testaments in der valentinianischen Gnosis. Texte und Untersuchungen zur Geschichte der altchristlichen Literatur.* Herausgegeben von Adolf Harnack und Carl Schmidt. Bd. 37,

of sand, while they endeavour to adapt (προσαρμόζειν) with an air of probability to their own peculiar assertions the parables of the Lord, the sayings of the prophets, and the words of the apostles, in order that their scheme may not seem altogether without support."[553] "Parables and allegories ... can frequently be drawn into various senses (εἰς πολλὰ ἕλκειν), according to the kind of exegesis to which they are subjected. And others of them, with great craftiness, adapted (ἐφαρμόζοντες) such parts of Scripture to their own figments."[554] Indeed, by employing this interpretation the Gnostics found in Holy Scripture whatever they tendentially sought there.[555] Predominantly in the first book of *Against Heresies* Irenaeus cites a whole series of Gnostic interpretations of various passages of Holy Scripture. We will cite a few of these interpretations by way of example. "Wherever the words *Æon* or *Æons* (αἰών, ἢ αἰῶνες)[556] occur, they at once refer them to these beings." The thirty aeons are indicated by the thirty years in which the Savior did nothing openly.[557] "The production, again, of the Duodecad of the Æons, is indicated by the fact that the Lord was twelve years of age when He disputed with the teachers of the law, and by the election of the apostles, for of these there were twelve. The other eighteen Æons are made manifest in this way: that the Lord, according to them, conversed (διατετριφέναι) with His disciples for eighteen months after His resurrection from the dead. They also affirm that these eighteen Æons are strikingly indicated by the first two letters of His name ['Ιησοῦς], namely Iota [ι] and Eta [η]. And, in like manner, they assert that the ten Æons are pointed out by the letter Iota, which begins His name;

Heft. 3 (Leipzig: 1911), 54–59.

553 Irenaeus, *Against Heresies* 1.8.1 (ANF 1:326; PG 7:520b–521a). Cf. Liechtenhan's remark (*Die Offenbarung im Gnosticismus*, 71, Anm. 1).

554 Idem 1.3.6 (ANF 1:320; PG 7:477b).

555 Cf. Liechtenhan, *Die Offenbarung im Gnosticismus*, 78; Th. Zahn, *Geschichte des neutestamentlichen Kanons*, Bd. 1.2, 720.

556 In Gnosticism, a living spirit or sphere of being that emanates from God. Most English translations of the Bible render this word as "age" or "world." – *Trans.*

557 Irenaeus, *Against Heresies* 1.3.1 (ANF 1:319; PG 7:469a, 468a).

while, for the same reason, they tell us the Saviour said, 'One Iota, or one tittle, shall by no means pass away until all be fulfilled.'"[558] The falling away of the twelfth aeon, according to the Gnostics, is indicated by the apostasy of Judas, the twelfth apostle, the Lord's suffering in the twelfth month, and the healing of the woman with an issue of blood after twelve years of affliction.[559]

Such were the interpretive methods of the Gnostics as characterized by St. Irenaeus. Nor was the saint exaggerating: a few surviving fragments of Gnostic exegesis paint for us a picture of absolute, unbridled arbitrary application of allegorical interpretation.[560] Sometimes different interpretations are given for a single passage.[561] In general, the Gnostics' explanation of the Scriptures was no less

---

558 Idem (ANF 1:319; PG 7:469a–b).

559 Idem (ANF 1:319; PG 469–473).

560 See Liechtenhan, *Die Offenbarung im Gnosticismus*, 72–75; C. Barth, *Die Interpretation des Neuen Testaments* TU 37.3, 46–52, 59–111.
Marcion, on the contrary, was a proponent of an exclusively literal understanding of Holy Scripture; consequently, in polemicizing with him Tertullian frequently defended the allegorical interpretation of various passages of Holy Scripture. See *Against Marcion* 2.19, 21–22; 3.5–6, 14–19; 4.15, 20; 5.1, etc. Cf. *Adamantius* 1.7: "Ὅπου παραβολὴ ἐπιγέγραπται, ἐκεῖνά ἐστι νοητά, τὰ δὲ ἄλλα ψιλά [wherever {a passage} is titled a parable, some of the things are noetic, while the rest are mere{ly what they are said to be}]" (GrchSch. 4:14.22–23). Concerning Marcion's method of interpretation, see Harnack, *Dogmengeschichte*[4] 1, 293. Anm. 3; Th. Zahn, *Geschichte des neutestam. Kanons*, Bd. 1, 587. Anm. 2.
At the same time, if necessary other Gnostics also sometimes insisted on a literal interpretation of Holy Scripture—for example, the prologue to the Gospel of John. See Irenaeus, *Against Heresies* 1.8.5 (PG 7:532). "As to their malignantly asserting that if heaven is indeed the throne of God, and earth His footstool, and if it is declared that the heaven and earth shall pass away, then when these pass away the God who sitteth above must also pass away, and therefore He cannot be the God who is over all." Here Irenaeus is admonishing the Gnostics for *putant Deum more hominis sedere*. (*Against Heresies* 4.3.1 [ANF 1:465; PG 7:979–980a]).

561 Thus, Mt. 10:38, Lk. 14:27, and Mk. 10:21, according to the Gnostic elucidation as cited by Irenaeus (*Against Heresies* 1.3.5, PG 7:476a), indicate the Horos (concerning it see 1.2.4)—namely, its supporting faculty (τὴν ἐδραστικήν). But in the *Excerpta ex Theod.* 42 (CrchSch. 17:120.1–7) Mt. 10:38 is given a different and very nebulous explanation, in which the Cross is juxtaposed to the body of Jesus. Vgl.: C. Barth, *Die Interpretation des Neuen Testaments* TU 37.3, 68–69, 86.

damaging to the truth than even [their] distortion of the text.[562]
Quite clearly, the doctrine concerning the Church as the custodian
of the truth, in the sense of the possessor of the authentic and inviolate apostolic Scriptures, was insufficient: certain standards had
to be set for the interpretation of those Scriptures. Occasionally
in the writings of St. Irenaeus we encounter immanent criticism,
so to speak, of the exegetic methods of the Gnostics: he speaks of
their inconsistency, their arbitrariness, the application of exegetical
principles only to certain passages of Holy Scripture and not to all
similar passages, etc.[563]

Simultaneously, Irenaeus and Tertullian attempted to establish
certain principles of ecclesiastical exegesis. First and foremost, the
teachers of the Church insist that not everything in Holy Scripture
is a parable, and not everything should be seen as allegory alone. In
the Scriptures of the prophets all is not figures and parables: they
say many things as clearly as day, with no allegory whatsoever. The
prophets employed allegories only at certain times and in certain
cases.[564] Besides, every allegory should first be understood literally:
it is necessary that a thing exist in and of itself before it is taken to
be a type of something else.[565] If we turn to the Gospel, here too we

---

562 Tertullian, *Prescription Against Heretics* 17: "Tantum veritati obstrepit adul-
ter sensus, quantum et corruptor stylus [Truth is just as much opposed by an
adulteration of its meaning as it is by a corruption of its text]" (PL 2:35a). Cf. *On
the Resurrection of the Flesh* 63: "Ipsum sermonem dei vel stilo vel interpretatione
corrumpens [destroying the very words of God whether by pen or by interpreta-
tion]" (CSEL 47:124.25–26).

563 Irenaeus, *Against Heresies* 2.23.1–2, 24.1–6, etc.

564 Tertullian, *On the Resurrection of the Flesh* 20 (CSEL 47:52.13–17, 53.13–15,
21–22).

565 Tertullian, *On the Resurrection of the Flesh* 30: "Nam etsi figmentum veritatis
in imagine est, imago ipsa in veritate est sui. Necesse est esse prius sibi, quo alii
configuretur. De vacuo similitudo non competit, de nullo parabola non convenit
[Now, although there is a sketch of the true thing in its image, the image itself
still possesses a truth of its own: it must needs be, therefore, that must have a prior
existence for itself, which is used figuratively to express some other thing. Vacuity
is not a consistent basis for a similitude, nor does nonentity form a suitable foundation for a parable]" (CSEL 47:68.11–14; cf. 20:52.11–15).

cannot agree that the Lord supposedly always spoke in parables.[566] Christ did not speak to everyone in parables, and since He did not, it follows that He did not always speak in parables, nor for all men, but only for some.[567] To be sure, the Lord sometimes spoke even to His disciples in parables, but Scripture always adds in these cases: He spoke to them in a parable. From this we may conclude that the Lord spoke more often without parables. Besides this, the Lord explained His parables.[568]

What should govern us in interpreting obscure and unclear passages of Scripture? In Holy Scripture much is expressed clearly and definitively. It is this clearly and definitively expressed material that should govern us in understanding that which is stated unclearly. The brief but expressive statement of Tertullian, "Incerta de certis et obscura de manifestis praejudicari,"[569] may be considered the chief thesis in the ecclesiastical exegesis then being established. Clear and definitively expressed truths must lie at the foundation. "Since parables admit of many interpretations, what lover of truth will not acknowledge, that for them to assert God is to be searched out from these, while they desert what is certain, indubitable, and true, is the part of men who eagerly throw themselves into danger, and act as if destitute of reason? And is not such a course of conduct not to build one's house upon a rock which is firm, strong, and

---

566 The Gnostics cited Mt. 13.34: "Without a parable spake he not unto them."

567 In the English source, "Since it was to the Jews that He spoke in parables, it was not then to all men; and if not to all, it follows that it was not always and in all things parables with Him, but only in certain things, and when addressing a particular class" (ANF 3:568). –*Trans.*

568 Tertullian, *On the Resurrection of the Flesh* 33 (CSEL 47:72). For more detail on the exegetical principles of Tertullian, see the work by Adhémar d'Alès, *La théologie de Tertulllien*, 245 et suiv.

569 Tertullian, *On the Resurrection of the Flesh* 21 (CSEL 47:54.2–3). Cf. *Against Praxeas* 20: "Secundum plura intellegi pauciora [to understand the few statements in the light of the many]" (CSEL 47:263.12–13), and *On Modesty* 17: "Pauca multis, dubia certis, obscura manifestis adumbrantur [The few are shadowed by the many, the doubtful by the certain, the obscure by the plain]" (CSEL 20.1:258.22–23).

placed in an open position, but upon the shifting sand?"⁵⁷⁰ One
must not interpret parables based on what is itself stated unclearly and obscurely. Otherwise there will be as many truths as there
are interpreters of parables (*qui absolvent parabolas*)—truths self-contradictory and affirming opposite teachings (*contraria sibimet dogmata
statuentes*).⁵⁷¹ Conversely, one who explains the obscure by means of
what is understandable safely interprets Holy Scripture: then the
parables are interpreted identically by all, and the truth (*veritatis corpus*) is preserved whole and inviolate.⁵⁷² That there are parables in
Holy Scripture is accepted, but not their blasphemous application
(τὴν βλάσφημον ὑπόθεσιν).⁵⁷³ St. Irenaeus additionally advises that
one not try to learn from Scripture all that one wishes. There is
much that we do not and cannot know, and so we must leave all this
to God.⁵⁷⁴ "If, therefore, according to the rule which I have stated,
we leave some questions (ζητημάτων) in the hands of God, we shall
both preserve our faith uninjured, and shall continue without danger; and all Scripture, which has been given to us by God, shall be
found by us perfectly consistent; and the parables shall harmonize
with those passages which are perfectly plain (διαρρήδην); and those
statements the meaning of which is clear, shall serve to explain the
parables (ἐπιλύσει τὰς παραβολάς); and through the many diversi-

---

570 Irenaeus, *Against Heresies* 2.27.3 (ANF 1:399; PG 7:803c–804a). The heretics, as St. Irenaeus puts it, "insert [in their speculations] a difficulty incapable of
solution (*nodum insolubilem*)—*Against Heresies* 2.10.2 (ANF 1:370; PG 7:735b). Cf.
Tertullian, *On Modesty* 9: "Non ex parabolia materias commentamur, sed ex ma-
teriis parabolas interpretamur [We, however, who do not make the parables the
sources whence we devise our subject-matters, but the subject-matters the sources
whence we interpret the parables]" (CSEL 20.1:235.25–26).

571 Idem 802c–803a. Cf. 2.10.1: "No question can be solved by means of
another which itself awaits solution; nor, in the opinion of those possessed of
sense, can an ambiguity be explained by means of another ambiguity, or enigmas
by means of another greater enigma, but things of such character receive their
solution from those which are manifest, and consistent and clear" (ANF 1:370;
PG 7:735a–b).

572 Idem (PG 7:802c).

573 Idem (PG 7:545b, 548a).

574 Idem (PG 7:804).

fied utterances [of Scripture] there shall be heard one harmonious melody in us, praising in hymns that God who created all things."[575]

Thus, the Church is the custodian of the truth, because it possesses Holy Scripture—not its text only, but also its **correct interpretation.**[576] Thus, establishing principles of interpretation served a practical need: it answered the question of how to derive truth from the books of Holy Scripture that were preserved in the Church. But naturally these principles were woefully insufficient. Scholarly principles of interpretation are all well and good, but they can be badly applied. Principles are always overly general, and it is difficult to live by principles alone. This is on the one hand. On the other hand, principles of interpretation could have particularly little significance at the time when Irenaeus was living and working. This was a time when the allegorical method of Philo reigned supreme—the only scholarly method of interpreting not only Holy Scripture, but also Homer,[577] and we see how St. Irenaeus, having established the aforementioned principles of interpretation, himself pays tribute to the thinking of his time. One need only look at several examples of Irenaeus's own interpretations—for example, his interpretation of Moses' marriage to the Ethiopian woman,[578] the story of Lot,[579] Christ's washing of the disciples' feet,[580] Balaam's ass,[581] and many others—to see that Irenaeus himself was unable

---

575 Idem (ANF 1:400; PG 806b–c).

576 Idem: in the Church there is "a lawful (*legitima*) and diligent exposition in harmony with the Scriptures, both without danger and without blasphemy; and [above all, it consists in] the preeminent gift of love, which is more precious than knowledge, more glorious than prophecy, and which excels all the other gifts [of God]" (ANF 1:508; PG 1077b–1078a).

577 Concerning this method, see the study by Dr. Paul Heinisch: *Der Einfluss Philos auf die äteste christliche Exegese (Barnabas, Iustin und Clemens von Alexandrien)* (W. Münster: 1908), 5–29, 52–125. Cf. remark by C. Barth (*Die Interpretation des Neuen Testaments* TU 37.3, 59).

578 Idem (PG 7:1042b).

579 Idem (PG 1068–1070).

580 Idem (PG 1046–1047).

581 Irenaeus, *Fragments* 23 (PG 7:1241b). See also his interpretations of Judges 16.26 (*Fragments* 27, PG 7:1244b), 2 Kgs. 6:5–7 (*Against Heresies* 5.17.4, *Fragments*

to renounce the allegorical method of interpretation.[582] In practice
St. Irenaeus quite frequently diverged from the exegetical principles
he himself established in polemics with the Gnostics, and in interpreting Holy Scripture he employed the method of his opponents
whom he so sharply censured.[583] It may even be asserted that in the
first centuries the allegorical method of interpreting Holy Scripture was essential for church writers.[584] In employing the allegorical method of interpretation St. Irenaeus even took a significant
step forward compared to the church writers who preceded him:
he extended this method of interpretation to the New Testament,
as well, whereas before him it had been customary to interpret only
the Old Testament allegorically.[585] Consequently, the principle of
interpreting was not consistently employed, and it was not the rules
of hermeneutics that guarded the church writers from error.[586]

From this alone we see that in defining herself as the custodian
of the truth of Christ the Church could not stop at claiming the
Holy Scriptures as her own property: in addition to general scholarly methods, a special ecclesiastical principle was needed to interpret
these Scriptures. This second token of the Church—the custodian
of the truth—was indicated in **Tradition.** But Gnosticism was un-
like certain later heresies, which openly and intentionally break with

---

28 [PG 7:1171a, 1244c]), Lk. 13:19 (*Fragments* 31 [PG 7:1245a]), Judg. 15:11
(*Fragments* 42 [PG 7:1260a]), Jn. 11:43, 44 (*Against Heresies* 4.13.1 [PG 7:1156b–
c]), the story of Jacob (4.21.3 [PG 7:1045–1046]), and the story of Tamar (4.25.2
[PG 7:1051a–b]).

582 We cannot agree with those who write that allegedly "in interpreting various passages of Scripture St. Irenaeus primarily adheres to the literal meaning
and in general tries to avoid the so-called figurative and allegorical method of
interpretation" (*Pravoslavny sobesednik* [1874], vol. 2, 226).

583 Böhringer, *Die alte Kirche*, 2-ter Teil., 411; Beuzart, *Essai sur la théologie
d'Irénée* (Paris: 1908), 25–26.

584 Concerning this see Heinisch, *Der Einfluss Philos Auf Die Älteste Christliche
Exe*, 30–36.

585 P. Heinisch, *Der Einfluss Philos Auf Die Älteste Christliche Exe*, 40. Concerning Tertullian see the observation of Adhémar d'Alès, *La théologie de Tertulllien*,
250–252, 254.

586 Vgl. Thomasisus, *Dogmengeschichte* 1, 135.

Tradition.[587] The Gnostics likewise constantly cite Tradition. But the Gnostics would cite a "secret tradition." This secret tradition was in the spirit of the time. The Judean scribe said that the people who knew not the law were ignorant (see Jn. 7:49). The Greek philosopher recognized only the sage as a complete person. In all mysteries there was a special secret tradition for each class of initiates. The Gnostic doctrine of a secret tradition was a phenomenon of the same order. The doctrine of a secret tradition was so widespread among the Gnostics that certain researchers of Gnosticism consider this teaching to be the core of Gnosticism (Lipsius). Indeed, nearly all the individual Gnostic sects are known to have cited a secret tradition. The Carpocratians asserted that Christ spoke in secret (ἐν μυστηρίῳ) with His disciples, separately from the others (κατ' ἰδίαν), and required of them that they too communicate this to those who were worthy and firmly established (τοῖς ἀξίοις καὶ τοῖς πειθομένοις ταῦτα παραδιδόναι).[588] The Valentinians and the Ophites said that after His resurrection Christ abode (*remoratum*) with the disciples for 18 months, and since knowledge had descended upon Him (*sensibilitate in eum descendente*) He taught that which was clear, and instructed a few of His disciples in the mysteries (*mysteriorum*) whom He knew to be capable of receiving them.[589] In the Gnostic work *Pistis Sophia*, the time Christ abode with the apostles was extended to fully 11 years.[590] The Gnostics traced their tradition either to certain individuals from the apostles' company or to the apostles' companions. The Naassenes said that the chief tenets of their teaching (κεφάλαια) were relayed by James, the brother of the Lord, to Mary the Mother of God.[591] They pointed to the apostle

---

587 "Der Gnosticismus verhält sich in dieser Hinsidit ganz anders, als die modernen Formen der Heterodoxie, welche mit der Ueberlieferung absichtlich brechen."—Ritschl, *Die Entstehung der altkath. Kirche*, 338–339.

588 Irenaeus, *Against Heresies* 1.25.5 (PG 7:685a). Cf. *Excerp. ex Theod.* 66, GrchSch 17, 128.24–26.

589 Idem (PG 7:703a). Cf. 1.3.2, 2.27.2 (PG 7:469a, 803c).

590 Liechtenhan, *Die Offenbarung im Gnosticismus*, 46.

591 Hippolytus, *The Refutation of all Heresies* 5.7 (PG 16:3126c).

Phillip[592] and to Judas' replacement Matthias, whom Christ allegedly instructed separately.[593] The apostle Paul (2 Cor. 12:2–4) says that
he was "caught up to the third heaven … and heard … words,
which it is not lawful for a man to utter," and the Gnostics claimed
that these words were relayed to them.[594] The Cainites even knew
of a composition entitled "Ἀναβατικὸν Παύλου [The Assumption
of Paul]"[595] Finally, Basilides considered his mentor to be Glaucius,
interpreter to the apostle Peter, and Valentinus, they said, listened
to Theudas, who was an intimate (γνώριμος) of the apostle Paul.[596]

Consequently, in the works of the church writers first and foremost we encounter a denial of any secret tradition. The apostles
all received a single, all-perfect knowledge from the Lord. "It is unlawful to assert that they preached before they possessed 'perfect
knowledge,' as some do even venture to say, boasting themselves as
improvers of the apostles." The apostles were invested with power

---

592 Epiphanius, Haer. 26.13 (PG 41:352d).

593 "Βασιλείδης τοίνυν καὶ Ἰσίδωρος… φασὶν εἰρηκέναι Ματθίαν αὐτοῖς
λόγους ἀποκρύφους, οὓς ἤκουσε παρὰ τοῦ Σωτῆρος κατ᾽ ἰδίαν διδαχθείς [Basi-
lides, therefore, and Isidorus… say that Matthias communicated to them secret
discourses, which, being privately instructed, he heard from the Saviour.]" (Hippolytus, *The Refutation of all Heresies* 7.20 [PG 16:3302b]). Cf. Clement of Alexandria, *Stromata* 2.9.45.4 (GrchSch. 15:137.2–3. 7.13.82.1; 7.17.108.1; GrchSch
17:58.20–21, 76.22 [PG 8:981a; 9:513b, 552b]).

594 Hippolytus, *Refutation of all Heresies* 5.8: "Ταῦτα, φησίν, ἐστὶ τὰ τοῦ
πνεύματος ἄρρητα μυστήρια, ἃ ἡμεῖς ἴσμεν μόνοι [these, the say, are the ineffable
mysteries of the Spirit, which only we know]" (PG 16:3146c–3147a). Cf. Tertullian, *Prescription Against Heretics* 24: "Hos se aliqua haeresis sequi affirmat [if any
heresy affirms that it does itself follow them" (PL 2:43a). Irenaeus, *Against Heresies*
2.30.7 (PG 7:819–820). The fifth-century Armenian writer Eznik attests to the
same with regard to the Marcionites (*Wardapet Eznik von Kolb*). See his composition
Against Sects 4.3. This composition has been translated by Ioh. Michael Schmid
(Bibliothek der alten armenichen Literatur in deutschen Üebersetzung, herausgegeben von der Wiener Mechitharisten-Congregation, Bd. 1 [Wien: 1900],
180–181).

595 Epiphanius, Haer. 38.2 (PG 41:656d).

596 Clement of Alexandria, *Stromata* 7.17.10.4. CrchSch. 17:75.15–18 (PG
9:549a). For more detail on the secret tradition of the Gnostics, see Liechtenhan,
Die Offenbarung im Gnosticismus, 45–50; A. Ritschl, *Die Entstehung der altkath. Kirche,*
339–340; Thomasius, *Dogmengeschichte* 1, 124–125.

from on high, received all the gifts of the Holy Spirit, received perfect knowledge, and then went forth to all the ends of the earth to preach.[597] And in preaching the apostles taught not something different, but only what they had received from the Lord.[598] Therefore through the apostles we have come to know the truth, that is, the teaching of the Son of God. To them also the Lord said: "He that heareth you heareth me; and he that despiseth you despiseth me and him that sent me" (cf. Lk. 10:16).[599]

In *The Prescription Against Heretics* Tertullian conducts a detailed analysis of the Gnostics' entire theory of a secret tradition. Tertullian demonstrates in detail that Christ hid nothing from any of the apostles: the Holy Spirit instructed them in every truth.[600] Knowing all, they imparted all things to all men. The words of the apostle Paul to Timothy, "Keep that which is committed to thy trust" (1 Tim. 6:20), pertain to the entire teaching of the apostle, and not to some secret Gospel (*occulti alicujus Evangelii*).[601] As Christ Himself concealed nothing, so also did the apostles: after all, in their epistles they themselves entreated that all speak the same things.[602]

These arguments must result in a disavowal of the Gnostic teaching of a secret tradition. Christ cannot be separated from the

---

597 Irenaeus, *Against Heresies* 3.1.1 (ANF 1:414; PG 7:844b).

598 Tertullian, *Prescription Against Heretics* 6: "Acceptam a Christo disciplinam fideliter nationibus assignaverunt [they faithfully delivered to the nations the doctrine which they had received from Christ]" (PL 2:21a). Cf. Irenaeus, *Against Heresies* 3.5.1: "The apostles ... are above all falsehood; for a lie has no fellowship with the truth, just as darkness has none with light, but the presence of the one shuts out that of the other" (ANF 1:417; PG 7:858a).

599 Irenaeus, cit. op. 3, preface (PG 7:834b–844a).

600 *Prescription Against Heretics* 22, 23, 24 (PL 2:39–43).

601 Ibid. 25 (PL 2:43–44). Cf. *Scorpiace* 12 (CSEL 20.1:172.5–12).

602 Ibid. 26: "Quanquam, etsi quaedam inter domesticos, ut ita dixerim, disserebant, non tamen ea fuisse credendum est, quae aliam regulam fidei superducerent, diversam et contrariam illi, quam catholice in medium proferebant [Although, even supposing that among intimate friends [domesticos], so to speak, they did hold certain discussions, yet it is incredible that these could have been such as to bring in some other rule of faith, differing from and contrary to that which they were proclaiming catholically]" (PL 2:45b). Cf. PL 2:44–46.

apostles; the apostles openly preached to the world all that Christ
had taught them.[603] "There is some one, and therefore definite,
thing taught by Christ, which the Gentiles are by all means bound
to believe, and for that purpose to 'seek,' in order that they may be
able, when they have 'found' it, to believe. However, there can be no
indefinite seeking for that which has been taught as one only definite
thing. You must 'seek' until you 'find,' and believe when you have
found. ... We have in our possession that which was taught (*quod
institutum est*) by Christ. ... Believe this besides, that nothing else is
to be believed, and therefore nothing else is to be sought, after you
have found and believed what has been taught by Him who charges
you to seek no other thing than that which He has taught."[604] In
repudiation of the doctrine of a secret tradition, Tertullian points
out the practical detriment, so to speak, of this doctrine. If one
occupies himself with seeking out a secret tradition, he may never come to believe, for the searching will never cease. "For where
shall be the end of seeking? ... (Shall it be) with Marcion? But even
Valentinus proposes (to us the) maxim, 'Seek, and ye shall find.'
(Then shall it be) with Valentinus? Well, but Apelles, too, will assail
me (*pulsavit*) with the same quotation (*pronuntiatione*); Hebion also,
and Simon, and all in turn, have no other argument wherewithal to
entice me, and draw me over to their side. Thus I shall be nowhere
... precisely as if I had no resting-place; as if (indeed) I had never
found that which Christ has taught—that which ought to be sought,
that which must needs be believed." Believing must put an end to
seeking (*omnem prolationem quaerendi et inveniendi credendo fixisti*).[605] "It is
not necessary to seek the truth among others which it is easy to obtain from the Church; since the apostles, like a rich man [depositing
his money] in a bank, lodged in her hands most copiously all things
pertaining to the truth: so that every man, whosoever will, can draw

---

603 Of great importance is the expression of Serapion of Antioch, recorded
by Eusebius. He writes, "We, brethren, receive both Peter and the other apostles
as Christ" (*Church History* 6.12.3 [NPNF² 1:258; GrchSch 9.2:544.15–16]).

604 Tertullian, *Prescription Against Heretics* 9 (ANF 3:248; PL 2:26–27).

605 Tertullian, *Prescription Against Heretics* 10 (ANF 3:248; PL 2:28–29).

from her the water of life. For she is the entrance to life; all others are thieves and robbers."[606]

Thus, the apostles left no special, secret tradition: they openly preached the whole truth and entrusted it to the Church. Consequently, only the Church can determine the truth. In establishing this thesis, the church writers thereby banish all arbitrariness and individualism in general from the sphere of faith. This individualism cannot as yet be banished either by precisely defining the canon of New Testament books, nor by establishing certain principles of interpretation, since any principle is always applied more or less individualistically.[607] Tertullian, with his customary bluntness, even puts forward the idea that debates based on Scripture alone can be of no benefit.[608] One should not appeal to Scripture or enter into debate only where there is no victory whatsoever, or where victory is uncertain or unlikely.[609] "We must discuss: ... 'From what and through whom, and when, and to whom, has been handed down that rule, by which men become Christians?' For wherever it shall be manifest that the true Christian rule and faith (veritas et disciplinae et fidei) shall be, there will likewise be the true Scriptures and expositions thereof, and all the Christian traditions."[610] Clearly, in the opinion of Tertullian, without church standards the Scriptures themselves may be reinterpreted however one pleases, and they cannot supply the truth.

---

606 Irenaeus, *Against Heresies* 3.4.1 (ANF 1:416–417; PG 7:855a–b).

607 Karl Adam says, "Tertullian's classic work *The Prescription Against Heretics* comes down directly to this thesis: in matters of faith, it is not subjective research that matters, but only the decision of the Church, because it infallibly preserves the apostolic and in general the ancient teaching." (*Der Kirchenbegriff Tertullians*, 26–27.)

608 Tertullian, *Prescription Against Heretics* 17: "Nihil proficiat congressio Scriupturarum, nisi plane ut stomachi quis ineat eversionem, aut cerebri [a controversy over the Scriptures can, clearly, produce no other effect than help to upset either the stomach or the brain]" (PL 2:35a).

609 In another place Tertullian says that if one disputes on the basis of Scripture alone, he will only be wasting his breath and gain nothing but vexation from the blasphemy of the heretics (*Prescription Against Heretics* 17 [PL 2:35b]).

610 Ibid. 19 (PL 2:36a–b).

Only the Church can unerringly understand Holy Scripture, for only the Church, and not the individual, is the custodian of the truth. The most general expression of the self-identification of the Church, and consequently the most general principle for interpreting Holy Scripture, is the **"Rule of Faith"** of the Church—the *regula fidei*, as Tertullian calls it,[611] or the "Rule of Truth"—Κανὼν τῆς ἀληθείας, as St. Irenaeus usually expresses it.[612] This "Rule" is none other than the Symbol of Faith that is read at baptism,[613] which developed from the baptismal formula bequeathed by the Lord Himself.[614] Tertullian also frequently compares this rule with the vow or oath that soldiers take upon entering the army, and calls it by the special term *sacramentum*. The Christian enters into the army of Christ when he reads the "Rule of Faith" at baptism[615] The content of this confession of the early

611 Ibid. 3, 13 (PL 2:17a, 30b). *Against Praxeas* 2 (CSEL 47:229.14), *On the Veiling of Virgins* 1 (PL 2:937b).

612 Irenaeus, *Against Heresies* 1.9.4, 22.1; 3.2.1, 15.1 (PG 7:545b, 669a, 847a, 918a). Cf. *veritatis regula* in Tertullian's *Against Hermogenes* 1 (CSEL 47:126.4). Cf. Irenaeus, *Demonstration of the Apostolic Preaching* 6.

613 Ibid. 1.9.4: "Ὃν (κανόνα) διὰ τοῦ βαπτίσματος εἴληφε [which {rule} he received through baptism]" (PG 7:545b). Tertullian, *To the Martyrs* 3 (PL 1:624a), *The Shows* 4, *On Idolatry* 6 (CSEL 20.1:6, 14, 35, 24–25).

614 Concerning this see Th. Zahn, *Glabensregel und Taufbekenntnis in der alten Kirche. Skizzen aus dem Leben der alten Kirche*, 2-te Aufl. (Erlangen und Leipzig: 1898), 248 ff.; Harnack, *Dogmengeschichte*[4] 1, 354 ff.; F. Loofs, *Leitfaden der Dogmengeschichte*[4] §11.6, 79.

615 *Prescription Against Heretics* 20: "Ejusden sacramenti una traditio [the one tradition of the selfsame mystery]" 32, *Chaplet.* 11, bis. 13 (PL 2:37b, 54a. Not. 48, 111c, 113b, 117a). *To the Martyrs* 3: "Cum in sacramenti verba respondimus [in our very response to the sacramental words]" (PL 1:624a). *On Idolatry* 6. *Scorpiace* 4. *Treatise on the Soul* 1 (CSEL 20.1:35.24, 153.14, 299.22). *Against Marcion* 1.28, 4.5: "De societate sacramenti confoederantur [they are united with them in the fellowship of the mystery]" (CSEL 47:329.28, 430.23–24). In general, the comparison of the baptismal Symbol with the military oath is frequently encountered among the writers of Africa. See Th. Zahn, *Skizzen...*, 250, 380). See also the work by S.P. Znamensky, "From the Life of Words (The Semasiological Fates of the Term *Sacramentum*)" ["Из жизни слов (Семасиологические судьбы термина *sacramentum*")], *Bogoslovsky vestnik* 1909, vol. 1, 565–570.

Church is related several times by St. Irenaeus[616] and three times by Tertullian,[617] both of whom present this "Rule" with anti-Gnostic overtones.[618]

This "Rule of Faith," then, is only one, and it is unchanging;[619] consequently, it is this "Rule" that we must follow in seeking the truth. Only by having an unadulterated (*inulteratam*) rule of truth can one be saved.[620] The greater or lesser knowledge of some to the measure of their understanding lies not in changing the actual content of the "Rule of Faith," but in carefully studying what is said in parables and reconciling it to the content of the faith (οἰκειοῦν τῇ τῆς πίστεως ὑποθέσει).[621] One who unswervingly maintains within him the rule of truth (ὁ τὸν κανόνα τῆς ἀληθείας ἀκλινῆ ἐν ἑαυτῷ κατέχων) that he received through baptism will reject the Gnostic fallacies.[622] "You may seek and discuss as much as you please, and give full rein to your curiosity," as long as you in no way contradict the "Rule of Faith." "Faith has been deposited in the rule. ... To know nothing in opposition to the rule (of faith), is to know all things."[623] The "Rule of Faith" unites all members of the Church.

---

616 Irenaeus, op. cit. 1.10.1, 3.4.2.

617 *Prescription Against Heretics* 13, *On the Veiling of Virgins* 1 (PL 2:31, 937), *Against Praxeas* 2 (CSEL 47:228–229).

618 Harnack, *Dogmengeschichte* 1, 362–365; Böhringer, *Die alt Kirche*, 2-tes Th., 417–418; Adhémar d'Alès, *La théologie de Tertullien*, 256–258; P. Batiffol, *L'église naissante et le catholicisme*, 320. K. Adam is inclined to see in Tertullian's *On the Veiling of Virgins* the official symbol of the Church of Carthage. In the *Regula fidei* in *The Prescription Against Heretics*, anti-Judean and anti-Gnostic elements abound, while Montanist and anti-Monarchianist ideas found their way into *Against Praxeas*. See *Der Kirchen Begriff Tertullians*, 28, 37–40.

619 Tertullian, *On the Veiling of Virgins* 1: "Una omnino est, sola immobilis et irreformabilis" (PL 2:937b). Cf. *The Prescription Against Heretics* 14 (PL 2:31b).

620 Irenaeus, *Against Heresies* 3.15.1 (PG 7:918a).

621 Idem 553b, 556a.

622 Idem 545b, 348a.

623 Tertullian, *Prescription Against Heretics* 14: "Manente forma eius in suo ordine quantumlibet quaeras et tractes et omnem libidinem curiositatis effundas. ... Fides in regula posita est. ... Aduersus regulam nihil scire omnia scire est" (PL 2:31b, 32a).

Being governed by a common rule, they can differ only in the depth and groundedness of their faith, but not in its content. "Nor will any one of the rulers in the Churches (ἐν ταῖς ἐκκλησίας προεστώτων), however highly gifted he may be in point of eloquence, teach doctrines different from these[624] (for no one is greater than the Master); nor, on the other hand, will he who is deficient in power of expression inflict injury on the tradition. For the faith being ever one and the same, neither does one who is able at great length to discourse regarding it, make any addition to it, nor does one, who can say but little diminish it."[625] The "Rule of Faith," as it were, connects the whole Church and is one of the primary manifestations of its oneness.[626] The oneness of the individual Churches is also expressed in "their peaceful communion, and title of brotherhood, and bond of hospitality," but all this is grounded specifically in having a single "Rule of Faith."[627] Consequently, the church writers are now able to speak of oneness of faith in the various Churches. The concept of the "Rule of Faith" extends to the concept of faith in general,[628] though this does not imply a verbatim equivalence of the theological views of church writers in various Churches. There was no verbatim equivalence even in the "Rule of Faith," yet this was no hindrance to the statement: "Regula fidei una omnino est [The Rule of Faith is altogether one]." This referred to oneness of Christian faith in its chief tenets.[629]

---

624 That is, those expressed in the "Rule of Faith." –*Trans.*

625 Irenaeus, *Against Heresies* 1.10.2 (ANF 1:330; PG 7:553a). Cf. 5.20.2: "Quanto pluris sit idiota religiosus a blasphemo et impudente sophista [of how much greater consequence is a religious man, even in a private station, than a blasphemous and impudent sophist]" (PG 7:1177c–1178a).

626 Concerning this, see Th. Zahn, *Skizzen...*, 243–245. Cf. R. Seeberg, *Studien zur Geschichte de Begriffes der Kirche*, 20–21, Anm.

627 Tertullian, *Prescription Against Heretics* 20: "Quae jura non alia ratio regit, quam ejusdem sacramenti una traditio [privileges which no other rule directs than the one tradition of the selfsame mystery]" (ANF 3:252; PL 2:37b). Cf. n82; Rigaltii. Et Albaspin, 38d.

628 See P. Batiffol, *L'église naissante et le catholicisme*[3] 239n2. Cf. Th. Zahn, *Skizzen...*, 380–381.

629 Cf. Th. Zahn, *Skizzen...*, 250–253.

But it was not enough to point to the doctrine of the Church as the κανὼν τῆς ἀληθείας [Rule of Truth]. It also had to be proven that the Church did indeed preserve the truth imparted to her by the apostles. And we see that the anti-Gnostic writers of the Church thoroughly demonstrate the thesis that **the Church is indeed the custodian of the truth: it not only received the truth from the apostles, but also preserves it pure and inviolate.**

The writers of the Church point to oneness of faith throughout the world. Having received the faith from the apostles, "the Church ... although scattered throughout the whole world (ἐν ὅλῳ τῷ κόσμῳ), yet, as if occupying but one house, carefully (ἐπιμελῶς) preserves it. She also believes[630] these points [of doctrine] just as if she had but one soul, and one and the same heart, and she proclaims them, and teaches them, and hands them down (παραδίδωσιν), with perfect harmony, as if she possessed only one mouth. For, although the languages (διάλεκτοι) of the world are dissimilar, yet the import of the tradition is one and the same. For the Churches which have been planted in Germany do not believe or hand down anything different, nor do those in Spain, nor those in Gaul, nor those in the East, nor those in Egypt, nor those in Libya, nor those which have been established in the central regions of the world.[631] But as the sun, that creature of God, is one and the same throughout the whole world, so also the preaching of the truth (κήρυγμα τῆς ἀληθείας) shineth everywhere, and enlightens all men that are willing to come to a knowledge of the truth."[632] In every Church one may see the Tradition of the apostles (*in omni Ecclesia adest respicere*).[633] "Many nations of those barbarians who believe in Christ [have] salvation written in their hearts by the Spirit, without paper or ink, and, carefully [preserve] the ancient tradition (*veteram traditionem*). ... Those who, in the absence of written documents, have believed this

---

630 In the Russian original, literally "She believes identically (ὁμοίως)." –*Trans.*

631 "Αἱ κατὰ μέσα τοῦ κόσμου." Some hold these to be the Churches in Palestine, others—the Churches in Italy. See PG 7:553d, note 1. P. Batiffol, *L'église naissante et le catholicisme*, 240n1.

632 Irenaeus, *Against Heresies* 1.10.2 (ANF 1:331; PG 7:552a–553).

633 Idem 3.3.1 (ANF 1:415; PG 7:848a). Cf. nn50–51, 847d.

faith, are barbarians, so far as regards our language; but as regards
doctrine, manner, and tenor of life, they are, because of faith, very
wise indeed; and they do please God, ordering their conversation in
all righteousness, chastity, and wisdom. If any one were to preach
to these men the inventions of the heretics (*adinventa*), speaking to
them in their own language, they would at once stop their ears,
and flee as far off as possible, not enduring even to listen to the
blasphemous address. Thus, by means of that ancient tradition of
the apostles (*per illam veterem apostolorum traditionem*), they do not suffer
their mind to conceive anything of the [doctrines suggested by the]
portentous language of these teachers."[634] "The preaching of the
Church is everywhere consistent, and continues in an even course
(*constantem et aequaliter perseverantem*)."[635] Throughout the whole world
the Church has one and the same faith, and throughout the whole
world it points to a single path of salvation.[636]

Thus, the doctrine of the Church is united throughout the universe, and **it is this universal nature of church doctrine
that proves its truth.** Error could not have occurred in the same
form and at the same time in various parts of the world. "Is it likely
that so many churches, and they so great, should have gone astray
into one and the same faith?"[637] "When ... that which is deposited
among many is found to be one and the same, it is not the result
of error, but of tradition."[638] St. Irenaeus constantly juxtaposes the
universal unity of church truth to the variety and inconstancy of
heretical teachings. Any two or three given heretics do not treat
the same subjects the same way, but rather contradict each other
both as to pragmatic elements (τοῖς πράγμασι) and as to names.[639]

---

634 Idem 3.4.2 (ANF 1:417; PG 7:855c, 856a–b).

635 Idem 1.24.1 (ANF 1:458; PG 7:966a).

636 Idem 1.10.3, 5.20.1 (PG 560a, 1177b).

637 Tertullian, *Prescription Against Heretics* 28: "Ecquid verisimile est, ut tot ac
tantae in unam fidem erraverint?" (ANF 3:256; PL 2:47a).

638 Ibid.: "Quod apud multos unum, non est erratum, sed traditum" (PL
2:47b).

639 Irenaeus, *Against Heresies* 1.11.1; 2, Preface (PG 7:560a, 707a–708a). Cf.
5.20.2: "Proceeding on their way variously, (*varie et multiformiter et imbecille*) inhar-

Concerning their depth they also have many differing opinions.[640] They also have many disagreements (πολλὴ μάχη) concerning the Savior.[641] There are as many redemptions as there are mystagogues (μυσταγωγοί) of their way of thinking.[642] St. Irenaeus characterizes the heretics as follows: "They differ ... widely among themselves both as respects doctrine and tradition, and ... those of them who are recognised as being most modern make it their effort daily to invent some new opinion, and to bring out what no one ever before thought of."[643] Tertullian characterizes heresies in similar fashion. The heretics differ in their reasoning; they are united only by a shared enmity toward the one truth.[644] They all begin by distorting the "Rule of Faith."[645] "Their very unity ... is schism. ... They ... swerve even from their own regulations[646] (*regulis suis*), forasmuch as every man, just as it suits his own temper, modifies the traditions he has received after the same fashion as the man who handed them down did, when he moulded them according to his own will. ... That was allowable to the Valentinians which had been allowed to

---

moniously, and foolishly, not keeping always to the same opinions with regard to the same things, as blind men are led by the blind, they shall deservedly fall into the ditch of ignorance lying in their path, ever seeking and never finding out the truth" (ANF 1:548; PG 7:1178a).

640 Idem (PG 7:569a).

641 Idem (PG 7:576a).

642 Idem (PG 7:657b).

643 Idem 1.21.5 (ANF 1:347; PG 7:667b, 670a). Cf. 3.24.2: "They ... [think] differently in regard to the same things at different times, and never [attain] to a well-grounded knowledge, being more anxious to be sophists of words than disciples of the truth. For they have not been founded upon the one rock, but upon the sand" (ANF 1:458; PG 7:967a). Cf. 5.20.1 (ANF 1:547–548; PG 7:1177a).

644 Tertullian, *Prescription Against Heretics* 41 (ANF 3:263; PL 2:68b).

645 Tertullian, *On Monogamy* 2: "Adversarius spiritus ex diversitate praedicationis appareret, primo regulam adulterans fidei [the adversary spirit would be apparent from the diversity of his preaching, beginning by adulterating the rule of faith]" (PL 2:981a). Cf. Irenaeus, *Against Heresies* 3.2.1; "Unus quisque ipsorum ... regulam veritatis depravans [every one of these men... depraving the system of truth]" (PG 7:847).

646 In the Russian source, "Rule of Faith." –*Trans.*

Valentinus; that was also fair for the Marcionites which had been done by Marcion—even to innovate on the faith (*fidem innovare*), as was agreeable to their own pleasure. In short, all heresies, when thoroughly looked into, are detected harbouring dissent in many particulars even from their own founders. The majority of them have not even churches. Motherless, houseless, creedless, outcasts, they wander about."[647] This variety and mutual contradiction of heretical teachings clearly attests that they are false and not in keeping with the teaching of the apostles.[648] Error produces variety.[649] Hence, the Church does not accept heretics due to their differences in creed (*ob diversitatem sacramenti*), which cannot be of the apostles.[650]

This, then, is the token of the apostolic dignity of church doctrine: this doctrine is of a universal nature; it is one throughout the world. The unity of the Church, as St. Irenaeus and Tertullian teach, is expressed in unity of the faith received from the apostles. The pledge of the truth of this faith is its universal nature. What is maintained identically everywhere is in fact the truth delivered to the Church by the apostles. Thus, in the doctrine concerning the Church as the custodian of the truth, catholicity presupposes apostolicity.[651]

---

647 Tertullian, *Prescription Against Heretics* 42 (ANF 3:264; PL 2:70a–b). Cf. *Against Hermogenes* 45 (CSEL 47:176.7–10).

648 Irenaeus, *Against Heresies* 1.9.5: "[They] differ among themselves, as if they were inspired by different spirits of error. For this very fact forms an *a priori* proof that the truth proclaimed by the Church is immoveable, and that the theories of these men are but a tissue of falsehoods (φευδηγορίαν)" (ANF 1:330; PG 7:548–549).

649 Tertullian, *Prescription Against Heretics* 28: "Variasse debuerat error doctrinae Ecclesiarum [Error of doctrine in the churches must necessarily have produced variety]" (PL 2:47a).

650 Tertullian, *Prescription Against Heretics* 32 (PL 2:54a).

651 "Tertullien ne sépare pas la catholicité de l'apostolicité" (E. Michaud, "L'ecclésiologie de Tertullien." See the *Revue internationale de théologie* (1905): 270. In establishing the principle that catholic (*quod apud multos unum invenitur*) = apostolic (*non est erratum, sed traditum*), Adhémar d'Alès holds that Tertullian made an important contribution to the historical development of Christian dogma. See *La théologie de Tertullien*, 261. Cf. P. Batiffol, *L'église naissante et le catholicisme*, 328–329.

It should also be noted that for the Church to be one, St. Irenaeus teaches, **oneness of faith is sufficent.** Disagreements in questions of faith destroy the unity of the Church, while disagreements in church practices and various local customs in no way hinder the unity of the Church. St. Irenaeus laid out these views in a letter to the Roman bishop Victor, who wanted to break ties with the Churches of Asia Minor, where the time of the celebration of Pascha differed from the practice of Rome.[652] Irenaeus wrote: "The controversy is not merely as regards the day, but also as regards the form itself of the fast. For some consider themselves bound to fast one day, others two days, others still more, while others [do so during] forty: the diurnal and the nocturnal hours they measure out together as their [fasting] day. And this variety (ποικιλία) among the observers [of the fasts] had not its origin in our time, but long before in that of our predecessors, some of whom probably, being not very accurate in their observance of it (παρὰ τὸ ἀκριβές), handed down to posterity the custom (καθ' ἁπλότητα καὶ ἰδιοτισμὸν συνήθειαν) as it had, through simplicity or private fancy, been [introduced among them]. And yet nevertheless all these lived in peace one with another, and we also keep peace together. Thus, in fact, the difference [in observing] the fast establishes the harmony of [our common] faith (ἡ διαφωνία τὴν ὁμόνοιαν τῆς πίστεως συνίστησιν).[653] In support of his opinions Irenaeus cites the fact that Polycarp likewise preserved peace with the Roman bishop Anicetus, though neither could convince the other of the necessity of either practice: "Neither could Anicetus persuade Polycarp not to observe what he had always observed with John the disciple of our Lord, and the other apostles

---

652 Concerning this see Professor V.V. Bolotov, *Lectures on the History of the Early Church* ["Лекции по истории древней Церкви"] 2, 428.

653 Irenaeus, *Fragments* 3 (ANF 1:568–569; PG 7:1228c–1229a); Eusebius, *Church History* 5.24.12–13 (GrchSch. 9.1:494.15–25). The same idea was also expressed by Polycrates of Ephesus on behalf of "a great multitude" of "bishops who were present." While defending his practice, at the same time Polycrates says that all those who had previously adhered to this practice did not fall away from the Rule of Faith, but adhered to it in all things, as he himself, Polycrates, does likewise (Eusebius, *Church History* 5.24.2–7 [NPNF² 1:242; GrchSch. 9.1:490, 492]).

with whom he had associated; neither could Polycarp persuade Anicetus to observe it as he said that he ought to follow the customs
of the presbyters that had preceded (πρὸ αὐτοῦ) him."[654] From this
we may see that the idea that oneness of faith alone was needed for
church unity was not the personal opinion of Irenaeus, but was in
fact part of the church consciousness of that time. The dispute over
the time of the celebration of Pascha put church unity to the test,
but apparently the idea that different practices and customs were
permissible in the Church was so firmly grounded in church consciousness that the proud Roman bishop refrained from insisting
on excommunicating the Churches of Asia Minor. Tertullian also,
as we have seen, particularly insists on unity of the "Rule of Faith"
alone. Only the heretics argue against the "Rule of Faith," which
is why they are heretics;[655] for apostasy from the "Rule of Faith" is
apostasy from the truth.[656]

The proof we have presented for the thesis that the Church
is the custodian of the truth may be called abstract, logical proof:
from oneness of faith one infers the inviolability of that faith and
its apostolic dignity. But the anti-Gnostic writers of the Church
also have other proof of this same truth—proof of a more pos-

---

654 Eusebius, *Church History* 5.24.14–17 (GrchSch. 9.1:494, 496). Cf. Irenaeus,
Fragments 3 (ANF 1:569; PG 7:1229b, 1232a)

655 Tertullian, *Prescription Against Heretics* 13: "Haec regula … nullas habet
apud nos quaestiones, nisi quas haereses inferunt et quae haereticos faciunt [This
rule… raises among ourselves no other questions than those which heresies introduce, and which make men heretics]" (PL 2:31b).

656 Idem (PL 2:17a). Michaud sees in Tertullian's writings the germ of the later well-known formula: "In necessariis unitas, in dubiis libertas, in omnibus car-
itas [in necessary things unity; in uncertain things liberty; in all things charity]"
("L'ecclésiologie de Tertullien," *Revue internationale de théologie* [1905]: 265). In the
Montanist period, as is seen from the reasoning in *Chaplet* (cfp. 3 [PL 2:98b–c]),
Tertullian thought somewhat differently (cf. Adhémar d'Alès, *La théologie de Tertul-
lien*, 258–259). But even then he wrote, "Una nobis et illis fides, unus Deus, idem
Christus, eadem spes, eadem lavacri sacramenta. Semel dixerim, una Ecclesia
sumus [They and we have one faith, one God, the same Christ, the same hope,
the same baptismal sacraments; let me say it once for all, we are one Church]"
(*On the Veiling of Virgins* 2 [PL 2:939a]). Cf. R. Seeberg, *Studien zur Geschichte des
Begriffes der Kirche*, 22.

itive, historical nature. This, first and foremost, is the *argumentum praescriptionis* already familiar to us, which, as we have seen, Tertullian employed to demonstrate the inviolability of the books of Holy Scripture accepted by the Church. The Church is more ancient than all heretics—such is the key tenet of this argument. This argument has already been briefly presentd by St. Irenaeus. "Prior to Valentinus, those who follow Valentinus had no existence; nor did those from Marcion exist before Marcion; nor, in short, had any of those malignant-minded people (*sensus maligni*), whom I have above enumerated, any being previous to the initiators and inventors of their perversity.[657] For Valentinus came to Rome in the time of Hyginus, flourished under Pius, and remained until Anicetus. Cerdon, too, Marcion's predecessor, himself arrived in the time of Hyginus, who was the ninth bishop. ... Marcion, then, succeeding him, flourished under Anicetus, who held the tenth place of the episcopate. But the rest, who are called Gnostics, take rise from Menander, Simon's disciple, as I have shown; and each one of them appeared to be both the father and the high priest (*antistes*) of that doctrine into which he has been initiated. But all these (the Marcosians) broke out into their apostasy much later, even during the intermediate period of the Church (*mediantibus iam Ecclesiae temporibus*)."[658]

But it is Tertullian who promotes the *argumentum praescriptionis* with particular insistance. *Id verius quod prius*—thus Tertullian briefly formulates his argument.[659] Truth always necessarily precedes falsehood.[660] The original always precedes the copy; imitation always occurs after the thing itself. Heresies could not occur earlier

---

657 The Russian source adds here: "The time when all the heretics lived is known."

658 Irenaeus, *Against Heresies* 3.4.3 (ANF 1:417; PG 7:856b–857b).

659 "That is true, which is earlier." Tertullian, *Against Marcion* 6.5 (CSEL 47:430.11). Cf. 4.4: "Id verius existimetur, quod est serius [how absurd it would be... that that should be thought to be the truer position which is the later one]" (429.6–7).

660 Tertullian, *Against Marcion* 4.5 (CSEL 47:432.10–11). Cf. *Treatise on the Soul* 5 (PL 1:617).

than true teaching.[661] The parable of the sower relates how first the good seed was sown, and only then the tares. In the matter of doctrine likewise, "that that which was first delivered is of the Lord and is true, whilst that is strange and false which was afterwards introduced."[662] The Church possesses the more ancient doctrine,[663] while heresies, having appeared later, consequently perverted the foundations of truth.[664] Against the heretics Tertullian puts forward his *praescriptio novitatis* [law of newness];[665] they may now be accused *de testimonio temporum*,[666] *de aetate sola*.[667] Their early[668] origin alone (*posteritas*) stands in accusation of all heretics.[669] Tertullian calls heresies recent[670] and new,[671] and says that the heretics are "of

---

661 Tertulian, *The Prescription Against Heretics* 29 (ANF 3:256; PL 2:48a). Cf. 35 (PL 2:58a).

662 Tertulian, *The Prescription Against Heretics* 31 (ANF 3:258; PL 2:51–52).

663 Tertulian, *Against Marcion* 5.19 (CSEL 47:642.27–643.1); *Against Hermogenes* 1 (Ibid., 126); *Prescription Against Heretics* 34 (PL 2:57a).

664 Tertullian, *Against Marcion* 3.1: "Illic scilicet pronuntiandam regulae interversionem, ubi posteritas invenitur [we are forced to declare that there is undoubtedly a subversion of the rule {of faith}, where any opinion is found of later date]" (CSEL 47:377.16–17). Cf. 1.1:292.4–6. Cf. *Against Praxeas* 2: "Id esse verum, quodcumque primum; id esse adulterum, quodcumque posterius [that whatever is first is true, whereas that is spurious which is later in date]" (CSEL 47:229.19–20).

665 Tertullian, *Against Marcion* 1.1 (CSEL 47:292.8). Cf. *Against Hermogenes* 1: "De posteritate praescribere [to lay down the rule {against heretics} of the lateness of their date]" (CSEL 47:126.3–4).

666 "By the testimony of time." Tertullian, *Against Marcion* 5.19 (CSEL 47:642.26–27).

667 "On the mere ground of the age [in which they lived]." Tertullian, *The Prescription Against Heretics* 34 (PL 2:57a).

668 A misprint, as the parenthetical *posteritas* indicates that the author is referring to the *late* origin of heretical doctrines. –*Trans.*

669 Tertullian, *Against Praxeas* 2 (CSEL 47:229.16).

670 Tertullian, *The Prescription Against Heretics* 35 (PL 2:57a).

671 Tertullian, *The Prescription Against Heretics* 6 (PL 2:21a). Cf. *Against Hermogenes* 1: "Novella est" (CSEL 47:126.8). *Against Praxeas* 2: "Ipsa novellitas Praxeae hesterni [the absolutely novel character of Praxeas of yesterday]" (CSEL 47:229.17).

yesterday" (*hesterni*).[672] The origin of the heretics is perfectly well known.[673] Marcion and Valentinus lived only recently, almost in the reign of Antoninus. At first [they] recognized the doctrine of the Church, then later they were excommunicated for spreading their doctrines. If we trace the geneological tree of Apelles, he proves to be no more ancient than his teacher Marcion. Nigidius and Hermogenes persist in error to this day.[674] At the time when the heretics were beginning to preach, the Church had already filled the whole world.[675] The heretics need to prove that they are the new apostles. "Let them maintain that Christ has come down a second time, taught in person a second time, has been twice crucified, twice dead, twice raised!"[676]

Tertullian himself ascribed great significance to the foregoing arguments, which is why he repeats them in nearly all his polemical works.[677] All these arguments Tertullian terms *praescriptio*. A *praescriptio* is a point of reasoning after which processes or disputes in general become pointless and must cease.[678] Tertullian expresses the thought that to denounce heresies this argument alone is suficient, *sine retractatu doctrinarum*.[679] But of course matters of faith are not the same as judicial legal proceedings, and Tertullian did not limit himself to the *praescriptio* alone, but was obliged to enter into a detailed

---

672 Tertullian, *Against Praxeas* 2 (ANF 3:598; CSEL 47:229.16, 17).

673 Tertullian, *Against Valentinus* 4 (CSEL 47:180.22–23).

674 Tertullian, *The Prescription Against Heretics* 30 (PL 2:48–50). Cf. *Against Hermogenes* 1: "Denique ad hodiernum homo in saeculo" (CSEL 47:126.8–9). *Against Marcion* 5.19 (CSEL 47:643).

675 Tertullian, *Against Marcion* 5.19 (CSEL 47:643.8–13).

676 Tertullian, *The Prescription Against Heretics* 30 (ANF 3:257; PL 2:51a).

677 Tertullian himself says, "Solemus praescribere" (*Against Hermogenes* 1, *Against Marcion* 5.19 [CSEL 47:126.3–4, 642.26–27].

678 See Adhémar d'Alès, *La théologie de Tertullien*, 201; P. Batiffol, *L'église naissante et le catholicisme*, 326–330. Cf. Migne (PL 2:1433).

679 "Without a consideration of their doctrines." *Against Marcion* 1.1 (CSEL 47:292.7).

analysis of the heretical systems, *etiam specialiter respondere, dare etiam, retractatibus locum.*[680]

Thus, heresies are a new creation of their originators; they are not of the apostles. The Church, however, is of a different origin. The Church is more ancient than all heresies and originates from the apostles of Christ. The apostles "obtained the promised power of the Holy Ghost for the gift of miracles and of utterance; and after first bearing witness to the faith in Jesus Christ throughout Judæa, and founding churches (there), they next went forth into the world and preached the same doctrine of the same faith to the nations. They then in like manner founded churches in every city, from which all the other churches, one after another, derived the tradition (*traducem*) of the faith, and the seeds of doctrine, and are every day deriving them, that they may become churches (*ut ecclesiae fiant*). Indeed, it is on this account only that they will be able to deem themselves apostolic, as being the offspring (*soboles*) of apostolic churches. Every sort of thing must necessarily revert to its original for its classification (*censeatur*). Therefore the churches, although they are so many and so great, comprise but the one primitive church, (founded) by the apostles, from which they all (spring). In this way all are primitive, and all are apostolic, whilst they are all proved to be one."[681]

The Churches are not only founded by the apostles: in them **apostolic succession** is preserved. The apostles have given the Church a particular organ for preserving inviolate the doctrine delivered to it. This is the **successive episcopate.** The Churches prove their apostolic origin and dignity specifically by the fact that the apostles appointed their successors in them. The heretics cannot prove the apostolic origin of their churches; they have no apostolic succession. "Let them unfold the roll (*ordinem*) of their bishops, running down in due succession from the beginning (*per successiones ab initio decurrentem*) in such a manner that [that first bishop of

---

680 "To give particular answers as well, to give space also to the things that have been withdrawn." Tertullian, *The Prescription Against Heretics* 45 (PL 2:74a). Cf. *Against Praxeas* 2, *Against Marcion* 1.1 (CSEL 47.229.21–22, 292.8–10).

681 Tertullian, *The Prescription Against Heretics* 20 (PL 2:37a–b).

theirs] bishop shall be able to show for his ordainer and predecessor (*auctorem et antecessorem*) some one of the apostles or of apostolic men,—a man, moreover, who continued stedfast (*perseveraverit*) with the apostles. For this is the manner in which the apostolic churches transmit their registers (*census suos deferunt*): as the church of Smyrna, which records that Polycarp was placed therein by John; as also the church of Rome, which makes Clement to have been ordained (*ordinatum*) in like manner by Peter. In exactly the same way the other churches likewise exhibit (their several worthies), whom, as having been appointed to their episcopal places by apostles, they regard as transmitters of the apostolic seed (*apostolici seminis traduces*)."[682] The apostles providentially (*providentius*) established the episcopacy.[683] The apostolic institution of the episcopacy in the Christian Church was so indubitable for Tertullian that even in his Montanistic works, though opposed at that time to the bishops of the Church, he refrains from raising any objections to it. In *On Modesty* Tertullian distinguishes between the apostolic gifts. One must distinguish between doctrine and power (*inter doctrinam apostolorum et potestatem*). The bishops inherited the right to teach from the apostles, and Tertullian does not deny his opponent this right.[684] Thus, Tertullian predominantly speaks only of the apostolic establishment of the episcopacy, although he hints at succession (*successio*) of the episcopacy in the Church.

The idea of episcopal succession as proof of the truth of church doctrine had already been expounded in particular detail by St. Irenaeus. Without exaggeration it may be stated that this idea predom-

---

682 Tertullian, *The Prescription Against Heretics* 32 (ANF 3:258; PL 2:52b–53a). "Confligant tale aliquid haeretici! [Let the heretics contrive something of the same kind!]" Tertullian exclaims. Cf. *On the Veiling of Virgins* 2: "Eas ego Ecclesias proposui, quas et ipsi apostoli vel Apostolici viri condiderunt [I have proposed (as models) those Churches which were founded by apostles or apostolic men]" (PL 2:939a).

683 Tertullian, *De Fuga* 13: "Hanc episcopatui formam apostoli providentius condiderunt" (PL 2:141a).

684 Tertullian, *On Modesty* 21 (ANF 4:98–101; CSEL 20.1:268–269). Cf. Schanz, "Der begriff der Kirche." *Theologische Quartalschrift* (1893): 571–572. I. Turmel, *Tertullien*, 57. K. Adam, *Der Kirchenbegriff Tertullian*, 41.

inates in the holy father's system of ecclesiological views. At every
opportunity St. Irenaeus briefly repeats his idea that the truth is preserved in the Church through episcopal succession.[685] "The succession of the bishops, by which [the apostles] have handed down the
Church which exists in every place," is the "distinctive manifestation
(*character*) of the body of Christ."[686] That the apostles appointed for
themselves successors Irenaeus cites when repudiating the Gnostic
teaching regarding a secret tradition. "We are in a position to reckon up those who were by the apostles instituted (*instituti*) bishops in
the Churches ... who neither taught nor knew of anything like what
these [heretics] rave about. For if the apostles had known hidden
mysteries (*recondita mysteria*), which they were in the habit of imparting to 'the perfect' apart[687] and privily from the rest, they would
have delivered them especially to those to whom they were also
committing the Churches themselves.[688] For they were desirous that
these men should be very perfect and blameless in all things, whom
also they were leaving behind as their successors (*successores*), delivering up their own place of government (*locum magisterii*) to these men;
which men, if they discharged their functions honestly (*emendate
agentibus*), would be a great boon [to the Church], but if they should

---

685 See *Against Heresies* 3.2.2: "Traditio, quae per successiones presbyterorum
in Ecclesiis custoditur [tradition... which is preserved by means of the succession of presbyters in the Churches]" (PG 7:847a). 3.3.2: "Fidem per successiones
episcoporum pervenientem usque ad nos [the Faith which comes down to our
time by means of the successions of the bishops]" (PG 7:848b). 3.3.3: "Τῇ αὐτῇ
διαδοχῇ (*successione*) ᾗτε ἀπὸ τῶν ἀποστόλων ἐν τῇ Ἐκκλησίᾳ παράδοσις, καὶ τὸ
τῆς ἀληθείας κήρυγμα κατήντηκεν εἰς ἡμᾶς [By this same succession, both the
tradition that is in the Church from the apostles and the preaching of truth have
come down to us]" (PG 7:851b). 4.33.8: "Character corporis Christi secundum
successiones episcoporum, quibus illi eam, quae in unoquoque loco est, Ecclesiam tradiderunt [the distinctive manifestation of the body of Christ according
to the successions of the bishops, by which they have handed down that Church
which exists in every place]" (PG 7:1077b). Cf. 4.26.2–5, 5.20.1 (PG 7:1053c,
1056a–b, 1177a–b).

686 Irenaeus, *Against Heresies* 4.33.8 (ANF 1:508; PG 7:1077b).

687 In the Russian source, "of imparting perfectly apart." –*Trans.*

688 In the Russian source, "to whom the Churches themselves were committing them." –*Trans.*

fall away, the direst calamity."[689] The apostolic doctrine is preserved among the presbyters of the Church.[690] St. Irenaeus then shifts to purely historical grounds, desiring to demonstrate the succession of the bishops. For the sake of brevity the holy father restricts himself to the Church of Rome,[691] which in the West was the sole apostolic Church, and he enumerates the Roman bishops. "The blessed apostles, then, having founded and built up the [Roman] Church, committed into the hands of Linus the office of the episcopate (τὴν τῆς ἐπισκοπῆς λειτουργίαν). Of this Linus, Paul makes mention in the Epistles to Timothy. To him succeeded (διαδέχεται) Anacletus; and after him, in the third place from the apostles, Clement was allotted the bishopric (τὴν ἐπισκοπὴν κληροῦται). This man, as he had seen the blessed apostles, and had been conversant with them, might be said to have the preaching of the apostles still echoing [in his ears], and their traditions (τὴν παράδοσιν) before his eyes. ... To this Clement there succeeded (διαδέχεται) Evaristus. Alexander followed Evaristus; then, sixth from the apostles, Sixtus was appointed (καθίσταται); after him, Telesphorus, who was gloriously martyred; then Hyginus; after him, Pius; then after him, Anicetus. Soter having succeeded Anicetus, Eleutherius does now, in the twelfth place from the apostles, hold the inheritance of the episcopate (τὸν τῆς ἐπισκοπῆς κλῆρον)."[692] Although St. Irenaeus promised to restrict himself to the Roman Church alone, he could not help but mention his native Church of Smyrna, and so he adds: "Polycarp also was not only instructed by apostles, and conversed with many who had seen Christ, but was also, by apostles in Asia, appointed bishop (ὑπὸ ἀποστόλων κατασταθεὶς ἐπίσκοπος) of the Church in Smyrna. ... To these things all the Asiatic Churches testify, as do also those men who have succeeded (διαδεγμένοι) Polycarp down to the present time."[693] St. Irenaeus also adds a brief note concerning the Church

---

689 Idem 3.3.1 (ANF 1:415; PG 7:848a–b).

690 Idem 4.32.1 (ANF 1:506; PG 7:1071a).

691 Idem (PG 7:848b).

692 Idem 3.3.3 (ANF 1:416; PG 7:849a–b). Irenaeus' testimony is also cited by Eusebius. See Eusebius, *Church History* 5.6.1–4 (GrchSch. 9.1:438).

693 Idem 3.3.4 (ANF 1:416; PG 7:851b–c, 852a–b). Eusebius, op. cit. 4.14.3–

of Ephesus: "The Church in Ephesus, founded by Paul, and having John remaining among them permanently until the times of Trajan, is a true witness of the tradition of the apostles."[694] The unbroken succession of the bishops from the apostles, St. Irenaeus holds, is the most important proof of true apostleship and of the Church. "In this order, and by this succession," says St. Irenaeus, "the ecclesiastical tradition from the apostles, and the preaching of the truth, have come down to us. And this is most abundant proof (*plenissima haec ostensio*) that there is one and the same vivifying faith, which has been preserved in the Church from the apostles until now, and handed down in truth (*in veritate*)."[695] **Thus, episcopal succession is the chief basis for recognizing this truth: that the Christian Church is the custodian of the truth.**[696]

In comparing St. Irenaeus's teaching on the succession of the apostolic Tradition in the Church with Tertullian's teaching on the same subject, a certain divergence between them may be discerned. Irenaeus bases his arguments almost entirely on episcopal succession in individual Churches. The bishops successively relay the apostolic teaching in inviolate form, and for this reason one and the

---

5 (GrchSch. 9.1:332).

694 Idem (PG 7:854b, 855a).

695 Idem 3.3.3 (ANF 1:416; PG 854b, 855a).

696 Among writers of the same period, appointment by the apostles and unbroken episcopal succession is considered proof of the truth of church doctrine. Eusebius cites an excerpt from a writer in Asia Minor in the late second century: "If after Quadratus and Ammia in Philadelphia, as they assert, the women with Montanus received the prophetic gift, let them show who among them received it from Montanus and the women" (*Church History* 5.17.4 [NPNF[2] 1:234; GrchSch. 9.1:470.19–21]). Here succession as the criterion of truth is acknowledged by both the Montanists and the ecclesiastical writer. The ecclesiastical writer Caius, who lived in the time of the Roman bishop Zephyrinus, wrote to Proclus, a Montanist: "I can show the trophies of the apostles. For if you will go to the Vatican or to the Ostian way, you will find the trophies of those who laid the foundations of [the Roman] church." In a letter to the Romans the Corinthian bishop Dionysius attests: "Both [Peter and Paul] planted and likewise taught us in our Corinth" (Eusebius, op. cit. 2.25.6–8 [NPNF[2] 1:130; GrchSch. 9.1:176, 178]). Thus, we find references to the bishops' succession from the apostles in the works of a writer of the East, one of the West, and one who lived between East and West.

same faith is found in different Churches scattered throughout the world. St. Irenaeus demonstrates the succession of the episcopacy and explains how the truth that the apostles delivered is preserved inviolate in the Church. Tertullian says nothing about episcopal succession, and does not enumerate a series of successive bishops, as does St. Irenaeus.[697] He focuses his attention primarily on the fact that the Church was founded by the apostles. That doctrine is united in different present-day Churches proves its inviolability, which is why all Churches may be called the one apostolic Church. St. Irenaeus and Tertullian emphasize different aspects of the same system of doctrine on church Tradition or the apostolicity of the Church. That at which one only hints (universal unity of faith in Irenaeus's works), the other develops in detail, while what one expounds in detail (episcopal succession in the writings of Irenaeus) the other only mentions in passing (Tertullian's *successio*). Irenaeus and Tertullian are mutually complementary.[698]

It must however be said that for church writers neither the Churches' founding by the apostles nor the succession of the bishops is a self-sufficient and absolute guarantee that the truth of Christ is preserved in the Church. In the previous essay we expounded in detail the teaching of St. Irenaeus on the action of the Holy Spirit in the Church. For the holy father, the whole life of the Church is the fruit of the Holy Spirit dwelling in the Church. Preservation of the truth likewise is not separate from this common church life: it is one of the manifestations of the grace-filled life of the Church. Through the Holy Spirit Christians see, hear, and speak.[699] The Holy Spirit bestows knowledge of the truth.[700] One who has the Holy Spirit may judge concerning heretical errors.[701] It is the Holy Spirit Who guards the Church from error. "The preaching

---

697 See Batiffol's remark in *L'église naissante et le catholicisme*,[3] 322.

698 Cf. Karl Adam, *Der Kirchenbegriff Tertullians*, 33–34. In our opinion, however, Adam exaggerates the difference between Irenaeus and Tertullian when he sees his writings as demonstrating the apostolicity of only the individual Church.

699 Irenaeus, *Against Heresies* 5.20.2 (PG 7:1178c).

700 Idem (PG 7:1077a).

701 Idem (PG 7:1072–1077).

of the Church is everywhere consistent, and continues in an even
course, and receives testimony from the prophets, the apostles, and
all the disciples ... through the entire dispensation of God, and that
well-grounded system which tends to man's salvation (*quae secundum salutem hominis est solidam operationem*), namely, our faith; which,
having been received from the Church, we do preserve, and which
always, **by the Spirit of God**, renewing its youth, as if it were
some precious deposit in an excellent vessel, causes the vessel itself containing it to renew its youth (*juvenescens*) also. For this gift
of God has been entrusted to the Church, as breath was to the
first created man, for this purpose, that all the members receiving
it may be vivified. ... 'For in the Church,' it is said, 'God hath set
apostles, prophets, teachers' [1 Cor. 12:28], and all the other means
through which the Spirit works (*universam reliquam operationem Spiritus*);
of which all those are not partakers who do not join themselves
(*concurrunt* or *currunt*) to the Church, but defraud themselves of life
through their perverse opinions and infamous behaviour. For where
the Church is, there is the Spirit of God; and where the Spirit of
God is, there is the Church, and every kind of grace; but the Spirit
is truth."[702] "Wherefore it is incumbent to obey the presbyters who
are in the Church,[703]—those who, as I have shown, possess the succession from the apostles (*qui successionem habent ab apostolis*); those
who, together with the succession of the episcopate, have received
the certain gift of truth, according to the good pleasure of the
Father (*quicum episcopates successione charisma veritatis certum, secundum
placitum Patris acceperunt*)."[704] "Where, therefore, the gifts of the Lord
have been placed (*charismata Domini posita sunt*), there it behoves us
to learn the truth, [namely,] from those who possess that succession

702 Idem 3.24.1 (ANF 1:458; PG 7:966a–c).

703 In the Russian source, "it is incumbent on them who are in the Church to
obey...." *–Trans.*

704 Idem 4.26.2 (ANF 1:497; PG 7:1053c–1054a). Cf. 4.26.4: "Adhaerere his
qui et apostolorum sicut praediximus, doctrinam custodiunt, et cum presbyterii
ordine sermonem sanum et conversationem sine offensa praestant [adhere to
those who, as I have already observed, do hold the doctrine of the apostles, and
who, together with the order of priesthood, display sound speech and blameless
conduct]" (Ibid. [PG 7:1055a]).

of the Church which is from the apostles (*quae est ab apostolis succes-sio*), and among whom exists that which is sound and blameless in conduct, as well as that which is unadulterated and incorrupt in speech. For these also preserve this faith of ours in one God who created all things; and they increase that love [which we have] for the Son of God ... and they expound the Scriptures to us without danger, neither blaspheming God, nor dishonouring the patriarchs, nor despising the prophets."[705] Thus, the episcopate is merely an organ, endowed with a particular charisma (*charisma veritatis*, the charisma of truth) of the Holy Spirit dwelling in the Church, Who Himself preserves the truth inviolate.[706] In general St. Irenaeus does not separate truth from church life: in this regard the Church is a kind of supernatural reality, though absolutely inseparable from its visible manifestation.[707] It nourishes (ἀνατρέφει) the presbyters with its powers of grace,[708] while these apparently possess the charisma of the truth only by virtue of their ecclesiastical position.

Tertullian likewise expresses the same idea fairly distinctly: in his writings the Holy Spirit is likewise depicted as dwelling continually in the Church by His power, which also preserves church doctrine inviolate. To be sure, Tertullian does not express this truth directly. "Grant, then, that all have erred; ... that the Holy Ghost had no such respect to any one (church) as to lead it into truth, although

---

705 Idem 4.26.5 (ANF 1:498; PG 7:1056a–b).

706 Schanz asserts that *charisma veritatis* does not [signify] the infallibility of the individual bishop, but rather [signifies] the infallibility of the episcopacy as a whole ("Der Begriff der Kirche," *Theologische Quartalschrift* [1893]: 567). Converse-ly, Adam sees here the personal charisma of the bishop, and sees this as a defect in the teaching of Irenaeus (*Der Kirchenbegriff Tertullians*, 34). But we are inclined to think that such a distinction ought not to be made in the teaching of Irenaeus. The Church is catholic, while *successio* always intimately affects the individual Church. But in the life of the Church the individual Church coincides with the entire ecumenical Church. See Batiffol, *L'église naissante et le catholicisme*, 244. Cf. also Schanz, op. cit., 568–569. P. Beuzart sees in St. Irenaeus's writings the germ of the same as yet unformed idea that in general the hierarchy in the Church is primarily an organ of the Holy Spirit (*Essai sur la théologie d'Irénée*, 161).

707 Cf. Beuzart, *Essai sur la théologie d'Irénée*, 151–152, 153.

708 Irenaeus, *Against Heresies* 4.26.5 (ANF 1:498; PG 7:1055c).

sent with this view by Christ [see Jn. 14:26], and for this asked of
the Father that He might be the teacher of truth (*doctor veritatis*) [Jn.
15:26]; grant, also, that He, the Steward (*villicus*) of God, the Vicar
of Christ, neglected His office, permitting the churches for a time to
understand differently, (and) to believe differently, what He Himself
was preaching by the apostles."[709] Despite this form of expression,
Tertullian's thinking is quite clear and coherent, the more so given
that in general Tertullian frequently speaks of the action and in-
dwelling of the Holy Spirit in the church community.[710] Even in his
apology addressed to the gentiles Tertullian speaks of the Spirit of
holiness with which Christian brotherhood is imbued.[711] Even Tertullian's "Rule of Faith" states that the Holy Spirit takes the place of
Christ and governs the faithful.[712] The Holy Spirit fortifies the martyrs[713] and makes the hearts of Christians a house of God.[714] Christians have a common hope, a common joy, common sorrow and
suffering, because they share a common Spirit from the common
Lord and Father.[715] Hence it may be said that the preservation of
truth in the Church is likewise an act of the Holy Spirit.[716] Tertul-

---

709 Tertullian, *The Prescription Against Heretics* 28 (ANF 3:256; PL 2:47a).

710 "Die Überzeugung von der erleuchtenden Tätigkeit des Hl. Geistes in der
Kirche durchdringt gerade ihn auf das tiefste" (Karl Adam, 35).

711 Tertullian, *Apology* 39: "Quanto dignius fratres et dicuntur et habentur, qui
unum Patrem Deum agnoverunt, qui unum Spiritum biberunt sanctitatis [how
much more fittingly they are called and counted brothers who have been led to
the knowledge of God as their common Father, who have drunk in one spirit of
holiness.]" It is noteworthy that Tertullian then goes on to say concerning the
truth: "Qui de uno utero ignorantiae, ejusdem ad unam lucem expaveruiint veritatis [who from the same womb of a common ignorance have agonized into the
same light of truth!]" (PL 1:471–472).

712 Tertullian, *The Prescription Against Heretics* 13: "Misisse vicariam vim Spiritus sancti, qui credetes agat" (PL 2:31a). Cf. 28: *Christi vicarius* (PL 2:47a).

713 Tertullian, *To the Martyrs* 3 (PL 1:624b).

714 Tertullian, *On the Apparel of Women* 2.1 (PL 1:1316a).

715 Tertullian, *On Repentance* 10: "Communis spes, metus, gaudium, dolor,
passio, quia communis Spiritus de communi Domino et Patri" (PL 1:1245a).

716 According to Adam, in the action of the Holy Spirit Tertullian saw the
final and supreme surety of all church doctrine: "Die letzte, höchste Garantie

lian does not develop this idea, perhaps because for the Gnostics it had no meaning. In general Tertullian prefers to conduct polemics on historical and philosophical grounds rather than theological.[717] In any case it may be thought that St. Irenaeus's idea of *charisma veritatis* is not entirely foreign to Tertullian.

On this point also, however, between St. Irenaeus and Tertullian a rather significant variance may be noted. St. Irenaeus linked *certum charisma veritatis* [the certain charisma of truth] with an episcopacy that traced its unbroken succession back to the apostles, by which means in the ecclesiological system of St. Irenaeus the episcopacy is intimately connected with the teaching of the Church. In the writings of Tertullian this is absent. As we have already seen, according to Tertullian's teaching the Holy Spirit governs the whole Church, and *charisma veritatis* does not belong to the episcopacy alone. Tertullian highly esteems the bishops as pastors of the Church, calling them *praesides*,[718] *pastores*,[719] *antistites*,[720] and *praepositi*;[721] he rebukes the heretics for failing to revere their own bishops,[722] and ascribes to the bishops a *jus docendi* that the rest do not possess.[723] But along with this in the writings of Tertullian we have seen too high a value set upon the "Rule of Faith" itself. For Tertullian, the Symbol becomes a **rule for faith,** as in a judicial codex, which he calls "a law"[724]—*Regula a Christo instituta*.[725] The Church received

---

aller Kirchenlehre" (*Der Kirchenbegriff Tertullians,* 35).

717 Cf. Adam, *Der Kirchenbegriff Tertullians,* 36.

718 "Guardians." Tertullian, *The Prescription Against Heretics* 42 (PL 2:70a).

719 "Shepherds." Tertullian, *Chaplet* 1 (PL 2:97a).

720 "Overseers." Idem (PL 2:97c).

721 "Presidents." Tertullian, *On Monogamy* 12 (PL 2:997c–998a).

722 Tertullian, *Prescription Against Heretics* 42 (PL 2:70a).

723 Tertullian, *On Baptism.*

724 Cf. Zahn, *Skizzen…,* 253 ff; Harnack, *Dogmengeschichte*[4] 1, 364.

725 Tertullian, *The Prescription Against Heretics* 14 (PL 2:31b). Cf. 9: "Unum utique et certum aliquid institutum esse a Christo quod credere omni modo debeant nationes [there is some one, and therefore definite, thing taught by Christ, which the Gentiles are by all means bound to believe]" (PL 2:26b–27a). 44: "Semel Evangelium et ejusdem regulae doctrinam apostolis meis delegaveram [I

the "Rule of Faith" from the apostles, the apostles from Christ, and
Christ from God;[726] it has come down from the very beginning of
the Gospel.[727] Consequently, there would appear to be no room left
for a more precise definition of the dogmas. The *Regula fidei* is dead
capital, as it were.[728] *Crede quod traditum est!*[729] But in that case the
teaching work of the episcopacy is apparently reduced to only two
separate types: to teach the "Rule of Faith" and to preserve it. For
Tertullian there is no room for dogmatic definitions of faith in the
Church through the episcopacy, and his ecclesiological system is less
favorable toward this doctrine than the system of St. Irenaeus.[730]

From all the foregoing teaching of St. Irenaeus and Tertullian
concerning the Church we may see that here first and foremost the
Church is presented as **a community that preserves in purity the truth handed down by the apostles from God.** The
Church is apostolic because only in it is the doctrine of the apostles
preserved. The apostolicity of the Church is substantiated by the ecumenical nature and oneness of the Church, on the one hand, and
on the other by the unbroken succession of the bishops, whom the
apostles made their vicars in the work of teaching and preserving

---

once gave the gospel and the doctrine of the said rule to my apostles]" (PL 2:73a).

726   Idem (PL 2:61a). Cf. *Against Marcion* 1:21: "dei regula [rule of God]"
(CSEL 47:317.29, 318.2).

727   Tertullian, *Against Praxeas* 2 (CSEL 47:229.14–15). All this is said concerning the Symbol in its definitive form. Cf. Zahn, *Skizzen...*, 251–252.

728   Adam, *Der Kirchenbegriff Tertullians,* 40.

729   "Believe what was handed down!" Tertullian, *On the Flesh of Christ* 2 (PL
2:801a). Cf. *Prescription Against Heretics* 9: "Nihil amplius, nisi custodiendum quod
credidisti [nor have you anything further to do but to keep what you have be-
lieved]" (PL 2:27a).

730   Karl Adam gives a detailed analysis of Tertullian's teaching on how the
episcopacy relates to the work of teaching in the Church (*Der Kirlchenbegriff Tertullians,* 36–45). "By stripping episcopal teachership as a whole of all dogmatic content, of all divine surety of doctrinal truth," Adam concludes, "without noticing
it Tertullian buried his Rule of Faith that he had substantiated with such effort
and skill, and even the authority of church dogma in general" (44–45). At the
same time, all of Adam's reasoning ultimately manifests the Catholic tendencies
of the author.

the truth in the Churches they had established. This general summary of their overall doctrine concerning the Church is distinctly expressed by the ecclesiastical writers themselves. To the Church is entrusted the light of God, she preaches the truth, and she is the seven-branched candlestick that bears the light of Christ.[731] The Church is the school of Christ Himself, and His chosen disciples are the teachers, who are able to teach all things.[732] In the Church, certain truth is clear;[733] therefore truth must be sought only in the Church.[734] The woman in the Gospel sought the drachma within her own house; in like manner truth must be sought only in one's own Church.[735] One must "flee to the Church, and be brought up in her bosom."[736] She received the truth from the apostles, and in all the world she alone, preserving it well, has transmitted it to her sons.[737] The Church transmits the truth, and only that which the Church transmits is true.[738] In the Church there is the living apostolic Tradition, directly assimilated from the apostles by their disciples, who personally (κατ᾽ ὄψιν) saw them.[739] Irenaeus himself cites

731 Irenaeus, *Against Heresies* 5.20.1 (ANF 1:548; PG 7:1177b).

732 Tertullian, *Scorpiace* 12: "Quis nunc medullas scripturarum magis nosset, quam ipsa Christi schola? Quos et sibi discipulos dominus adoptavit, omnia utique edocendos et nobis magistros adordinavit, omnia utique docturos [Who, now, should know better the marrow of the Scriptures than the school of Christ itself?— the persons whom the Lord both chose for Himself as scholars, certainly to be fully instructed in all points, and appointed to us for masters to instruct us in all points]" (CSEL 20.1:172.5–8).

733 Tertullian, *The Prescription Against Heretics* 9 (ANF 1:247–248; PL 2:26b–27a).

734 Irenaeus, *Against Heresies* 3.4.1 (PG 7:855a).

735 Tertullian, *The Prescription Against Heretics* 12: "Quaeramus ergo in nostro, et a nostris, et de nostro [Let our "seeking," therefore be in that which is our own, and from those who are our own: and concerning that which is our own]" (PL 2:30b).

736 Irenaeus, *Against Heresies* 5.20.2 (ANF 1:548; PG 7:1178a).

737 Ibid, Preface (ANF 1:526; PG 7:1119a).

738 Idem (PG 7:852a, 853a, according to the Greek text).

739 Idem 5.5.1, 30.1, 36.2 (PG 7:1135a–b, 1203b, 1223b).

the words of a certain presbyter who listened to those who saw the apostles and by the apostles were taught.[740]

From all this a practical rule emerges.

"Suppose there arise a dispute relative to some important (*modica*) question among us, should we not have recourse (*recurrere*) to the most ancient Churches with which the apostles held constant intercourse, and learn from them what is certain and clear (*certum et liquidum*) in regard to the present question?"[741] "Now, what that was which [the apostles] preached—in other words, what it was which Christ revealed to them—can, as I must here likewise prescribe, properly be proved (*probari*) in no other way than by those very churches which the apostles founded in person, by declaring the gospel to them directly themselves, both *vivâ voce*, as the phrase is, and subsequently by their epistles. ... All doctrine which agrees (*conspiret*) with the apostolic churches, those moulds and original sources of the faith (*matricibus et originalibus fidei*), must be reckoned for truth, as undoubtedly containing that which the (said) churches received from the apostles, the apostles from Christ, Christ from God. Whereas all doctrine must be prejudged as false which savours of contrariety to the truth of the churches and apostles of Christ and God."[742] "Come now, you who would indulge a better curiosity, if you would apply it to the business of your salvation, run over the apostolic churches, in which the very thrones of the apostles are still pre-eminent in their places (*suis locis praesident*, or *praesidentur*), in which their own authentic writings are read (*ipsae autenticae litterae*), uttering the voice and representing the face (*facies*) of each of them severally. Achaia is very near you, (in which) you find Corinth. Since you are not far from Macedonia, you have Philippi; (and there too)

---

740 Idem 4.27.1 (PG 7:1056b).

741 Idem 3.4.1 (PG 7:855b): "Modica quaestio"; consequently, this refers to tradition in the broadest sense of the word.

742 Tertullian, *The Prescription Against Heretics* 21 (ANF 3:252; PL 2:38a–b). Cf. *Against Marcion* 1.21: "Non alia agnoscenda erit traditio apostolorum quam quae hodie apud ipsorum ecclesias editur [no other teaching will have the right of being received as apostolic than that which is at the present day proclaimed in the churches of apostolic foundation]" (CSEL 47:318.2–3).

you have the Thessalonians. Since you are able to cross (*tendere*) to Asia, you get Ephesus. Since, moreover, you are close upon (*adjaces*) Italy, you have Rome, from which there comes even into our own hands the very authority (of the apostles themselves) (*auctoritas prae-sto est*). How happy is its church, on which apostles poured forth all their doctrine along with their blood! where Peter endures a passion like (*adaequatur*) his Lord's! where Paul wins his crown in a death like John's, where the Apostle John was first plunged, unhurt, into boiling oil, and thence remitted to his island-exile!"[743] St. Irenaeus likewise cites "that tradition derived from the apostles, of the very great, the very ancient, and universally known Church founded and organized at Rome by the two most glorious apostles, Peter and Paul. ... For to this Church, on account of its superior pre-eminence, must needs come (necesse est convenire) the whole Church, that is, the faithful who exist from everywhere, in which [Church] the Tradition from the apostles has always been preserved by those [faithful] who exist from everywhere."[744]

---

743 Ibid. 36 (PL 2:58b–60). Cf. *Against Marcion* 4.5: "Id esse ab apostolis traditum, quod apud ecclesias apostolorum fuerit sacrosanctum. Videamus quod lac a Paulo Corinthii hauserint; ad quam regulam Galatae sint recorrecti; quid legant Philippenses, Thessalonicenses, Ephesii; quid etiam Romani de proximo sonent, quibus Evangelium et Petrus et Paulus sanguine quoque suo signatum reliquerunt [that comes down from the apostles, which has been kept as a sacred deposit in the churches of the apostles. Let us see what milk the Corinthians drank from Paul; to what rule of faith the Galatians were brought for correction; what the Philippians, the Thessalonians, the Ephesians read by it; what utterance also the Romans give, so very near (to the apostles), to whom Peter and Paul conjointly bequeathed the gospel even sealed with their own blood]" (CSEL 47:430.13–18). It may be thought that in the excerpts cited (especially from *The Prescription Against Heretics*) Tertullian is referring to Tradition in a broader sense than the *regula fidei* alone.

744 Irenaeus, *Against Heresies* 3.3.2 (ANF 1:415–416; PG 7:848b, 849a). This is a new translation based on the Latin and in agreement with the Russian translation. The translation in the ANF is significantly different, as St. Hilarion will proceed to discuss; it reads, "For it is a matter of necessity that every Church should agree with this Church, on account of its pre-eminent authority, that is, the faithful everywhere, inasmuch as the apostolical tradition has been preserved continuously by those [faithful men] who exist everywhere."

The latter words of Tertullian and St. Irenaeus which we have cited deserve special attention. A proper understanding of them may still better highlight the general nature of the doctrine concerning the Church as the custodian of the truth, whereas a tendential interpretation of them may greatly distort their nature. Roman Catholic theologians desire to see the words cited as evidence that St. Irenaeus of Lyons taught **the supremacy and infallibility of the Roman Church**: the Roman Church alone and in isolation is the custodian of the truth, and the entire ecumenical Church must agree with the latter.

Let us first analyze the words of St. Irenaeus as briefly as possible.[745]

The words cited above survive only in the Latin translation, and read as follows: "Ad hanc enim Ecclesiam propter potiorem principalitatem necesse est omnem convenire Ecclesiam, hoc est eos qui sunt undique fideles, in qua semper ab his, qui sunt undique, conservata est ea quae est ab apostolis Traditio." Confessional differences raise disputes concerning how to understand this passage, and these

---

745 An entire body of literature has developed around this question. But even in Russian scholarly literature this question has been parsed with nearly full sufficiency. See [the work] by Archimandrite Sylvester, *The Doctrine Concerning the Church* ["Учение о Церкви"], 184–187, note; the work by Archimandrite (Archbishop) Nikanor, *An Analysis of the Roman Teaching Concerning Apparent (Papal) Supremacy in the Church* ["Разбор римского учения о видимом (папском) главенстве в Церкви"], 2nd ed. (Kazan: 1871), 171–188. Of particular [importance] is the brochure of Prof. F.A. Kurganov, "Did St. Irenaeus, Bishop of Lyons, Attest to the Primacy and Infallible Teachership of the Roman Church, and Particularly of its Pontiff?" ["Свидетельствовал ли св. Ириней, епископ Лионский, о приматстве и непогрешимом учительстве Римской Церкви, в частности—ее первосвященникеа?"] (Kazan: 1893). Here the entire body of literature on the matter is listed (naturally, through 1893). Cf. F.X. Funk, *Der Primat der römischen Kirche nach Ignatius und Irenäus.* Kirchengeschichtliche Abhandlungen und Untersuchungen, 1-er Band. (Paderborn: 1897), 14, Anm. See also [the work by] H. Boehmer, "Zu dem Zeugnisse des Irenäus von dem Ansehen der römischen Kirche," *Zeitschrift für die neutestamentliche Wissenschaft und die Kunde des Urchristentums*, herausgeg. von E. Preuschen (1906), 193–201. The latest foreign literature is listed by Dr. Otto Bardenhewer. See *Patrologie*, 3-te Aufl. (Freiburg im Breisgau: 1910), 99.

disputes predominantly hinge on the word *convenire*.[746] Scholars of a strictly Catholic school ordinarily supplement the word *convenire* so as to produce the following: "convenire et concordare in rebus fidei cum Ecclesia Romana."[747] Orthodox authors likewise translate *convenire* as "to agree."[748] There are no grounds, however, for imposing upon *convenire* a meaning which it cannot possibly have. *Convenire* means "to come together," "to assemble," and this is its meaning here also—all the more so since further on we find the word *undique*—"from everywhere," which specifically indicates space. *Undique* signifies the place from which all the faithful come together to the Roman Church: they come together from everywhere,[749] and thus the whole Church (*omnis Ecclesia*) assembles together.[750]

The reason or occasion for this assembly is indicated in the words *propter potiorem principalitatem*. *Principalitas* is sometimes under-

---

746 Funk, *Kirchengeschichtliche Abhandlungen und Untersuchungen* 1, 15.

747 "To agree and in matters of Faith with the Church of Rome." See *De Irenaei doctrina* 3.31, Migne (PG 7:278c). I. Schwane, *Dogmengeschichte der vornicäischen Zeit*, 468–469. Harnack, *Dogmengeschichte*[4] 1, 487, Anm. Cf. Prof. Kurganov in the brochure cited, 30–31. Note by Batiffol, *L'église naissante et le catholicisme*, 250. Harnack also supports a figurative understanding of the word *convenire* (*Dogmengeschichte*[4] 1, 487, Anm. 1). O. Bardenhewer, *Patrologie*[3], §32.3, 98: *convenire = übereinstimmen*.

748 Such is the [supposition] of Archpriest P. Preobrazhensky, translator of the works of St. Irenaeus into Russian (*Collected Works*, 222 [Rus. ed.]) and Archimandrite Nikanor (op. cit., 184–186).

749 *Convenire* is translated as "come together" by Prof. F. Kurganov (see the brochure cited, 27–30) and S. Sushkov (*Against the False Teaching on the Ecumenical Supremecy of the Roman Church* ["Против лжеучения о вселенском главенстве Римской Церкви"] (Saint Petersburg: 1891), 207, 210, 215–216. In the early 18th century Grabe wrote, "Intellegendum esse confluxum eorum, qui ab omni Ecclesia Romam mittebantur [We must understand the confluence of those who were being sent to Rome from the whole Church]" (Migne, PG 7:280c). Many Catholics likewise translate *convenire* via *zusammenkommen*, such as Funk (*Kirchengesch. Abh. Und Untersuch.* 1, 15–19). See also Kurganov, 22-23n30.1. H. Boehmer asserts that the word *convenire* can only mean "to agree" with regard to persons when followed by the preposition *cum*, not *ad*, as in the passage at hand (*Zeitschrift fur die neutestam. Wissenschaft* [1906], 196).

750 Incidentally, Batiffol considers *omnis ecclesia* a synonym for *unaquaeque ecclesia* [each Church] (*L'église naissante et le catholicisme*, 251n2).

stood to mean antiquity, which produces the following meaning:
the Roman Church is consulted regarding matters of faith because
it has greater antiquity (*potiorem principalitatem*).[751] To be sure, somewhat previously St. Irenaeus termed the Roman Church *antiquissima*, but here this is clearly a purely honorary epithet, since St.
Irenaeus naturally knew that it was not the Roman Church that was
antiquissima in the literal sense of the word: in the same third book
of *Against Heresies* St. Irenaeus says of the Church of Jerusalem that
from it the whole Church received its beginning, and hence it is the
metropolis of the citizens of the New Testament.[752] If the antiquity
of a Church were the sole and sufficient reason for the faithful from
everywhere to come together to it, their meeting place would indisputably have to be Jerusalem.[753] It must therefore be acknowledged
that although *potior principalitas* pertains specifically to the Roman
Church, and not to the city of Rome,[754] it signifies the privilege
that the Roman Church enjoys specifically as the Church of the
capital city. Rome was then the center of the world, and hence the
Roman Church naturally was a sort of meeting place for Christians
from every place.[755] The words that follow—"in qua semper ab his,

---

751 Archimandrite Nikanor, op. cit., 183; A. Ritsehl, *Die Entstehung der altkath.
Kirche*, 573–574: "Wegen des hervorragenden Alters." See also Chr. Wordsworth,
St. Hippolytus and the Church of Rome in the Earlier Part of the Third Century (London:
1853), 200n8. It is surmised that the Latin translator used the word *principalitas* to
render the Greek words πρωτεῖον, πρωτεία [first place], ἀρχαιότης [antiquity],
αὐθεντία [authority], and the word *potiorem* (or *potentiorem*) to render τὸ ἐξαίρετον,
τὸ ὑπέρτερον. See Funk, 14 (Migne, PG 7:278d). But naturally this back translation can be of no scholarly significance, since it is nothing more than than a con-
strual (see Kurganov, brochure cited, 24–26). The text of St. Irenaeus's writings
give no grounds for adopting either translation, since the Latin translator uses the
word *principalitas* to render various Greek words.

752 Irenaeus, *Against Heresies* 3.12.5 (PG 7:897b).

753 See Archimandrite Nikanor, op. cit., 188.

754 *De Irenaei doctrina* 3.34.2 (Migne, PG 7:281b); Kurganov, brochure cited,
28; note of Funk, *Kirchenegesch. Abh. Und Untersuch* 1, 20–21.

755 Cf. Kurganov, brochure cited, from 33 on. Harnack holds that *necesse est*
= "es kann nicht anders sein" (*Dogmengeschichte*[4] 1, 487, Anm. 1). Boehmer understands *principalitas* to mean apostolic institution, and *potentior* to indicate the
institution of the Roman Church by two apostles, which Tertullian also sees as its

qui sunt undique, conservata est ea quae ab apostolis traditio [in which [Church] the Tradition from the apostles has always been preserved by those [faithful] who exist from everywhere]"—have customarily been applied to the Roman Church, so that this passage took on the following meaning: in the Roman Church the apostolic tradition was preserved by the faithful of the whole world, who when necessary would converge in Rome as the capital city. The Roman Church was under the constant supervision of all the other Churches, which themselves verified their doctrine in Rome, where the whole Ecumenical Church was in a way represented.[756] Today, however, even most Catholic scholars have begun applying *in qua* (etc.) to *omnis ecclesia*,[757] with some even surmising the second *qui sunt undique* to be an error of the copyist, who substituted these words for others that designated the bishops, in which case the authentic reading would have been as follows: "Ab his, qui (praesunt ecclesiis?) conservata est ... traditio,"[758] or "ab his qui successionem habent ab apostolis."[759] If we accept this, the meaning of the pas-

---

advantage (*Prescription Against Heretics* 36; *Against Marcion* 4.5; *Zeitschr. Für die neutestamentliche Wissenschaft* [1906], 198). Beuzart, while holding that *potentiorem principalitatem* cannot be replaced with the concept of primacy, nevertheless notes that in any case by these words Irenaeus wishes "assigner le premier rang" (*Essai sur la théologie d'Irénée*, 156), "une situation prééminente" (174), to the Roman Church and its bishop. In the opinion of O. Bardenhewer, *propter potiorem principalitatem* = "ihrer höheren Autorität wegen" (*Patrologie* §32.3, 98).

756 See Kurganov, brochure cited, 39, 43–44. Vgl. Harnack, *Dogmengeschichte* 1, 487, Anm. 1.

757 Harnack, "Das Zeugniss des Irenäus über das Ansehen der römischen Kirche," *Sitzungsberichten der Königlich-preussischen Akademie der Wissenschaften zu Berlin* (1893). Vgl. *Dogmengeschichte* 1, 487, Anm. 1. Funk, *Kirchengesch. Abhandlungen.* 1, 12 ff. Cf. Batiffol, *L'église naissante et le catholicisme*,[3] 251.

758 Dom Morin, "Une erreur de copiste dans le texte d'Irénée sur l'eglise romaine," *Revue bénédictine*, 25 (1908): 515–520. Batiffol, *L'église naissante et le catholicisme*,[3] 251.

759 "The tradition... was preserved by them who (preside over the Churches?)." Boehmer, *Zeitschrift für die neutestamentliche Wissenschaft*, 200–201. Incidentally, Boehmer is inclined to think that these words pertain to *ad hanc ecclesiam*. Consequently, here we have an indication of the Roman bishops, whose succession is listed in the very next paragraph.

sage in question becomes the following: the apostolic Tradition is preserved in the whole Church (by the bishops?),[760] but from every Church (the Christians) continually travel to the Church of Rome as being that of the capital.

Let us now put the passage we have analyzed into context. The holy father has just said that all who desire to see the truth in every Church may learn (*in omni Ecclesia adest respicere*) the Tradition of the apostles, which is revealed throughout the world, and we can list the bishops appointed by the apostles in the Churches, and their successors (*successores*) down to our day. But since it would be very lengthy (*valde longum*) to enumerate the succession of all the Churches, St. Irenaeus decides to confine himself to the tradition that the very great, very ancient, and universally known Church of Rome had from the apostles.[761] As though justifying his choice of example, St. Irenaeus goes on to say that to this Church (*ad hanc enim*) the faithful from everywhere come together as to the capital Church. It is perfectly clear that here St. Irenaeus is merely citing the Roman Church by way of example, the more so since here he also references Smyrna and Ephesus.[762] Naturally, this example was not selected arbitrarily: the Roman Church had to be cited,[763] but for purely historical rather than dogmatic reasons, since at that time, as the capital Church, it was the most well known (*omnibus cognita*), and by natural necessity[764] all the Churches of the known world at that time had dealings with it. Consequently, there are no grounds for interpreting the current passage from St. Irenaeus in the sense that the Church of Rome is acknowledged to be the supreme mother Church.[765] Regarding the Roman Church, from St. Irenaeus's

---

760 "By them who have succession from the apostles." This produces a complete parallel to *Against Heresies* 4.26.2 (PG 7:1053c–1054a).

761 Irenaeus, *Against Heresies* 3.3.1–2 (ANF 1:415; PG 7:848a, b).

762 Vgl. Seeberg, *Studien zur Geschichte des Begriffs der Kirche*, 17–18.

763 Harnack, *Dogmengeschichte* 1, 487.

764 Surmising that in the Latin text *necesse est* replaces the Greek ἀνάγκη, it is asserted that *necesse est* specifically signifies natural necessity, not dogmatic or moral necessity. Vgl. Wordsworth, *St. Hippolytus and the Church of Rome*, 202–204.

765 Vgl. Harnack, *Sitzungsberichten…* (1893), 948; Funk, *Kirchengeschichtliche Ab-*

words we can say only that it is *inter pares,* no more,[766] and *prima* according to its situation in the empire's capital (and while Rome remains the capital of the world).

According to the exhortation of St. Irenaeus, if any confusion arises regarding any matter, one must go not necessarily to Rome, but to the apostolic Churches in general. Consequently, 3.3.2 can hardly be considered even a parallel to 3.4.1: in the former instance *convenire* is contingent upon historical reasons, while in the second *decurrere* is contingent on reasons of dogma.[767]

While not acknowledging the Roman Church to have any particular infallibility, immediately after listing the Roman bishops St. Irenaeus says that life-giving faith has been preserved from the apostles in the Church (*in Ecclesia*)—that is, in the whole ecumenical Church. And it is perfectly logical that the church historian Eusebius, for whom episcopal succession had such importance,[768] presents lists of the bishops of various Churches, taking from Irenaeus only the lists of the Roman bishops, and omitting the words where Irenaeus explains why he confines himself to lists of the bishops of the Roman Church alone.

Funk proposes that the word *convenire* and the entire passage in question be understood in light of church history. He points out that immediately after the passage under comment St. Irenaeus recalls the journey of St. Polycarp of Smyrna to Rome.[769] But one cannot

---

handlungen und Untersuch 1, 21.

766 Together with Harnack, and contrary to Funk. See Funk, *Kirchengeschichtliche Abhandlungen und Untersuch* 1, 22–23.

767 Batiffol is therefore incorrect when in *convenire ad* he sees "l' idée d'une démarche active à la recherche de la vérité" (*L'église naissante et le catholicisme,* 250). One could agree with Batiffol if he did not place dogmatic significance in his words. Historically, however, in the second century *démarche active à la recherche de la vérité* could lead to Rome, where the self-identification of the ecumenical Church was as though more fully expressed, as at the center of the world. Here there was a kind of continual common Council. See Kurganov, brochure cited, 51.

768 Eusebius, *Church History* 1.1.1.4 (GrchSch 9.1:6.1, 8.14–17). Concerning this see Franz Overbeck, *Die Bischofsliaten und die apostolische Vachfolge in der Kirchengeschichte des Eusebius* (Basel: 1898), 8 ff.

769 Funk, *Kirchengeschichtliche Abhandlungen und Untersuch* 1, 18.

help but notice that in this instance the reference to Polycarp is a
most unfortunate one for defenders of the Roman Catholic understanding of St. Irenaeus's teaching. St. Irenaeus depicts Polycarp of
Smyrna as the most reliable of witnesses to the apostolic Tradition.
Here also St. Irenaeus writes of Polycarp: "He it was who, coming
to Rome in the time of Anicetus caused many to turn away from
the aforesaid heretics to the Church of God, proclaiming that he
had received this one and sole truth from the apostles,—that, namely, which is handed down by the Church."[770] In Rome Polycarp was
not an obedient disciple of the Roman bishop, but a person who by
his own authority, as it were, sanctioned the doctrine of the Roman
Church, teaching and converting heretics. According to the report
of Eusebius, Polycarp came to Rome "and had a conference with
Anicetus on a question concerning the day of the paschal feast."[771]
The details of this conference emerge from a fragment of a letter
from Irenaeus to the Roman bishop Victor, which states: "Anicetus
[could not] persuade Polycarp to forego the observance [in his own
way], inasmuch as these things had been always [so] observed by
John the disciple of our Lord, and by other apostles with whom
he had been conversant."[772] Where here are the grounds for interpreting *convenire* to mean agreeing, or even to mean verifying one's
doctrine? Finally, the whole account of the disputes concerning the
time of the celebration of Pascha, in which St. Irenaeus likewise
took part, attest with utter clarity that the latter did not consider the
Roman bishop alone to be the infallible custodian of the truth.[773]
This custodian, St. Irenaeus teaches, can only be the entire Ecumenical Church.

---

770 Irenaeus, *Against Heresies* 3.3.4 (ANF 1:416; PG 852b–853a).

771 Eusebius, *Church History* 4.14.1 (GrchSch. 9.1:332.3–6).

772 Irenaeus, *Fragments* 3 (ANF 1:569; PG 7:1229b, 1232a). Eusebius, *Church History* 5.24.16 (GrchSch. 9.1:496.10–13).

773 See Eusebius, *Church History* 5.23–24. The negative effect of these disputes for the doctrine of the primacy of the Roman bishop is pointed out by Friedrich Iaskowski ("Die Kirchengeschichte des Eusebius von Cäsarea und der Primat," *Revue internationale de théologie* [1909]: 345–348).

Catholic theologians sometimes attempt to ascribe the idea of the primacy of the Roman Church to Tertullian also, based on his words cited above. In listing the apostolic Churches in which one may learn the true Tradition, Tertullian naturally specifies the Church of Rome as well, and calls it "happy" because in her the apostles Peter, Paul, and John preached, and bore witness to their teaching even to the shedding of their blood.[774] In any case, it is perfectly clear that the grounds for citing Tertullian's words in support of the primacy of the Roman Church is far too paltry. Even Catholic scholars admit that Tertullian sets the Roman Church not above the other apostolic Churches, but rather on the same level with them. In terms of doctrine, in Tertullian's view the Churches of Corinth, Phillipi, or Thessalonika are just as independent as Ephesus or Rome.[775] Concerning the Roman Church Tertullian says, "Since ... you are close upon (*adjaces*) Italy, you have Rome,"[776] or, "Let us see ... what utterance also the Romans give, so very near (to the apostles), to whom Peter and Paul conjointly bequeathed the gospel."[777] Clearly, to the mind of Tertullian, the Roman Church can only have a certain degree of doctrinal authority for those non-apostolic Churches nearest her, such as that of Africa. "The Roman Church is the same kind of nearest available authority for the Italian or the inhabitants of North Africa as is Corinth or Phillipi for the inhabitants of Achaea, Macedonia, or Asia Minor."[778] Any primacy of the Roman Church is simply out of the question.[779]

---

774 Tertullian, *The Prescription Against Heretics* 36 (ANF 3:260; PL 2:59a). *Against Marcion* 4.5 (CSEL 47:430.16–18). For an analysis of Catholic citations of Tertullian, see Archimandrite Nikanor, op. cit. 189–201, 201–206; Michaud, "L'ecclésiologie de Tertullien," 345–348.

775 Adam, *Der Kirchenbegriff Tertullians,* 45–47. Adam sees this as a manifestation of the overarching shortcoming in the entire system of Tertullian—a one-sided understanding of the teachership of the bishop in the sense of preserving the doctrine handed down to him while remaining silent on credal definition.

776 Tertullian, *Prescription Against Heresies* 36 (ANF 3:260; PL 2:59a).

777 Tertullian, *Against Marcion* 4.5 (ANF 3:350; CSEL 47.430.14, 16–18).

778 Archim. Nikanor, op. cit., 202–203.

779 While admitting that Tertullian says nothing of the primacy of the Roman Church, Catholic authors nevertheless imply in passing that the idea of the

While rejecting all tendential Catholic citations of the writings of St. Irenaeus and Tertullian as distorting the teaching of these ancient writers concerning the Church, we must reiterate our conclusion from an analysis of their ecclesiology. Unbroken succession of the episcopacy is cited as the cause of the inviolate preservation of apostolic doctrine in the Church, and for this reason all individual Churches are in agreement with each other. **The ecumenical mind of the Church, guided by the Holy Spirit, is itself the sole expression of the truth of Christ.**

Thus, the Church is the custodian of the truth. To be outside the Church is to be outside the truth.[780] St. Irenaeus and Tertullian envision and condemn heresy first and foremost specifically as false doctrine, as a decimation of the truth. Heresies defile by fornication the virginal doctrine conveyed by Christ,[781] and by corrupting doctrine they inflict harm upon the Church.[782] Heresy is a choice,

---

infallibility of "happy Rome" is at least not foreign to Tertullian. See Adam, op. cit., 46, and Adhémar d'Alès, *La théologie de Tertullien*, 216. Catholic authors more insistently allege that Tertullian speaks of the preeminence of the apostle Peter, the founder of the Roman Church (in particular see Adhémar d'Alès, op. cit., 216–218; cf. Batiffol, *L'église naissante et le catholicisme*, 333n1; Turmel, *Tertullien*, 281). Even Adam, however, acknowledges that Tertullian bases the apostolic dignity of the Roman Church on the preaching and suffering of three apostles, and not of Peter alone (op. cit., 46). It is revealing that Tertullian never mentions the Roman Church as having been founded by the apostle Peter alone—in general a foreign concept for the early Church. See the article cited by Iaskowski, *Revue internationale de théologie* (1909): 335–336. Cf. final conclusion of Michaud: "La doctrine romaine sur le pape comme fondemant infaillible de l'église et comme dépositaire de l' autorité divine et absolue du Christ est fausse et antichrétienne" (*Revue internationale de théologie* [1905]: 270).

780 Irenaeus, *Against Heresies* 4.33.7: "Qui sunt extra veritatem, id est extra Ecclesiam" (ANF 1:508; PG 7:1076b–c).

781 Tertullian, *Prescription Against Heretics* 44: "Quid ergo dicent, qui illam stupraverint adulterio haeretico, virginem traditam a Christo? [What, then, will they say who shall have defiled it, even the virgin which Christ committed to them with the adultery of heretics?]" (PL 2:72a).

782 Tertullian, *The Prescription Against Heretics* 4: "Nunc sunt haereses, non minus doctrinarum perversitate Ecclesiam lacessantes [Heresies, at the present time, will no less rend the church by their perversion of doctrine]" (PL 2:18b). Cf. 42: "de veritatis destructione [destruction of the truth]" (PL 2:69b).

which is the meaning of the Greek word αἵρεσις. The effect of heresy is specifically perversion of the faith (*adulterae doctrinae*), and by perversion of the faith the apostle Paul specifically means heresies.[783] Heresy is doctrine contaminated with poison.[784] "All [heretics] have fallen from the truth. And the heretics ... bring strange fire to the altar of God. ... [They] rise up (*exsurgunt*) in opposition to the truth, and exhort others against the Church of God."[785] They "are neither nourished into life from the mother's breasts, nor do they enjoy that most limpid fountain which issues from the body of Christ; but they dig for themselves broken cisterns out of earthly trenches, and drink putrid water out of the mire, fleeing from the faith of the Church lest they be convicted; and rejecting the Spirit, that they may not be instructed. Alienated thus from the truth, they do deservedly wallow in all error, tossed to and fro by it, thinking differently in regard to the same things at different times, and never attaining to a well-grounded knowledge (*sententiam stabilitam*), being more anxious to be sophists of words than disciples of the truth."[786]

Consequently, the church writers strictly condemn heresies and heretics, "who give rise to schisms, who are destitute of the love of God (κένους ὄντας τοῦ Θεοῦ ἀγάπης), and who look to their own special advantage rather than to the unity of the Church; and who for trifling reasons, or any kind of reason which occurs to them, cut

---

783 Tertullian, *The Prescription Against Heretics* 6: "Sed et in omni pene epistola de adulterinis doctrinis fugiendis inculcans, haereses taxat: quorum opera sunt adulterae doctrinae [Indeed, in almost every epistle, when enjoining on us (the duty) of avoiding false doctrines, he sharply condemns heresies. Of these the practical effects are false doctrines]" (PL 2:20b). Cf. Tertullian, *The Prescription Against Heretics* 3.3.4 (PG 7:854a).

784 Tertullian, *On Baptism* 1: "venenatissima doctrina [most venomous doctrine]" (CSEL 20.1:201.9).

785 Irenaeus, *Against Heresies* 4.26.2 (ANF 1:497; PG 7:1054a).

786 Irenaeus, *Against Heresies* 3.24.1–2 (ANF 1:458; PG 7:966c–967a). K. Kellner, translator of the works of Tertullian into German, says of him that, based on his linguistic usage, heresy differs from the Church not in doctrine, but in organization. See *Terltullians sämtliche Werke*, Bd. 2 (Köln: 1882), 9. But naturally those who assert the opposite are more correct. See Adam, *Der Kirchenbegriff Tertullians*, 24, Vgl.: 24, Anm. 2; Thomasius, *Die Dogmengeschichte* 1, 115; Harnack, *Dogmengeschichte*⁴ 1, 407–408.

in pieces and divide the great and glorious body of Christ, and so far as in them lies, [positively] destroy it,—men who prate of peace while they give rise to war, and do in truth strain out a gnat, but swallow a camel [see Mt. 23:24]. For no reformation of so great importance (κατόρθωσις—*correctio*) can be effected by them, as will compensate for the mischief arising from their schism."[787] "The heretics … shall be burned up by the fire from heaven, as were Nadab and Abiud. But such as rise up in opposition to the truth, and exhort others against the Church of God, [shall] remain among those in hell (*apud inferos*), being swallowed up by an earthquake, even as those who were with Chore, Dathan, and Abiron. But those who cleave asunder, and separate the unity of the Church, [shall] receive from God the same punishment as Jeroboam did."[788] The heretics are not Christians: they did not receive from Christ the doctrine that they pursue by choice, from which pursuit they received the name of heretics.[789] Christians and heretics do not have one God and one Christ.[790] The heretics are occupied less with converting the heathen than with corrupting the members of the Church: they tear down all that is of the Church so as to build what is their own.[791] For this reason St. Irenaeus exhorts people to flee heretical doctrines, and to watch carefully lest they suffer harm from them.[792] He cites the example of how John, the disciple of the Lord, fled from the bath in Ephesus when he saw Cerinthus, and how Polycarp called Marcion the first-born of Satan. "Such was the horror (εὐλάβεια)

---

787 Irenaeus, *Against Heresies* 4.33.7 (ANF 1:508; PG 7:1076a–b).

788 Irenaeus, *Against Heresies* 4.26.2 (ANF 1:497; PG 7:1054a).

789 Tertullian, *The Prescription Against Heretics* 37: "Si enim haeretici sunt, christiani esse non possunt, non a Christo habendo, quod, de sua electione sectati, haereticorum nomine admittunt. Ita non Christiani" (ANF 3:261; PL 2:61b). Cf. 16: "non est christianus" (Ibid., PL 2:34b).

790 Tertullian, *On Baptism* 15: "Non idem deus est nobis et illis, nec unus Christus, id est idem [they and we have not the same God, nor one—that is, the same—Christ]" (CSEL 20.1:214.2–3).

791 Tertullian, *The Prescription Against Heretics* 42: "Hoc sit negotium illis, non ethnicos convertendi sed nostros evertendi. Nostra suffodiunt, ut sua aedificent" (PL 2:69a–b).

792 Irenaeus, *Against Heresies* 5.20.2 (PG 7:1178a).

which the apostles and their disciples had against holding even verbal communication with any corrupters (παραχαρασσόντων) of the truth."[793] Tertullian fancies that at the Last Judgment also the Lord will say to the faithful, "I forbade you to listen to heretics."[794]

Without a doubt, the chief point in the foregoing teachings of St. Irenaeus and Tertullian concerning the Church is their clearly and definitively expressed view of Tradition, successively preserved in the Church from the apostles on, as the constant criterion of truth. In opposition to Gnostic individualism they insistently promoted the authority of the Church. **It is the whole Church alone, and not the individual, that is the bearer of the truth.**[795] But how does this teaching relate to the earliest elucidation of the idea of the Church? The Church, naturally, has always lived by Tradition, for each individual person lives by tradition, and every society must necessarily live by tradition.[796] There is no need to speak of the early history of Tradition; the question must be **whether in the early period there was a scholarly and theological principle of Tradition**. Was the very principle of tradition first established by St. Irenaeus in his polemics with gnosis, or was it a long-existent and previously known principle, which was merely expressed more precisely and in greater detail in accordance with the needs of the day? At the same time, was the doctrine concerning the Church as the custodian of the truth a late second-century novelty in church literature, or was this too an intrinsic, fully realized conviction of Christians? The answer to these questions is all the more essential in that some are inclined to see the principle of tradition specifically as a novelty, introduced into church theology merely in opposition to the Gnostic doctrine of a secret tradition, and thereby they make the Gnostics the first to establish the principle of tradition. Ritschl considers baseless the presumption that the

---

793 Irenaeus, *Against Heresies* 3.3.4 (ANF 1:416; PG 7:853–854).

794 Tertullian, *The Prescription Against Heretics* 44: "Prohibueram vos aurem accommodare haereticis" (PL 2:73a).

795 Cf. remark by Bardenhewer (*Patrologie*[3], §50.4, 161).

796 See the reasonable observation of Ritschl in *Die Entstehung der altkath. Kirche*, 340).

apostles themselves established the principle of a tradition that was
to be used to understand their own writings.[797] Naturally, the apostles could not have dictated this, since in their teaching they made
no distinction between oral and written teaching. The apostle Paul
terms "tradition" all that he taught the Christians. "Brethren, stand
fast, and hold the traditions (τὰς παραδόσεις) which ye have been
taught, whether by word, or our epistle" (2 Thess. 2:15), writes the
apostle Paul. The Church does not view oral and written Tradition
as absolutely separate and distinct from one another. Only after the
apostles' death did it become possible to delineate written and oral
Tradition; but without a doubt **the authority of the Church** as
the custodian of Tradition in general was already clearly defined by
the apostles themselves.[798] The important significance of Tradition
from a fundamental standpoint is naturally realized when a blatant
distortion of that Tradition occurs. We have seen that the doctrine
concerning church Tradition was expressed by church writers specifically in combating the second-century Gnosticism that perverted apostolic Tradition. But is Gnosticism really the first error with
which the Church had to contend? The fight against heresies was
begun by the apostle Paul himself. In former times some scholars
did not recognize that there were Gnostics in the age of the apostles. Ritschl, for example, stated that apostolic-era Gnosticism is a
hypothesis invented to explain the pastoral epistles, and that it contradicts all historical data.[799] Gnosis, they say, could not have existed
prior to the Gnostics, and we know that the Gnostics appeared in
the second century.[800] But today the question of whether Gnosti-

---

797 Ritschl, *Die Entstchung der altkath. Kirche*, 339, 340.

798 "Authorities are given in the very concept of the Church" (Harnack, *Entstehung und Entwickelung der Kirchenverfassung und des Kirchenrechts*, 13 ff.).

799 Ritschl, *Die Entstchung der altkath. Kirche*, 342.

800 All these opinions are presented by D. Bogdashevsky in *The False Teachers
Denounced in the First Epistle of the Apostle John* ["Лжеучители, обличаемые в Пер-
вом послании апостола Иоанна"] (Kiev: 1890), 113–114. See also Alexander
Klitin, *The Authenticity of the Epistles of the Holy Apostle Paul to Timothy and Titus*
["Подлинность посланий святого апостола Павла к Тимофею и Титу"]
(Kiev: 1887), from 152 on.

cism existed in apostolic times may be held to have been answered in the affirmative.[801]

The historical data that Ritschl cites and which, in his opinion, contradict the hypothesis of apostolic-era Gnosticism,[802] pertain to the appearance of renowned Gnostic false teachers and entire schools in the second century;[803] but like any phenomenon Gnosis developed gradually, and the degree to which it came to flourish in the second century necessarily presupposes a preliminary stage in its development.[804] Indeed, indications of Gnosticism may be found

---

801   See the above cited studies by D.I. Bogdashevsky and A. Klitin. Also cf. Hieromonk (bishop) Evdokim, *The Holy Apostle and Evangelist John the Theologian* ["Святой апостол и евангелист Иоанн Богослов"] (Sergiev Posad: 1898), 249–253. See also V.N. Myshtsyn, *The Organization of the Christian Church* ["Устройство христианской Церкви"], 219–221; N. Sagard, *The First General Epistle of the Holy Apostle and Evangelist John the Theologian* ["Первое соборное послание святого апостола и евангелиста Иоанна Богослова"] (Poltava: 1903), from 142 on. Cf. the exegetical article by Prof. D.I. Bogdashevsky in *Works of the Kiev Theological Seminary* [ТКДА] (1904), vol. 2, 310–314; Harnack, *Dogmengeschichte*[4] 1, 262 ff., *Die Mission und Ausbreitung des Christentums*[2] 1, 23–30; Thomasius, *Die Dogmengeschichte* 1, 70 ff.; Knopf, *Das nachapostolische Zeitalter*, 290 ff., 339; Batiffol, *L'église naissante et le catholicisme*, 118n2.

802   Ritschl, *Die Entstehung der altkath. Kirche*, 342, Anm. 1.

803   The testimony of Clement of Alexandria which Ritschl cites (*Stromata* 7.17:106.4–107.1 [GrchSch. 17:75–76]) concerning the appearance of "inventors of heresies about the time of the reign of Hadrian" pertains to the specific heresies of Vasilidas, Valentinus, and Marcion. Hegesippus, however, explicitly attests to the existence of Gnostic errors in apostolic times: "The Church ... remained a pure and uncorrupted virgin, since, if there were any that attempted to corrupt the sound norm of the preaching of salvation, they lay until then concealed in obscure darkness (ἐν ἀδήλῳ τοῦ σκότους). But when the sacred college of apostles had suffered death in various forms, and the generation of those that had been deemed worthy to hear the inspired wisdom with their own ears had passed away, then the league of godless error took its rise as a result of the folly of heretical teachers, who, because none of the apostles was still living, attempted henceforth, with a bold face (γυμνῇ κεφαλῇ), to proclaim, in opposition to the preaching of the truth, the 'knowledge which is falsely so-called'" (Eusebius, *Church History* 3.32.7–8 [NPNF[2] 1:164; GrchSch 9.1:270.7–18]).

804   Harnack, *Dogmengeschichte*[4] 1, 262: "Gnosticismus hat Vorstufen gehabt." Bogdashevsky, 115–116; Klitin, 133–135; Hieromonk Evdokim, op. cit., 252.

in many epistles of the apostle Paul—to the Corinthians,[805] the Colossians,[806] the Ephesians,[807] and especially the pastoral epistles.[808] The false teachers spread their teaching, distorting the teaching of Christ (καπηλεύοντες τὸν λόγον τοῦ Θεοῦ).[809] Hence, in the fight against that same Gnosticism **the principle of Tradition and the authority of the Church was already established in apostolic times.**[810]

How are the faithful to guard themselves against error? The apostle Paul gives a single answer: they are to hold fast to the teaching delivered to them. This answer appears identically throughout all his epistles. He exhorts the Thessalonians to hold fast to the Traditions,[811] to "withdraw ... from every brother that walketh disorderly (ἀτάκτως), and not after the tradition which he received of us (μὴ κατὰ τὴν παράδοσιν ἣν παρελάβετε παρ᾽ ἡμῶν)" (2 Thess. 3:6). [He] praises the Corinthians for holding to the Tradition[812] as he delivered it to them (καθὼς παρέδωκα ἡμῖν τὰς παραδόσεις κατέχετε) (1 Cor. 11:2). [He] exhorts the Philippians to do "those things, which ye have learned, and received, and heard, and seen" (Phil. 4:9).[813] He entreats the Romans to beware of "them which cause divisions and offenses contrary to the doctrine (παρὰ τὴν διδαχήν) which ye have learned" (Rom. 16:17).[814] And then there is

805 See 1 Cor. 1:18–31; 6:12; 8:1, 4–13; 5:1–5.

806 See Col. 2, 8, 18, 21, 23.

807 See Eph. 4:14; 1:8–9, 12–18; 3:2–3.

808 See 1 Tim. 1:4–16; 6:20; 6:4. 2 Tim. 2:23. Tit. 1:10, 11, 14, 15; 3:9; and many others. Data on the Gnosis that the apostle Paul denounced have been compiled by Bogdashevsky, 144–150.

809 2 Cor. 2:17.

810 Cf. Knopf, *Das nachapostolische Zeitalter*, 395.

811 Cf. 2 Thess. 2:15: "κρατεῖτε τὰς παραδόσεις [hold the traditions]." Cf. 1 Thess. 4:1.

812 In the Russian source, as in the Greek, the word rendered "ordinances" in KJV is the same as that rendered "tradition" elsewhere. *–Trans.*

813 See Col. 2:7: "βεβαιούμενοι τῇ πίστει καθὼς ἐδιδάχθητε [stablished in the faith, as ye have been taught]." Cf. 1:7.

814 See Rom. 6:17: "εἰς ὃν παρεδόθητε τύπον διδαχῆς [that form of teaching

the most expressive passage from the epistle to the Galatians: "But though we, or an angel from heaven, preach any other gospel unto you than that which we have preached unto you, let him be accursed. As we said before, so say I now again, if any man preach any other gospel unto you than that ye have received, let him be accursed" (Gal. 1:8–9).[815] It is quite clear that here the criterion for a dissenting view cannot be considered the writings of the apostle, but only Tradition in the broad sense of the word. This, quite obviously, is the living self-identification of the Church, the possessor and custodian of apostolic truth. This Tradition is obligatory. Disagreement with it is a sign of fallacy. **This principle of Tradition was positively established in the earliest epistles of the apostle Paul.**[816] But the clearest and most detailed teaching regarding tradition is set forth by the apostle Paul in the epistles of the final period of his life—the pastoral epistles. The holy apostle knew that the time of his departure was approaching: he had finished his course, and a crown of righteousness was prepared for him (see 2 Tim. 4:7).[817] He had traversed the earth end to end, preaching the Gospel and founding many Churches. And when at the sunset of his life he gazed upon his work, involuntarily his thoughts turned to the future, and trepidation crept into the heart of the apostle to the gentiles. The events of the apostle's own life convinced him that after his death cruel times would follow: "in latter times" many would "depart from the faith, giving heed to seducing spirits, and doctrines of devils; speaking lies in hypocrisy; having their conscience seared with a hot iron" (1 Tim. 4:1–2).[818] All that Hegesippus says concerning the post-apostolic times[819] was foreseen by the holy apostle. And so in the epistles to Timothy and to Titus we see the apostles' concern for the future. He continually repeats his exhortation and

whereunto ye were delivered {ASV}]."

815 See 2 Jn. 1:10.

816 In the late fifties apostolic Tradition (*paradosis*) was recognized as an authority. See Loofs, *Leitfaden der Dogmengeschichte*[4] §11.6, 78.

817 See 2 Tim. 4:6–8.

818 See 2 Pet. 2:1–3.

819 Eusebius, op. cit. 3.32.8 (GrchSch. 9.1:270.11–18).

admonition to hold fast unswervingly to the truth[820] and to turn
away from false teachings.[821] The apostle reminds Timothy how he
besought him "to abide still at Ephesus," when he "went into Macedonia," and to "charge some that they teach no other doctrine (μὴ
ἑτεροδιδασκαλεῖν), neither give heed to fables and endless genealo-
gies" (1 Tim. 1:3–4), and exhorts him to "lay hold on eternal life,"
to profess "a good profession (καλὴν ὁμολογίαν) before many witnesses, and to "keep this commandment without spot, unrebukable,
until the appearing of our Lord Jesus Christ" (1 Tim. 6:12, 14);
to continue "in the things which thou hast learned and hast been
assured of (ἐν οἷς ἔμαθες καὶ ἐπιστώθης)" (2 Tim. 3:14). The apostle commands Titus likewise to speak "the things which become
sound doctrine (ἃ πρέπει τῇ ὑγιαινούσῃ διδασκαλίᾳ)," "in doctrine
shewing uncorruptedness" and "sincerity" (Tit. 2:1, 7). The degree
of the apostle's concern and to which preserving doctrine inviolate
was continually on his mind may be seen from how at the end of the
first epistle to Timothy he exclaims, "O Timothy, keep that which
is committed to thy trust [παρακαταθήκην], avoiding profane and
vain babblings, and oppositions of science falsely so called" (1 Tim.
6:20).[822] To Timothy again the apostle writes, "The things that thou
hast heard of me among many witnesses, the same commit thou
(παράθου) to faithful men, who shall be able to teach others also"
(2 Tim. 2:2). The apostle likewise enjoins the more reliable of the
faithful to guard the truth inviolate. Men may teach, if they are
able; the apostle forbids only women to teach.[823] "The church of
the living God, the pillar and ground of the truth" (1 Tim. 3:15)—

---

820 See 1 Tim. 1:18–20; 3:15; 4:11-16; 6:12, 14, 20; 2 Tim. 1:6, 8, 13; 2:2, 15;
3:14; 4:2, 5; Tit. 1:9; 2:1, 7–8, 15.

821 See 1 Tim. 1:3–4, 4:7; 6:3–5, 6, 20; 2 Tim. 2:14, 16, 23–26; 3:5; Tit.
1:10–11, 13–14; 3:10.

822 "Let it not suffer diminution. It is not thy own. Thou art intrusted with
the property of another, do not lessen it" (John Chrysostom, *Homilies on 1 Timothy*
18 [NPNF¹ 1:472]).

823 See 1 Tim. 2:12–15. In Tit. 2:3, "teachers of good things"
(καλοδιδασκάλους) naturally refers to worldly teaching; the subjects of this teaching are then listed in the two verses that follow.

that is, truth is upheld, as it were, by the self-identification of the entire Church, guarded by the Holy Spirit.[824]

Thus, the principle of the tradition and **authority of the Church** were already clearly and definitively **established by the apostle Paul.**[825] Regarding the time that followed, it should first of all be noted that no psychology would allow for the supposition that the successors of the apostles could have severed ties with them. This supposition is the more strange in that for a long time the Church, in the absence of a canon of sacred books, lived by Tradition exclusively. Without paper or ink the ancient Tradition was preserved.[826] There was no thoroughly developed theological scholarly concept of Tradition, or rather we do not find it in church literature prior to the mid-second century; but the moment the opportunity arose church writers made mention of Tradition and of the authority of the Church. And this we encounter from the very outset of Christian literature.[827] For example, the Didache contains this injunction: "You must not forsake (μὴ ἐγκαταλίπῃς) 'the Lord's commandments,' but 'observe' the ones you have been given, 'neither adding nor subtracting (μήτε ἀφαιρῶν) anything.'"[828] According to the Didache, the community must test wandering teachers.

---

824 See 2 Tim. 1:14: "τὴν καλὴν παραθήκην φύλαξον διὰ Πνεύματος Ἁγίου τοῦ ἐνοικοῦντος ἐν ἡμῖν [That good thing which was committed unto thee keep by the Holy Ghost which dwelleth in us]."

825 "Although in church life the apostle Paul leaves considerable room for freedom and independent action on the part of the faithful, for manifestation of individual spiritual gifts, for revelation in the Spirit, nevertheless he is far from recognizing unlimited freedom and individualism in the realm of faith. He sets boundaries for them in beginnings of the church Tradition that is forming around him. ... This concept, of important significance in the history of the organization of the Church, as may be seen from the other pastoral epistles, is overlooked by many scholars, though it is already quite clearly expressed in the first epistles of the apostle Paul" (V.N. Myshtsyn, *The Organization of the Christian Church* ["Устройство христианской Церкви"], 97–98, 99). Cf. Batiffol, *L'église naissante et le catholicisme*, 118, 136–139.

826 Irenaeus, *Against Heresies* 3.4.2 (ANF 1:417; PG 7:855c).

827 Vgl. Harnack, *Dogmengeschichte*⁴ 1, 181. Vgl. 273 ff.

828 *Didache* 4.13 (ECF 173). Cf. 4.3: "οὐ ποιήσεις σχίσμα [thou wilt not create a schism {division}]."

"Now, you should welcome anyone who comes your way and teaches you all we have been saying (τὰ προειρημένα). But if the teacher proves himself a renegade and by teaching otherwise (ἄλλην διδαχήν) contradicts all this (that has been said—εἰς τὸ καταλῦσαι), pay no attention to him."[829] "Everyone 'who comes' to you 'in the name of the Lord' must be welcomed. Afterward, when you have tested him (δοκιμάσαντες), you will find out about him, for you have insight (σύνεσιν γὰρ ἕξετε) into right and wrong."[830] For this reason true and false prophets and teachers are constantly discussed.[831] It is clear that in the Didache, aside from moral criteria (that he do as he teaches) there is also another, as we see from the following words: "Every prophet who teaches the truth (διδάσκων τὴν ἀλήθειαν) but fails to practice what he preaches is a false prophet."[832] Here the moral criterion is applied to the person of the prophet, while the teaching can be true regardless of his moral character. If the prophet himself does not do as he teaches, he is merely a false prophet; nothing is said about his teaching. The community verifies the

---

829 *Didache* 11.1–2 (ECF 176).

830 The Russian source reads, "for you must distinguish between right and false." –*Trans.Didache* 12.1 (ECF 177). Cf. Rev. 2:2: "Thou hast tried them which say they are apostles, and are not, and hast found them liars."

831 *Didache* 11.5, 6, 8, 9, 10, 11; 13.1, 2.

832 *Didache* 11.10. The words that follow—"Πᾶς δὲ προφήτης δεδοκιμασμένος, ἀληθινός, ποιῶν εἰς μυστήριον κοσμικὸν ἐκκλησίας μὴ διδάσκων δὲ ποιεῖν, ὅσα αὐτὸς ποιεῖ, οὐ κριθήσεται ἐφ' ὑμῶν [And every prophet, proved true, working unto the mystery of the Church in the world, yet not teaching others to do what he himself does, shall not be judged among you]" (11.11)—are difficult to interpret. Metropolitan Philotheos Bryennios understands "μυστήριον κοσμικὸν ἐκκλησίας [the mystery of the Church in the world]" to mean the symbolic actions of a prophet. Harnack, recalling Eph. 5:22–23, understood these words to mean celibacy on the part of the prophet, which he did not make obligatory for all. See Harnack, *Die Lehre der zwölf Apostel*, TU 2.1, 44–47, Anm. A. Karashev, *On the Newly Discovered Historical Manuscript* The Teaching of the Twelve Apostles [О новооткрытом памятнике "Учение двенадцати апостолов"] (Moscow: 1896), appendices, XXXV–XXXVII. But here it is important that we note the adjacent words "δεδοκιμασμένος" and "ἀληθινός" ("tested by the Church" = "true").

truth of the teaching as well.[833] Confirmation of this is also found in Revelation, which appeared about the time of the Didache, where the community in Pergamos is reproached because there are "there them that hold the doctrine of Balaam" and "the doctrine of the Nicolaitanes," and the community in Thyatira because it permitted "that woman Jezebel, which calleth herself a prophetess, to teach" (Rev. 2:14, 15, 20). Conversely, the Church of Ephesus does well in that it hates the works of the Nicolaitanes.[834] According to the Didache, the Christian may learn the word of God (τὸν λόγον τοῦ Θεοῦ) in the preaching of an apostle, a prophet, or a teacher,[835] and can recognize when he is being taught outside of God (ἐπεὶ παρεκτὸς Θεοῦ σε διδάσκει).[836] All these injunctions on testing teachers obviously bespeak the existence of a Tradition preserved in the Church, and this Tradition is a definite authority and a reliable criterion of truth or falsehood.

From the late first century (A.D. 95–97) we have the epistle of Clement of Rome to the Corinthians concerning the disturbances that occurred there. Researchers of this epistle note that it is particularly noteworthy for its lack of any opinions foreign to church Tradition.[837] Its author clearly cites the principle of a tradition that has guarded him from diverging into deviant thinking. "Let us give up vain and fruitless cares," he writes, "and approach to the glorious and venerable rule (κανόνα) of our tradition."[838] These words

---

833 In regard to the community, it cannot be presumed to possess any special charisma for testing prophets. They tested them based on a definite authority. Cf. Batiffol, *L'église naissante et le catholicisme*³, 127, 128, 131.

834 See Rev. 2:6.

835 *Didache* 4.1.

836 Idem 6.1.

837 Harnack, *Der erste Klemensbrief. Sitzungsberichte der Königlich-Preussischen Akademie der Wissenschaften* (1909) 3, 53.

838 Clement of Rome, *First Epistle to the Corinthians* 7.2 (ANF 1:7): "Ἔλθωμεν ἐπὶ τὸν εὐκλεῆ καὶ σεμνὸν τῆς παραδόσεως ἡμῶν κανόνα" Here Harnack understands "παραδόσεως" in a general sense, extending to all everything delivered and belonging to Christianity (*Der erste Klemensbrief*, 53, Anm. 4).

clearly recognize the principle of tradition, whatever the extent of that Tradition may be understood to be.[839]

Ignatius the God-bearer praises the Ephesians because, stopping their ears, they did not permit the dissemination of evil doctrine among them,[840] and he advises that error be countered with steadfastness in the faith.[841] He considers desirable the lot of the Christians of Ephesus, who by the power of Jesus Christ were always of one mind with the apostles.[842] For St. Ignatius, faith is something quite definite, and for this reason he strictly condemns those who corrupt the faith of God (ἐὰν πίστιν Θεοῦ ἐν κακῇ διδασκαλίᾳ φθείρῃ). Both one so defiled (ῥυπαρός) and one who hearkens to him will go away into everlasting fire.[843] Christians must be united in one faith.[844] St. Ignatius exhorts the Magnesians to become firm in the teaching (ἐν τοῖς δόγμασι) of the Lord and the apostles.[845] To the Trallians he speaks of the necessity of consuming only Christian food and turning away from strange herbage, which is heresy:[846] one who partakes of heresy immediately dies.[847] They will be able to refrain from heretical errors if they do not become conceited and do not separate from Jesus Christ God, the bishop, and the commandments of the apostles (διαταγμάτων τῶν ἀποστόλων).[848] In his epistle to the Philadelphians St. Ignatius extols their bishop

---

839 Vgl. G. Hoennicke, *Das Iudenchristentum…*, 350–351.

840 Ignatius, *Epistle to the Ephesians* 11.1.

841 Idem 10.2: "Πρὸς τὴν πλάνην αὐτῶν ὑμεῖς ἑδραῖοι τῆς πίστεως" Cf. 12.

842 Idem 11.2: "Οἳ καὶ τοῖς ἀποστόλοις πάντοτε συνῄνεσαν ἐν δυνάμει Ἰησοῦ Χριστοῦ."

843 Idem 16.2. Cf. 17.2: "Λαβόντες Θεοῦ γνῶσιν [having received knowledge of God]."

844 Idem 20.2.

845 Ignatius, *Epistle to the Magnesians* 13.1.

846 Ignatius, *Epistle to the Trallians* 6.1.

847 Idem 11.1. Cf. 6.2: "Λαμβάνει ἐν ἡδονῇ κακῇ ἀποθανεῖν [he takes, with a fatal pleasure leading to his own death.]."

848 Idem 7.1. In chapter 9 St. Ignatius even presents a kind of short symbol of faith: "One ought not even to listen to anyone who speaks at variance with this symbol."

for being in harmony with the commandments as the strings are with the harp.[849] Calling the Christians of Philadelphia children not only of the light, but of the truth,[850] he exhorts them to flee from evil doctrines. Many wolves take captive those who walk the path of God.[851] Those who follow a schismatic (σχίζοντι) or who adhere to strange doctrine (ἐν ἀλλοτρίᾳ γνώμῃ περιπατεῖ) do not inherit the kingdom of God."[852] "I flee to the Gospel as to the flesh of Jesus, and to the apostles as to the presbytery of the Church (ὡς πρεσβυτερίῳ ἐκκλησίας)."[853] In his epistle to the Smyrnaeans, as in that to the Trallians, St. Ignatius sets forth Tradition in the form of a sort of "Rule of Faith,"[854] and likewise exhorts them not only not to receive heretics, but if possible not even to meet with them.[855] In the life of St. Ignatius there were instances reminiscent of the disputes of the later writers Irenaeus and Tertullian with the Gnostics regarding Holy Scripture. He writes: "When I heard some saying, If I do not find it in the ancient Scriptures (ἐν τοῖς ἀρχείοις), I will not believe the Gospel[856]; on my saying to them, It is written, they answered me, That remains to be proved (ὅτι πρόκειται). But to me Jesus Christ is in the place of all that is ancient (ἀρχεῖα) [Scripture]: His cross, and death, and resurrection, and the faith which is by Him, are undefiled monuments of antiquity (τὰ ἄθικτα ἀρχεῖα); by which I desire, through your prayers, to be justified."[857] Like Tertullian, who refused to converse with the heretics based on Scripture, St. Ignatius wishes to end the debate with the heretics and cites his

---

849 Ignatius, *Epistle to the Philadelphians* 1.2: "Συνευρύθμισται γὰρ ταῖς ἐντολαῖς χορδαῖς κιθάρα."

850 Idem 2.

851 Idem 2.

852 Idem 3.2.

853 Idem 5.1 (ANF 1:82).

854 Ignatius, *Epistle to the Smyrnaeans* 1, 2.

855 Idem 4.1, 7.2.

856 In the Russian, "the ancient Scriptures—that is, the Gospel—I will not believe."

857 Ignatius, *Epistle to the Philadelphians* 8.2 (ANF 1:84).

personal faith in Christ.[858] But this faith was of course specifically that of the Church. St. Ignatius did not separate himself from the Church, and so it may be thought that in the passage cited the living self-identification of the Church or of one who belongs to her is considered a sufficient standard of truth, regardless of Holy Scripture, the words of which were already being reinterpreted in the time of St. Ignatius.[859] In general, all Ignatius's speeches on heretics and on true faith specifically depict the Church as the custodian of the truth in contrast to heresies.[860]

In the epistle of Ignatius's disciple Polycarp, bishop of Smyrna, to the Philippians, we find some very clear indications of the principle of tradition. In his epistle he says that he does not wish to teach them anything. Why? "For neither I, nor any other such one, can come up to the wisdom of the blessed and glorified Paul. He, when among you, accurately and stedfastly taught the word of truth (τὸν περὶ ἀληθείας λόγον) in the presence of those who were then alive. And when absent from you, he wrote you a letter, which, if you carefully study, you will find to be the means of building you up in that faith which has been given you, and which … 'is the mother of us all.'"[861] In another place Polycarp enjoins the Phillipians to serve God as He Himself commanded together with the apostles and prophets who preached to us the good news, fore-

---

858 Such is Zahn's understanding of this passage (*Geschichte des neutestamentlichen Kanons*, Bd. 1.2, 846–847. Bd. 2.2, Erlangen und Leipzig [1892], 14.1d, 945–948); Batiffol, *L'église naissante et le catholicisme*[3], 163. But Knopf [thinks] otherwise (*Das nachapost. Zeitalter*, 309).

859 Concerning this see Zahn, *Geschichte des neutestamentlichen Kanons*, Bd. 1.2, 842; Batiffol, *L'église naissante et le catholicisme*[3], 164: "La foi qui fait foi est la foi dont témoigne l'église on tante que telle … la foi écrite n'est pas toute la foi."

860 There are no grounds for thinking that Ignatius viewed the community outside of its link to its historical past, as Myshtsyn asserts. See *Organization of the Christian Church*, 311.

861 Polycarp, *Epistle to the Phillipians* 3.2–3 (ANF 1:33). Cf. 11 (ANF 1:35): "… among you, in the midst of whom the blessed Paul laboured, and who are commended in the beginning of his Epistle. For he boasts of you in all those Churches which alone then knew the Lord; but we [of Smyrna] had not yet known Him."

telling to us the coming of our Lord.[862] Polycarp exhorts them to adhere to Tradition: "Forsaking the vanity of many, and their false doctrines (ψευδοδιδασκαλίας), let us return to the word which has been handed down to us from the beginning."[863] [He] entreats them to submit to the word of righteousness,[864] and to be united in the truth.[865] Polycarp calls the "first-born of Satan" one who interprets the Lord's words however he wishes (ὃς ἂν μεθοδεύει τὰ λόγια τοῦ κυρίου πρὸς τὰς ἰδίας ἐπιθυμίας), making them to contradict church doctrine.[866] Thus, in this epistle of Polycarp we find information of considerable import. Already he is speaking of Tradition. In his eyes, the founding of a Church by the apostle Paul himself is significant: this founding elevates the Church to such a height that there is no need to teach her, for Tradition is especially alive in her. The antiquity of the Church is also a token of her authority ("but we [of Smyrna] had not yet known Him" [11]). Here we have nearly all the elements of the doctrine of Tradition that would later be developed in detail.[867]

The doctrine of Tradition is very clearly expressed in the last two chapters of the *Epistle to Diognetus*, but as we know these two chapters, being homiletical in nature, are quite foreign to the rest of the epistle. Even in manuscripts these chapters are located separately,[868] and hence they must be considered a later addition and cannot be used to typify views in the first half of the second century. But even in the indisputably authentic chapters we read, "Chris-

---

862 Ibid. 6.3. This can be understood to mean only the apostles who were immediate disciples of the Lord. This is indicated by the fact that only the Old Testament prophets are mentioned.

863 Ibid. 7.2 (ANF 1:34): "Ἐπὶ τὸν ἐξ ἀρχῆς ἡμῖν παραδοθέντα λόγον ἐπιστρέψωμεν."

864 Idem 9.1: "Πειθαρχεῖν τῷ λόγῳ τῆς δικαιοσύνης."

865 Idem 10.1: "State ... in veritate sociati."

866 Idem 7.1.

867 Concerning Polycarp, cf. Batiffol, *L'église naissante et le catholicisme*[3], 191–198.

868 Funk, *Die apostolischen. Väter*, XXXI; Archpriest P. Preobrazhensky, *Works of St. Justin the Philosopher* ["Сочинения св. Иустина Философа"], 365–366.

tians dwell as sojourners in corruptible [bodies],[869] looking for the incorruptibility in the heavens. ... For, as I said, this was no mere earthly invention which was delivered to them (παρεδόθη), nor is it a mere human system of opinion (ἐπίνοιαν), which they judge it right to preserve so carefully, nor has a dispensation of mere human mysteries been committed to them (οὐδὲ ἀνθρωπίνων οἰκονομίαν μυστηρίων πεπίστευνται)."[870]

Eusebius of Caesarea says of Hegesippus that he wrote down in five books the authentic tradition of the preaching of the apostles (τὴν ἀπλανῆ παράδοσιν τοῦ ἀποστολικοῦ κηρύγματος).[871] Once again, in these words we can see evidence of Tradition. Similar evidence is also found in fragments of the writings of Hegesippus preserved by Eusebius. "The church of Corinth," Hegesippus writes, "continued in the true faith (ὁ ὀρθὸς λόγος) until Primus was bishop in Corinth. I conversed with them on my way to Rome, and abode with the Corinthians many days, during which we were mutually refreshed in the true doctrine (τῷ ὀρθῷ λόγῳ)." Hegesippus goes on to state that the Church possessed the truth: "They called the Church a virgin, for it was not yet corrupted by vain discourses (ἀκοαῖς ματαίοις)." Each author of heresies "introduced privately and separately his own peculiar opinion (ἰδίως καὶ ἑτέρως ἰδίαν δόξαν)." The false Christians "divided the unity of the Church (τὴν ἕνωσιν τῆς ἐκκλησίας) by corrupt doctrines (φθοριμαίοις λόγοις) uttered against God and against his Christ."[872] Consequently, according to Hegesippus, the Church is the custodian of the truth, and heresy is an innovation of its authors. The truth of the Church is imparted to her, while the content of a heresy belongs to its author. This means that, for Hegesippus, antiquity and oneness of faith in different Churches is proof of the one truth of the Church.[873] In his

---

869 The Russian source reads, "in a corruptible world." −*Trans.*

870 *Epistle to Diognetus* 6, 7; Funk, cit. ed., 138; *Works of St. Justin,* 377.

871 Eusebius, *Church History* 4.8.2 (GrchSch. 9.1:314.8−10).

872 Eusebius, *Church History* 4.22.2, 4−6 (NPNF² 1:198−199; GrchSch. 9.1:370, 372).

873 Cf. Henri Dannreuther, *Du témoingnage d' Hégésippe sur l'église chrétienne aux deux premiers siècles* (Nancy: 1878), 59−60, 62, 67; Batiffol, *L'église naissante et le ca-*

travels to various Churches he saw how in every place the faith was the same, and therefore the faith of the Church is in fact true. Separation from the Church is a distortion of true doctrine. Hegesippus points to the authors of heresies just as St. Irenaeus and Tertullian would do later.

Polycrates of Ephesus, as we have already seen, in disputing with the Roman bishop Victor, explicitly cites the tradition of his kinsmen and the tradition received from the apostles Phillip and John the Theologian. In his epistle, as it is recorded by Eusebius, we encounter not only the term *Tradition* but also *Rule of Faith* (ὁ κανὼν τῆς πίστεως).[874]

Justin the Philosopher and Hermas provide brief confessions of faith.[875] Justin says that doctrine is delivered by Jesus Christ,[876] and proclaimed in every nation through the apostles.[877] The doctrine of the Church of his day, which is the same throughout the world, Justin closely links to the apostles. The Church proclaims what she has been taught by the apostles.[878] In preserving the doctrine of the apostles, the Church is consequently the possessor of the truth. Heresies are the spawn of the demons.[879] Christians are the disciples of the true and pure doctrine of Jesus Christ, while heretics are known by the names of the originators of the given doctrine and opinion:[880] they only bear the name of Christians, but if they are

---

tholicisme[3], 208–209; Zahn, *Geschichte des neutestam. Kanons*, Bd. 1.2, 461; Harnack, *Dogmengeschichte*[4] 1, 367, Anm. 2; 407, Anm. 1.

874 Eusebius, op. cit. 5.24.6 (GrchSch. 9.1:492.8).

875 Justin, *First Apology* 6; *Dialogue with Trypho* 80 (CAG 1.1:20, 22; 1.2:288 sqq.).

876 Justin, *First Apology* 6, 23, 42, 66, 67 (CAG 1.1:20, 118, 180, 182, 184, 186).

877 Justin, *First Apology* 42. Cf. *Dialogue with Trypho* 109, 119 (CAG 1.1:118, 1.2:386, 428).

878 Idem 1.13, 14, 67 (CAG 1.1:40, 46, 188).

879 Idem 1.26; *Dialogue with Trypho* 82 (CAG 1.2:298).

880 Justin, *Dialogue with Trypho* 35 (ANF 1:212; CAG 1.2:118 sqq.): "They style themselves Christians, just as certain among the Gentiles inscribe the name of God upon the works of their own hands."

On the Dogma of the Church

not in accord with Christian doctrine (which Justin expounds here in brief), do not consider them Christians.[881]

The period surrounding the life and work of St. Irenaeus provides evidence of Tradition in every corner of the world. Concerning Dionysius of Corinth Eusebius relates that he amply extended his inspired activity not only to his subordinates, striving to benefit all by means of the catholic epistles that he wrote to the Churches. His epistle to the Lacedæmonians contains instruction in the Orthodox faith and an exhortation to peace and unity. In his epistle to the Nicomedians, repudiating the heresy of Marcion, Dionysius firmly upholds the rule of truth (τῷ τῆς ἀληθείας κανόνι). Dionysius is also aware of men who had dared to distort the Scriptures of the Lord.[882]

Theophilus of Antioch compares the Churches with fruitful islands abundant with water, with calm places and harbors in which to find refuge from the storm. "So God has given to the world which is driven and tempest-tossed by sins, assemblies (τὰς συναγωγάς)— we mean holy churches—in which survive the doctrines of the truth (αἱ διδασκαλίαι τῆς ἀληθείας), as in the island-harbours of good anchorage; and into these run those who desire to be saved, being lovers of the truth, and wishing to escape the wrath and judgment of God." Conversely, St. Theophilus likens heresies to islands that are "rocky and without water, and barren, and infested by wild beasts ... on which ships are wrecked, and those driven among them perish." "There are doctrines of error (αἱ διδασκαλίαι τῆς πλάνης)—I mean heresies—which destroy those who approach them. For they are not guided by the word of truth."[883] This clearly expresses the doctrine of the Tradition that abides in the Churches, and Harnack says that Theophilus has the same understanding of the Church as St. Irenaeus.[884]

---

881 Justin, *Dialogue with Trypho* 80 (ANF 1:239; CAG 1.2:288–292): "right-minded (ὀρθογνώμοντες) Christians on all points." For more detail concerning Justin, see Batiffol, *L'église naissante et le catholicisme*[3], 224–231.

882 Eusebius, op. cit. 4.23.1–2, 4, 12 (GrchSch. 9.1:374, 378).

883 Theophilus of Antioch, *To Autolycus* 2.14 (CAG 8:98, 100).

884 Harnack, *Dogmengeschichte* 1, 367, Anm. 2.

From the historical literature of the Church of Rome we may point out an anonymous writer who wrote against the Monarchians that without fear they distorted Divine Scripture and rejected "the rule of ancient faith" (πίστεως ἀρχαίας κανόνα).[885]

Finally, we will cite two illustrations of how apostolic Tradition was preserved in the Church. Papias of Hieropolis, who wrote five volumes entitled *Exposition of the Sayings of the Lord*, says of himself: "But I shall not hesitate also to put down for you along with my interpretations whatsoever things I have at any time learned carefully from the elders and carefully remembered, guaranteeing their truth. For I did not, like the multitude, take pleasure in those that speak much, but in those that teach the truth; not in those that relate strange commandments, but in those that deliver the commandments given by the Lord to faith, and springing from the truth itself (τοῖς τὰς παρὰ τοῦ Κυρίου τῇ πίστει δεδομένας καὶ ἀπ᾽ αὐτῆς παραγινομένας τῆς ἀληθείας). If, then, any one came, who had been a follower of the elders, I questioned him in regard to the words of the elders (τοὺς τῶν πρεσβυτέρων ἀνέκρινον λόγους),— what Andrew or what Peter said, or what was said by Philip, or by Thomas, or by James, or by John, or by Matthew, or by any other of the disciples of the Lord, and what things Aristion and the presbyter John, the disciples of the Lord, say."[886]

Here we have remembrances from the early childhood of St. Irenaeus in his own letter to Florinus: "These doctrines (τὰ δόγματα), O Florinus, to speak mildly, are not of sound judgment. These doctrines disagree with the Church (ἀσύμφωνά ἐστι τῇ ἐκκλησίᾳ). ... These doctrines, the presbyters who were before us, and who were companions of the apostles, did not deliver to thee. For when I was a boy, I saw thee in lower Asia with Polycarp. ... I remember the events of that time more clearly than those of recent years. For what boys learn (μαθήσεις), growing with their mind, becomes joined with it; so that I am able to describe the very place in which the blessed Polycarp sat as he discoursed, and his goings out and his

---

885 Eusebius, op. cit. 5.28.13 (NPNF² 1:248; GrchSch. 9.1:504.11–12).

886 Idem 3.39.3–4 (NPNF² 1:170–171; GrchSch. 9.1:286); *Fragments* 2; Funk, *Die apostolischen Väter,* 126.

comings in, and the manner of his life, and his physical appearance, and his discourses to the people, and the accounts which he gave of his intercourse with John and with the others who had seen the Lord. And as he remembered their words, and what he heard from them concerning the Lord, and concerning his miracles and his teaching, having received them[887] (παρειληφώς) from eyewitnesses of the 'Word of life,' Polycarp related all things in harmony with the Scriptures."[888]

Here we have before us two portraits. Papias traverses earth and sea to collect the sayings of the Lord, in order to learn the details of the apostolic Tradition. Discoursing with the people at the sunset of his life, the blessed Polycarp recalls the Tradition of the apostles with whom he personally companied, and there listening to him, laying up all his words in his heart, is a young man—the future bishop of Lyons and contender with Gnosticism, who for the first time would begin to speak clearly, definitively, and insistently about Tradition. These two portraits draw aside for us the curtain that conceals from us the life of the early Church, and we see how carefully and with what love the apostolic Tradition in the Church was guarded.

From all the data cited we may rightfully conclude that the Church has always thought of herself as the custodian of the truth delivered by the apostles, and that the consciousness of her unbreakable, living link with the apostolic teaching has always dwelt in the Church.[889] Apostolic Tradition, however formulated, was the criteria of truth or falsehood. This principle of tradition was present in church consciousness from the very beginning. The conflict with Gnosticism that intensified in the second century naturally spurred church writers to expound the principle of church Tradition in greater detail and to more precisely substantiate it. This task was first undertaken by St. Irenaeus and Tertullian, in whose

---

887 In the Russian source, "having received the Tradition." –*Trans.*

888 Idem 5.20.4–6 (NPNF[2] 1:238–239; GrchSch. 9.1:482, 484); *Fragments* 1 (PG 7:1225a, 1228a–b).

889 Vgl.: Knopf, *Das nachapostolische Zeitalter,* 393.

writings the doctrine of Tradition holds such an important place.[890] After them, when the thinking of church writers encountered the question of Tradition, they were able to respond to it more thoroughly and homogeneously. For anyone can observe in his own life how an idea previously held becomes more definite when expressed in words, and especially when written down. This same process of definition occurred with the Church's doctrine on Tradition after the anti-Gnostic polemical literary activity of St. Irenaeus and Tertullian. But the data we have cited regarding the preceding period in church history justifies us in asserting that **this doctrine was not created out of nothing in the second half of the second century**. The doctrine of Tradition, formerly encountered in fragmentary comments and often merely in hints, was merely developed into a more or less complete system of thought.[891]

As we have seen, however, for the anti-Gnostic writers the doctrine of the Church as the custodian of the truth is inseparably linked to the idea of the hierarchical structure of the Church itself. The Churches were founded by the apostles, and those same apostles appointed bishops for them. In each individual Church an unbroken chain of successive bishops can be traced back to the apostles. The task of the bishop is also to guard the true doctrine against distortion. The bishops even have a special charisma of truth (*charisma veritatis*). All this together substantiates the truth of the apostolicity of the Church—the truth that the Church preserves inviolate the doctrine of Christ which the apostles delivered to her. Consequently, a successive episcopacy is a token of the true Church, and without the hierarchy there is no Church. Was this point of doctrine concerning the Church something completely new in the history of the dogma concerning the Church? The scholarly answer to this question is tied to the question of the origin of the episcopacy, and hence is extremely difficult. This difficulty is due to a lack of precise historical data. In addition to being quite limited, all these historical data are also distinctly ambiguous, and therefore subject to highly

---

890 See Myshtsyn, *Organization of the Christian Church in the First Two Centuries*, 358.

891 See Schanz, "Der Begrift der Kirche," *Theologische Quartalschrift* (1893): 565–566; Batiffol, *L'église naissante et le catholicisme*³, 195, 235–236.

varied interpretations. In the history of the early Church one could
hardly point to a more convoluted matter for scholarly resolution
than the question of the origin of the episcopacy. Scholars have
advanced innumerable opinions on the matter. In Western Protestant academia, however, over the past fifty years a more or less
universal view of the origin of the episcopacy has emerged. The
foundation of this view was laid by Albrecht Ritschl,[892] whom many
scholars follow, down to the renowned Harnack.[893] These more or
less general views may be briefly summarized as follows.[894] From
the very beginning of the existence of the Christian Church it had
a twofold form of organization. The work of teaching fell to the
duty of specific charismatic persons—evangelists, apostles, prophets, and teachers. The work of these persons was not limited to any
particular community: on the contrary, these were wandering missionaries and teachers. Along with this Church-wide charismatic
organization, individual communities had their own organization.
These communities, naturally, were initially headed by elders. Out
of these there grew the presbyterate (πρεσβυτέριον), from whom
select persons soon came to be distinguished—the bishops and deacons. These persons were not involved in teaching: their duties were
related to administration and economy. The performance of the
Eucharist and managing property—this comprised the entire work
of the bishops and deacons. It was only in the second century that
the episcopacy received a special position in the church organization. Gradually a monarchical episcopacy developed. There was a
prolonged struggle between the charismatics and the bishops, from
which the episcopacy emerged victorious. Following this victory
the bishops took the teaching work of the charismatics upon them-

---

892   His book, *Die Entstehung der altkatholischen Kirche,* Sohm calls "a study that
defined the current predominant views without exception." See the note in *Church
Structure in the First Two Centuries* ["Церковный строй в первые два века"], 28–29.

893   Harnack himself says, "Wir, auf Ritschl's Schultern stehend…" (*Das Neue
Testament um das Jahr 200* [Freiburg i. B.: 1889), 23.

894   Since the history of the origins of the episcopate have no direct bearing
upon the issue at hand, we will summarize the general views expressed by Western scholarship briefly, without citing individual scholarly works.

selves. The fight against Gnosis in the second half of the second century created favorable conditions for the episcopacy to conquer everywhere. By the end of the second century the church structure that we see in the writings of St. Irenaeus and Tertullian had taken shape. All these are "provisions that have now become commonly accepted in academic circles, which can only be refuted with a certain degree of risk to one's scholarly reputation."[895]

But if we accept all these provisions of Protestant scholarship, what does this entail for the issue at hand? Theory ordinarily follows practice. Historical developments elevated the episcopacy: it in fact came to head the Church and, in justification of this usurpation of sorts, a theory of the apostolic institution and unbroken succession of the episcopacy is created. In justification of this theory, the more determined scholars add, so-called pastoral epistles were compiled about the mid-second century, falsely superscribed with the name of the apostle Paul, or at any rate the authentic epistles of the apostle were interpolated in the interests of the hierarchy. What then of the teaching of St. Irenaeus concerning the apostolic succession of the episcopacy? It is an invention of Irenaeus himself, one not at all in line with the facts. St. Irenaeus says that the first bishops were appointed by the apostles, while in actuality the apostles appointed no bishops. St. Irenaeus says that the successive series of bishops can be traced back to the apostles without a break. But in actuality the series of successive bishops could only have been traced back 50 or 60 years (and that by no means universally) from the time when Irenaeus himself lived and worked. In general, the teaching concerning the important significance of the hierarchy for the Church is an innovation of the late second century, quite unknown to the first, in which the thinking differed drastically.

---

895 Words of Prof. A.I. Pokrovsky in response to the dissertation of V.N. Myshtsyn. See the *Journals of the Collections of the Council of the Moscow Theological Academy for 1909* ["Журналы собраний Совета Московской духовной академии за 1909 год"], 104. Cf. study by Prof. N.A. Zaozersky, "The Hierarchical Principle of Church Organization," *Bogoslovsky vestnik* (1911): vol. 1, 63–66. The Protestant theories are presented and analyzed by Batiffol in *L'église naissante et le catholicisme*[3], 172–193.

This representation of all the consequences for the question at hand is by no means an exaggeration. We find similar reasoning in the writings of Protestant scholars themselves. Consider for example what Ritschl writes: "This theory of the episcopacy (of St. Irenaeus and Tertullian) is at once dogmatic and historical. Dogmatically, it is a significant point in catholic Christianity, while historically it is the supreme authority on the historical views of the Church. We would be rejecting the entire development heretofore represented if we accepted this provision or added only a little in repudiation of this historical theory. From the most ancient or simultaneous sources it has been established that the theory of the episcopacy developed by Irenaeus and Tertullian could not have signified from the beginning. The content of the "Rule of Faith" (*Regula fidei*) accepted as apostolic, which is specifically an antithesis to the heretical Gnosis of the second century, proves that the idea of the episcopacy to which it is most intimately linked could only have spread and gained traction as a reaction to Gnosis."[896] F. Böhringer, who in the main repeats Ritschl verbatim, expresses the same idea still more bluntly. "That on which (this theory) must rely—namely, historical corroboration—is historical fiction. The allegation that the apostles appointed bishops in the Churches which they founded

---

896 Ritschl, *Die Entstehung der altkatholischen Kirche*, 444–445. Ritschl goes on to demonstrate his own premise based on the writings of Clement of Alexandria (445–449). But at the same time Ritschl points to the Church of Jerusalem, over which community the apostle James presided. In citing the testimony of Hegesippus, "διαδέχεται τὴν ἐκκλησίαν μετὰ τῶν ἀποστόλων ὁ ἀδελφὸς τοῦ κυρίου Ἰάκωβος [after the apostles the brother of the Lord James succeeded to the church]" (Eusebius, *Church History* 2.23.4), Ritschl reasons that in Jesus' stead he (James) is taking on the governance of the entire community or Church, which naturally at the time of this communication was geographically limited to Jerusalem (416). Hegesippus however attests that after James's death, Simon, also a kinsman of the Lord (ἀνεψιὸς τοῦ κυρίου), became bishop. This permits Ritschl to posit the following: James and his successors comprise successors not of the apostles, but of the Lord (417). Thus, according to Ritschl, there was a succession of bishops of sorts in the Church of Jerusalem, where they were successive vicars of Christ, but this succession perished along with the Church of Jerusalem itself (435–436). At the same time, Ritschl sees a certain vestige of the practices of the Church of Jerusalem at a later time in Alexandria (434–435). This opinion of Ritschl finds no sympathy, "and rightly so," adds Sohm (29n).

as their successors with the power to teach ... is a supposition—one which, as we see from the earliest writings of the apostolic fathers, is completely unknown to the history of the period, and which was only ascribed to the earlier history retrospectively in the Church's fight with Gnosis in the last third of the second century, albeit not by Irenaeus alone, in whose writings this (un)historical concept is first encountered."[897] It is quite clear that from the outset the Orthodox researcher cannot concur with opinions of this sort. The Orthodox researcher may rather risk his scholarly reputation and acknowledge premises that contradict the data of modern Western science, rather than relinquish his conviction of the veracity of the Tradition of the ecumenical Orthodox Church. In addition to the fragmentary testimony of church literature that is subject to widely varied interpretation, the Orthodox researcher also has a source of **scholarly** knowledge. This is the Tradition of the Orthodox Catholic Church, and he can always prefer the latter source to the former.[898]

But the contradiction between Tradition and scholarly data is not in fact so stark as it may seem upon first acquaintance with works by those scholars who have most bluntly expressed their

---

897 F. Böhringer, *Die alte Kirche*, 2-ter. Teil, 424–425. Vgl. Nitzsch, *Grundriss der christlichen Dogmengeschichte*, 255: the authority of the bishops is declared "auf Grund der Fiction, dass der Episcopat an die Stelle des Apostolats getreten sei." Knopf says essentially the same, although less bluntly. See *Das nachapostolische Zeitalter*, 396: "Die bischöflich monarchische Verfassung wurde als apostolische augegeben und den Bischöfen die Qualität von Nachfolgern der Apostel erteilt." In the opinion of F. Loofs, Irenaeus's argumentation is pseudohistorical rather than historical, because it specifies fictitious people, "qui ab apostolis instituti sunt episcopi in ecclesiis [who were instituted by the apostles as bishops in the churches]" (*Leitfaden der Dogmengeschichte*[4], §19.3, 135. Vgl. 3-te Aufl., 88). Regarding Irenaeus's theory of the episcopacy, Dr. Ioh. Leipoldt observes: "Das ist gewiss keine Lüge; aber ebenso gewiss ist es ein Irrtum" (*Geschichte des neutestamentlichen Kanons* 1, 161). Harnack likewise finds it possible to call the doctrine of the apostolic institution of the episcopacy a legend (*Die Chronologie der altchristlichen Litteratur bis Eusebius* 1, 200).

898 Here we permit ourselves to cite the authoritative and persuasive demonstration of "the lofty and truly scholarly significance of the Tradition of the Orthodox Catholic Church," developed by Prof. M.D. Muretov in his work *Ernest Renan and His "Life of Jesus"* (Saint Petersburg: 1908), 139–156.

extreme views on the origins of the episcopacy in the Christian
Church. If we delve deeper into the state of affairs, we find that
neither is everything quite so favorable in Protestant scholarship:
not everything is so very decisively resolved as to render all objections devoid of any scholarly basis. We may even say that the very
state of the sources of historical knowledge discussed above do not
permit a scholarly answer to the question of the origin of the episcopacy that would leave no room whatsoever for doubt.[899] Consequently, "for the Church's scholarly self-authentication, Orthodox
scholarship must satisfy only the following two conditions: the first
is to expose the unsubstantiated nature of negative willful thinking
and sophism, and the second is to demonstrate that certain truth,
subjected to enemy attacks, has always comprised and represents
the **essential** content of the ecumenical mind of the Church."[900]
In our question the first task is the duty of the sciences of church
history or church law, and we can divest ourselves of the obliga-
tion to "expose the unsubstantiated nature of negative sophism"
as regards the origin of the episcopacy, especially since this task
has already been successfully carried out in Russian scholarship.[901]

---

899 "In this problem there are too many indefinite values for it to be at all
possible to hope for its exhaustive elucidation, even in the distant future" (V.N.
Myshtsyn, *The Organization of the Christian Church*, V). Writes Prof. A.A. Spassky:
"In the history of the question at hand, due to the meager data available to science and the possibility of their reinterpretation, every conception of the original
structure of the Church, however compelling it may seem, can only serve as
an attempt to **clarify** this complex and troublesome problem, and can by no
means claim to be its ultimate resolution." (*Journal of the Collections of the Council
of the Moscow Theological Academy* for 1909, 97). Cf. remark by Prof. V.V. Bolotov
(*Lectures on the History of the Early Church* 2, 458); Heinrich Bruders, *Die Verfassung
der Kirche von den ersten Jahrzehnten der apostolischen Wirksamkeit an bis zum Jahre 175 n.*
Vgl. *Forschungen zur Christlichen Literatur-und Dugmengeschichte*, herausgeg. von Dr. A.
Ehrhard und Dr. I.P. Kirsch, 4.1–2 (Mainz: 1904), 69, 128–129; Schanz, "Der
Begriff der Kirche," *Theologische Quartalschrift* (1893): 550: "Die Frage, wie aus der
kollegialen Gemeindeleitung eine monarchische geworden werde, wenn nicht
neue Quellen gefunden werden sollten, ungelöst bleiben, und sich für alle nähere
Einzelheiten mit einem 'ignoramus et ignorabimus' begnügen...."

900 Muretov, op. cit., 155.

901 Here we refer to Myshtsyn's *The Organization of the Christian Church in the*

The second task is historical and dogmatic in nature, and hence we must now examine whether early Christian literature contains any evidence that the idea of the apostolic institution of the episcopacy and its unbroken succession as the foundation and surety of the inviolability of apostolic Tradition in the Church was not foreign to church consciousness in the earliest times.

First of all we may make the following observation. The doctrine of the unbroken succession of the episcopacy from the apostles as a token of the true apostolic Church was expressed by St. Irenaeus in the fight against Gnosis. This circumstance, as stated above, gives grounds for Western scholars to assert that this doctrine was almost wholly invented by St. Irenaeus alone. To us it appears that, on the contrary, this circumstance can only serve to disprove such an assertion. Could St. Irenaeus really have cited "historical fiction" in the fight against Gnosis? Aside from the fact that this presumption that St. Irenaeus resorted to certifiably unscrupulous falsehood is absolutely inadmissible with regard to this great father of the Church,[902] this prompts the bewildered question: could such referencing of "historical fiction" have had in any way facilitated polemical success? Less than a century had passed since the death of the apostles; their Tradition was still alive in all Christian communities; and even the children were still living of those who had talked with the apostles themselves, heard their teaching, and naturally passed it on to their children.[903] To cite "historical fiction" in

---

First Two Centuries. This work fairly thoroughly shows the substantial problems and defects of the typical western scholarly answer to the question of the origin of the episcopacy in the early Christian Church. Nearly all the author's conservative conclusions may be accepted for use in Orthodox scholarship, since they do not at all dissent from the principles of the Orthodox Church. Concerning the significance of this work, see the note by Prof. A.A. Spassky in *The Journals of the Collections of the Council of the Moscow Theological Academy* for 1909, 98.

902 See Zahn, *Geschichte des neutestamentlichen Kanons,* Bd. 1.2, 436. Vgl. Harnack, *Das Neue Testament um das Jahr 200,* 18. Vgl. *Einige Bemerkungen zu Adolf Harnack's Prüfung der Geschichte des neutestamentlichen Kanons,* von Theodor Zahn (Erlangen und Leipzig: 1889), 32–33. Zahn decisively (and quite rightly!) emphasizes a similar idea and considers it particularly important (33).

903 Cf. Irenaeus, *Against Heresies* 4.27.1 (PG 7:1056b).

polemics and under such circumstances would have meant not only to fail to convince his opponents, but also to plant seeds of doubt in his own followers. If the argumentation of St. Irenaeus had been "pseudohistorical," as F. Loofs called it, its untenability would have been obvious to all at the time, and it would have been completely pointless.[904] Overall, it is very difficult to fathom how St. Irenaeus could have been caught manipulating the facts and creating "historical fiction" not by the Gnostics of the second century, but only by those of the second half of the nineteenth.

If we turn to surviving literary data, first of all **in the Gospel** we find the doctrine that **Christ Himself was sent by His Father.**[905] His food and drink are to do the will of the Father Who sent Him.[906] He Who was sent by God (ὃν ἀπέστειλεν ὁ Θεός) speaks the words of God.[907] His teaching belongs to Him Who sent Him;[908] consequently, one who receives Him receives Him Who sent Him.[909] His miracles are intended so that people might believe that the Son was sent.[910]

Being Himself sent by the Father, **Jesus Christ chooses and sends the apostles**, first to the Jews only,[911] and then to the whole world.[912] This sending of the apostles is seemingly linked to the sending of Jesus Christ Himself: it is as though both sendings comprise a single chain. As the Father sent His Son, so also the Son sends His disciples.[913] One who receives the apostles receives Christ, and those

---

904 Vgl. Dr. F.X. Funk, *Die Echtheit der ignatianischen Briefe* (Tubingen: 1883), 56. Vgl. Zahn, *Einige Bemerkungen...*, 30.

905 See Mt. 15:24, 21:37. Mk. 12:6. Lk. 4:18, 43. Jn. 3:17; 5:29, 36; 6:29, 44, 57; 11:42; 17:18, 21. Acts 3:20. 1 Jn. 4:9, 14.

906 See Jn. 4:34.

907 See Jn. 3:34, 5:31.

908 See Jn. 7:16.

909 See Mt. 10:40, Mk. 9:37, Lk. 9:48. Cf. Lk. 10:16.

910 See Jn. 5:36, 6:29, 11:42, 16:30.

911 See Mt. 10:5, 16; Mk. 3:14, 6:7; Lk. 9:2, 10:1.

912 See Mt. 28:16–20, Mk. 16:15, Lk. 24:47–49.

913 See Jn. 17:18, 20:21.

who receive Christ receive Him that sent Him.[914] "He that heareth you heareth me; and he that despiseth you despiseth me; and he that despiseth me despiseth him that sent me" (Lk. 10:16).

In the same way the apostle Paul received this sending directly from the Lord Jesus Christ,[915] and for this reason he constantly calls himself an apostle of Jesus Christ, called to be an apostle (κλητὸς ἀπόστολος),[916] and not appointed by men.[917] The apostle Paul was directly taught by Christ,[918] and he himself says that preaching was committed to him.[919] In the late second century St. Irenaeus and Tertullian said regarding church truth: *Quod ecclesiae ab apostolis, apostoli a Christo, Christus a Deo accepit* [that the church received from the apostles, the apostles from Christ, Christ from God]. In the New Testament we now have the last two links in the chain by means of which divinely revealed truth is preserved and spread in the world by right of succession. The first link is not yet mentioned, because in reality it did not yet exist. But already from the history of the apostles and from the apostolic epistles we learn of the succession that followed: the succession of the episcopacy from the apostles.

The science of church history can cite considerable data in support of the apostolic origin of the episcopacy in the Christian Church.[920] But our purpose is to learn whether the bishop was considered a successor to the apostles in the work of teaching and preserving the truth, as he appears in the teaching of St. Irenaeus that we have presented. Concerning this we may point out several

---

914 See Mt. 10:40, Jn. 13:20.

915 See Acts 9:3–6, 16–17. Cf. Acts 26:17.

916 See Rom. 1:1, 11:13. 1 Cor. 1:1, 9:1, 2, 5; 15:9. 2 Cor. 1:1, 8:23; 11:5; 12:11. Eph. 1:1. Col. 1:1. 1 Thess. 2:7. 1 Tim. 1:1; 2:7. 2 Tim. 1:1, 11. Tit. 1:1. The apostle Peter calls himself the same: 1 Pet. 1:1, 2 Pet. 1:1.

917 See Gal. 1:1. The other apostles likewise acknowledged Paul to possess the dignity of an apostle. See Gal. 2:7–9.

918 See Gal. 1:12, 16–22. 1 Cor. 11:23. Eph. 3:3. Concerning the apostle Paul, see Bruders, *Die Verfassung der Kirche*, 181–183, 89–92.

919 See Tit. 1:3.

920 Concerning this, see the dissertation of V.N. Myshtsyn, *The Organization of the Christian Church*, particularly 144–155 and from 229 on.

testimonies in the earliest epistles of the apostle Paul. In the epistle to the Philippians the apostle writes, "I beseech Euodias, and beseech Syntyche, that they be of the same mind in the Lord (τὸ αὐτὸ φρονεῖν ἐν Κυρίῳ). And I intreat thee also, true yokefellow (σύζυγε γνήσιε), help those women (συλλαμβάνου αὐταῖς) which laboured with me in the gospel, with Clement also, and with other my fellow-labourers" (Phil. 4:2–3).[921] Here the apostle addresses two women with an exhortation to be of one mind,[922] wishing to remove all disagreement in the matter of faith. At the same time he addresses his sincere fellow laborer, apparently with a request to aid Euodias and Syntyche to achieve oneness of mind. Consequently, in Philippi there was a person whose task it was to see that the faithful were of one mind and to confirm those who were wavering. Many scholars attempt to learn the name of this person, but this is of course a pointless undertaking. All that matters is that the apostle Paul is giving the primate of the Church of Phillipi the right and authority to confirm the members of that Church in oneness of mind. The apostle first exhorts them to oneness of mind himself, and then asks his good fellow laborer to exhort them likewise. The apostle is extending his own work of teaching to the primate of the community.

We find a still more important testimony in the book of the Acts of the Apostles, in the parting discourse of the apostle Paul with the presbyters in Ephesus. Here *presbyters* need not be understood to mean the college of presbyters of the Church of Ephesus alone, because the text says nothing of this. "And from Miletus he sent to Ephesus, and called the elders of the church (τῆς ἐκκλησίας)" (Acts 20:17). But we know how long the apostle Paul lived in Ephesus, and naturally in the environs of Ephesus he founded many Churches.[923] The apostle himself mentions in his address that he had "gone

---

921 For a more detailed analysis of this passage, see V.N. Myshtsyn, 144–146.

922 Previously the same epistle hinted somewhat at dissension in Philippi (2:2–3).

923 "All they which dwelt in Asia heard the word of the Lord Jesus, both Jews and Greeks" (Acts 19:10). Demetrius the silversmith said, "Not alone at Ephesus, but almost throughout all Asia, this Paul hath persuaded and turned away much people" (Acts 19:26).

preaching the kingdom of God (ἐν οἷς διῆλθον κηρύσσων)" (Acts 20:25). These words become clearer if we suppose that the apostle beheld before him the primates of the various Churches he had founded. All the Churches of Asia were in a sense united around Ephesus: it is from Ephesus that the apostle relays a greeting on behalf of all the Churches of Asia to the Corinthians,[924] and it is therefore quite natural that, in passing through Ephesus and wishing to meet with the primates of the Churches, the apostle sends them specifically to Ephesus.[925] What then does the apostle say to the primates of the Churches of Asia? The apostle calls to mind his teaching work: "For I have not shunned to declare unto you all the counsel of God" (Acts 20:27),[926] and then immediately continues: "Take heed therefore (οὖν) unto yourselves, and to all the flock (ποιμνίῳ), over the which the Holy Ghost hath made you overseers (ἐπισκόπους), to feed the church of God, which he hath purchased with his own blood" (Acts 20:28). The apostle then gazes into the future: "I know this, that after my departing shall grievous wolves enter in among you, not sparing the flock. Also of your own selves shall men arise, speaking perverse things, to draw away disciples after them. Therefore watch, and remember, that by the space of three years I ceased not to warn (νουθετῶν)[927] every one night and day with tears. And now, brethren, I commend you to God, and to the word of his grace, which is able to build you up (ἐποικοδομῆσαι), and to give you an inheritance among all them which are sanctified" (Acts 20:29–32). These words of the apostle are most telling. He exhorts the primates of the Churches of Asia, having a presentiment of the "bonds and afflictions" foretold to him (Acts

924 See 1 Cor. 16:19.

925 The opinion that bishops came not only from Ephesus to the apostle Paul at Miletus was already expressed by St. Irenaeus of Lyons: "When the bishops and presbyters who came from Ephesus and the other cities adjoining had assembled in Miletus..." (*Against Heresies* 3.14.2 [ANF 1:438; PG 7:914b]; cf. Migne, note 1, 914d).

926 Cf. also Acts 20:20: "I kept back nothing that was profitable unto you, but have shewed you, and have taught you publicly, and from house to house."

927 In the Russian, учить (to teach). *–Trans.*

20:23). He desires for the last time to give them instruction, a final testament. It is clear that the apostle sees the primates of the Churches specifically as keepers of his own work and successors of his teachership. Not by accident does the apostle twice mention his ceaseless work of teaching in his address. He likewise speaks to his listeners of cruel wolves who will not spare the flock. The pastors of the Church must guard the Church from wolves, naturally, by words of preaching and teaching. The Holy Spirit appointed the bishops, and the purpose of this appointment is to shepherd the Church. This passage clearly contradicts the delimitation promoted by certain scholars, who separate administrative posts from those of pastors and teachers in the early Christian Church.[928] On the contrary, Jewish and Christian writers are more inclined to combine the concepts of pastorship and episcopacy (oversight). In the Old Testament likewise ἐπίσκοπος does not solely signify an external overseer or steward, but at times also signifies one who sees—the heart of man, for example.[929] In the New Testament we need only point to the words of the apostle Peter: "Ye were as sheep going astray; but are now returned unto the Shepherd and Bishop of your souls (ἐπὶ τὸν ποιμένα καὶ ἐπίσκοπον τῶν ψυχῶν ὑμῶν)" (1 Pet. 2:25).[930] Consequently, combining episcopacy and pastorship is quite conceivable for the New Testament writers, as may be seen from the discourse of the apostle Paul in Miletus. Consequently, we

---

928 In the *Prolegomena* to the *Didache* (TU 2.1), Harnack marks this strict delimitation (103, 120, 144, 145, 149). Cf. note to the *Didache*, 56–57. Vgl. Ritschl, *Die Entstehung der altkath. Kirche*, 358. Sohm says the following of this delimitation: "Our modern understanding, which thinks of teaching and administration as opposites, has been projected upon antiquity" (*Church Structure*, 139). H. Bruders likewise decisively opposes this delimitation of charisma and office (see *Die Verfassung der Kirche*, 70–73).

929 See Wisd. 1:6. Cf. Is. 60:17, Ezek. 34:11–12, Num. 4:16, 31:14, etc. An analysis of the concept of ἐπίσκοπος, albeit a brief one, [is] given by V.N. Myshtsyn, 142–144. See also Sohm, 143–144n13. In secular language, ἐπίσκοπος is an extraordinarily ambiguous expression of many meanings.

930 In pointing out this passage from the epistle of the apostle Peter, Sohm observes: "Christ the Lord is Himself denoted as Bishop (although doubtless not as financial officer!)" (*Church Structure*, 144n13).

have sufficient grounds to acknowledge that bishops in the Church were appointed as continuers of the apostolic work of teaching and as guardians of Christian doctrine against injury.[931] Finally, in the discourse of the apostle Paul it should be noted that he foresees the falling away of some of the primates themselves, and hence he commits them all to the particular protection of God and to the word of God's grace. Thus, the apostle is clearly speaking of a particular grace which, even if it were to permit the falling away of individual leaders of the Churches, would guard them all together against falling away as a group.

Next, we may judge regarding the views of the apostolic age on the question of the apostolic succession of the bishops based on the so-called pastoral epistles of the apostle Paul. These epistles, as we know, are the subject of endless controversy in Protestant scholarlship. Some authoritative scholars, such as Zahn and Weiss, consider them authentic epistles of the apostle Paul, and date them to approximately A.D. 65. Others (such as Goltzman and Jülicher) either date their composition to the first half of the second century, or else (like Harnack) split the epistles into different parts and date these parts to different times, ranging from A.D. 90 to A.D. 145. Consequently, they either completely disregard these epistles, or else use them to characterize the structure and views of the Church in the post-apostolic period. For the Orthodox researcher there is no question as to when the pastoral epistles were written: the final argument from the mouth of the Orthodox researcher is to cite

---

931 "The combining of teachership and governance, while indisputable for later periods, will remain an unsolved mystery until this combination is recognized as having been firmly fixed in the understanding of the very first Christians. For in that case there can be no doubt that the catholic bishop, in his capacity of teacher of his community (and successor of the apostles), also received the authority to govern the community" (Sohm, *Church Structure*, 64–65n. See also 138–144). At the same time, these arguments of Sohm are tinted by his own particular tendencies: the idea that teachership and governance could be opposites was unthinkable in early Christianity, because governance in the *ekklesia* cannot be governance in the name of some corporately organized society, but governance in the name of God—that is, governance by means of the word of God (64n).

church Tradition.[932] To all the questions of Protestant scholarship the Orthodox Church can answer in the words of Tertullian: "I am the heir of the apostles. Just as they committed [the faith] ... even so do I hold it."[933] Without entering into a study of the authenticity of the pastoral epistles,[934] we will merely note that in [this] matter

---

932 See A. Klitin, *The Authenticity of the Epistles of the Holy Apostle Paul to Timothy and Titus* ["Подлинность Посланий св. апостола Павла к Тимофею и Титу"], 298. See Muretov, *Ernest Renan and His "Life of Jesus,"* 154–155.

933 Tertullian, *Prescription Against Heretics* 37 (ANF 3:261; PL 2:61c).

934 In brief, see Myshtsyn, *Organization of the Christian Church*, 214–218. See also the work cited by Klitin, devoted primarily to an analysis of Goltzman's views. Here we will note only the earliest testimonies to the authenticity of the pastoral epistles. The first epistle of Clement, 2.7: "εἰς πᾶν ἔργον ἀγαθόν" (cf. Tit. 3:1); 7.3: "καὶ ἴδωμεν, τί καλὸν καὶ τί τερπνὸν καὶ τί προσδεκτὸν ἐνώπιον τοῦ ποιήσαντος ἡμᾶς" (cf. 1 Tim. 5.4, 2.3). Cf. also 1 Clem. 29.1 and 1 Tim. 2:8. Polycarp of Smyrna composed his epistle to the Philippians under the direct influence of the pastoral epistles. After mentioning the apostle Paul in chapter 3, in the beginning of chapter 4 Polycarp cites 1 Tim. 6:10, 7. Then he cites several fairly clear quotes in chapters 4 and 5, namely 1 Tim. 5:5, 3:8, and 2 Tim. 2:12. Chapter 9 contains a verbatim quote from 2 Tim. 4:10. Cf. also Polycarp 12.3 and 1 Tim. 2:1, 2 and 4:15. (For a detailed analysis of Polycarp's testimony, see Myshtsyn, 215–218). Theophilus of Antioch says, "Concerning subjection to authorities and powers, and prayer for them, the divine word gives us instructions, in order that 'we may lead a quiet and peaceable life (ὅπως ἤρεμον καὶ ἡσύχιον βίον διάγωμεν)'" (*To Autolycus* 3.14 [ANF 2:115; CAG 8:222])—that is, he quotes 1 Tim. 2:1–2 verbatim, calling it Θεῖος λόγος (divine word). Cf. *To Autolycus* 2.16 (ANF 2:101; CAG 8:104): "remission of sins, through the water and laver of regeneration" (Tit. 3:5). Irenaeus of Lyons quotes the epistles together with the name of the apostle Paul: *Against Heresies* I, preface (1 Tim. 1:4); 3.3.3, 3.3.4 (Tit. 3:10). The Muratorian fragment recognizes all three pastoral epistles (59–64). Clement of Alexandria in his *Stromata* ascribes the epistles to Paul (*Stromata* 2.11, 52.5–7 [GrchSch. 15:141]). According to Tertullian, the epistles were ascribed to Paul even by the heretics, who cited 1 Tim. 6:20 and 2 Tim. 2:2 in justification of their doctrine of a secret tradition (*The Prescription Against Heretics* 25 [PL 2:43–44]). Tertullian himself expresses amazement at the absence of the pastoral epistles in the canon of Marcion, and sees this as further proof of the heretic's arbitrary treatment of Holy Scripture: "Miror tamen, cum ad unum hominem litteras factas receperit, quod ad Timotheum duas, et unam ad Titum de ecclesiastico statu compositas, recusaverit [I wonder, however, when he received (into his Apostolicon) this letter (to Philemon) which was written but to one man, that he rejected the two epistles to Timothy and the one to Titus, which all treat of

one is struck by *circulus vitiosus in demonstrando*. Incidentally, the authenticity of the pastoral epistles is denied based on the claim that they evince a theory that appeared only later. But it would be better to judge the views and theories of the era to which the epistles date based on the epistles themselves. If we consider the pastoral epistles to be the authentic compositions of the apostle Paul, on their basis we can outline with considerable clarity the view of the significance of the bishop that he expresses in them. We must of course acknowledge that the pastoral epistles do not discuss the bishop in detail, speaking predominantly of the bishop's moral qualities; but certain of the qualities specified are highly telling, and from them we may judge concerning the holy apostle's dogmatic views of the significance of the bishop in the Church.[935]

As we can see from the pastoral epistles, the apostle Paul does not consider preserving the faith pure and inviolate to be the exclusive calling of individual persons or any one ecclesiastical office.[936] The entire Church is "the pillar and ground of the truth" (1 Tim. 3:15). At the same time we also cannot help but note that the apostle appoints the primates of the communities to head the work of guarding the teaching delivered to them.[937] Among the qualities of a bishop the apostle lists the work of teaching, which he describes in greater detail. A bishop must hold fast "the faithful word as he hath

---

ecclesiastical discipline]" (*Against Marcion* 5.21 [CSEL 47:649.19–22]). Protestant scholarship is allowing for an inexplicable miracle in supposing that the Church in the mid-second century could have mistaken later works of recent and unknown authorship for the epistles of Paul.

935 For a demonstration of the apostolic institution of the episcopacy based on the pastoral epistles, see Myshtsyn, from 229 on.

936 Ibid., 222.

937 Protestant scholars likewise sometimes recognize this (Ritschl, *Die Entstehung der altkath. Kirch*, 352, 358, but cf. 350), particularly if the pastoral epistles are dated to the post-apostolic period. See C. Weizsäcker, *Das apostolishe Zeitalter*, 621–622; H.I. Holzmann, *Lehrbuch der historisch-kritischen Einleitung in das Neue Testament*, 3-te Aufl. (Freiburg i. B.: 1892), 290–291; Harnack, *Die Entstehung und Entwickelung der Kircheverfassung und des Kirchenrechts*, 50–51. Harnack surmises that 1 Tim. 3:1–3 and Tit. 1:7–9 are interpolations. Cf. note by Batiffol (*L'église naissante et le catholicisme*, 141–142, paragraph 2).

been taught (ἀντεχόμενον τοῦ κατὰ τὴν διδαχὴν πιστοῦ λόγου), that he may be able by sound doctrine both to exhort (ἐν τῇ διδασκαλίᾳ τῇ ὑγιαινούσῃ) and to convince the gainsayers. For there are many unruly and vain talkers and deceivers ... whose mouths must be stopped (ἐπιστομίζειν)" (Tit. 1:9–11). Preserving the true Tradition and repudiating false teachers, according to the apostle, is primarily the duty of the bishop.[938]

In the epistle to Timothy, among the other qualities of a bishop the ability to teach—διδακτικόν—is once again specified.[939] The apostle requires of the bishop that he be "not greedy of filthy lucre" and "not covetous" (1 Tim. 3:3). The mention of these qualities compels us to suppose that that the bishop had the charge of managing church property. Furthermore, the bishop is called Θεοῦ οἰκονόμος [steward of God]. He "must be blameless, as the steward of God (ὡς Θεοῦ οἰκονόμον)" (Tit. 1:7). But it is therefore useless to consider the bishop a steward of property only.[940] We must take note of many other qualities, which it would be odd to require of a steward or a treasurer. For example, what could the requirement of monogamy, the well-known "μίας γυναικὸς ἀνήρ", have to do with the office of treasurer?[941] To the above requirements that the bishop be able to teach—requirements quite inexplicable with regard to a treasurer—we must also add that he be peaceable, gentle, humble, and not given to anger.[942] That all these qualities are listed indicates specifically that the bishop was not a steward of property alone, and that among the faithful he had to deal not only with matters of

---

938 "He who knows not how to combat the adversaries ... and to beat down reasonings, he who knows not what he ought to teach with regard to right doctrine, far from him be the Teacher's throne. For the other qualities may be found in those under his rule. ... But that which characterizes the Teacher is this, to be able to instruct in the word" (Chrysostom, *Homilies on Titus* 2 [NPNF[1] 13:526]).

939 See 1 Tim. 3:2.

940 "It would be a gross error to consider management of communal property to be not only the exclusive but even the chief function of the bishop." (Myshtsyn, *The Organization of the Christian Church*, 231.)

941 See 1 Tim. 3:2, Tit. 1:6.

942 See 1 Tim. 3:3–6, Tit. 1:7.

housekeeping. That the bishop is called the steward (οἰκονόμος) of God, if taken in the context of the apostle's entire line of thought, is highly revealing. Various passages from the epistles of the apostle Paul himself superbly illustrate for us this designation of the bishop. The house of God is what apostle calls the Church of the living God. All his exhortations to Timothy have but one goal: that he know "how ... to behave (ἀναστρέφεσθαι) ... in the house of God" (1 Tim. 3:15)—that is, that he know his tasks and duties as the steward of God, the overseer of the Church.[943] The apostle's thinking is constantly in a realm far removed from finances. In other passages also he applies οἰκονόμος to himself and to others in the expression "stewards of the mysteries of God" (οἰκονόμοι μυστηρίων Θεοῦ),[944] while the apostle Peter called all believers "stewards of the manifold grace (οἰκονόμοι ποικίλης χάριτος)" (1 Pet. 4:10).[945] The Greek word οἰκονομία [oikonomia] in the same epistle signifies edification in the faith.[946] It is worth noting that the apostle uses the same exact words to denote the bishop's stewardship of his own house and of the Church. The apostle denotes stewardship of a house and stewardship of the Church using the same term: πτοῖστασθαι.[947] In general, the apostle speaks simultaneously of the bishop's stewardship of his

---

943 Among the Greeks, an οἰκονόμος (steward) was not limited to the sphere of economics. The *oikonomos* was one who managed a household, not only income and expenditures. See Myshtsyn, 232. Cf. Lk. 12:42–46. Concerning the meaning of οἰκονόμος see Cremer, *Biblisch-theolog. Wörterbuch*[9], 746.

944 See 1 Cor. 4:1.

945 See also Gal. 4:2: "ὑπὸ οἰκονόμους [under *governors*]" refers to upbringing. Cf. the meaning of οἰκονομία [*oikonomia*] in 1 Cor. 9:17: "οἰκονομίαν πεπίστευμαι [a *dispensation*... is committed unto me]"; Eph. 3:2: "τὴν οἰκονομίαι τῆς χάριτος τοῦ Θεοῦ [the *dispensation* of the grace of God]"; 3:9: "τίς ἡ οἰκονομία τοῦ μυστηρίου [what is the *fellowship* of the mystery]".

946 1 Tim. 1:4: "οἰκονομίαν Θεοῦ τὴν ἐν πίστει [the dispensation of God which is in faith]." Incidentally, this passage occasionally reads οἰκοδομίαν and οἰκοδομήν [edifying] instead of οἰκονομίαν. See Tischendorf, *Novum Testamentum graece*, Ed. Octava, vol. II (Lipsiae: 1872), 841.

947 See 1 Tim. 3:4: "τοῦ ἰδίου οἴκου καλῶς προϊστάμενον [One that ruleth well his own house]." 3:5: "τοῦ ἰδίου οἴκου προστῆναι [to rule his own house]." 5:17: "οἱ καλῶς προεστῶτες πρεσβύτεροι [the elders that rule]."

own house and his stewardship of the Church. The bishop must be "one that ruleth (προϊστάμενον) well his own house, having his children in subjection with all gravity; (for if a man know not how to rule (προστῆναι) his own house, how shall he take care of the church of God?)" (1 Tim. 3:4–5). This link between stewardship of the Church and stewardship of one's house is especially visible in the epistle to Titus. No sooner has the apostle outlined the bishop's family life—he must have "faithful children, not accused of riot or unruly"—than the apostle's thoughts promptly turn to the Church: "For a bishop must be blameless, as the steward of God (οἰκονόμον)" (Tit. 1:6–7). Clearly, the apostle views the bishop specifically as the overseer of the community. As in one's own home each is master of all parts, so also all branches of church life are subject to the bishop. In his own house the bishop watches over his children, that they might be good Christians, of right belief (τέκνα ἔχων πιστά) and well-behaved; the children must be submissive to their father. And this is how the apostle envisions the work of the bishop in the Church. He must consider all men his children, and see to it that they hold fast to true doctrine and be chaste. It is to this work of the bishop that the apostle assigns the chief place; indeed, it was necessitated by the circumstances of the time. The life of Christians in that time was not so very filled with material interests. Christian communities ought never to be pictured as economically based societies. On the contrary, first and foremost it was their religious and moral life that needed guidance, and danger chiefly threatened the faith and morals of Christians. With good reason the pastoral epistles are filled with the apostle's words concerning numerous false teachers, those cruel wolves who did not spare the flock. The work of teaching, overseeing believers in the sphere of their faith, keeping inviolate the teaching committed to them—these were the duties with which the apostle charged the bishops.

Such is the position of the bishop within the Christian community. But the apostle envisions the bishop as a person who heads the community for those outside it, as well. The Churches of Ephesus could have had all kinds of contact with gentile society. Clearly, the apostle considers these interactions the task of the bishop, when he requires that the bishop be a respectable person not only for Christians, but also for those outside the Church. He must "have a good report of them which are without (μαρτυρίαν καλὴν ἔχειν ἀπὸ τῶν ἔξωθεν); lest he fall into reproach and the snare of the devil" (1 Tim. 3:7).

Thus, the position of the bishop in the Church, according to the apostle, is a very high one. The apostle himself reasons thus when he considers the episcopacy a thing to be sought[948] and allows for the possibility that the bishop may be tempted by lust for power and pride. For this reason the bishop must be "not a novice (μὴ νεόφυτον), lest being lifted up with pride he fall into the condemnation of the devil" (1 Tim. 3:6).[949] The episcopacy required one tried in the faith, tried in Christian humble-mindedness, for whom the temptation of pride would present no threat. But the very possibility of becoming prideful is indicative of the bishop's headship in the Christian community.

Although Timothy and Titus cannot be considered bishops in the proper sense, nevertheless their position essentially differed little from that of the bishop. For a whole series of churches they were what the bishop was in each individual[950] city, in each individual Christian community. But Timothy and Titus combined the governance of all branches of church life: they taught,[951] saw to the propagation and preservation of true doctrine,[952] denounced false

---

948 See 1 Tim. 3:1: "Εἴ τις ἐπισκοπῆς ὀρέγεται, καλοῦ ἔργου ἐπιθυμεῖ [if a man desire the office of a bishop, he desireth a good work]."

949 The epistle to Titus contains no such requirement, which is quite logical. In the communities of Crete, where Titus labored (1:5), there may not have been anyone who had converted to the faith particularly long ago. Conversely, in Ephesus it must be presumed that there were believers who had long ago joined the Church.

950 See Tit. 1:5.

951 See 1 Tim. 4:13: "Πρόσεχε τῇ ἀναγνώσει, τῇ παρακλήσει, τῇ διδασκαλίᾳ." Cf. 4:11: "Παράγγελλε καὶ δίδασκε" 2 Tim. 4:2, Tit. 2:1, 7; 3:8.

952 2 Tim. 2:2: "The things that thou hast heard of me among many witnesses, the same commit thou to faithful men (παράδου πιστοῖς), who shall be able to teach (διδάξαι) others also." Cf. 1 Tim. 6:20, 2 Tim. 1:13–14.

teachers,[953] cut off heretics from the Church,[954] appointed people to church offices,[955] and so on.[956]

The apostle Peter speaks similarly concerning the duties of a hierarch: "The elders which are among you (πρεσβυτέρους ἐν ὑμῖν) I exhort, who am also an elder, and a witness of the sufferings of Christ: ... feed (ποιμάνατε) the flock of God which is among you (τὸ ἐν ὑμῖν), taking the oversight[957] thereof, not by constraint, but willingly; not for filthy lucre, but of a ready mind; neither as being lords over God's heritage (τῶν κλήρων), but being examples to the flock" (1 Pet. 5:1–3).[958] As in the apostle's speech at Miletus, the relationship between the hierarchy and the church communities is likened to that between a shepherd and his flock. This comparison only makes sense when we presume that a presbyter or bishop appointed by the apostles had all branches of church life at his disposal. Here too the apostle calls himself a fellow elder or presbyter. Once again, this indicates that in the Churches of Pontus, Galatia, Cappadocia, Asia, and Bithynia, to which the first epistle of Peter was addressed, there were overseers whose authority was just as complete as that of the apostles.

---

953 See 1 Tim. 1:3–5; 4:6, 11–12. 2 Tim. 2:14, 16–17, 25–26. 2 Tit. 2:15.

954 See Tit. 3:10–11.

955 See 1 Tim. 3:15, 5:19–20, 22. Tit. 1:5.

956 It may even be supposed that the pastoral epistles were written for the express purpose of providing an example for bishops in the persons of Timothy and Titus, so fundamentally similar were the positions of the former and the latter in the Church. See Myshtsyn, 238; Knopf, *Das nachapostolische Zeitalter,* 203–204. Cf. W.M.H. Hay, M.A. Aitken, *Apostolical Succession Considered in the Light of the Facts of the History of the Primitive Church* (London: 1903), 182–184; H. Bruders, *Die Verfassung der Kirche,* 242–255, 96–97. But cf. Klitin, op. cit., 239: "The post held by Timothy and Titus was none other than that of bishop."

957 Ἐπισκοποῦντες—not considered authentic by all critics of the text. See Tischendorf, *Novum testamentum graece*[8] 2, 297.

958 For a detailed analysis of this passage, see the article by Prof. N.A. Zaozersky, "The Hierarchical Principle in Church Organization" ["Иерархический принцип в церковной организации"], *Bogoslovsky vestnik* (1911), vol. 1: from 70 on.

As may be seen from the above, it was the bishops to whom the apostles entrusted the governance of the Churches in the full sense of the word: the episcopacy was an office that was not limited merely to administrative and economic functions, but also included the work of teaching and the preservation of the truth. It was this all-encompassing church office that the apostles instituted. The author of the book of Acts relates concerning the apostles Paul and Barnabas that when the Churches were first founded they ordained presbyters in every Church (χειροτονήσαντες δὲ αὐτοῖς κατ' ἐκκλησίαν πρεσβυτέρους).[959] The author of the books of Acts makes a passing reference to this. It is clear that for him and his readers the ordination of presbyters at the foundation of the Church was a perfectly natural and ordinary occurrence. To Titus the apostle Paul wrote: "For this cause left I thee in Crete, that thou shouldest set in order the things that are wanting, and ordain elders in every city (καταστήσης κατὰ πόλιν πρεσβυτέρους), as I had appointed thee (διετάξαμεν—more precisely, 'established the order')" (Tit. 15). In the epistles to Timothy there is no such injunction, but the detailed enumerations which we read of the necessary qualities of a bishop become logical only if we assume that the apostle Paul wishes to give Timothy guidelines of a sort for appointing bishops.[960]

In the apostolic epistles we find mention of a special act of the laying on of hands, which imparted a particular gift to the person appointed to an office.[961]

In the apostolic and post-apostolic age, in addition to hierarchical individuals, in the Christian Church we also see charismatics, free teachers and preachers—apostles, evangelists, prophets, and teachers.[962] After the discovery of *The Teaching of the Twelve Apos-*

---

959 See Acts 14:23.

960 If 1 Tim. 5:22, "Χεῖρας ταχέως μηδενὶ ἐπιτίθει [Lay hands suddenly on no man]," refers to ordination in general, it appears to us that there are no grounds to see this as referring to the bishop's ordination exclusively of presbyters, as Knopf for example believes (*Das nachapostilische Zeitalter,* 197, 204).

961 See 1 Tim. 4:14, 2 Tim. 1:6–7. Cf. Acts 13:2–3, 14:23; 1 Tim. 5:22.

962 Concerning these in Russian literature see the essay by Prof. A.P. Lebedev, "Charismatic Teachers of the Initial Church in the 1st and 2nd Centuries" ("Xa-

tles,[963] scholarly, predominantly Protestant literature ascribed rather
too great a significance to these charismatics: all teaching activity
in the Church was ascribed exclusively to the charismatics, and in
this regard they were juxtaposed to the members of the hierarchy,
who allegedly were wholly estranged from the work of teaching.
In the first century there were allegedly two church organizations:
the hierarchical (local) and the charismatic (church-wide). Representatives of the former included administrators and treasurers,
while representatives of the second included teachers and those
who conducted worship services.[964] From this viewpoint, properly
speaking the successors of the apostles were specifically the charismatic teachers, whereas the hierarchy only declared itself successor
to the apostles after it had supplanted the charismatics.[965] Consequently, even those scholars who do not deny the apostolic institution of the episcopacy do not recognize the apostolic succession
of the later episcopacy A. Ritschl, for example, while recognizing
the historicity of the apostolic institution of the episcopacy and the
hierarchy in general, simultaneously considers hierarchal offices the
polar opposite of apostleship.[966] But the information we have cited
from the New Testament books of Holy Scripture do not permit

ризматические учители первенствующей Церкви I и II века"), in *Collected
Church History Compositions* ("Собрание церковно-исторических сочинений"),
vol. 10 (Moscow: 1905), 3–26.

963 *The Didache —Trans.*

964 These views are discussed in particular detail by Harnack in his *Prolegomena* to the edition of *The Teaching of the Twelve Apostles.* Cf. notes to the text of the
Didache (56–59). Harnack also delineates the patriarchal organization (*Prolegomena,*
148). Vgl. *Entstehung und Entwickelung der Kirchenverfassung und des Kirchenrechts,* 57–59.

965 Stripped of their work in the church, in Harnack's opinion, the charismatics became ascetics, thereby establishing the beginnings of monasticism (*Prolegomena TU* 2.1, 156–157, Anm. 86).

966 Ritschl, *Die Entstehung d. altkath. Kirche,* 358–359. In Russian literature the
priest Mikhail Fiveisky expresses a similar view. See *Spiritual Gifts in the Initial Christian Church* ("Духовные дарования в первоначальной христианской Церкви")
(Moscow: 1907), 42: "Only missionaries who traverse the earth preaching the
Gospel can be considered the successors of the apostles. ... The apostles and the
bishops belonged to two classes of ministers that differed significantly from each
other."

us to agree, first and foremost, that members of the hierarchy were wholly estranged from the work of teaching. On the contrary, it is the members of the hierarchy who alone are ordained and designated for service in the Church: no mention is made of any kind of ordination of charismatics. We must therefore acknowledge that the charismatics were specifically and exclusively free and voluntary teachers and preachers alongside the regular office of hierarch, which likewise included the right to teach. In and of itself, the gift of the Holy Spirit (χάρισμα) did not render its bearer an appointed official, a representative of the organization, and we have to speak not of a charismatic organization, but only of charismatics who acted under the governance of a single hierarchical church organization. It should be further noted that in the books of the New Testament χάρισμα is a broad concept: it also encompasses all church ministries in general, even charitable activity.[967]

Consequently, in the New Testament books we find no extensively developed theory of the apostolic succession of the episcopacy, but we do see this very succession at its outset. In founding the Churches, the apostles wholly transferred their governance (including the work of teaching) to the hierarchy they had established (see Tit. 1:5: διετάξαμεν), who were ordained sometimes by the apostles themselves, and sometimes through their deputies, such as Timothy and Titus. The theory of apostolic succession is declared "imprecise and even incorrect," but when this claim is made, the theory of the apostolic succession of the bishops is understood to mean a theory "by which the bishops are successors of the apostles in the full sense of the word, who have fully inherited their competencies."[968] But neither St. Irenaeus nor Tertullian expressed such a theory. Both St. Irenaeus and Tertullian declare the ministry of the apostles to be unique. The apostles founded the Churches, then entrusted the

---

967 For more detail, see Bruders, *Die Verfassung der Kirche*, 63–64, 69–73; Prof. N.A. Zaozersky, *The Hierarchical Principle in Church Organization*, especially from 80 on. "The apostle does not differentiate between systematically extraordinary and ordinary actions of the Spirit." (Prof. P.P. Glubokovsky, *The Evangelism of the Holy Apostle Paul in its Origin and Essence* ["Благовестие св. апостола Павла по его происхождению и существу"], book 2, 673n862.)

968 Myshtsyn, *The Organization of the Christian Church*, 206.

governance of these Churches and the guardianship of Tradition to the bishops.[969] This is aptly put by A.V. Gorsky when he says that "the ministry of the apostles was without succession: in the proper sense, the apostles had no successors, nor could they have. Irenaeus states that Peter and Paul imparted to Linus not apostolicity, but episcopacy."[970] In the opinion of Myshtsyn, "the fact that the apostles instituted the episcopacy and appointed bishops does not prove the apostolic succession of the bishops, just as the appointment of deacons gives no grounds for this conclusion."[971] But this opinion positively cannot be accepted. The apostles not only instituted the episcopacy and appointed bishops, but, as the author himself repeatedly states, along with governance they entrusted to them the work of teaching in the Church—something they did not entrust to the deacons. For this reason deacons cannot be called successors of the apostles with regard to preserving the truth of Christ. The bishops are successors of the apostles not in the sense of absolute equality with them, but only in that, being initially appointed by the apostles, they successively preserve from the apostles the true doctrine in the Church. Through the succession of her bishops the Church proves her apostolicity.[972] The theory of the apostolic succession of

---

969 Irenaeus, *Against Heresies* 3.3.3, 4. Tertullian, *Prescription Against Heretics* 32 (PL 2:53a). Here Tertullian traces the succession in Smyrna back to Polycarp, and in Rome to Clement, whom the apostles appointed.

970 A.V. Gorsky, *The History of the Gospel and the Apostolic Church* ["История евангельская и Церкви апостольской"], 120. Myshtsyn is quite wrong in citing A.V. Gorsky (206). For Gorsky, as we see, substantiates his opinion using the words of Irenaeus of Lyons, which Myshtsyn somehow omitted when citing the excerpt from Gorsky. From Gorsky see also 428–434. Cf. Th. Zahn, *Das Evangelium des Matthäus*, 547.

971 Myshtsyn, *The Organization of the Christian Church*, 206–207.

972 The objections of the priest Mikhail Fiveisky against the apostolic succession of the bishops are likewise completely groundless. See his work, *Spiritual Gifts in the Initial Christian Church*, 42. (1) "The successors of the apostles would also have had to be called apostles." But the apostolic ministry was not the episcopacy, and the episcopacy is not the apostolic ministry. Their work completed, the apostles committed the communities they had formed to the oversight of the bishops, and there is nothing remarkable about the fact that these bishops received a different name. (2) "Episcopacy in the person of James, the brother of the Lord, as we may

the bishops, first developed in detail by St. Irenaeus, is one proof of the thesis that "the Church is the custodian of the truth." This theory may briefly be outlined as follows: Christ imparted the truth to the apostles, and the apostles to the Church, which through the succession of her bishops preserves this truth in inviolate form. Just as the apostles did not become equal to Christ when they received the truth from Him, so also the bishops, although successors of the apostles, need not necessarily be apostles themselves. As the apostles were chosen by the Lord to spread the Gospel "unto the ends of the earth," so also the episcopacy was established by the holy apostles to preserve the truth in the Church unto the end of the age.[973] The doctrine of the divine institution in the Church of the episcopacy that continues the work of the apostles is clearly expressed by the apostle Paul. Thus, in the New Testament we find the following concept. The Lord Jesus Christ was sent into the world by God the Father. Jesus Christ sent the apostles. The apostles instituted the episcopacy, entrusting it with the complete oversight of the Churches that they themselves had founded.

---

deduce from the testimonies of Eusebius and Hegesippus, arose during the time of the apostles themselves. If the apostolic ministry and the episcopacy had existed simultaneously, naturally the representatives of the latter could not have been considered successors of the former." This objection is already rendered invalid by the fact that successors can exist even during the lifetime of the person whose place they fill. After founding a Church, the apostles committed it to a bishop, while they themselves continued on preaching the gospel (cf. Tit. 1:5).

973 "If Goltzman is trying especially hard to prove that we must not see the bishops as direct successors of the apostolic ministry according to their gift, here he may be quite certain of success. That the apostolic ministry was extraordinary and unique, there can be no doubt: only Catholic theologians defending the idea of papal supremacy may stubbornly insist otherwise. Nevertheless, this non-succession of the apostolic ministry cannot be an argument against the divine origin of the church hierarchy, just as the non-succession of the ministry of Jesus Christ cannot be an argument against the divine institution and extraordinariness of the apostolic ministry" (Klitin, op. cit., 253). In general it should be noted that quite early on in church literature the twelve apostles were set apart from among the other builders of the Church of Christ. The ministry of the twelve apostles is seen as something unique and extraordinary. See Harnack, *Prolegomena* TU 2.1, 101. Vgl. *Die Mission und Ausbreitung des Christentums²* 1, 267–274.

From the end of the apostolic age we have yet another excellent testimony, from which we can see what the bishop was in each
individual community. We are referring to the **third epistle of
the apostle John.** Despite its modest length, this epistle contains
considerable data for characterizing the significance of the bishop, and for this reason it attracts scholarly attention.[974] We will attempt to extract from this epistle only what pertains expressly to the
present question of the apostolic succession of the bishops. From
the epistle we can see that Diotrephes, the head of the community,
did not receive in his Church missionaries who wandered about
preaching, and even forbade those who wished to receive them (see
3 Jn. 1:10). Gaius, to whom the letter is addressed, received missionaries despite this, but apparently he was uneasy at disobeying
his primate, and for this reason in his supreme authority the apostle
John approves his actions (see 3 Jn. 1:5–6). The apostle wrote that
preachers of the Church be received, but Diotrephes did not accept
these epistles (see 3 Jn. 1:9). From this we see that, once again, all interactions between the Church and external people or communities
took place through Diotrephes. The epistle states that Diotrephes
loves to have preeminence (ὁ φιλοπρωτεύων—see 3 Jn. 1:9). It cannot be thought therefore that he was assuming a preeminence that
was not his own.[975] The apostle does not in the least reproach him
for preeminence, but reproaches him only for his particular love
of preeminence, and for his jealousy of his power.[976] Diotrephes's

---

974 See A. Harnack, *Über den dritten Iohannesbrief: Texte und Untersuchungen zur
Geschichte der altchristlichen Literatur, herausgeg. von Oscar von Gebhardt und Adolf Harnack,*
15.3b (Leipzig: 1897). A fairly detailed analysis has been made by V.N. Myshtsyn
(*The Organization of the Christian Church,* 249–259).

975 See Ritschl, *Die Entstehung der altkath. Kirche,* 408: "Diese Gewalt als eine
ordnungswidrige, usurpirte und nicht rechtlich gesicherte dargestellt wird."

976 Th. Zahn quite rightly calls Diotrephes a hierarch greedy for honor, who
did not follow the words of Christ (Mt. 10:44) and the example and exhortations
of the apostles (*Einleitung in das Neue Testament,* Bd. 2, 3-te Aufl. [Leipzig: 1907],
589, 592–593, Anm. 6). Vgl. Knopf, *Das nachapostolische Zeitalter,* 206: "Der Presbyter versucht nicht, die Stellung, die der mann einnimmt, grundsätzlich anzu-
greifen, nur die Art, wie er seit Amt führt, tadelt er heftig." Cf. Batiffol, *L'église
naissante et le catholicisme,* 146: "Il serai plus historique de se demander, non pas si

love of power caused him to reject even the authority of the apostle himself, and to revile him with "malicious words" (3 Jn. 1:10). The apostle John, like the apostle Paul, appointed bishops in the Churches,[977] but while he lived he considered himself the supreme overseer of all the Churches. Diotrephes however began to deny the authority of the apostle, and this betrayed his love of power. But the position of Diotrephes as depicted in the epistle was very high indeed: he was foremost in the community, its absolute overseer and steward, even its superior. He even excommunicates from the Church (ἐκ τῆς ἐκκλησίας ἐκβάλλει—see 3 Jn. 1:10). For this reason the incident with Diotrephes may be considered proof of the high position that bishops held in the Churches by the late apostolic period: it was they who were the absolute overseers of the Churches. If we turn our attention to the reasons for Diotrephes's action, we must consider him first and foremost the guardian of doctrinal purity. Why did Diotrephes not receive the missionaries? One must assume that there was a motive. In his second epistle the apostle John says that among wandering teachers there are many deceivers (see 2 Jn. 1:7). The apostle provides the token by which false teaching may be discerned (see 2 Jn. 7), and urges his readers not to receive false teachers into their house and not to salute them (see 2 Jn. 10), for one who salutes a false teacher "is a partaker of his evil deeds" (2 Jn. 1:11). Perhaps these false teachers even arose from among the

---

la primauté de Diotrephes est une usurpation, mais si son cas est seulement celui d' une maladroit."

977 Clement of Alexandria attests that upon returning from the isle of Patmos the apostle John visited the regions nearest to Ephesus, where he appointed bishops, organized entire Churches, and received certain persons indicated by the Holy Spirit into the clerical ranks: "ὅπου μὲν ἐπισκόπους καταστήσων, ὅπου δὲ ὅλας ἐκκλησίας ἁρμόσων ὅπου δὲ κλῆρον ἕνα γέ τινα κληρώσων τῶν ὑπὸ τοῦ πνεύματος σημαινομένων [here to appoint bishops, there to set in order whole Churches, there to ordain such as were marked out by the Spirit.]" (*Salvation of the Rich Man* 42.2 [GrchSch. 17:188.3–7]). This testimony is also cited by Eusebius. See *Church History* 3.23.6 (GrchSch. 9:1:238.14–19). Cf. information concerning the interactions between the apostle John and the bishops of Asia Minor in Harnack's *Über den dritten Iohannesbrief,* TU 15.3b, 23–24.

apostle John's former disciples.[978] To this testimony may be added information from *The Teaching of the Twelve Apostles*—a historical
manuscript that is quite close chronologically. For there too we find
constant exhortations to look to the doctrinal purity and morals of
wandering preachers. Clearly, among missionary preachers various
abuses had arisen.[979] It may be that the community of Diotrephes
had already suffered in some way at the hands of these missionaries, and so they did not resist the bishop when he forbade receiving
them. But for us this paints Diotrephes specifically as one standing
guard over the Church, defending it against possible errors. He is a
successor of the apostles in the full sense of the word, possibly even
appointed by the apostles themselves. All this, however, in no way
justifies Diotrephes's hostile attitude toward the apostle.[980]

In the book of Revelation likewise it is the bishop whom we
find holding exactly the same position in the individual community.
The second and third chapters of Revelation contain revelations
concerning the seven Churches of Asia Minor—those of Ephesus,
Smyrna, Pergamum, Thyatira, Sardis, Philadelphia, and Laodicea.
Each revelation is preceded by the words, "Unto the angel of the

---

978 See 1 Jn. 2:19: "They went out from us, but they were not of us."

979 Concerning this, see Harnack's *Prolegomena*, TU 2.1, 144, 122.

980 Harnack offers a different interpretation of the third epistle of John. In
Harnack's opinion, here we see the ancient patriarchal and provincial missionary
organization struggling to prevent the segregation of the individual community,
and for this very purpose the former produced the monarchical episcopacy. Di-
otrophes is the first monarchical bishop whose name we know. But the "elder" is
attempting to block this organization that is being reestablished: he sees in it only
the ambition of a particular individual. Diotrephes demonstrated an independence that the bishops did not yet have in the time of the apostle Paul (*Über den 3
Iohannesbrief,* 21, 24.) Cf. *Entstehung und Entwickelung d. Kirchenverf. und d. Kirchenrechts,*
48–49. From this standpoint, naturally, one might see the story of Diotrephes as
a negative in speculating on the apostolic succession of the episcopacy, as does
Aitken (*Apostolical Succession,* 185–186). The episcopacy arises, as it were, contrary to the will of the apostle. But Harnack's interpretation is not accepted by
Knopf (*Das nachapostolische Zeitalter,* 206–207), Bruders (*Die Verfassung der Kirche,*
122, Anm. 1.224), Batiffol (*L'église naissante et le catholicisme³,* 144–146), Myshtsyn
(*The Organization of the Christian Church,* from 249 on), and Zahn (*Einleitung in das
Neue Testament³,* Bd. 2, 589).

church of ... write."⁹⁸¹ If these angels refer to the bishops,⁹⁸² the

---

981 Rev. 2:1, 8, 12, 16; 3:1, 7, 3.

982 Whom to see in these "angels" of the Churches is a matter of considerable dispute. In the history of exegesis we may note three most typical readings. (1) The angels are bishops; (2) the angels are actual guardian angels of the Churches, just as Holy Scripture teaches that there are angels of individual persons (Mt. 18:10, Acts 12:15) or individual nations (Deut. 32:8, Acts 10:13, 20); (3) the angels are a personification of the Church itself. For a detailed exposition and analysis of the various opinions on this question, see Alexander Zhdanov, *The Revelation of the Lord Concerning the Seven Churches of Asia: An Attempt to Explain the First Three Chapters of Revelation* ("Откровение Господа о семи асийских Церквах [опыт изъяснения превых трех глав Апокалипсиса]") (Moscow: 1891), 100–112. Zhdanov himself accepts the third opinion: "The angel of the Church is the personification of a real spiritual moral power that manifests its activity in the history of the Church, or this power itself, presented in the form of a man." Cf. Weizsäcker, *Das apostolische Zeitalter,* 612: "die Personifikation der Gemeinde." Ritschl understands the angels to be the primates of the Churches, but not bishops (*Die Entstehung d. altkath. Kirche,* 408–409). Vgl. Harnack, *Entstehung und Entwick. der Kircheverfassung und des Kirchenrechts,* 48. Knopf is inclined to acknowledge them to be bishops (*Das nachapostolische Zeitalter,* 207–209). Zahn decisively acknowledges the angels to be bishops (*Einleitung in das Neue Testament³* 2, 613–616). See also Myshtsyn, *The Organization of the Christian Church,* 260–262. Cf. Bolotov, *Lectures on the History of the Early Church* 2, 458. The following grounds may also be cited [in support of] understanding the angels to mean bishops. When Scripture says "write," this implies an addressee, which cannot be either an angel (but cf. Origen, *Homilies on Luke* 23 [PG 13:1863a–b]) or the abstract concept of a Church, symbolically expressed. Although the content of the letters pertains to the whole Church (an objection made by Zhdanov, op. cit., 102–103), the letter itself is written specifically to a bishop. For 3 Jn. also states, "I wrote unto the church," but apparently via Diotrephes, who did not impart the apostle's epistles to his community. The letters conclude with "... what the Spirit saith unto the churches" (Rev. 2:7, 11, 17, 29; 3:6, 13, 22)—apparently through the bishop, who will read this letter in the congregation of the Church. Furthermore, at 2:20 after τὴν γυναῖκα the Alexandrian, Vatican, and other codices add σου [thy] (Tischendorf, *Novum Testamentum graece³* 2, 919), thus presenting the angel of Thyatira as having a wife, which is of course only applicable to a bishop. See Zahn, *Einleitung in das Neue Testament³* 2, 620–621. But cf. Emil Schürer, *Die Prophetin Isabel in Thyatira. Theologische Abhandlungen Carl von Weizsäcker zu seinem siebzigsten geburtstage,* 11 December 1892 gewidmet (Freiburg i.B.: 1892), 39–41. In any case, the words of the mystic are extremely obscure, for which reason even Catholic scholars sometimes pass over the testimony of Revelation in silence. See Batiffol, *L'église naissante et le catholicisme³,* 145–146n2.

information that we have in Revelation outlines the position of the
bishop quite explicitly. The bishop heads the church community.
He receives the epistles from the apostle and imparts them to the
Church (as in the third epistle of the apostle John). He is also the
keeper of doctrinal purity. He tests those who call themselves apostles—that is, wandering missionary preachers.[983] The angel of the
Church of Smyrna combats the heretical Judaizers (see Rev. 2:9).
The angel of the Church of Pergamum is confronted with the fact
that it has within itself "them that hold the doctrine of Balaam"
(Rev. 2:14–15),[984] and the angel of the Church of Thyatira—that it
permits "that woman Jezebel, which calleth herself a prophetess, to
teach and to seduce" the servants of God (Rev. 2:20). All the others
in Thyatira are exhorted to hold fast to what they have (see Rev.
2:24–25). To the angel of the Church of Sardis the apostle writes,
"Be watchful, and strengthen the things ... that are ready to die.
... Remember therefore how thou hast received and heard, and
hold fast, and repent" (Rev. 3:2–3). Via the bishop the apostle writes
not regarding economic or administrative affairs, but specifically regarding doctrine and the preservation of good morals. The apostle
considers the bishop fully his successor, over whom he watches only
while he himself is still alive. Here to be sure the *theory* of apostolic
succession is absent, but we do find the succession itself, which is of
course no less important.

From the late first century we have yet another surviving testimony of considerable importance as to the position of the bishop in
the Christian Church. This is the epistle of Clement of Rome to the
Corinthians. This historical manuscript must be highly esteemed
indeed, as it is by Harnack in one of his last works, in which he calls
the epistle one of the most important, if not the most important, ex-

---

983 Rev. 2:2. Cf. 1 Jn. 2:19, 2 Jn. 9–11, 3 Jn. 5–8. Diotrephes did the same as
the angel of the Church of Ephesus, but later prohibited receiving missionaries
and wanderers in general without testing them anew each time.

984 Rev. 2:16: "Repent; or else I will come unto thee quickly, and will fight
against them with the sword of my mouth" (ἐν τῇ ῥομφαίᾳ τοῦ στόματός μου).
Could this not be a promise from the apostle to come himself to the aid of the
bishop of Pergamum if he does not uproot the errors? But ordinarily this verse
is interpreted to mean the chastisement of God. See Zhdanov, op. cit., 189–191.

ample of post-apostolic literature, due to its time, origin, form, and significance.[985] Indeed, in addition to the Greek original, this epistle exists in Latin, Syrian, and Coptic translations. One of the two Greek manuscripts in which the epistle survives is the renowned Alexandrian Codex. In the Syrian manuscript the epistle is also linked to the books of the New Testament, among the general epistles and the epistles of the apostle Paul, and it is even divided into liturgical pericopes.[986] The early Church likewise esteemed this epistle very highly. In his letter to the Roman bishop Soter (about A.D. 170), Dionysius of Corinth relates that the epistle of Clement was read in the church: "To-day," writes Dionysius, "we have passed the Lord's holy day, in which we have read your epistle. From it, whenever we read it, we shall always be able to draw advice, as also from the former epistle, which was written to us through Clement."[987] St. Irenaeus reports as follows: "No small dissension (στάσεως γενομένης) having occurred among the brethren at Corinth, the Church in Rome dispatched a most powerful (ἱκανοτάτην) letter to the Corinthians, exhorting them to peace, renewing their faith, and declaring the tradition which it had lately received from the apostles (ἣν νεωστὶ ἀπὸ τῶν ἀποστόλων παράδοσιν εἰλήφει)."[988] Consequently, Irenaeus sees this epistle as containing, as it were, the essential content of the apostolic Tradition.[989] The epistle was written on behalf of the most important Church in the West, addressed to a renowned Church of the East.[990] We must therefore view it as an expression of

---

985 "Der erste Klemensbrief," *Sitzungsberichte der Königl* 3 (Preussischen Akademie der Wissenschaften: 1909), 39.

986 Zahn, *Geschichte des neutestamentlichen Kanons*, Bd. 1.1, 352; Funk, *Die apostolisclien Väter*, XVII–XIX; Harnack, "Der erste Klemensbrief," 39.

987 Eusebius, *Church History* 4.23.11 (GrchSch. 9.1:378.7–10).

988 Irenaeus, *Against Heresies* 3.3.3 (ANF 1:416; PG 7:850a–b). This passage is preserved in the original Greek by Eusebius. See *Church History* 5.6.3 (GrchSch. 9.1:438.15–19).

989 Harnack holds this opinion of St. Irenaeus to be entirely correct (40, Anm. 1).

990 The existence of this epistle is sometimes interpreted to mean the primacy of the Roman Church, and its historical and dogmatic significance is viewed primarily in that it offers actual proof of the primacy of the Roman Church (O.

authentic apostolic Tradition. But in this epistle we can even find a
certain theory of the apostolic succession of the church hierarchy.

The epistle was written regarding "that shameful and detestable
sedition, utterly abhorrent to the elect of God, which a few rash
and self-confident persons have kindled to such a pitch of frenzy,
that your venerable and illustrious name, worthy to be universally
loved, has suffered grievous injury."[991] It may be supposed that this
sedition consisted in that the Corinthians had ceased to obey their
superiors (ἡγουμένοις) and to render due honor to the presbyters
(πρεσβυτέροις),[992] and had deprived certain irreproachable bishops
of their ministry.[993] This sedition was headed by several persons;
from several remarks in the epistle it may be concluded that these
were charismatic preachers, who are described here the same way
as in *The Teaching of the Twelve Apostles.*[994] Consequently, under the
oversight of these people a sort of rebellion flared up against the
former primates of the community. In his epistle Clement exhorts
the addressees to submit to the hierarchy. It should be noted that
Clement has no occasion to speak of various hierarchical ranks: he
exhorts the laity to submit to the hierarchy in general.[995]

Bardenhewer, *Patrologie* §8.2, 25; Schwane, *Dogmengeschichte* 1, 441; Batiffol, *L'église
naissante et le catholicisme*[3], 141. Cf. *Clement de Rome: L'Eptre aux Corinthiens et l'Ho-
mélie du II-e siècle, texte grec., trad. Française, introduction et notes par H. Hemmer* (Paris:
1909). The author echoes M. Duchesne, stating that if the Roman Church could
through its bishop exhort the Church of Corinth to peace, this is an acknowledgment of its primacy. But to this E.M. objects that this assertion is pure fiction:
mere solidarity in spiritual fellowship would be fully sufficient to send this epistle.
See *Revue internationale de théologie* (1910): 141.

991 1 Clem. 1:1.

992 Idem 1:3.

993 Idem 44. Cf. 47, 54.

994 Idem 38: "him that is pure in the flesh"; that is, an ascetic. 48: "pure in
all his deeds." 54: "I will depart, I will go away whithersoever ye desire" (consequently, they were wanderers). 57: "the ... arrogant self-confidence of your
tongue" may indicate eloquence. Cf. 21: "those men who are ... lifted up, and
who glory in the pride of their speech."

995 Concerning this see Ritschl, *Die Entstehung d. altkath. Kirche*, 360–361.
Myshtsyn provides more detail (*The Organization of the Christian Church*, 194–201).

Among the reasoning concerning submissiveness and humility that suffuses the greater part of the epistle, Clement cites the
apostolic institution and succession of the hierarchy. Here are his
own words: "The apostles have preached the Gospel to us (ἡμῖν
εὐηγγελίσθησαν) from the Lord Jesus Christ; Jesus Christ [has done
so] (ἐξεπέμπφθη) from God. Christ therefore was sent forth by God,
and the apostles by Christ. Both these appointments, then, were
made in an orderly way (εὐτάκτως), according to the will of God.
Having therefore received their orders, and being fully assured by
the resurrection of our Lord Jesus Christ, and established in the
word of God, with full assurance (μετὰ πληροφορίας) of the Holy
Ghost, (the apostles) went forth proclaiming that the kingdom of
God was at hand. And thus preaching through countries and cities, they appointed the first-fruits [of their labours] (καθίστανον
ἀπαρχὰς αὐτῶν), having first proved them by the Spirit, to be bishops and deacons of those who should afterwards believe. Nor was
this any new thing (καὶ τοῦτο οὐ καινῶς), since indeed many ages
before it was written concerning bishops and deacons. For thus saith
the Scripture in a certain place, 'I will appoint their bishops in righteousness, and their deacons in faith'" (see Is. 60:17).[996] "Our apostles also knew, through our Lord Jesus Christ, and there would be
strife on account of the office of the episcopate (ἐπὶ τοῦ ὀνόματος
τῆς ἐπισκοπῆς). For this reason, therefore, inasmuch as they had obtained a perfect foreknowledge of this, they appointed those [minis-
ters] already mentioned (τοὺς προειρημένους), and afterwards gave
instructions (ἐπινομῆς), that when these should fall asleep, other approved men should succeed (διαδέξωνται) them in their ministry
(λειτουργίαν). We are of opinion, therefore, that those appointed
by them (that is, by the apostles), or afterwards by other eminent
men, with the consent of the whole Church (συνευδοκησάσης τῆς
ἐκκλησίας πάσης), and who have blamelessly served the flock of
Christ in a humble, peaceable, and disinterested spirit, and have
for a long time possessed the good opinion of all, cannot be justly

---

996 1 Clem. 42. Cf. 43:1: "And what wonder is it if those in Christ who
were entrusted with such a duty by God, appointed those [ministers] before mentioned?" The author then goes on to speak of the rod of Aaron.

dismissed from the ministry. For our sin will not be small (ἁμαρτία οὐ μικρά), if we eject from the episcopate (τῆς ἐπισκοπῆς) those who have blamelessly and holily fulfilled its duties."[997]

This is how Clement resolves the dispute that had arisen in Corinth because of the episcopate (ἐπισκοπή). He points to the fundamental reason why those persons against whom the charismatics had roused the sedition must not be stripped of their ministry. This fundamental reason is that they were appointed to ministry by eminent men, who had themselves been appointed by the apostles to head the Churches. Every dispute over the episcopate (ἐπισκοπή) must cease, because the church offices are instituted by God,[998] and their present bearers received lawful appointment to these offices. Consequently, those who rebel against the hierarchy are stripped of hope, and Clement threatens them with punishment.[999] The apostles themselves gave instructions (ἐπινομήν) that the hierarchical ministry not cease in the Church, but that it be successively conveyed from generation to generation. This is the succession that distinguishes the true overseers of the community from all others. The succession of these superiors (ἡγούμενοι) may easily be traced back to the apostles. The holders of ecclesiastical offices in Corinth were appointed by eminent men (ὑφ' ἑτέρων ἐλλογίμων ἀνδρῶν) or the first-fruits of faith; these latter were appointed by the apostles. The apostles were sent by the Lord Jesus Christ, and Christ—by God. It is on this successive appointment that the hierarchical structure of the Church is founded: personal charisma without appointment does not give one the right to be a lawful overseer of the Church.[1000]

In Protestant scholarly literature, the occurrence at Corinth which occasioned Clement's epistle is seen as one particular instance of the struggle that the episcopacy allegedly conducted against representatives of the more ancient charismatic organization, when it

---

997 Idem 44.

998 In another place also Clement calls the hierarchical structure a divine institution. See 1 Clem. 40:3 (ANF 1:16): "Where and by whom He desires these things to be done, He Himself has fixed (ὥρισεν) by His own supreme will."

999 1 Clem. 57:1–7. Here Clement is citing Prov. 1:23–33.

1000 For more detail see Bruders, *Die Verfassung der Kirche*, 74–81, 100–102.

began appropriating their long-standing right of teachership exclusively for itself.[1001] But there are greater grounds for believing that
it was the charismatics who rebelled against the hierarchy that had
existed since the very beginning. By virtue of their special gifts they
could at times acquire greater respect in the communities, so that
their bishops, who lacked [these] extraordinary gifts, lost their significance.[1002] This sparked the misunderstanding in Corinth also,
and Clement is writing not of some new thing unknown to the Corinthians: he is only exhorting them not to renounce the hierarchy
instituted by the apostles in favor of the charismatics.[1003] Clement
substantiates his exhortation specifically by pointing out the apos-

---

1001 Weizsäcker, *Das apostolische Zeitalter*, 621; I.T.F. Farquhar, "The Visible
Church in the Light of History," *Revue internationale de théologie* (1904): 474–475.

1002 Vgl. Bruders, *Die Verfassung der Kirche*, 121.

1003 In essence the same is also encountered in the *Didache*. With their gift
the λαλοῦντες ἐν πνεύματι (those speaking in the spirit, 11.7) could sometimes
seem to overshadow the representatives of the hierarchy who dwelt permanently
in the community. For this reason the author writes, "Appoint (χειροτονήσατε),
therefore, for yourselves, bishops and deacons worthy of the Lord, men meek,
and not lovers of money, and truthful and proved; **for they also render to you
the service of prophets and teachers** (ἡμῖν γὰρ λειτουργοῦσι καὶ αὐτοὶ τὴν
λειτουργίαν τῶν προφητῶν καὶ διδασκάλων). Despise them not, therefore, for
they are your honoured ones (τετιμημένοι ὑμῶν), **together with the prophets
and teachers** (μετὰ τῶν προφητῶν καὶ διδασκάλων)" (15.1–2). A community
might perhaps have no prophet in its midst (13.4). But even if there were a prophet, the bishops ought not to be despised, though their gift be more humble in its
manifestations. For they are the constant teachers of the communities. There
is no essential distinction between their ministry and the ministry of the charismatics. The bishops are esteemed just as are the prophets and teachers (μετὰ
τῶν), and not less (not μετὰ τοὺς). Thus, the *Didache* essentially provides the same
defense of the hierarchy against communities becoming temporarily enamored
with wandering charismatics as does the epistle of Clement. Cf. Bruders, *Die
Verfassung der Kirche*, 120, Anm. 224. Cf. Sohm, *Church Structure…*, 142–144. Zahn
eschews a literal understanding of *Didache* 15.1, and with no apparent grounds
weakens the significance of 15.2, and consequently he persists in differentiat-
ing between hierarchs and charismatics. On the one hand, among them there is
"kein förmlicher Rangunterschied," while on the other the prophets and teachers "in erster Linie der Ehre werth sind" (and yet—μετὰ τῶν!). (*Forschungen zur
Geschichte de neutestamentlichen Kanons und der altkirchlicher Literatur*. 3. Th. [Erlangen:
1884], 302–303.)

tles' institution of the ecclesiastical offices, which are to be preserved in the Church by succession.

To be sure, Clement does not develop the doctrine of the succession of the episcopacy in the same detail as St. Irenaeus would do later, but this is perfectly natural. For the dispute in Corinth was not over matters of faith, but over church administration: it was a dispute over the **episkope**.[1004] Clement had no need to speak in detail of the succession of the bishops as guardians of the truth. But though he had no explicit need, Clement nevertheless expressed the doctrine of episcopal succession fairly definitively. In the epistle of Clement we already see the same chain of succession as in the writings of St. Irenaeus and Tertullian: God, Christ, the apostles, the bishops.[1005] Consequently, the origin and invention of the theory of the apostolic succession of the bishops must be ascribed not to St. Irenaeus, but to Clement, and it must be dated not to the second half of the second century, but to the late first century. In recent times some indeed do exactly this, such as Sohm. As we know, this scholar constructed the hypothesis of a Church without law in the initial period, when there was some sort of unclear charismatic administration.[1006] In his opinion, the epistle of Clement takes the ju-

---

1004 Myshtsyn, *The Organization of the Christian Church*, 194.

1005 Clement says nothing of succession specifically with respect to the work of teaching. Consequently it is customarily opined that Clement is speaking only of the continuation of a church hierarchy stripped of the work of teaching. See Ritschl, *Die Entstehung der altkath. Kirche*, 358–363, 414–415; Knopf, *Das nachapostolische Zeitalter*, 167, 171; Weizsäcker, *Das apostolische Zeitalter*, 619; Harnack, *Entstehung und Entwick. der Kircheverfassung und des Kirchenrechts*, 54. But this opinion is depends wholly on that contradistinction between office and charismatic teachership which Protestant scholars so assiduously impose on the early Church. In our opinion, however, in Clement's words we can specifically see the theory of the apostolic succession of the episcopacy, since he does not separate teachership from the episcopacy. Even Harnack himself acknowledges that in the epistle of Clement is rooted the entire teaching of the latter Church regarding church authority and offices. If Christ received the authority of God, and the apostles received the authority of Christ, it is a small step to conclude that the officials appointed by the apostles possess the authority of the apostles ("Der erste Klemensbrief," 54–55).

1006 Harnack makes the following valid observation: "The strongest impres-

dicial structure of the community in Rome with its episcopal organization and traces it back to divine decree. In the organization of the community in Rome we see before us the form of organization that comprises the sole point of origin of the entire subsequent history of church structure. In this lies the tremendous significance of the epistle of Clement for the history of church structure. Here we see before us the form of organization that produced all that later followed.[1007] But it is perfectly impossible to grant that the epistle of Clement introduced something new, something heretofore nonexistent,[1008] and became a new point of church doctrine. Clement was perhaps himself a contemporary of the holy apostles;[1009] he wrote his epistle a mere 30 years after the death of the apostles Peter and Paul. As we see from the epistle itself,[1010] the apostles were examples

---

sion made by this epistle is that this new religion was first and foremost not based on cults, not enthusiastic, still less gnostic or theoretical and mysterial, but a moral movement" ("Der erste Klemensbrief," 42. Vgl. 55).

1007 Sohm, 171, 172–173. Cf. Knopf, *Das nachapostolische Zeitalter,* 164. See also the emphatic arguments of Ernest Renan: "Our epistle resolves the matter in a spirit of pure Catholicism. The apostolic rank is everything. It might be said that Catholicism originated in Rome, since the Church of Rome outlined the rules for it. Primacy belongs not to spiritual gifts: it belongs to the hierarchy, the authority conveyed by means of canonical consecration, linked by an unbroken chain to the apostles. It was felt that a free Church, as Jesus had designed it, and as Paul continued to envision it, was an anarchistic utopia, of which nothing could come in the future." (*Histoire des Origines du Christianisme,* vol. 5: *Les Évangiles et la Seconde Génération Chrétienne.* Published in Russian as *The History of the First Centuries of Christianity,* vol. 5: The Gospel and the Second Generation of Christianity ["История первых веков христианства. Т. 5. Евангелие и второе поколение христианства"], E.A. Serebryakov, trans. [Saint Petersburg: N. Glagolev Publishing], 195.)

1008 Indeed, Sohm theorizes that it is even something completely contrary to the nature of Christianity itself, meaning that authority stands in contrast to the essence of the Church. See 11, etc.

1009 Concerning this, see Myshtsyn, *The Organization of the Christian Church,* 186–187.

1010 1 Clem. 5:1: "But not to dwell upon ancient examples, let us come to the most recent spiritual heroes (ἐπὶ τοὺς ἔγγιστα γενομένους ἀθλητάς). Let us take the noble examples furnished in our own generation (ἡμῶν τὰ γενναῖα)." He then goes on to discuss Peter and Paul.

whom everyone still remembered. In Corinth, as we have seen from
the words of the epistle itself, there were primates appointed by
the apostles themselves. The apostolic Tradition was still very much
alive in the memory of Christians, for not even a whole generation had passed. How could one possibly think that Clement and
the entire community at Rome dared in an official epistle to pass
off something obviously new, something of their own invention, for
something that was of Christ? Still more unclear is how an epistle
with a new teaching, one that even contradicted the apostolic doctrine still fresh in the memory of all, could have been in any way significant for the Corinthians in its content, and even have acquired
among them the high authority indicated by Dionysius's letter to
Soter.[1011] Furthermore, in the epistle Clement himself clearly states
that prior to the sedition the Corinthians had a proper structure
in accordance with the commandment of the apostles. Thus, the
doctrine of the apostolic succession of the episcopacy expressed in
the epistle of Clement[1012] cannot be considered the beginning of
church doctrine on the subject in general, but only a link in the Tra-

---

1011 Myshtsyn, *The Organization of the Christian Church*, 205–206. Could Clement have written in this manner to the Corinthians concerning their primates,
when some of them undoubtedly themselves witnessed the appointment of their
presbyters? To us this appears improbable. "If the theory of Clement's epistle
had not coincided with the views of the Christians of Corinth, the epistle of
Clement would have met with no success whatsoever: it would have been considered an innovation, a falsehood, and perhaps would have perished forever. Yet
the reality bespeaks quite the opposite."—Prof. N.A. Zaozersky, "On the Essence
of Church Law" ["О сущности церковного права"] in *Bogoslovsky vestnik* (1909),
vol. 3: 336. This article also contains a detailed analysis of Sohm's theory of "a
Church without law." Harnack likewise provides a detailed critique of Sohm's
theory in the book *Entstehung und Entwick. d. Kirchenverfas. und d. Kirchenrechts.*

1012 For some reason Myshtsyn ultimately does not see this doctrine in Clement when he writes, "A century later (?), under the influence of particular historical circumstances, this gave rise to the theory of the apostolic succession of the
bishops. But, we repeat, it would be a mistake to ascribe it to Clement" (207). Yet
the author himself says on the same page that "the first indications of this theory
are already visible in his writings," and that Clement "concentrated the entire
ministry of the Church in the concept of the ecclesiastical representation instituted by the apostles. Consequently, he naturally arrived at a unilateral (?) and
unidimensional succession: God, Christ, the apostles, and the bishops."

dition delivered successively from the apostles.[1013] "The elevation of Clement to the status of the founder of Catholicism is a hypothesis of Sohm, one devoid of any historical basis." "Yes, that Saint Clement, an apostolic man, was a precise zealot, and even preserved the apostolic institutions in writing, is a fact attested by Church-wide Tradition."[1014]

Thus, in the epistle of Clement of Rome we see how already in the first century, although the teaching of this century is not well known, one way or another the Church in its self-identification and the dogma concerning the Church already understood the apostolic succession of the episcopacy to be a token of the true Church.[1015]

A mere two decades separates the epistle of Clement from a tremendously important historical work in which we find constant mention of the Church. This is the epistles of St. Ignatius the God-bearer. In certain respects the epistles of St. Ignatius the God-bearer are highly noteworthy and even stand out from other second-century church literary works. In the history of recent church historical science these were fated to have tremendous significance—namely, in resolving the question of how the Christian Church was originally organized. The most radically negative authors to write regarding the origin of the church hierarchy, such as Ritschl or Böhringer, proceeded from a denial of the authenticity of the epistles of St. Ignatius, which they dated to the late second century.[1016] This left

---

1013 "Who, then, distorted the apostolic structure of the Church: Sohm, or Clement, bishop of Rome in the first century? The answer is not difficult" (Zaozersky, *Bogoslovsky vestnik* [1909], vol. 3: 336).

1014 Zaozersky, ibid, 338.

1015 Vgl. Knopf, *Das nachapostolische Zeitalter,* 172.

1016 Some divided the epistles of Ignatius into two groups, one of which was declared authentic, and the other—of later origin. Some recognized as authentic the shortest edition of these epistles—the Syrian. Nevertheless, in the authentic epistles they specifically saw testimony concerning the earlier organization of the Church. Conversely, in the surreptitious epistles they detected clear traces of its later organization. This juxtaposition is made in detail by Böhringer (*Die alte Kirche,* Bd. 1. Th. 1., 33–46). In the four epistles that he held to have been added later, a clear purpose is evident: to exalt and glorify in a specifically hierarchical sense the episcopacy that had set itself apart from the presbyterate (41).

Protestant scholars an entire century (from the holy apostles to St. Irenaeus) in which to fit their fictitious process of the formation of a monarchical episcopate. In recent decades the authenticity of the epistles of St. Ignatius has been universally recognized in Protestant scholarly circles, marking a trend toward orthodoxy even in Protestant scholarly works. The recognition of the authenticity of the epistles of St. Ignatius gave rise to the nearly insurmountable difficulty of fitting the entire process of the purported development of episcopal authority in the Church into a mere half a century.[1017] This forced them to either reject their former vehement hypothesis or to create new ones, which in any case are considerably closer to the Orthodox teaching on the inherence of a divinely instituted hierarchy in the Church.[1018] In the history of the dogma concerning the Church, on the one hand the epistles of St. Ignatius are of great importance, and on the other their significance is fairly limited. Certain ideas in these epistles are expressed most decisively and are frequently repeated, but other ideas are completely undeveloped. The epistles are marked by a certain tendency to leave things unsaid; such is the impression left with the reader. The researcher is therefore duty-bound to avoid two possible extremes: not to misuse the argument *e silentio*, of which Protestant authors are habitually guilty, and not to supplement the ideas of the holy father with their own, which they wish to see in him in support of their preconceived theories.[1019] For this reason we will expound St. Ignatius's teaching concerning the Church and the significance of its hierarchy in the form in which it is found in the epistles, and will attempt to explain the particularities of this teaching as far as possible.

1017 This period ought to be shortened by another twenty years since, as we have seen, upon analyzing the first epistle of Clement of Rome even Harnack and Sohm admit that it already contains all the elements of later Catholicism.

1018 The value of the epistles of Ignatius in the history of the question of how the Christian Church was organized is also noted in the introduction to the work by Myshtsyn, II–V.

1019 See for example Archimandrite Sylvester, *The Doctrine Concerning the Church*, 119–120.

St. Ignatius most frequently repeats the idea of oneness of mind among the members of the Church. He says of himself that he pursued his work as a man appointed to unify.[1020] St. Ignatius describes this oneness of people in the Church both with words and with apostolic comparisons. Gentiles and Jews are united in the one Body of the Church of Christ (ἐν ἑνὶ σώματι τῆς ἐκκλησίας αὐτοῦ).[1021] St. Ignatius calls the Church of Antioch a lesser Body (σωματεῖον).[1022] The Church of Ephesus he likens to an edifice of God the Father.[1023] "Do ye therefore," writes St. Ignatius to the Magnesians, "all run together as into one temple of God, as to one altar, as to one Jesus Christ."[1024] As for the Church, St. Ignatius likens it to a choir singing a hymn in harmony.[1025]

In exactly the same way St. Ignatius clearly expresses the universal thinking of the Church: the whole Church is a society living the new life of Christ. This life St. Ignatius calls true life, another life (ἄλλος βίος),[1026] and this life he links inseparably to Christ. Without Christ there is no true life.[1027] Christ Himself is the union of the

1020   Ignatius, *To the Philadelphians* 8.1: "Ὡς ἄνθρωπος εἰς ἕνωσιν κατηρτισμένος." Concerning union or unanimity see also *To the Ephesians* 2.2, 4.1–2, 5.1–2, 13.1–2, 14.1. *To the Magnesians* 1.2, 6.1–2, 7.1–2, 13.2, 15. *To the Trallians* 12.2, 13.2. *To the Philadelphians,* preface, 2.1–2, 3.1–2, 7.2, 11.2. *To the Smyrnaeans* 12.2. *To Polycarp* 1.2, 8.3. Concerning St. Ignatius Archpriest P. Preobrazhensky writes: "The idea of the internal and external unity of the Church, along with exhortations to Christians to maintain it, is encountered so frequently in the epistles of St. Ignatius, and so profoundly occupied his soul, permeating all his injunctions, that St. Ignatius may rightly be called a teacher of unity" (*The Writings of the Apostolic Men* [Saint Petersburg: 1895], 267).

1021   Ignatius, *To the Smyrnaeans* 1.2.

1022   Idem, 11.2.

1023   Ignatius, *To the Ephesians* 9.1: "Ὡς ὄντες λίθοι ναοῦ πατρός." Cf. the teaching of the apostle Paul—e.g., 1 Cor. 3:9, Eph. 2:21.

1024   Ignatius, *To the Magnesians* 7.2: "Ὡς εἰς ἕνα ναὸν συντρέχετε Θεοῦ, ὡς ἐπὶ ἓν θυσιαστήριον, ἐπὶ ἕνα Ἰησοῦν Χριστόν."

1025   Ignatius, *To the Ephesians* 4.2.

1026   Idem 9.2, 11.1; *To the Trallians* 2.1; *To the Smyrnaeans* 4.1.

1027   Ignatius, *To the Trallians* 9.2. Cf. *To the Magnesians* 9.2, *To the Smyrnaeans* 1.1.

members of the Church;[1028] He is the common life of Christians.[1029] Christian life shone forth through Christ and through His death.[1030] Those who do not believe in the reality of the Flesh of Christ bear death in themselves.[1031] Christ is the Head of the Church, the believers are His members (μέλη αὐτοῦ),[1032] and the Church is the society of God (τὸ ἐν Θεῷ πλῆθος).[1033] Men are united into this society by faith, which is the Lord's Flesh, and love, which is the Blood of Jesus Christ.[1034] All is perfection in faith and love, and there is nothing higher than these.[1035] Christians are companions of one another,[1036] children of the Light of truth (τέκνα φωτὸς ἀληθείας),[1037] and they do all things in Jesus Christ.[1038] Unbelievers are the image of this world, but believers in love are the image of God the Father through Jesus Christ.[1039] Christians leave the old, sour leaven and are changed into the new leaven (εἰς νέαν ζύμην).[1040] The unity of Christians is both bodily and spiritual:[1041] they have an undivided Spirit, Who is Jesus Christ.[1042]

St. Ignatius also teaches concerning the Holy Spirit as the principle of new grace-filled life at work in the Church. By the Holy Spirit Christians are elevated to the height of moral perfection.[1043]

1028 Idem 11.2.

1029 Ignatius, *To the Ephesians* 3.2.

1030 Ignatius, *To the Magnesians* 9.1.

1031 Ignatius, *To the Smyrnaeans* 5.2.

1032 Ignatius, *To the Trallians* 11.2, *To the Ephesians* 4.2.

1033 Idem 8.2.

1034 Idem 8.1. Cf. *To the Romans* 7.3.

1035 Ignatius, *To the Smyrnaeans* 6.1.

1036 Ignatius, *To the Ephesians* 9.2. Cf. *To Polycarp* 6.1.

1037 Ignatius, *To the Philadelphians* 2.1.

1038 Ignatius, *To the Ephesians* 8.2. Cf. *To the Magnesians* 6.2, 7.1.

1039 Ignatius, *To the Magnesians* 5.2.

1040 Idem 10.2.

1041 Idem 13.2.

1042 Idem 15. Cf. *To the Philadelphians* 6.2.

1043 Ignatius, *To the Ephesians* 9.1.

They are God-bearers and bearers of holiness,[1044] they prosper in faith and love, in the Father, the Son, and the Spirit.[1045] The perfect Christian has God within himself.[1046]

Here we have compiled incidental statements scattered throughout the various epistles of St. Ignatius. The chief idea that permeates all the epistles is the idea that the one Church is the custodian of the truth. This doctrine we have already outlined above, but it must be supplemented by St. Ignatius's teaching on the significance of the hierarchy in the Church. In the epistles of St. Ignatius the church hierarchy is closely connected specifically with preserving true doctrine in the Church. For all the epistles of St. Ignatius were occasioned by the false teaching of the Docetists that threatened the Christian Churches. It is against false teachers that St. Ignatius constantly warns the Christians of Asia Minor.[1047] In light of this impending danger, Christians had to be given some definite criterion for recognizing truth and falsehood. It is this criterion that St. Ignatius gives in his epistles. It may briefly be expressed as follows: one must be in complete accord with the bishop and submit to him unconditionally. The hierarchy in the person of the bishop is a reliable—and, in the opinion of St. Ignatius, the only—surety of the veracity of church doctrine. This thesis, as we will subsequently see, St. Ignatius has little inclination to prove: for him it is a truth that requires no proof.[1048] Accord with the bishop and submission to him—this is the chief idea of St. Ignatius, which he tirelessly re-

---

1044 Idem 9.2.

1045 Ignatius, *To the Magnesians* 13.1. Cf. above, 94–95.

1046 Ignatius, *To the Romans* 6.2.

1047 The Docetist false teachers are invariably mentioned in nearly all the epistles of St. Ignatius. See for example *To the Ephesians* 7, 9, *To the Magnesians* 8, 10, 11; *To the Trallians* 6, 8, 9, 10; *To the Philadelphians* 6; *To the Smyrnaeans* 2, 4, 7; etc. For more detail concerning the predominating sentiment in St. Ignatius's disposition, under the effect of which he wrote to the Churches of Asia Minor, see Myshtsyn, op. cit., from 295 on.

1048 See Myshtsyn, 299: "For him the bishop, like church authority in general, being in and of himself an obvious fact in need of no substantiation, is a fully reliable and indeed the sole bulwark of the true faith, which localizes in itself true Christianity that is not subject to any doubt."

iterates in all his epistles in various turns of phrase. "It is fitting that
ye should run together in accordance with the will of your bishop,
which thing also ye do," writes St. Ignatius to the Ephesians.[1049]
"Let us be careful, then, not to set ourselves in opposition to the
bishop, in order that we may be subject to God."[1050] "It is well to
reverence both God and the bishop."[1051] "We ought to receive every
one whom the Master of the house sends to be over His household,
as we would do Him that sent him. It is manifest, therefore, that
we should look upon the bishop even as we would upon the Lord
Himself."[1052] St. Ignatius praises the deacon Sotio "inasmuch as he
is subject to the bishop as to the grace of God, and to the presbytery as to the law of Jesus Christ."[1053] To the Trallians St. Ignatius
likewise writes: "Continue subject to the bishop, as to the command
[of God], and in like manner to the presbytery."[1054] One must not
despise the age of the bishop, but must show him all reverence.
One who submits to the bishop submits not to him, but rather to
the Father of Jesus Christ, the bishop of all. One must submit to
the bishop without any hypocrisy, since one who does not submit
deceives not the visible bishop, but Him that is invisible.[1055] "Give ye
heed to the bishop, that God also may give heed to you. My life be
given for them that are submissive to the bishop, to the presbyters,
and to the deacons."[1056] Those who do not submit to the bishop do
not have a good conscience (οὐκ εὐσυνείδητοι).[1057] "He who does
anything apart from the bishop, and presbytery, and deacons, such

---

1049 Ignatius, *To the Ephesians* 4.1 (ANF 1:50), 20.2; *To the Magnesians* 6.2; *To
the Smyrnaeans* 8.1.

1050 Idem 5.3 (ANF 1:51); *To the Magnesians* 13.2.

1051 Ignatius, *To the Smyrnaeans* 9.1 (ANF 1:90). Cf. *To Polycarp* 8.3 (ANF 1:96;
see n12): "Continue ye in the unity ... of God [and of the bishop]."

1052 Ignatius, *To the Ephesians* 6.1 (ANF 1:51).

1053 Ignatius, *To the Magnesians* 2.

1054 Ignatius, *To the Trallians* 13.2; *To the Smyrnaeans* 8.1.

1055 Ignatius, *To the Magnesians* 3.1–2. Cf. *To the Trallians* 12.2: "Ἀναψυχεῖν τὸν
ἐπίσκοπον."

1056 Ignatius, *To Polycarp* 6.1 (ANF 1:95).

1057 Ignatius, *To the Magnesians* 4 (ANF 1:61).

a man is not pure in his conscience."[1058] "He who honours the bishop has been honoured by God; he who does anything without the knowledge of the bishop, does [in reality] serve the devil."[1059] "Do ye [nothing] without the bishop and presbyters. Neither endeavour that anything appear reasonable and proper to yourselves apart."[1060] [1061] On the contrary, "Be ye subject to the bishop as to the Lord," for then "ye appear to me to live not after the manner of men, but according to Jesus Christ."[1062] Without the hierarchy there is no Church.[1063] Where the bishop is, there the people must also be.[1064] "Where the shepherd is, there do ye as sheep follow."[1065] Christians will be able to guard against error only when they are not puffed up and do not separate from Jesus Christ our God and the bishop.[1066] "As many as are of God and of Jesus Christ are also with the bishop."[1067] "If [anyone] begins to boast"—in reference to virgins—"he is undone; and if he reckon himself greater than the bishop, he is ruined."[1068] "There is one flesh of our Lord Jesus Christ, and one cup to [show forth] the unity of His blood; one altar; as there is one bishop, along with the presbytery and deacons."[1069] "Let that be deemed a proper Eucharist, which is [administered] either by the bishop, or by one to whom he has entrusted it. ... It is not lawful without the bishop either to baptize or to celebrate a love-feast; but

---

1058 Ignatius, *To the Trallians* 7.2 (ANF 1:69).

1059 Ignatius, *To the Smyrnaeans* 9.1 (ANF 1:90). *To Polycarp* 4: "Let nothing be done without thy consent" (ANF 1:94).

1060 In the Russian, "Do not think to produce anything praiseworthy if you do this on your own." *–Trans.*

1061 Ignatius, *To the Magnesians* 7.1 (ANF 1:62); *To the Smyrnaeans* 8.1.

1062 Ignatius, *To the Trallians* 2 (ANF 1:66).

1063 Idem 3.1.

1064 Ignatius, *To the Smyrnaeans* 8.2.

1065 Ignatius, *To the Philadelphians* 2 (ANF 1:80).

1066 Iganitus, *To the Trallians* 7.1 (ANF 1:68–69).

1067 Ignatius, *To the Philadelphians* 3.2 (ANF 1:80).

1068 Ignatius, *To Polycarp* 5.2.

1069 Ignatius, *To the Philadelphians* 4 (ANF 1:81).

whatsoever he shall approve of, that is also pleasing to God, so that everything that is done may be secure and valid."[1070] "It becomes both men and women who marry, to form their union with the approval of the bishop, that their marriage may be according to God, and not after their own lust."[1071]

For more detail see Specht, *Die Lehre von der Kirche*, 89–94.

Thus, St. Ignatius teaches that the bishop and the hierarchy as a whole are the watchmen of the Church.[1072] It is also perfectly clear that the epistles of Ignatius contain no grounds for limiting the function of the hierarchy solely to the economic aspect of church life. In the epistle to Polycarp St. Ignatius presents a sort of portrait of the bishop. Here the bishop is envisioned as the absolute overseer of the community entrusted to his care. Apostasy from the bishop is apostasy from the Truth.[1073] According to St. Ignatius, the hierarchy commands the entire life of the church communities, and is not mere judicial administration. It shepherds not only the bodies of the faithful, but primarily their souls.[1074] St. Ignatius makes no mention of any other persons who were at the level of the hierarchy. To be sure, St. Ignatius particularly connects the bishop and the

---

1070 Ignatius, *To the Smyrnaeans* 8.1–2 (ANF 1:89–90).

1071 Ignatius, *To Polycarp* 5.2 (ANF 1:95).

1072 "In the eyes of Ignatius, all representatives of church authority comprise an indivisible whole by virtue of their position in the church hierarchy. Being fellow laborers and helpers of the bishop, the presbyters and deacons cannot violate the unity of church authority, exercised primarily by the bishop. This unity is attained by their submission to the bishop." "In his view, harmony among all representatives of church authority appears perfectly natural." See Myshtsyn, *The Organization of the Christian Church*, 303.

1073 Cf. Ignatius, *To the Philadelphians* 3.2–3: "As many as are of God and of Jesus Christ are also with the bishop. ... If any man follows him that makes a schism in the Church (σχίζονται), he shall not inherit the kingdom of God. If any one walks according to a strange opinion (ἐν ἀλλοτρίᾳ γνώμῃ περιπατεῖ), he agrees not with the passion [of Christ] (τῷ πάθει οὐ συγκατατίθεται)."

1074 For more detail see Knopf, *Das nachapostolische Zeitalter*, 212–213. It does seem to us, however, that Knopf imputes a significance to a passage from the epistle to the Ephesians (6.1) that is not there.

whole hierarchy with the Eucharist,[1075] but this by no means implies that the Eucharist was the sole occupation of the hierarchy. It could even be said that here the eucharistic work of the hierarchy is intimately connected with its teaching work.[1076] The epistles of Ignatius are directed against the Docetians: the hierarchy must guard believers against the Docetian error not only by preaching the truth, but also by performing the Eucharist, which Docetism denied. The bishop must entreat all to work out their salvation,[1077] and preach on various aspects of faith and piety.[1078] A pious bishop even when silent is more powerful (apparently in his teaching) than those who vainly talk (μάταια).[1079] At the same time the bishop must assemble congregations and call all members of the community to assemble.[1080] The Eucharist is therefore the measure of the orthodoxy of a member of the Church: to stray from the Eucharist meant to stray into Docetism.[1081] Consequently, it must be firmly posited that **in the teaching of St. Ignatius, the hierarchy is specifically the guardian of the purity and inviolability of Christian doctrine in the Church.** An unbiased reading of the epistles of Ignatius must produce this conclusion.[1082]

1075 Concerning this see Myshtsyn, op. cit., 307–308.

1076 This idea is also superbly developed by Knopf (*Das nachapostolische Zeitalter,* 213–214). In Knopf's opinion, for St. Ignatius the centralization of worship assemblies and their subjection to the bishop are a panacea against all heresies, even if the bishop should be unskilled in teaching.

1077 Ignatius, *To Polycarp* 1.2.

1078 Idem 5. In the epistle to the Philippians (chapter 6), Polycarp likewise states that the presbyters have a duty to convert those in error.

1079 Ignatius, *To the Philadelphians* 1.1.

1080 Ignatius, *To Polycarp* 4.2: "πυκνότερον συναγωγαὶ γινέσθωσαν ἐξ ὀνόματος πάντας ζητεῖ."

1081 Ignatius, *To the Smyrnaeans* 7.1: "They abstain from the Eucharist and from prayer, because they confess not the Eucharist to be the flesh of our Saviour Jesus Christ, which suffered for our sins" (ANF 1:89).

1082 In Protestant scholarly literature this position elicits vehement objections. See Ritschl, *Die Entstehung der altkath. Kirche* 404–405, 409–410. But Böhringer is particularly abrupt when he writes, "We find no trace of the communal office having been customarily and invariably linked to preaching the Gospel and to

St. Ignatius likewise does not allow for thinking that the bishop could err: this concept is completely outside his perspective. It is therefore perfectly logical that St. Ignatius would also say nothing of any norms to which the bishop must adhere.[1083] To Polycarp St. Ignatius writes that he be governed only by the will of God.[1084] In the epistles of St. Ignatius, the local Church is presented as self-sufficient, and is treated outside any connection with the other Churches. The power of the bishop is limited to the confines of his Church. This particularity of the epistles of St. Ignatius is accentuated with particular emphasis by Protestant scholars, who wish to find in St. Ignatius the doctrine of the unity of the invisible Church of Christ. Only individual communities without any ties between them exist visibly.[1085]

Indeed, on the one hand in his epistles St. Ignatius has the local Christian community headed by the bishop, and on the other— the whole Church together headed by Jesus Christ Himself. To the Ephesians St. Ignatius writes, "You ... are so joined to [the bishop] as the Church is to Jesus Christ, and as Jesus Christ is to the Father."[1086] To the Smyrnaeans he writes, "Wherever the bishop shall appear, there let the multitude [of the people] also be; even as, wherever Jesus Christ is, there is the Catholic Church."[1087] Here for

---

the work of teaching by virtue of the office itself—a specifically apostolic duty. On the contrary, rather, St. Ignatius once again disassociates the communal office from the work of teaching. The latter is not yet formally linked to any office whatsoever, but remains at the disposal of each believer who is capable of it" (*Die alte Kirche*, 1-er Bd. 1-ter Teil, 36–37). At the same time, Böhringer writes this only regarding those epistles of St. Ignatius which he recognizes as authentic, and states himself that "ganz anders dagegen ist Alles im faschen Ignatius" (37).

1083 Concerning this see several comments by Myshtsyn, op. cit., 313–314.

1084 Ignatius, *Epistle to Polycarp* 4.1. Cf. also the foreword to the epistle to Polycarp.

1085 Seeberg, *Studien zur Geschichte des Begriffs der Kirche*, 11–14; Harnack, *Dogmengeschichte*⁴ 1, 405 ff. Vgl. Thomasius, *Dogmengeschichte* 1, 101–102; Ritschl, *Die Enstehung d. altkath. Kirche*, 407.

1086 Ignatius, *To the Ephesians* 5.1 (ANF 1:51).

1087 Ignatius, *To the Smyrnaeans* 8.2 (ANF 1:89): "Ὅπου ἂν ᾖ Χριστὸς Ἰησοῦς, ἐκεῖ ἡ καθολικὴ ἐκκλησία."

the first time in church literature we encounter the term ἡ καθολικὴ ἐκκλησία ("the catholic church"), and this term, it must be thought, specifically denotes the whole totality of the Christian Church as opposed to the individual, self-contained community.[1088] It may be supposed that in the same epistle to the Smyrnaeans St. Ignatius is giving an explanation for the term καθολικὴ ἐκκλησία ("catholic church") here used: "ἐν ἑνὶ σώματι τῆς ἐκκλησίας αὐτοῦ."[1089]

We cannot, however, speak of the existence of an invisible Church on these grounds. For, as has already been stated at the outset of our study, from these same epistles of St. Ignatius we learn of the liveliest commerce among the individual Churches. That there were no judicial norms linking one Church to the next is a fact; but the absence of external judicial norms does not mean that St. Ignatius understood Christianity to exist (or that it actually existed) solely in the form of communities isolated from one another. St. Ignatius did not envision Christianity solely as his own visible Church of Antioch: there is one Christianity in all the Churches, and to all the Churches St. Ignatius writes the same message. In his epistle to the Ephesians St. Ignatius even speaks of bishops appointed to the utmost bounds of the earth (οἱ κατὰ τὰ πέρατα ὁρισθέντες).[1090] Here we see the whole visible Church governed by the bishops. Here we can even find an indication of a single episcopacy for the whole Church.[1091] According to St. Ignatius's teaching, the whole

---

1088 Concernig the meaning of the words "ἡ καθολικὴ ἐκκλησία" in Ignatius, see Harnack, *Dogmengeschichte* 1, 406, Anm. 3; Myshtsyn, 306n1. M.D. Muretov sees the words of Ignatius as indicating the entirety of the Church or its catholicity—a living, effectual union of Christ, the hierarchy, and the people. Concerning the term καθολικός [catholic], see the appendix to the treatise *The Ancient Hebrew Prayers Under the Name of the Apostle Peter* ["Древнееврейские молитвы под именем апостола Петра"] (Trinity-Sergius Lavra: 1905), 30.

1089 Ignatius, *To the Smyrnaeans* 1.2. See Muretov, op. cit., 153.

1090 Ignatius, *To the Ephesians* 3.2. All scholarly conjecture regarding the word πέρατα [ends] is completely groundless, the more so since in the epistle to the Romans (6.1) Ignatius uses the expression τὰ πέρατα τοῦ κόσμου [the ends of the world]. Cf. Preobrazhensky, *The Writings of the Apostolic Men*, 293n2; Myshtsyn, 316–317n2.

1091 Knopf does not rule out the possibility of this understanding, but in this

Church is united to Christ. Christ is its Head. This teaching wholly
coincides with the teaching of the apostle Paul. But from both the
teaching of the apostle Paul and the teaching of St. Ignatius it does
not at all follow that the one Church headed by Christ is thought
to be merely invisible. On the contrary, in the headship of Christ,
which is one for the one Church, individual Churches can only find
an incentive for visible union.[1092] St. Ignatius envisions the Church
as a real unity. The one Church is dispersed to the ends of the earth.
In this respect the epistles of St. Ignatius elucidate the chronologically proximate[1093] *Martyrdom of Polycarp*, where the holy catholic
Church is presented as dispersed throughout the whole universe
(κατὰ τὴν οἰκουμένην), so that local Churches are simply like par-
ishes (παροικίαι) of this one Church.[1094]

We must also take note of the fact that St. Ignatius was of course
writing to individual communities. He had no occasion to speak of
the unity of the whole Church. Consequently, in a strictly scholarly
sense we can only state that his brief and more or less random epis-

instance he characterizes the thinking of St. Ignatius as "eine handgreifliche,
dogmatisierende Übertreibung" (*Das nachapostolische Zeitalter*, 221, Anm). But cf.
Ritschl, *Die Entstehung der altkath. Kirche*, 407–408.

1092 Cf. Archimandrite Sylvester, *The Doctrine Concerning the Church*, 131–133.
Seeberg gives particular attention to the epistle to the Magnesians 3.2, where
Christ is called ἐπίσκοπος ἀόρατος [invisible bishop] as opposed to ἐπίσκοπος
βλεπόμενος [visible bishop] (op. cit., 13). But here too there is no doctrine of
an invisible Church, because Christ can only be called the invisible Head of the
Church, though the Church itself were visible. St. Ignatius talks, for example,
about the union between Christ and the individual person (*To the Romans* 6.3).
Can we really conclude from this that this person is invisible?

1093 Funk, *Die apostolischen Väter*, XXVII–XXVIII.

1094 See the *Inscription*: "Τῆς ἁγίας καὶ καθολικῆς ἐκκλησίας." 8.1: "κατὰ τὴν
οἰκουμένην καθολικῆς ἐκκλησίας" as well as 19.2, where Jesus Christ is called the
pastor "τῆς κατὰ τὴν οἰκουμένην καθολικῆς ἐκκλησίας [of the catholic Church
{dispersed} throughout the inhabited world]." See also 5.1, 16.2. For an analysis
of all these expressions, see Muretov, op. cit., 30–31. Concerning the *Inscription*
the author writes: "Here we see the following distinctions: the individual communities in Smyrna and Philomelium; all communities in every place (ecumenicity
or territoriality); the Church that is Holy (truth, orthodoxy, authenticity, canonic-
ity), and, finally, Catholic: in contrast to all other definitions, apparently she alone
is Catholic, in unity and entirety abiding in all communities in every place" (31).

tles say nothing of the hierarchical unity of the visible Church. But
to state that St. Ignatius supposedly speaks in favor of some invisible
Church would be to impose one's own reasoning on the author's
ideas, thereby abusing the *ex silentio* argument.[1095]

For these *ex silentio* arguments the epistles of Ignatius offer considerable leeway, since in their brevity they do not always speak
precisely and definitively on the same subjects.[1096] Catholic scholars, citing the numerous epithets which Ignatius bestows upon the
Church of Rome in his epistle, and the expression "Jesus Christ
alone will oversee it [the Church of Syria], and your love,"[1097] claim
that St. Ignatius taught the primacy of the Church of Rome.[1098] But
once again we must note that far more is being read into St. Ignatius's words than they communicate. In this instance the words of
St. Ignatius are highly ambiguous, and may be interpreted to mean
anything whatsoever.[1099] In any case, St. Ignatius says nothing of
the Church of Syria being judicially dependent on that of Rome.
He writes, "Remember in your prayers the Church in Syria, which
now has God for its shepherd, instead of me."[1100] If the Church of
Rome had possessed any judicial authority, Ignatius would not have
mentioned prayer only.

1095 It is most telling that Böhringer, while declaring the complete edition of
the epistles of Ignatius to be of later origin, finds in them all the elements of the
later doctrine of the hierarchy. The bishop is not only the vicar of God and the
organ of unity for the individual community, but the **organ of the Church,** the
representative of **church unity.** In *To the Smyrnaeans* 8.2, where some wish to see
the doctrine of the invisible Church, Böhringer reads the implicit concept that
the episcopacy is what unites the individual communities into a single Church.
See *Die alte Kirche,* vol. 1, 43–44.

1096 Concerning this see Myshtsyn, op. cit., 314.

1097 Ignatius, *To the Romans* 9.1 (ANF 1:77).

1098 Concerning this, see F.X. Funk, *Der Primat der römischen Kirche nach Ignatius
und Irenäus. Kirchengeschichtliche Abhandlungen und Untersuchungen,* 1-er Bd., 2–12; Batiffol, *L'église naissante et le catholicisme,* 167–170; Harnack, *Dogmengeschichte*⁴ 1, 486.

1099 Vgl. Funk, *Kirchengesch. Abh. und Untersuch,* 1. See several observations in
the treatise cited by Archimandrite Nikanor, 96–98.

1100 Ignatius, *To the Romans* 9.1 (ANF 1:77).

But the Catholic point of view apparently sees in Ignatius's epistles the episcopal organization of the whole Church under the headship of Rome. At the same time, on the basis of this same epistle of Ignatius to the Romans it is claimed that in the early second century in Rome there was not even a monarchical episcopacy at all.[1101] But to this also we may say in the words of F. Loofs: adherents of the historical method "frequently work with a slew of highly dubious *ex silentio* arguments. Who, for example, would vouch for the accuracy of the conclusion that, since Ignatius does not mention a single bishop, there was no monarchical episcopacy at the time when Ignatius wrote his epistle to the Romans?"[1102]

So as not to see in the epistles of St. Ignatius what is not actually there, we must recognize them as establishing one chief thesis: in the community the guardian of purity of faith is the bishop, and all must unite around him in oneness of mind.[1103] Why does St. Ignatius consider the bishop to be the guardian of purity of faith? Does he offer any grounds for doing so? We have already stated that St. Ignatius states this concept almost peremptorily. His epistles do not show there to have been debates in any place regarding the authority of the bishop. For St. Ignatius the episcopacy is a firmly established institution, not one in its inception. Though a bishop be young, as in the Church of Magnesia,[1104] there is not a shadow of a doubt as to his legitimacy. Consequently, St. Ignatius had no need to *prove* the necessity of submitting to the bishop: he had only to admonish and exhort to this submission. Only a reminder was required, without any particular proof whatsoever.[1105] Next, St. Ig-

---

1101 Concerning this see Myshtsyn, op. cit., 318–321, where an analysis of this conjecture is also given.

1102 Loofs, *Theolog. Studien und Kritiken* (1890), 657; Myshtsyn, 320n1.

1103 On one occasion St. Ignatius even uses the following expression: "Be ye subject to the bishop, and to one another, as Jesus Christ to the Father, according to the flesh, and the apostles to Christ, and to the Father, and to the Spirit" (*To the Magnesians* 13.2 [ANF 1:64–65]).

1104 Ignatius, *To the Magnesians* 3.1.

1105 Funk holds that the absence of tendencies in the epistles of St. Ignatius is the best proof of their authenticity: it cannot be said that they were falsified in

natius was writing to communities that he knew, where the bishops were persons known to him, to whom he was bound by close bonds of friendship.[1106] Indeed, these bishops were guardians of doctrinal purity even before the epistles were written. Men tried and true, whose youth may sometimes even have been spent in apostolic times, these persons could not have betrayed the truth and fallen into such an error as Docetism. The true position of the bishops and their own personal qualities rendered superfluous, at least for St. Ignatius, any detailed theory in justification of their ecclesiastical and doctrinal authority. Furthermore, the epistles of St. Ignatius cannot be viewed from an absolute standpoint: their significance was only relative, by virtue of their very purpose and nature. Being private letters, their significance was both local and temporal. Indeed, these works only make sense in the context in which they were written. The bishop of Antioch is going to Rome under convoy, where torture and death await him. Taking advantage of the opportunity, he sends brief letters to the Churches that were deeply concerned over his fate. There are therefore no grounds whatsoever to demand and expect St. Ignatius to provide precise, detailed dogmatic treatises on any subject at all. All theories justifying the authority of the hierarchy, arguments regarding church organization, and so forth were now far from the mind of St. Ignatius. One need only read the epistle to the Romans to judge to what degree the holy father had already renounced earthly life and earthly relations.

Nonetheless, in St. Ignatius we encounter brief comments that seem to express a certain theory. These comments are random and brief, and for this reason cannot serve as the basis for any complete theory, lest we risk substituting our own ideas for those of the holy father. We will therefore merely gather all these comments together.

First and foremost, St. Ignatius clearly speaks of the hierarchy as a divine institution. "Jesus Christ, our inseparable life, is the [manifested] will of the Father; as also bishops, settled (οἱ ὁρισθέντες) everywhere to the utmost bounds [of the earth], are so by the will

---

the interests of elevating the episcopacy. See *Die Echtheit der ignatianischen Briefe*, 61. Cf. 62, 64. Cf. Bardenhewer, *Patrologie*[3] §9.3, 32.

1106 Ignatius, *To the Ephesians* 5.1.

of Jesus Christ."[1107] The bishop is sent by God. "We ought to receive every one whom the Master of the house sends (πέμπει) to
be over His household, as we would do Him that sent him. It is
manifest, therefore, that we should look upon the bishop even as we
would upon the Lord Himself."[1108] In his salutation to the Church
of Philadelphia St. Ignatius refers to bishops, presbyters, and deacons "who have been appointed according to the mind of Jesus
Christ, whom He has established in security, after His own will, and
by His Holy Spirit."[1109] St. Ignatius sometimes refers to the deacons
as the institution of God.[1110]

In these admittedly few phrases of St. Ignatius we may see the
doctrine of the divinely instituted hierarchy—a divine institution
not in the dogmatic sense alone, but also in the historical sense, as
attested by the passage cited from the epistle to the Ephesians.[1111]
The bishop is said to be sent to govern the house of God, that is,
the Church. In this respect St. Ignatius is very close to Clement of
Rome: for both of them the hierarchical church offices are a divine institution that is essential for the true Church.[1112] Already this
phrase in the salutation of the epistle to the Philadelphians hints
at the idea of a particular grace-filled power imparted to the hierarchy. In his epistle to Polycarp also, St. Ignatius places the bishop
in a direct relationship to God and to Jesus Christ, Who as it were

---

1107 Idem 3.2 (ANF 1:50).

1108 Idem 6.1 (ANF 1:51–52).

1109 Ignatius, *To the Philadelphians*, inscription: "Σὺν τῷ ἐπισκόπῳ καὶ τοῖς σὺν
αὐτῷ πρεσβυτέροις καὶ διακόνοις ἀποδεδειγμένοις ἐν γνώμῃ Ἰησοῦ Χριστοῦ, οὓς
κατὰ τὸ ἴδιον θέλημα ἐστήριζεν ἐν βεβαιωσύνῃ τῷ ἁγίῳ αὐτοῦ πνεύματι."

1110 Ignatius, *To the Trallians* 3.1; *To the Smyrnaeans* 8.1.

1111 "The bishop of Antioch, a disciple of the apostles, naturally knew what
he was saying, and knew by virtue of whose institution he bore upon himself that
great rank."—Archpriest A.V. Gorsky, *The Formation of the Canon of the Sacred Books
of the New Testament* ("Образование канона священных книг Нового Завета")
(Moscow: 1871), 17 (=Addendae to the Edition of the Works of the Holy Fathers
["Прибавления к изданию творений святых отцов"] [1871], part 24, 313).

1112 Vgl. Bruders, *Die Verfassung der Kirche* 87, 102; Batiffol, *L'église naissante et le
catholicisme*, 157–158. But cf. Ritschl, *Die Entstehung der altkath. Kirche*, 408.

oversees the bishop.[1113] It would however be too perilous to ascribe to St. Ignatius an idea akin to the teaching of St. Irenaeus of Lyons concerning *charisma veritatis* [the charisma of truth].

The historical argument which later anti-Gnostic writers employed in their struggle with the heretics, when they pointed to the ministry of the episcopacy in the true Church successively received from the apostles, is one that we do not find in the writings of St. Ignatius.[1114] St. Ignatius says nothing about episcopal succession from the apostles;[1115] on the contrary, in his writings we find a parallel which, being a unique feature of the ecclesiological views of St. Ignatius, even in a sense replaces the theory of episcopal succession. Namely, in St. Ignatius we find phrases such as these: "Your bishop presides in the place of God, and your presbyters in the place of the assembly of the apostles, along with your deacons, who are most dear to me, and are entrusted with the ministry of Jesus Christ."[1116]

1113 Ignatius, *To Polycarp*, inscription, 1.3, 2.3, 4.1.

1114 In the words from *To the Ephesians* 3.2 cited above a certain succession may be discerned: Jesus Christ is the will of the Father, as the bishops themselves are by the will of Jesus Christ. But this faint suggestion seems to us to be wholly insufficient grounds to ascribe to St. Ignatius a positive theory of apostolic succession, as Bruders does when he asserts that in the mind of St. Ignatius the first messengers and vicars of God the Father—namely, Christ and His apostles—were replaced by others, and that their charge extends to the bishops and the presbyters of A.D. 113 (see *Die Verfassung der Kirche*, 84–85.) On the other hand, we must deem extreme the opinion of Ritschl—that in Ignatius there is allegedly no suggestion of the episcopacy being a continuation of the apostolic ministry, and that the phrase in *To the Romans* 4.2–3, where Ignatius compares himself to the apostles Peter and Paul, even proves that he could not have held himself to possess apostolic fullness of authority (see *Entstehung d. altkath. Kirche*, 407). Above we have already stated that the ministry of the twelve apostles was always considered special and extraordinary, but the theory of apostolic succession should not be divorced from the fact of the apostles having established an unbroken hierarchy.

1115 Vgl. Schanz, "Der Begriff der Kirche," *Theologische Quartalschrift* (1893): 554; Aitken, *Apostolical Succession*, 195: "We observe too that these startling documents yield no real support to the doctrine of Apostolical succession by the imposition of hands."

1116 Ignatius, *To the Magnesians* 6.1 (ANF 1:61): "Προκαθημένου τοῦ ἐπισκόπου εἰς τόπον Θεοῦ καὶ τῶν πρεσβυτέρων εἰς τόπον συνεδρίου τῶν ἀποστόλων, καὶ τῶν διακόνων τῶν ἐμοὶ γλυκυτάτων πεπιστευμένων διακονίαν Ἰησοῦ Χριστοῦ."

"Ye are subject to the bishop as to Jesus Christ. … And be ye subject also to the presbytery, as to the apostles of Jesus Christ, who is our hope."[1117] "See that ye all follow the bishop, even as Jesus Christ does the Father, and the presbytery as ye would the apostles."[1118] "Let all reverence the deacons as Jesus Christ, and the bishop as being a type of the Father, and the presbyters as the sanhedrin of God, and assembly of the apostles."[1119] From above the phrases of St. Ignatius we cannot however conclude that he had supposedly created a new theory according to which the bishop inherited the place of Jesus Christ, and the presbyters—the place of the apostles.[1120] In this instance St. Ignatius's discourse on succession cannot be called historical; it is rather typological. During the life of Jesus Christ the Church could be divided specifically as follows: Jesus Christ, the apostles, and believers. Christ is the Head and Center of the whole Church, and the apostles are His most intimate disciples, through whom He disseminates His teaching. This image, for perfectly logical reasons, came to the mind of St. Ignatius. Every local Church was as though a reflection of this first Christian community of believers: at the head of the Church stood the bishop,[1121] surrounded his close circle of the "well-woven spiritual crown of [the] presbytery,"[1122] which stood between the bishop and the laity. It is this analogy that St. Ignatius presents in his epistles. But it is essential to recognize that the significance of the analogy itself is historical, not typological, as the Protestants would wish to see it, proceeding from their idea of an invisible Church. In the Protestant interpretation, St. Ignatius's thinking is as follows: the bishop is as a symbol (*Typos*) of Christ or God, and the presbyters are symbols of

---

1117 Ignatius, *To the Trallians* 2.1–2 (ANF 1:66–67).

1118 Ignatius, *To the Smyrnaeans* 8.1 (ANF 1:89).

1119 Ignatius, *To the Trallians* 3.1 (ANF 1:67): "Πάντες ἐντρεπέσθωσαν τοὺς διακόνους ὡς Ἰησοῦν Χριστόν, ὡς καὶ τὸν ἐπίσκοπον ὄντα τύπον τοῦ πατρός, τοὺς δὲ πρεσβυτέρους ὡς συνέδριον Θεοῦ καὶ ὡς σύνδεσμον ἀποστόλων."

1120 Cf. Böhringer, *Die alte Kirche* 1.1, 42.

1121 Let us recall the admonitions of St. Ignatius cited above—that nothing be done without the will of the bishop.

1122 Ignatius, *To the Magnesians* 13.1 (ANF 1:64; see ANF 1:64n16).

the apostles. From this it follows that an organized individual community is a reflection (*Abbild*) of the whole Church that is spiritually united to Christ: each individual community must be a reflection of the celestial Church.[1123] But in the writings of Ignatius there is no concept of a celestial Church in which there is a semblance of earthly relations within the confines of the individual community. Harnack says that the concept of a celestial Church is based on the expressions used by Ignatius,[1124] but this is only conjecture, as the holy hierarch Ignatius offers no such concept. Furthermore, we will now see that the thinking of the holy hierarch Ignatius is too indefinite, and consequently there are no grounds for ascribing too great a significance to it.

Already in the passages we have cited one cannot help but note the remarkable imprecision of the holy father's expressions. For example, the bishop is said to preside in place of God, yet in another place we find an exhortation to submit to the bishop as to Jesus Christ, though it is stated that the ministry of Jesus Christ is entrusted to the deacons. If we find reference to the presbyters as to apostles, the bishop can be likened only to Jesus Christ; yet St. Ignatius likens him to God the Father also, and God the Father naturally cannot be called ἐπίσκοπος ἀόρατος (invisible bishop), as Jesus Christ is called on one occasion. Furthermore, the admonition to follow the bishop as Jesus Christ followed the Father is clearly at odds with the usual comparisons: here believing laypersons are likened to Jesus Christ.

But this imprecision increases still greatly in our eyes if we take note of St. Ignatius's other sayings. "Be ye subject to the bishop, and to one another, as Jesus Christ to the Father, according to the flesh, and the apostles to Christ, and to the Father, and to the Spirit."[1125] Here our familiar parallels and chain of command are re-

---

1123 Seeberg, *Studien zur Geschichte des Begriffs der Kirche*, 13; Harnack, *Dogmengeschichte*[4] 1, 406: "Jede einzelne Gemeinde soll ein Abbild der himmlischen Kirche sein." Vgl. 406, Anm. 2. Vgl. Thomasius, op. cit., 100–101; A. Harnack, *Die Mission und Aubreitung des Christentums* 1, 362 ff.

1124 Harnack, *Dogmengeschichte*[4] 1, 406, Anm. 2.

1125 Ignatius, *To the Magnesians* 13.2 (ANF 1:64–65).

jected: only the idea of submission is taken from from individual examples of obedience—Christ to God the Father, and the apostles to Christ—and a moral lesson is given. The first chapters of the epistle to the Trallians, as we have seen, most strikingly outlines the comparison of the bishop with Christ, and of the presbyters with the apostles,[1126] but at the end of the same epistle we encounter a phrase that is wholly at odds with the foregoing comparison. "It becomes every one of you, and especially the presbyters, to refresh the bishop, to the honour of the Father, of Jesus Christ, and of the apostles."[1127] Here the bishop is simultaneously likened to God the Father, to Jesus Christ, and to the apostles. The likening of the bishop to the apostles is a particularly jarring departure from our familiar comparison of the apostles with the presbyters alone. We also must not fail to observe that on the one hand St. Ignatius compares the bishop with God the Father or with Jesus Christ, as though exalting him above the apostles, but on the other hand he strictly differentiates between himself as a bishop and the apostles, refusing even to compare himself to them.[1128]

If we always keep in mind this constant imprecision that we have noted in how St. Ignatius expresses the same ideas, any talk of his having an original theory justifying episcopal authority will be severely limited. Had St. Ignatius possessed a clear and definite idea of the private Christian community as the reflection of a celestial Church or a reflection of those who believed in Christ during His life, he could not have employed expressions so very contrary to this concept. While in the epistles of St. Ignatius we do not encounter the doctrine of episcopal succession, neither do they contain any theory to supplant this doctrine. We cannot view his comparison of the bishop with God or with Jesus Christ and of the presbyters with

---

1126 Incidentally, in *To the Trallians* 3.1 the presbyters are called not only σύνδεσμος ἀποστόλων [assembly of the apostles], but also συνέδριον Θεοῦ [sanhedrin of God].

1127 Ignatius, *To the Trallians* 12.2 (ANF 1:72): "Ἀναψυχεῖν τὸν ἐπίσκοπον εἰς τιμὴν πατρὸς Ἰησοῦ Χριστοῦ καὶ τῶν ἀποστόλων."

1128 See Ignatius, *To the Romans* 4.3, *To the Trallians* 3.3; cf. *To the Ephesians* 3.1.

the apostles as a fully developed, definite dogmatic theory. When St. Ignatius outlines the ideal image of the Church, he is envisioning the historical image of the "little flock," whose Shepherd was Jesus Christ, and no more. At times, as we have seen, St. Ignatius takes only the idea of submission and oneness of mind, and cites examples in confirmation of his tireless exhortations to submit to the bishop. In his epistles St. Ignatius clearly and definitively expresses but a single thought: in order not to stray from the truth and not to distort the Christian faith, the bishop must be followed in all things. Consequently, the hierarchy is treated as the organ for preserving the Christian faith pure and inviolate. St. Ignatius offers no detailed doctrine concerning the Church, and this is perfectly logical. Credal doctrine and definitions always follow after. In the early centuries, all members of the Church too vividly identified as living members of the single living organism of the Church. The idea of the Church "bubbled up as a living spring, so to speak, in the life of the Church, not yet enclosed in the granite of creed or code, and it was life itself, without any formula." "No need had yet ripened for any special formulation of this particular aspect of Christianity, since it was directly experienced by believers and was provided for them in the very essence of the faith."[1129] The epistles of St. Ignatius serve as a brilliant and convincing example of this very experience. A more detailed definition of a member of the Church only arose when the living practice of the concept of the Church began to diminish. In this respect, the doctrine concerning the Church of St. Irenaeus of Lyons is the next step in the history of the dogma concerning the Church, although he shares the same central idea as St. Ignatius. Both St. Ignatius and St. Irenaeus alike express the idea that the truth can only be preserved in a living union with the organism of the Truth. St. Ignatius does not substantiate this idea, but merely exhorts all to abide in oneness of mind and to submit to the bishop. St. Irenaeus then substantiates this general concept in detail, and in justification of it he points to the episcopal succession in the Churches founded by the apostles and to the unity of

---

1129 Cf. M.D. Muretov, *On the Significance of the Term Καθολικός* ["О значении термина *καθολικός*"], 116–117.

the faith in the Churches of all the world. In matters of the faith,
St. Ignatius depicts the individual Christian community as self-contained; St. Irenaeus then speaks of a universal Church, for the most
ancient apostolic Churches are for him the inheritance of the whole
Church, and should be consulted in uncertain situations. But both
St. Ignatius and St. Irenaeus alike speak of the doctrinal authority
of the bishop.

In the significant intervening time from St. Ignatius to St. Irenaeus we may point out yet another testimony to the importance which
the early Church ascribed to episcopal succession. This testimony
is that of Hegesippus, of whom Eusebius says that he wrote "the
true tradition (τὴν ἀπλανῆ παράδοσιν) of apostolic doctrine,"[1130] he
himself being one of the nearest successors to the apostles.[1131] First
and foremost Hegesippus attests that the Church of Jerusalem was
successively governed from the very beginning. First the Church
of Jerusalem was received by James, the brother of the Lord, together with the other apostles.[1132] When James the Just suffered his
martyric death, his cousin Simon, son of Cleophas, was appointed
bishop (καθίσταται ἐπίσκοπος).[1133] The same Hegesippus writes of
his sojourn in Rome: "When I had come to Rome I compiled a list
of the (episcopal) succession through Anicetus, whose deacon was
Eleutherus. And Anicetus was succeeded by Soter, and he by Eleutherus. In every succession, and in every city that is held which is
preached by the law and the prophets and the Lord."[1134]

1130 Eusebius, *Church History* 4.8.2 (NPNF[2] 1:180; GrchSch. 9.1:314.8–10).

1131 Idem 2.23.3. "Ὁ Ἡγήσιππος ἐπὶ τῆς πρώτης τῶν ἀποστόλων γενόμενος διαδοχῆς" (GrchSch. 9.1:166.6–7).

1132 Idem 2.23.4: "Διαδέχεται τὴν ἐκκλησίαν μετὰ τῶν ἀποστόλων ὁ ἀδελφὸς τοῦ κυρίου Ἰάκωβος [James, the brother of the Lord, succeeded to {the govern-
ment of} the Church in conjunction with the apostles]" (GrchSch. 9.1:166.9–10). Jerome translates μετὰ τῶν ἀποστόλων as *post apostolos* [after the apostles] (*On Illustrious Men* 2 [PL 23:609b]), but Rufinus renders it as *cum apostolis* [with the apostles] (GrchSch. 9.1:167.1).

1133 Idem 4.22.4 (GrchSch. 9.1:370.9–11).

1134 Idem. 4.22.3: "Γενόμενος δὲ ἐν Ῥώμῃ, διαδοχὴν ἐποιησάμην μέχρις Ἀνικήτου · οὗ διάκονος ἦν Ἐλεύθερος, καὶ παρὰ Ἀνικήτου διαδέχεται Σωτήρ, μεθ᾽ ὃν Ἐλεύθερος. ἐν ἑκάστῃ δὲ διαδοχῇ καὶ ἐν ἑκάστῃ πόλει οὕτως ἔχει ὡς ὁ

Hegesippus's own words do not reveal what motivated him to compile a list of the Roman bishops,[1135] and why he discusses the episcopal succession in the Church of Jerusalem. It would therefore be risky to see any sort of developed, detailed theory of episcopal succession in the words cited.[1136] If however we take the passages cited in context, we may make several highly probable suppositions. In the first instance, after pointing out the episcopal succession in the Church of Jerusalem, Hegesippus immediately goes on to say that the Church was not corrupted by vain teachings, and then indicates a whole series of false teachers who engendered various heresies. In the second instance, having just stated that "the church of Corinth continued in the true faith (ἐν τῷ ὀρθῷ λόγῳ) until Primus was bishop in Corinth," at the end of the words we have cited he

---

νόμος κηρύσσει καὶ οἱ προφῆται καὶ ὁ κύριος [And when I had come to Rome, I compiled a list of the succession through Anicetus, whose deacon was Eleutherus. And Anicetus was succeeded by Soter, and he by Eleutherus. In every succession, and in every city that is held which is preached by the law and the prophets and the Lord]" (GrchSch. 9.1:370.9–11).

1135   The conjecture of some who wish to read διατριβὴν ἐποιησάμην [I remained there] instead of διαδοχὴν ἐποιησάμην [I compiled a list of the succession] (H. Dannreuther, *Du temoignage d' Hégésippe*, 24n2; Louis Duchesne, *Early History of the Christian Church* [New York: Longmans, Green & Co., 1912] 1, 175n1) must be decisively rejected: it is supported only by the translation of Rufinus (GrchSch. 9.1:371.2: *permansi inibi*), who according to Duchesne (ibid.) is often random in his interpretations, but it completely contradicts the context, as Duchesne also states. Furthermore, as Tillemont also points out, Eusebius (*Church History* 4.11.8 [GrchSch. 9.1:324.8–10]) and Jerome (*On Illustrious Men* 22 [PL 23:641a]) unanimously report that Hegesippus came to Rome in the time of Anicetus, where he abode until Eleutherus was bishop. See *Memoires pour servir a l' histoire ecclesiastique des six premiers siecles*, vol. 3 (Paris: 1695), 610. See also Migne (PG 5:1322b) and Batiffol, *L'église naissante et le catholicisme*[3], 208n1. At the same time, Tillemont declines to understand διαδοχὴν to mean a list of bishops, and gives an entirely artificial interpretation of the expression διαδοχὴν ἐποιησάμην: "Il mit par ecrit la doctrine que luivoit alors l' Église Romaine, et qu'elle avoit toujours tenue par une succession continuelle depuis les Apôtres" (*Memoires*, vol. 3, 611; cf. 48).

1136   "Hégésippe n'est pas un théoricien de la catholicité et de l' apostolicité: il en est un témoin, parce que la catholicité et l' apostolicité ont été dans les faits avant de devenir des arguments" (Batiffol, *L'église naissante et le catholicisme*[3], 208).

then indicates that the truth was preserved in the Church everywhere ("in every city") and at all times ("in every succession").[1137]
In both cases we cannot fail to note that Hegesippus somehow links
the preservation of truth in the Church and the succession of the
bishops. Episcopal succession in the Church is as though juxtaposed
to heresies originating from their progenitors, with no link to the
apostles.[1138] Consequently, without making any tendential suppositions, it may nevertheless be thought that from Hegesippus we have
something akin to Irenaeus's theory of the apostolic succession of
the episcopate.[1139] Twenty years before Irenaeus wrote *Against Heresies* we find traces of his theory at the opposite end of the world of
the day.

If we cast our gaze over the brief comments of the writers of the
first two centuries regarding the doctrine concerning the Church,
we will have to acknowledge that St. Irenaeus's teaching concerning the Church is the conclusion and completion of all the ecclesiological views expressed in pieces and fragments in anti-Gnostic
literature. The actual teaching of St. Irenaeus is firmly based in the
doctrine of the holy apostle Paul concerning Tradition, and the
doctrine of the apostle Paul was always alive in church consciousness, as clearly witnessed by the data we have extracted from the
remnants of early church literature. When at last the need arose, in
the late second century this doctrine was developed and substantiated more or less in detail.[1140]

1137 Eusebius, *Church History* 4.22.2 (ANF 1:198). −*Trans.*

1138 Cf. Batiffol, *L'église naissante et le catholicisme*, 209.

1139 Funk is inclined to acknowledge that in the matter of preserving apostolic tradition Hegesippus ascribes the same significance to the episcopacy, and
that, in citing a catalog of bishops, his motivations were the same as those of St.
Ireneaeus. See *Die Echtheit der ignatianischen Brief*, 55. Cf. Dannreuther, *Du temoignage
d' Hégésippe*, 59–60, 62, 67.

1140 Concerning this Harnack rightly observes: "The thesis that the bishops
per successionem received the gospel truth from the apostles as charisma, and that
consequently they, as teachers, collectively represent the apostles and that only by
this means *veritas in ecclesiis custoditur* [truth in the churches is preserved]—this thesis would have been established even without the conflict with Gnosis, although
it did in fact develop as a result of this conflict" (*Entstehung und Entwickelung der*

It is of course entirely appropriate and allowable to ask: was the doctrine concerning the Church as expounded by St. Irenaeus and Tertullian the common heritage of the Church at that time? To answer this question we must turn to writers of their day whose activities were conducted in other parts of the world. Of these writers, the first who stands out is Clement of Alexandria. Unfortunately, the surviving writings of Clement contain too little information to provide any definite answer. That Clement says nothing specific regarding the Church, Tradition, and the hierarchy already must prevent us from giving any decisive answer, which in any case could be given no scholarly substantiation. Regarding Clement's views on the question at hand we can judge only by chance phrases, encountered but rarely and as though in passing in writings devoted to entirely different subjects. It is quite logical that evaluations of these scattered ideas would differ considerably. Untroubled by the lack of clear and definite data, many Protestant scholars nevertheless glibly and decisively pass judgment regarding Clement's views. In Clement they find no concept of church Tradition with any definite content and with its formula firmly established in the church Symbol. The hierarchy, according to Clement, likewise has no role in guarding church truth, and the concept of unbroken episcopal succession as the pledge of the inviolability of Christ's teaching in the Church is not only absent in his writings, but is also completely foreign to the entire structure of his views. Consequently, in Clement they find none of the fundamental concepts of the ecclesiological system of St. Irenaeus and Tertullian. The explanation given is of course that Clement still holds the perspective of the oldest concept of the Church, when neither the hierarchical structure nor the monarchical episcopate were known.[1141] "No echo of the strife[1142] penetrated the tranquil seclusion in which Clement lectured and

---

Kirchenverfassung und des Kirchenrechts, 89).

1141 We have presented the views of Harnack (*Dogmengeschichte*[4] 1, 367–371, 404–405, Anm. 412–413), which are customarily repeated in Protestant scholarly literature. Cf. Loofs, *Leitfaden der Dogmengeschichte*[4] §23.1, 167.

1142 At this point the Russian source inserts the explanatory words "caused by the victory of the hierarchy". *–Trans.*

composed. He reflects with calm fidelity the image of the antique
times in which he had himself been reared. His heart is with the
Republic; he is the Samuel of the new monarchy."[1143]

All these arguments and others like them concerning the ecclesiology of Clement are too decisive to allow for agreement. It
must be acknowledged that in Clement's fragmentary and isolated
comments concerning the Church, a great many statements may be
found that fully coincide with the chief provisions of the ecclesiology of St. Irenaeus and Tertullian. First and foremost, for Clement
it is the Church which is the custodian of the truth[1144] in contrast
to heresy,[1145] which does not have true knowledge of God.[1146] The
token of this true Church is its unity. This is the catholic Church;
in it people unite in unity of faith.[1147] The apostolic doctrine was
one, as was their Tradition.[1148] In the whole Church there was one

---

1143 Charles Bigg, *The Christian Platonists of Alexandria* (Oxford: 1886), 100.
Quoted from Batiffol, *L'église naissante et le catholicisme*[3], 315.

1144 Clement, *Stromata* 7.15.92.3: "Ἐν μόνῃ τῇ ἀληθείᾳ καὶ τῇ ἀρχαίᾳ ἐκκλησίᾳ
ἥ τε ἀκριβεστάτη γνῶσις [in the truth alone and in the ancient Church is both
the exactest knowledge…]" (GrchSch. 17:65.20–21; PG 9:528b). 7.16.100.7: "ὃ
ἐν τῇ ἐπιστήμῃ ἡ ἐκκλησία ἡ ἀληθής [those who are in knowledge are the true
Church]" (GrchSch. 71.4–5; PG 9:540a).

1145 Idem 7.15.92.7 (GrchSch. 17:65.31–35; PG 9:528c).

1146 Idem 7.16.93.4 (GrchSch. 17:66.13–14; PG 9:529b).

1147 Idem 7.17.107.5: "Κατά τε οὖν ὑπόστασιν κατά τε ἐπίνοιαν κατά τε
ἀρχὴν κατά τε ἐξοχὴν μόνην εἶναί φαμεν τὴν ἀρχαίαν καὶ καθολικὴν ἐκκλησίαν,
εἰς ἑνότητα πίστεως μιᾶς, τῆς κατὰ τὰς οἰκείας διαθήκας, μᾶλλον δὲ κατὰ τὴν
διαθήκην τὴν μίαν διαφόροις τοῖς χρόνοις, ἑνὸς τοῦ θεοῦ τῷ βουλήματι δι' ἑνὸς
τοῦ Κυρίου συνάγουσαν τοὺς ἤδη κατατεταγμένους οὓς προώρισεν ὁ Θεός,
δικαίους ἐσομένους πρὸ καταβολῆς κόσμου ἐγνωκώς [Therefore in substance
and idea, in origin, in pre-eminence, we say that the ancient and Catholic Church
is alone, collecting as it does into the unity of the one faith—which results from
the peculiar Testaments, or rather the one Testament in different times by the will
of the one, God, through the one, the Lord—those already ordained, whom God
predetermined, knowing before the foundation of the world that they would be
righteous]" (GrchSch 17.76:10–16; PG 9:552a–b).

1148 Idem 7.17.108.1: "Μία γὰρ ἡ πάντων γέγονε τῶν ἀποστόλων ὥσπερ
διδασκαλία, οὕτως δὲ καὶ ἡ παράδοσις [for as was the teaching, so also the tradition of the apostles was one]" (GrchSch. 17:76.22–24; PG 9:552c).

mind and, as it were, one breath.[1149] Conversely, the doctrines of the heretics are diverse and contradictory. It is of heresies that Solomon the Wise said: "He who is grounded in falsehood soweth the wind and chaseth after winged birds. For he hath forsaken the ways of his own vineyard, and wandered in the tracks of his own husbandry" (see Prov. 9:12). Such are the heresies that desert the Church.[1150] Among heresies a spirit of contention prevails. They disdain and mock each other. The same idea held in honor by some, while others find it foolish.[1151]

Clement then appears to repeat Tertullian's *argumentum praescriptionis*. Namely, he considers the fact that the Church is more ancient than the heretics to be the token of its authenticity. "That the human assemblies which they held (τὰς ἀνθρωπίνας συνηλώσεις) were posterior to the Catholic Church requires not many words to show. For the teaching of our Lord at His advent, beginning with Augustus and Tiberius, was completed in the middle of the times of Tiberius.[1152] And that of the apostles, embracing the ministry of Paul, ends with Nero. It was later, in the times of Adrian the king, that those who invented the heresies arose; and they extended to the age of Antoninus the elder, as, for instance, Basilides, though he claims (as they boast) for his master, Glaucias, the interpreter of Peter. ... Marcion, who arose in the same age with them, lived as an old man with the younger [heretics]. And after him Simon heard for a little the preaching of Peter. Such being the case, it is evident that these later heresies, and those yet subsequent to them in time, were new inventions (κεκαινοτομῆσθαι) falsified (παραχαραχθείσας) from the oldest and most authentic Church. From what has been said, then, it is my opinion that the true Church, that which is really ancient, is one."[1153] For Clement, the true Church is specifically [the

---

1149 Idem 7.6.32.1–4 (GrchSch. 17:24; PG 9:444b–c).

1150 Idem 1.19.95.5–7 (GrchSch. 15:61; PG 8:812b–c).

1151 Idem 7.16.101.1–2 (GrchSch. 15:71; PG 9:540a–b).

1152 The Russian and Greek sources read "was completed in the middle of the times of Augustus." See ANF 2:554n10 for a discussion of the translator's decision to depart from the Greek source. –*Trans.*

1153   Idem 7.17.106.3–107.3 (ANF 2:554–555; GrchSch. 17:75–76; PG

ancient Church] (ἡ ἀρχαία ἐκκλησία, τῷ ὄντι ἀρχαία).[1154] Consequently, for Clement the custodian of the truth is the visible, ancient
catholic Church founded by the apostles.[1155]

Being the treasury of the truth, the Church has certain standards. In Clement we frequently encounter the expressions κανὼν
τῆς πίστεως, κανὼν τῆς ἀληθείας, κανὼν ἐκκλησιαστικός, κανὼν
τῆς παραδόσεως ("rule of the faith, rule of the truth, ecclesiastical
rule, rule of the tradition") and the like.[1156] Although to be sure
there are not sufficient grounds to assert that by these terms Clement meant the "Rule of Faith" of which St. Irenaeus and Tertullian
spoke, nevertheless it cannot be denied that Clement does use these
terms to signify certain Church-wide standards. In speaking of the
heretics' departure at the consecration of the Eucharist, Clement
says that they are acting μὴ κατὰ τὸν κανόνα τῆς ἐκκλησίας [not in
accordance with the rule of the Church].[1157] By distorting the truth,
the heretics are defrauding τὸν κανόνα τῆς ἐκκλησίας [the rule of
the Church].[1158] Clement wishes to introduce his own work κατὰ
τὸν εὐκλεῆ καὶ σεμνὸν τῆς παραδόσεως κανόνα [the glorious and
venerable rule of tradition].[1159] All members of the Church in general must not violate τὸν ἐκκλησιαστικὸν κανόνα [the ecclesiastical
rule].[1160] Clement even speaks of interpreting Holy Scripture in ac-

---

9:548–549, 552).

1154 Idem 7.15.92.3 (GrchSch 17:65.20), 7.17.107.3 (GrchSch 17:76.6; PG
9:528b, 529b).

1155 Harnack likewise notes in Clement an emperical concept of the Church,
by virtue of which the Church itself is the institution of true doctrine; but he
attempts to temper this acknowledgment by pointing out that Clement expresses
this only polemically (see *Dogmengeschichte*[4] 1, 413). But this comment naturally
changes nothing whatsoever, since both St. Irenaeus and Tertullian express their
doctrine concerning the Church in polemics with the Gnostics.

1156 The pertinent materials are compiled by Harnack (see *Dogmengeschichte*[4]
1, 369, Anm.).

1157 Clement of Alexandria, *Stromata* 1.19.96.1 (GrchSch. 15:61.30; PG
8:813a).

1158 Idem 7.16.105.5 (GrchSch. 17:74.22-23; PG 9:545b).

1159 Idem 1.1.15.2 (GrchSch. 15:11.14–15; PG 8:704c).

1160 Idem 7.15.90.2 (GrchSch. 17:64.5–6; PG 9:525a).

cordance with the Lord's teaching and with pious Tradition, and of interpreting according to the church rule (τῶν γραφῶν ἐξήγησις κατὰ τὸν ἐκκλησιαστικὸν κανόνα). Here Clement also provides a certain definition of this exegetical principle of the Church, possibly hinting at Marcion: "The church rule is the concord and harmony of the law and the prophets in the covenant delivered at the coming of the Lord."[1161] From the phrases cited we can see that by κανὼν ἐκκλησιαστικός [ecclesiastical rule] Clement specifically means a definite ecclesiastical doctrine;[1162] otherwise his arguments would make no sense at all.

Clement is therefore no stranger to Tradition either, which he says is of the Church, of Christ, of the Lord, and so on.[1163] Church tradition originates from the Lord Himself: it is revealed by the Son of God Himself and delivered to the apostles,[1164] and it is they who were the true Gnostics.[1165] True knowledge has reached us through succession, being delivered by the apostles to a few without being committed to writing.[1166] In the foreword to the *Stromata* Clement appears to note the historical successions through which Tradition came down to him from the apostles. He promises to expound what

---

1161 Clement of Alexandria, *Stromata* 6.15.125.2–3 (ANF 2:509; GrchSch. 15:495.3–7; PG 9:349a).

1162 Batiffol, *L'église naissante et le catholicisme*[3], 300: "C' est une doctrine ferme et exclusive." Vgl. Harnack, *Dogmengeschichte*[4] 1, 369, Anm.: "Jedenfalls aber zeigt die Stelle, welch' einen eiten Gebrauch Clemens von dems Audruck 'kirchlicher Kanon' gemacht hat."

1163 See Harnack, *Dogmengeschichte*[4] 1, 369, Anm.

1164 Clement of Alexandria, *Stromata* 6.7.61.1: "Τὴν γνωστικὴν παράδοσιν,... ὡς αὐτὸς κατὰ τὴν παρουσίαν τοὺς ἁγίους ἐδίδαξεν ἀποστόλους... ἡ γνῶσις... παρὰ τοῦ Υἱοῦ τοῦ Θεοῦ παραδοθεῖσα [the gnostic tradition {i.e. the tradition of knowledge}... as He Himself taught the apostles during His presence... the knowledge {gnosis}... having been imparted by the Son of God]." (GrchSch. 15:462; PG 9:284a).

1165 Idem 6.8.68.2 (GrchSch. 15:466.8–9; PG 9:289c).

1166 Idem 6.7.61.3: "Ἡ γνῶσις αὕτη, ἡ κατὰ διαδοχὰς εἰς ὀλίγους ἐκ τῶν ἀποστόλων ἀγράφως παραδοθεῖσα κατελήλυθεν [this knowledge is that which has descended by in succession to a few, having been imparted unwritten by the apostles]." (GrchSch. 15:462.28–30; PG 9:284a).

he has heard from blessed and honorable men. "They preserving the tradition of the blessed doctrine derived directly from the holy apostles, Peter, James, John, and Paul, the sons receiving it from the father ... came by God's will to us also to deposit those ancestral and apostolic seeds."[1167] But nowhere do we see Clement draw any connection between the Tradition successively preserved in the Church and the hierarchy.[1168] It must however be noted that Clement explicitly speaks of the apostolic institution of the episcopate. He calls James the Just specifically the first **bishop** of Jerusalem.[1169] Likewise, in relating concerning the holy apostle John, he says that the latter traveled throughout the localities surrounding Ephesus, appointing bishops (ὅπου ἐπισκόπους καταστήσων).[1170] Although Clement says very little about the hierarchy, he depicts the position of the bishop in the Church as being a very lofty one. The bishop is the primate of the whole Church (τῆς ἐκκλησίας ἁπάσης προΐστασθαι);[1171] he is the chief commander of the Church (τῆς ἐκκλησίας ἀφηγεῖσθαι).[1172]

Thus, in Clement of Alexandria we find nearly all the elements of the ecclesiology of the Western opponents of Gnosticism. In his

---

1167 Idem 1.1.11.1–3 (ANF 2:301; GrchSch. 15:8–9; PG 8:697, 700). Cf. this fragment in Eusebius: "The Lord after his resurrection imparted knowledge to James the Just and to John and Peter, and they imparted it to the rest of the apostles, and the rest of the apostles to the seventy, of whom Barnabas was one" (*Church History* 2.1.4 [NPNF² 1:104; GrchSch. 17:199.21–24]).

1168 Harnack is particularly insistent on this point (see *Dogmengeschichte* 1, 370, Anm. 404, Anm.). But Harnack is not justified in reading in *Stromata* 7.19.104.1— "Ὁ γνωστικὸς... τὴν ἀποστολικὴν καὶ ἐκκλησιαστικὴν σώζων ὀρθοτομίαν τῶν δογμάτων [The gnostic... maintaining apostolic and ecclesiastic orthodoxy in doctrines]" (GrchSch. 17:73.15–17; PG 9:544a)—the idea that the truth is supposedly preserved by the Gnostics: the preservation of apostolic and ecclesiastical doctrine is specifically the **token** of the true gnostic.

1169 Clement of Alexandria, *Fragments* 10 (GrchSch. 17:198.23–24 [=Eusebius, *Church History* 2.1.3]).

1170 Clement of Alexandria, *Salvation of the Rich Man* 42.2 (GrchSch. 17:188.4–5).

1171 Clement of Alexandria, *Stromata* 3.12.79.6 (GrchSch. 15:232.1–2; PG 8:1180a).

1172 Idem 3.18.108.2 (GrchSch. 15:246.19; PG 8:1212b).

writings only the doctrine of the hierarchy, which was generally not extensively developed, is not linked to the doctrine of Tradition. But we ought not of course to draw from this such broad conclusions as those customary among Protestant historians;[1173] indeed, on the whole the surviving writings of Clement bear little resemblance to the works of Western writers.

We have examined the outcome at which, having passed through various preceding stages, church thinking arrived in the second half of the second century regarding the question of the Church as the custodian of the truth. Even then this doctrine was not yet decisively formulated: in the works of later writers this doctrine would be more fully expressed. But the subsequent dogmatic thinking of the Church was roused by other conditions of church life, and the grounds for subsequent definition of the concept of the Church likewise differed. The outcome we have set forth was reached by church thought in the fight against Gnosis primarily in the second century. Gnosis, as we have already stated, was not an exclusively Christian phenomenon: rather, it was an extra-Christian movement, which intruded from without into the system of Christian thinking, introducing foreign elements into it and thereby damaging the original apostolic teaching of the faith. In its fight with Gnosis the Church more precisely formulated the confession of the faith, introducing anti-Gnostic elements into it and establishing the principle of a church tradition continuously preserved in the Church since the apostles by means of the successive ministry of the episcopate. But differences in thinking were also possible among people who acknowledged both the "Rule of Faith" and the doctrinal authority of the episcopate. Differences in thinking were possible in the very heart of the Church.

Historically, any given concept of the Church was closely linked to church life itself. Any given form of church life would influence the definition of the concept of the Church, and vice versa: any given concept of the Church would influence church life, rousing people to put theoretical definitions of the qualities of the Church into

---

1173 For a somewhat more detailed treatment of Clement, see Batiffol, *L'église naissante et le catholicisme*[3], 295–316.

practice. In its history the dogma concerning the Church is closely linked to the history of ecclesiastical discipline, and a new period in the development of the dogma concerning the Church began at the very point in time when this question shifted to disciplinary grounds. Chronologically this period follows immediately after the one we have just examined: only in the second half of the second century did the intense struggle with Gnosticism finally end, and the time of intensified and prolonged disciplinary disputes ensued.

FOURTH ESSAY

The Doctrine
of the Sanctity of the Church
and the Conflict with Montanism

Our Lord Jesus Christ came to earth to renew mankind, whom He called to infinite moral perfection. Mankind sets out upon this path of moral perfection by rejecting his former life, altering his entire spiritual visage (μετανοέω). In this respect those who set out on the path of Christian perfection become people set apart, separated out from the sphere of natural, sinful life.[1174] It is in this sense, as we have already seen in outlining the New Testament doctrine concerning the Church, that the books of the New Testament call Christians saints[1175] (ἅγιοι). By this same token, however, moral perfection is not considered obligatory for the Christian to any specific degree, and in any case in the matter of moral perfection one can hardly speak of an equal degree of this perfection for all. The idea of moral perfection within the bounds of this earthly life is foreign to the sacred writers of the New Testament. "If we say that we have no sin, we deceive ourselves, and the truth is not in us" (1 Jn. 1:8). And it is worth noting that the apostle John says these words along with an exhortation to walk in the light. Consequently, Christians

---

1174 See Justin Martyr, *Dialogues* 119: "We have left already the way of living (ἀπὸ τῆς πολιτείας) in which we used to spend our days, passing our time in evil after the fashions of the other inhabitants of the earth" (ANF 1:259; CAG 1.2:426).

1175 Literally, "holy ones." *—Trans.*

may be said to be **in the process** of moral perfection. It is the
community of these persons in the process of moral perfection that
comprises the close-knit organism of the Church. In the exposition
of the New Testament doctrine concerning the Church, primarily
of the apostle Paul, we have seen that the Church is specifically
depicted as an organism continually advancing in perfection according to the image of Christ the God-man. The existence of
the Church is specifically οἰκοδομὴ τοῦ σώματος τοῦ Χριστοῦ and
καταρτισμὸς τῶν ἁγίων.[1176] Christians gradually attain to moral
perfection, becoming saints in the proper sense, which state is expressed in the Greek words ἅγιος[1177] or, more frequently, καθαρός.
The word καθαρός in the New Testament is specifically used to
denote either physically pure objects[1178] or moral purity and blamelessness.[1179] Although καθαρός can be called a synonym of ἅγιος,
a distinction must be made between them.[1180] In the works of the
church writers of the first two centuries, above all other epithets the
Church is predominantly termed "Holy"—specifically, ἁγία. We
find this title in the epistle that bears the name of Barnabas,[1181] in

---

1176 Eph. 4:12.

1177 Concerning the meaning of ὅσιος see Cremer, *Bibl.-theol. Wörterburh*[9],
780–782.

1178 Mt. 27:59: "Σινδόνι καθαρᾷ"; Jn. 13:10: "Ἔστι καθαρὸς ὅλος"; Rev.
15:16: "Γίνον καθαρόν»; Rev. 19:8: "Βύσσινον λαμπρὸν καὶ καθαρόν"; Rev.
19:14: "Βύσσινον λευκὸν καθαρόν"; etc. See the *Concordance* of C.H. Bruder (Lipsiae: MDCCCLXXXVIII), 449–450. Cremer, *Bibl.-theol. Wb.*[9], 528–529.

1179 Mt. 5:8: "Οἱ καθαροὶ τῇ καρδία"; 1 Tim. 1:5; 2 Tim. 2:22: "Ἀγάπη ἐκ
καθαρᾶς καρδίας"; 1 Tim. 3:9; 2 Tim. 1:3: "ἐν καθαρᾷ συνειδήσει." Cf. 1 Pet.
1:22. See the *Concordance* by Bruder, 449–450; Cremer, *Bibl.-theol. Wörterburh*[9], 528.

1180 Concerning the relationship between ἅγιος and καθαρός (or more
precisely between the verbs ἁγιάζειν and καθαρίζειν), see the reasoning of the
priest E.A. Vorontsov (*Bogoslovsky vestnik* [1910], vol. 1: 1–4). See also D. Kasitsyn:
*Schisms of the Early Centuries of Christianity: Montanism, Novatianism, Donatism, and
Their Influence on the Development of the Doctrine Concerning the Church* ("Расколы первых веков христианства. Монтанизм, новацианство, донатизм и влияние
их на раскрытие учения о Церкви") (Moscow: 1889), 8–9n5 (=Addendae, 43).

1181 *Epistle of Barnabas* 13:6: "Λαὸν ἅγιον." Cf. Justin Martyr, *Dialogue with
Trypho* 119 (CAG 1.2:426).

the epistles of St. Ignatius,[1182] in *The Pastor of Hermas*,[1183] the writings of Theophilus of Antioch[1184] and Apollonius,[1185] in *The Martyrdom of Polycarp*,[1186] and in many other early works of church literature.[1187]

What meaning did church consciousness associate with calling the Church "holy"?

This question should first and foremost be answered [as follows]: this term was never connected with the idea of the Church as a community **of those who have achieved perfection**—of saints in the modern sense of the word. This idea is completely incomprehensible and contradicts many passages of Holy Scripture, where even one who has entered the Church is still considered subject to sin and a constant sinner. The entire process of the spiritual life, in the thinking of the New Testament, is a continual struggle with sin, and in this struggle there is always room for falling and getting back up. In his epistle the holy apostle James writes, "Confess (ἐξομολογεῖσθε) your faults one to another" (Jas. 5:16), and the holy apostle John likewise writes, "If we confess (ὁμολογῶμεν) our sins, he is faithful and just to forgive (ἀφῇ) us our sins, and to cleanse (καθαρίσῃ) us from all unrighteousness" (1 Jn. 1:9). Examples of repentance are also given in apostolic times. The apostle Paul commanded that the incestuous Corinthian be excommunicated from the Church,[1188] but he then permits him to be received back again, though he had so gravely sinned.[1189] We also know of the moving account first encountered in the writings of Clement of Alexan-

---

1182 Ignatius, *To the Trallians*, inscription: "Ἐκκλησία ἁγία."

1183 *The Pastor of Hermas* 1.1.1.6: "Ἕνεκεν τῆς ἁγίας ἐκκλησίας." 1.1.3.4: "κτίσας τὴν ἁγίαν ἐκκλησίαν."

1184 Theophilus of Antioch, *To Autolycus* 2.14 (CAG 8:98).

1185 Eusebius, *Church History* 5.18.5 (GrchSch. 9.1:474.18–19).

1186 Inscription: "Τῆς ἁγίας καὶ καθολικῆς ἐκκλησίας." Funk, *Die apostolischen Väter*, 115.

1187 See Harnack, *Dogmengeschichte*⁴ 1, 407–408, Anm. 2.

1188 See 1 Cor. 5:5.

1189 See 2 Cor. 2:6–11.

dria, concerning how the holy apostle John restored to the path
of salvation a young man whom he had baptized, but who in his
absence had become a robber.[1190] This narrative ends with these
words: "The [apostle] pledging, and assuring him on oath that he
would find forgiveness for himself from the Saviour, beseeching and
falling on his knees, and kissing his right hand itself, as now purified
by repentance, led (ἐπανήγαγε) him back to the church. Then by
supplicating with copious prayers, and striving along with him in
continual fastings, and subduing his mind by various utterances of
words, did not depart, as they say, till he restored (ἐπιστῆσαι) him to
the Church, presenting in him a great example of true repentance
and a great token of regeneration (παλιγγενεσίας)."[1191]

In consulting the earliest works of church literature, we most
first of all note that initially the concept of the "sanctity" of the
Church was not just a concept: no, rather, this concept was intimately linked with the life of the Christian Church. This society
was holy not merely in words, **but also in its very life. The
Church was specifically Holy.** The entire moral content of
early Christian literary works is permeated throughout with purely
ascetic ideas. The ascetic nature of the early Christian worldview
may already be seen in reading *The Teaching of the Twelve Apostles.*
In the so-called "second epistle of Clement" the ascetic worldview
in the moral sphere is grounded in the unique dogmatic doctrine
of the sanctity of the Church. "I do not, however, suppose ye are
ignorant that the living Church is the body of Christ. ... Now the
Church, being spiritual, was manifested in the flesh of Christ, thus
signifying to us that, if any of us keep her in the flesh and do not

---

1190 This account is also repeated by many later writers. Clement of Alexandria precedes his account with this comment: "Ἄκουσον μῦθον οὐ μῦθον, ἀλλά
ὄντα λόγον περὶ Ἰωάννου τοῦ ἀποστόλου παραδεδομένον [Listen to a legend
that is no legend but a true account handed down concerning John the apostle]"
(*Salvation of the Rich Man* 42.1 [GrchSch. 17:188.1–2]). From this we may see that
Clement himself has no doubt of the veracity of this account. Concerning the
historicity of this story see Hieromonk Evdokim, *The Holy Apostle and Evangelist
John the Theologian* ["Св. апостол и евангелист Иоанн Богослов"], 393n121.

1191 Clement of Alexandria, *Salvation of the Rich Man* 42.15 (ANF 2:603–604;
GrchSch. 17:190.12–19). Cf. Eusebius, op. cit. 3.23.19.

corrupt her, he shall receive her again in the Holy Spirit: for this flesh is the copy (ἀντίτυπον) of the spirit. No one then who corrupts the copy, shall partake of the original. This then is what He meaneth, 'Keep the flesh, that ye may partake of the spirit.' But if we say that the flesh is the church and the spirit Christ, then he that hath shamefully used the flesh hath shamefully used the Church. Such a one then shall not partake of the spirit, which is Christ."[1192] It is in this doctrine of the sanctity of the Church, based on the classical realistic concept of the symbol, that the author sees the basis of his exhortations to continence.[1193] The moral teaching of the epistle itself is strictly ascetic in nature. "Brethren, leaving willingly our sojourn (τὴν παροικίαν) in this present world, let us do the will of Him that called us, and not fear to depart out of this world.[1194] ... Consider, brethren, that the sojourning (ἡ ἐπιδημία) in the flesh in this world is but brief and transient, but the promise (ἐπαγγελία) of Christ is great and wonderful, even the rest of the kingdom to come, and of life everlasting."[1195] We must consider the good things of this earth as belonging to others, and must not desire them.[1196] "If we desire ... to serve both God and mammon, it will be unprofitable (ἀσύμφορον) for us.[1197] ... This world and the next are two

---

1192   *Second Epistle of Clement* 14.2, 3–4: "Οὐκ οἴομαι δὲ ὑμᾶς ἀγνοεῖν, ὅτι ἐκκλησία ζῶσα σῶμά ἐστιν Χριστοῦ... ἡ ἐκκλησία δὲ πνευματικὴ οὖσα ἐφανερώθη ἐν τῇ σαρκὶ Χριστοῦ, δηλοῦσα ἡμῖν, ὅτι ἐὰν ἡμῶν τηρήσῃ αὐτὴν ἐν τῇ σαρκὶ καὶ φθείρῃ, ἀπολήψεται αὐτὴν ἐν τῷ πνεύματι τῷ ἁγίῳ· ἡ γὰρ σὰρξ αὕτη ἀντίτυπός ἐστι τοῦ πνεύματος· οὐδεὶς οὖν τὸ ἀντίτυπον φθείρας τὸ αὐθεντικὸν μεταλήψεται, ἄρα οὖν τοῦτο λέγει, ἀδελφοί, τηρήσατε τὴν σάρκα, ἵνα τοῦ πνεύματος μεταλάβητε· εἰ δὲ λέγομεν εἶναι τὴν σάρκα τὴν ἐκκλησίαν καὶ τὸ πνεῦμα Χριστόν, ἄρα οὖν ὁ ὑβρίσας τὴν σάρκα ὕβρισεν τὴν ἐκκλησίαν. Ὁ τοιοῦτος οὖν οὐ μεταλήψεται τοῦ πνεύματος, ὅ ἐστιν ὁ Χριστός."

1193   Idem 15.1: "Οὐκ οἴομαι δὲ ὅτι μικρὰν συμβουλίαν ἐποιησάμην περὶ ἐγκρατείας, ἣν ποιήσας τις οὐ μετανοήσει, ἀλλὰ καὶ ἑαυτὸν σώσει κἀμὲ τὸν συμβουλεύσαντα."

1194   2 Clem. 5:1 (ANF 7:518).

1195   Idem 5:5, 19:3 (ANF 7:518).

1196   Idem 5:6: "Τὰ κοσμικὰ ταῦτα ὡς ἀλλότρια ἡγεῖσθαι καὶ μὴ ἐπιθυμεῖν αὐτῶν."

1197   Idem 6:1 (ANF 7:518).

enemies.[1198] ... We cannot ... be the friends of both; and it behoves us, by renouncing the one (τούτῳ ἀποταξαμένους), to make use of the other[1199] (ἐκείνῳ χράσθαι). Let us reckon that it is better to hate the things present (τὰ ἐνθάδε), since they are trifling, and transient, and corruptible; and to love those which are to come, as being good and incorruptible."[1200] The author emphatically condemns those who prefer the present pleasures to the future promise.[1201]

This ascetic ideal for living[1202] was particularly suited to the idea of the sanctity of the Church, and it is quite logical that the doctrine that the Church is Holy was a perfectly ordinary definition of it. We should not however exaggerate the import of this doctrine. The possibility that members of the Church would sin was never denied, and the very authors who expound the general ascetic ideal for living also speak of confession of sins. For example, in the *Didache* we find this injunction: "At the church meeting you must confess your sins, and not approach prayer with a bad conscience."[1203] The Eucharist must always be preceded by confession of sins.[1204] In his epistle to the Romans, Clement of Rome writes the following concerning repentance: "Let us turn to every age that has passed, and learn that, from generation to generation (ἐν γενεᾷ καὶ γενεᾷ), the Lord has granted a place of repentance to all such as would be converted unto Him. Noah preached repentance, and as many as listened to him were saved. Jonah proclaimed destruction to the Ninevites; but they, repenting of their sins, propitiated God by prayer, and obtained salvation, although they were aliens [to the

---

1198 Idem 6:3 (ANF 7:518).

1199 In the Russian source, "to live by the other." —*Trans.*

1200 Idem 6:5–6 (ANF 7:518).

1201 Idem 10:3: "Προῃρημένοι μᾶλλον τὴν ἐνθάδε ἀπόλαυσιν ἢ τὴν μέλλουσαν ἐπαγγελίαν."

1202 In outlining the ascetic ideal for living in the early Church we have cited only limited data. Pierre Batiffol provides certain additional data. See *Etudes d' histoire et de théologie positive*, 2-me éd. (Paris: 1902), 47–54.

1203 *Didache* 4.14 (ECF 173).

1204 Idem 14.1: "Εὐχαριστήσατε προεξομολογησάμενοι τὰ παραπτώματα ὑμῶν." Cf. *Epistle of Barnabas* 19.12: "ἐξομολογήσῃ ἐπὶ ἁμαρτίας σου."

covenant] of God (ἀλλότριοι τοῦ Θεοῦ ὄντες).[1205] The ministers of the grace of God have, by the Holy Spirit, spoken of repentance; and the Lord of all things has himself declared with an oath regarding it.[1206] ... Desiring, therefore, that all His beloved should be partakers of repentance, He has, by His almighty will, established [these declarations]."[1207] Clement also exhorts the Corinthians to repentance.[1208] St. Ignatius the God-bearer expresses this conviction: "To all them that repent, the Lord grants forgiveness, if they turn in penitence to the unity of God, and to communion with the bishop. I trust [as to you] in the grace of Jesus Christ, who shall free you from every bond."[1209] In the epistle of Polycarp of Smyrna to the Philadelphians we find strict condemnation of the presbyter Valentius, who had fallen into acquisitiveness: "If a man does not keep himself from covetousness, he shall be defiled by idolatry, and shall be judged as one of the heathen."[1210] At the same time, Polycarp speaks of the possibility of repentance for such sinners: "I am deeply grieved, therefore, brethren, for him (Valens) and his wife; to whom may the Lord grant true repentance! And be ye then

---

1205 1 Clem. 7:5–7 (ANF 1:7).

1206 1 Clem. 8:1–4 (ANF 1:7). This is followed by quotes from Ez. 33:11, 18:30, 32:12; Is. 1:16–20.

1207 1 Clem. 8:5 (ANF 1:7).

1208 Idem 51:1, 3: "Καλὸν ἀνθρώπῳ ἐξομολογεῖσθαι περὶ τῶν παραπτωμάτων ἢ σκληρῦναι τὴν καρδίαν αὐτοῦ [it is better that a man should acknowledge his transgressions than that he should harden his heart]." "At the same time," says F.X. Funk, "in his epistle to the Corinthians Clement of Rome speaks of repentance in such general terms that no conclusion on the matter—that is, on the matter of early Christian discipline—may be drawn from his words" (see *Zur altchristlichen Bussdisciplin: Kirchengeschichtliche Abhandlungen und Untersuchungen* 1, 172). Iohann Stufler does not agree with this opinion of Funk, instead drawing broad conclusions from the epistle of Clement on the matter of discipline also (see "Die bussdisziplin der abendländischen Kirche bis Kallistus," in *Zeitschrift für katholische Theologie* [1907], 451). At present our goal is to note in Clement the general idea of repentance in conjunction with the definition of the sanctity of the Church.

1209 Ignatius, *To the Philadelphians* 8.1 (ANF 1:84).

1210 Polycarp, *Epistle to the Philippians* 11.2 (ANF 1:35): "Si quis non se abstinuerit ab avaritia, ab idololatria coinquinabitur et tamquam inter gentes judicabitur."

moderate in regard to this matter, and 'do not count such as enemies,' but call them back as suffering and straying members (*sicut
passibilia membra et errantia*), that ye may save your whole body."[1211] In
a homily ascribed to Clement of Rome we again find a teaching on
repentance: "As long ... as we are upon earth, let us practice repentance, for we are as clay in the hand of the artificer (τοῦ τεχνίτου).
For as the potter, if he make a vessel, and it be distorted or broken
in his hands, fashions it over again; but if he have before this cast
it into the furnace of fire, can no longer find any help for it: so let
us also, while we are in this world, repent with our whole heart of
the evil deeds we have done in the flesh, that we may be saved by
the Lord, while we have yet an opportunity of repentance. For after
we have gone out of the world, no further power of confessing or
repenting will there belong to us."[1212] The time of this earthly life
is envisioned as a time of repentance, and only after death does the
possibility of repentance cease: then people are vessels placed in the
furnace, and it is too late to correct them. This historical work mentions repentance several times more,[1213] with Christians constantly
viewed as being in the process of perfection.[1214] Only a life spent in
struggle with sin and in virtue leads to perfect salvation (εἰς τέλος
σωθῶμεν).[1215] It should be remembered that the so-called "second
epistle of Clement" comprises a homily, and consequently it is addressed specifically to members of the Church who have already
been cleansed of their sins in baptism.

The testimonies to repentance in the early years that we have
cited are however highly uncertain. It is perfectly clear that the
question of early penitential discipline in church historical science is
nearly beyond resolution. This question is visited and revisited, and

---

1211 Polycarp, *Epistle to the Philippians* 11.4 (ANF 1:35):

1212 2 Clem. 8:1–3 (ANF 7:519).

1213 Idem 13:1, 17:1, 19:1.

1214 Idem 7:1–4, 9:7: "Ἇς ἔχομεν καιρὸν τοῦ ἰαθῆναι, ἐπιδῶμεν ἑαυτοὺς τῷ
θεραπεύοντι θεῷ." 11:1, 16:4, 17:3.

1215 Idem 19:2–3. Cf. Barn. 4:11 (ANF 1:139): "Let us be spiritually-minded:
let us be a perfect temple to God. As much as in us lies (ἐφ' ὅσον ἐστὶν ἐν ἡμῖν), let
us meditate upon the fear of God, and let us keep His commandments."

new views are constantly put forward, which however are backed by very little data from historical sources.[1216]

In approaching the question from a dogmatic rather than a historical perspective, we do not experience so insurmountable a difficulty, if for no other reason than that we can point to a perfectly obvious fact: the dogmatic doctrine of the sanctity of the Church was not yet a topic of discussion. The sanctity of the Church lay more in life than in dogma, and in life the soil was still being prepared for the emergence of the dogmatic doctrine of the sanctity of the Church.

Here we will merely note that the data cited, wherein a member of the Church is presented as sinful and penitent, gives us grounds not to accept without objection the assertion frequently encountered in historic and dogmatic literature that from the very beginning the Christian Church considered itself a society of saints.[1217] Nowhere in historical sources is this idea clearly expressed.[1218] We have already said that the elucidation of the dogmatic doctrine of the sanctity of the Church was preceded by the holy life of Christians. There was a force that for a long time maintained Christian life at the peak of perfection: this was the enthusiasm of the first Christians, which also manifested itself in an abundance of spiritual

---

1216 Concerning this see S.I. Smirnov, *The Spiritual Father in the Early Eastern Church* ("Духовный отец в древней Восточной Церкви"), part 1 (Sergiev Posad: 1906), from 220 on.

1217 Ernst Rolffs, *Das Indulgenz Edict des römischen Bischofs Kallist,* TU 11.3 (Leipzig: 1893), 10; Smirnov, op. cit., 220; Harnack, *Dogmengeschichte*[4] 1, 406, 414.

1218 [There is much that contradicts this.] See for example the epistle of Barnabas 4:14 (ANF 1:139), which states: "Let us beware lest we be found [fulfilling that saying], as it is written, 'Many are called, but few are chosen.'" Consequently, Christians are not yet chosen, but only called. 2 Clem. 20:3: "The saints are appointed as an example for Christians." The typical tendential Protestant concept of the Church in the early centuries is disputed by Catholic scholars, and not without justification. "The so-called 'ancient concept of the Church,' according to which it was only a society of perfected saints, rather than an institution (*Anstalt*) intended for the sanctification (*Heiligung*) of sinful mankind, is one of the many fictions with which Harnack's history of the dogmas abounds" (Iohann Stufler, "Die Sündenvergebung bei Origenes," in *Zeitschrift für katholische Theologie* [1907], 195–196).

gifts. Small Christian communities, sprinkled throughout a pagan world, were under the vigilant oversight of their pastors, and virtue blossomed in the fertile soil of a common brotherly love. In the very worldview of the early Christians there was much that continually fanned the flame of this enthusiasm. In reading the earliest works of Christian literature we constantly observe how [their] writers are permeated with the anticipation of the imminent end of the world.[1219] Indeed, we encounter the idea that the world would soon end even among the New Testament writers.[1220] Here we should also add the chiliastic tendencies of certain writers. The expectation of the swift end of the world and the advent of an earthly kingdom of Christians naturally had considerable significance for maintaining the ascetic enthusiasm of the early Christians. This expectation gave Christians the strength to disdain the good things of the visible world for the sake of impending bliss in the Kingdom of Christ.[1221] But time passed, and the world remained. In vain Chris-

---

1219 In the *Didache* the prayer, "Let this world pass away" (10.6); Barn. 4:3: "The final stumbling-block ... (or source of danger) (τὸ τέλειον) approaches," [followed] by quotes from Dan. 9:24–27; Mt. 24:22; Dan. 7:24, 8. Barn. 21:3: "The day is at hand on which all things shall perish with the evil [one]. The Lord is near, and His reward [Is. 40:10]" (ANF 1:149). 1 Clem 23:5: "Of a truth, soon and suddenly shall His will be accomplished, as the Scripture also bears witness, saying, 'Speedily will He come, and will not tarry;' and, 'The Lord shall suddenly come to His temple, even the Holy One, for whom ye look' [Is. 14:1; Mal. 3:1. Cf. Hab. 2:3, Heb. 10:37]" (ANF 1:11). 2 Clem. 12:1: "Let us expect, therefore, hour by hour, the kingdom of God" (ANF 7:520). At 16:3 we read, "γινώσκετε δέ, ὅτι ἔρχεται ἤδη ἡ ἡμέρα τῆς κρίσεως [Know that the day of judgment already draws near]"; that is, in quoting Mal. 4:1 the author inserts ἤδη [already]. Concerning the Second Coming see also 17:4–6. Likewise, in *To the Ephesians* 11.1 Ignatius the God-bearer writes, "The last times are come upon us" (ANF 1:54). Hermas beheld a tower that was nearly completed (*The Pastor of Hermas,* 3.9.5.1, 3.9.32.1), and people **hastened** to build the tower (3.9.3.2, 3.9.5.7).

1220 For example, Jas. 5:9: "The judge standeth before the door"; 1 Pet. 4:7: "The end of all things is at hand." Cf. 1 Cor. 1:7, 8; 15:51, 52; 1 Thess. 4:15; Phil. 4:5; Rev. 1:3, 22:10.

1221 The expectation that the world would soon end was a highly important element of the early Christian worldview. Concerning this see Ritschl, *Die Entstehung der altkath. Kirche,* 509, 519, 522. Cf. Harnack, *Das Mönchtum, seine Ideale und seine Geschichte: Reden und Aufsätze,* 1-er Band (Giessen: 1904), 88; *Mission und*

tians lifted their gaze heavenward: no approaching Judge was to be seen upon the clouds. The expectation of His imminent coming lost all intensity, and along with it ascetic enthusiasm waned.[1222] In addition, great changes took place in the situation of the Christian Church. It embraced the whole world, and to it were joined people from every social stratum. Christians dwelt in both palaces and hovels; slaves and masters alike joined the Church. But of every society it may be stated that the greater and more varied its membership, the less unity it has, and the lower its **overall quality** becomes. Inevitably, the same had to befall the Church. In the earliest communities there flourished a strict ascetic ideal of life, and the sanctity of the Church was felt with particular clarity. But the new elements that had entered the Christian Church were less and less governed by the ascetic ideal, and "nominal Christians" appeared.[1223] In an environment of this type of Christians, naturally, the idea of the sanctity of the Church diminished. Thus, very early on two directions emerged in the Church, each of which was governed by its own idea of the sanctity of the Church, and which in accordance with this idea outlined a particular preferred structure of church discipline. But naturally these two directions did not immediately enter into conflict. Initially this difference in thinking was merely an undetermined concept of the sanctity of the Church, which allowed for a variety of opinions among different people.

[It is this] state of the dogmatic doctrine of the sanctity of the Church [that is outlined] in *The Pastor of Hermas*, where the idea of the Church is in fact its focus.[1224] We will now analyze *The Pastor* in somewhat greater detail.

Ausbreitung des Christentums 1, 293. See Prof. A.A. Spassky's note on the Russian translation of this book (Kharkov: 1907), 219. Bolotov, *Lectures on the History of the Early Church*, 2nd ed., 349–350. Knopf, *Das nachapostolische Zeitalter*, 396 ff. Th. Zahn, *Der Hirt des Hermas*, 316–326, 344–350.

1222   See Knopf, *Das nachapostolische Zeitalter*, 398–399.

1223   Harnack describes this well (see *Das Mönchtum: Reden und Aufsätze* 1, 89–92). See also Smirnov, *The Spiritual Father*, 221–222; Harnack, *Die Mission und Usbreitung des Christentumes* 1, 172 ff, especially 184–185.

1224   See Zahn, *Der Hirt des Hermas*, 139; R. Seeberg, *Studien zur Geschichte des Begriffs der Kirche*, 7.

The worldview we encounter in *The Pastor of Hermas* is a strictly ascetic one. The pastor tells Hermas that the servants of God are sojourners. Their city lies far from the cities of the earth. There is no need therefore here on earth to purchase estates, to build magnificent buildings and needless dwellings. One who acquires anything in an earthly city gives no thought to returning to his homeland. He is an irrational, double-minded, pitiful man, who does not understand that everything earthly is not his own, and is under the authority of another. "For the Lord of this country justly says to thee, 'Either obey my laws or depart from my dominion.' What, then, dost thou intend to do, having a law in thine own city, on account of thy lands, and the rest of thy possessions? Thou shalt altogether deny thy law.[1225] ... If thou shalt desire to return to thy city, thou wilt not be received, because thou hast denied the law of thy city, but wilt be excluded from it. Have a care, therefore: as one living in a foreign land, make no further preparations for thyself than such merely as may be sufficient; and be ready, when the master of this city shall come to cast thee out for disobeying his law, to leave his city, and to depart to thine own, and to obey thine own law without being exposed to annoyance, but in great joy."[1226] These words require no explanation: they can only be supplemented with one very telling passage. A woman appears to Hermas and says to him: "Is it not your opinion that a righteous man commits sin when an evil desire arises in his heart? There is sin in such a case, and the sin is great ... for the thoughts of a righteous man should be righteous."[1227]

In accordance with this general ascetic ideal of Christian life, *The Pastor of Hermas* speaks a great many times of the sanctity of the Church. The tower in which from Hermas beheld the Church was built of "splendid square stones.[1228] ... The stones which were

---

1225 In the Russian source the end of the former sentence is appended to the latter, in the form of a question: "On account of thy lands, and the rest of thy possessions, shalt thou altogether deny thy law?" –*Trans.*

1226 *The Pastor of Hermas* 3.1.1–6 (ANF 2:31).

1227 Idem 1.1.8 (ANF 2:9).

1228 Idem 1.3.2.4; 3.9.3.3; 3.9.4.5.

placed in the building just as they were ... were polished and fitted exactly into the other stones, and became so united one with another that the lines of juncture could not be perceived."[1229] "Square white stones which fitted exactly into each other"[1230] were used for the construction of the tower. Less perfect stones, which signified sinful men, were not placed in the tower, but were set aside, while some were even broken apart and cast far away from the tower.[1231] There were stones that were white and round, but which nevertheless were not used for the building.[1232] These are those who have faith, but who also possess the riches of this age. They will only be pleasing to the Lord when their riches have been cut off.[1233] Only perfect stones are taken for the building of the tower.

Consequently, in speaking of the Church, out of all her qualities Hermas particularly emphasizes her sanctity. But this discussion of sanctity does not hinder him from being primarily a preacher of repentance.[1234]

The teaching in *The Pastor of Hermas* on repentance is quite remarkable. Hermas beheld stones brought from the earth, which were set aside.[1235] Hermas asked the old woman who accompanied him, "Who then are those whom they rejected and cast away?" She replied: "These are they who have sinned, and wish to repent. On this account they have not been thrown far from the tower, because they will yet be useful in the building, if they repent. Those then who are to repent, if they do repent, will be strong in faith, if they now repent while the tower is building. For if the building be

---

1229 Idem 3.2.6 (ANF 2:13).

1230 Idem 3.5.1 (ANF 2:14).

1231 Idem 3.2.7 (ANF 2:13).

1232 Idem 3.2.8.

1233 Idem 3.6.5–6.

1234 "*The Pastor of Hermas* is a historic penitential work in the proper sense. From beginning to end the author is occupied by a single idea: to exhort all his contemporaries and all environs of the Church in no uncertain terms to swift repentance." Such is Stufler's characterization of *The Pastor of Hermas* (*Zeitschrift für katholische Theologie* [1907], 452).

1235 *The Pastor of Hermas* 1.3.2.7.

finished, there will not be more room for any one, but he will be rejected. And they only have this, that they lie near the tower."[1236] This clearly refers to the possibility of repentance for one who has sinned. Repentance only becomes impossible once the building of the Church is complete—that is, when the earthly existence of the Church shall cease. Another passage presents this same building of the tower-Church in a different form. Namely, it is represented that certain stones placed in the building did not become shining, but remained as they were when laid. These stones were unsuitable in the building of the tower, and the stones were removed and returned to the place from which they were taken.[1237] But even after this, before the very end of construction, the building process is paused. The Lord of the tower must come and test the building, so that if any stones within it are found unsuitable they might be replaced.[1238] This testing of the building by the Lord is then described. The Lord tested each stone, striking each stone thrice with a staff which He held in His hand. Some stones became black as soot following the blows; some were neither black nor white; others were uneven and were not in keeping with the other stones; still others became covered with a great many stains. The Lord commanded that all these stones be taken out from the tower and laid down beside it.[1239] But even after this the Lord gives the "pastor" a command to cleanse all these rejected stones and to place in the tower those that can be fitted to the rest. The pastor expresses the hope that the majority of the stones may be corrected and employed for the building.[1240] Indeed, many stones were corrected, and when they were placed in the building the tower appeared to be made of a single stone.[1241] This entire semblance is interpreted as follows: "After they had entered into the same place, and became one body, certain of these defiled

---

1236 Idem 3.5.5 (ANF 2:14).

1237 *The Pastor of Hermas* 3.9.4.6–7.

1238 *The Pastor of Hermas* 1.3.6.1. Cf. 13.8–9.

1239 Idem 9.6.1–5.

1240 Idem 9.7.1–2, 4–5.

1241 Idem 9.8–9.

themselves, and were expelled from the race of the righteous, and became again what they were before, or rather worse."[1242] "He that has known God, ought not any longer to do evil, but to do good. ... They who have known God ... and still continue in evil, shall be chastised doubly, and shall die for ever. In this way, then, will the Church of God be purified. ... In like manner also shall it be with the Church of God, after it has been purified, and has rejected the wicked, and the hypocrites, and the blasphemers, and the waverers, and those who commit wickedness of different kinds. After these have been cast away, the Church of God shall be one body, of one mind, of one understanding, of one faith, of one love. And then the Son of God will be exceeding glad, and shall rejoice over them, because He has received His people pure."[1243] In these words cited from *The Pastor of Hermas* the blameless state of the Church is envisioned only in the future. Then there will be none in her who work unrighteousness of various kinds, and then the people of God will be pure. But the earthly Church is a society still in the process of perfection. Repentance is possible for those who fall. Only the sons of iniquity (οἱ υἱοὶ τῆς ἀνομίας) are completely rejected.[1244] For all this Hermas gave thanks to the Lord, "because He had pity on all that call upon His name; and sent the angel of repentance to us who sinned against Him, and renewed (ἀνεκαίνισεν) our spirit;

1242 Idem 9.17.5. Cf. 13.8–9.

1243 Idem 9.18.1–4 (ANF 2.50).

1244 *The Pastor of Hermas* 1.3.6.1. Cf. 3.9.8.1–5. This concept of the possibility of rebirth is also expressed in the vision of the vine from which the angel distributed branches. For many these branches dried up. The angel watered them abundantly, after which several branches proved to be green and to have offshoots, and even to be bearing fruit (see 3.8, especially 3.8.5.6). The vision concludes with this command (3.8.11.1, 3): "Go and tell them to every one, that they may repent, and they shall live unto God. Because the Lord, having had compassion on all men, has sent me to give repentance, although some are not worthy of it on account of their works; but the Lord, being long-suffering, desires those who were called by His Son to be saved. ... All who with their whole heart shall purify themselves from their wickedness before enumerated, and shall add no more to their sins, will receive healing from the Lord for their former transgressions, if they do not hesitate at these commandments; and they will live unto God" (ANF 2:43).

and when we were already destroyed, and had no hope of life, He restored us to newness of life."[1245]

Thus, *The Pastor of Hermas* speaks of the possibility of repentance even for one who has faltered in spirit and lost the hope of life. The historic work in question is speaking figuratively; it is hard to draw specific historical information from it. The pastor constantly speaks of repentance, but is forgiveness possible for every sin? *The Pastor of Hermas* gives no exact answer to this question, but it does contain certain grounds for an answer.[1246] Here is what it says concerning apostates. "Apostates and traitors (οἱ ἀποστάται καὶ προδόται) of the Church, who have blasphemed the Lord in their sins, and have, moreover, been ashamed of the name of the Lord by which they were called ... these to the end (εἰς τέλος ἀπώλοντο) were lost unto God."[1247] But from what follows it is clear that the cause of this perishing is not the quality of the sin, but lack of remorse on the part of the sinners.[1248] "Not a single one of them repented, although they heard the words which I spake to them, which I enjoined upon you" (that is, the words concerning repentance). "From such life departed."[1249] For them repentance is possible if they have not apostatized from their heart, "but if any one is found to have denied

---

1245 *The Pastor of Hermas* 3.9.14.3 (ANF 2:48).

1246 Concerning the question of repentance in *The Pastor of Hermas*, F.X. Funk offers several observations. See *Zur altchristlichen Bussdisciplin: Kirchengeschichtliche Abhandlungen und Untersuchungen*, 1-er Bd., 168–171. See also S.I. Smirnov, *The Spiritual Father*, 221n1. See also the work by Prof. Gusev, "Readings on Patrology: Saint Hermas and his book *The Pastor*" ("Чтения по патрологии. Святой Ерм и его книга 'Пастырь'"), in *Pravoslavny sobesednik* (1896) 1, 111–115. The views of *The Pastor of Hermas* receive a wide variety of interpretations in scholarly literature. Some see the author of *The Pastor* as a rigorist, while others conversely see in him an opponent of Montanist strictness. See Stufler, *Zeitschrift für katholische Theologie* (1907), 452–454. Stufler says that Hermas is not a predecessor or an opponent of Montanism, but a preacher of repentance, who adheres to the viewpoint of ecclesiastical orthodoxy.

1247 *The Pastor of Hermas* 3.8.6.4 (ANF 2:41). Cf. 9.19.1, 26.5.

1248 Vgl. Schwane, *Dogmengeschichte der vornicäischen Zeit*, 449; Knopf, *Das nachapostolische Zeitalter*, 433 Anm. 2.1; Stufler, "Die Bussdisziplin der abendländischen Kirche bis Kallistus," *Zeitschrift für kath. Theologie* (1907), 455–456.

1249 *The Pastor of Hermas* 3.8.6.4 (ANF 2:41).

from the heart, I do not know if he may live."[1250] The same may be seen in another passage of *The Pastor of Hermas,* which refers to the possibility of repentance for the children of Hermas, whom he did not admonish and whom he permitted to become terribly corrupted (ἀφῆκες καταφθαρῆναι δεινῶς). The corruption of the house of Hermas is defined as impiety against God and the parents.[1251] Nevertheless it is said that the Lord will heal all the evils that have been done.[1252] "Cease not therefore to admonish your sons; for I know that, if they will repent with all their heart, they will be enrolled in the Books of Life with the saints."[1253] Forgiveness even for adultery is described quite clearly: "If the woman put away should repent, and wish to return to her husband. ... If the husband do not take her back, he sins, and brings a great sin upon himself (ἁμαρτάνει καὶ μεγάλην ἁμαρτίαν ἑαυτῷ ἐπισπᾶται); for he ought to take back the sinner who has repented. But not frequently (μὴ ἐπὶ πολὺ δέ). For there is but one repentance to the servants of God.[1254] ... [Let him] who has sinned ... sin no more.[1255] But with regard to his previous transgressions, there is One who is able to provide a cure; for it is He, indeed, who has power over all."[1256] Experience had shown Hermas that those who had sinned gravely rarely proved capable of repentance,[1257] but from a dogmatic standpoint, in the views of

---

1250 Idem 9.26.5 (ANF 2:52).

1251 *The Pastor of Hermas* 1.1.3.1 (ANF 2:10). The sins of the children of Hermas are described as follows (1.2.2.2): "Your seed, O Hermas, has sinned against God, and they have blasphemed against the Lord, and in their great wickedness they have betrayed their parents. And they passed as traitors of their parents, and by their treachery did they not reap profit. And even now they have added to their sins lusts and iniquitous pollutions" (ANF 2:11).

1252 Idem 1.3.1. Cf. 3.8.11.1.

1253 Idem 1.3.2.

1254 *The Pastor of Hermas* 2.4.1.7–8. The same is true for the wife: she too must receive a husband who has sinned.

1255 Bracketed words are those of the current translator, due to slight differences between the Russian source and the English. –*Trans.*

1256 Idem 2.4.1.11.

1257 See above, 3.8.6.4. Cf. 1.3.7.2: "Nor does the thought of repentance ever come into their hearts, on account of their devotion to their lusts and to the

The Pastor of Hermas, even forgiveness for grave sins—specifically, adultery—is possible. It was for this reason, incidentally, that in the early third century Callistus, bishop of Rome, cited *The Pastor of Hermas* in justification of his edict concerning forgiveness of sins of the flesh.[1258]

But even in the author's own writings this lenient view[1259] is not entirely conformed to the concept of the sanctity of the Church. The following discourse takes place between Hermas and the "pastor": "I heard, sir, some teachers maintain that there is no other repentance than that which takes place, when we descended into the water and received remission of our former sins." The pastor responds: "That was sound doctrine (καλῶς) which you heard; for that is really the case. For he who has received remission of his

---

crimes which they committed" (ANF 2:15).

1258 See concerning the sins of the children of Hermas, 1.2.2.2. Tertullian is known to have reacted sharply to *The Pastor of Hermas* for this condescension. *On Modesty* 10: "Scriptura Pastoris, quae sola moechos amat, divino instrumento meruisset incidi, si non ab omni concilio ecclesiarum, etiam vestrarum, inter apocrypha et falsa judicaretur, adultera et ipsa et inde patrona sociorum [if the scripture of "the Shepherd," which is the only one which favours adulterers, had deserved to find a place in the Divine canon; if it had not been habitually judged by every council of Churches (even of your own) among apocryphal and false (writings); itself adulterous, and hence a patroness of its comrades]" (CSEL 20.1:240.11–14). Furthermore, Tertullian calls *The Pastor of Hermas* "Pastor moechorum [shepherd of adulterers]" (*On Modesty* 20 [CSEL 20.1:266.21]). Cf. Stufler's argument in *Zeitschr. Für kath. Theologie* (1907), 457; Friedrich Frank, *Die Bussdisciplin der Kirche von den Apostelzeitben bis zum siebenten Jahrhundert* (Mainz: 1867), 420, 836–837; Schwane, *Dogmengeschichte der mornic. Zeit,* 487.

1259 It must however be noted that even this lenient view of the author requires moral labors on the part of the penitent. 3.7.4–5; cf. 1.1.2.1: "Do you think, however, that the sins of those who repent are remitted? Not altogether, but he who repents must torture (βασανίσαι, "to test using a stone," from βάσανος, "touchstone") his own soul, and be exceedingly (ἰσχυρῶς) humble in all his conduct, and be afflicted with many kinds of affliction (ἐν πάσαις θλίψεσι); and if he endure the afflictions that come upon him, He who created all things, and endued them with power, will assuredly have compassion, and will heal him; and this will He do when He sees the heart of every penitent pure from every evil thing" (ANF 2:38–39).

sins ought not to sin any more, but to live in purity.[1260] ... For those who have now believed, and those who are to believe, have not repentance for their sins; but they have remission of their previous sins [that is, in baptism]. For to those who have been called before these days, the Lord has set repentance. For the Lord, knowing the heart, and foreknowing all things, knew the weakness of men and the manifold wiles of the devil, that he would inflict some evil on the servants of God, and would act wickedly towards them. The Lord, therefore, being merciful, has had mercy on the work of His hand, and has set repentance for them; and He has entrusted to me power over this repentance. And therefore I say to you, that if any one is tempted by the devil, and sins after that great and holy calling in which the Lord has called His people to everlasting life, he has opportunity to repent but once. But if he should sin frequently after this (ὑπὸ χεῖρα), and then repent, to such a man his repentance will be of no avail; for with difficulty will he live (δυσκόλως γὰρ ζήσεται)."[1261] Here we have cited the most characteristic passage from *The Pastor of Hermas*. In the Christian Church at that time there were apparently teachers who denied the possibility of repen-

---

1260 Cf. Justin Martyr, *Dialogue with Trypho* 44: "There is no other [way] than this—to become acquainted with this Christ, to be washed in the fountain spoken of by Isaiah for the remission of sins; and for the rest, to live sinless lives" (ANF 1:217).

1261 *The Pastor of Hermas* 2.4.3.1–6 (ANF 2:22). Cf. Funk's observation concerning this in *Kirchengeschictliche Abhandlungen und Untersuchungen*, 1-er Bd., 169–170. The same is also repeated in 1.2.2.4–8: "Then shall they be forgiven all the sins which in former times they committed, and forgiveness will be granted to all the saints [that is, the Christians—*auth.*] who have sinned even to the present day, if they repent with all their heart, and drive all doubts from their minds. For the Lord has sworn by His glory, in regard to His elect, that if any one of them sin after a certain day which has been fixed [ὡρισμένης τῆς ἡμέρας ταύτης], he shall not be saved. For the repentance of the righteous has limits. Filled up are the days of repentance to all the saints; but to the heathen, repentance will be possible even to the last day. ... Those who denied their Lord have abandoned their life in despair, for even now these are to deny Him in the days that are coming. To those who denied in earlier times, God became gracious, on account of His exceeding tender mercy" (ANF 2:11). Cf. also 3.9.26.5.

tance.[1262] In their opinion, one who entered the Church through baptism received remission of his former sins, and ought to have broken off all ties with his sinful life. And the pastor fully approves of this view.

But the words that follow are concessionary in their tone. Both human weakness and the temptations of the devil are taken into account, and consequently repentance is appointed for those who have sinned. Once again, however, a limit is set: only those who have sinned prior to his preaching can repent, while henceforth all who receive forgiveness of sins in baptism must lead a sinless life. Here we encounter a stricter view than before, when repentance was said to be possible for all, and only the uselessness of constantly recurring repentance was pointed out.[1263] Hermas is therefore a preacher of a particular Church-wide repentance, after which there must be no place for repentance.[1264] But the very possibility of this repentance and the fact that this repentance was preached tells us that the sanctity of the Church was not understood strictly in the sense of a society of saints. In the Church there may be different people, **and not all within her are holy to the same degree.**[1265] Hermas sometimes refers to Christians as saints (ἅγιοι),

---

1262 E. Preuschen attempted to prove that the διδάσκαλοι mentioned by Hermas were not of his generation, but before him, so that 2.4.3.1 may be even seen as a reference to Heb. 6:4–6, and the opinion of the Didascalians may be held to express the ideal of the early Church. See "Zur Kirchenpolitik des Bischofs Kallist," in *Zeitschrift für die neutestamentliche Wissenschaft und die Kunde des Urchristentums* (1910), 148–149. But all the evidence presented by Preuschen is highly unconvincing. The Didascalians of whom we read in Hermas should be considered adherents of a rigoristic movement in Hermas's own time.

1263 *The Pastor of Hermas* 2.4.3.6.

1264 Hermas's denial of future repentance is naturally due to his expectation of the impending end of the world. Concerning this see Stufler, *Zeitschr. für kath. Theologie* (1907), 461–463. Vgl. Bardenhewer, *Patrologie*[3] §37.1, 108. Furthermore, this denial is not maintained consistently (Stufler, ibid., 463–465).

1265 When the angel of the Lord demanded of the people the branches they had been given, he received different kinds of branches from them (3.8.1.1–18). The pastor however, upon seeing before him stones of various kinds, said (3.9.7.4–5), "The greater part of these stones … I will hew, and put into the building, and they will harmonize (ἁρμόσουσι) with the others." Hermas asked:

but, as may be seen from the foregoing, for him this is by no means tied to the idea that the members of the Church are exclusively holy. For Hermas, the sanctity of the Church is not the sanctity of each individual member thereof. Nevertheless, in Hermas we encounter a very significant compound concept: "the saints who have sinned" (τοῖς ἁγίοις τοῖς ἁμαρτήσασιν).[1266] This expression gives us grounds to ascribe to *The Pastor of Hermas* the idea that the Church is not exclusively a society of saints. *The Pastor of Hermas* does not confound ἅγιος and καθαρός. Individuals may progress toward perfection, as may the whole Church. This moral transfiguration of the Church was the objective of Hermas's own preaching. And this is the highly significant vision in which the moral renewal of the Church is depicted. The first time the Church appeared in the form of an old woman. In the second vision she had a young face, but an elderly body and hair; nevertheless she was more merry than before. In the third vision she was far younger in her entirety, with a lovely face, and she was quite merry.[1267] The first vision signified that the spirit of Christians had become decrepit and had no strength because of the sins and doubts of the heart. Burdened with their daily affairs, Christians had fallen into negligence and did not place their cares upon the Lord. Their spirit had become broken, and they had grown old in their sorrows.[1268] The second vision is interpreted as follows: the Lord took pity upon Christians and renewed their spirit; they set aside their infirmities, and vigour came to them. They grew

---

"'How, sir ... can they, after being cut all round about, fill up the same space?' He answered, 'Those that shall be found small (μικροί) will be thrown into the middle of the building, and those that are larger will be placed on the outside, and they will hold them together'" (ANF 2:45). And indeed, two days later certain stones were placed outside, because they were found to be strong and able to hold together the stones thrown in the middle, for nothing was was cut off in them. ... Other stones were cut round about and placed in the middle of the building of the tower, for they were weaker. Certain stones were short, and were also thrown in the middle of the building (3.9.8.3–5, 7).

1266 *The Pastor of Hermas* 1.2.2.4 (ANF 2:11). Cf. 3.9.13.2, which assumes the possibility of bearing the name of the Son of God without possessing His power.

1267 *The Pastor of Hermas* 1.3.10.3–5. Cf. 1.1.2.2.

1268 *The Pastor of Hermas* 1.3.11.2, 3.

strong in the faith, and the Lord rejoiced at seeing their strength.[1269] The third vision also signifies the complete renewal of Christians souls. Those who repent from their whole heart will be rejuvenated and grow strong.[1270]

This vision of the younger Church clearly and definitively presents the idea that the members of the Church in various eras of her historical existence may veer more or less from the ideal of the sanctity of the Church; while at other times the whole Church may be set aright and renewed, and may approach the goal, unreachable in this earthly life, of the perfect sanctity of her members.[1271] On this dogmatic sort of basis alone hangs Hermas's entire preaching of repentance. Hermas opens the door of repentance very wide. Sometimes he seems to forget what has been said about repentance being possible only for former sins. We have seen that going forward Hermas wishes to close the doors of repentance completely for those who have sinned. Nevertheless, in his writings we find severe condemnation of those who deny repentance, whom Hermas places not far from apostates. Concerning the former he continues: "They who gave [their branches] in withered and undecayed, these also were near to them; for they were hypocrites, and introducers of strange doctrines (διδαχὰς ξένας), and subverters of the servants of God, especially of those who had sinned, not allowing them to repent, but persuading them by foolish doctrines (ταῖς διδαχαῖς ταῖς μωραῖς πείθοντες αὐτούς)."[1272]

We have set forth the doctrine on the sanctity of the Church found in *The Pastor of Hermas*. In this doctrine we cannot help but notice certain points that are not reconciled with each other, and there would seem to be no firm grounds for any definitive reconciliation of them. Hermas is a preacher of repentance; to deny repentance, in his own words, is to preach a foolish doctrine; yet

---

1269 Idem 3.12.3.

1270 Idem 3.13.2, 4.

1271 Cf. observation of Zahn, *Der Hirt des Hermas*, 191, 192–193, 206, 222, 223, 285, 288, 291–292. See also Seeberg, *Studien zur Geschichte des Begriffs der Kirche*, 9–10.

1272 *The Pastor of Hermas*, 3.8.6.5 (ANF 2:41).

he himself approves the opinion of certain teachers who said that repentance is not possible after baptism. Hermas is frequently considered an advocate of particularly lenient views.[1273] Indeed, all rigorism is foreign to *The Pastor of Hermas*, but in it we may also find the strictest of stances. Hermas is governed by a strict ascetic ideal of the sanctity of the Church, but reality was far from this ideal. The preacher of repentance wishes to morally renew the Church, so that at least in the future the ideal he holds dear might be realized. This ideal is quite understandable for an ascetic such as Hermas was, but it is noteworthy that he does not immediately cast out from the Church people who do not meet this ideal and who sinned after baptism, as ought to have been done if the author were governed by a rigoristic concept of the sanctity of the Church. Rather, he calls them to repentance, after which they may prove suitable for the construction of the building of the Church.[1274] Ideally, of course, it is best that people sin no more and have no need of repentance after their rebirth in baptism. But to make this ideal a positive law of

---

1273 Such is the opinion of Batiffol, for example (*Etudes d' histoire et de théologie positive*², 60–61). Cf. D. Kasitsyn, *Schisms of the Early Centuries of Christianity*, 73: "*The Pastor* of Hermas, who was primarily a preacher of repentance, teaches with particular force that all sins, however great, can be remitted and cleansed in the Church."

1274 A highly detailed analysis of the doctrine of *The Pastor of Hermas* on repentance has been made by Stufler ("Bussdisziplin der abendländischen Kirche bis Kallistus," in *Zeitschr. Für katholische Theologie* [1907], 451–473). Here Stufler thoroughly defends the following four theses: 1. All sins committed after baptism, even the gravest, may be forgiven, meaning that only those perish who voluntarily shun repentance and harden their hearts. 2. The forgiveness proclaimed by the angel of repentance is not only the otherworldly forgiveness of God, but also comprises reconciliation with the Church and reception back into her. 3. After the deadline for repentance that God proclaims through *The Pastor of Hermas*, secondary repentance—that is, repentance after baptism and forgiveness of subsequent grave sins—must indeed cease, but not absolutely and unconditionally, but only based on the assumption that the end of the world is at hand. 4. Secondary repentance existed even before Hermas, and the forgiveness of sins proclaimed by *The Pastor of Hermas* is not an innovation. Preuschen raises several objections to Stufler. See "Zur Kirchenpolitik des Bischofs Kallist," in *Zeitschrift für die neutestamentliche Wissenschaft und die Kunde des Urchristentums* (1910), 146–149.

the Church would be "to subvert the servants of God, persuading them by foolish doctrines."[1275]

Despite the ambiguity of the dogmatic doctrine in *The Pastor of Hermas,* the doctrine of the sanctity of the Church may nevertheless be formulated as follows: Christians who join the Church thereby renounce their sinful life, and must therefore live henceforth in purity and blamelessness. But due to the weakness of sinful human nature they may sin again, and even gravely so. A man may reform and be a worthy member of the Church of Christ. **The sanctity of the Church does not lie in a sanctity acquired once and for all by its individual members, but specifically in that they have embarked upon the path of sanctity, and are governed in their lives by the ideal of holiness, which they achieve by means of constant struggle with sin and the temptations of the devil.**[1276]

The Pastor of Hermas presents the doctrine of the sanctity of the Church to us in a form that is still far from definite. Once again, this attests that at that time the Christian Church had not yet elucidated the concept of the sanctity of the Church. But this could not [continue] for long. St. Hermas expressed the desire that all contradictions between his ideal of the sanctity of the Church and the actual life of Christians might cease. In his time, Christian enthusiasm had already waned, and in the future rather the reverse was to be anticipated: holiness of life was likely to decrease still further. Deprived of their former enthusiasm, Christians were more inclined to heed the crafty seductions of the enemy of the human race. The contradiction between the ideal and reality which motivated the preacher

---

1275 Cf. Batiffol, *Etudes d' histoire et de théologie positive*, 67–68.

1276 The doctrine of *The Pastor of Hermas* concerning the Church in terms of its sanctity is rightly noted by Archimandrite Sylvester, although his analysis of *The Pastor* is highly superficial and incomplete. Namely, the author defines the purpose of the Church according to the teaching of Hermas as follows: "The purpose for which the Church exists on earth is spiritual and moral prosperity and sanctity, which the faithful achieve to the best of their abilities, entering into an inner union with the Church and availing themselves of her resources for sanctification" (*The Doctrine Concerning the Church*, 114–115). The latter words, as will be seen, require considerable delimitation.

of repentance could only become more acute in the future. History itself urged that the dogmatic doctrine of the sanctity of the Church be elucidated and developed in greater detail. We have seen that Hermas already speaks of the Didascalians, who positively denied repentance for members of the Church who had sinned. Consequently, the question of repentance and of its compatibility with the idea of the sanctity of the Church had already arisen in church society. Some were already refusing to reconcile the sanctity of the Church with the presence of past sinners and penitents in the Church, and rather than seeking a solution to the problem they severed the two and denied the second element—that is, repentance. A dogmatic doctrine of the sanctity of the Church in the sense of the sanctity of its composite members was taking shape.[1277] The question would intensify as it moved to practical grounds, when the abstract dogma would give way to real relations, and church doctrine to church discipline.[1278] The second century bequeathed to the third this now matured contradiction, which would be resolved only after a certain conflict, and this resolution would result in a more thoroughly and more definitively expounded doctrine on the sanctity of the Church. In the history of the dogma concerning the Church, the better part of the third century consists namely of the history of the conceptual development of the sanctity of the Church. This particular concept was central: entire ecclesiastical movements formed around it, and it was a subject of discussion among church writers.

As the second century gave way to the third, as we see from the writings of Tertullian, in order to reconcile the idea of the sanctity of the Church with the sinfulness of its members, some deemed it sufficient to declare some sins forgivable and others unforgivable. These held that a mutual agreement on this division of sins was

---

1277 Cf. the work by Archpriest A.M. Ivantsov-Platonov, *Heresies and Schisms of the First Three Centuries of Christianity* ["Ереси и расколы первых трех веков христианства"] (Moscow: 1877), 106–107.

1278 Vgl. Zahn, *Der Hirt des Hermas*, 310. Zahn surmises that for Hermas the διδάσκαλοι [teachers] were in a sense authoritative, as he speaks of them with respect, and not as of his other opponents (310, Anm. 1).

permissible. A mild sin did not sever one from the Church; such a
sin could be forgiven by a bishop.[1279] But there were grave sins that
could not be forgiven, even if the sinner should repent. Repentance
of mild sins resulted in the penitent's complete reunification to the
Church, but the repentance of one who had sinned mortally did not
open the doors to communion with the Church.[1280] Consequently,
certain sins were compatible with the sanctity of the Church. The
sanctity of the Church demanded at least that all its members be
pure of mortal sins.

But in vain would we search Tertullian for any definitive and
fully satisfactory answer to the question: what is a mortal sin? According to *On Modesty*, a mortal and unforgivable sin is one committed against God,[1281] but this definition can hardly be called clear
and precise. Tertullian himself lists the mortal sins several times, but
each time he does so their number differs and the sins themselves
vary. In *On Modesty* 19 Tertullian lists seven mortal sins "quae veniam
non capiunt—homicidia, idololatria, fraus, negatio, blasphemia un-
tique et moechia et fornicatio [which are incapable of pardon —

1279 Tertullian, *On Modesty* 18: "Levioribus delictis veniam ab episcopo consequi poterit [lighter sins will be able to obtain pardon from the bishop]" (CSEL
20.1:261.26–27).

1280 Tertullian, *On Modesty* 2: "Haec dividimus in duos exitus. Alia erunt
remissibilia, alia inremissibilia [These we divide into two issues: some will be
remissible, some irremissible]." Then, concerning repentance: "Secundum hanc
differentiam delictorum paenitentiae quoque condicio discriminatur. Alia erit
quae veniam consequi possit, in delicto scilicet remissibili, alia quae consequi
nullo modo possit, in delicto scilicet inremissibili [According to this difference of
sins, the condition of repentance also is discriminated. There will be a condition
which may possibly obtain pardon — in the case, namely, of a remissible sin:
there will be a condition which can by no means obtain it — in the case, namely,
of an irremissible sin]" (CSEL 20.1:223.29, 224.1–2, 13–16).

1281 Tertullian, *On Modesty* 2: "Delicta mundantur, quae quis in fratrem, non
deum admiserit [The sins which are (thus) cleansed are such as a man may have
committed against his brother, not against God]" (Csel 20.1:223.13–14). 21:
"Mortalia, quae in ipsum (Deum) fuerint admissa et in templum ejus [mortal
sins, such as have been committed against {God} Himself, and against His tem-
ple]" (269.4–5). "Praejudicatur non dimittenda in Deum delicta, cum in homine
admissa donantur [For the forgiveness of {sins} committed in the case of a man
is a prejudgment against the remission of sins against God.]" (270.31–32).

murder, idolatry, fraud, apostasy, blasphemy; (and), of course, too, adultery and fornication]."[1282] In *Against Marcion* 4.9 there are also seven sins (*septem maculis capitalium delictorum*): "idololatria, blasphemia, homicidium, adulterium, stuprum, falsum testimonium, fraus [idolatry, blasphemy, murder, adultery, fornication, false-witness, and fraud]."[1283] In *On Modesty*, however, Tertullian demonstrates in detail that only three sins cannot be forgiven: apostasy from the faith (*idololatria*), fornication and adultery (*moechia et fornicatio*), and murder (*homicidia*). Only these three sins comprise an inseparable chain: forgiveness is possible either for all of them or for none,[1284] and Tertullian dedicates one of his most powerful and eloquent pages to elucidating the interconnection between these particular three sins in life.[1285] But in another place, reasoning on the link between these sins, Tertullian joins to them a fourth, *fraus*, calling it mortal as well.[1286] Furthermore, in *On Modesty* 19, after listing the seven mortal sins, Tertullian adds an ambiguous "et si alia violatio templi Dei [and if there be any other violation of the temple of God],"[1287] and

---

1282 CSEL 20.1:265.23–25.

1283 Idem 47.441.28–442.1. Vgl. Harnack, *Dogmengeschichte*[4] 1, 439, Anm. 1.

1284 Tertullian, *On Modesty* 5: "Adsistit idololatres, adsistit homicida, in medio eorum adsistit et moechus. ... Idololatrem quidem et homicidam semel damnas, moechum uero de medio excipis, idololatrae successorem, homicidae antecessorem, utriusque collegam? [hard by {the door of the church} stands an idolater, hard by stands a murderer; in their midst stands, too, an adulterer... Do you once for all condemn the idolater and the murderer, but take the adulterer out from their midst?— {the adulterer,} the successor of the idolater, the predecessor of the murderer, the colleague of each?]" (CSEL 20.1:227.21–22, 28–228.1).

1285 Tertullian, *On Modesty* 5, 226–227. Cf. *Scorpiace* 3: "idololatrian moechiae sororem [idolatry, sister to adultery]" (CSEL 20.1:151.17).

1286 Tertullian, *On Idolatry* 1: "Quodsi tam fraus quam stuprum atque adulterium mortem afferunt, iam in his aeque idololatria de homicidii reatu non liberatur. Post talia crimina, tam exitiosa, tam deuoratoria salutis... [But if fraud, just as much as fornication and adultery, entails death, then, in these cases, equally with the former, idolatry stands unacquitted of the impeachment of murder. After such crimes, so pernicious, so devouring of salvation]" (CSEL 20.1:30.22–31, 1).

1287 CSEL 20.1:265.24–25. Concerning the meaning of *violatio templi dei*, see E. Rolffs, *Das Indulgenz-Edict*, TU 11.3, 45. Cf. Adhémar d' Alès, *La Théologie De Tertullien*, 274–275n5, 485–486; Gerhard Esser, *Die Busschriften Tertullians "De*

in *On Repentance* Tertullian demonstrates that spiritual sins and sins of the flesh are equal, so that the concept of adultery also extends to *aspectus concupiscentia* [the concupiscence of one's gaze].[1288] It should also be noted that in Tertullian's writings the very concept of *peccatum inremissibile* [irremissible sin] is only found in his Montanist writings, while in *On Repentance* it is absent.[1289]

Incidentally, it must be stated that it was these three sins that were chiefly considered mortal—not only by Tertullian, but also by his contemporary Hippolytus of Rome, for example.[1290] But early Christian literature does not specify the exact extent of each mortal sin, nor do they have any definite extent in and of themselves, with the possible exception of murder.[1291]

This is why we are bound to recognize that **the concept of mortal sin in the second and early third centuries was ambiguous:**[1292] **the division of sins into mortal and non-mor-**

---

paenitentia" und "De pudicitia" und das Indulgenzedikt des Papstes Kallistus (Bonn: 1905), 14, Anm. 1.

1288 Tertullian, *On Repentance* 3: "Adulterum non eum solum definit (Dominus), qui cominus in alienum matrimonium cecidisset, verum etiam ilium, qui aspectus concupiscentia contaminasset [He defines not only the man who had actually invaded another's wedlock to be an adulterer, but likewise him who had contaminated {a woman} by the concupiscence of his gaze]" (PL 1:1232b–c).

1289 Cf. Batiffol, *Etudes d' histoire et de théologie positive²*, 83. Preuschen rightly states: "The casuistry regarding forgivable and unforgivable sins was only just beginning, and it first took shape in Montanist circles" ("Zur Kirchenpolitik des Bischofs Kallist," in *Zeitschrift für die neutestam. Wissenschaft* [1910], 152. Cf. 151.)

1290 Hippolytus of Rome, *Fragments: On Proverbs*. "Τρεῖς θυγατέρες ἦσαν τῇ ἁμαρτίᾳ ἀγαπώμενοι ἀγαπήσει, ἡ πορνεία, ὁ φόνος καὶ εἰδωλολατρεία · διὰ τούτων τῶν πράξεων νεκροῦσα ἡ ἁμαρτία τὸν ἄνθρωπον, μηδέποτε ἠλλιωμένη, ἀλλὰ πάντοτε ἐπαύξουσα [There were three daughters fondly loved by sin— fornication, murder, and idolatry... In destroying man by these actions, sin never varies, but only grows continually.]" (PG 10:621a).

1291 Concerning this, see *Das Indulgenz Edict des römischen Bischofs Kallist kritisch untersucht und reconstruirt von der Theol. Ernst Rolffs*, TU 11.3, 49–50.

1292 Vgl. Döllinger, *Hippolytus und Kallistus oder die römische Kirche in der ersten Hälfte des dritten Jahrhunderts* (Regensburg: 1853), 136; Rolffs, *Das Indulgenz-Edict* TU 11.3, 43; Knopf, *Das nachapostolische Zeitalter*, 433; Ritschl, *Die Entstehung der altkath. Kirche*, 371, 514; Böhringer, *Die alte Kirche*, 3-ter Th., 458–459; Shternov,

tal was not Church-wide and was not linked to any definite dogmatic idea of the sanctity of the Church.[1293]

If we turn to the church history and church literature of the earliest times, it will become still more clear to us that the division of sins into mortal and non-mortal is not something intrinsic and precisely defined. We lack sufficient historical data to answer the question: how did this division of sins into two classes originate? Experts on the subject of church history vary in their responses to this question.[1294] Tertullian himself sees the definition of three mortal sins as an apostolic institution, finding this institution in the epistle of the Apostolic Council to the Christians in Antioch.[1295] But this understanding is wholly contradicted by the canonical text of the New Testament: ἀπέχεσθαι εἰδωλοθύτων καὶ αἵματος καὶ πνικτῶν καὶ πορνείας.[1296] This text says nothing whatsoever about mortal sins: it only prohibits eating things sacrificed to idols and blood, and

---

Tertullian, 310; Adam, *Der Kirchenbegriff Tertullians*, 181, Anm. 3; Frank, *Die Bussdisciplin der Kirche*, 419 ff.

1293 Vgl. Rolffs, *Das Indulgenz-Edict*, 43; Loofs, *Leitfaden der Dogmengeschichte*, §29.2a, 205; Batiffol, *Etudes d' histoire et de théologie positive*, 82, 96.

1294 See Rolffs, *Das Indulgenz-Edict*, 46–47, Anm. 2; Harnack, *Dogmengeschichte*[4] 1, 440–441; Smirnov, *The Spiritual Father*, 222n2.

1295 Acts 15:29; Tertullian, *On Modesty* 12: "Hanc regulam de auctoritate spiritus sancti apostoli emittunt ad eos qui iam ex nationibus allegi coeperant. Visum est, inquiunt, spiritui sancto et nobis nullum amplius uobis adicere pondus quam eorum a quibus necesse est abstineri, a sacrificiis et a fornicationibus et sanguine, a quibus obseruando recte agetis. ... Haec sola praeponant utique non remissibilia [this is the rule which the apostles, on the authority of the Holy Spirit, send out to those who were already beginning to be gathered to their side out of the nations: "It has seemed (good)," say they, "to the Holy Spirit and to us to cast upon you no ampler weight than (that) of those (things) from which it is necessary that abstinence be observed; from sacrifices, and from fornications, and from blood: by abstaining from which you act rightly,"... these alone they put in the foremost rank, of course as not remissible" (CSEL 20.1:241.26–242.3, 10).

1296 "[A]bstain from meats offered to idols, and from blood, and from things strangled, and from fornication" (Acts 15:29). For textological notes, see the book *Des Aposteldecret nach seiner ausserkanonischen Textgestalt untersucht von Gotthold Resch*, TU 28.3 (Leipzig: 1905), 8. Tishendorf also accepts the reading cited in the text (*Novum Testamentum graece*[8] 2, 134).

also fornication. Tertullian translates εἰδωλόθυτον [meats offered to idols] via the word *sacrificium* or *idololatria*,[1297] and αἷμα [blood] as *sanguis*, understanding it to mean murder.[1298] The meaning of the decree of the Apostolic Council is customarily determined in close connection with determining the significance of the Council itself.[1299] Though this decree is understood variously, Tertullian's interpretation is acknowledged to be the least admissible of all. In the late second century and thereafter, this understanding had considerable significance when resolving questions of ecclesiastical discipline, but it is completely foreign to the spirit and intentions of the Apostolic Council.[1300] In Tertullian's day, his understanding of the apostles' conciliar decree is encountered only among Western authors, and is unknown to those of the East. For example, in the decree of the Apostolic Council Origen sees only a prohibition against eating things sacrificed to idols and things strangled, and against fornication.[1301] Consequently, in the East the decree of the

---

1297 In addition to the quote from *On Modesty* 12, 242.2, see also *On Idolatry* 24 (CSEL 20.1:57.26).

1298 Tertullian, *On Modesty* 12: "moechiae et fornicationi locum ... inter idololatriam et homicidium [the place of adultery and fornication... between idolatry and murder]" (CSEL 20.1:242.4–5). Vgl. Dr. Karl Ad. Heinrich Kellner, *Tertullians sämtliche Schriften*, 1-er Bd. (Köln: 1882), 422, Anm. 2.

1299 See Resch, *Das Aposteldecret*, 68 ff. See Prof. N.N. Glubokovsky, *The Message of Christian Freedom in the Epistle of the Holy Apostle Paul to the Galatians* ("Благовестие христианской свободы в Послании св. апостола Павла к Галатам") (St. Petersburg: 1902), 76; N.N. Glubokovsky, "The Apostolic Council of Jerusalem" ("Иерусалимский Собор Апостольский") in *The Orthodox Encyclopedia of Theology* ("Православная богословская энциклопедия") vol. 6, from col. 436 on.

1300 G. Resch, *Das Aposteldecret* TU 28.3, 143–147; E. Preuschen, *Zeitschrift für die neutestam. Wissenschaft* (1910), 152. G. Esser sees Tertullian's interpretation of the decree of the Apostolic Council as extremely arbitrary and no more. See *Die Busschriften Tertullians*, 25–26. Adhémar d' Alès likewise considers Tertullian's exegesis highly suspect ("fort suspecte"). See "Tertullien et Calliste," *Revue d'histoire ecclésiastique* 13 (1912): 249.

1301 Origen, *Commentary on Matthew* 10: "Eestatur Epistola apostolorum in Actibus, quam miserunt ad gentes, ut nihil servent ex lege nisi immolatum, et fornicationem [... the epistle of the apostles in Acts, which they sent to the nations, that they keep nothing from the law except the meats offered to idols, and fornication]" (PG 13:1613d–1614a).

Apostolic Council could have had no influence on ecclesiastical discipline in the sense of dividing sins into those that could and could not be forgiven.[1302]

The historical facts also give us no clear and definite guidance for resolving the issue of where the division of sins into mortal and non-mortal originated. Indeed, is this not contradicted by the fact that the church literature of the first two centuries contains no clear division of sins into these two particular classes? Tertullian speaks of this division in the third century, but is this sufficient grounds to assert that the church practice of the first two centuries was solely that described by Tertullian? On the contrary, in the historical reports of the first two centuries one may find data proving that the

---

1302   In the study cited above, Resch demonstrates that preference should be given to the Western formulation of the apostolic decree, but even in this formulation the decree has nothing to do with defining mortal sins: idolatry seems to designate all sins against God in general, murder—all sins against one's neighbor in general, and fornication—sins against oneself (41–44, 53, 72–73, 75–79, 102–106, 126–127, 141–143, 151, 169). Thus, the apostolic decree is nothing less than the briefest possible compendium of Christian ethics: "das kürzeste zystematische Compendium der christlichen Ethik" (52). Harnack echoed this view (in his most recent works, *Die Apostelgeschichte. Beiträge zur Einleitung in das Neue Testament* 3 [1908], 188–198, and *Neue Untersuchungen zur Apostelgeschichte und zur Abfassungszeit der synoptischen Evangelien. Beiträge zur Einleitung in das Neue Testament*, 4 Heft [Leipzig: 1911], 22–24), although formerly he thought differently concerning the apostolic decree (*Das Aposteldekret und die Blasssche Hypothese. Sitzungsberichte der königlich-Preussischen Akademie der Wissenschaften* [1899]. Vgl. *Lukas der Arzt der Verfasser des dritten Evangeliums und der Apostelgeschichte* [Leipzig: 1906], 91 ff). A detailed analysis of this view and criticism of its argumentation are presented in the article by H. Coppieters, "Le décret des Apôtres (Act. XV, 28.29)," *Revue biblique internationale* (1907): 34–58. The author gives preference to the Eastern version of the decree (50 et suiv). H. Diehl likewise spoke out emphatically against this same view of Resch and Harnack. See "Das sogenannte Aposteldekret. Ein Beitrag zur Kritik von A. Harnack. «Apostelgeschichte,»" in *Zeitschrift für die neutestamentliche Wissenschaft und die Kunde des Urchristentums* (1909), 277–296. Vgl. Zahn, *Einleitung in das Neue Testament²*, Bd. 2, 345–347, 354–356. K. Six (S.J.) likewise sees the decree of the Apostolic Council as prohibiting certain kinds of food, and not mortal sins: *Das Aposteldekret (Act 15, 28, 29). Seine Entstehung und Geltung in den ersten vier Jahrhunderten* (Innsbruck: 1912). See the review of E.N. in the publication *Internationale Kirchliche Zeitschrift* (1912), 138–140. See also W. Sanday, "The Apostolic Decree (Acts XV. 20–29)," in *Theologische Studien. Theodor Zahn dargebracht* (Leipzig: 1908), 321–325.

division of sins into mortal and venial was not always in evidence.
We have already cited how St. John the Theologian received the
young man turned robber. Although this instance is exceptional—it
is no mere hierarch, but an apostle who receives him[1303]—it would
be hard to suppose that the apostle was not behaving as he himself taught others to do. We have also seen that Clement of Rome
discusses repentance at length in his epistle to the Corinthians, yet
it contains not a trace of dividing sins into any particular classes.
He says nothing about lifetime excommunication for any particular
sins: on the contrary, he speaks of restoring all who have strayed.[1304]
Dionysius, bishop of Corinth (approx. A.D. 170), in his epistle to
the Church of Amastris, commands that all who convert after falling away and transgressing or even after heretical error be received
again.[1305] In the account of the suffering of the martyrs of Lyon
we read: "Through their continued life the dead were made alive.
... And the virgin mother [the Church] had much joy in receiving alive those whom she had brought forth (ἐξέτρωσε) as dead.
For through their influence many who had denied were restored,
and re-begotten, and rekindled with life."[1306] Concerning restoring

---

1303 Vgl. Funk, *Kirchengeschichtliche Abhandlungen und Untersuchungen* 1, 173: "Bei
dem «geretteten Jüngling» darf die Besondere Obhut, in die der Apostel genom-
men hatte, jedenfalls nicht ganz ausser Acht gelassen werden."

1304 1 Clem. 59:4: "Τοὺς πλανωμένους τοῦ λαοῦ σου ἐπίστρεφον [the wandering ones of Thy people turn]." Ioh. Stufler even asserts that Clement recognizes forgiveness of all sins without exception. See *Zeitschrift für katholische Theologie*
(1907), 451. Vgl. Frank, *Die Bussdisciplin der Kirche*, 835–836.

1305 Eusebius, *Church History* 4.23.6: "Καὶ τοὺς ἐξ οἵας δ' οὖν ἀποπτώσεως,
εἴτε πλημμελείας εἴτε μὴν αἱρετικῆς πλάνης, ἐπιστρέφοντας δεξιοῦσθαι
προστάττει [...and commands them to receive those who come back again after
any fall, whether it be delinquency or heresy]" (GrchSch. 9.1:374.27, 376.1–2).
Harnack, it seems, has no grounds for his attempt to weaken the force of this
testimony by pointing out the ambiguity of the term δεξιοῦσθαι. See *Dogmengeschichte*⁴ 1, 440, Anm. Vgl. Döllinger, *Hippolytus und Kallistus*, 131.

1306 Eusebius, op. cit. 5.1.45–46 (NPNF² 1:216, GrchSch. 9.1:420.5–9). Here
we merely note the concept of the possibility of "the dead" being restored to
life, without resolving the question of the form in which this rebirth takes place.
Incidentally, cf. [the work by] Ioh. Stufler in the edition of *Zeitschrift für katholische
Theologie* (1907), 445. But it is indisputable that even in the second century the

those who had sinned gravely to communion with the Church, certain information is also found in the writings of St. Irenaeus of Lyons.[1307] Eusebius records the following information from the time when Zephyrinus was bishop in Rome. The heretics Asclepiodotus and Theodotus had persuaded Natalius to accept a post as their bishop. Miraculously brought to his senses, "he put on sackcloth and covered himself with ashes, and with great haste and tears he fell down before Zephyrinus, the bishop, rolling at the feet not only of the clergy, but also of the laity; and he moved with his tears the compassionate Church of the merciful Christ; and having used much supplication, and shown the welts of the stripes which he had received, yet scarcely was he taken back into communion."[1308] If the situation in the second-century Church of Syria is to be judged by the Syrian *Didascalia*, it must be acknowledged that the Church of Syria knew nothing of a division of sins into two classes.[1309]

---

intercession of the martyrs was taken into consideration with regard to those who had lapsed from the faith. See Eusebius, op. cit. 5.2.5–7.

1307 See *Against Heresies* 1.6.3, 10.1, 13.5.7; 3.4.3; 4.40.1 (PG 7:508b, 552a, 588a–b, 592a, 857a–b, 1112b–c). The conclusions which Ioh. Stufler draws from the reports of Irenaeus (*Zeitschrift für katholische Theologie* [1907], 440–441, 447–448), in any case, can always be disputed. Cf. Harnack, *Dogmengeschichte* 1, 440, Anm. 1. Prof. Dr. Hugo Koch considers Irenaeus an adherent of rigoristic views on the forgiveness of sins ("Sündenvergebung bei Irenaus," in *Zeitschrift für die neutestamentliche Wissenschaft und die Kunde des Urchristentums* [1908], 35–46). In defense of his opinion, Koch cites *Against Heresies* 4.27.1–4, 28.1–2 (41–44), and holds that the testimony of Irenaeus may even be applied to the Eastern Church as well (46). But in our opinion there are far stronger grounds for challenging these broad conclusions from Irenaeus's words cited than even the opposite conclusions of Stufler, who did not allow the article by H. Koch to go uncritiqued. See *Zeitschrift für katholische Theologie* (1908), 488–497. E. Preuschen fully shares the opinion of Koch (*Zeitschrift für die neutestam. Wissenschaft* [1910], 149).

1308 Eusebius, *Church History* 5.28.9–12 (NPNF² 1:248; GrchSch. 9.1:502, 504).

1309 In the Syrian Didascalia we read: "O bishop, so far as thou canst, keep those that have not sinned, that they may continue without sinning; and those that repent of (their) sins heal and receive. But if thou receive not him who repents, because thou art without mercy, thou shalt sin against the Lord God; for thou obeyest not our Saviour and our God, to do as He also did with her that had sinned, whom the elders set before Him." (Here the text of Jn. 8:9–11 is quoted.) "In Him therefore, our Saviour and King and God, be your pattern,

Above we have already noted that the concept of mortal sin was somewhat unclear in Tertullian's own writings, which in our opinion lends [this] very division of sins into forgivable and unforgivable a merely relative meaning and significance. In evaluating the data and information just cited, even scholars of the same confession differ significantly among themselves.

Protestant authors predominantly, and Catholic writers only partially, ascribe no significance to these facts.[1310] The majority of Catholic scholars and a few of their Protestant colleagues[1311] consider these data sufficient to substantiate the supposition that in the first two centuries the division of sins into two classes was not Church-wide and in general is not something inherent to the Church. We wholeheartedly join the latter group of scholars in their opinion, and this justifies us in supposing, not without good cause, that **in the first two centuries the sanctity of the Church was not**

O bishops" (*Didascalia Apostolorum*, R.Hugh Connolly, trans. (Oxford: Clarendon Press, [1929], 76). See *Die Syrische Diadascalia, übers. und erklärt von Hans Achelis und Iohs. Flemming. Texte und Untersuchungen zur Geschichte der altchristlichen Literatur. XXV. 2* (Leipzig: 1904), 38–39. The authors rightly note: "The author knows of no sins that cannot be forgiven—furthermore, he has never heard of certain instances being too grave for the episcopal authority to forgive sins. In Syria there existed no law that would separate out mortal sins" (306–307). Stufler decisively states that in general there can hardly be any doubt with regard to the Eastern Church: rigorism never predominated in it. See *Zeitschrift für katholische Theologie* (1907), 438. Vgl. Döllinger, *Hippolytus und Kallistus*, 131.

1310 Of Catholic authors [and their works, the following may be listed]: F.X. Funk, "Das Indulgenzedikt des Papstes Kallistus," *Theologische Quartalschrift* (1906): 541 ff. *Zur altchristlichen Bussdisciplin. Kirchengensch. Abh. und Untersuch* 1, 155 ff.; Ioseph Turmel, *Histoire de la théologie positive depuis l'origine jusqu'au concile de Trente*, 3-me éd. (Paris: 1904), 141: "cas exceptionnels qu'on peut négliger."

1311 Of Protestant works [we shall name], for example: Loofs, *Leitfaden der Dogmengeschichte* §29.2b, 205–206. Vgl. Harnack, *Dogmengeschichte*[4] 1, 440, Anm. 1. Of Catholic works the following could be named: Frank, *Die Bussdisciplin der Kirche*, 840 ff.; Ios. Schwane, *Dogmengeschichte der vornic. Zeit*, 453, 489; I. Stufler, "Die Bussdisziplin der abendländischen Kirche bis Kallistus," in *Zeitschrift für katholische Theologie* (1907), 438; Adhémar d' Alès, *La Théologie de Tertullien*, 487–489; *La Théologie de saint Hippolyte* (Paris: 1906), 41–42; "Tertullien et Calliste," *Revue d'histoire ecclésiastique*, vol. 13 (1912): 246. Of Russian works, see D. Kasitsyn, *Schisms of the Early Centuries of Christianity*, 70–81.

dogmatically and inseparably linked to any particular degree of sanctity among the individual members of the Church, and that this degree was not, at any rate, an absence of mortal sins.

To be sure, in his polemical work directed against the Church Tertullian declares that the Church does not grant communion to those who have fallen into mortal sins,[1312] but this declaration of his can hardly be called accurate even with regard to the Western Churches:[1313] a mere thirty years later St. Cyprian attests that only a few of the earliest African bishops refused forgiveness for sins of adultery, yet even these did not break the peace with those who followed a different practice.[1314] This would have been completely unthinkable if there had originally prevailed a concept of the Church as a society of saints, or at least of those who had not fallen into mortal sins.

Finally, let us turn once again to the writings of Tertullian. Beginning at the seventh chapter in his treatise *On Repentance*, albeit sorrowfully (*piget*), Tertullian speaks of secondary repentance, that is, of repentance after baptism. Here Tertullian seems to echo the reasoning of Hermas. It is best of course not to sin after baptism, but the devil constantly tempts a man, and "he is never deficient in stumbling blocks nor in temptations"; consequently, "in the vestibule (*in vestibulo*) [God] has stationed the second repentance (*poenitentiam*

1312 Tertullian, *On Modesty* 12: "Neque idololatriae neque sanguini pax ab ecclesiis redditur [there is no restoration of peace granted by the Churches to "idolatry" or to "blood."]" (CSEL 20.1:242.26–27).

1313 Vgl. Frank, *Die bussdisciplin der Kirche*, 422, 840; Adhémar d' Alès, "Tertullien et Calliste," *Revue d'histoire ecclésiastique*, vol. 13 (1912): 246, 250: "L'histoire du II-e Siècle proteste contre une assertion aussi génerale."

1314 Cyprian of Carthage, *Epistle 55 [51] to Antonianus*, 21: "Apud antecessores nostros quidam de episcopis istic in provincia nostra dandam pacem moechis non putaverunt et in totum poenitentiae locum contra adulteria clauserunt, non tamen ... quia apud alios adulteris pax dabatur, qui non dabat de ecclesia separaretur [And, indeed, among our predecessors, some of the bishops here in our province thought that peace was not to be granted to adulterers, and wholly closed the gate of repentance against adultery. Still... because by some peace was granted to adulterers, he who did not grant it should be separated from the Church]" (CSEL 3.2:638–639).

secundam)." This repentance is a second benefit (*iteratum beneficium*), a repeated medicine for a repeated sickness (*iteratae valentudinis ite-randa medicina est*).[1315] This second repentance can be permitted but once,[1316] and must be accompanied by various penitential labors, which are collectively called *exomologesis*.[1317] In Tertullian's opin-ion, this repentance is essential, and he extensively demonstrates its validity, wishing to dispel all doubt on the matter.[1318] Tertullian gives no clear indication of whether even mortal sins may be for-given through secondary repentance, but ultimately there is great-er evidence to support that even mortal sins are not excluded.[1319] Secondary repentance resulted in complete reunification with the Church,[1320] as evidenced by the very fact that in the parable of the

---

1315 Tertullian, *On Repentance* 7 (ANF 3:663, PL 1:1240b–1242a passim).

1316 Ibid: "Secundae, imo jam ultimae spei ... sed jam semel, quia jam se-cundo [a second— nay, in that case, the last— hope... but now once {for all}, because now for the second time]" (PL 1:1240b, 1241b). Idem 9: "poenitentiae secundae et unius [second and only {remaining} repentance]" (1243b).

1317 Idem 9 (PL 1:1243 sq). Cf. the observations of E. Rolff in his work *Das In-dulgenz—Edict...*, 33. See also Adhémar d' Alès, *La Théologie de Tertullien*, 340–344.

1318 Idem 8 (PL 1:1242 sq).

1319 Idem 4: "Omnibus delictis seu carne, seu spiritu, seu facto, seu voluntate commissis, qui poenam per judicium destinavit, idem et veniam per poeniten-tiam spondidit [To all sins, then, committed whether by flesh or spirit, whether by deed or will, the same {God} who has destined penalty by means of judgment, has withal engaged to grant pardon by means of repentance]" (PL 1:1233a). At the same time, the devil attempts "fidem terrenae potestatis formidine ever-tere [to subvert his faith by fear of earthly power]" (Idem 7, PL 1:1241b). Does this not indicate apostasy from the faith? Cf. Loofs, *Leitfaden der Dogmengeschichte* §29.2b, 206; Harnack, Lapsi, Hauck RE 3, Bd. 11, 286. Batiffol, *Etudes d' histoire et de théologie positive*, 84. G. Esser holds that beyond a doubt even grave sins were forgiven. See *Die Bussschriften Tertullians*, 15, 18.

1320 Some object to this. See E. Preuschen, *Tertullians Schriften «De paenitentia» und «De pudicitia» mit Rücksicht auf die Bussdisziplin untersucht* (Glessen: 1890), 12 ff.; Rolffs, *Das Indulgenz—Edict*, TU 11.3, 38–40, 51; Funk, *Kirchengeschichtliche Abhand-lungen und Untersuchungen* 1, 166; Harnack, *Dogmengeschichte* 1, 441, Anm. 1. But see Loofs, *Leitfaden der Dogmengeschichte*[4] §29.2b, 206–207, Anm. 11. Adhémar d' Alès, *La théologie de Tertullien*, 340n1. Schanz, "Die Absolutionsgewalt in der alten Kir-che," *Theologische Quartalschrift* (1897): 46; O. Bardenhewer, *Patrologie* §50.5, 163; Iohann Stufler, "Die verschiedenen Wirkungen der Taufe und Busse nach Tertul-

drachma that was lost and then found Tertullian sees "**restituti** peccatoris exemplum,"[1321] *restituti* being the term by which Tertullian denotes specifically reception back into the Church.[1322] The fact that a so-called **second repentance** existed in the second century, in our opinion, likewise attests that the Christian Church of that time did not consider itself a society of saints made perfect.[1323] It can only be asserted that the idea of the sanctity of the Church, as yet undeveloped, motivated certain bishops to completely excommunicate persons who had fallen into mortal sins. But **this was a matter of their own pastoral wisdom,**[1324] **and not an inevitable consequence of the general dogmatic doctrine of the sanctity of the Church.**[1325]

Nevertheless, the question of ecclesiastical discipline was becoming increasingly acute. Differences in practice could have easily developed into fundamental dogmatic dissension. All that was needed was the impetus to set the theological mind of the Church

---

lian," in *Zeitschrift für Katholische Theologie* (1907), 372–376. Esser provides the most detailed evidence in *Die Bussschriften Tertullians*, 12, Anm. 1, 19–24. Of late even Preuschen is inclined to acknowledge that "Tertullian's silence in *On Repentance* on the matter of there supposedly being certain sins that cannot be redeemed through the act of repentance arguably forces the conclusion that all sins were viewed as forgivable." *Tertullian. De Paenitentia. De Pudicitia. Herausgegeben von Erwin Preuschen.* 2-te, neugearbeitete Auflage (Tübingen: 1910), Einleitung. S.V.

1321   "An example of a restored sinner." Tertullian, *On Repentance* 8 (PL 1:1242b).

1322   See *On Modesty* 6, 7 (four times), 9, 15, 19, 20 (CSEL 20.1:229.9; 230.24–25; 232.12, 17; 233.5–6; 238.15; 251.10–13; 262.24; 266.11–14. Concerning the meaning of the term *restitutio* in the writings of Tertullian, see Adhémar d' Alès, "Tertullien et Calliste," *Revue d'histoire ecclésiastique*, vol. 13 (1912): 253.

1323   Harnack sees this allowance for secondary repentance as the start of a change in the ancient belief that Christianity is a society of saints. See *Dogmengeschichte*[4] 1, 442.

1324   "The practice of receiving those who had sinned varied in different Churches and circumstances, as being a matter of pastoral wisdom" (Prof. V.V. Bolotov, *Lectures on the History of the Early Church*, 2nd ed., 364).

1325   Frank, *Die Bussdisciplin der Kirche*, 841: "Es war also diese Härte ein Gegenstand rein praktischer und nicht dogmatischer Natur."

in motion specifically with regard to the sanctity of the Church. And this impetus was provided by Montanism.

There is no need for us to examine in detail the complex issue of the origin of Montanism and its history, as a vast body of literature exists on the subject.

We may join numerous church historians in recognizing that the essence of Montanism lay not in its rigoristic disciplinary requirements as such, but in a new kind of prophecy.[1326] This is precisely how the essence of Montanism is presented in the few surviving historical accounts. Eusebius cites the words of an anonymous personage regarding the origins of Montanism. "A recent convert, Montanus by name, through his unquenchable desire for leadership, gave the adversary opportunity against him. And he became beside himself, and being suddenly in a sort of frenzy and ecstasy (ἐν κατοχῇ τινι καὶ παρεκστάσει), he raved, and began to babble and utter strange things, prophesying in a manner contrary to the constant custom of the Church handed down by tradition from the beginning."[1327] Epiphanius considers the sole distinguishing characteristic of the Cataphrygians to be specifically their recognition of other prophets after the prophets.[1328] "Concerning the Father, the Son, and the Holy Spirit their thinking is the same as that of the Holy Ecumenical Church: but those who heeded 'seducing spirits, and doctrines of devils' (1 Tim. 4:1) separated from her, saying, 'We too ought to receive the gifts.'"[1329] Tertullian quite decisively states that what renders the Montanists spiritual is their recognition of spiritual gifts,[1330] which the materialists do not accept,[1331] and that

---

1326 Ritschl, *Die Entstehung der altkath. Kirche*, 462 ff.; Harnack, *Dogmengeschichte* 1, 427, 432; Adam Karl, *Der Kirchenbegriff Tertullians*, 134; Bolotov, *Lectures* 2, 356–357, 366.

1327 Eusebius, *Church History* 5.16.7 (ANF 2:231; GrchSch. 9.1:462).

1328 Epiphanius, Haer.: "Ἑτέρους προφήτας παρεισφέρουσι μετὰ τοὺς προφήτας" (PG 41:845d).

1329 Epiphanius, Haer. 48.1 (PG 41:856b).

1330 Tertullian, *On Monogamy* 1: "Penes nos autem, quos spirituales merito dici facit agnitio spiritualium charismatum [Among us, however, whom the recognition of spiritual gifts entitles to be deservedly called Spiritual]" (PL 2:979b).

1331 Idem 1: "Psychicis non recipientibus spiritum [to the Psychics, since they

it is this recognition of the Paraclete that separated them from the Church.[1332]

Of what sort exactly was this prophecy?

Certain scholars have suggested that the Montanist prophets are supposedly the direct continuers of the spiritual gifts that existed in apostolic times of old, and that Montanist prophecy differed not at all from the prophetic gift that had existed in the early Christian Church.[1333] Without going into a detailed analysis of this view, we will say only that all historical sources attest to the contrary. Both the words cited by Eusebius and the writings of Epiphanius specifically contest the form of Montanist prophecy itself. The Montanist prophets specifically prophesied "in a manner contrary to the constant custom of the Church handed down by tradition from the beginning" (παρὰ τὸ κατὰ παράδοσιν καὶ κατὰ διαδοχὴν ἄνωθεν τῆς ἐκκλησίας ἔθος).[1334] Epiphanius extensively demonstrates specifically the unusual nature of this new kind of prophecy. According to historical data, Montanist prophecy was exclusively ecstatic in nature; in it the person was only the "lyre."[1335] The Mon-

---

receive not the Spirit,]" (PL 2:980a).

1332 Tertullian, *Against Praxeas* 1: "Et nos quidem postea agnitio paracleti atque defensio disjunxit a psychics [We indeed, on our part, subsequently withdrew from the carnally-minded on our acknowledgment and maintenance of the Paraclete]" (CSEL 47:228.19–20).

1333 For a detailed discussion of the form of this new gift of prophecy, see Ritschl, *Die Entstehung der altkath. Kirche*, 465–477. But this view is developed in particular detail by Schwegler. See *Der Montanismus und die Christliche Kirche des zweiten Jahrhunderts* (Tübingen: 1841). D. Kasitsyn presents Schwegler's view and provides a fairly detailed analysis of it in his study *Schisms of the Early Centuries of Christianity*, 25–42 (=Addendae, part 43, 25–42).

1334 Eusebius, op. cit. 5.16.7 (ANF 2:231; GrchSch. 9.1:462.13–14). Cf. 5.17.3: "Τοῦτον δὲ τὸν τρόπον οὔτε τινὰ τῶν κατὰ τὴν παλαιὰν οὔτε τῶν κατὰ τὴν καινὴν πνευματοφορηθέντα προφήτην δεῖξαι δυνήσονται [They cannot show that one of the old or one of the new prophets was thus carried away in spirit]" (470.12–14).

1335 "Behold, the human lyre (ὡσεὶ λύρα), and I touch him as a tambourine; the man sleeps, but I keep vigil; behold, the Lord brings ecstasy (ὁ ἐκστάνων) upon the hearts of men and gives to men a heart" (Epiphanius, Haer. [PG 41:861a, part 2, 308]). Cf. Nitzsch, *Grundriss der christlichen Dogmengeschichte* 1, 261.

tanist prophets were not in command of themselves, observed no consistency in their thinking,[1336] "talked wildly and unreasonably and strangely";[1337] their words were the words of ecstatics.[1338] It is worthy of note that both opponents and defenders of Montanism refer to this prophecy as "new,"[1339] and Tertullian himself says that it is specifically the form of Montanist prophecy that is the subject of debate with the psychics.[1340] "Traits not encountered in regard to other heresiarchs, such as in the description of the founders of Gnostic sects, are quite vividly depicted in the eccentric figures of the Phrygian prophets, who apparently quite strongly resembled lunatics."[1341] Consequently, Montanist prophecy must be declared a morbidly sectarian phenomenon, originating in Phrygia, possibly not without the influence of Eastern cults, as Neander indicated

---

1336   Epiphanius, Haer. 48.3: "οὐδ' εὐσταθοῦντες φανοῦνται, οὔτε παρακολουθίαν λόγου ἔχοντες" (PG 41:860d).

1337 Anonymous quotation in Eusebius, *Church History* 5.16.9 (NPNF[2] 1:231; GrchSch. 9.1:464.2).

1338 Epiphanius, Haer. 48.4: "Ἐκστατικοῦ ῥήματα" (PG 41:861a).

1339 Eusebius, op. cit. 5.16.4 (GrchSch. 9.1:460.16). In his epistle to Caricus and Pontius, Serapion writes of "this lying band of the new prophecy (νέας προφητείας), so called" (Eusebius, op. cit. 5.19.2 [NPNF[2] 1:237; GrchSch. 9.1:478.27]). Tertullian, *Against Praxeas* 30: "sermones novae prophetiae" (CSEL 47:288.11); *Against Marcion* 3.24: "novae prophetiae sermo testatur [the word of the new prophecy... attests]" (CSEL 47:419.25–26); *Against Marcion* 4.22: "novae prophetiae gratiae extasin, id est amentiam, convenire? [...the new prophecy, that to grace ecstasy or rapture is incident?]" *On the Resurrection of the Flesh* (CSEL 47:492.28); 63: "per novam prophetiam de paracleto inundantem [through the new prophecy, which descends in copious streams from the Paraclete]" (CSEL 47:125.14–15); *On Monogamy* 14: "nova prophetia" (PL 2:1000b).

1340 Tertullian, *Against Marcion* 4.22: "In spiritu enim homo constitutus, praesertim cum gloriam dei conspicit vel cum per ipsum deus loquitur, necesse est excidat sensu, obumbratus scilicet virtute divina. De quo inter nos et psychicos quaestio est [For when a man is rapt in the Spirit, especially when he beholds the glory of God, or when God speaks through him, he necessarily loses his sensation, because he is overshadowed with the power of God — a point concerning which there is a question between us and the carnally-minded{psychicos}]" (CSEL 47:493.1–4). Vgl. Bardenhewer, *Patrologie*[3] §31.1, 101.

1341 Bolotov, *Lectures on the History of the Early Church*, 2nd ed., 352. See also 356–358. Cf. F. Loofs, *Leitfaden der Dogmengeschichte* §24.2–3, 172–174.

in his day.[1342] Placing Montanist prophecy on the same level as the prophetic gift of the early Christians is something that Bonwetsch, a historian of Montanism, flatly refuses to do,[1343] as does Harnack.[1344]

New prophecy presupposes a new revelation, and indeed, Montanism surfaces with a new doctrine concerning revelation. The matter therefore now concerns a highly significant point: that of Christian Revelation.[1345]

We may judge how this new prophecy regarded New Testament revelation from the writings of Tertullian. Tertullian attempts to prove that the Paraclete introduces nothing new.[1346] The Montanists and the psychics have one faith, one God, the same Christ, the same hope, the same baptism—in a word, they are one Church.[1347] The prophets—Montanus, Princilla, and Maximilla—do not preach another God, do not reject Jesus Christ, and do not distort the "Rule of Faith."[1348] The Paraclete introduces nothing against the catholic Tradition, whereas heresy always distorts the "Rule of Faith" (*regulam adulterans fidei*).[1349] The Paraclete speaks not of himself, but that which Christ entrusts to him:[1350] the Paraclete is the vicar of the Lord.[1351]

1342 See Kasitsyn, *Schisms of the Early Centuries of Christianity* 18n1 (=Addendae, part 43, 18n1). Cf. Bolotov, *Lectures on the History of the Early Church,* 2nd ed., 351–352: "Within the somewhat morose natural attitude of the Phrygians there lay a profound religiousness, one that manifested itself in a particular ecstatic cult of the mother of the gods, which was considerably widespread in these parts."

1343 Gottlieb Nathanael Bonwetsch, *Die Geschichte des Montanismus* (Erlangen: 1881), 63 ff.

1344 Harnack, *Dogmengeschichte*⁴ 1, 430–431, Anm. 2. Cf. 429, Anm. 1. But see *Die Lehre d. zwölf Apostel,* TU 2.1, 122–126.

1345 For a detailed study of how the "new prophecy" relates to Church-wide revelation, see Adam, *Der Kirchenbegriff Tertullians,* 151 ff.

1346 Tertullian, *On Monogamy* 3: "Nihil novi Paracletus inducit" (PL 2:983b).

1347 Tertullian, *On the Veiling of Virgins* 2 (PL 2:939a).

1348 Tertullian, *On Fasting* 1 (CSEL 20.1:274.23–24). Cf. 11, 289–290.

1349 Tertullian, *On Monogamy* 2 (PL 2:980–981).

1350 Tertullian, *On the Veiling of Virgins* 1 (PL 2:938b).

1351 Ibid. (PL 2:937c).

But there are weighty grounds for disagreement with Tertullian on this point. In the pre-Montanist period of his life, as we have seen, Tertullian was a zealous defender of the apostolic Tradition preserved in the Church. He himself, in polemicizing against the Gnostic doctrine of a secret tradition, demonstrated that Christ imparted the fullness of the truth, which was assimilated by the apostles and by all believers. Naturally, even in the Montanist period of his life Tertullian could not flatly contradict what he himself had formerly expressed.[1352] In actuality, the preaching of the Montanist prophets emerged specifically as a new revelation. St. Hippolytus says that the Montanists considered their prophetesses superior to the apostles, and that they believed them to say things beyond even that which Christ Himself had spoken.[1353] Concerning the Montanists the writer who supplemented Tertullian's treatise *The Prescription Against Heretics* reports that they said the Holy Spirit was in the apostles, but the Paraclete was not; and that the Paraclete said more through Montanus than Christ did in the Gospel, and not only more, but even better and superiorly.[1354] Even Tertullian's own writings contain much that can hardly be reconciled with his assurances that the Paraclete supposedly introduced nothing new.

The Paraclete, according to Tertullian's own teaching, is essential to bring Christian doctrine to perfection.[1355] Tertullian even

---

1352 Cf. Kasitsyn, *The Schisms of the Early Centuries* 44–45 (=Addendae, part 43, 435).

1353 Hippolytus, *The Refutation of All Heresies* 8.19: "Ὑπὲρ δὲ ἀποστόλους καὶ πᾶν χάρισμα ταῦτα τὰ γύναια δοξάζουσι, ὡς τολμᾶν πλεῖόν τι Χριστοῦ ἐν τούτοις λέγειν τινὰς αὐτῶν γεγονέναι" (PG 16:3366d).

1354 52 (PL 2:91a): "Paracletum plura in Montano dixisse, quam Christum in Evangelium protulisse, nec tantum plura, sed etiam meliora atque majora." "Here the view that Christianity could be improved was asserted in the broadest possible way, despite the fact that in its entire spirit Montanism may also be understood as a kind of retrograde movement" (Bolotov, *Lectures on the History of the Early Church*, 2nd ed., 366). Cf. Harnack, *Dogmengeschichte*[4] 1, 429, Anm. 4.

1355 Tertullian, *De Fuga in Persecutione* 14: "Paracletus necessarius deductor omnium veritatum, exhortator omnium tolerantiarum [the Comforter is requisite, who guides into all truth, and animates to all endurance]" (PL 2:142a–b). *On Modesty* 11: the Paraclete "ipsius disciplinae determinator [the Determiner of discipline itself]." (PL 2:1054a). *On the Resurrection of the Flesh* 63 (CSEL 47:125).

presents an entire theory of how revelation gradually develops in the world. "To every thing there is a season" (Eccles. 3:1–8). In nature, a tree gradually develops from a grain. So also the truth of God was first in its infancy; then the law and the prophets brought it to a childlike state; then the Gospel brought it to adolescence; and now the Paraclete has brought it to maturity.[1356] This later theory of developing revelation differs strongly from the earlier theory, according to which all development ends with the doctrine of Christ and the apostles.[1357] But if the Paraclete is to the teaching of Christ as maturity is to adolescence, clearly this new teaching revokes the old doctrine: the Paraclete revokes Christ, just as Christ did the law of Moses. Tertullian only avoids naming Christ, substituting the apostles for Him. If Christ rejected what Moses taught, why cannot the Paraclete revoke the institutions of Paul?[1358] For even in human institutions later laws (*decreta*) supersede those that are older.[1359]

It may be noted that even Tertullian himself experienced a certain unease at withdrawing from what he himself had formerly preached.[1360] At times he tries to prove that the Paraclete institutes nothing new, and merely restores what was before.[1361] But all such

---

1356 Tertullian, *On the Veiling of Virgins* 1: "Sic et justitia (nam idem Deus justitiae et creaturae) primo fuit in rudimentis, natura Deum metuens: dehinc per legem et Prophetas promovit in infantiam: dehinc per Evangelium efferbuit in juventutem: nunc per Paracletum componitur in maturitatem [So, too, righteousness — for the God of righteousness and of creation is the same — was first in a rudimentary state, having a natural fear of God: from that stage it advanced, through the Law and the Prophets, to infancy; from that stage it passed, through the Gospel, to the fervour of youth: now, through the Paraclete, it is settling into maturity]" (PL 2:938a–b).

1357 Tertullian, *To His Wife* 1.2 (PL 1:1277a–b). Vgl. Adam, *Der Kirchenbegriff Tertullians* 152, Anm. 2.

1358 Tertullian, *On Monogamy* 14: "Cur non et Paracletus abstulerit, quod Paulus indulsit?" (PL 2:1000a).

1359 Tertullian, *Exhortation to Chastity* 6 (PL 2:970b).

1360 In *Against the Jews* (8.11 [PL 2:654a–b, 672a) in Tertullian's own writings one may find the idea that prophecy and all development of revelation had already ended in the time of Christ.

1361 Tertullian, *On Monogamy* 4: "Hoc ipsum demonstratur a nobis, neque novam, neque extraneam esse monogamiae disciplinam, imo et antiquam et

interpretations naturally could not convincingly prove that the new Montanist revelation was founded on the teaching of Christ.[1362] Tertullian found himself facing a dilemma: Christ and the apostles, or the Paraclete? For himself Tertullian resolves this dilemma by sharply delimiting the sphere of faith and the sphere of morality, dogma, and discipline. The "Rule of Faith" is invariable.[1363] The work of the Paraclete concerns the interpretation of Scripture and the sphere of discipline, which he brings to greater perfection.[1364] The Paraclete only alters discipline,[1365] but he confirms the teaching of Christ.[1366]

In actuality, all these reflections on the part of Tertullian are merely an artificially constructed theory designed with the prejudiced intent of proving that the Paraclete does not revoke Christ.

---

propriam Christianorum; ut Paracletum restitutorem potius sentias ejus, quam institutorem [This very thing is demonstrable by us: that the rule of monogamy is neither novel nor strange, nay rather, is both ancient, and proper to Christians; so that you may be sensible that the Paraclete is rather its restitutor than institutor]" (PL 2:983c).

1362 Vgl. K. Adam, *Der Kirchenbegriff Tertullians* 153: "Seine Versuche, die neuen Gebote in die Intention des Alten uud Neuen Testamentes hineinzudeuten, sind denn auch zu gekünstelt, um vernüftig zu sein. Trotz dieser exegetischen Kunststücke vermag er Christus nicht als Prinzip und Grund der neuen Prophetic, sondern nur als deren Vorläufer festzuhalten."

1363 Tertullian, *On the Veiling of Virgins* 1: "Regula fidei una omnino est, sola immobilis, et irreformabilis [The rule of faith, indeed, is altogether one, alone immoveable and irreformable]" (2:937b).

1364 Ibid: "Quae est ergo Paracleti administratio nisi haec, quod disciplina dirigitur, quod Scripturae revelantur, quod intellectus reformatur, quod ad meliora proficitur? [What, then, is the Paraclete's administrative office but this: the direction of discipline, the revelation of the Scriptures, the reformation of the intellect, the advancement toward the better things?]" (PL 2:938a).

1365 Concerning Tertullian's views on the invariability of discipline, see V. Kiparisov, *On Church Discipline* ("О церковной дисциплине") (Sergiev Posad: 1897), 137.

1366 Tertullian, *On Monogamy* 2: "Ipsum primo Christum contestabitur, qualem credimus, cum toto ordine Dei Creatoris et ipsum glorificabit, et de ipso commemorabit [bearing emphatic witness to Christ, {as being} such as we believe {Him to be}, together with the whole order of God the Creator, and will glorify Him, and will 'bring to remembrance' concerning Him]" (PL 2:981b).

This view produces a purely formalistic regard for the "Rule of Faith": it is merely a collection of abstract formulas. Christ is declared to be merely a theoretical Teacher of Christianity, while His moral teaching was a product of His particular place and time. Apparently in the sphere of moral teaching, if not completely removed, Christ recedes into the background, yielding precedence to the Paraclete.[1367] For Tertullian, the sphere of discipline sometimes broadens greatly, and the Paraclete not only alters certain disciplinary requirements, but even gives new strength to courageously endure persecution,[1368] and it is he that gives power to abstain from remarriage.[1369] We cannot even say that Montanism left the dogmatic aspect of Christianity completely inviolate,[1370] although naturally its chief import lay not in the sphere of dogma.[1371]

All this gives grounds to assert that Montanism wished to be a new stage of revelation—one superior to that given through Jesus Christ and the apostles.[1372] The Montanists even composed new

---

1367 This is [described] in greater detail in Karl Adam's *Der Kirchenbegriff Tertullians*, 154–157, 163–165.

1368 Tertullian, *De Fuga in Persecutione* 14: "Quem qui receperunt, neque fugere persecutionem, neque redimere noverunt, habentes ipsum, qui pro nobis erit sic et locutus in interrogatione, ita juvaturus in passione [they who have received Him will neither stoop to flee from persecution nor to buy it off, for they have the Lord Himself, One who will be our mouth when we are put to the question, as well as stand by us to aid us in suffering]" (PL 2:142b).

1369 Tertullian, *On Monogamy* 14: "Tempus ejus donec Paracletus operaretur fuit, in quem dilata sunt a Domino, quae tunc sustineri non poterant, quae jam nemini competit portare non posse; quia per quem datur portare posse, non deest [The time for its indulgence was {the interval} until the Paraclete began His operations, to whose coming were deferred by the Lord {the things} which in His day 'could not be endured;' which it is now no longer competent for any one to be unable to endure, seeing that He through whom the power of enduring is granted is not wanting]" (PL 2:1000c).

1370 See Ritschl, *Die Entstehung der altkath. Kirche*, 479–497. Cf. Tillemont, *Memoires*, vol. 4, 474–478.

1371 Cf. Bolotov, *Lectures on the History of the Early Church*, 2nd ed., 359.

1372 Vgl. Ritschl, *Die Entstehung der altkath. Kirche*, 521. "Clearly, the Montanist doctrine of a 'new revelation of the Paraclete' not only pertained to intensifying church discipline, but comprised an explicit denial of Christian revelation at its

scriptures[1373] that were quite numerous—βίβλους ἀπείρους [count-
less books], in the words of Hippolytus—from which more was to
be learned than from the law, the prophets, and the Gospels.[1374] The
opponents of Montanism had grounds to assert that the Montanist
prophets denied Jesus Christ, despite Tertullian's venomous protests
to the contrary.[1375] The Church at that time was firmly grounded
upon an apostolic foundation. In its fight against Gnosticism somewhat earlier the Church had defined itself specifically as Apostolic,
and it was for this that the adherents of Montanism reviled the entire catholic Church under heaven.[1376] The Montanist is a *spiritalis
homo*.[1377] One who does not acknowledge the Paraclete is a psychic,
devoid of the Spirit, having only flesh and a soul.[1378] The faith of
psychics is an animal faith.[1379] In general, in the writings of Tertullian we find a great many sharply accusatory statements against the
Church of the psychics.[1380] V.V. Bolotov has made a highly interesting and insightful comparison of Montanism and Gnosis, in which
the author sees them to have one common trait that sets them apart
from all later heresies: "They readily conceded that to this day the
catholic Church maintains the same doctrine proclaimed to it by

---

very core" (Kasitsyn, *Schisms of the Early Centuries*, 47–48 [=Addendae, part 43,
438–439]). Vgl. Nitzsch, *Grundriss der christlichen Dogmengeschichte* 1, 261; Harnack,
Dogmengeschichte[4] 1, 429, Anm. 4.

1373 Eusebius, *Church History* 5.120.3 (GrchSch. 9.2:566.16–18).

1374 Hippolytus, *The Refutation of All Heresies* 8.19: "πλεῖόν τι δι' αὐτῶν
φάσκοντες μεμαθηκέναι ἢ ἐκ νόμου καὶ προφητῶν καὶ τῶν Εὐαγγελίων" (PG
16:3366c–d).

1375 Tertullian, *On Fasting* 16 (CSEL 20.1:274.21–25).

1376 Eusebius, op. cit. 5.16.9 (NPNF[2] 1:232).

1377 Tertullian, *On Fasting* 16 (CSEL 20.1:295.13); *On Modesty* 21 (CSEL
20.1:271.9).

1378 Ibid. 17: "Merito homines solius animae et carnis spiritalia recusatis
[Men of soul and flesh alone as you are, justly do you reject things spiritual]"
(CSEL 20.1:297.5–6).

1379 Ibid. 1: "fides animalis" (CSEL 20.1:274.11).

1380 See for example his *On Modesty* 1 (CSEL 20.1:220); *On Fasting* 12 (CSEL
20.1:290–291).

the apostles, and that even now the Church adheres to the same doctrine and practice as it had in the apostolic age. But they were convinced that they had a source of revelation far superior to that which the Church possesses. Thus, for them the catholic Church was not so much fallible and erring as it was behind the times."[1381]

Given the Montanist attitude toward the New Testament revelation of Christianity, in combating Montanism the Church was faced with a question: should it stay with the Tradition which in both doctrine and morality had come down to it by succession from the eyewitnesses of the Lord, the apostles? Or should it place its trust in the ecstatic "new" prophecy, although this would require breaking with apostolic tradition on many points? In other words, was the Church to remain Apostolic, or to become Montanistic? Montanism with its "new" revelation was reevaluating Tradition, and in so doing it roused the church writers to undertake a detailed examination of the doctrine concerning the Church. In the fight against Gnosticism, the principle of tradition was established to counter arbitrary **rationalistic** interpretations of Christianity. Montanism raised the question of how tradition regarded charismatic revelations. For this reason in polemics with Montanism one may find supplementation of the doctrine concerning the Church as the custodian of the Truth that was developed to combat Gnosticism.

"Against the so-called Phrygian heresy, the power which always contends for the truth raised up a strong and invincible weapon, Apolinarius of Hierapolis ... and with him many other men of ability." A great many writings of these opponents of Montanism survived to the time of Eusebius.[1382] But very few manuscripts of anti-Montanist literature remain, these being almost exclusively fragments preserved by Eusebius.[1383] Only recently, by means of

---

1381 Bolotov, *Lectures on the History of the Early Church*, 2nd ed., 367.

1382 Eusebius, op. cit. 5.16.1 (NPNF[2] 1:229–230).

1383 This is why D. Kasitsyn's refutation of the Montanist doctrine of a "new revelation" is not that offered by church writers contemporary with Montanism, but his own, on the basis of Christian revelation in general. See *Schisms of the Early Centuries of Christianity*, 57–63 (=Addendae, part 43, 448–455).

analyzing several early Christian literary works, has church historical science uncovered a few additional remnants of anti-Montanist literature.[1384]

At the outset of its emergence in Asia Minor, Montanism immediately met with resistance from representatives of the Church. "The faithful in Asia met often in many places throughout Asia to consider this matter, and examined the novel utterances and pronounced them profane, and rejected the heresy, and thus these persons were expelled from the Church and debarred from communion." [1385] The Church had never been an ecstatic, sectarian phenomenon;[1386] consequently, Montanism was rejected. In polemical literature, church doctrine on charismas and how Tradition regarded them was more extensively developed. The most noteworthy specimen of anti-Montanist literature in reworked form[1387] is recorded by Epiphanius. The authorship of this work is naturally difficult to determine. This anonymous work is ascribed to Rhodon, excerpts of whose writings are cited by Eusebius[1388] and Apollonius,[1389] and whom Jerome[1390] and Hippolytus[1391] mention. But

---

1384 We refer to [the work by] Heinrich Gisbert Voigt, *Eine verschollene Urkunde des Antimontanistischen Kampfes* (Leipzig: 1891). See also Ernst Rolffs, *Urkunden ausdem antimontanistischen Kampfe des Abendlandes. Texte und Untersuchungen zur Geschichte der altchristlichen Literatur, herausg. von Oscar von Gebhardt und Adolf Harnack.* XII.4 (Leipzig: 1895). We shall subsequently be employing these studies.

1385 Eusebius, op. cit. 5.16.10 (NPNF² 1:232; GrchSch. 9.1:464).

1386 Vgl. Harnack, *Der erste Klemensbrief*, 42.

1387 Concerning how Epiphanius reworked his sources, see Voigt, *Eine verschollene Urkunde*, 135–136, Anm. 1–5.

1388 So asserts Lipsius [in his compositions] *Zur Quellenkritik des Epiphanies* and *Die Quellen der ältesten Ketzergeschichte*. See Voigt, 208–215. Here [may also be found] an analysis of Lipsius's conjectures.

1389 Hilgenfeld, *Ketzergeschichte des Urchristenthums*. See Voigt, 221–222. Here also see references to other anti-Gnostic writers known only by name: Apollinaris, Soterius, Miltiades, and Serapion (222–223).

1390 Voigt, op. cit., 224–233.

1391 Rolffs Bonwetsch, *Urkunden*, TU 12.4, 100 ff.; Prof. Karl Johannes Neumann, *Hippolytus von Rom in seiner Stellung zu staat und Welt* (Leipzig: 1902), 119. Hippolytus's authorship was opposed by Voigt (216–221), and also Harnack, *Die*

Voigt rightly observes: "To find the author of something composed in antiquity that has come down to us nameless is a doubtful undertaking, even if that composition has reached us completely in its original text. How much more bold, then, must we think the advancement of an opinion concerning the author of a work that lies before us only in reworked form!"[1392] Whoever the author of this anti-Montanistic work may be, from it we may judge the tenets that church writers developed to counter the Montanists.[1393]

First and foremost, church writers rejected the ecstatic form of prophecy.[1394] Eusebius cites an anonymous account concerning Miltiades: "He shows that a prophet ought not to speak in ecstasy."[1395] The saints of God, being filled with the Holy Spirit, according to the measure of the gifts that the Spirit bestowed to each, and "according to the proportion of faith" (Rom. 12:6) "to profit withal" (1 Cor. 12:7), all prophesied in the true spirit, in their right mind (ἐρρωμένη διανοία) and with consistency of thought (νῷ).[1396] The prophet spoke all things with a calm (καταστάσεως) and consistent train of thought, and proclaimed (ἐφθέγγετο) that which was of the Holy Spirit, speaking all things sensibly (ἐρρωμένως).[1397] The words of a prophet are the words of a man who speaks consistently, and not of one in ecstasy (ἐξισταμένου).[1398] These are the traits of true prophets: that when the Holy Spirit is at work, both their

---

Chronologie der altchristlichen Literatur bis Evsebius, Bd. II (Leipzig: 1904), 229–230.

1392 Voigt, 208. Vgl. Bardenhewer, *Patrologie*³ §33.5, 102.

1393 Cf. P. de Labriolle, "La Polémique antimontaniste centre la prophétie estatique," in *Revue d'histoire et de littéerature religieuses*, vol. 11 (1906), 118–119.

1394 Cf. Tertullian, *Against Marcion* 4.22 (CSEL 47:493).

1395 Eusebius, *Church History* 5.17.1: "μὴ δεῖν προφήτην ἐν ἐκστάσει λαλεῖν" (GrchSch. 9.1:470.5–6). "The Eastern polemicists against Montanism merely demonstrated a profound understanding of the very essence of this movement when they attacked this particular aspect of Montanism—its recognition of a new prophecy that the Church had rejected" (Bolotov, *Lectures on the History of the Early Church*, 2nd ed., 367).

1396 Epiphanius, Haer. 48.3 (PG 41:857d).

1397 Idem 48.3 (PG 41:860a).

1398 Idem 48.3 (PG 41:860b).

teaching and their speech is sensible.[1399] The Montanist prophets, though they promise to prophesy, prove not to be their own masters (εὐσταθοῦντες) and not to maintain consistency in their words.[1400] Next follows a detailed examination of various passages from the Holy Scripture of the Old and New Testaments which the Montanists could cite in defense specifically of the ecstatic form of their prophecies.[1401] In denying the ecstatic form of the Montanist prophecies, the church writers developed their own broader view of spiritual gifts in the Church—the same view expressed by the apostle Paul.[1402]

1399 Idem 48.3 (PG 41:860c). Cf. Eusebius, op. cit. 5.17.3.

1400 Idem 48.3 (PG 41:860d).

1401 Idem 48.4–8. In *On Monogamy* Tertullian does not provide an in-depth defense of the ecstatic form of prophecy. This defense was probably made in his work *On Ecstasy*, which Jerome mentions (*On Illustrious Men* 40): "Tertullianus sex voluminibus adversus ecclesiam editis, quae scripta περὶ ἐκστάσεως, septimum proprie adversus Apollonium elaboravit, in quo omnia quae ille arguit, conatur defendere [Tertullian added to the six volumes which he wrote On ecstasy against the church a seventh, directed especially against Apollonius, in which he attempts to defend all which Apollonius refuted]" (PL 23:655b). Cf. PL 23:663a. This work is discussed by Rolffs in *Urkunden*, TU 12.4, 71–74, where among other things Rolffs says, "*On Ecstasy*, without a doubt, was a justification of the ecstatic form of Montanist prophecy, and simultaneously a defense of its content. It was a multifaceted defense of the revelation of the Paraclete" (73). Vgl. Nitzsch, *Grundriss der chr. Dogmengeschichte* 1, 262. Vgl. Harnack, *Chronologie* 2, 275–276.

1402 It should be noted that in the writings of the apologists of the early Church we encounter statements characterizing prophecy as ecstatic. Justin the Philosopher writes: "When you hear the utterances of the prophets spoken as it were personally, you must not suppose that they are spoken by the inspired themselves, but by the Divine Word who moves them (ἀπὸ τοῦ κινοῦντος αὐτοὺς θείου λόγου)" (*The First Apology* 36 [CAG 1.1:106]). The author of the *Hortatory Address to the Greeks* says: "The Divine Spirit [as a] divine plectrum ... descending from heaven, and using righteous men as an instrument like a harp or lyre ... [reveals] to us the knowledge of things divine and heavenly" (8 [ANF 1:276; CAG 3:40]). Athenagoras asserts that the Spirit of God moved the lips of the prophets as instruments (ὡς ὄργανα), and that the prophets, moved by the Spirit of God in an ecstasy (κατ᾽ ἔκστασιν) of their minds, proclaimed that with which they were inspired, for the Spirit employed them just as a musician plays a flute (*Legatio* 7.2; Geffcken, *Zwei griechische Apologeten*, 125, 127; *Works of the Apologists* ["Сочинения апологетов"], 60, 61). Theophilus of Antioch calls the prophets the musical in-

The question of spiritual gifts was also discussed by St. Hippolytus,[1403] who, as far as we can tell from historical sources, was also an opponent of Montanism.[1404] Although the writings of Hippolytus

---

struments of God (*Theophilus to Autolycus* 2.9 [CAG 8:76]). Cf. Justin Martyr, *Dialogue with Trypho* 115 (CAG 1.2:412); Clement of Alexandria, *Stromata* 6.18.168.3: "προφήτας θεοῦ... ὄργανα θείας γενομένους φωνῆς" (GrchSch. 15:517.23–24). In order to correctly understand and properly evaluate all these statements, it must not be forgotten that they were made by apologists for polemical purposes and do not comprise any particular theory such as that of the Montanists. The prophecy of the Church, as may be judged from 1 Cor. 14, the *Didache*, and *The Pastor of Hermas*, was not ecstatic in nature. For more detail see P. d. Labriolle, *La polémique antimontaniste contre la prophétie exatique Revue d'histoire et de littérature religieuses*, vol. 11 (1906), 122–127. Cf. Nitzsch, *Grundriss der christlichen Dogmengeschichte* 1, 261; Thomasius, *Die Dogmengeschichte* 1, 130–131, 132; P. Heinisch, *Der Einfluss Philos auf die älteste christliche Exegese*, 44–46; Bolotov, *Lectures on the History of the Early Church*, 2nd ed., 358, 367.

1403 The caption of Hippolytus's composition devoted to the question of spiritual gifts is preserved in a monument to Hippolytus discovered in Rome, a cast of which is located in the Moscow Historical Museum. Lines 9–11 of the surviving inscription read as follows:
ΕΡΙΧΑΡΙΣΜΑΤΩΝ
ΠΟΣΤΟΛΙΚΗΠΑΡΑΔΟ
ΣΙΣ
These lines are interpreted variously. Some see them as two captions: (π)ερὶ χαρισμάτων and (Ἀ)ποστολικὴ παράδοσις ['On Charismata' and 'Apostolic Tradition'], while others combine both lines and read the caption as follows: (π)ερὶ χαρισμάτων (ἀ)ποστολικὴ παράδοσις ['The Apostolic Tradition on Charismata']. Hans Achelis, *Hippolytstudien. – Texte und Untersuchungen zur Geschichte der altchristlichen Literatur, herausgegeben von Oscar von Gebhardt und Adolf Harnack* 16.1 (Leipzig: 1897), 4, 7.

1404 Voigt surmises that Hippolytus was lenient toward Montanism, and in proof of this cites the observation of Stephen Gobar in Photius: "τίνας ὑπολήψεις εἶχεν ὁ ἁγιώτατος Ἱππόλυτος περὶ τῆς τῶν Μοντανιστῶν αἱρέσεως [what opininos the most holy Hippolytus had regarding the heresy of the Montanists]" (*Eine verschollene Urkunde*, 216, Anm. 3. Vgl. 220). Rolffs rightly notes that it is hard to deduce a lenient stance on the Montanists from these words (*Urkunden* TU 2.4, 109, Anm. 1). Those passages of the *The Refutation of All Heresies* that refer to the Montanists cannot be termed lenient. See *The Refutation of All Heresies* 10.25 [21]: "οἱ δὲ Φρύγες ἐκ Μοντανοῦ τινος καὶ Πρισκίλλης καὶ Μαξιμίλλης τὰς ἀρχὰς τῆς αἱρέσεως λαβόντες [The Phrygians, however, derive the principles of their heresy from a certain Montanus, and Priscilla, and Maximilla]" (PG 16:3439b). In another passage Hippolytus expresses himself still more strictly (*The Refuta-

περὶ χαρισμάτων [on charismas] have been lost, it is supposed that
his views on the χαρίσματα were reflected in the eighth book of
the *Constitutions of the Holy Apostles*.[1405] In any case, it must be supposed [that] when the Apostolic Constitutions speak of gifts, they
are referring to the false Montanist doctrine concerning them.[1406]
The Apostolic Constitutions state first and foremost that the gifts
exist only for unbelievers, so that those not persuaded by the word
might be persuaded by the power of signs.[1407] Consequently, the
gifts are of temporary and limited significance,[1408] and "there is no
man who has believed in God through Christ, that has not received
some spiritual gift (χάρισμα πνευματικόν): for this very thing, having
been delivered from the impiety of polytheism, and having believed
in God the Father through Christ, this is a gift of God. ... Let not,
therefore, any one that works signs and wonders judge any one of
the faithful who is not vouchsafed the same: for the gifts of God
which are bestowed by Him through Christ are various; and one
man receives one gift, and another another. For perhaps one has
the word of wisdom, and another the word of knowledge; another, discerning of spirits; another, foreknowledge of things to come;

---

tion of All Heresies 8.18: "αὐτοὶ αἱρετικώτεροι τὴν φύσιν [even more heretical in
nature]"). Consequently, G. Volkmar is quite wrong in considering Hippolytus a
semi-Montanist (*Hippolytus und die römischen Zeitgenossen* [Zürich: 1855], 111). But
even according to Volkmar Hippolytus denies the individual and spontaneous
aspect that the *ecclesia spiritualis* connected solely with the ecstatic form and with
particular individuals, in contrast to the psychics and in limitation of the prophetic gifts. See Adhémar d' Alès, *La théologie de saint Hippolyte*, 69, 169.

1405 Concerning this, see Voigt, *Eine verschollene Urkunde*, 216–217, Anm. 6);
Christian Carl Iosias Bunsen, *Hippolytus und seine Zeit*, 1-er Bd. (Leipzig: 1852),
434 ff.; F.X. Funk, *Didascalia et constitutiones apostolorum*, vol. 1 (Paderbernae: 1906):
Prolegomena, 17–18; *St. Hippolytus, Bishop of Rome: Works in Russian Translation* ["Св.
Ипполит, еп. Римский. Творения в русск. перев."], published by the Kazan
Theological Academy, 1st ed. (Kazan: 1898), XLIV; Harnack, *Chronologie* 2, 503–
507.

1406 See Kasitsyn, *Schisms of the Early Centuries of Christianity*, 61n2 (Addendae,
part 43, 452n2).

1407 *The Constitutions of the Holy Apostles* 8.1.1.2 (ANF 7:479).

1408 Idem 8.1.1.17 (ANF 7:480). Here it is explicitly stated that the power of
signs may eventually prove superfluous (περιττή).

another, the word of teaching; another, long-suffering; another, continence according to the law (ἔννομον)."[1409] Consequently, the concept of "the gifts" applies to ministry in the Church and even to the virtues of individual persons.[1410]

The church writers do not reject gifts in the Church, but they do provide a criterion for determining their authenticity. This criterion was set by apostolic Tradition: "The Holy Church of God also likewise accepts gifts, but gifts valid and already tested in the Holy Church of God by the power of the Holy Spirit on the basis of the prophets, the apostles, and the Lord Himself."[1411] The church writers absolutely refused to accept the position alleging that a prophet can say something that contradicts the word of God. A true prophet can only be in the Church, and he must be in full accord with church Tradition. "The Lord sealed (ἐσφράγισε) the Church, and imbued her with the fullness of gifts (ἐπλήρωσεν αὐτὴ τὰ χαρίσματα)."[1412] The church writers constantly disprove the Montanist prophecies by citing Holy Scripture, apparently viewing Holy Scripture as a reliable criterion of the truth, and as a higher authority than the "new" prophets. "In all things Montanus proved at odds with the Divine Scriptures, as is clear to every intelligent reader. Hence, if he is at odds, he is a stranger to the Holy universal Church; likewise

---

1409 Idem 8.1.1.10, 12 (ANF 7:480).

1410 Vgl. Chr. Bunsen, *Hippolytus und seine Zeit* 1, 436, 437; *The Constitutions of the Holy Apostles* 8.1.1.21 (ANF 7:480): [here] the episcopacy is called "charisma."

1411 Epiphanius, Haer. 48.1: "Καὶ ἡ ἁγία τοῦ Θεοῦ ἐκκλησία ὁμοίως τὰ χαρίσματα δέχεται ἀλλὰ τὰ ὄντως χαρίσματα, καὶ τῇ ἁγίᾳ Θεοῦ Ἐκκλησίᾳ διὰ Πνεύματος ἁγίου δεδοκιμασμένα παρά τε προφητῶν καὶ ἀποστόλων, καὶ αὐτοῦ τοῦ Κυρίου" (PG 41:856b–c; part 2, 303). See Haer. 48.2: "μετὰ τὰς προφητείας τὰς διὰ τῶν ἁγίων ἀποστόλων ἐν τῇ ἁγίᾳ Ἐκκλησίᾳ δοκιμασθείσας [after the prophecies that were tested through the holy apostles in the holy Church]" (PG 41:857a; part 2, 304). *The Constitutions of the Holy Apostles* discuss false prophecy and false prophets: "We say these things, not in contempt of true prophecies, for we know that they are wrought in holy men (ἐν τοῖς ὁσίοις) by the inspiration (κατ' ἐπίπνοιαν) of God, but to put a stop to the boldness of vainglorious men; and add this withal, that from such as these God takes away His grace" (8.1.2.7 [ANF 7:481]). The last words, of course, are clearly hinting at the Montanist prophets.

1412 Epiphanius, Haer. 48.3 (PG 41:857d; part 2, 306).

foreign to her is his heresy, which boasts of having prophets and gifts: it did not receive them, but is removed from them. Who then, reasoning consistently (παρακολουθῶν), would dare to call them prophets?"[1413] In another place, along with Holy Scripture, the entire body of church Tradition is named as a criterion for prophecies. "By all things you see their discord with Divine Scripture and the otherness of their opinions and conjectures compared to the faith of God and correct doctrine."[1414] "Silas and Agabus"—prophets of apostolic times—"did not equal (οὐ παρεξέτειναν) themselves to the apostles, nor did they exceed their own measures (τὰ ἑαυτῶν μέτρα). … Women prophesied also. … Yet were not these elated against their husbands, but preserved their own measures."[1415] Montanist prophecy, which set itself higher than apostolic Tradition and broke with it, was declared a false prophecy by the church writers,[1416] and the source of this prophecy was declared to be the devil.[1417] **In combating the new prophecy, once again the Church affirmed herself as Apostolic.** In combating Gnosticism the doctrine of a secret tradition was rejected, and it was stated that Jesus Christ delivered the truth to the apostles, who in turn delivered it in its entirety to the Church. Montanism offered a new era of revelation, but the Church held to the former legacy of Christ and the apostles. In combating Montanism the church writers began citing the words of the apostle Paul: "But though we, or an angel

---

1413 Idem, Haer. 48.11 (PG 41:872b; part 2, 320).

1414 Epiphanius, Haer. 48.13: "καὶ ὁρᾷς κατὰ πάντα τρόπον τὴν πρὸς τὸ θεῖον γράμμα τούτων διαφωνίαν, καὶ τὴν ἀλλοίαν ὑπόνοιάν τε καὶ ὑπόληψιν παρὰ τὴν τοῦ Θεοῦ πίστιν καὶ ἀκολουθίαν" (PG 41:876; part 2, 325).

1415 *The Constitutions of the Holy Apostles* 8.2.8–9 (ANF 7:481).

1416 Tertullian, *On Fasting* 1.11–12 (CSEL 20.1:275.9; 289.15, 23; 291.10).

1417 Idem 11: "spiritus diaboli est, dicis, o psychice [It is the spirit of the devil, you say, O Psychic]" (CSEL 20.1:289.26–27); *On Monogamy* 2: "ab adversario spiritu" (PL 2:981a); *The Constitutions of the Holy Apostles* 8.3.1: "ἀλλοτρίῳ πνεύματι κινουμένων moved by an alien spirit]" (Ed. Funk, 470.13–14). See also Eusebius, *Church History* 5.16, where the same is repeatedly stated by an anonymous author cited. Cf. *Epistles of Cyprian* 74.7 (epistle of Firmilian to Cyprian): "non veritatis spiritum sed erroris fuisse [to have been the spirit not of truth but of error]" (ANF 5:392; CSEL 3.2:814.25).

from heaven, preach any other gospel unto you than that which we have preached unto you, let him be accursed" (Gal. 1:8). Tertullian heard this text from his opponents.[1418] From an anonymous source in Eusebius we likewise read, "It is impossible for one who has chosen to live according to the Gospel, either to increase or to diminish [it]."[1419] All of Christian revelation has already been given in the age of the apostles. The words of Revelation (see Rev. 22:18–19) likewise safeguard the Holy Scripture of the New Testament,[1420] just as the words of Deuteronomy (see Deut. 4:2) safeguarded the Old Testament from amendment. The author of the Muratorian fragment is an opponent of Montanism,[1421] and he clearly expresses the idea that the New Testament is complete, and consequently *The Pastor of Hermas*, although beneficial for reading, can never be included with the writings of the apostles and the prophets, as being of recent authorship.[1422] In the life of the Church, the apostolic age

---

1418 Idem 1: "Novitatem igitur objectant, de cujus inlicito praescribant aut haeresin judicandam, si humana praesumptio est, aut pseudoprophetiam pronuntiandam, si spiritalis indictio est, dum quaqua ex parte anathema audiamus, qui aliter adnuntiamus [They are therefore constantly reproaching us with novelty; concerning the unlawfulness of which they lay down a prescriptive rule, that either it must be adjudged heresy, if {the point in dispute} is a human presumption; or else pronounced pseudo-prophecy, if it is a spiritual declaration; provided that, either way, we who reclaim hear {sentence of} anathema]" (CSEL 20.1:275.7–11). Morcelli and Bonwetsch also surmised that in *On Fasting* Tertullian is refuting a particular anti-Montanist work. This view is substantiated in detail by E. Rolffs. See *Urkunden* TU 12.4, 19–21. In analyzing *On Fasting* (21–31), Rolffs notes those passages that may be considered more or less literal quotations from the work being refuted, and offers a reconstruction of the work itself. The passage cited, in Rolff's opinion, is specifically a quote from this anti-Montanist writer.

1419 Eusebius, op. cit. 5.16.3 (NPNF[2] 1:230; GrchSch. 9.1:460.13–14).

1420 See Tertullian, *Against Hermogenes* 22 (CSEL 47:151.18–19).

1421 Lines 84–85.

1422 Lines 73–80: "Legi eum quidem oportet, se publicare vero in ecclesia populo neque inter profetas completum numero neque inter apostolos in finem temporum potest." Cf. Th. Zahn, *Geschichte des neutestamentlichen Kanons*, Bd. 2.1, 116. Cf. Origen, *Commentary on Matthew* 47: "A Genesi usque ad apostolicos libros, post quos nullis scripturis ita credendum est sicut illis" (PG 13:1668b–c).

was exceptional and inimitable, and no "new" revelation such as that of the Montanists will be accepted by the Church.[1423]

From the doctrine of the new revelation of the Paraclete the Montanists derived their doctrine of the Church as a sacred society of spiritual people, in contrast to whom those who do not accept the revelation of the Paraclete are merely *glorissima multitudo psychicorum*.[1424] In his Montanist writings Tertullian places the Church in a particular relationship with the Holy Spirit. Formerly he had taught: where the Three are—that is, the Father, the Son, and the Holy Spirit—there the Church is, which is the Body of the Three.[1425] But Tertullian establishes a particularly intimate link between the Church and Christ. Not only is Christ the Head of the Church[1426]—the Church itself *is* Christ.[1427] In his Montanist writings Tertullian goes so far as to state that the Church is primarily the Spirit, in Whom is the whole Trinity of the One Godhead, the Father, the Son, and the Holy Spirit.[1428] From this doctrine concerning

---

1423 Cf. Zahn, *Geschichte des neutestamentlichen Kanons* 1.1, 115–117.

1424 "An overboastful multitude of Psychics." Tertullian, *On Fasting* 11 (CSEL 20.1:289.1–2).

1425 Tertullian, *On Baptism* 6: "Ubi tres, id est Pater et Filius et Spiritus Sanctus, ibi ecclesia, quae trium corpus est" (CSEL 20.1:206.26–27). Cf. *Exhortation to Chastity* 7: "Ubi tres, Ecclesia est, licet laici [Where three are, a church is, albeit they be laymen]" (PL 2:971a). These words of Tertullian are subjected to various interpretations, concerning which see E. Michaud, "L'ecclésiologie de Tertullien," *Revue internationale de théologie* (1905): 267–268.

1426 Tertullian, *Against Marcion* 5.18 (CSEL 47:640, 15 sqq.).

1427 Tertullian, *On Repentance* 10: "In uno et altero Ecclesia est, Ecclesia vero Christus [In a company of two is the church; but the church is Christ]" (PL 1:1245b).

1428 Tertullian, *On Modesty* 21: "Ipsa ecclesia proprie et principaliter ipse est spiritus, in quo est trinitas unius divinitatis, pater et filius et spiritus sanctus ecclesia spiritus" (CSEL 20.1:271.3–5, 6). Cf. *On Modesty* 11: "Nemo perfectus ante repertum ordinem fide, nemo Christianus ante Christum coelo resumptum, nemo sanctus ante spiritum sanctum de coelo repraesentatum ipsius disciplinae determinatorem [None was perfect before the discovery of the order of faith; none a Christian before the resumption of Christ to heaven; none holy before the manifestation of the Holy Spirit from heaven, the Determiner of discipline itself]" (CSEL 20.1:241.14–17).

the Church as a society of spiritual, holy people there followed all the Montanist requirements of stricter church discipline. A Christian lives in the light, but if he sins he has already fallen away from the light. While living in the light, a Christian cannot sin.[1429] One might expect that Tertullian would deny repentance completely.[1430] But even the Montanists, proceeding from their idea of the sanctity of the Church, did not demand that all those who had sinned be excluded from the Church. For minor sins even the Montanists allowed for repentance:[1431] they required strict observation of the custom, not unknown in the early Church, by which only those who had fallen into mortal sins were excommunicated. This point was the focus of Tertullian's literary battle with his contemporary, the Roman bishop Callistus, who immediately upon his enthronement in Rome advanced several measures regarding church discipline.[1432] Callistus is a practical man,[1433] and for such people the circumstances of the time are always highly significant. In Rome at that time moral laxity was rampant,[1434] and, influenced by this laxity, the strict morals of Christians likewise collapsed. Callistus openly announced a certain mitigation of church discipline, apparently not finding this

1429 Ibid. 19: "Emundabimur a delicto in lumine incedentes, in quo delictum agi non potest, a Deo sic emundari nos ait, non quasi delinquamus, sed quia non delinquamus [we shall be utterly purified from sin {by} "walking in the light," in which sin cannot be committed. The sense in which he says we "are utterly purified" by God is, not in so far as we sin, but in so far as we do not sin]" (CSEL 20.1:263.24–27).

1430 Vgl. Adam, *Der Kirchenbegriff Tertullians*, 123–124.

1431 Tertullian, *On Modesty* 19: "Si nulla sit venia istorum, nemini salus competat [if there were no pardon for such sins as these, salvation would be unattainable to any]" (CSEL 20.1:265.20–21). Vgl. Adam, *Der Kirchenbegriff Tertullians*, 181–182.

1432 Hippolytus provides a biography of Callistus (*On the Refutation of All Heresies* 9.12 [PG 16:3379 sqq.]). See Döllinger, "Die Geschichte de Kallistus," in *Hippolytus und Kalliustus*, 115–125. See the reasoning of Böhringer [in his work] *Die alte Kirche* 3, 416, 473–474.

1433 As Döllinger says of him, "Von der Natur mit dem χάρισμα κυβερνήσεως ausgestattet" (124).

1434 Concerning this laxity see, for example, Tacitus, *The Annals* 14.20, in *Taciti libri qui supersunt*, vol. 1 (Lipsiae: 1861), 262.

contradictory to the existing concept of the sanctity of the Church. Callistus issued an edict declaring forgiveness of sins against chastity: "Ego et moechiae et fornicationis delicta paenitentia functis dimitto."[1435] In this instance, *dimitto* specifically signified restoration

---

1435 "I remit, to such as have discharged (the requirements of) repentance, the sins both of adultery and of fornication." Tertullian, *On Modesty* 1 (CSEL 20.1:220.5–6). Since the majority of Tertullian's literary work falls during the episcopacy of Zephyrinus in Rome (A.D. 200–217), for a long time Zephyrinus was considered the author of the edict. So thought Pamelius, Baronius, Dion, Petavius, Albaspinus, Morinus, and Jacob Sirmond. Protestant historians—the authors of the Magdeburg Centuries, Basnage, Gottfried Arnold, Spanheim— take no notice of the edict, perhaps deliberately, failing to understand Tertullian's irony in saying "Pontifex maximus, episcopus episcoporum" with respect to the bishop of Rome. More recent church historians—Schrökh, Schwegler, Ritschl, Baur, Lipsius—also name Zephyrinus as the author of the edict, but they differ in their understanding of the significance of the decree. A few, such as Cardinal Orsi in his later writings and Gieseler, held the edict to have been authored by an unknown bishop of Carthage—an African. Morcelli follows Orsi in additionally specifying a specific author in Africa—Cyrus, bishop of Carthage (cf. Tillemont, *Memoires*, vol. 3, 224). Böhringer surmises that the author may have been Optatus, bishop of Carthage, and that the edict may have been published in A.D. 205 (see *Die alte Kirche*, 3-ter Th., 458). After the discovery of Hipploytus's *The Refutation of All Heresies*, De Rossi, their discoverer, began to consider Callistus the author of the edict. In 1878 Harnack came to the same conclusion, followed in 1884 by Jungmann. Nöldechen bolstered this opinion with a new study on the time when Tertullian's writings were composed. Preuschen declared the question conclusively resolved. See Rolffs, *Das Indulgenz-Ed.*, TU 11.3, 1–9. Today Callistus is unanimously recognized as the author. See Adhémar d' Alès, *La théologie de Tertullien*, 478n1; S.I. Smirnov, *The Spiritual Father*, 226n; Funk, *Kirchengesch. Abhandlungen und Untersuch* 1, 156–157; the note by Prof. Brilliantov in *The Lectures of Bolotov* ("Лекции Болотова"), 2nd ed., 568; E. Preuschen, *Zeitschrift für die neutestam. Wissenschaft* (1910), 138 ff. Many opinions have been voiced concerning the composition of the edict. See Migne, PL 2:1031c–d; Rolffs, *Das Ind. Ed.*, TU 11.3, 11–12. Preuschen, Harnack, and Nöldechen have made attempts to restore the edict, and Rolffs provided a reconstruction (see *Das Ind.-Ed.*, TU 11.3, 104–116). [The text is provided] on the even-numbered pages, with the German translation on the odd-numbered. Preuschen renounces his own attempt at reconstruction in his earlier work, *Tertullians Schriften «De paenitentia» und «De pudicitia»*," and places little value on Rolfft's reconstruction. See *Zeitschrift für die neutestam. Wissenschaft* (1910), 141. Cf. Esser Gerhard, *Die Bussschriften Tertullians «De paenitentia» und «De pudicitia»*, 5, Anm. 2; 12, Anm. 2. Döllinger adopts the original view that sins against chastity had been absolved by Zephyrinus, and Callistus then absolved

to communion with the Church, since Tertullian quite frequently replaces *dimitto* with the words *communicare* and *communicatio*. We also encounter the combinations *recipere in communicationem, communicationem restituere*, and so forth.[1436] It was against this edict of the Roman bishop that Tertullian wrote his treatise *On Modesty*. It should be noted that a characteristic trait of Tertullian's polemical writings is an abundance of argumentation. Tertullian piles on proofs of every possible nature, giving preference to quantity over quality.[1437] It may be that in *On Modesty* he is conveying and refuting not only what he read in the edict, instead examining the question in greater detail, but at any rate only from *On Modesty* do we learn the thought process of Tertullian's opponents. *On Modesty* is presented as a dispute between a psychic and a Montanist. Tertullian presents many texts of Holy Scripture cited by his opponent. If we presume that all these texts were in the edict of Callistus,[1438] this means that for the first time the edict presented detailed argumentation of the possibil-

---

other mortal sins. See *Hippolytus und Callistus*, 126–138. Döllinger's view is shared by Hagemann (Rolffs, *Das Ind.-Ed.*, 8) and G. Volkmar (*Hippolytus und die römische Zeitgenossen*, 107), who apparently follows Döllinger. Döllinger's opinion is partially shared by Archpriest Ivantsov-Platonov—see [his work] *Heresies and Schisms*, 92–93. In the literature of the history of the Russian Church to this day Zephyrinus has been unquestioningly considered the author of the edict. See K.M. Mazurin, *Tertullian and His Works* ["Тертуллиан и его творения"] (Moscow: 1892), 315–316; F.W. Farar, *Lives of the Fathers*, published in Russian as *The Life and Works of the Holy Fathers and Teachers of the Church* ("Жизнь и труды святых отцов и учителей Церкви"), A.P. Lopukhin, trans. (St. Petersburg: 1891), 120, 932. But cf. Smirnov, *The Spiritual Father*, 225. Bolotov (*Lectures*, 2nd ed., 369) considered Zephyrinus the author of the edict.

1436 Tertullian, *On Modesty* 15, 18, 22 (CSEL 20.1:251.4; 252.6–7; 259.3; 260.24; 261.2; 272.30; 273.4–5).

1437 See I.V. Popov, *Tertullian: An Essay in Literary Characterization* ["Тертуллиан. Опыт литературной характеристики"] (Sergiev Posad: 1893), 32–34. "Tertullian cited proofs from Holy Scripture, disputed the interpretation of the text, appealed to Tradition, left not a single objection of his opponent unrefuted, and ultimately resorted to rationalistic arguments" (32).

1438 Vgl. Rolffs, *Das Indulgenz—Edict*, TU 11.3, 12.

ity for granting church communion to those who had sinned mortally, without violating the sanctity of the Church in the process.[1439]

Complete forgiveness of sins against chastity is demonstrated first and foremost from the properties of God. Goodness and mercy are qualities of God, as seen from many passages of Scripture.[1440] The children of God must likewise be merciful and peacemakers, as Scripture requires of them.[1441] Tertullian also indicates the justice of God (*tamen et justus*). God not only pardons, but also punishes; people likewise not only can but must judge, as we see from Holy Scripture (see 1 Cor. 5:3–5). One who has sinned mortally must remain outside the Church.[1442] Tertullian's opponents held that if a penitent is not vouchsafed communion with the Church, his repentance is in vain.[1443] This seems to express the idea that salvation is impossible outside of communion with the visible Church. The Church must receive the penitent into her bosom, that his repentance not be to no effect. Tertullian, however, thinks differently. He sees this view of the psychics as an usurpation of the power of God.[1444] In the

---

1439 Cf. I. Turmel, *Histoire de la théologie positive* 1, 142–143. Incidentally, Tertullian offers some justification for "secondary repentance" in chapter 8 of his early work *On Repentance*. For more detail see Adhémar d' Alès, *La théologie de Tertullien*, 479 et suiv. P. Patiffol, Études d'histoire et de théologie positive,[2] 33; Preuschen, *Zeitschrift für die neutestam. Wissenschaft* (1910), 136–137; Esser, *Die Bussschriften Tertullians...*, 12, Anm. 1.

1440 Joel 2:13; Hos. 33:11; 1 Tim. 4:10. Tertullian, *On Modesty* 2: "Deus inquiunt, bonus et optimus et misericors et miserator et misericordiae plurimus ["But," say they, "God is 'good,' and 'most good,' and 'pitiful-hearted,' and 'a pitier,' and 'abundant in pitiful-heartedness,'"]" etc. (CSEL 20.1:222.9 sqq). It should be noted that in *Against Marcion* 4.10 Tertullian himself demonstrates the mercy of God based on the Scriptures of the Old Testament.

1441 Many passages of Holy Scripture are cited: Tertullian, *On Modesty* 2 (CSEL 20.1:222–223).

1442 Tertullian, *On Modesty* 2.

1443 Ibid. 3: "Si enim, inquiunt, aliqua paenitentia caret venia, jam nec in totum agenda tibi est. Nihil enim agendum est frustra ['Why, if,' say they, 'there is a repentance which lacks pardon, it immediately follows that such repentance must withal be wholly unpractised by you. For nothing is to be done in vain.']" (CSEL 20.1:224.21–23).

1444 Ibid. 3: "Hujus quoque paenitentiae fructum, id est veniam, in sua potes-

Montanist worldview, only God—and not the Church—can grant forgiveness.[1445] Repentance without reception back into the Church is not in vain, because the penitent can receive the fruit of repentance from God. Although he will not achieve communion with the Church, he will find peace with God.[1446] Thus, salvation is achievable even outside communion with the visible Church.[1447]

The demand that one who has sinned mortally not be restored to communion with the Church is one that Tertullian substantiates specifically using a dogmatic doctrine of the sanctity of the Church. If fornicators are received back into communion with the Church, the Church cannot then be called the Body of Christ or the temple of God, and believers are no longer the members of Christ.[1448] No sooner does Tertullian cite the first words of Callistus's edict than he exclaims: "But it is in the church that this (edict) is read, and in the church that it is pronounced; and (the church) is a virgin! Far, far from Christ's betrothed be such a proclamation! She, the true, the modest, the saintly, shall be free from stain even of her ears."[1449] Thus, in Tertullian's view, restoring those who have sinned mortally to communion with the Church is wholly incompatible with her

---

tate usurpaverunt [since they have usurpingly kept in their own power the fruit of this as of other repentance — that is, pardon]" (CSEL 20.1:224.27–28).

1445 Ibid. 3: "Quantum autem ad nos, qui solum dominum meminimus delicta concedere [As regards us, however, who remember that the Lord alone concedes {the pardon of} sins]" (CSEL 20.1:224.29–225.2).

1446 Ibid. 3: "Non frustra agetur ... et si pacem hic non metit, apud dominum seminat. Nec amittit, sed praeparat fructum [It will not be practiced in vain.... if it reaps not the harvest of peace here, yet it sows the seed of it with the Lord; nor does it lose, but prepares, its fruit]" (CSEL 20.1:225.2, 9–11).

1447 Tertullian acknowledges the possibility of pardon for those who have mortally sinned even without the intercession of Christ, when he states that "horum ultra exorator non erit Christus [For these Christ will no more be the successful Pleader]" (Ibid. 19 [CSEL 20.1:265.25]).

1448 Ibid. 6: "Non corpus Christi, non membra Christi, non templum dei vocabatur, cum veniam moechiae consequebatur" (CSEL 20.1:230.13–14).

1449 Ibid. 1: "Sed hoc in ecclesia legitur, et in ecclesia pronuntiatur, et virgo est. Absit a sponsa Christi tale praeconium! Illa, quae vera est, quae pudica, quae sancta, carebit etiam aurium macula" (ANF 4:74; CSEL 20.1:220.10–13).

sanctity. The sanctity of the Church requires the exclusion of those who have mortally sinned.[1450]

Callistus and those of like mind with him held a different view of the Church. In justification of his decree he cited the parables of the lost sheep and the lost drachma,[1451] understanding the lost sheep and the lost drachma specifically to mean Christians who had sinned, sheep of the flock of Christ, which is the Church. Such Christians, the parable teaches, must be restored to the Church, that they might not perish utterly by wandering too long abroad.[1452] For this reason the historical objective of the Church has been specifically to restore fallen men to moral health. One who has joined the Church may stray from her, like a sheep from the flock; such a one must be returned to the fold of the Church.

Tertullian objects, arguing that the parables refer to the conversion of gentiles, not sinners, although in *On Patience* and *On Repentance* he himself applied those same parables to the repentance of sinners.[1453] But even if the parables did refer to sinners, they cannot be used to justify the restoration of sinners to the Church. If the sheep had not merely wandered off, but had perished utterly, and if the drachma had not merely been lost, but had been completely

---

1450 Tertullian gives a unique interpretation of 1 Cor. 5:5: "Eum spiritum dixerit, qui in ecclesia censetur, salvum id est integrum praestandum in die domini ab immunditiarum contagione ejecto incesto fornicatore [that spirit which is accounted to exist in the Church must be presented 'saved,' that is, untainted by the contagion of impurities in the day of the Lord, by the ejection of the incestuous fornicator]" (Ibid. 13; CSEL 20.1:246.8–11).

1451 Cf. the observation of Rolffs in *Das Indulg.-Edict,* TU 11.3, 69.

1452 Tertullian, *On Modesty* 7: "Ovis proprie Christianus et grex domini ecclesiae populus et pastor bonus Christus et ideo Christianus in ove intelligendus, qui ab ecclesiae grege erraverit [But a 'sheep' properly means a Christian, and the Lord's 'flock' is the people of the Church, and the 'good shepherd' is Christ; and hence in the 'sheep' we must understand a Christian who has erred from the Church's flock.]" (CSEL 20.1:231.6–8).

1453 Tertullian, *On Patience* 12 (CSEL 47:19.3 sqq); *On Repentance* 8 (PL 1:1242b–1243a). The difference in how the parables are interpreted in *On Patience* and *On Repentance* is vividly presented by Adhémar d'Alès. See "Tertullien et Calliste," *Revue d'histoire ecclésiastique* (1912): 229.

destroyed, clearly there would be no need to seek them.[1454] The fornicator and adulterer, therefore, are specifically dead, and one cannot justify by parables their restoration to the Church.[1455] This latter thought of Tertullian's clearly conforms very little to his former reasoning on the benefits of repentance even outside the Church.

Pastors who justified the restoration of sinners to communion with the Church applied to themselves the words of Ezekiel (see Ezek. 34:3–4), where the Lord reproaches the shepherds of Israel for not having supported the weary, nor converted the erring, nor sought the perishing. Once again, here too we see a general view of the Church not as a closed society of saints, but rather as having the purpose of supporting the weary and erring. Tertullian evades this argument of his opponents with a sophistic interpretation: the Lord is censuring the shepherds for having permitted the sheep to perish, but not for failing to restore again those that have been devoured by wild beasts.[1456] This idea of Tertullian's likewise contradicts his own words about how God Himself is able to forgive one who has mortally sinned.

The views of the Roman bishop Callistus and those of like mind with him may also be judged by several other arguments cited in defense of their practice. These include the parable of the prodigal son and the story of the incestuous man of Corinth. The parable of the prodigal son is interpreted not in the historical sense upon which Tertullian insists,[1457] but in a moral sense. The Chris-

---

1454 Tertullian, *On Modesty* 7 (CSEL 20.1:232.15 sqq).

1455 Ibid. 7: "Moechum vero et fornicatorem quis non mortuum statim admisso pronuntiavit? Quo ore mortuum restisues in gregem ex parabolae ejus auctoritate, quae non mortuum pecus revocat? [But, for the adulterer and fornicator, who is there who has not pronounced him to be dead immediately upon commission of the crime? With what face will you restore to the flock one who is dead, on the authority of that parable which recalls a sheep not dead?]" (CSEL 20.1:233.4–7).

1456 Ibid. 7 (CSEL 20.1:233.7–16).

1457 Ibid. 8: "Quos enim populos in duobus filiis collocant, Iudaicum majorem, Christianum minorem [For they set down, as represented in the two sons, two peoples—the elder the Jewish, the younger the Christian]" (CSEL 20.1:234.9–10).

tian, represented by the younger son in the parable, departed far from his Father and squandered the riches received from God the Father—in baptism, naturally—on heathen living. If he, stripped of rational blessings, having placed himself in the service of the prince of this world and receiving from him the command to herd swine, comes to his senses and returns to the Father, he will receive his former vesture, the clothing of the Holy Spirit, and once again the ring—a sign of purification.[1458] This interpretation of the parable of the prodigal son[1459] was only possible if the Church was viewed not as a society of the saints and the saved, but as a society

---

1458 This is the interpretation of the parable that Tertullian places into the mouth of Callistus. See *On Modesty* 9: "Christianus est qui acceptam a deo Patre substantiam utique baptismatis, utique Spiritus sancti et exinde spei aeternae longe evagatus a patre prodigit ethnice vivens, si exutus bonis mentis etiam principi saeculi servitium suum tradidit et ab eo porcis alendis, immundis scilicet spiritibus curandis praepositus resipuit ad patrem reverti ... recuperabit vestem priorem, indumentum spiritus sancti, et annulum denuo, siguaculum lavacri... [it is a Christian who, after wandering far from his Father, squanders, by living heathenishly, the "substance" received from God his Father — (the substance), of course, of baptism—(the substance), of course, of the Holy Spirit, and (in consequence) of eternal hope; if, stripped of his mental "goods," he has even handed his service over to the prince of the world — who else but the devil?— and by him being appointed over the business of "feeding swine" — of tending unclean spirits, to wit — has recovered his senses so as to return to his Father... will recover his former "garment," the robe of the Holy Spirit; and a renewal of the "ring," the sign and seal of baptism]" (CSEL 20.1:236.28–237.1, 7–9). These words are also included in Rolffs's reconstruction of the edict of Callistus. See *Das Indulg-Edict*, TU 11.3, 106, 108.

1459 This interpretation, as noted above, Tertullian emphatically rejected, thereby explicitly contradicting what he himself said in *On Repentance* 8: "Illum etiam mitissimum patrem non tacebo, qui prodigum filium revocat, et post inopiam poenitentem libens suscipit. Immolat vitulum praeopimum, convivio gaudium suum oxornat. ... Is ergo te filium suum, etsi acceptam ab eo prodegeris, etsi nudus redieris, recipiet [That most gentle father, likewise, I will not pass over in silence, who calls his prodigal son home, and willingly receives him repentant after his indigence, slays his best fatted calf, and graces his joy with a banquet... He, then, will receive you, His own son, back, even if you have squandered what you had received from Him, even if you return naked]," etc. (PL 1:1242c–1243a). This interpretation is almost literally identical to that which the "psychics" give to the parable, according to *On Modesty.*

of those working out their salvation and sanctification. Through repentance a person returns to the fold of the Church, where once again he receives all the gifts of the Holy Spirit, formerly given him in the Sacrament of Baptism, but lost through a sinful life. We have already seen that baptism in the early Church was frequently called repentance: it was a reversal of one's whole life and one's entire way of thinking. Now emphasis is redoubled on the significance of repentance for moral perfection in the bosom of the Church. For Montanism this significance did not exist: one who repented of a mortal sin stood outside the Church, hoping for forgiveness from God. Callistus considers repentance a means of man's cleansing from sin. Sin does not cut a person off from the Church, but merely moves the Church to prescribe for him a suitable remedy, as repentance is in fact called.[1460] Repentance is for Christians, not for pagans. "Remedies are unintelligible to such to whom the perils themselves are unintelligible: ... the principle of repentance finds there its corresponding place where sin is committed with conscience and will, where both the fault and the favour are intelligible; that he who mourns, he who prostrates himself, is he who knows both what he has lost and what he will recover if he makes to God the offering of his repentance."[1461]

The view of repentance specifically as a means of the sinner's correction, as an aid for his restoration to moral health, is particularly revealed in the interpretation of the story of the incestuous man of Corinth. In the second epistle to the Corinthians the apostle Paul speaks of restoring to communion with the Church that incestuous man whom in the first epistle he had commanded "to deliver ... unto Satan for the destruction of the flesh (εἰς ὄλεθρον τῆς σαρκός)" (1 Cor. 5:5).[1462] This "destruction of the flesh" (*interitus carnis*) Callistus and his supporters understood to mean the act of

---

1460 "Remedium" (Tertullian, *On Modesty* 10 [CSEL 20.1:239.6]). In another place repentance is called an aid for one who has sinned (*On Modesty* 19: "Fornicationi posuerit poenitentiae auxilium [he has assigned to fornication the auxiliary aid of repentance]" [CSEL 20.1:261.30]).

1461 Tertullian, *On Modesty* 10 (ANF 4:84; CSEL 20.1:239.7 sqq).

1462 See 2 Cor. 2:5–11.

repentance—to mean the *exomologesis* which existed in the church practice of the day. The destruction of the flesh is specifically fasting, penitential mourning (*sordes*), withdrawal from every evil deed, and so on. Through this penitential act the sinner is cleansed of sin, and hence he must be restored to communion with the Church.[1463] Consequently, repentance is specifically the healing of a morally infirm member of the Church.[1464]

Such are all the data that may be gleaned from Tertullian's polemics with Callistus for characterizing the early third-century views of the Church from the standpoint of its stance on members who had sinned. These polemics are pursued not regarding the dogma concerning the Church itself: they deal with a different subject—namely, the restoration to communion with the Church of those who had fallen into the mortal sins of adultery and fornication. It

---

1463 Tertullian, *On Modesty* 13: "Hic jam carnis interitum in officium poenitentiae interpretantur, quod videatur jejuniis et sordibus et incuria omni et dedita opera malae tractationis carnem exterminando satis Deo facere; ut ex hoc argumententur fornicatorem, imo incestum illum, non in perditionem satanae ab apostolo traditum, sed in emendationem, quasi postea veniam ob interitum, id est conflictationem carnis, consecuturum, igitur et consecutum [Here they go so far as to interpret "destruction of the flesh" of the office of repentance; in that by fasts, and squalor, and every species of neglect and studious ill-treatment devoted to the extermination of the flesh, it seems to make satisfaction to God; so that they argue that that fornicator — that incestuous person rather — having been delivered by the apostle to Satan, not with a view to "perdition," but with a view to "emendation," on the hypothesis that subsequently he would, on account of the "destruction" (that is, the general affliction) "of the flesh," attain pardon, therefore did actually attain it]" (CSEL 20.1:244.22–29). Tertullian understands the destruction of the flesh to mean death. "Incestum fornicatorem non in emendationem, sed in perditionem tradidit satanae. ... Denique in interitum, inquit, carnis, non, in cruciatum; ipsam substantiam damnans, per quam exciderat [So, therefore, the incestuous fornicator, too, he delivered, not with a view to emendation, but with a view to perdition, to Satan... Finally, he says, "for the destruction of the flesh," not its torture, condemning the actual substance through which he had fallen out]" (ibid. 13; CSEL 20.1:245.26–246.2).

1464 Concerning the meaning of deliverance to Satan in early Church literature, see Dr. Anton Seitz, *Die Heilsnotwendigkeit der Kirche nach der altchristlichen Literatur bis dzur Zeit des hl. Augustinus* (Freiburg im Breisgau: 1903), 111–116. The general sense is precisely that expressed by Callistus; Tertullian is alone in his view (113).

is quite clear, however, that differing views on the Church lies at the heart of all these polemics. One who has sinned mortally cannot remain in communion with the Church, for otherwise the sanctity of the Church will be compromised: the Church is comprised solely of people of a high moral plane, who do not permit mortal sins to occur. Such are the fundamental principles of Montanist ecclesiology. It may be noted that in the ecclesiological system of the Montanists the significance of the Church is drastically reduced. The Church imparts the grace of the Holy Spirit only to those entering it, in the Sacrament of Baptism. These gifts must be preserved: if a person loses them, the Church can give him no further assistance by means of grace. Church discipline merely safeguards the sanctity of the Church itself; it offers nothing for the moral perfection of individuals.[1465] The views of Tertullian's opponents are not yet so precisely formulated, but it is perfectly clear that Callistus did not consider restoring even those who had sinned mortally to communion with the Church to be incompatible with the concept of the sanctity of the Church. For him the Church is not a society of saints, but a hospital for the morally infirm. The purpose of church discipline is not to safeguard the sanctity of the Church by cutting off those who have mortally sinned; rather, its focus is specifically the moral upbringing of the members of the Church.

The edict of the Roman bishop Callistus is frequently overestimated in the history of the discipline of the early Church. There is a tendency to view it as the first stone in the edifice of a new disciplinary practice that stands in stark contrast to the entire structure of how the early Church viewed the essence of the Church.[1466] Formerly the Church was envisioned as no less than a society of perfect saints; but now the groundwork is laid for a new doctrine on the sanctity of the Church, according to which she merely serves to further the moral perfection of Christians, for which reason the sanctity of the Church is in no way contradicted by her inclusion of members who have fallen even into mortal sins. At the same time,

---

1465 Vgl. Adam, *Der Kirchenbegriff Tertullians*, 184 ff.

1466 This opinion is considered almost universal. See F.X. Funk, "Das Indulgenzedikt des Papstes Kallistus," *Theologische Quartalschrift* (1906): 541–542.

Tertullian's treatise *On Modesty* is considered an apology for the general practice of the early Church and the ancient concept of the Church. We have already demonstrated in detail that from the very beginning the Church did not see itself as an exclusive society of perfect saints; consequently it must not be thought that the edict of Callistus introduced any decisive reform of the dogmatic doctrine of the sanctity of the Church. It was Montanism that wished to enact such a reform, based on the new revelation of the Paraclete,[1467] but this attempt merely resulted in the Church likewise defining its stance on those who had mortally sinned, clearly and definitively declaring in the edict of Callistus that restoring those who had sinned mortally to communion neither violates nor contradicts the sanctity of the Church. With respect to discipline, the edict of Callistus, though grounded in earlier tradition,[1468] is nevertheless something new: what was formerly a rare occurrence it enacted as law, providing certain grounds for leniency of practice,[1469] but this produced no change in the dogmatic doctrine of the sanctity of the Church.[1470]

The question of absolution of mortal sins was closely linked to another—the right of the bishop to absolve mortal sins, or who in the Church possessed "**the power of the keys**." At the heart of this question lies the same division of sins into forgivable and

---

1467 Tertullian himself sees ecclesiastical progress in his arguments when he says, "Nemo proficiens erubescit [No one blushes at his own improvement]" (*On Modesty* 1 [CSEL 20:220.24]). Ritschl states that neither Montanism nor the bishop of Rome were grounded in tradition, but that each was introducing a novelty of its own. See *Die Entstehung der altkatholischen Kirche*, 514, 516. Vgl. Stufler, *Zeitschrift für katholische Theologie* (1907), 440; Adhémar d' Alès, *La théologie de Tertullien*, 491.

1468 Vgl. Loofs, *Leitfaden der Dogmengeschichte* §29.2b, 208; Jos. Schwane, *Dogmengeschichte der vornic. Zeit*, 453, 499; Paul Monceaux, *Histoire littéraire de L'Afrique Chrétienne depuis les origines jusqu'a l'invasion arabe*, vol. 1 (Paris: 1901), 432; Adhémar d'Alès, "Tertullien et Calliste," *Revue d'histoire ecclésiastique* (1912): 256; Bardenhewer, *Patrologie* §56.1, 195.

1469 Cf. Adhémar d' Alès, *La Théologie de saint Hippolyte*, 48; Adam, *Der Kirchenbegriff Tertullians*, 179–180, Anm. 4. Cf. Stufler, *Zeitschrift für katholische Theologie* (1907), 325.

1470 Vgl. Schanz, "Der Begriff der Kirche," *Theologische Quartalschrift* (1893): 581. See also Gerhard Esser, *Die Busschriften Tertullians* 8, 28.

unforgivable that we have previously discussed. In Tertullian, in the same treatise *On Modesty*, we find the idea that the bishop may forgive only non-mortal, less grave sins, and that God alone can forgive mortal sins.[1471] The edict of the Roman bishop Callistus shows that he viewed the matter differently: in his edict he states, "Ego et moechia et fornicationis delicta paenitentia functis dimitto."[1472] The question of to whom "the power of the keys" belongs in the Church is resolved quite decisively: it belongs to the bishop. In the treatise *On Modesty* we see that the bishop of Rome substantiated his statement with a certain theory. The Lord said to Peter, "Upon this rock I will build my church. I will give (*dedi*) unto thee the keys of the kingdom of heaven: and whatsoever thou shalt bind or loose on earth shall be bound or loosed in heaven" (cf. Mt. 16:18–19). This power to bind and to loose, which the Lord gave to the apostle Peter, Callistus extends to himself and to the whole Church of the apostle Peter. The Church, in the person of its bishop, may bind and loose.[1473] Consequently, the bishop is the successor not only of the apostolic authority to teach, but also of the power to bind and to loose.

Tertullian, proceeding from Montanist views, naturally could not agree with this theory of Callistus,[1474] and he rejects it completely. Tertullian says that one must differentiate between the teaching

---

1471 Tertullian, *On Modesty* 18: "Aut levioribus delictis veniam ab episcopo consequi poterit aut maioribus et inremissibilibus a Deo solo" (CSEL 20.1:261.26–27).

1472 "I remit, to such as have discharged (the requirements of) repentance, the sins both of adultery and of fornication."

1473 Ibid. 21: "Idcirco praesumis et ad te derivasse solvendi et alligandi potestatem, id est ad omnem ecclesiam Petri propinquam [you therefore presume that the power of binding and loosing has derived to you, that is, to every Church akin to Peter]" (CSEL 20.1:270.1–6), and "Sed habet, inquis, potestatem ecclesia delicta donandi ['But,' you say, 'the Church has the power of forgiving sins.']" (CSEL 20.1:269.22–23). Cf. note 1 of Turmel, *Tertullien*, 215.

1474 Concerning Tertullian's stance on episcopal authority, see Adam, *Der Kirchenbegriff Tertullians*, 157–160. It must be acknowledged that in Tertullian's Montanist writings one may observe an evaluation of and stance on the hierarchy that differed significantly from those previous. See Heinrich Bruders, "Mt. 16, 19; 18, 18 und In. 20, 22–23 in frühchristlicher Auslegung," in *Zeitschrift für katholische Theologie* (1910), 664–668.

and the authority of the apostles (*inter doctrinam apostolorum et potestatem*). The authority to absolve mortal sins belongs to God alone
(*majoribus et inremissibilibus a Deo solo*), and if the apostles did sometimes absolve these sins, they did so by their own authority, and not
by their right as teachers (*non ex disciplina, sed ex potestate fecisse*).[1475] In
the apostles the authority to bind and to loose was combined with
the power to work miracles. Ananias, for example, was stricken with
death, and Elymas with blindness. As proof of his authority to bind
and to loose, the bishop ought to exhibit similar miracles.[1476] The
bishops inherited only the duty of teaching (*disciplinae*)—the ministry, not the authority—and hence he cannot loose and bind. Tertullian does not deny that the Church has the power to loose sins.[1477]
One of the Montanist prophets said that the Church has the power
to forgive offenses, but it will not do so, lest people fall into other
offenses.[1478] The Paraclete is able to grant forgiveness even for sins
of fornication, but it does not wish to, lest a greater evil result.[1479] If
the bishop appropriates the power to bind and to loose, he usurps
the right of the Church (*hoc jus ecclesiae usurpes*). Even the apostle Peter bound what had to be bound, and loosed what was permitted to
loose. It was in this sense that the Lord said to him the words cited;

1475 Here *disciplina* apparently corresponds to *doctrina*, used above. Cf. Kiparisov, *On Church Discipline* ("О церковной дисциплине"), 16, 18n27.

1476 Tertullian, *On Modesty* 21: "Exhibe igitur et nunc mihi, apostolice, pro-
phetica exempla, ut agnoscam divinitatem, et vindica tibi delictorum ejusmodi
remittendorum potestatem [Exhibit therefore even now to me, apostolic sir, prophetic evidences, that I may recognise your divine virtue, and vindicate to yourself the power of remitting such sins!]" (CSEL 20.1:269.2–19).

1477 Ibid. 21: "Hoc ego magis et agnosco et dispono [This I acknowledge
and adjudge more {than you do}]" (CSEL 20.1:269.23). But a little further on
we read, "Dabo tibi claves, non ecclesiae ['I will give to you the keys,' not to the
Church]" (CSEL 20.1:270.9–10).

1478 Tertullian, *On Modesty* 21: "Potet ecclesia donare delictum, sed non faciam, ne et alia delinquant ['The Church has the power to forgive sins; but I will
not do it, lest they commit others withal.']" (CSEL 20.1:269.22–25). Harnack for
his part reads *alii* in place of *alia*. Cf. Adam, *Der Kirchenbegriff Tertullians*, 221–222.

1479 Ibid. 21: "Spiritus veritatis potest quidem indulgere fornicatoribus veniam, sed cum plurium malo non vult" (CSEL 20.1:269.29–31).

consequently, the example of the apostle Peter cannot be used to prove the right of the bishop to loose even mortal sins.[1480] "For, in accordance with the person of Peter, it is to spiritual men [*spiritalibus*, in the Montanist sense –*Auth.*] that this power will correspondently appertain, either to an apostle or else to a prophet." Tertullian then summarizes his objections: "Accordingly 'the Church,' it is true, will forgive sins: but (it will be) the Church of the Spirit, by means of a spiritual man; not the Church which consists of a number of bishops (*sed ecclesia spiritus per spiritalem hominem, non ecclesia numerus episcoporum*). For the right and arbitrament is the Lord's, not the servant's; God's Himself, not the priest's."[1481]

Thus, two different practices regarding mortal sins were each accompanied by a particular theory. According to the theory of Callistus, the authority to bind and to loose in the Church belongs to the bishop, which authority he inherited from the apostles. According to the theory of Tertullian, the authority to bind and to loose belongs not to the bishop, but to the spiritual man, the charismatic, through whom God Himself forgives sins in the proper sense.[1482] In the theory of Callistus we now see the fulfillment of the

---

1480 Ibid. 21: "Adeo nihil ad delicta fidelium capitalia potestas solvendi et alligandi Petro emancipata [Hence the power of loosing and of binding committed to Peter had nothing to do with the capital sins of believers]" (CSEL 20.1:270).

1481 Ibid. 21 (CSEL 20.1:271.1–11). "C'est le disciple de Montan qui parle en ce moment," observes Turmel (*Tertullien*, 218).

1482 We will cite the interesting reasoning of Böhringer: "This testimony shows us that at that time the bishops, by virtue of apostolic succession, had already begun to consider themselves not only the possessors of true doctrine, but also the stewards of 'the power of the keys.' Tertullian acknowledged the former, but opposed the latter. In any case, it was a novelty when the bishops usurped for themselves this right which hitherto had been exercised by the Church (the community). Here Tertullian was of course inconsistent, since whoever had already acknowledged the authority of the bishop to teach by virtue of apostolic succession ought to have acknowledged the episcopal 'power of the keys' by virtue of that same succession. If he did not wish to acknowledge it, he ought to have rejected the former also, since the same non-historical justification exists for both. In any case, given this opposition to bishops' 'power of the keys,' which resulted in ascribing to God the exclusive authority to absolve sins, the question constantly focused solely on mortal sins, since Tertullian does not deny the bishop's right

earlier church teaching concerning apostolic succession from the
apostles. The bishop is not only the guardian of the purity of the
faith, but also the guardian of the sanctity of the Church. From the
apostles he inherited not only the power to teach (*locus magisterii*), but
also "the power of the keys."

Certain additional features of the history of the dogma concerning the Church in the early third century are provided in the
writings of Hippolytus of Rome. The disciplinary decrees of Callistus, it must be supposed, were one of the motivating factors for the
occurrence of the so-called schism of Hippolytus in Rome.[1483] Between Hippolytus and Callistus there were several points of contention on questions of disciplinary practice.[1484] Hippolytus undoubt-

---

and authority to absolve sins of lesser gravity. Is this not once again doing things
by halves? It very nearly appears that opposition only to the liberal discipline
of the bishop evoked this opposition to 'the power of the keys' (for mortal sins).
If the bishops had shifted to the stricter discipline of the Montanists, Tertullian
and his Montanist friends would probably not have denied them the right of
absolution, at least in principle. The very idea of absolution of sins by God,
which was contrasted to absolution by the bishop, is one that Tertullian does not
pursue consistently—not only in that he applies it solely to mortal sins, but also
in that he ascribes forgiveness of mortal sins, at least *in abstracto*, to the Church.
To be sure—and this is another truth in a controversial point—he spiritualized
the concept of this Church, replacing the episcopal Church with a spiritual one.
But this idea also immediately becomes tainted and partisan, because who is
this spiritual Church, if not Tertullian and his Montanist confederates?" (*Die alte
Kirche* 3, 476–477.)

1483 The chief catalyst, of course, was the trinitarian disagreements. See
Funk, "Das Indulgenzedikt des Papstes Kallistus," *Theologische Quartalschrift* (1906):
561; Döllinger, *Hippolytus und Kallistus*, 229–230.

1484 The schism of Hippolytus left hardly any traces in church literature,
and the fate of Hippolytus himself is very unclear. The works of Hippolytus are
known in many languages—Greek, Latin, Syrian, Arabic, Ethiopian, Slavonic
(Achelis, *Hippolytstudien*, TU 16.4, 1). In recent times fragments of his works have
also been discovered in the Georgian language (N. Marr, *Texts and Research on
Armenian and Georgian Philology. Book 3: Hippolytus. Explanation of the Song of Songs,
According to a 10th-century Manuscript* ["Тексты и разыскания по армяно-грузинской филологии, кн. III. Ипполит. Толкование Песни песней, по рукописи
X века"]). He is also a saint venerated by the entire Church (Achelis, 35–62). But
at the same time Eusebius does not know where he was bishop (*Church History*
6.22), nor do Jerome (*On Illustrious Men*, 61) and others (Achelis 11, 14–15). In

edly was also aware of Callistus's edict, though he does not mention it in his later work, *The Refutation of All Heresies*.[1485] Hippolytus relates that Callistus was the first to begin to show leniency toward sins against chastity, saying that he would grant forgiveness of sins to all.[1486] Hippolytus rebukes Callistus for doing little to safeguard the morals of his flock, not preserving Tradition, not discerning with whom to commune, but granting communion with the Church indiscriminately to all.[1487] Hippolytus also relates another argument which Callistus cited in defense of his disciplinary practice. It was Callistus who applied to the Church Christ's instructions to leave the tares to grow among the wheat—that is, to leave sinners in the Church—and who compared the Church to the ark of Noah, in which were dogs, wolves, ravens, and all things both clean and unclean. In the Church, Callistus said, it must be the same.[1488] This

---

the words of Döllinger, in church history Hippolytus stands ἀπάτωρ, ἀμήτωρ, ἀγενεαλόγητος [fatherless, motherless, without genealogy] (*Hippolytus und Kallistus*, 54). Achelis diligently compiled all traces of Hippolytus in historic manuscripts (42–43, 44, 32–34), but these traces are very few. Archpriest Ivantsov-Platonov attempts to explain this circumstance in *Heresies and Schisms*, 100–102. Of the disputes between Hippolytus and Callistus we learn only from the reports of Hippolytus himself. See *The Refutation of All Heresies* 9.11–12. A fairly detailed commentary on these reports is presented in the work cited by Döllinger, 115 ff.

1485 Vgl. Rolffs, *Das Indulg.-Edict*, TU 11, 88, 134–135.

1486 Hippolytus, *The Refutation of All Heresies* 9 [7].12: "πρῶτος τὰ πρὸς τὰς ἡδονὰς τοῖς ἀνθρώποις συγχωρεῖν ἐπενόησε, λέγων πᾶσιν ὑπ' αὐτοῦ ἀφίεσθαι ἁμαρτίας [he first invented the device of conceding to men their indulgence in sensual pleasures, saying that all had their sins forgiven by himself]" (PG 16:3386a). The word πρῶτος [first] can hardly serve as sufficient grounds to suppose that Hippolytus likewise attests that the disciplinary measures of Callistus were a break with earlier church tradition. Cf. Esser, *Die Bussschriften Tertullians*, 28.

1487 Idem: "Ταῦτα μὲν οὖν ὁ θαυμασιώτατος Κάλλιστος συνεστήσατο, οὗ διαμένει τὸ διδασκαλεῖον φυλάσσον τὰ ἔθη καὶ τὴν παράδοσιν, μὴ διακρῖνον, τίσι δεῖ κοινωνεῖν, πᾶσι δ' ἀκρίτως προσφέρων τὴν κοινωνίαν [that most astonishing Callistus established, whose school continues, preserving its customs and tradition, not discerning with whom they ought to communicate, but indiscriminately offering communion to all]" (PG 16:3387b).

1488 Idem (PG 16:3386c). Rolffs includes the comparison of the Church with the ark in his reconstruction of the edict of Callistus, surmising that it is this Old Testament likeness of the Church which Tertullian is contrasting to the New Tes-

comparison vividly conveys Callistus's concept of the Church as a
society not only of saints, but also of sinners.[1489] Callistus apparently expressed this view bluntly, and this concept of the Church is
linked to the lenient disciplinary decrees of Callistus of which Hippolytus relates. These highly lenient disciplinary decrees of Callistus and the abuses that accompanied these decrees evoked a protest
from Hippolytus, who headed a separate community.[1490] He does
not even call the community of Callistus a Church, but a school,

---

tament figure of "the Body of Christ" (*Das Indulgenz-Edict*, TU 11.3, 68, Anm. 3).

1489 "In diesem Satze erscheint der Abfall von dem alten Kirchenbegriff
vollendet," says Harnack (*Dogmengeschichte* 1, 409). Cf. also Harnack's observations that follow. But regarding the comparison of the Church with Noah's ark
which Callistus employed it should be noted that Tertullian also was not unfamiliar with this comparison in his earlier works. There we read, "Ecclesia est
arcae figura [the Church is a type of the ark]" (*On Baptism* 8 [CSEL 20.1:208.1]).
"Navicula illa figuram ecclesiae praeferebat, quod in mari id est saeculo, flucti-
bus id est persecutionibus et tentationibus inquietatur [But that little ship did
present a figure of the Church, in that she is disquieted "in the sea," that is, in
the world, "by the waves," that is, by persecutions and temptations]" (Ibid. 12
[CSEL 20.1:212.3–5]). Christian thinking employed the image of Noah's ark
very early on to elucidate the idea of the Church (see Archimandrite Christopher,
Early Christian Iconography as an Expression of the Credal Identity of the Early Church
["Древнехристианская иконография как выражение древнецерковного ве-
росознания"] [Moscow: 1887], 205). This symbol is encountered in the earliest
catacomb depictions (Maurus Wolten, *Die römischen Katakomben und ihre Bedeutung
für die katholische Lehre von der Kirche* [Frankfurt a. M.: 1866], 28–30). This symbol,
naturally, expresses first and foremost the thought that salvation is impossible
outside the Church (cf. M. Wolter, op. cit., 29)—that is, the thought with which
Tertullian's Montanist arguments in *On Modesty* are not in agreement, which is
why they cannot be viewed as a reflection of the early Church-wide view of
the Church. But the idea which Callistus emphasizes in the image of the ark is
likewise not foreign to the mind of the early Church. Tertullian himself wrote:
"Viderimus enim si secundum arcae typum et corvus et milvus et lupus et canis
et serpens in ecclesia erit certe idololatres in arcae typo non habetur [We will see
to it, if, after the type of the Ark, there shall be in the Church raven, kite, wolf,
dog, and serpent. At all events, an idolater is not found in the type of the Ark]"
(*On Idolatry* 24 [CSEL 20.1:58.4–6]). Cf.: "De arca Noë Ecclesiae typo patrum
sententiae. Sanctorum patrum opuscula selecta in usum praesertim studiosorum
theologiae edidit." H. Hurter, vol. 3 (Oeniponti: 1868), 217 sqq.; Loofs, *Leitfaden
der Dogmengeschichte* §29.2b, 208.

1490 Cf. Adhémar d' Alès, *La Théologie de saint Hippolyte*, 46–47.

as the heretical communities were called.[1491] Hippolytus calls only his own community a Church, and suggests that the followers of Callistus be called Callistians.[1492]

But this division between Hippolytus and Callistus over questions of church discipline was of an entirely different nature than the disagreement between Callistus and Tertullian.[1493] There we see a profound and fundamental difference: a difference in the dogmatic doctrine concerning the Church. *The Refutation of All Heresies* by no means shows Hippolytus to have based his denial of Callistus's disciplinary institutions on the same concept of the Church which Tertullian contrasts to Callistus. Hippolytus disapproves of the disciplinary measures of Callistus **not for dogmatic reasons**, but more for practical ones. He holds these decrees to be harmful to the moral state of the members of the Church.[1494] Hippolytus believed that no concessions should be made to the spirit of the times. He was a zealot of higher Christian ideals, strict with himself and others, and recognized no allowances for circumstances.[1495] But even he saw with grief and chagrin that strict ideals for living attract few devotees. The strict discipline of his community seemed too heavy a burden to many, and its numbers steadily decreased, while the

---

1491 Hippolytus, *The Refutation of All Heresies* 9 [7].12: "Τοιαῦτα ὁ γόης, τολμήσας συνεστήσατο διδασκαλεῖον κατὰ τῆς Ἐκκλησίας [The impostor Callistus, having ventured on such opinions, established a school of theology in antagonism to the Church]" (PG 16:3386a). Concerning the name διδασκαλεῖον see Döllinger, 102 and Anm. 118; Ivantsov-Platonov, *Heresies and Schisms,* 93–94n44.

1492 Idem (3387–3388b): "ἀφ' οὗ καὶ τὴν τοῦ ὀνόματος μετέσχον ἐπίκλησιν καλεῖσθαι διὰ τὸν πρωτοστατήσαντα τῶν τοιούτων ἔργων Κάλλιστον καλλιστιανοί [And from him they have derived the denomination of their cognomen; so that, on account of Callistus being a foremost champion of such practices, they should be called Callistians.]."

1493 Cf. Adhémar d' Alès, *La Théologie de saint Hippolyte,* 68–70; Schwane, *Dogmengeschichte der vornic. Zeit,* 484.

1494 Hippolytus, *On the Refutation of All Heresies* 9 [7].12: "οὗ διαμένει τὸ διδασκαλεῖον φυλάσσον τὰ ἔθη καὶ τὴν παράδοσιν [whose school continues, preserving its customs and tradition]" (PG 16:3387b). Vgl. G. Volkmar, *Hippolytus und die römischen Zeitgenossen,* 107.

1495 Ivantsov-Platonov, *Heresies and Schisms,* 106.

community of Callistus with its more lenient discipline continued to grow.[1496]

In Tertullian's works, denying 'the power of the keys' to the bishop is inseparably linked to the overarching doctrine concerning the Church. In Hippolytus not only do we not find the same, but on the contrary he is wholly in agreement with his opponent on the question of episcopal authority.[1497] In the foreword to *The Refutation of All Heresies* Hippolytus calls bishops the successors of the apostolic grace of "high-priesthood and the office of teaching": the bishops are "guardians of the Church," and "must not be found deficient in vigilance."[1498]

Thus we see that in the first quarter of the third century there was a doctrine expressed concerning the Church as **a society that constantly advances in perfection by the aid of the grace**

1496   Hippolytus, *On the Refutation of All Heresies* 9 [7].12: "Οὗ τῷ ὅρῳ ἀρεσκόμενοι πολλοὶ συνείδησιν πεπληγότες ἅμα τε καὶ ὑπὸ πολλῶν αἱρέσεων ἀποβληθέντες, τινὲς δὲ καὶ ἐπὶ καταγνώσει ἔκβλητοι τῆς Ἐκκλησίας ὑφ' ἡμῶν γενόμενοι, προσχωρήσαντες αὐτοῖς ἐπλήθυναν τὸ διδασκαλεῖον αὐτοῦ [And many persons were gratified with his regulation, as being stricken in conscience, and at the same time having been rejected by numerous sects; while also some of them, in accordance with our condemnatory sentence, had been by us forcibly ejected from the Church. Now such disciples as these passed over to these followers of Callistus, and served to crowd his school]" (PG 16:3386b).

1497   Cf. Harnack, *Dogmengeschichte*⁴ 1, 403, Anm. 2.

1498   Hippolytus, *On the Refutation of All Heresies. The Proœmium*: "Ταῦτα δὲ ἕτερος οὐκ ἐλέγξει, ἢ τὸ ἐν Ἐκκλησίᾳ παραδοθὲν ἅγιον Πνεῦμα οὗ τυχόντες πρότεροι οἱ ἀπόστολοι μετέδοσαν τοῖς ὀρθῶς πεπιστευκόσιν· ὧν ἡμεῖς διάδοχοι τυγχάνοντες τῆς τε αὐτῆς χάριτος μετέχοντες ἀρχιερατείας τε καὶ διδασκαλίας καὶ φρουροὶ τῆς Ἐκκλησίας λελογισμένοι οὐκ ὀφθαλμῷ νυστάζομεν, οὐδὲ λόγον ὀρθὸν σιωπῶμεν... ἀλλὰ τοῦ ἰδίου καιροῦ τὰ μέτρα ἐπιτελοῦντες, καὶ ὅσα παρέξει τὸ ἅγιον Πνεῦμα πᾶσιν ἀφθόνως κοινωνοῦντες [But none will refute these, save the Holy Spirit bequeathed unto the Church, which the Apostles, having in the first instance received, have transmitted to those who have rightly believed. But we, as being their successors, and as participators in this grace, high-priesthood, and office of teaching, as well as being reputed guardians of the Church, must not be found deficient in vigilance, or disposed to suppress correct doctrine... but careful to complete the measure of our particular opportunity, and to impart to all without grudging whatever the Holy Ghost supplies]" (ANF 5:10; PG 16:3020c).

of God. The Montanist doctrine on the sanctity of the Church in the sense of the moral purity of the members comprising it was condemned as a heresy. The Church opened the door of repentance to all sinners, and the bishop is declared to be the organ of repentance.[1499]

The thoughts expressed by Callistus and in part by Hippolytus arouse numerous objections from Protestant church historians. In the polemics between Tertullian and Callistus, Protestant scholarship takes the side of the zealous African rigorist, which is quite logical. For, as we have already had occasion to state, in modern Western church historical scholarship the almost universally accepted view is that the Christian Church of the first two centuries was a series of sectarian groups with a charismatic organization, or rather with no organization at all. The Church conceived itself as a society of perfect saints, which excluded any member who had gravely sinned. Given this view it makes perfect sense that Tertullian and Montanism in general are represented as being almost unshakably grounded in the more ancient thinking of the Church—grounded in Tradition. He was the reaction of early Christian piety to the secularization of the Church, which is necessarily linked to consolidation of the position of the catholic Church. To reject and condemn Montanism would be for the Church to condemn its own past.[1500] The episcopacy formed in the second century, which supplanted the charismatic organization, caused a transformation of the concept of the Church. In particular, the declaration of a right to "the power of the keys" is merely the ambitious claim of an episcopacy that was gaining momentum, but which had no historical

----

1499 Böhringer compares the significance of Montanism with the significance of Gnosticism: "In opposition to the Montanist idea of a Church whose sanctity was contingent on the purity of life of its members, it was contended that the sanctity of the Church depends on possessing the means of sanctification—that is, the sacraments. Gnosticism was an intellectual phenomenon, and it resulted in the bishop being acknowledged to possess the authority to teach by virtue of apostolic succession. The disciplinary phenomenon of Montanism resulted in 'the power of the keys' likewise being connected with the episcopacy" (*Die alte Kirche* 3, 482–483).

1500 Loofs, *Leitfaden der Dogmengeschichte*[4] §24, 172.

basis.[1501] In the first two centuries the episcopacy had hardly any of
the rights of the apostles; the Church was governed by the charismatics. It was to them, not the bishops, that "the power of the keys"
belonged. Consequently, when in *On Modesty* Tertullian declared
that the Church could forgive sins only *per spiritalem hominem*,[1502] and
not through the bishop, he was grounded in the history of the early
Church. Consequently, the question of the bishop's "power of the
keys" is inseparably linked to one more overarching and fundamental: did the Church of the first two centuries think of itself as a sectarian spiritual society of saints; or, in accordance with the apostolic
teaching, since the very beginning of its historical existence had it
always conceived itself to be a moral organization (the Body), in
which its members, closely united to one another, led by the Holy
Spirit, attain unto the measure of the stature of Christ? Protestant
scholarship almost unanimously supports the former understanding of church consciousness in the first two centuries, denies the
bishop's "power of the keys," and in general rejects the inherence
of the Sacrament of Repentance in the Christian Church. But are
the historical data really so indisputable and self-evident as to place
history and dogmatic theology in so adversarial a position? The historical data are so incomplete and ambiguous that not only people
of different confessions, but even scholars of the same creed are
at odds in their interpretations. In any case, the question of "the
power of the keys" in the first two centuries cannot be conclusively
resolved in the Protestant sense: considerable data can be found to
support the opposite conclusion, and nothing compels us to assume

---

1501 "Diese Ansicht wird durch die Geschichte wideilegt, und die ihr zu Grun-
de liegende Deutung der Aussprüch Christi ist unrichtig" (Ritschl, *Die Entstehung
der altkath. Kirche*, 372. Vgl. 372–388). Harnack, *Dogmengeschichte* 1, 403, Anm. 2;
Tertullian, *De paenitentia. De pudicitia.* Herausgegeben von Lie. Erwin Preuschen
(Freiburg i. B.: 1891), Einleitung, VII–VIII. (In the foreword to the new edition—
Tübingen: 1910, V–VI—Preuschen speaks considerably less decisively.) Cf. E.
Preuschen, "Zur Kirchenpolitik des Bischofs Kallist," in *Zeitschrift für die neutestam.
Wissenschaft* (1910), 154–158.

1502 "By means of a spiritual man." Tertullian, *On Modesty* 21:17.

this radical change in the history of the concept of the Church of which the Protestants speak.[1503]

First and foremost it must be noted that **nowhere are there any positive data that speak of the charismatics possessing "the power of the keys."**[1504] To judge the situation in the second century based on Tertullian, who apostatized from the Church, is groundless at best. Based on what we have in *On Modesty* we can only surmise the following: the Church considered "the power of the keys" the right of the bishop, while Montanism denied the bishop this right. Tertullian's reasoning in *On Modesty* (21) does not echo the common conviction of the early Church, but is merely the fruit of his Montanist delusion.[1505] But if we subject the testimony of Tertullian to an in-depth analysis, it says much in favor of "the power of the keys" belonging to the bishop even in the first centuries. We have already cited testimony from Tertullian where he asserts the right of the bishop to forgive less grave sins. It is worth noting that this testimony is given in his Montanist work *On Modesty*. But if in the first two centuries "the power of the keys" was solely in the hands of the charismatics, it is quite unclear why the bishop was still able to absolve lesser sins. If in the first two centuries the bishop only celebrated the liturgy and served as financial officer of the Christian community, it would have been more natural for him to possess no "power of the keys" whatsoever, with regard to sins of any kind. Tertullian limits the bishop's "power of the keys" to less grave sins; to mortal sins this power does not extend. But, as we have already demonstrated, the difference between mortal and non-mortal sins was very, very relative: at any rate, it was not a definite rule, founded upon any dogmatic theory. But if there was ever

---

1503 Catholic scholarship raises some very serious objections to the customary view among Protestant scholars, and introduces radical changes to it. See for example the article by Prof. Dr. Schanz, "Die Absolutionsgewalt in der alten Kirche," *Theologische Quartalschrift* (1897): 27–69. Here the essence of the Protestant views on the matter are presented in brief (27–29).

1504 Schanz gives an analysis of the pertinent passages of Holy Scripture, albeit with Catholic tendencies. See *Theologische Quartalschrift* (1897): 30–43.

1505 Vgl. F. Frank, *Die Bussdisciplin der Kirche*, 79, 81.

a place where mortal and non-mortal sins were not differentiated, Tertullian's entire construct collapses. If a bishop ever forgave a mortal sin, from a dogmatic standpoint this completely destroys the Protestant concept of the charismatic element as an essential condition for possession of "the power of the keys" in the early Church.

Next we must observe the following. Tertullian is aware of the right of the Church to forgive even mortal sins. In confirmation of this, as we have seen, he even quotes a Montanist prophet.[1506] But Tertullian limits this right to the church of the Montanists, where "the power of the keys" belongs solely to the spiritual man.[1507] In Tertullian, the terms *spiritalis ecclesia* and *spiritalis homo* signify a Montanist who acknowledges the revelation of the Paraclete. But this revelation of the Paraclete is a new era in the life of the Christian Church. The Church that does not acknowledge this revelation, obviously, had been a *multitudo psychicorum* even before this. Prior to Montanus there were no spiritual men and there was no spiritual church, and at that time, obviously, it was the *ecclesia numerus episcoporum* [the Church which consists of a number of bishops] that was able to forgive sins. In his work *Scorpiace* Tertullian considers the Church the holder of "the power of the keys"; nothing at all is said of any limitations to this authority.[1508] Furthermore,

---

1506 Tertullian, *On Modesty* 21: "Sed habet, inquis, potestatem ecclesia delicta donandi. Hoc ego magis et agnosco et dispono, qui ipsum paracletum in prophetis novis habeo dicentem: potest ecclesia donare delictum, sed non faciam, ne et alia delinquant ['But,' you say, 'the Church has the power of forgiving sins.' This I acknowledge and adjudge more {than you do; I} who have the Paraclete Himself in the persons of the new prophets, saying, 'The Church has the power to forgive sins; but I will not do it, lest they commit others withal.']" (CSEL 20.1:269.22–25). Bolotov is therefore right in observing: "In not allowing for forgiveness of 'mortal' sins, Tertullian is proceeding not from any dogmatic presumptions that would limit the authority of the Church. ... This strictness is merely a matter of the pastoral wisdom of the Montanist primates" (*Lectures*, 2nd ed., 365). Cf. P. Batiffol, *Études d'histoire et de théologie positive*, 97.

1507 Tertullian, *On Modesty* 21 (CSEL 20.1:270.1–11).

1508 Tertullian, *Scorpiace* 10: "Memento claves ejus hic dominum Petro et per ejum ecclesiae relinquisse, quas hic unusquisque interrogatus atque confessus feret secum [remember that the Lord left here to Peter and through him to the Church, the keys of it, which every one who has been here put to the question,

it should be remembered that Montanist prophecy is not a phenomenon identical to the charismatic element of early Christianity; and if Tertullian ascribes "the power of the keys" exclusively to the prophets of the Paraclete it by no means follows that prior to Tertullian this authority in the Church belonged to the charismatics.[1509] For Tertullian himself calls the discipline of the Paraclete "new." After all, Tertullian does not employ against Callistus his favorite *argumentum praescriptionis,* which he employs in other instances! In *On Modesty* Tertullian is not disputing the "novelty" of Callistus, but rather his own pre-Montanist views on questions of church discipline. Between his *On Modesty* and *On Repentance* there is a clear contradiction—one which quite astonished the blessed Jerome,[1510] and which many recent scholars observe.[1511] The Church did not alter its understanding of its own sanctity: it was Tertullian who, having strayed into Montanism, altered his former convictions regarding the Church. He himself admits that he formerly thought as the psy-

---

and also made confession, will carry with him]" (CSEL 20.1:167.24–26). Does this not contradict what Tertullian wrote previously? "Dabo tibi claves, non ecclesiae ['I will give to you the keys,' not to the Church]" (*On Modesty* 21 [CSEL 20.1:270.9–10]).

1509 Schanz rightly notes: "Caution should be exercised in supposing that in this pseudo-prophetic movement we are dealing with the last vestiges of the ancient doctrine of forgiveness of sins through spiritual men" ("Die Absolutionsgewalt in der alten Kirche," *Theologische Quartalschrift* [1897]: 46–47). See Smirnov, *The Spiritual Father,* 242: "The great Church probably never adhered to a doctrine alleging that the right to bind and to loose belonged solely to one who was 'spiritual'—an apostle or a prophet."

1510 Jerome, *Letter of Jerome to Pope Damasus* 21.3.2: "Vehementer admiror Tertullianum in eo libro, quem de pudicitia adversum paenitentiam scripsit et sententiam veterem nova opinione dissolvit [I am extremely astonished at Tertullian in that book, in which he wrote on modesty against repentance and refuted an old way of thinking by a new opinion]" (CSEL 54:115.17–19).

1511 Tillemont, *Memoires,* vol. 3, 220; P. Monceaux, *Histoire littéraire de l'Afrique chrét,* vol. 1, 432–433; Esser, *Die Bussschriften Tertullians,* 8 ff., 12; Preuschen, "Zur Kirchenpolitik des Bischofs Kallist," *Zeitschrift für die neutestamentliche Wissenschaft* (1910): 135, 143–144; Bruders, "Mt. 16, 19; 18, 18 und In. 20, 22, 23 in frühchristlicher Ausegung," *Zeitschrift für katholische Theologie* (1910): 668; Bardenhewer, *Patrologie* §50.5, 163; Adhémar d'Alès, "Tertullien et Calliste," *Revue d'histoire ecclésiastique* (1912): 227, 241, 256.

chics, and that he expects to be reproached for thoughtlessness for having altered his views.[1512] Why depict Tertullian, a Montanist, as an adherent of the views of the early Church on the sanctity of the Church, when he himself does not consider himself to be one?! He himself makes it clear that the first two centuries of church history are on the side of his opponents.

In church historical scholarship, recently the **martyrs** or **confessors** have been cited as the chief proof of the thesis that in the Church of the first two centuries "the power of the keys" belonged only to the charismatics, and not to the hierarchy. In ancient times the confessors or martyrs were viewed specifically as a particular kind of spiritual men—as charismatics. We see this view in the account of the martyrs of Lyon,[1513] in Tertullian's epistle to the martyrs,[1514] and in many later historical manuscripts.[1515] It is known that the martyrs were intimately involved in the forgiveness of grave sins. From this it is concluded that only the martyrs or charismatics in general possessed "the power of the keys," and that it was only after contending with the charismatics that the hierarchy appropriated for itself this power which it had not formerly possessed.

1512 Tertullian, *On Modesty* 1: "Erit et hic adversus psychicos titulus, adversus meae quoque sententiae retro penes illos societatem, quo magis hoc mihi in notam levitatis obiectent [This too, therefore, shall be a count in my indictment against the Psychics; against the fellowship of sentiment also which I myself formerly maintained with them; in order that they may the more cast this in my teeth for a mark of fickleness]" (CSEL 20.1:220.17–19). One can hardly agree with Funk when he alleges that the change in convictions to which Tertullian here refers pertains not to the question of repentance, but to his general stance on the Church after his transition to Montanism. See *Kirchengeschichtliche Abhandlungen und Untersuchungen* 1, 166. Vgl. *Theologische Quartalschrift* (1906): 545. For an analysis of this view, see Adhémar d'Alès, *Revue d'histoire ecclésiastique* (1912): 236–240.

1513 Eusebius, *Church History* 5.1.9, 10, 29 (GrchSch. 9.1:404.20–21; 406.2, 3; 412.28–29).

1514 Tertullian, *To the Martyrs* 1, 3 (PL 1:620a, 624b). Cf. *On Modesty* 22: "Christus in martyre est [Christ is in the martyr]" (CSEL 20.1:272.10).

1515 Concerning the charismatism of the martyrs, see Smirnov, *The Spiritual Father*, 236–237; Rolffs, *Das Ind.-Ed.*, 42; Schanz, *Theologische Quartalschrift* (1897): 55–57; Harnack, *Dogmengeschichte* 1, 441, Anm. 1.

But this citation of the martyrs is highly unconvincing, as well. Very few historical accounts exist, and they contain no data to support such broad generalizations.

The first report of the martyrs receiving the lapsed back into the Church is found in the aforementioned account of the martyrs of Lyon. There we read the following: "[The martyrs] defended all, but accused none. They absolved all, but bound none (ἔλυον ἅπαντας, ἐδεσμεύον δὲ οὐδένα). And they prayed for those who had inflicted cruelties upon them, even as Stephen, the perfect witness. ... They did not boast over the fallen, but helped them in their need with those things in which they themselves abounded, having the compassion of a mother, and shedding many tears on their account before the Father. They asked for life, and he gave it to them, and they shared it with their neighbors. Victorious over everything, they departed to God. Having always loved peace, and having commended peace to us they went in peace to God, leaving no sorrow to their mother, nor division or strife to the brethren, but joy and peace and concord and love."[1516] But here there are no grounds whatsoever to suppose that only the martyrs, and not the hierarchs, possessed "the power of the keys." On the contrary, no mention is made of independent forgiveness of sins whatsoever: the martyrs merely defended and prayed for all. This testimony may rather be seen as an indication that the confessors **merely interceded** for the lapsed to be received: they commended peace, and left behind joy, peace, concord, and love.[1517] In any case, from a historical standpoint this testimony is highly ambiguous, and to reconstruct a picture of second-century church discipline from this indistinct piece of the mosaic is risky at best.[1518]

1516 Eusebius, *Church History* 5.2.5–8 (NPNF² 1:218; GrchSch. 9.1:430–431). Eusebius cites these words "on account of the inhuman and unmerciful disposition of those who, after these events, acted unsparingly toward the members of Christ."

1517 Vgl. Schanz, *Theologische Quartalschrift* (1897): 51. Harnack makes this observation: "Er sucht dem Briefe Zeugnisse zu entnehmen, dass die Konfessoren die Wiederaufnahme definitiv Gefallener betrieben und erreicht hätten, aber die von ihm beigebrachten Stellen reden davon nicht." (*Lapsi*, RE 3, Bd. 11, 286.)

1518 Smirnov gives a supremely contradictory depiction of second-century

Already the anti-Montanist writer Apollonius, after describing the mores of adherents of the new prophecy, inquires with irony: "Which of these forgives the sins of the other? Does the prophet the robberies of the martyr, or the martyr the covetousness of the prophet?"[1519] These words mock the Montanist principle by which the power to forgive sins in the Church belongs not to the hierarchy, but to adherents of the "new" prophecy. The Church, clearly, acknowledged no such principle.[1520] Finally, we find certain data on the same question in Tertullian. He too is aware of the martyrs' part in penitential discipline.[1521] Tertullian also speaks of the Holy

---

discipline. See *The Spiritual Father,* 231–232: "It is surmised that in maintaining strict discipline toward the lapsed, in order to relax it the Church resorted to special revelations, as well as to the intervention of the martyrs on behalf of the lapsed" (231). Cf. Harnack, *Lapsi* RE 3, BD 11, 286: "It is clear that the martyrs alone were the stewards of this affair, because it was they who began to mitigate the strictness of the third-century Church toward the lapsed. There was obviously no higher authority than they that could have verified and affirmed their decision: the bishops did not consider this their right." A mere three lines later we read: "But, on the other hand, the decision of the martyrs was not of a universally binding and absolute nature: it merely authorized, but did not necessarily compel, the church community to receive one who had lapsed. ... This latter decision remained in the power of the bishop."

1519 Eusebius, op. cit. 5.18.7 (NPNF² 1:236; GrchSch. 9.1:476.3–5).

1520 Vgl. Schanz, *Theologische Quartalschrift* (1897): 52.

1521 Tertullian, *On Modesty* 22: "Statim ambiunt moechi, statim adeunt fornicatores, jam preces circumsonant, jam lacrimae circumstagnant maculati cujusque, nec ulli magis aditum carceris redimunt quam qui ecclesiam perdiderunt [immediately adulterers beset him, fornicators gain access to him; instantly prayers echo around him; instantly pools of tears of all the polluted surround him; nor are there any who are more diligent in purchasing entrance into the prison than they who have lost the Church]" (CSEL 20.1:271.14–17). According to *On Repentance* 9, a penitent must "presbyteris advolvi, et caris Dei adgeniculari [throw himself before the presbyters and fall prostrate before the knees of the dear ones of God]" (PL 1:1244a, c). In a comment Le Prieur explains: "Putarim ego per caros Dei intelligendos esse martyres [I would that that 'the dear ones of God' are to be understood as being the martyrs]." Preuschen echoes this same view. See *Zeitschrift für die neutestam. Wissenschaft* (1910): 154–155. *Cari Dei* could be taken to mean people of exalted life in general, whose prayer "availeth much" (Jas. 5:16); but of course this does not exclude the martyrs. Vgl. Rolffs, *Das Indulg-Ed.* TU 11.3, 33, Anm. 3; Böhringer, *Die alte Kirche* 3, 477–478. See also the mate-

Spirit living in the martyrs. But it is noteworthy that nowhere does Tertullian consider the martyrs the exclusive organ for remission of sins: he lists them along with members of the hierarchy, listing the actions of the Holy Spirit in the martyrs, but saying nothing of forgiveness of sins.[1522] But particular attention should be given to Tertullian the Montanist. Sometimes Callistus is portrayed as placing the decision of the bishop between the martyrs' decree that a sinner be received and his reception by the community.[1523] But historical sources utterly refute this concept. Tertullian rebukes Callistus not only for appropriating for himself the right to forgive sins—a right belonging to the Paraclete alone—but also because he extends this authority to the martyrs of the "sensual" Church.[1524] If the martyrs had formerly been the exclusive organ of remission of sins by virtue of their charisma, Tertullian would have defended this right of theirs and would have admonished Callistus for appropriating that which belonged to the martyrs. But Tertullian disputes the right of the martyrs to have any part in forgiving mortal sins. Even the martyrs have no right to forgive mortal sins, and the bishop cannot permit them to do so.[1525] "Let it suffice to the martyr to have purged his own sins: it is the part of ingratitude or of pride to lavish upon others also what one has obtained at a high price. Who has redeemed another's death by his own, but the Son of God alone?" The Son of God was "Himself pure from sin. ... If, however, you are a sinner, how will the oil of your puny torch (*faculae*) be able to suffice for you and for me? ... If Christ is in the martyr for this reason, that the

---

rial collected by Carl Holl, in *Enthusiasmus und Bussgewalt beim griechischen Mönchtum* (Leipzig: 1898), 129, Anm. 1.

1522 Vgl. Schanz, *Theologische Quartalschrift* (1897): 57: "In general, wherever the charismatism of the martyrs is mentioned, nothing is said to imply that their charisma served as the basis of their power to forgive sins."

1523 Smirnov, *The Spiritual Father*, 233.

1524 Tertullian, *On Modesty* 22: "At tu jam et in martyras tuos effundis hanc potestatem [But you go so far as to lavish this power upon martyrs withal!]" (CSEL 20.1:271.12). See the observation of Schanz (*Theologische Quartalschrift* [1897]: 52–53).

1525 Ibid. 22: "Quis permittit homini donare quae Deo reservanda sunt? [Who permits man to bestow what is to be reserved for God?]" (CSEL 20.1:271.27).

martyr may absolve adulterers and fornicators, let him tell publicly
the secrets of the heart. ... For thus it was that the Lord Jesus Christ
showed His power" in healing the paralytic (see from Mt. 9:4 on).
He showed His power by a miracle, and without this proof no one
may be believed to have the power to forgive sins. Christ was able
to demonstrate His power, whereas the martyrs cannot. Martyrdom
is another baptism; and if I can forgive sins after the second baptism, why can I not do the same after the first?[1526] Thus, Tertullian
disputes the right of the confessors to participate in any way in the
forgiving of mortal sins.[1527]

This fact decisively contradicts the modern view of Protestant
scholars, according to which "the power of the keys" in the first
two centuries was linked to spiritual gifts. Both Tertullian and the
Montanists in general, who denied the hierarchy "the power of the
keys," adhered to the doctrine that, following its secularization, hierarchical church authority in its entirety appropriated the rights
of the charismatics. If this had been so, if Tertullian the Montanist
had indeed been grounded in the purported tradition of the early
Church, he would not have written the twenty-second chapter of
On Modesty, where he disputes the rights of the martyrs to forgive
mortal sins. For then, from the standpoint of Tertullian, the martyrs' part in forgiveness of sins would have been a remnant of the
ancient, exclusively charismatic organization so dear to the hearts
of Protestant scholars, which the psychics had distorted.[1528] This
circumstance astonishes Preuschen, who acknowledges that there

---

1526 Ibid. 22 (ANF 4:100; CSEL 20.1:272.1–28).

1527 Although Tertullian highly esteems confessorship, Böhringer states that
his stance changed if a confessor wished to release others from sins, and even
mortal sins, at that. In Tertullian's eyes this undermined discipline and intruded
on the domain of divine authority in a way that was no better than forgiveness of
sins by a bishop. See *Die alte Kirche* 3, 478–479. See Bolotov, *Lectures*, 2nd ed., 365.

1528 The particularly close connection between the martyrs and penitential
discipline, Harnack opines, is namely "ein archäistischer Rest, der sich aber bis
zum Ende des 3. Jahrhunderts gehalten hat" (*Novatian*, RE 3, Bd. 14, 229). Cf.
Tertullian. De paenitentia. De pudicitia. Herausgeg. von Erwin Prleuschen (Freiburg I. B.:
1891). Einleitung, VIII, "Reste enthusiastischer Verfassung." The second edition
from 1910 no longer contains anything of the sort.

is no possible explanation for it, since the Montanists as such did not deny the possibility of forgiving sins.[1529] There can be but one explanation: the Church of Christ was never a charismatic organization, and "the power of the keys" was not connected with spiritual gifts in the early Church. All this was invented by German Protestants seventeen centuries after these historical events, based on limited and very vague evidence that could even be interpreted to mean the opposite.

The martyrs were highly venerated in the early Church, and it may be they whom Tertullian terms *cari Dei* [the dear ones of God]. It is quite logical that their intercession and mediation had great significance for the restoration to communion with the Church of a member who had sinned and then repented, but there are no grounds for ascribing to them "the power of the keys."[1530] This power belonged to the bishop as a successor of the apostles. The Roman bishop Callistus did not introduce a new doctrine about "the power of the keys" in the Church belonging to the bishop, and the Montanists disputed this doctrine not because they held the viewpoint of the second-century Church, but only because they were heretics who had introduced the new "revelation" of the Paraclete, which the Church rejected. If Callistus had created a new, hitherto unknown dogmatic doctrine, this doctrine could hardly have been silently accepted by everyone but the Montanists, and Montanism would not have elicited such swift and decisive condem-

---

1529 Preuschen, *Zeitschrift für die neutestamentliche Wissenschaft* (1910), 158–159. Vgl. Schanz, "Die Absolutionsgewalt in der alten Kirche," *Theologische Quartalschrift* (1897): 57.

1530 Funk, having briefly indicated the historical accounts of the martyrs' participation in penitential discipline, states that certain accounts do indeed contain words that suggest an authority to remit sins. Sometimes the martyrs expressed claims to that right, and sometimes it was practiced. But this as a rule is difficult to accept, as the evidence cited is insufficient for this. The evidence would also make sense in another instance, since intercession with certainty of what was expected and what previously nearly always met with success could be denoted as a bestowal of peace or as remission of sins. ... Furthermore, on the other hand, the right of the bishop is also expressed. See *Zur altchristlichen Bussdisciplin. Kirchengeschichtliche Abhandlungen und Untersuchungen* 1, 180–181. Vgl. 176.

nation in both East and West.[1531] Montanism was not the Church
of the first and second centuries in the third century. True, it stood
in opposition to the increasing decline of Christian morals, but like
all rigorism it founded its demand for greater moral strictness upon
dogmatic grounds unknown to the early Church. Such were the
doctrine of the sanctity of the Church in the sense of the moral perfection of her members, the ascribing of "the power of the
keys" solely to the Montanist prophets, and the denial of this power
to the hierarchy of the psychics.[1532] These points were as yet almost
undeveloped in the dogmatic theology of the Church; the concept
of the sanctity of the Church had not been precisely and definitively formulated. But when Montanism definitively and abruptly
formulated its false doctrine of the sanctity of the Church, church
thought focused on this subject, and the Orthodox development
of the concept of the sanctity of the Church was undertaken, in
connection with the question of who in the Church possessed "the
power of the keys." In the first quarter of the third century, only the
first steps had been taken. We can see how little positive dogmatic
content the surviving anti-Montanist manuscripts yet contain, and
how the dogmatic thinking of the Church as yet had no well-trod-
den paths and ready arguments.

This we have said primarily of the **Western** representatives
of church theological thought. But then it was Western theological

---

1531 The Antiochian bishop Serapion, a contemporary of Montanism, wrote
in his letter to Caricus and Pontius that the brotherhood throughout the world
considered the Montanist new prophecy an abomination. See Eusebius, *Church
History* 5.19.2 (NPNF[2] 1:237).

1532 Schanz is therefore correct when he writes, "The few testimonials of
post-apostolic times concerning forgiveness of sins by the spiritually gifted cannot be considered sufficient grounds for a theory that overturns every right of
the Church, in spite of the apostolic succession intensely emphasized from the
time of Callistus of Rome; and this is the more true given that the significance
of these testimonials is a subject of debate to this day." A little lower he makes a
most astute and sharp-witted observation: "It would be wrong for anyone to ascribe (*zurückdatiert*) a later institution to the beginning with no further discussion;
but it would be equally false for anyone to wish to find a remnant (*Überbleibsel*) of
early Christianity in heretical movements." ("Die Absolutionsgewalt in der alten
Kirche," *Theologische Quartalschrift* (1897): 68–69.

thought that focused on elucidating the concept of the sanctity of the Church: there the disciplinary controversies so closely connected specifically with the idea of the sanctity of the Church were already known. In the **East** these controversies were unknown, and the Eastern writers had no occasion to make a point of examining the dogmatic question of the sanctity of the Church. Their concept of the sanctity of the Church can only be reconstructed based on scattered, fragmentary comments encountered in works devoted to different questions entirely. If we turn to the writings of those eminent Eastern writers of the second and early third centuries, Clement of Alexandria and Origen, we find a completely different treatment of questions relating to the idea of the sanctity of the Church than those we have seen among Western writers of the same period. In all the reasoning of the Western writers it is impossible not to notice their rather legalistic nature: for them sin is first and foremost a **crime**, and *exomologesis* is **satisfaction**, which is followed by **"pardon."** Mortal sins are too great a crime. The Church cannot forgive sins against God. In Clement of Alexandria we find a completely different understanding of sin. Sins are passions, contrary to human nature; sin is a corruption of nature.[1533] The goal of a man's life is presented as the purification from sinful inclinations, and as advancement in moral and even physical perfection (ἠθικῶς τε καὶ φυσικῶς).[1534] The true gnostic, as Clement describes him, is continually moving forward (προκοπή).[1535] The work of the gnostic, which Clement compares to the art of the physician, must be focused on perfecting others as well (εἰς τὴν τῶν ἀνθρώπων ἐπανόρθωσιν).[1536]

1533 Clement of Alexandria, *Stromata* 2.13.59.6: "Παρὰ φύσιν οὖν κίνησις ψυχῆς κατὰ τὴν πρὸς τὸν λόγον ἀπείθειαν τὰ πάθη [Passions, then, are a perturbation of the soul contrary to nature, in disobedience to reason]" (GrchSch. 15:145.5–6; PG 8:997b).

1534 Idem 4.26.163.1–4 (GrchSch. 15:320–321; PG 8:1373a).

1535 Idem 4.26.170.4 (GrchSch. 15:323.31–324.5; PG 8:1380a).

1536 Idem 7.1.3.4: "Αὐτὸς ὁ γνωστικός, ἀνθρώποις τὴν βελτιωτικὴν ἐνδυκνύμενος θεωρίαν, ὅπως ἂν καὶ παιδεύειν ᾖ τεταγμένος εἰς τὴν τῶν ἀνθρώπων ἐπανόρθωσιν... [and the gnostic himself... exhibits to men the scheme of improvement, in the way in which he has been appointed to discipline men for their amendment]" (GrchSch. 17:4.21–24; PG 9:405a–b).

Clement speaks not of "forgiveness" of sins, but of their healing; furthermore, the more perfect can guide the less perfect, and the latter must seek this guidance.[1537] Clearly, in the system of Clement the Montanist idea of the sanctity of the Church in the sense of the sanctity of its composite members does not and cannot exist.[1538] Only God is perfect (τέλειος), whereas the followers of Christ are inexperienced babes.[1539] The Logos alone is sinless,[1540] but it is typical of all men (ἔμφυτον καὶ κοινόν) to sin.[1541] There are several levels of moral perfection.[1542] To the best of their abilities men must try to sin less (ἐλάχιστα ἁμαρτάνειν), and above all they must strive to become free of passions and vices (τῶν παθῶν καὶ νοσημάτων).[1543] One can only wonder that some make so bold as to call themselves perfect, setting themselves higher than the apostle. Clement cites the words of the apostle Paul (see Phil. 3:12–14) and reasons: he considers himself perfect (τέλειον) because he has renounced his former life and has begun to strive for one that is better—not as one perfect in gnosis, but as one who aspires to perfection. Clearly, by "perfection" he meant renunciation of sins and a rebirth unto faith in the only Perfect One, and the complete abandonment of

---

1537 Clement of Alexandria, *Who is the Rich Man that shall be Saved?* 41.1: "Δεῖ πάντως σε τὸν σοβαρὸν καὶ δυνατὸν καὶ πλούσιον ἐπιστήσασθαι ἑαυτῷ τινα ἄνθρωπον θεοῦ καθάπερ ἀλείπτην καὶ κυβερνήτην [it is by all means necessary for you, who art pompous, and powerful, and rich, to set over yourself some man of God as a trainer and governor.]" (GrchSch. 17:187.8–10; PG 9:645c). Cf. *The Instructor* 1.1; 3.3 (GrchSch. 12:91, 11 ff.; PG 8:252a–b).

1538 Archimandrite Sylvester views the doctrine concerning the Church in Clement and Origen specifically in connection with Montanism. See *The Doctrine Concerning the Church...*, from 224–225 on.

1539 Clement of Alexandria, *The Instructor* 1.7.53.1 (GrchSch. 12:121.23 ff.; PG 8:312c).

1540 Idem 3.12.93.3: "Μόνος γὰρ ἀναμάρτητος αὐτὸς ὁ λόγος" (GrchSch. 12:287.9; PG 8:672c). Cf. *The Instructor* 1.2; 4.1–2 (GrchSch. 12:91.22, 28; PG 8:252c, d).

1541 Idem 3.12.93.3 (GrchSch. 12:287.10–11; PG 8.672c).

1542 Idem 1.2.4.2–3 (GrchSch. 12:91–92; PG 8:253a). Vgl. P. Heinisch, *Der Einfluss Philos auf die älteste christliche Exegese*, 277–278.

1543 Idem 1.2.4.2 (GrchSch. 12:91.28–92.2; PG 8:293a).

former sins.[1544] For Clement, as for the apostle Paul, the Church is a continually maturing organism—a Body.[1545] The Church is holy,[1546] and Christ has her for His bride.[1547] She belongs to Christ alone.[1548] Strict oneness is in keeping with her sanctity. The Church surpasses all things; there is nothing like or equal to her.[1549] But believers will achieve complete perfection only in the celestial Church, where Christ will be in all things. In the temple of God, that is, in the universal Church (ἡ πᾶσα ἐκκλησία), there are also lower mansions.[1550] The earthly Church is only a likeness (εἰκών) of the celestial Church. The earthly Church aspires to perfection, and for this reason we pray that God's will be done on earth as it is in heaven.[1551] In this lies the historical task of the Church—in training up the human race, and in leading it to perfection.[1552] Only in the Church,

---

1544 Clement of Alexandria, *The Instructor* 1.6.52.2–3 (GrchSch. 12:121.8 ff.; PG 8:312c).

1545 Vgl. Harnack, *Dogmengeschichte* 1, 412. For more detail on Clement, see Dr. Karl Holl, *Enthusiasmus und Bussgewalt beim griechischen Mönchtum*, 226–230. Among other things the author writes that, before any other place, it was in Alexandria that people arrived at the idea that "dass der Gläubige nicht ein Fertiger, sondern ein Werdender ist" (226). Indeed, this is of course Clement's idea, but no one arrived at it: rather, the Church had it from the beginning.

1546 Clement of Alexandria, *The Instructor* 1.6.42.1: "ἀκήρατος ὡς παρθένος [pure as a virgin]" (GrchSch. 12:115.14–15; PG 8:300b).

1547 Clement of Alexandria, *Stromata* 3.6.49.3: "τὴν ἰδίαν νύμφην εἶχεν, τὴν ἐκκλησίαν [He had His own bride, the Church]" (GrchSch. 15:218.27–28; PG 8:1152c). Cf. 3.12.80.2 (232.11–12; PG 8:1180b).

1548 Idem 3.11.74.2 (GrchSch. 15:229.19–20; PG 8:1173d).

1549 Idem 7.17.107.6 (GrchSch. 17:76.16 ff.; PG 9:552b).

1550 Idem 6.14.114.1 (GrchSch. 15:489.6–7; PG 9:337b).

1551 Idem 4.8.66.1: "εἰκὼν δὲ τῆς οὐρανίου ἐκκλησίας ἡ ἐπίγειος, ὅπερ εὐχόμεθα καὶ ἐπὶ γῆς γενέσθαι τὸ θέλημα τοῦ θεοῦ ὡς ἐν οὐρανῷ" (GrchSch. 15:278.10–12; PG 8:1277b). Cf. *Stromata* 4.26.172.2 (GrchSch. 15:324.28 ff.; PG 8:1381a).

1552 Clement of Alexandria, *The Instructor* 1.6.27.2: "τὸ βούλημα αὐτοῦ ἀνθρώπων ἐστὶ σωτηρία καὶ τοῦτο ἐκκλησία κέκληται" (GrchSch. 12:106.10–11; PG 8:281b).

having Christ as its Head, do men attain unto perfection.[1553] The
Church gains strength and increases by assimilating the gifts of
God.[1554] "The universal Father is one, and one the universal Word;
and the Holy Spirit is one and the same everywhere, and one is the
only virgin mother. I love to call her 'Church'. This mother, when
alone, had not milk, because alone she was not a wife. But she is at
once virgin and mother—pure as a virgin, loving as a mother. And
calling her children to her, she nurses them with holy milk, viz., with
the babe-like (βρεφώδει) Word. Therefore she had not milk; for the
milk was this child fair and comely, the body of Christ, which nourishes by the Word the young nation (τὴν νεολαίαν). ... The Word
is all to the child, both father and mother and tutor and nurse."[1555]
All this guidance of the members of the Church by the Logos has
a single goal: purification from fleshly passions (ἵνα καταργήσωμεν
τῆς σαρκὸς ἡμῶν τὰ πάθη).[1556] Repentance is one resource for the
moral perfection of the members of the Church, and the church hierarchy serves for this same advancement in perfection.[1557] Clement
cites discourses on repentance from *The Pastor of Hermas* and adds:
he who from among the heathen and from his former life has converted to faith, obtains forgiveness of sins once (ἅπαξ). But he who
has sinned after this, in repenting, even if he should obtain pardon
(κἂν συγγνώμης τυγχάνῃ), ought to be ashamed, since he cannot
be washed (by baptism) unto the remission of sins. True repentance
and spiritual rebirth occur when a person does not return to his

1553 Idem 1.5.18.4: "τελειούμεθα τότε, ὅτε ἐσμὲν ἐκκλησία τὴν κεφαλήν,
τὸν Χριστὸν, ἀπειληφότες [we are then made perfect, when we are the church,
having received Christ the head]" (GrchSch. 12:101.3–4; PG 8:272a).

1554 Idem 1.6.38.3: "δι' ὧν (σχ. τῆς πίστεως καὶ τῆς ἐπαγγελίας) ἡ ἐκκλησία,
καθάπερ ἄνθρωπος ἐκ πολλῶν συνεστηκυῖα μελῶν, ἄρδεταί τε καὶ αὔζεται [by
means of which [sc. the faith and the promise] the Church, like a human being
consisting of many members, is refreshed and grows]" (GrchSch. 12:113.2–4;
PG 8:266b). Cf. 1.6.42.3; 43.1 (GrchSch. 12:115.20 ff.; PG 8:301a).

1555 Idem 1.6.42.1–43.1 (GrchSch. 12:115.10–22, 29; PG 8:300b–c, 301a).

1556 Idem.

1557 Clement of Alexandria, *Stromata* 7.11.3.3: "κατὰ τὴν ἐκκλησίαν τὴν
μὲν βελτιωτικὴν οἱ πρεσβύτεροι σῴζουσιν εἰκόνα" (GrchSch. 17:4.18–19; PG
9:405a).

former sins. Moral vacillation (ἐπιτηδειότης εἰς εὐτρεψίαν) comes from want of training—from lack of asceticism (ἐξ ἀνασκησίας) To frequently ask forgiveness for those things in which we often sin is only words of repentance (δόχησις), and not repentance itself.[1558] Consequently, Clement is aware of a forgiveness of sins that can apparently be requested of members of the church hierarchy, but he takes a more profound view of repentance: his words have as their object the moral rebirth of members of the Church, and not just the forgiveness of sins.

Regarding the second highly renowned representative of the Church of Alexandria—Origen—opinions vary. It is surmised that Origen knew of the disciplinary disputes occurring in the West. His writings even explicitly hint at the decrees of Callistus—decrees of which Origen does not approve. In the polemics between Callistus and Hippolytus he sided with the latter. This idea, already expressed by Döllinger,[1559] is frequently repeated in church historical scholarship.[1560] That Origen did not approve of the measures taken by Callistus comes as no surprise. Origen is as much an ascetic as Hippolytus. The overly lenient practice of Callistus could not evoke sympathy in one who himself lived on just a few oboli[1561] per day. But Origen, like Hippolytus, did not promote the Montanist doctrine of the sanctity of the Church.

Origen reasons concerning the Church in a way that would have been impossible if he had adhered to the Montanist doctrine of the sanctity of the Church. "The whole Church of God" is the Body of Christ, vivified by the Son of God, "and the members of this body—considered as a whole— ... consist of those who are believers; since, as a soul vivifies and moves the body, which of itself

---

1558 Idem 2.13.56.1–2; 57.1–2; 58.1–3; 59.1 (GrchSch. 15:143.15–144.22; PG 8:996c).

1559 Döllinger, *Hippolytus und Kallistus*, 256–257.

1560 See Harnack, *Dogmengeschichte*[4] 1, 416, 442–443, 447–449, 484; Rolffs, *Das Indulgenz-Edict*, TU 11.3, 127 ff.; Ios. Turmel, *Histoire de la théologie positive* 1, 144; Batiffol, *Études d' histoire et de théologie positive*[2], 110.

1561 An obol was a silver coin equal to one sixth of a drachma, used in ancient Greece. –*Trans.*

has not the natural power of motion like a living being, so the Word, arousing and moving the whole body, the Church, to befitting action, awakens, moreover, each individual member belonging to the Church, so that they do nothing apart from the Word."[1562] Origen speaks of the true Church (τῆς κυρίως ἐκκλησίας) which has no taint, but is holy and unsullied.[1563] The sinner is excommunicated from the Church, even if men do not excommunicate him.[1564] But along with this doctrine on the sanctity of the Church Origen says that the Church is renewed each day to the image of Him Who created her.[1565] The Church is not always at the same height.[1566] "The face of the Church is declared to be comely or ugly (*turpis*) according to the virtues and aspirations of her believers."[1567] In his homilies on the book of Genesis, Origen compares the Church with the ark. "This people, therefore, which is saved in the Church, is compared to all those whether men or animals which are saved in the ark. But since neither the merit of all nor the progress in faith (*in fide profectus*) is one, therefore, also that ark does not offer one abode for all, but there are two lower decks and three upper decks and compartments are separated in it to show that also in the Church, although all are contained within the one faith and are washed in the one baptism, progress, however, is not one and the same for all, 'but each one in

1562 Origen, *Against Celsus* 6.48 (PG 11:1373b; GrchSch. 3:119.28–120.5).

1563 Origen, *On Prayer* 20.1 (PG 11:477c; GrchSch. 3:343.13–15).

1564 Origen, *Homilies on Jeremiah* 29.4 (PG 13:577b).

1565 Origen, *On Canticles* 4. Though he spoke of the daily renewal of the Church, here Origen says that Christ presented the Church to Himself holy and without blemish—that is, the souls of those who have reached perfection (*quae ad perfectionem venerunt*), who all collectively form the Body of the Church. And this Body must be presented beautiful and comely, if the souls of which it is formed abide in all the beauty of perfection (*in omni perfectionis decore permanserint*) (PG 13:191b).

1566 For example, Origen speaks of his own time as considerably worse than the time that preceded it, in *On Jeremiah* 4.3 (PG 13:288d; GrchSch. 6:25.16 ff.). *Commentaries on Matthew*, vol. 17, n. 24 (PG 13:1548c–1549a).

1567 Origen, *On Canticles* 4 (PG 13:191c; *Origen: The Song of Songs. Commentary and Homilies*, R.P. Lawson, trans. [New York, NY and Mahwah, NJ: Newman Press, 1957]).

his own order' (*unusquisque in suo ordine*)."[1568] Concerning the Lord's parable of the net (see Mt. 13:47–48), Origen says: "It is fitting that in the 'fishing-net' of the whole Church, there are both good and bad. If all things are already pure, what do we leave behind for the judgment of God? And according to another parable, both grain and chaff are kept together on the threshing-floor, although only the grain is to be collected in Christ's storehouses (Lk. 3:17). ... I do not claim that the 'threshing-floor' is the whole world; rather, I understand the threshing-floor to be the gathering of the entire Christian community. For just as each and every threshing-floor is enclosed, and is full of grain or chaff, but not all grain or again all chaff, so also in the Churches on earth (*in Ecclesiis terrestribus*), one person is grain, another chaff. ... If someone at some time sees a sinner in our congregations, he should not be scandalized or say, 'Look! There is a sinner in the assembly of the saints.' ... While we are in the present world, that is, in the threshing-floor and in the fishing-net, both good and bad are contained in it."[1569] In comparing the members of the Church to the pagans, Origen says that they are like lights in the world, but that among them some are better while others are worse.[1570] In explaining the fact that in Jerusalem the sons of Judah and the Jebusites dwelt together (see Josh. 15:63), Origen recalls Christ's words concerning the tares: "Let both grow together" (Mt. 13:30). "As the weeds are permitted in the Gospel to grow up together with the wheat, in the same manner even here in Jerusalem—that is, in the Church—there are certain Jebusites who lead an ignoble and degenerate (*ignobilem et degenerem*) life, and who are perverse not only in their faith, but in their actions, and in every manner of living. For while the Church is on earth, it is not possi-

---

1568   Origen, *Homilies on Genesis* 2.3 (from *The Fathers of the Church, vol. 71: Origen. Homilies on Genesis and Exodus,* Ronald E. Heine, trans. [Washington, D.C.: CUA Press, 1981], 78; PG 12:150c).

1569   Origen, *Homilies on Ezekiel* 1.11 (from *Origen of Alexandria: Exegetical Works on Ezekiel,* Mischa Hooker, trans., Roger Pearse, ed. [Ipswich, MA: Chieftan Publishing, 2014], 52–53; PG 13:677b–c). Cf. *Homilies on Numbers* 27.6 (PG 12:779c).

1570   Origen, *Against Celsus* 3.26 (GrchSch. 2:227). Cf. the observation of Harnack in *Dogmengeschichte*[4] 1, 448–449, Anm.

ble to cleanse it to such purity (*ad liquidum*) that neither an ungodly person nor any sinner seems to reside in it, where everyone is holy and blessed and no blot of sin is found in them."[1571] In the Church, vessels of wrath are often also concealed. The time will come when the Church will be cleansed: this is the time of the judgment (κατὰ τὸν καιρὸν τῆς κρίσεως). But for now she contains within her the vessels of wrath together with the vessels of mercy, the tares are found together with the wheat, and a single net contains fish both cast away and chosen.[1572] In his application of Christ's parable of the tares to the Church, Origen resembles Callistus of Rome.[1573]

Thus, in the opinion of Origen, in the Church there are not only saints. The members of the Church gradually attain to perfection, and the purpose of the Church is to guide people in this, their process of perfection. "The Church ... is full of brightness from the east even to the west, which is full of the true light, which is the pillar and ground of the truth."[1574] "For just as the moon is said to receive light from the sun so that the night likewise can be illuminated by it, so also the Church, when the light of Christ has been received, illuminates all those who live in the night of ignorance. But if someone progresses in this so that he is already made a 'child of the day,' so that 'he walks honestly in the day,' as 'a child of the day and a child of light,' this person is illuminated by Christ him-

---

1571 Origen, *Homilies on Joshua* (from *The Fathers of the Church, vol. 105: Origen. Homilies on Joshua*, Barbara J. Bruce, trans., Cynthia White, ed. [Washington, D.C.: CUA Press, 1984]; PG 12:928c–d). Cf. *Homilies on Matthew* 10.13: "μὴ ξενιζώμεθα, ἐὰν πρὸ τοῦ ἀφορισθῆναι τοὺς ἐκ μέσου τῶν δικαίων, ὑπὸ τῶν ἐπὶ τοῦτο ἐξαποστελλομένων ἀγγέλων, ὁρῶμεν ἡμῶν τὰ ἀθροίσματα πεπληρωμένα καὶ πονηρῶν [let us be not surprised if, before those who are in the midst of the righteous have been separated by the angels sent to this end, we see our gatherings filled also with evil men]" (PG 13:865b).

1572 Origen, *Fragments on Jeremiah* 31 (GrchSch. 6:215.6–13; PG 13:597d).

1573 Vgl. Seeberg, *Studien zur Geschichte des Begriffs der Kirche*, 30; Harnack, *Dogmengeschichte* 1, 697, Anm. 2.

1574 Origen, *Commentary on the Gospel of Matthew* 47 (PG 13:1669c; quoted from Darwell Stone, *The Christian Church* [New York: Edwin S. Gorham, 1906], 103).

self just as the day is illuminated by the sun."[1575] Consequently, the Church is thought of as an intermediary between Christ and men in the task of their illumination.[1576]

If Origen presents even the entire Church as a single organism advancing in perfection, all the more so each individual of which the Church is comprised. To be sure, in his allegorical interpretations of Holy Scripture Origen sometimes speaks as though one who has sinned departs from the Church. For example, Origen sometimes interprets the words of the prophet Jeremiah concerning the Babylonian captivity as follows: the sinner is given over to Nebuchadnezzar, that is, the devil, who leads him away from Jerusalem (that is, the Church) into Babylon.[1577] More often, however, when speaking of the sanctity of a member of the Church Origen represents him not so much as having achieved a state of sanctity as taking thought for his sanctity (*sanctitatis stadium gerat*). "Those who are not saints die in their sins; but those who are saints do penance for their sins, put up with their wounds, understand their faults, and so they search out the priest, and ask for a cure; they look forward to a purification through the bishop. That is why therefore the word of the law cautiously and with significance states that the bishops and priests receive the sins not of anyone, but of the saints alone; for he is a 'saint' who attends to his sin through the bishop."[1578] It is in this that the righteous man differs from the unrighteous: that if falls into sin occur he hastens to repent and knows how he ought to do so, like unto David.[1579]

1575 Origen, *Homilies on Genesis* 1.5 (from *The Fathers of the Church, vol. 71: Origen. Homilies on Genesis and Exodus,* 54; PG 12:150c).

1576 See Archimandrite Sylvester, *The Doctrine Concerning the Church,* 242–245.

1577 Origen, *Homilies on Jeremiah* 1.3; (19); 18.14 (PG 13:257b–c, 492; GrchSch. 6:3.3 ff.; 170 ff.).

1578 Origen, *Homilies on Numbers* 10. t. (PG 12:638a, from Ernest Latko, *Origen's Concept of Penance* [Diss.: Université Laval, 1949)]. Cf. *Homilies on Leviticus* 5.3 (PG 12:450b–c).

1579 Origen, *Homilies on Psalm 36* 4.2 (PG 12:1351c–d). Cf. *Homilies on Psalm 37*, Rom. 2:2 (PG 12:1382c).

But does Origen allow for repentance of all sins, culminating in restoration to communion with the Church? Scholars vary widely in their views of how Origen regarded mortal sins. Some assert that Origen absolutely did not acknowledge forgiveness of mortal sins to be possible here on earth: mortal sins can be forgiven by God.[1580] Others surmise that Origen's views changed toward the end of his life under the influence of later events with which he was well acquainted in the Western Church; in his earlier writings, regarding the disciplinary disputes between Hippolytus and Callistus, he declared himself a supporter of Hippolytus.[1581] Finally, a third group considers Origen an adherent of a more lenient view, according to which the Church here on this earth can forgive any sin; consequently, even restoring those who have sinned mortally to communion with the Church in no way contradicts the sanctity of the Church.[1582]

One could of course surmise that Origen's austere ascetic views had softened as his life drew to a close. His former strictly ascetic views of the whole Church were greatly mitigated by the circumstances of historical existence. The important thing for us to note is that Origin did not adhere to the doctrine, supposedly universal to the early Church, which the Montanists and (as we shall see) the Novatians defended in the third century. It must be noted that the Montanist doctrine that forgiveness of mortal sins can only come from God Himself after the death of the sinner could hardly have come from the mouth of Origen: for he taught apocatastasis,[1583] which leaves no room whatsoever for evil and suffering. Consequently, Origen's words concerning forgiveness of sins may rather

---

1580 See Funk, *Kirchengesch. Abhandlungen und Untersuch* 1, 159, 163.

1581   As per Döllinger, *Hippolytus und Kallistus,* 256; Holl, *Enthusiasmus und Bussgewalt,* 230–231; Turmel, *Histoire de la théologie positive*[3] 1, 144n2, 147n1; Loofs, *Leitfaden der Dogmengeschichte*[4] §29.2b, 207, Anm. 7. Cf. 208, Anm. 2.

1582 Frank, *Die Bussdisciplin der Kirche,* 838–840; Adhémar d' Alès, *La Théologie de saint Hippolyte,* 44–46; Stufler, "Die Sündenvergebung bei Origenes," *Zeitschrift für katholische Theologie* (1907): 205 ff.

1583 Apocatastasis: A form of Christian universalism teaching that the punishments of hell will have an end allowing for everyone ultimately to be saved. —*Trans.*

be seen as indicating that the Church can forgive even grave sins. Origen frequently refers to forgiveness of mortal sins.

Mortal sins—not only murder or adultery, but also theft, bearing false witness, plundering, and rape—Origen calls the treasure of the devil, his coin, the money with which he purchases his slaves.[1584] The devil constantly sows tares among the wheat. But even one who has fallen into the gravest of sins must not despair: through repentance, weeping, and good works he may atone for his deed and be made whole.[1585] The soul, swallowed up by the abyss of debauchery, may still escape destruction, as Jonah escaped the belly of the whale;[1586] one who repents ought not to despair, for a multitude of sins cannot surpass the mercy of God.[1587] In his composition

---

1584 Origen, *Homilies on Exodus* 6.9: "Haec omnia diaboli census est et diaboli thesaurus. Talis enim pecunia de ejus moneta procedit. Hac igitur pecunia emit ille, quos emit, et efficit sibi servos omnes, qui de hujuscemodi censu ejus quantulumcunque susceperint [All these are the devil's riches and the devil's treasure. For such wealth proceeds from his mint. Accordingly, it is by using this wealth that he buys those whom he buys, and makes them all his slaves, who from such riches of his have received ever so little]" (PG 12:338b–c).

1585 Idem 6.9: "Paenitendo, flendo, satisfaciendo deleat, quod admissum est. Dicit enim propheta, quia si conversus ingemueris, tunc salvus eris [By repenting, by lamenting, by making amends, let him erase what was committed. For the prophet says, Because then thou wilt be saved]" (PG 12:338d).

1586 Idem 6.6: "Si quem videris luxuriae carnis et voluptatibus corporis deditum, in quo animus nihil valet, sed totum libido carnis obtinuit, dicito et de hoc, quia devoravit eum terra. ... Nec tamen penitus desperandum est. Possibile namque est, ut si forte resipiscat, qui devoratus est, rursum possit evomi, sicut Ionas [If you see one given to the luxury of the flesh and to the pleasures of the body, in whom the rational soul is not strong at all but who is wholly possessed by the desire of the flesh, let it be said also concerning him that the earth has swallowed him up... Nevertheless the penitent must not despair. For it is possible, if perchance he that was swallowed up would come to himself, it is possible for him to be vomited out like Jonah]" (PG 12:335d–336a).

1587 Origen, *Homilies on Leviticus* 9.8: "Nihil desperandum est his qui compugnuntur et convertuntur ad Dominum. Non enim superat bonitatem Dei malitia delictorum [Those who are battled against and turned back toward the Lord must not at all despair; for the badness of sins does not surpass the goodness of God]" (PG 12:520d–521a). Cf. *Homilies on Judges* 3.2 (PG 12:963b), *Homilies on Leviticus* 16.2 (PG 12:561a).

Against Celsus Origen compares penitents with men raised from the dead. There Origen says that those who have fallen into grave sins of the flesh are considered as dead in the Christian Church, but if they display due remorse, they are considered as raised from the dead, and after lengthy testing they are received as new converts; nevertheless even then they are given no authority or office in the Church.[1588] Origen knows of mortal sins, *quae dicuntur ad mortem*, but he speaks of the possibility of repentance even for one who has fallen into sins of this kind. Even one who has fallen into mortal sins must have recourse to repentance: if he has sinned once, let him not sin again; and if twice or even thrice, let him not add new sins to these.[1589] Even a mortal sin may be healed: one who confesses his sin and atones for it by works of repentance (*per exomologesin*) may earn forgiveness.[1590] It is of course preferable for a person of exalt-

---

1588 Origen, *Against Celsus* 3.51: "Οὗτοι ὡς ἀπολωλότας καὶ τεθνηκότας τῷ θεῷ τούς ὑπ' ἀσελγείας ἤ τινος ἀτόπου νενικημένους ὡς νεκροὺς πενθοῦσι, καὶ ὡς ἐκ νεκρῶν ἀναστάντας, ἐὰν ἀξιόλογον ἐνδείζωνται μεταβολήν, χρόνῳ πλείονι τῶν κατ' ἀρχὰς εἰσαγομένων ὕστερόν ποτε προσίενται, εἰς οὐδεμίαν ἀρχὴν καὶ προστασίαν τῆς λεγομένης ἐκκλησίας τοῦ θεοῦ καταλέγοντες τοὺς φθάσαντας μετὰ τὸ προσεληλυθέναι τῷ λόγῳ ἐπταικέναι [the Christians lament as dead those who have been vanquished by licentiousness or any other sin, because they are lost and dead to God, and as being risen from the dead (if they manifest a becoming change) they receive them afterwards, at some future time, after a greater interval than in the case of those who were admitted at first, but not placing in any office or post of rank in the Church of God those who, after professing the Gospel, lapsed and fell]" (GrchSch 2:247.22–248.5; PG 11:988b–c). Concerning these words Loofs observes that Origen considers the possibility of receiving excommunicated adulterers back again to be the universal Christian practice. See *Leitfaden der Dogmengeschichte*[4] §29.2b, 208, Anm. 2.

1589 Origen, *Homilies on Leviticus* 11.2 (PG 12:533c, d): "Si aliquis est qui forte praeventus est in hujuscemodi peccatis, admonitus nunc verbo Dei, ad auxilium confugiat poenitentiae: ut si semel admisit, secundo non faciat, aut si et secundo, aut etiam tertio praeventus est, ultra non addat." In *Homilies on Leviticus* 16.2, however, we read: "In gravioribus criminibus semel tantum poenitentiae conceditur locus [In the graver crimes, only once is a place granted for repentance]" (PG 12:561a).

1590 Origen, *Homilies on the Psalms* 1.5 (PG 12:1328b). Cf *Homilies on Jeremiah* 19.9. Here Origen presents two adulterers—one who has repented, another who has despaired—and asks: "τίνα λέγεις ἐλπίδας ἔχειν παρὰ θεῷ; ἀρ' ἐκεῖνον τὸν

ed piety and virtue (*athleta pietatis ac virtutis*) never to fall. But should a fall occur, let him hasten to atone for the sin committed through repentance (*poenitentiae suae satisfactione*).[1591]

Like the apostle Paul, Origen speaks quite frequently of delivering a sinner to Satan.[1592] In Origen, this "deliverance unto Satan" is a sort of *terminus technicus* to denote the excommunication of a sinner from the Church. "Jerusalem ... is interpreted as the Church, which is a city of God built from living rocks, from which anyone who sins, when delivered to Nebuchadnezzar, to Satan, is cast out."[1593] But Origen interprets this deliverance to Satan very differently from Tertullian in *On Modesty*. One who has been excommunicated from the Church must undergo penitential labors during his time outside the Church; otherwise he will not be received back into the Church. The Hebrews returned to Jerusalem after their captivity; likewise one who has sinned mortally may be received back if only he repents.[1594] The duration of penitential labors must

---

πορνεύσαντα καὶ μὴ φροντίσαντα, ἀλλ' ἀπαλγοῦντα ὡς καὶ παραδόντα αὐτὸν τῇ ἀσελγείᾳ ἢ τοῦτον τὸν μετὰ τὴν μίαν ἁμαρτίαν πενθοῦντα, θρηνοῦντα, οὗτος (δηλονότι) ἐλπίδων (κρειττόνων) ἐστίν [Who do you say has hopes with God? That one who fornicated and cared not, who puts away sorrow so much so as to have surrendered himself to licentiousness, or this one who after sinning once mourns, laments? Clearly this latter one has better hopes]" (PG 13:521b–c; GrchSch. 6:191.31–192.3).

1591 Origen, *Homilies on the Psalms* 4.2 (PG 12:1533b–c).

1592 Origen, *Homilies on Leviticus* 14.4; *Homilies on Numbers* 19.3; *Homilies on Joshua* 7.6; *Homilies on Judges* 2.5; *Homilies on Psalm 37* 1.2 (PG 12:558b–c, 724c, 861a–b, 961a–b, 1375a); *Homilies on Jeremiah* 1.3; *Homilies* 18.14; *Homilies* 19.9; *Homilies on Ezekiel* 12.3 (PG 13:257b–c, 492b–c, 521c–d, 755c–d).

1593 "Ἡ Ἰερουσαλὴμ εἰς τὴν ἐκκλησίαν μεταλαμβάνεται, ἥτις ἐστὶ πόλις τοῦ θεοῦ, οἰκοδομηθεῖσα ἐκ λίθων ζώντων, αφ' ἧς τις ἁμαρτάνων ἐκβάλλεται παραδιδόμενος Ναβουχοδονόσορ, τῷ σατανᾷ." (Origen, *Fragments on Jeremiah* 48, from *The Fathers of the Church, vol. 97. Origen: Homilies on Jeremiah; Homily on 1 Kings 28*, John Clark Smith, trans. [Washington, D.C.: CUA Press, 1998] 305 [GrchSch. 6:222.7–10; PG 13:577a]). Cf. *Homilies on Joshua* 21.1: "Neque dicimus de iis qui manifeste et evidenter criminosi sunt, ut non de Ecclesia expellantur [And we are not speaking of those who are manifestly and obviously slanderous, that they should not be expelled from the Church]" (PG 12:929a).

1594 "Ἴστω δὲ ὁ τῆς Ἰερουσαλὴμ ἐκβληθεὶς ὡς, ἐὰν μὴ ποιήσῃ χρόνον

be commensurate with the gravity of the sin.[1595] "Origen viewed excommunication of sinners who posed a danger to the Church as a pedagogical measure, similar to the penal exile employed in civil society, and leaving open the possibility for the sinner's correction and his restoration to the Church."[1596] The destruction of the flesh, for which the apostle delivered the incestuous Corinthian to Satan, Origen understands to mean death to sin,[1597] a destruction of sensuality.[1598] The destruction of the flesh is specifically its purification from sin—the same ordinarily practiced by penitents.[1599] That is to say, Origen understands the destruction of the flesh in the sense of *exomologesis* as it was interpreted in the edict of Callistus which Tertullian disputed.

αὐτάρκη πράττων ἔξω τῆς ἐκκλησίας ἃ δεῖ, οὐκ ἐπάνεισιν ἐπὶ τὴν Ἰερουσαλήμ. Δεῖ δὲ αυτὸν ἔξω γεγονότα μὴ ἀμελεῖν τοῦ οἰκοδομεῖν οἰκίαν καὶ φυτεύειν παραδείσους. Ταῦτα γὰρ μὴ ποιῶν μηδὲ πληρώσας, τὸν συμβολικὸν ἀριθμὸν τῶν ἐτῶν τῶν ἑβδομήκοντα σαββάτου καὶ ἀναπαύσεως ὄντα, οὐκ ἐπάνεισι κοινωνήσων τῇ ἐκκλησίᾳ, μένει δὲ καταδεδικασμένος ἔξω τῆς Ἰερουσαλήμ [But let the one expelled from Jerusalem know that, unless he spend sufficient time doing outside of the church what must be done, he shall not return to Jerusalem. And when he has gone out, he must not neglect to build a house and to plant gardens. For if he has not done these things nor fulfilled the number of seventy years, which is a symbol of the sabbath and of rest, he will not return to commune with the Church; but he remains outside of Jerusalem condemned]." (Origen, *Fragments on Jeremiah* 48 [GrchSch. 6:222.14–22]). Cf. *Homilies on Ezekiel* 3.8 (PG 13:694d).

1595 Origen, *Homilies on Judges* 3.2: "Quanto tempore deliquisti, tanto nihilominus tempore humilia te ipsum Deo. Et satisfactio ei in confessione poenitentiae" (PG 12: 963b).

1596 Archimandrite Sylvester, *The Doctrine Concerning the Church in the First Three Centuries*, 259.

1597 Origen, *Commentaries on the Epistle to the Romans* 4.6: "Apostolus peccatorem tradebat in interitum carnis, ut spiritum faceret salvum, hoc est, ut moreretur peccato et vivetur Deo" (PG 14:1068c).

1598 Origen, *Homilies on Psalm 37* 1.2: "Tradi ergo in interitum carnis, hoc est in afflictionem corporis, quae solet a poenitentibus expendi, eumque carnis interitum nominavit, qui tamen carnis interitus, vitam spiritui conferat" (PG 12:558c).

1599 Origen, *Homilies on Leviticus* 14.4: "Tradidi in interitum carnis, hoc est in afflictionem corporis, quae solet a poenitentibus expendi, eumque carnis interitum nominavit, qui tamen carnis interitus, vitam spiritui conferat" (PG 12:558c).

In his foreword to his commentary on the epistle to the Corinthians[1600], when determining the period between the writing of the first and second epistles to the Corinthians, Origen says that in the second epistle the apostle Paul receives back again the same incestuous man whom he delivered to Satan in the first.[1601] And the apostle's reason for commanding that he be received is that over the course of his excommunication he has brought forth the fruits of repentance.[1602] In speaking of excommunication from the Church for sins, at the same time Origen clearly and definitively attests that through repentance the sinner can be restored again to the people of God **in this life.**[1603]

Thus, in Origen we find very clear testimony that forgiveness of mortal sins is possible. When he does speak of sins being unforgivable, these passages only *appear* to contradict the general thesis that we have established: these passages specifically presume a lack of remorse on the part of the sinner himself. The cause therefore lies not in God or in the properties of the Church, but in the unrepentance of the sinner himself.[1604] If we consider this teaching of Origen regarding repentance, we are obliged to acknowledge that in the dogmatic doctrine of the sanctity of the Church Origen retains no traces of the supposed early universal doctrine of the Church as a society of saints. According to Origen, the Church is not a society

---

1600 Interestingly, the author does not specify which.

1601 "In prima Epistola ejectum eum qui fuerat incesti scelere pollutus ... in secunda jam revocat" (PG 14:834b). It is worth noting that, according to Tertullian, in his time adherents of the lenient approach believed that "apostolum paulum in secunda ad Corinthios eidem fornicatori veniam dedisse quem in prima dedendum satanae in interitum carnis pronuntiarit" (*On Modesty* 13 [CSEL 20.1:243.2–4]).

1602 Ibid.: "Quod utique non faceret, nisi processu temporis dignos in eo fructus pervidisset, et quod jam caro interitum, quem designaverat Apostolus sucepisset, peccato scilicet et vitiis mortua, ut ita demum viveret Deo" (PG 14:834b–c).

1603 Origen, *Homilies on Ezekiel* 3.8: "Iuste autem proictur, qui digna fecit abjectione ut auferatur a populo Dei et eradicetur ab eo et tradatur satanae. Et in praesenti quidem potest quis egrediens de populo Dei rursum per poenitentiam reverti" (PG 13:694d).

1604 Vgl. Stufler, *Zeitschr. für kathol. Theologie* (1907): 225–226.

of saints, but **a hospital** established by Christ **for the human race that lies sick with sin.**

This healing work of the Church, according to Origen, is entrusted to the pastors of the Church. The supreme Physician is the Savior Himself: in the Old Testament He is followed by the prophets, and in the New—by the apostles Peter and Paul and all those appointed after them in the Church, who are charged with church discipline for the healing of wounds and whom God appointed to be physicians in the Church.[1605] The apostles and those like them, priests after the image of the great High Priest, trained in divine therapy (τῆς τοῦ Θεοῦ θεραπείας), being taught by the Holy Spirit, know for which sins sacrifices may be offered, and when, and in what manner, and they know for which this should not be done.[1606] Like Christ, Who instituted the priesthood in the Church, the bishops must take upon themselves the sins of the people and grant them forgiveness of sins.[1607] God grants forgiveness to men through other men,[1608] and only in the Church.[1609] "The power of the keys" belongs to *qui praesunt Ecclesiae* [those who preside over the Church]; definitions of this power are given *per episcopi vocem* [by the voice of the bishop].[1610] Christ gave to the apostle Peter "the power of the

---

1605 Origen, *Homilies on Psalm 37* 1.1: "... Et hi omnes qui post apostolos in Ecclesia positi sunt, quibusque curandorum vulnerum disciplina commissa est, quos voluit Deus in Ecclesia sua esse medicos animarum" (PG 12:1369b—c).

1606 Origen, *On Prayer* 28.9: "Οἱ ἀπόστολοι καὶ οἱ τοῖς ἀποστόλοις ὡμιωμένοι, ἱερεῖς ὄντες κατὰ τὸν «μέγαν» «ἀρχιερέα», ἐπιστήμην λαβόντες τῆς τοῦ θεοῦ θεραπείας, ἴσασιν, ὑπὸ τοῦ πνεύματος διδασκόμενοι, περὶ ὧν χρὴ ἀναφέρειν θυσίας ἁμαρτημάτων καὶ πότε καὶ τίνα τρόπον, καὶ γινώσκουσι, περὶ ὧν οὐ χρὴ τοῦτο ποιεῖν" (PG 11:529a; GrchSch. 3:381.2–6).

1607 Origen, *Homilies on Leviticus* 5.3: "Consequens est, secundum imaginem ejus, qui sacerdotium Ecclesiae dedit, etiam ministri et sacerdotes ecclesiae peccata populi accipiant, et ipsi imitantes magistrum, remissionem peccatorum populo tribuant" (PG 12:451c).

1608 Origen, *On Prayer* 28.9: "τὸ νοηθῆναι τὴν δι᾽ ἀνθρώπων ἄφεσιν ὑπὸ θεοῦ γινομένην ἀνθρώποις ἁμαρτημάτων" (PG 11:528d; GrchSch. 3:380.23–24).

1609 Origen, *Homilies on John* 6.(59).38.304 (GrchSch. 10:168.20; PG 14:304b).

1610 Origen, *Homilies on Leviticus* 14.3 (PG 12:556a).

keys," and here is how Origen reasons concerning the succession of this power in the Church:

> Consider how great power the rock has upon which the church is built by Christ, and how great power every one has who says, "Thou art the Christ, the Son of the living God" [Mt. 16:16], so that the judgments of this man abide sure, as if God were judging in him, that in the very act of judging (ἐν αὐτῷ τὸ κρίνειν) the gates of Hades shall not prevail against him. But when one judges unrighteously, and does not bind upon earth according to the Word of God, nor loose upon earth according to His will, the gates of Hades prevail against him. ... Wherefore he has the keys of the kingdom of heaven, opening to those who have been loosed on earth that they may be also loosed in heaven, and free; and shutting to those who by his just judgment have been bound on earth that they also may be bound in heaven, and condemned. But when those who maintain the function of the episcopate (τὸν τόπον τῆς ἐπισκοπῆς) make use of this word as Peter, and, having received the keys of the kingdom of heaven from the Saviour, teach that things bound by them, that is to say, condemned, are also bound in heaven, and that those which have obtained remission by them are also loosed in heaven, we must say that they speak wholesomely (ὑγιῶς) if they have the way of life on account of which it was said to that Peter, "Thou art Peter" [Mt. 16:18]; and if they are such that upon them the church is built by Christ, and to them with good reason this could be referred; and the gates of Hades ought not to prevail against him when he wishes to bind and loose. But if he is tightly bound with the cords of his sins, to no purpose does he bind and loose.[1611]

These last words cited are interpreted variously. Sometimes people wish to see in these words the idea that "purity of faith and life on the part of the bishop are an essential condition for 'the pow-

---

1611 Origen, *Commentary on Matthew* 12.14 (PG 13:1013b–c).

er of the keys,' which he possesses by virtue of his office, to be effectual in his hands."[1612] But purity of life is of course a highly relative
concept, and it is hard to allow that Origen inseparably linked "the
power of the keys," which in his opinion is of such importance in
the life of the Church, with the ever-relative and conventional concept of purity of life. The context of Origen's words justifies seeing
these last words also as expressing only the idea that is expressed
in a different form at the beginning of the excerpt cited—namely,
that unjust (perhaps biased) condemnation or forgiveness is of no
significance in the eyes of God.[1613] The sanctity of the office, naturally, compels every priest to behave as befits his office; for even the
Old Testament priests consumed the sacrifice for sins in a sacred
place.[1614]

But Protestant scholars concentrate their particular attention
upon a very few select passages from the writings of Origen, and
draw conclusions that match their overarching perception of early
church history—namely, they ascribe to Origen the opinion that

1612 Smirnov, *The Spiritual Father,* 244.

1613 Origen says quite definitively that abuses can occur in the exercising of
church discipline, "quando sine judicio et sine ratione non propter peccata quae
faciunt, excommunicant quosdam, sed propter aliquem zelum et contentionem
prohibent intrare frequenter et meliores quam sunt ipsi [when they excommunicate certain men without judgement and without reason, not on account of sins
which they do, but on account of some jealousy and strife they prohibit even better men than themselves from entering frequently]" *(Commentaries on Matthew 14*
[PG 13:1620b]). In Origen's words on justice in exercising the right to bind and
to loose, Stufler sees an echo of the offenses he personally suffered at the hands
of an unjust bishop. See *Zeitschrift für katholische Theologie* (1907), 198.

1614 Origen, *Homilies on Leviticus* 5.3: "Decent ergo et ipsi Ecclesiae sacerdotes
ita perfecti esse, ut in officiis semper sacerdotalibus eruditi, ut peccata populi in
loco sancto, in atriis tabernaculi testimonii, ipsi non peccando consumant" (PG
12:451c–d). We consider highly artificial the interpretation of A. Katansky, according to which "the bonds of one's own sins should be understood to mean not
crimes of the priest against morality, or (in other words) his sins as an individual,
but crimes against the faith and the church canons, or crimes as a member of the
hierarchy" *(The Dogmatic Doctrine on the Seven Sacraments of the Church in the Works of
the Early Fathers and Writers of the Church Through Origen* ["Догматическое учение
о семи церковных Таинствах в творениях древнейших отцев и писателей
Церкви до Оригена включительно"] [Saint Petersburg: 1877], 247n).

charismatism is the sole basis for "the power of the keys." Of these passages, *On Prayer* 28.8 is most frequently cited. Here is the passage:

> It is when a man is inspired (ἐμπνευσθείς) by Jesus as were the apostles, when he can be known from his fruits to have received the Spirit that is Holy and to have become spiritual through being led by the Spirit after the manner of a Son of God unto every reasonable duty, that he forgives whatsoever God has forgiven and holds those sins that are irremediable (ὁ δὲ ἐμπνευσθεὶς ὑπὸ τοῦ Ἰησοῦ ὡς οἱ ἀπόστολοι καὶ «ἀπὸ τῶν καρπῶν» γινώσκεσθαι δυνάμενος, ὡς χωρήσας τὸ Πνεῦμα τὸ ἅγιον καὶ γενόμενος πνευματικὸς τῷ ὑπὸ τοῦ Πνεύματος ἄγεσθαι τρόπον υἱοῦ Θεοῦ ἐφ᾽ ἕκαστον τῶν κατὰ λόγον πρακτέων, ἀφίησιν ἃ ἐὰν ἀφῇ ὁ Θεὸς καὶ κρατεῖ τὰ ἀνίατα τῶν ἁμαρτημάτων), and as the prophets served God in speaking not their own message but that of the divine Will, so he too serves the God who alone has authority to forgive.[1615] ... I know not how it is, but there are some who have taken upon themselves what is beyond priestly dignity, perhaps through utter lack of accurate priestly knowledge, and are proud of their ability to pardon even acts of idolatry and to forgive acts of adultery and fornication, claiming that even sin unto death is absolved through their prayer for those who have dared to commit such. They do not read the words: There is sin unto death; not for it do I say that a man should ask [1 Jn. 5:16]."[1616]

The above words of Origen are subjected to a wide variety of interpretations, some of them quite decisive. First and foremost some wish to see this as Origen teaching that the power to bind and to loose belongs only to persons who possess spiritual gifts, charismas, and that this power is not given to a man according to his hierachical position in the Church, but depends exclusively upon his personal charismas.[1617] Along with this the opinion it is even opined

1615 Origen, *On Prayer* 28.8 (PG 11:528c; GrchSch. 3:380.8 ff.).

1616 Ibid. 18.10 (PG 11:529b; GrchSch. 3:381.12–18).

1617 This view is decisively expressed by K. Holl. See *Enthusiasmus und Bussge-*

that in these words Origen is protesting against interference in the matter of forgiving sins on the part of persons with no call to do so—namely, the confessors and the martyrs.[1618] First and foremost it must be noted that Origen says nothing to suggest that individual charismas are fully sufficient for one to possess "the power of the keys."[1619] Origen constantly speaks of the church hierarchy; and of this hierarchy, in addition to its ecclesiastical dignity, Origen makes certain moral demands. In his reasoning Origen presumes the apostolic dignity of the person who forgives sins, but that person, by his conviction, must possess certain personal qualities. Not that these qualities are conditions for even possessing "the power of the keys," but they enable one who holds this power not to abuse it, but to use it in accordance with the will of God.[1620] Such a man absolves those sins that God would have absolved. One who absolves sins must know and be able to discern from the very state of the sinner which sins may be absolved and which may not. Thus, the first half of the excerpt cited from *On Prayer* 28.8 contains the same idea as in the excerpt from the commentary on the Gospel of Matthew that we cited somewhat previously: only the judgment of one who is worthy is as unshakable as the judgment of God Himself Who judges within him. Juxtaposing both passages, we may formulate Origen's thinking as follows: **a member of the hierarchy possesses "the power of the keys" by virtue of his ecclesiastical position, but this power, like all things human, is not absolute, for its bearer can sometimes be unjust**, with the result that one who does not deserve punishment is excommunicated from the Church, or that within the Church there are people

---

walt, 232–233. Cf. Rolffs, *Das Indulgenz—Edict*, TU 11.3, 127.

1618 Such is the opinion of Redepenning. See *Origenes* (Bonn: 1841), Bd. 2, 416. Others see in the words cited a prohibition against ordinary priests forgiving mortal sins: mortal sins may be forgiven only by a bishop. Concerning this see Stufler, *Zeitschr. für kathol. Theologie* (1907): 218–219.

1619 See Smirnov, *The Spiritual Father*, 243.

1620 Vgl. Schanz, "Die Absolutionsgewalt in der alten Kirche," *Theologische Quartalschrift* (1897): 49. Vgl. Holl, *Enthusiasmus und Bussgewalt*, 233–234.

who will be condemned by God Himself.[1621] Origen's words indicate no inseparable connection between charisma and "the power of the keys," but they are of great importance in determining how Origen understands the Church. If the judgment of hierarchical authority does not always correspond to the judgment of God, clearly belonging to the earthly Church does not equate to certain salvation in heaven. Outside the Church there is no salvation,[1622] but even in the Church one may perish—ideas completely foreign to the Montanists.

The second half of the words cited from Origen in *On Prayer* 28.10 do indeed appear to deny the right of the bishops to forgive mortal sins: this right is said to be beyond priestly dignity.[1623] But to correctly understand Origen's words we must take them not in isolation, as is customarily done, but in context. Citing the evangelist (see Jn. 20:22–23), Origen says that the apostles received from Christ the power to forgiven sins. But, Origen surmises, some may reproach the apostles, asking why they did not forgive all men; on the contrary, some they bound, so that they are bound in heav-

---

1621 Origen, *Homilies on Leviticus* 14.3: "Exiit a veritate, exiit a timore Dei, a fide, a charitate, sicut superius diximus, quomodo per haec quis exeat de castris Ecclesiae, etiamsi per episcopi vocem minime abjiciatur. Sicut e contrario interdum sit, ut aliquis non recto judicio eorum, qui praesunt Ecclesiae depellatur, et foras mittatur. ... Et ita sit ut interdum ille qui foras mittitur, intus sit: et ille foris, qui intus retinere videtur" (PG 12:556a). Cf. *Commentary on Matthew* 14 (PG 13:1620): "Quamvis vetiti, tamen intrant et haereditant regnum coelorum."

1622 Origen, *Homilies on Joshua* 3.5: "Nemo sibi persuadeat, nemo semetipsum decipiat: extra hanc domum, id est extra Ecclesiam nemo salvatur [Let no one persuade himself, let no one deceive himself: outside of this house, that is, outside the Church, no one is being saved]" (PG 12:841c–842a). It would be futile to see in these words any contradiction to the words cited in the previous note, where particular attention should be given to the words *non recto judicio eorum, qui praesunt Ecclesiae depellatur* [he is expelled by the not right judgement of those who preside over the Church]. In other words, this refers to an abuse that shows that the gates of hell have prevailed against the bearer of "the power of the keys." Cf. *Commentary on Matthew* 14 (PG 13:1620b).

1623 In the opinion of Rolffs (*Das Indulgenz-Edict,* TU 11.3, 127), in these words Origen is specifically polemicizing with Callistus—a tendency which Preuschen likewise sees in the words of Origen (see *Zeitschrift für die neutestamentliche Wissenschaft* [1910]: 154).

en also. Origen deflects this rebuke by pointing out that even the Old Testament priests did not offer sacrifices for all sins; so also the apostles did not their own will, but acted in accordance with the will of God. Both the apostles and the bishops who succeed them know which sins should be forgiven and which must not.[1624] If we consider the context of Origen's words in examining the passage in question, we must read it not as a denial of the bishop's "power of the keys,"[1625] but only as a statement of how that power should be properly understood. "The power of the keys" is the power to bind and to loose. But some "are proud (αὐχοῦσι) of their ability to pardon even acts of idolatry and to forgive acts of adultery and fornication." If the bearer of "the power of the keys" boasts that he can forgive any sin he wishes (as indicated by the words μηδὲ ἀκριβοῦντες τὴν ἱερατικὴν ἐπιστήμην [and do not]), this is already an improper understanding of "the power of the keys." The power to bind and to loose as one pleases, and not according to the state of the sinner, is naturally beyond the priestly dignity. Consequently, Origen does not deny "the power of the keys" to members of the hierarchy, but rather he protests against its indiscriminate usage. Even a denial of the bishop's authority to forgive mortal sins, if Origen ever did express it, from his point of view would have been only a confirmation of the bishop's right to bind. Members of the hierarchy not only loose, but also bind, having inherited this dual authority from the apostles. The power to bind is manifested in excommunicating from the Church those who have sinned gravely; excommunication is itself a demonstration of the power to bind, given by the apostles to their successors.[1626]

1624 Origen, *On Prayer* 28.9 (PG 11:528d–529a; GrchSch. 3:380–381).

1625 Smirnov asserts that, in reflecting on the power to bind and to loose, Origen "did not consider all bishops, whom he calls priests (ἱερεῖς, *sacerdotes*), its possessors: he asserted that personal sanctity and grace-filled enlightenment—spirituality—was an essential condition for this" (*The Spiritual Father,* 259–260).

1626 Origen, *Homilies on Judges* 2.5: "Vides ergo, quia non solum per apostolos suos. Deus tradidit delinquentes in manus inimicorum, sed et per eos, qui ecclesiae praesident et potestatem habent non solum solvendi; sed et ligandi [So you see that God hands sinners over into the hands of enemies not only by means of His own apostles but also by those who preside over the church and have the power,

We must also take note of another expression from Origen's words in *On Prayer* 28.10. He upbraids those who boast of their power to forgive sins, "claiming that even sin unto death is absolved **through their prayer** for those who have dared to commit such. They do not read the words: There is sin unto death; not for it do I say that a man should ask [1 Jn. 5:16]." Those who boasted of their power to forgive sins apparently alluded to the power of their prayer, saying that **through their prayer** even mortal sins are loosed. Consequently, here too Origen is not saying that a bishop cannot forgive mortal sins at all: rather, **mere prayer for the sinner alone** is not sufficient for this. For a mortal sin to be forgiven the sinner must first be excommunicated from the Church for a time, and only after works of repentance must he be restored to communion with the Church. Can it therefore be surmised that in the words cited Origen is requiring only *exomologesis* [act of repentance] for the forgiveness of mortal sins?[1627] Do not the "deliverance unto Satan" and the *interitus carnis* [destruction of the flesh] which we have seen in Origen suggest an answer in the affirmative?

Other passages from Origen in support of the inseparable link between spiritual gifts and "the power of the keys" which he allegedly espoused are cited very rarely, and they contain no grounds for ascribing to Origen any such opinion.[1628]

---

not only of loosing, but also of binding]" (PG 12:961a).

1627 Stufler decisively advances this opinion: "«*De orat.*» 28, tadelt Origenes einige Bischöfe, nicht deswegen, weil sie überhapt die Sünden der Unzucht, des Ehebruchs und Götzendienstes nachlassen, sondern weil sie sich rühmen, dies zu vermögen «διὰ τῆς εὐχῆς», durch ihr Gebet allein, ohne vorausgegangene vollwertige Bussleistung" (*Zeitschr. für katholische Theol.* [1907]: 220–221). According to this interpretation of Origen's words, his reproach does not even apply to Callistus, who declared only *paenitentia functis* in his edict on the forgiveness of sins against chastity [see note 1435 above —ED.]. It may be conjectured that in the East in the first half of the third century an even more lenient practice was encountered (naturally, in the capacity of an abuse) than that which Callistus instituted in Rome. This is precisely the conjecture made by Stufler (Ibid., 227–228).

1628 Concerning this, see Stufler (*Zeitschr. für katholische Theol.* [1907]: 224 flg.), who puts it quite emphatically: "Es besteht aber kein Grund, dem Origenes auch diese Häresie aufzubürden."

Consequently, there are not sufficient grounds to consider Origen a defender of the rigoristic view of the Church as a society of saints. Nor are there grounds to attribute to him the error of the Montanists, alleging that mortal sins can be forgiven only by one who possesses particular **spiritual** gifts.[1629]

We may now summarize the findings of our research in this essay.

The apostolic doctrine of the sanctity of the Church is not a doctrine of the particular sanctity of individual members of the Church. The apostle Paul presents the Church as an organism that is constantly maturing in moral perfection. In the early Church there prevailed not the self-satisfied and haughty consciousness of one's own sanctity so typical of all sectarians, but a humble consciousness of one's sinfulness and the need for correction and repentance. This is why in nearly all historic works of early church literature we find the indefatigable preaching of repentance. But the general ascetic worldview that predominated in the early Church maintained a strict disciplinary practice, according to which in several Churches those who had sinned mortally were excommunicated from the Church, although this proceeded **not from a dogmatic** doctrine of the essential sanctity of the members of the Church. Discipline varied, and a division of sins into mortal and non-mortal was not known in all places. Soon, however, influenced by a general moral decline, discipline with respect to mortal sins began to be relaxed, and it was explicitly stated that those who had fallen into these sins could be restored to communion with the Church. This was merely a change in disciplinary practice: **the dogmatic doctrine of the sanctity of the Church remained unalterable.** The relax-

---

1629 Over the course of several centuries, however, certain writers have expressed requirements that persons who absolve sins possess particular moral qualities. Frequently the power to bind and to loose is also ascribed to persons whose office is not hierarchical in nature. Concerning this see Smirnov, *The Spiritual Father*, 170–172. Here the words of Barsanuphius the Great are cited, and the author rightly deems them a personal opinion. See also 200–208. A certain popularity of this opinion is quite understandable psychologically, if not dogmatically, but we are writing a history of dogma, and not of repentance.

ation of discipline met with protest from people of a strictly ascetic bent. But some denied this mitigated discipline because, under the influence of the sectarian, ecstatic "new" revelation of the Paraclete in the Montanist prophets, strictness was taken to the point of rigorism and a new dogmatic view of the Church was advanced, according to which the Church is a society of perfected saints. A grave sinner had to be completely cut off from the communion of the Church; he had to spend the remainder of his life in penitential labors, and this repentance was to culminate in the sinner's posthumous forgiveness by God Himself. Others, such as Hippolytus of Rome, disputed the relaxation of discipline for practical reasons, and did not incorporate either the new prophecies or the new dogmatic concept of the Church into their polemics. In connection with their doctrine of a new revelation, the Montanists denied the authority of the bishops to bind and loose mortal sins, ascribing this power to God alone and to their own prophets, in whom God Himself spoke. At the same time, however, the edict of Callistus, bishop of Rome, quite emphatically expressed the idea that in the Church "the power of the keys" belonged to the bishop. The attempt of modern scholars to present the Montanists as defenders of the ancient Church-wide views of the Church and "the power of the keys" cannot be accepted. The doctrine of the sanctity of the Church in the sense of the sanctity of its individual members was unknown in the early Church, and there are no grounds for ascribing "the power of the keys" exclusively to the charismatics or to confessors who were counted as such. Upon analysis of the data cited in its defense, the appeal to the Eastern writers Clement and Origen, alleging that in the East they professed views similar to those of the Montanists, must be conclusively rejected. In Origen we find a doctrine not of the sanctity of the individual members of the Church, but of their gradual perfection within the Church. The data cited in defense of the thesis that Origen denied that the bishops possessed "the power of the keys" are also insufficient. Thus, although a detailed dogmatic doctrine of the sanctity of the Church had not yet been developed, data from the history of penitential discipline and of the doctrine of repentance in general show that **the**

apostolic doctrine of the maturing Body of the Church formed the foundation of ecclesiastical concepts of the sanctity of the Church from the very beginning of the existence of the Church and survived until the third century, when the scholarly theological development of the concept of the sanctity of the Church was undertaken.

FIFTH ESSAY

The Teaching
of Saint Cyprian of Carthage
Concerning the Church

The name of Saint Cyprian of Carthage has become closely linked with the history of the doctrine concerning the Church. The historical circumstances surrounding the life of the Carthaginian saint, his pastoral work, and his own personal practice all made him a church writer who focused primarily on developing the doctrine concerning the Church. Before him this doctrine had already been a topic of discussion among church writers, and the formulation of the doctrine concerning the Church was already taking shape and maturing; but few points had been precisely and fully elucidated. We have presented the doctrine concerning Tradition up to and including St. Irenaeus and Tertullian, and their teaching on the Church as the custodian of the truth of Christ. But we have already seen that even in St. Irenaeus and Tertullian each individual church community is viewed as something independent and self-sufficient with regard to doctrine. Unity of the faith among various Churches is cited only as a logical proof of the truth and authenticity of that faith. Both St. Irenaeus and Tertullian contended with Gnosticism, which distorted the dogmatic doctrine of the Church, and quite logically they insist on the need to preserve the "Rule of Faith." But contention and discord proved entirely possible even when the "Rule of Faith" was preserved unalterable by all. It was therefore necessary to specify other tokens of church unity. We have already seen how in the epistles of St. Ignatius the God-bearer the bishop was placed at the head of the church community, and all things were subordinate to him. But the possibility of error, of diverging from the truth and from the bishop, was as though beyond the realm of comprehension for second-century church writers. In the mid-third century, for the first time church writers found themselves facing the reality of obstinate separation from the Church on the part of a bishop and of entire communities. The fight against Montanism made it necessary to clarify the doctrine of the sanctity of the Church. But the fight against Montanism produced too few manuscripts, and we know very little of the dogmatic formulae created by Montanism's opponents in the Church. We have already noted the lack of a positive dogmatic doctrine of the sanctity of the Church. In our exposition of the disciplinary disputes of the first quarter of the third century, to the best of our ability we have avoided ascribing a precise formulation of a dogmatic doctrine of the sanctity of the Church to the church writers of that period. Nevertheless we fear lest we have introduced anything inspired by later dogmatic formulae, but unknown to the ecclesiastical thought of the early third century. Callistus, bishop of Rome, decisively declared that those who had sinned against chastity could be restored to communion with the Church. But quite logically the question of whether to receive all who had sinned mortally without exception sooner or later had to be answered in the affirmative. Tertullian had grounds to reproach Callistus for inconsistency, saying that his arguments sooner justify restoring apostates than adulterers to communion with the Church.[1630] In the early third century the work of resolving

---

1630 Tertullian, *On Modesty* 9: "Iam non moechi et fornicatores, sed idololatrae et blasphemi et negatores et omne apostatarum genus ... patri satisfacient [not adulterers and fornicators, but idolaters, and blasphemers, and renegades, and every class of apostates, will... make satisfaction to the Father]" (CSEL 20.1:237.1–3). "Aut et cetera delicta pariter capitalia concedi opportebit aut paria quoque eorum moechiam et fornicationem inconcessibilia servari [it will be fitting either that all other crimes equally capital should be conceded remissible, or else that their peers, adultery and fornication, should be retained inconcessible]" (CSEL 20.1:238.21–23). Cf. Döllinger's note on the meaning of Tertullian's objection, in *Hippolytus und Kallistus*, 130; Rolffs, *Das Indulgenz-Edict*, 11.3, 75 and

the question of restoring mortal sinners to church communion was undertaken, but this question itself remained almost entirely without due connection to the idea of the sanctity of the Church. Consequently, by the time of St. Cyprian's life and work many questions of church doctrine had come to a head, together with new questions that arose in his own time and pertained intimately to the doctrine concerning the Church. St. Cyprian combined all the results reached by previous ecclesiastical dogmatic thought, further developed them, and augmented them with new dogmatic theses, with the result that his teaching concerning the Church emerged as a more cohesive system.

The life and work of St. Cyprian—namely, his teaching concerning the Church—has already been the subject of detailed monographic works.[1631] In studying the history of the dogma concerning the Church we cannot of course pursue a study of monographic completeness. We must turn our attention primarily to the

Anm. 1. Cf. also the German translation by Kellner, *Tertullians sämtliche Schriften*, Bd. 1 (Köln: 1882), 417.

1631 In writing our essay, aside from general courses and the studies previously cited, we have employed the following works devoted exclusively to St. Cyprian: Johann Eduard Huther, *Cyprians Lehre von der Kirche* (Hamburg und Gotha: 1839); Dr. Friedrich Wilhelm Rettberg, *Thascius Cäcillus Cyprianus, Bischof von Carthago* (Gottingen: 1831); Iohannes Peters, *Der heilige Cyprian von Karthago, Bischof. Kirchenvater und Blutzeuge Christi, in seinem Leben und Kirken dargestellt* (Regensburg: 1877); Lic. Bernhard Fechtrup, *Der hl. Cyprian. Sein Leben und seine Lehre* (Münster: 1878); Dr. Ioseph Hub. Reinkens, *Die Lehre des heiligen Cyprian von der Einheit der Kirche* (Würzburg: 1873); Friedrich Böhringer, *Cyprianus, Bischof von Karthago, der das moderne spezifisch hierarchische Episcopat im Kampfe um seine Würde und sein Recht. Die alte Kirche*, 4-ter Teil (Stuttgart: 1874); Priest Alexey Molchanov, *St. Cyprian of Carthage and His Teaching on the Church* ["Св. Киприан Карфагенский и его учение о Церкви"] (Kazan: 1888); Dr. Bernhard Poschmann, *Die Sichtbarkeit der Kirche nach Lehre des hl. Cyprian. Forschungen zur Christlichen Literatur und Dogmengeschichte, herausgeg. von Dr. A. Ehrhard und Dr. I. P. Kirsch*, Bd. VIII, Heft. 3 (Paderborn: 1908); E. Michaud, "L' ecclésiologie de St. Cyprien," *Revue internationale de théologie* (1905): 34–35; 1906, 125–130; Hugo Koch, *Cyprian und der römische Primat. Texte und Untersuchungen zur Geschichte der altchristlichen Literatur. Herausgeg. von Adolf Harnack und Karl Schmidt*. XXXV, 1 (Leipzig: 1910); Dr. Anton Seitz, *Cyprian und der römische Primat oder Urchristliche Primatsentwicklung und Hugo Kochs modernistisches Kirchenrecht* (Regensburg: 1911).

significance of St. Cyprian's teaching on the Church in the history
of the dogma concerning the Church as a whole. A study of just the
historical events in the life of St. Cyprian would likewise lead us too
far afield. We therefore will not dwell on the historical details, but
will focus our attention on those dogmatic theses that in part dictated events and in part developed under the influence of events that
occurred. In expounding the views of St. Cyprian we will be guided
by systematic rather than chronological considerations.

Since the earliest days of his episcopal ministry St. Cyprian
encountered discord in the Church. For the bishop of Carthage
this church discord was, by his own admission, akin to a new persecution.[1632] To reconcile this discord and preach the unity of the
Church—this was the historical objective of St. Cyprian.[1633] Already Cyprian had a considerable legacy from the preceding centuries which he could employ in combating divisions in the Church.
Even St. Ignatius the God-bearer, who said of himself that he was
appointed for unity, spoke insistently of the need for peace in the
Church and for the preservation of true faith and submission to the
bishop. St. Ignatius also provides a certain basis for this particular
central position of the bishop in the Church. In St. Irenaeus and
Tertullian, as in St. Clement of Rome previously, we have already
seen the doctrine of the divine institution of the hierarchy and the
unbroken apostolic succession of the bishops. Here we see how Cyprian likewise assimilates all these ideas.[1634] Cyprian only expounds
and substantiates them with arguments, but at the same time he
highlights another aspect of the position of the bishop. The earliest
writers viewed the bishop primarily as the guardian of the truth of

---

1632 Cyprian of Carthage, *Epistles* 43-39.3, "To the People" (ANF 5:317;
CSEL 3.2:592). In quotations from the epistles of Cyprian we will include two
different numerations: the first number signifies the number of the epistle in
CSEL, volume 3, pars 2, and the second—the numbering in *The Ante-Nicene Fathers*, volume 5 (Grand Rapids, MI: Eerdmans, 1885).

1633 "Le fond de son caractère peut se résumer dans ces deux mots: Paix et
Unité" (Michaud, *Revue internationale de théologie* [1905]: 34). Vgl. Seeberg, *Studien
zur Gesch. Des Begr. der Kirche*, 84; Poschmann, *Die Sichtbarkeit der Kirche*, 4.

1634 For more detail see Poschmann, *Der Kirchenbegriff des hl. Cyprian und die
altere Tradition*, op. cit. 61 ff. Cf. Harnack's note in *Dogmengeschichte* 1, 405.

Christ entrusted to the Church. The schismastics with whom St. Cyprian had to contend did not distort doctrine, but introduced strife and discord. Consequently, for Cyprian agreement with the bishop is essential first and foremost for preserving peace in the Church.

St. Cyprian speaks clearly and decisively of the **divine institution of the hierarchy** in the Church. Our Lord Jesus Christ Himself said that nothing, not even the most insignificant of events, occurs without the knowledge and permission of God (see Mt. 10:29). Can one really think that God's priests are ordained (*ordinari*) in the Church without His knowledge? "For to believe that they who are ordained (*qui ordinantur*) are unworthy and unchaste, what else is it than to believe that his priests are not appointed (*constituantur*) in the Church by God, nor through God?"[1635] "Christ ... by His decree and word, and by His presence (*arbitrio et nutu ac praesentia*), both rules prelates themselves, and rules the Church by prelates."[1636] "The Lord ... condescends to elect and appoint for Himself priests in His Church. ... [He protects] them also when elected and appointed by His good-will and help, inspiring them to govern, and supplying ... vigour for restraining the contumacy of the wicked."[1637] The apostles, that is, bishops and overseers, were chosen by the Lord, Who appoints the bishops.[1638] Not only is each bishop ordained by particular volition, but God instituted the very principle of the hierarchy. The dignity of the bishop is the dignity of the apostles, successively preserved in the Church. "Our Lord, whose precepts and admonitions we ought to observe, describing the honour of a bishop and the order of His Church (*episcopi honorem*

1635   Idem 66-68.1, "To Florentius Pupianus" (ANF 5:373; CSEL 3.2:727). Cf. 66-68.5 (ANF 5:373–374; CSEL 3.2:730). Cf. *Epistles* 59-54.5 (ANF 5:340–341; CSEL 3.2:672).

1636   Idem 66-68.9, "To Florentius Pupianus" (ANF 5:375; CSEL 3.2:733).

1637   Idem 48-44, "To Cornelius" (ANF 5:322; CSEL 3.2:608). The Lord God made Cornelius bishop: *Epistles* 55-51, "To Antonianus" (ANF 5:329; CSEL 3.2:629). Cornelius was made bishop by the judgment (*judicio*) of God and his Christ (Ibid.), by the will of God (Ibid.; CSEL 3.2:630.3, 630–631).

1638   Cyprian of Carthage, *Epistles* 3-64.3, "To Rogatianus" (ANF 5:366; CSEL 3.2:471); *Epistles* 71-70.3, "To Quintus" (ANF 5:377–378; CSEL 3.2:774).

et ecclesiae suae rationem), speaks in the Gospel, and says to Peter: 'I say unto thee, That thou art Peter, and upon this rock will I build my Church; and the gates of hell shall not prevail against it. And I will give unto thee the keys of the kingdom of heaven: and whatsoever thou shalt bind on earth shall be bound in heaven: and whatsoever thou shalt loose on earth shall be loosed in heaven' [Mt. 16:18–19]. Thence, through the changes of times and successions (*per temporum et successionum vices*), the ordering (*ordinatio*) of bishops and the plan (*ratio*) of the Church flow onwards (*decurrit*); so that the Church is founded upon the bishops (*ecclesia super episcopos constituatur*), and every act of the Church is controlled by these same rulers (*praepositos*). ... This ... is founded on the divine law."[1639] The bishops, as successors of the apostles, appointed by God to the place of the

---

1639 Cyprian of Carthage, *Epistles* 33-36.1 (ANF 5:305; CSEL 3.2:566). Cf. *Epistles* 42-41, "To Cornelius": "unitatem a domino et per apostolos nobis successoribus traditam [unity delivered by the Lord, and through His apostles to us their successors]" (ANF 5:321; CSEL 3.2:602.18–19). The idea of the apostolic succession of the episcopacy was also clearly expressed by one of the bishops who was present at the Council of Carthage in 256: "Clarus a Mascula dixit: Manifesta est sententia Domini nostri Iesu Christi apostolos suos mittentis et ipsis solis potestatem a patre sibi datam permittentis, quibus nos successimus eadem potestate ecclesiam Domini gubernantes [Clarus of Mascula said: The sentence of our Lord Jesus Christ is plain, when He sent His apostles, and accorded to them alone the power given to Him by His Father; and to them we have succeeded, governing the Lord's Church with the same power]" (*Seventh Council of Carthage* 79:459). It should also be noted that in the words of Christ (Mt. 16:18–19) Cyprian sees merely the idea of founding the episcopacy in general. Every bishop is, as it were, a successor of the apostle Peter. Firmilian of Caesarea reasoned likewise in his letter to Cyprian. Citing the Gospel (Mt. 16:19, Jn. 20:22–23), he continues: "Potestas ergo peccatorum remittendorum apostolis data est et ecclesiis quas illi a Christo missi constituerunt et episcopis qui eis ordinatione vicaria successerunt [Therefore the power for remitting sins was given to the apostles, and to the churches which they, sent by Christ, established, and to the bishops who succeeded them by vicarious ordination]" (Cyprian of Carthage, *Epistles* 75-74.16 [ANF 5:394; CSEL 3.2:820–821]).

apostles,[1640] Cyprian sometimes even calls apostles.[1641] To the bishops, as successors of the apostles, belongs the right to teach in the Church. The bishops must both adhere to the faith and truth of the catholic Church themselves and teach it to others, demonstrating by all the rules of the Gospel and the apostles the validity of the divine dispensation of unity.[1642] The bishops are the chief guardians of faith and truth.[1643] The priests of God keep the divine precepts. If in anyone the truth should begin to waver and vacillate, they should immediately return to the origin which is of the Lord—to the evangelical and apostolical tradition (*ad originem dominicam et ad evangelicam atque apostolicam traditionem revertamur*).[1644] In this doctrine of the successive authority of the bishops from the apostles in the Church there is nothing essentially new, but it cannot be overlooked that in this instance Cyprian has a slightly different point of view on the matter. In St. Irenaeus, for example, the succession of the bishops is a historical argument in support of the truth of church Tradition. St. Cyprian's thinking, however, is in a purely dogmatic sphere: he speaks in general of the divine institution of a successive hierarchy in the Church.

The divinely established bishop, in the teaching of St. Cyprian, is that organ which first and foremost unites the individual com-

---

1640 "Christ ... says to the apostles, and thereby to all chief rulers, who by vicarious ordination succeed to the apostles: 'He that heareth you, heareth me; and he that heareth me, heareth Him that sent me; and he that despiseth you, despiseth me, and Him that sent me' [Lk. 10:16]" (Cyprian of Carthage, *Epistles* 66-68.4, "To Florentius Pupianus" [ANF 5:373; CSEL 3.2:729–730]). Cf. *Epistles* 69-75.5, "To Magnus": "ordinationi succedanea praesidens [presiding over {the Church} by successive ordination]" (ANF 5:398; CSEL 3.2:753).

1641 Cyprian of Carthage, *Epistles* 3-64.3, "To Rogatianus" (ANF 5:366; CSEL 3.2:471).

1642 Cyprian of Carthage, *Epistles* 73-72.20, "To Jubaianus" (ANF 5:384; CSEL 3.2:794).

1643 Cyprian of Carthage, *Epistles* 73-72.22, "To Jubaianus": "Qui fidei et veritati praesumus" (ANF 5:385; CSEL 3.2:796.7).

1644 Cyprian of Carthage, *Epistles* 74-73.10, "To Pompey" (ANF 5:389; CSEL 3.2:803.13 sqq).

munity around himself.[1645] "They are the Church who are a people united to the priest, and the flock which adheres to its pastor.
Whence you ought to know that the bishop is in the Church, and
the Church in the bishop (*episcopum in ecclesia esse et ecclesiam in episcopo*); and if any one be not with the bishop, that he is not in the
Church."[1646] The bishop is the one shepherd of the one flock (see Jn.
10:16).[1647] The bishop in the local Church possesses full authority;
"The bishop ... is one and rules over the Church;"[1648] the presbyters
or deacons who share his labors must submit to him, and only at
his charge must they perform all that their ministry in the church
requires.[1649] Like St. Ignatius the God-bearer, St. Cyprian tirelessly
speaks of obedience to the bishop. "Nor let them think," he writes
concerning virgins, "that the way of life or of salvation is still open
to them, if they have refused to obey the bishops and priests."[1650]
His writings contain a whole series of proofs that this obedience is
essential and pleasing to God. He cites all passages from the Holy
Scriptures of both Old and New Testaments wherever obedience

1645 The significance of the bishop for the community is depicted by Dr.
Johann Adam Möhler (*Die Einheit in der Kirche oder das Prinzip des Katholicismus, dargestellt in Geiste der Kirchenväter der drei ersten Jahrhunderte* (Tübingen: 1843), 175 ff., esp.
187–195); Poschmann, *Die Sichtbarkeit der Kirche*, 6.

1646 Cyprian of Carthage, *Epistles* 66-68.8, "To Florentius Pupianus" (ANF
5:374–375; CSEL 3.2:733). They therefore vainly flatter themselves who, not
being at peace with the priests, think by ingratiation to incline some to secret
fellowship with them.

1647 Cyprian of Carthage, *Epistles* 76-75.5, "To Magnus" (ANF 5:398; CSEL
3.2:753).

1648 Cyprian of Carthage, *Epistles* 66-68.5, "To Florentius Pupianus" (ANF
5:373–374; CSEL 3.2:730).

1649 Cyprian of Carthage, *Epistles* 5-4, "To the Presbyters and Deacons"
(ANF 5:282; CSEL 3.2:510). *Epistles* 3-64.3, "To Rogatianus": "Deacons [are the]
ministers of [the] episcopacy and of the Church" (ANF 5:366; CSEL 3.2:510).
Epistles 34-27.3, "To the Presbyters and Deacons": one who disobeys the will of
the bishop must be excommunicated and given over to judgment (ANF 5:306;
CSEL 3.2:570). *Epistles* 40-39.5: "Let them alone be without bishops who have
rebelled against bishops" (ANF 5:318; CSEL 3.2:594–595).

1650 Cyprian of Carthage, *Epistles* 4-61.4, "To Pomponius" (ANF 5:359;
CSEL 3.2:476).

to the priests is mentioned. Several times he cites the words of Deuteronomy (see 17:12–13), where the penalty for disobedience to the priest is death.[1651] The example of Christ is cited, Who rendered honor to the chief priests and scribes, though they had neither the fear of God nor the knowledge of Christ. "He [thereby] taught that true priests were lawfully and fully to be honoured (*legitime et plene honorari*)."[1652] Obedience to the bishop is essential for the peace and wholeness of the Church. "If, according to divine teaching, the whole fraternity should obey [him], no one would stir up anything against the college of priests; no one, after the divine judgment (*judicium*), after the suffrage (*suffragium*) of the people, after the consent (*consensum*) of the co-bishops, would make himself a judge, not now of the bishop, but of God. No one would rend the Church by a division of the unity of Christ. No one, pleasing himself, and swelling with arrogance, would found a new heresy, separate and without [the Church]."[1653] To all those who resist the authority of the bishop St. Cyprian cites the fate of Korah, Dathan, and Abiram, who began to consider themselves equal to the presiding priest and received the penalty for their sacrilegious audacity. This punishment of the rebels showed that He who appoints the priests will avenge them,[1654] and that whatever wicked men undertake in order by their own will to overthrow God's appointment (*ordinationem*) is done in opposition to God.[1655] Finally, in his epistle to Florentius Pupianus,

---

1651 Cyprian of Carthage, *Epistles* 4-61.4, "To Pomponius" (ANF 5:359; CSEL 3.2:476); *Epistles* 3-64.1, "To Rogatianus" (ANF 5:366; CSEL 3.2:469–470); *Epistles* 59-54.4, "To Cornelius" (ANF 5:340; CSEL 3.2:670). *Epistles* 66-68.3, "To Florentius Pupianus" (ANF 5:373; CSEL 3.2:728).

1652 Cyprian of Carthage, *Epistles* 3-64.3, "To Rogatianus" (ANF 5:366; CSEL 3.2:471).

1653 Cyprian of Carthage, *Epistles* 59-54.5, "To Cornelius" (ANF 5:340; CSEL 3.2:672).

1654 Cyprian of Carthage, *Epistles* 3-64.3, "To Rogatianus" (ANF 5:366; CSEL 3.2:470).

1655 Cyprian of Carthage, *Treatises* 1, "On the Unity of the Church" (ANF 5:427; CSEL 3.2:226). Here also mention is made of the king Uzziah, who took a censer and refused to obey and yield it to the priest Azariah when he tried to prevent him, and for this was stricken with leprosy upon his brow, being marked

which St. Cyprian wrote with intensity and strong feeling, we read: "Bees have a king, and cattle a leader, and they keep faith to him. Robbers obey their chief with an obedience full of humility. How much more simple and better than you are the brute cattle and dumb animals, and robbers, although bloody, and raging among swords and weapons! The chief among them is acknowledged and feared, whom no divine judgment has appointed, but on whom an abandoned faction and a guilty band have agreed."[1656] Obedience to the bishop—this indeed is the foundation of unity in the Church! Conversely, disobedience is the beginning of division and heresy. "For these things are the beginnings of heretics, and the origins and endeavours of evil-minded schismatics;—to please themselves, and with swelling haughtiness to despise him who is set over them. Thus they depart from the Church—thus a profane altar is set up out-side—thus they rebel against the peace of Christ, and the appoint-ment (*ordinatio*) and the unity of God."[1657] This idea is expressed repeatedly in various forms in the works of St. Cyprian. "Certain persons, proud, contumacious, and enemies of God's priests, either depart from the Church or act against the Church."[1658] In general,

---

(*notatus*) by an offended God upon that part of the body upon which those who please the Lord are anointed (*signantur*).

1656 Cyprian of Carthage, *Epistles* 66-68.6, "To Florentius Pupianus" (ANF 5:374; CSEL 3.2:730–731).

1657 Cyprian of Carthage, *Epistles* 3-64.3, "To Rogatianus" (ANF 5:366; CSEL 3.2:471–472). Cf. *Epistles* 66-68.5, "To Florentius Pupianus": "From this have arisen, and still arise, schisms and heresies, in that the bishop who is one and rules over the Church (*qui unus est et ecclesiae praeest*) is contemned by the haughty presumption of some persons; and the man who is honoured by God's conde-scension, is judged unworthy by men. For what swelling of pride is this, what arrogance of soul, what inflation of mind, to call prelates and priests to one's own recognition!" (ANF 5:373; CSEL 3.2:730). *Epistles* 59-54.5, "To Cornelius": "Neither have heresies arisen, nor have schisms originated, from any other source than from this, that God's priest is not obeyed; nor do they consider that there is one person for the time priest in the Church, and for the time judge in the stead of Christ" (ANF 5:340; CSEL 3.2:672). Cf. *Treatises* 1.10, "On the Unity of the Church" (ANF 5:424; CSEL 3.2:218).

1658 Cyprian of Carthage, *Epistles* 59-54.7, "To Cornelius" (ANF 5:341; CSEL 3.2:674).

early church literature considers pride to be the cause of heresy or schism. In St. Ignatius the God-bearer and St. Irenaeus of Lyons we have already seen a very semantically similar condemnation of heresy.[1659] But compared to the church writers who preceded him, here too St. Cyprian evinces a certain singularity. Formerly, pride was considered the source of opposition to the "Rule of Faith" or of its distortion.[1660] In the writings of St. Cyprian, heretical pride primarily produces rebellion against the hierarchy, against the bishop, to whom all in his sphere must submit. Consequently, in part St. Cyprian is supplementing the doctrine that preceded him concerning the authority of the bishop and the necessity of submission to him.[1661]

At the same time, St. Cyprian does not represent the bishop as an autocratic administrator of all church affairs, so that his statement that "the Church is in the bishop" could be interpreted to mean that the bishop replaces the Church. "The Church," says St. Cyprian, "is established in the bishop and the clergy, and all who stand fast in the faith."[1662] Quite frequently in the epistles of Cyprian we find accounts of the bishop resolving matters jointly with the clergy and the people.[1663] He himself writes to the presbyters

---

1659 Ignatius the God-bearer, *Epistle to the Philadelphians* 8, *Epistle to the Trallians* 7; Irenaeus of Lyons, *Against Heresies* 4.33.7. The views of early church writers on the source of heresies are presented in the book by Seitz, *Die Heilsnotwendigkeit der Kirche*, 84–86. Cf. also 87 ff. Vgl. Harnack, *Dogmengeschichte*⁴, 423.

1660 Cf. Tertullian, *The Prescription Against Heretics* 6: "Quorum opera sunt adulterae doctrinae [Of these the practical effects are false doctrines" (PL 2:20b); *On Monogamy* 2: "Adversarius spiritus ... primo regulam adulterans fidei [the adversary spirit... beginning by adulterating the rule of faith]" (PL 2:980–981). Cf. Irenaeus, *Against Heresies* 3.24.1–2.

1661 The teaching of St. Cyprian on the bishop is expounded in detail by the priest A. Molchanov (see *St. Cyprian of Carthage* ["Св. Киприан Карфагенский"], 208–248), and also by Huther (*Cyprians Lehre von der Kirche*, 59 ff.). We shall limit ourselves to an outline thereof. Concerning the bishop we will speak more later on.

1662 Cyprian of Carthage, *Epistles* 33-26.1, "To the Lapsed": "Ecclesia in episcopo et clero et in omnibus stantibus constituta" (ANF 5:305; CSEL 3.2:566.15–16).

1663 Cyprian of Carthage, *Epistles* 14-5.1, "To the Presbyters and Deacons" (ANF 5:282–283; CSEL 3.2:510); *Epistles* 19-13.1, "To the Clergy" (ANF 5:293;

and deacons: "From the first commencement of my episcopacy, I made up my mind to do nothing on my own private (*privatim*) opinion, without your advice and without the consent of the people."[1664] And concerning Cornelius, bishop of Rome, Cyprian relates that he always read the letters which he received to the distinguished clergy who preside with him (*tecum praesidenti*) and to his very holy and renowned congregation.[1665]

Certain scholars of church history fail to reconcile these two theses of St. Cyprian: "the Church [is] in the bishop" and "the Church is established in the bishop and the clergy, and all who stand fast in the faith." These latter wish to see two elements in the works of St. Cyprian: one earlier, one later.[1666] It is alleged that in Cyprian there are glimpses of the old idea that the Church is first and foremost a community,[1667] and a later, even unexpected trace of communal autonomy is encountered.[1668] Due to his circumstances, Cyprian was unable to eliminate this autonomy, but he was able to use it to his advantage.[1669] It is conjectured that he changed his view,[1670] or even

---

CSEL 3.2:525); *Epistles* 34-27.1, "To the Presbyters and Deacons" (ANF 5:306; CSEL 3.2:568–569).

1664 Cyprian of Carthage, *Epistles* 14-5.4, "To the Presbyters and Deacons" (ANF 5:283; CSEL 3.2:512).

1665 Cyprian of Carthage, *Epistles* 59-54.20, "To Cornelius" (ANF 5:346; CSEL 3.2:689).

1666 Harnack says that the passages in which Cyprian defined the Church as *constituta in episcopo et in clero et in omnibus credentibus* [established in the bishop and the clergy, and all the faithful] pertain to an earlier time, when he himself essentially professed the old concept of the Church, and that the definition of the Church as a community governed by the bishop is a product of the Novatian crisis. See *Dogmengeschichte*⁴, 417, Anm. 2.

1667 Seeberg, *Studien zur Geschichte des Begriffs der Kirche*, 34.

1668 Ritschl, *Die Entstehung der altkath. Kirche*, 558: "Er (Cyprian) zeigt sich also als Vertreter der Autonomie der Gemeinde, in einer Zeit, in welcher nach unserer Darstellung der Geschichte der Gedanke daran nicht mehr zu erwarten wäre." Cf. Böhringer, *Die alte Kirche* 4, 950: "Wir erkennen hierin" (*Epistles* 33-26.1) einen Rest der alten Gemeindeautonomie."

1669 Böhringer, *Die alte Kirche* 4, 950.

1670 Seeberg, *Studien zur Geschichte des Begriffs der Kirche*, 34–35. But cf.

that Cyprian was supposedly a supporter of episcopal absolutism at heart, but he disguised his views by speaking of the mutual concord of the bishop, the clergy, and the people.[1671]

The latter suspicion is groundless, however. In the writings of St. Cyprian himself the expressive testimony to the authority of the bishop stands side by side with the definition of the Church as consisting of the bishop, the clergy, and the faithful.[1672] Although it is rightly noted that St. Cyprian himself does not explain how he reconciles the two,[1673] there can be no doubt whatsoever that both these points are organically interconnected. St. Cyprian establishes the unity of the individual Church upon the authority and significance of the bishop: the bishop is the center and buttress of that unity.[1674] But the thinking of the holy father runs in the sphere of the dogmatic, not of the judicial. His teaching on the unity of the individual Church has no judicial overtones: St. Cyprian never descends from the exclusive basis of Christian morality. Given this nature of his teaching, the authority of the bishop and his constant connection with the community are not only not mutually exclusive, but on the contrary even complement each other. Through agreement with the bishop the Church abides in unity, and in agreement with the whole community the bishop finds moral grounds for his authority.[1675]

Poschmann's argument concerning this in *Die Sichtbarkeit der Kirche*, 64, Anm. 2. See also 6, Anm. 2.

1671 Ritschl, *Die Entstehung der altkath. Kirche*, 559: "Mit dem angeführten Grundsatz über die Harmonie von Bischof, Klerus, Gemeinde hat jedoch Cyprian seine eigentliche Ansicht nur sehr schwach maskirt."

1672 Cyprian of Carthage, *Epistles* 33-26.1, "To the Lapsed" (ANF 5:305; CSEL 3.2:566.15–16).

1673 Böhringer, *Die alte Kirche* 4, 950.

1674 "L'évêque est donc l'organe de l'église, mais il n'est pas l'église; il est le Symbole visible de son unité, mais il n'est pas l'unité même" (E. Michaud, "L' ecclésiologie de St. Cyprien," *Revue internationale de théologie* [1905]: 37).

1675 Cf. the reasoning of Michaud: "La notion de l'ordre dans l'église non de l'ordre factice qui résulte de la phantaisie et de l'absolutisme des chefs, mais de l'ordre vérilable, fondé sur le main-tien de la doctrine et des institutions du Christ." ("L' ecclésiologie de St. Cyprien," *Revue internationale de théologie* [1905]:

Such, in general terms, is the teaching of St. Cyprian on the unity of each individual Church, under the governance of a bishop. But, as previously stated, it is not this teaching that comprises the defining trait of the ecclesiological views of the holy father: this point in the doctrine concerning the Church had already been decisively made by church writers since the very beginning of Christian literature. And it is not this subject which St. Cyprian pursues with particular urgency. His favorite idea is the idea **of the unity of the entire Church of Christ.** We must not suppose, of course, that St. Cyprian created this teaching on the unity of the entire Church of Christ out of nothing. No; the idea of the unity of all Christianity had always dwelt in church consciousness; but in historical manuscripts this consciousness is glimpsed as if by chance: it was not the subject of detailed treatises.[1676] What Cyprian did was give clear and systematic expression to the dogmatic doctrine of the unity of the Church—a unity previously comprehended as an intrinsic necessity, which in one way or another received outward implementation.[1677]

Having established this general view of Cyprian's stance on the church thinking that preceded him, we now turn to a more de-

---

37). Cf. Batiffol, *L'eglise naissante et le catholicisme*, 422n2.

1676 At the outset of our study we outlined this early Christian idea of the unity of the Church. Orthodox and Catholic scholars always defend the thesis that the Church of Christ always thought of itself as a single whole. For brief notes on this awareness of the Church prior to Cyprian of Carthage, see the study by the priest A. Molchanov, *St. Cyprian of Carthage*, 187–190. The subject is discussed in somewhat greater detail, with lists of works cited, by Poschmann (*Die Sichtbarkeit der Kirche*, 71–75) and Möhler (*Die Einheit in der Kirche*, 213–220). The singular Protestant theory of Zohm should also be included here.

1677 Poschmann likewise arrives at nearly the same result (*Die Sichtbarkeit der Kirche*, 75). Möhler says the same (*Die Einheit in der Kirche*, 222): "What had long since existed in the Church was clearly and systematically expressed; for, after all the development that has been described, who can still claim that the Church was infiltrated by a new doctrine, a new phenomenon, or even that Cyprian alone and his composition on the unity of the Church introduced this doctrine into the Church?" See Poschmann (75, Anm. 2) for the opinions of other scholars. Cf. Loofs, *Leitfaden der Dogmengeschichte*⁴ §29.1, 204.

tailed exposition of his teaching concerning the unity of the entire
Church of Christ.

Christ sent His apostles forth to preach.[1678] His disciples, in accordance with the command of their Teacher and God, dispersed
throughout the world in order to impart the commandments unto
salvation, so as to lead men out of the darkness of error to the path
of light—to enlighten the blind and ignorant unto the knowledge
of the Truth.[1679] But the Church, established by the apostles to the
ends of the earth, is one. The apostles delivered only one Church
to the bishops.[1680] The Church is one at its very foundation; it is the
catholic Church.[1681] The Lord has established (*constituta*) the catholic
Church, which is one and alone (*una et sola*).[1682] "[Christ] beseeches
the Father for all, saying, 'Neither pray I for these alone, but for
them also which shall believe on me through their word; that they
all may be one; as Thou, Father, art in me, and I in Thee, that
they also may be one in us' [Jn. 17:20–21]. The Lord's loving-kind-
ness, no less than His mercy, is great in respect of our salvation,
in that, not content to redeem us with His blood, He in addition
also prayed for us. Behold now what was the desire of His petition,
that like as the Father and Son are one, so also we should abide in
absolute unity (*in ipsa unitate*)."[1683] "The Lord says, 'I and the Father
are one' [Jn. 10:30], and again it is written of the Father, and of
the Son, and of the Holy Spirit, 'And these three are one' [1 Jn.
5:7]. And does any one believe that this unity which thus comes

---

1678 Cyprian of Carthage, *Epistles* 74-73.2, "To Pompey" (ANF 5:386–387;
CSEL 3.2:800).

1679 Cyprian of Carthage, *Treatises* 6.14, "On the Vanity of Idols" (ANF
5:468; CSEL 3.2:31).

1680 Cyprian of Carthage, *Epistles* 73-72.13, "To Jubaianus" (ANF 5:382;
CSEL 3.2:787).

1681 Cyprian of Carthage, *Epistles* 73-72.20, "To Jubaianus" (ANF 5:384;
CSEL 3.2:794); *Epistles* 45-51.1, "To Cornelius" (ANF 320; CSEL 3.2:599).

1682 Cyprian of Carthage, *Epistles* 65-63.5, "To Epictetus" (ANF 5:365;
CSEL 3.2:725). Cf. *Epistles* 42-?.1, "To Cornelius" (CSEL 3.2:600).

1683 Cyprian of Carthage, *Treatises* 4.30, "On the Lord's Prayer" (ANF 5:455;
CSEL 3.2:288–289). Cf. 4.23 (ANF 5:453–454; CSEL 3.2:284–285).

from the divine strength (*de divina firmitate*) and coheres in celestial sacraments, can be divided in the Church, and can be separated by the parting asunder of opposing wills? He who does not hold this unity does not hold God's law, does not hold the faith of the Father and the Son, does not hold life and salvation."[1684] "The Lord, suggesting to us a unity that comes from divine authority, lays it down, saying, 'I and my Father are one' [Jn. 10:30]. To which unity reducing His Church, He says again, 'And there shall be one flock, and one shepherd' [Jn. 10:16]."[1685] In addition to the unity of the Persons of the most Holy Trinity, St. Cyprian grounds the unity of the Church in the oneness of God and Christ. "There is one God, and Christ is one, and there is one Church."[1686] "'And there shall be one flock and one shepherd.' And does any one believe that in one place there can be either many shepherds or many flocks?"[1687] The Church is particularly closely linked with Christ. The Church is the bride of Christ,[1688] conjoined and united (*adunata*) with Christ[1689] as her bridegroom.[1690] "The blessed apostle ... with his sacred voice testifies to the unity of Christ with the Church, cleaving to one an-

---

1684 Cyprian of Carthage, *Treatises* 1.6, "On the Unity of the Church" (ANF 5:423; CSEL 3.2:215).

1685 Cyprian of Carthage, *Epistles* 69-75.5, "To Magnus" (ANF 5:398; CSEL 3.2:753).

1686 Cyprian of Carthage, *Epistles* 43-39.5, "To the People" (ANF 5:318; CSEL 3.2:594). The same is found in *Treatises* 1.23, "On the Unity of the Church" (CSEL 3.2:231). Cf. CSEL 3.2:214. In his words in Eph. 4:4–6 the apostle Paul shows the sacrament of unity (*sacramentum unitatis*).

1687 Cyprian of Carthage, *Treatises* 1.8, "On the Unity of the Church" (ANF 5:423–424; CSEL 3.2:217).

1688 Cyprian of Carthage, *Treatises* 1.6, "On the Unity of the Church" (ANF 5:423; CSEL 3.2:216); *Epistles* 69-75.2, "To Magnus" (ANF 5:397–398; CSEL 3.2:751); *Epistles* 52-48.1, "To Cornelius" (ANF 5:325; CSEL 3.2:617); *Epistles* 74-73.6, "To Pompey" (ANF 5:388; CSEL 3.2:804).

1689 Cyprian of Carthage, *Epistles* 74-73.6, "To Pompey" (ANF 5:389; CSEL 3.2:804).

1690 Cyprian of Carthage, *Epistles* 73-72.11, "To Jubaianus" (ANF 5:382; CSEL 3.2:786).

other with indivisible links."[1691] St. Cyprian speaks of the marriage of Christ and the Church.[1692]

St. Cyprian likens the mystical union of Christ with the Church to the mingling of wine and water in the Cup of the Lord. As the wine and water are closely and inseparably united and cannot be separated from each other, in the same way nothing can separate Christ from the Church—that is, from the people who comprise the Church (*plebem in ecclesia constitutam*), who faithfully and firmly persevere in the faith, united by continual, undivided love.[1693] In the words that follow concerning the Sacrament of the Eucharist, to denote the union of the faithful in this Sacrament St. Cyprian employs the same imagery that we have already seen in *The Teaching of the Twelve Apostles*. "The body of the Lord cannot be flour alone or water alone, unless both should be united and joined together and compacted in the mass of one bread; in which very sacrament our people are shown to be made one, so that in like manner as many grains, collected, and ground, and mixed together into one mass, make one bread; so in Christ, who is the heavenly bread, we may know that there is one body, with which our number is joined and united."[1694] Naturally, this mystical union of the members of the Church in the Sacrament of the Eucharist could also be applied to the individual Church alone. But St. Cyprian, in agreement with the apostle, also calls the entire ecumenical Church the Body. He writes to Cornelius that every effort be made "to bring the members

---

1691 Cyprian of Carthage, *Epistles* 52-48.1, "To Cornelius" (ANF 5:325; CSEL 3.2:617). Here St. Cyprian is referring to Eph. 5:31–32.

1692 Cyprian of Carthage, *Epistles* 63-62.12, "To Caecilius" (ANF 5:361; CSEL 3.2:711).

1693 Cyprian of Carthage, *Epistles* 63-62.13, "To Caecilius" (ANF 5:362; CSEL 3.2:711). "Thus, therefore, in consecrating the cup of the Lord, water alone cannot be offered, even as wine alone cannot be offered. For if any one offer wine only, the blood of Christ is dissociated from us; but if the water be alone, the people are dissociated from Christ; but when both are mingled, and are joined with one another by a close union, there is completed a spiritual and heavenly sacrament" (ANF 5:362; CSEL 3.2:711–712).

1694 Cyprian of Carthage, *Epistles* 63-62.13, "To Caecilius" (ANF 5:362; CSEL 3.2:712). Cf. *The Didache* 10.5.

of the divided body into the unity of the Catholic Church (*ad catholicae ecclesiae unitatem*), and associate them into the bond of Christian charity."[1695] The Church "is one ... and the people are joined into a substantial unity of body (*in solidam corporis unitatem*) by the cement of concord."[1696] In another place St. Cyprian applies the very image of the Bread of the Eucharist to the whole Christian people.[1697] All the Churches scattered throughout the world are linked by the bonds of unity.[1698] It is noteworthy that the Roman clergy likewise, who in their epistle to Cyprian speak of "the body of the whole Church, whose members are scattered through every various province," speak of the entire ecumenical Church as one Body.[1699]

This theme of the unity of all separate Churches in the one ecumenical Church of Christ is developed most thoroughly in the excellent treatise by St. Cyprian, *On the Unity of the Catholic Church*. This treatise appears to expound the most fervent ideas of the holy father. His other treatises, especially his epistles, constantly repeat the same ideas as in *On the Unity of the Church*—sometimes verbatim. Hardly anything is omitted in this treatise; on the question of the unity of the Church, St. Cyprian's other works introduce hardly anything new. This work compiles everything from Holy Scripture

---

1695 Cyprian of Carthage, *Epistles* 45-41.1, "To Cornelius" (ANF 320; CSEL 3.2:599).

1696 Cyprian of Carthage, *Treatises* 1.23, "On the Unity of the Church" (ANF 5:429; CSEL 3.2:231). Cf. 1.5, 12, 23 (CSEL 3.2:214, 220, 230); *Epistles* 41-?.3: *Catholicae ecclesiae corpus unum* (CSEL 3.2:598). *Epistles* 66-68.8, "To Florentius Pupianus" (ANF 5:374–375; CSEL 3.2:732).

1697 Cyprian of Carthage, *Epistles* 69-75.6, "To Magnus": "When the Lord calls bread, which is combined by the union of many grains, His body, He indicates our people whom He bore as being united; and when He calls the wine, which is pressed from many grapes and clusters and collected together, His blood, He also signifies our flock linked together by the mingling of a united multitude" (ANF 5:398; CSEL 3.2:754).

1698 Cyprian of Carthage, *Epistles* 66-68.8, "To Florentius Pupianus" (ANF 5:374; CSEL 3.2:732).

1699 Cyprian of Carthage, *Epistles* 36-29.4: "Corpus totius ecclesiae, cujus per varias quasque provincias membra digesta sunt" (ANF 5:308; CSEL 3.2:575).

that could possibly be interpreted with application to the Church. Here also we see a whole series of various likenesses and analogies.

Already the Old Testament prophecies and prefigurations present the truth of the unity of the Church. The ark of Noah prefigured the one Church.[1700] The house of Rahab in the Old Testament served as the sole refuge during the destruction of the inhabitants of Jericho (see Josh. 2:18–19); but the house of Rahab prefigured the Church.[1701] The sacrament of the Passover required that the lamb slain as an image of Christ should be eaten in one house. There is no other home for believers than the one Church. The Church is the household of unanimity, and only those of one mind dwell in the house of God, in the Church of Christ.[1702] The Church is a garden enclosed and a fountain sealed,[1703] the vineyard of the Lord of hosts.[1704] Likewise, in the Song of Songs the Holy Spirit signifies the one Church, saying on the Lord's behalf: "My dove, my undefiled is but one; she is the only one of her mother, she is the choice one of her that bare her" (Song of Sol. 6:8).[1705]

1700 Cyprian of Carthage, *Treatises* 1.6, "On the Unity of the Church" (ANF 5:423; CSEL 3.2:214); *Epistles* 74-73.11, "To Pompey" (ANF 5:389; CSEL 3.2:809): "The Church ... is established in the unity of the Lord according to the sacrament of the one ark." *Epistles* 69-75.2, "To Magnus": "Peter himself, showing and vindicating the unity" of the Church (1 Pet. 3:20), cited the ark of Noah, attesting "that the Church is one ... attesting that the one ark of Noah was a type of the one Church" (ANF 5:398; CSEL 3.2:751).

1701 Cyprian of Carthage, *Treatises* 1.8, "On the Unity of the Church" (ANF 5:424; CSEL 3.2:217); *Epistles* 69-75.4, "To Magnus" (ANF 5:398; CSEL 3.2:752–753).

1702 Cyprian of Carthage, *Treatises* 1.8, "On the Unity of the Church" (ANF 5:424; CSEL 3.2:217); *Epistles* 69-75.4, "To Magnus" (ANF 5:398; CSEL 3.2:753–754).

1703 Cyprian of Carthage, *Epistles* 74-73.11, "To Pompey" (ANF 5:389; CSEL 3.2:808); *Epistles* 69-75.2, "To Magnus" (ANF 5:398; CSEL 3.2:751).

1704 Cyprian of Carthage, *Epistles* 63-62.12, "To Caecilius" (ANF 5:362; CSEL 3.2:711).

1705 Cyprian of Carthage, *Treatises* 1.4, "On the Unity of the Church" (ANF 5:422; CSEL 3.2:213); *Epistles* 69-75.2, "To Magnus" (ANF 5:398; CSEL 3.2:750–751).

This sacrament of unity, this union of unbroken accord, is signified in the Gospel account of the coat of our Lord Jesus Christ.
The coat was not divided and torn apart, but went entire to one to
whom it fell by lot, and was possessed by him uninjured and undivided (see Jn. 19:23–24). It had a unity that came down from above,
that is, from heaven and the Father. "When at Solomon's death his
kingdom and people were divided, Abijah the prophet, meeting Jeroboam the king in the field, divided his garment into twelve sec-
tions [see 1 Kgs. 11:30–36)]. ... But because Christ's people cannot
be rent, His robe, woven and united throughout, is not divided by
those who possess it; undivided, united, connected, it shows the coherent concord of our people who put on Christ. By the sacrament
and sign of His garment, [the Lord] has declared the unity of the
Church."[1706]

The catholic Church is one; it must not be severed or divided.[1707]
The sacrament of unity is inseparable.[1708] The unity of the Church
in no way contradicts the existence of individual communities dispersed throughout the world, under the governance of bishops. St.
Cyprian illustrates this truth by means of analogies. "The Church
... is one, which is spread abroad far and wide into a multitude by
an increase of fruitfulness. As there are many rays of the sun, but
one light; and many branches of a tree, but one strength based in
its tenacious root; and since from one spring flow many streams,
although the multiplicity seems diffused in the liberality of an over-
flowing abundance, yet the unity is still preserved in the source.
Separate a ray of the sun from its body of light, its unity does not
allow a division of light; break a branch from a tree—when broken,
it will not be able to bud; cut off the stream from its fountain, and

---

1706 Cyprian of Carthage, *Treatises* 1.4, "On the Unity of the Church" (ANF
5:422; CSEL 3.2:215–216).

1707 Cyprian of Carthage, *Epistles* 66-68.8, "To Florentius Pupianus" (ANF
5:375; CSEL 3.2:733). The Church is one, and cannot be divided. *Epistles* 74-
73.4, "To Pompey" (ANF 5:387; CSEL 3.2:802); *Epistles* 51-46.2, "To Cornelius"
(ANF 5:324; CSEL 3.2:615).

1708 Cyprian of Carthage, *Epistles* 69-75.6, "To Magnus" (ANF 5:399; CSEL
3.2:754).

that which is cut off dries up. Thus also the Church, shone over with the light of the Lord, sheds forth her rays over the whole world, yet it is one light which is everywhere diffused, nor is the unity of the body separated. Her fruitful abundance spreads her branches over the whole world. She broadly expands her rivers, liberally flowing, yet her head is one, her source one; and she is one mother, plentiful in the results of fruitfulness."[1709] In this animated and tenderly poetic excerpt we see clearly expressed the idea that the individual Christian community is alive and lives the life of Christ insofar as it is united with the entire ecumenical Church. For a local Church to isolate itself, to withdraw into seclusion, is the same for it as for a ray of light to separate itself from the sun, or a stream from its source, or a branch from the trunk. Life can only exist when there are organic ties with the ecumenical Church. If these ties are broken, Christian life dries up.

Finally, we must also examine another highly controversial argument of St. Cyprian by which he demonstrates the unity of the Church. St. Cyprian writes: "The Lord speaks to Peter, saying, 'I say unto thee...'" and so on (Mt. 16:18–19). "And again to the same He says, after His resurrection, 'Feed my sheep' [Jn. 21:16]. [Thus (He) establishes the Church upon one.][1710] And although to all the apostles, after His resurrection, He gives an equal power (*parem potestatem*), and says, 'As the Father hath sent me, even so send I you: Receive ye the Holy Ghost: Whose soever sins ye remit, they shall be remitted unto him; and whose soever sins ye retain, they shall be retained' [Jn. 20:21–23]; yet, that He might set forth unity (*ut unitatem manifestaret*), He arranged by His authority the origin of that unity, as beginning from one. Assuredly the rest of the apostles were also the same as was Peter, endowed with a like partnership both of honour and power (*hoc erant utique et ceteri apostoli quod fuit Petrus, pari consortio paediti et honoris et potestatis*); but the beginning proceeds from

---

1709 Cyprian of Carthage, *Treatises* 1.5, "On the Unity of the Church" (ANF 5:423; CSEL 3.2:214).

1710 The phrase in brackets is present in the Russian translation, but not *The Ante-Nicene Fathers*. Translation from the Russian by current translator. *–Trans.*

unity[1711] (*exordium ab unitate proficiscitur, ut ecclesia una monstretur*)."[1712]
And in another place St. Cyprian writes: "The Church founded by
Christ the Lord upon Peter, by a source and principle of unity (*origine et ratione unitatis*), is one."[1713] One can well imagine what considerable attention these passages from the works of Cyprian command
among Roman Catholic scholars and theologians. In their opinion,
here by one means or another St. Cyprian is attesting to **the primacy of the apostle Peter.** This understanding of St. Cyprian's
words has always been and continues to be disputed by Orthodox
and Protestant theologians. This controversy naturally will not end
as long as Catholicism with its teaching of papal primary continues
to exist. The polemical literature on both sides has already stated
all that can be said. If we bethought ourselves to thoroughly analyze this Catholic conviction, it would lead us far afield.[1714] We will

---

1711 In the Russian source, "but in the beginning one is indicated to denote
one Church." –*Trans.*

1712 Cyprian of Carthage, *Treatises* 1.4, "On the Unity of the Church" (ANF
5:422; CSEL 3.2:212–213).

1713 Cyprian of Carthage, *Epistles* 70-69.3, "To Januarius" (ANF 5:376;
CSEL 3.2:769). All similar phrases are compiled by Harnack in *Dogmengeschichte*[4]
1, 420–421, Anm. 2.

1714 We think it not superfluous to mention the literature pertaining to this
matter. One may learn the Catholic understanding of the passage cited from
Poschmann's book *Die Sichtbarkeit der Kirche,* 13–21. See also Karl Adam, "Cyprians Commentar zu Mt. 16, 18 in dogmengeschichtlicher Beleuchtung," *Theologische Quartalschrift* (1912): 99 ff., 203 ff., or the *nhel* by Seitz's *Cyprian und der
römische Primat,* 30 ff. The most detailed anti-Catholic interpretation [may be
found] in the specialized work by Koch, *Cyprian und der römische Primat,* TU 35.1,
6-22, 31–38. In Russian literature an analysis of Catholic references to Cyprian [is found] in the "Opinion on Proofs of a Defender of the Roman Catholic
Church in support of the Primacy of the Bishop of Rome" ["Мнение на доказательства защитника Римско-католиченской Церкви о главенстве риского
епископа"], in *Collected Opinions and Reviews of Philaret, Metropolitan of Moscow and
Kolomna,* under the editorship of the Most Reverend Savva, archbishop of Tver
["Собрание мнений и отзывов Филарета, митрополита Московского и Коломенского," изд. под редакцией преосв. Саввы, архиеп. Тверского"], vol.
2 (Saint Petersburg: 1885), 131–134; Archimandrite Nikanor, *An Analysis of the
Roman Doctrine of Visible (Papal) Primacy in the Church* ["Разбор римского учения
о видимом (папском) главенстве в Церкви"], 206–236; Kasitsyn, *Schisms of the*

merely note that the words cited state explicitly that all the apostles are equal in authority and honor. When the Lord spoke to the apostle Peter alone, He did so with the particular goal of showing the oneness of the Church (*ut unitatem manifestaret, ut ecclesia una monstretur* ["that He might set forth unity, that the Church might be shown to be one"]). In the same chapter St. Cyprian cited numerous testimonies in proof of the fact that the Church must be one. For St. Cyprian, the reference to Matthew (see 16:18–19) is just one out of this series of testimonies. That Christ founded the Church on the apostle Peter alone is, for St. Cyprian, merely a symbol of church unity—nothing more.[1715]

First Centuries of Christianity, 162–166 (Addendae, part 44, 365–370); Molchanov, *St. Cyprian of Carthage*, 254–262. We shall also note that the reading of the fourth chapter of *On the Unity of the Church* differs in various codices: later codices include a number of interpolations, part of which are retained in the Migne edition (PL 4:499–500). See Michaud, *Revue internationale de théologie* [1905]: 44–48; Batiffol, *L'eglise naissante et le catholicisme*, 440–447; Koch, "Cyprian und der römische Primat," 158–169; Bruders, "Mt. 16, 19; 18, 18 und Io 20, 22, 23 in frühchristlicher Auslegung," *Zeitschrift für katholische Theologie* (1911): 93 ff.

1715 This is precisely how nearly all non-Catholic scholars interpret the words cited from *On the Unity of the Church* 4. See Ritschl, *Die Entstehung der altkath. Kirche*, 573; Böhringer, *Die alte Kirche* 4, 592; Huther, *Cyprians Lehre von der Kirche*, 93; Reinkens, *Die Lehre des hl. Cyprian*, 5: "Petrus ist die persönliche Veranschaulichung der Idee der Einheit" (cf. 9). Benson, *Cyprian: His Life, His Times, His Work* (London: 1897), 198: "The origo, exordium, of unity starts (*proficiscitur*) from one as a manifestation or demonstration (*manifestaret, monstretur*) of unity" (quoted from Poschmann, 15, Anm. 1). Loofs, *Leitfaden der Dogmengeschichte*⁴ §29.3, 209. Cf. Batiffol, *L'eglise naissante et le catholicisme*, 431; Archimandrite Nikanor, op. cit., 211; Molchanov, *St. Cyprian of Carthage*, 261. Koch decisively defends this same understanding. See *Cyprian und der römische Primat*, 22: "Peter is the temporal beginning of the Church, and its unity rests upon unity with him and him specifically. **The actual principle, the effectual cause for the Church and its unity both at its beginning and thereafter is Christ Himself alone, and not Peter.** He is not the beginning of the Church, is not the beginning of unity, but he is the numerical unity (*unitas*) from which Christ blessed that His Church begin (*ab uno incipientem disposuit, exordium ab unitate proficiscitur*). By this beginning the Establisher showed most clearly that His Church must forever be one and alone. This—and nothing else—is the thinking of Cyprian." Cf. 11, 14, 16–17, Anm. 21, 27, 30, 43, 137–138. Koch sees this same meaning in Epistle 70-69.3 and 73-72.7 (42–45). But cf. Adam, *Theologische Quartalschrift* (1912): 108–109, 118–119.

Thus, St. Cyprian demonstrates the truth of the unity of the Church in particular detail and with particular expressiveness. But how does this unity manifest itself? If we trace St. Cyprian's own answer to this question in his works, we will see much that is already familiar to us from the works of earlier church writers. He takes care that all the Churches preserve constant oneness of mind.[1716] All Christians have a fellowship of confession (*confessionis consortium*),[1717] a common faith (*fides communis*),[1718] and St. Cyprian calls this faith a universal[1719] faith (*catholica fides*).[1720] Unity of faith comes through Tradition from God the Father and from our Lord and God Jesus Christ.[1721] Pure faith is found only in the Church,[1722] and unity of faith cannot be separated from unity of the Church.[1723] One who does not maintain the unity of the Church must not think that he keeps the faith. The apostle Paul speaks of one faith (see Eph. 4:5), and this unity should be firmly maintained and defended.[1724] Consequently, heresy is not only separation from the Church, but also is always a distortion of the faith: "[The enemy] has invented heresies and schisms, whereby he might subvert the faith, might corrupt the truth, might divide the unity. ... His ministers ... maintain ... per-

---

1716 Cyprian of Carthage, *Epistles* 32-31, "To the Carthaginian Clergy": "una fida consensio." Others read "una fide consensio" (ANF 5:311; CSEL 3.2:565).

1717 Cyprian of Carthage, *Treatises* 1.22, "On the Unity of the Church" (ANF 5:428; CSEL 3.2:230).

1718 Cyprian of Carthage, *Epistles* 13-6.2, "To Rogatianus" (ANF 5:284; CSEL 3.2:505).

1719 It should be noted that here the Russian source renders the Latin *catholica* as вселенский (ecumenical, universal), rather than кафолический (catholic), translating rather than transliterating it. –*Trans.*

1720 Cyprian of Carthage, *Epistles* 25-19, "To Caldonius" (ANF 5:297; CSEL 3.2:538).

1721 *Epistles* 74-73.4, "To Pompey" (ANF 5:387; CSEL 3.2:802).

1722 Cyprian of Carthage, *Epistles* 69-75.12, "To Magnus" (ANF 5:401; CSEL 3.2:760). Cf. *Epistles* 71-70.2, "To Quintus" (ANF 5:401; CSEL 3.2:773).

1723 *Epistles* 74-73.4, "To Pompey" (ANF 5:387; CSEL 3.2:802). Cf. *Epistles* 70-69.3, "To Januarius" (ANF 5:376; CSEL 3.2:770).

1724 Cyprian of Carthage, *Treatises* 1.4, "On the Unity of the Church" (ANF 5:422; CSEL 3.2:213).

fidy under the pretext of faith, antichrist under the name of Christ; so that, while they feign things like the truth, they make void the truth by their subtlety."[1725] As the devil is not Christ, although he deceives by His name, so also one who does not abide in the truth of His Gospel and faith cannot be considered a Christian.[1726] The heretic divides the Church and destroys the faith;[1727] "he bears arms against the Church ... for the faith faithless, for religion profane, a disobedient servant, an impious son, a hostile brother."[1728] "We ought to consider their faith who believe without [the Church]. ... Widely different is the faith ... with the other heretics; nay, with them there is nothing but perfidy, and blasphemy, and contention, which is hostile to holiness and truth."[1729]

Thus, to the mind of St. Cyprian, the unity of the Church is manifested in unity of the true faith. St. Cyprian does not remove Christianity from the ecumenical Church; in his writings both these concepts coincide perfectly.[1730] To be outside the catholic Church is to be outside the fold of Christ.[1731] All who are outside the Church

---

1725 Cyprian of Carthage, *Treatises* 1.3, "On the Unity of the Church" (ANF 5:422; CSEL 3.2:211–212).

1726 Cyprian of Carthage, *Treatises* 1.14, "On the Unity of the Church" (ANF 5:426; CSEL 3.2:223).

1727 Ibid., 1.15 (ANF 5:426; CSEL 3.2:224). Cf. Cyprian of Carthage, *Epistles* 73-72.4, "To Jubaianus": "Pests, and swords, and poisons of heretics for subverting the truth" (ANF 5:380; CSEL 3.2:781).

1728 Cyprian of Carthage, *Treatises* 1.17, "On the Unity of the Church" (ANF 5:427; CSEL 3.2:226). *Epistles* 51-46.1, "To Cornelius": Heretics are traitors to the faith and the catholic Church (ANF 5:324; CSEL 3.2:615). *Epistles* 43-39.4, "To the People": "With their adulterous doctrines ... [they] corrupt the chastity of the Church and violate the truth of the Gospel" (ANF 5:317–318; CSEL 3.2:593).

1729 Cyprian of Carthage, *Epistles* 73-72.4–5, "To Jubaianus" (ANF 5:380–381; CSEL 3.2:781, 782).

1730 Poschmann speaks of this in greater detail. See *Die Sichtbarkeit der Kirche*, 43–52. But Poschmann is not justified in titling this section "Die Heilsnotwendigkeit der sichtbaren Kirche." In our opinion, the necessity of the Church for salvation should be discussed in connection with the question of the sanctity of the Church.

1731 Cyprian of Carthage, *Epistles* 51-46.1, "To Cornelius" (ANF 5:324; CSEL 3.2:614–615).

must be considered its opponents and antichrists. St. Cyprian cites
the words of the Lord (see Lk. 11:23; Mt. 18:17) and the words of
the holy apostle John (see 1 Jn. 2:19), using them to substantiate
this thesis: all who have departed from the Church and act against
the Church are antichrists and heathens.[1732] For example, St. Cyprian writes the following to Antonianus concerning Novatian: "In
reference, however, to the character of Novatian, dearest brother,
of whom you desired that intelligence should be written you what
heresy he had introduced; know that, in the first place, we ought not
even to be inquisitive as to what he teaches, so long as he teaches out
of the pale of unity.[1733] Whoever he may be, and whatever he may
be, he who is not in the Church of Christ is not a Christian (*christianus non est qui in Christi ecclesia non est*)."[1734] In his treatise *On the Unity
of the Church* St. Cyprian likewise expresses the same idea, exclaim-
ing forcefully: "He can no longer have God for his Father, who has
not the Church for his mother."[1735] Consequently, as conditions for
belonging to Christianity St. Cyprian sets not only recognition of
the **teaching** of Christ, but first and foremost **concord with the
Church founded by Christ and submission to it.**[1736]

It may be supposed that those who separated from the Church
in the time of St. Cyprian continued to call themselves "Christi-

---

1732 Cyprian of Carthage, *Epistles* 69-75.1, "To Magnus": "If they who despise the Church are counted heathens and publicans, much more certainly is it
necessary that rebels and enemies ... should be counted among heathens and
publicans" (ANF 5:397; CSEL 3.2:749–750).

1733 In the Russian source, "outside the Church." *–Trans.*

1734 Cyprian of Carthage, *Epistles* 55-51.24, "To Antonianus" (ANF 5:333;
CSEL 3.2:642). Concerning Novatus St. Cyprian says the same. *Epistles* 52-48.1,
"To Cornelius": "How can he be with Christ who is not with the spouse of Christ,
and in His Church?" (ANF 5:325; CSEL 3.2:617).

1735 Cyprian of Carthage, *Treatises* 1.6, "On the Unity of the Church" (ANF
5:423; CSEL 3.2:214). Ibid., 1.17: "Does he think that he has Christ, who acts
in opposition to Christ's priests, who separates himself from the company of His
clergy and people?" (ANF 5:427; CSEL 3.2:226).

1736 This is naturally not the view of Cyprian alone. Cf. the sayings of writers
of the early Church, compiled by Seitz (*Die Heilsnotwendigkeit der Kirche*, 21–25,
83–86). Cf. Harnack, *Dogmengeschichte*⁴ 1, 423–425.

ans" and even "a church." St. Cyprian presents and analyzes one of their arguments: "Nor let any deceive themselves by a futile interpretation, in respect of the Lord having said, 'Wheresoever two or three are gathered together in my name, there am I in the midst of them' [Mt. 18:20]."[1737] St. Cyprian quite substantially disproves this usage of Christ's words: "Corrupters and false interpreters of the Gospel quote the last words, and lay aside the former ones, remembering part, and craftily suppressing part: as they themselves are separated from the Church, so they cut off the substance of one section." In this passage Christ speaks of unanimity; but "how can two or three be assembled together in Christ's name, who, it is evident, are separated from Christ and from His Gospel?" Christ promised to be with those who are unanimous, as he was with the three youths in the furnace and with the two imprisoned apostles. "When, therefore, in His commandments He lays it down, and says, 'Where two or three are gathered together in my name, I am with them,' He does not divide men from the Church, seeing that He Himself ordained and made the Church; but rebuking the faithless for their discord, and commending peace by His word to the faithful, He shows that He is rather with two or three who pray with one mind, than with a great many who differ, and that more can be obtained by the concordant[1738] prayer of a few, than by the discordant supplication of many. ... Do they deem that they have Christ with them when they are collected together, who are gathered together outside the Church of Christ?"[1739]

St. Cyprian does not limit the unity of the Church to unity of faith, but also speaks in detail of a living unity among the members of the Church, which earlier writers also mentioned in brief. Unity

---

1737 Böhringer takes note of these words and makes a very odd comment: "Noch aber war die altchristliche Ansicht von der Kirche nicht ganz ausgestorben" (*Die alte Kirche* 4, 957). But there are hardly any grounds to declare these words to be the early Christian view of the Church.

1738 In the English source cited, mistranslated as "discordant"; error corrected. —*Trans.*

1739 Cyprian of Carthage, *Treatises* 1.12–13, "On the Unity of the Church" (ANF 5:425; CSEL 3.2:220–222). Cf. *Epistles* 11-7.3, "To the Clergy" (ANF 5:286; CSEL 3.2:497–498).

of theoretical and dogmatic theses would not have met the needs of St. Cyprian's time either, when strife in the Church did not occur solely on these grounds. Consequently, according to the teaching of St. Cyprian, the unity of the Church must be manifested not in unity of faith alone, but also in unity of common love. To put it better, St. Cyprian did not separate faith and love. Faith enlivens only when it is preserved in life.[1740] The Church is "the unanimous and accordant people of God."[1741] "It behoves the sons of God to be peacemakers, gentle in heart, simple in speech, agreeing in affection, faithfully linked to one another in the bonds of unanimity. This unanimity formerly prevailed among the apostles; and thus the new assembly of believers, keeping the Lord's commandments, maintained its charity. Divine Scripture proves this, when it says, 'But the multitude of them which believed were of one heart and of one soul' [Acts 4:32]."[1742] In St. Cyprian we find a highly poetic description of the ideal of common Christian love: "In the house of God, in the Church of Christ, men dwell with one mind, and continue in concord and simplicity. Therefore also the Holy Spirit came as a dove, a simple and joyous creature, not bitter with gall, not cruel in its bite, not violent with the rending of its claws, loving human dwellings, knowing the association of one home; when they have young, bringing forth their young together; when they fly abroad, remaining in their flights by the side of one another, spending their life in mutual intercourse, acknowledging the concord of peace with the kiss of the beak, in all things fulfilling the law of unanimity. This is the simplicity that ought to be known in the Church, this is the charity that ought to be attained, that so the love of the brotherhood may imitate the doves, that their gentleness and meekness may be like the lambs and sheep. ... Bitterness cannot

---

1740 Cyprian of Carthage, *Epistles* 13-6.2, "To Rogatianus" (ANF 5:284; CSEL 3.2:505).

1741 Cyprian of Carthage, *Epistles* 72-71.2, "To Stephen" (ANF 5:379; CSEL 3.2:777).

1742 Cyprian of Carthage, *Treatises* 1.24–25, "On the Unity of the Church" (ANF 5:429; CSEL 3.2:231–232); *Treatises* 8.25, "On Works and Alms" (ANF 5:483; CSEL 3.2:393).

consist and be associated with sweetness, darkness with light, rain with clearness, battle with peace, barrenness with fertility, drought with springs, storm with tranquility."[1743] "Even the Lord's sacrifices themselves declare that Christian unanimity is linked together with itself by a firm and inseparable charity."[1744] "God commands us to be peacemakers, and in agreement, and of one mind in His house; and such as He makes us by a second birth (*secunda nativitate*), such He wishes us when new-born to continue, that we who have begun to be sons of God may abide in God's peace, and that, having one spirit, we should also have one heart and one mind. ... Our peace and brotherly agreement is the greater sacrifice to God—and a people united in one in the unity of the Father, and of the Son, and of the Holy Spirit."[1745] The members of the divided Body are brought into the unity of the ecumenical Church, and are bound together with the bonds of Christian love.[1746] The violation of common love and common accord is a violation of the unity of the Church. "The inexpiable and grave fault of discord is not even purged by suffering. ... Christ gave us peace; He bade us be in agreement, and of one mind. He charged the bonds of love and charity to be kept uncorrupted and inviolate. ... To the rewards of Christ ... he cannot attain who has violated the love of Christ by faithless dissension. He who has not charity has not God. ... They cannot dwell with God who would not be of one mind in God's Church."[1747] If the one Church is a bond of love, any separation from the Church, any heresy, at the core of which lie pride and self-will, attests to a

---

1743 Cyprian of Carthage, *Treatises* 1.8-9, "On the Unity of the Church" (ANF 5:424; CSEL 3.2:217–218).

1744 Cyprian of Carthage, *Epistles* 69-75.6, "To Magnus" (ANF 5:398; CSEL 3.2:754).

1745 Cyprian of Carthage, *Treatises* 4.23, "On the Lord's Prayer" (ANF 5:454; CSEL 3.2:284–285).

1746 Cyprian of Carthage, Epistles 45-41.1, "To Cornelius" (ANF 320; CSEL 3.2:599–600).

1747 Cyprian of Carthage, *Treatises* 1.14, "On the Unity of the Church" (ANF 5:425–426; CSEL 3.2:222–223); *Treatises* 4.24, "On the Lord's Prayer" (ANF 5:454; CSEL 3.2:285); *Epistles* 55-51.29, "To Antonianus" (ANF 5:335; CSEL 3.2:647).

lack of love. It could be said that the chief idea of the entire treatise on the unity of the Church is specifically that **heretics lack love, while the unity of the Church is a direct consequence of love.**[1748] A heretic or schismatic does not maintain either ecclesiastical unity or brotherly love,[1749] and he acts in opposition to the love of Christ.[1750] The heretics "are known to have departed from charity and from the unity of the Catholic Church."[1751] "What unity does he keep, what love does he maintain or consider, who, savage with the madness of discord, divides the Church, destroys the faith, disturbs the peace, dissipates charity, profanes the sacrament?"[1752]

This idea of the unity of the entire Church in love was, of course, not merely abstract. At the very outset of our study we spoke of how the self-identification as a Church that all of Christianity experienced was always manifested outwardly. St. Cyprian likewise speaks of this living expression of the idea of the unity of the Church in love.[1753] **The expression of Church-wide love, first and foremost, was prayer,** as Cyprian says on that subject. "Before all things, the Teacher of peace and the Master of unity would not have prayer to be made singly and individually, as for one who prays to pray for himself alone. For we say not 'My Father, which art in heaven,' nor 'Give me this day my daily bread;' nor does each one ask that only his own debt should be forgiven him; nor does he request for himself alone that he may not be led into temptation, and delivered from evil. Our prayer is public and

1748 Harnack says that this idea "ist ein Grundgedanke, ja die Spitze der Schrift de unitate" (*Dogmengeschichhte*⁴ 1, 418, Anm. 4).

1749 Cyprian of Carthage, *Epistles* 55-51.24, "To Antonianus" (ANF 5:333; CSEL 3.2:642); *Epistles* 72-71.2, "To Stephen": "Unmindful of evangelical peace and love ... [heretics] have fought with the madness of hostile discord against the unanimous and accordant people of God" (ANF 5:379; CSEL 3.2:777).

1750 Cyprian of Carthage, *Epistles* 69-75.1, "To Magnus" (ANF 5:397; CSEL 3.2:749). *Epistles* 68-66.4, "To Father Stephenus" (ANF 5:369; CSEL 3.2:748).

1751 Cyprian of Carthage, *Epistles* 69-75.1, "To Magnus" (ANF 5:397; CSEL 3.2:750).

1752 Cyprian of Carthage, *Treatises* 1.15, "On the Unity of the Church" (ANF 5:426; CSEL 3.2:224).

1753 Vgl. Harnack, *Dogmengeschichte*⁴ 1, 418, Anm. 4.

common (*publica et communis*); and when we pray, we pray not for one, but for the whole people, because we the whole people are one (*totus populus unum sumus*). The God of peace and the Teacher of concord, who taught unity, willed that one should thus pray for all, even as He Himself bore us all in one."[1754] "Let each one of us pray God not for himself only, but for all the brethren, even as the Lord has taught us to pray, when He bids to each one, not private prayer (*privatam precem*), but enjoined them, when they prayed, to pray for all in common prayer and concordant supplication."[1755] Heresies hinder prayer.[1756]

This same **common love, which unites the Christian Church, is expressed in almsgiving.** St. Cyprian wrote a separate book *On Works and Alms*, in which he especially exhorts Christians to mutual works of charity. In speaking of the unity of the Church he also takes the opportunity to talk of almsgiving: he is saddened, seeing that unanimity has waned and generosity in giving has diminished.[1757] The epistles of St. Cyprian provide a wealth of material for portraying the charitable work of the Church in the mid-third century. St. Cyprian speaks of aid to widows, the infirm, and the poor, and of providing for strangers.[1758] His writings speak of organized charitable work,[1759] of ransoming captives,[1760] and so on. Mutual support among the members of the individual commu-

---

1754 Cyprian of Carthage, *Treatises* 4.8, "On the Lord's Prayer" (ANF 5:449; CSEL 3.2:271). Concerning the prayer of one Church for another, see *Epistles* 62-59, "To the Numidian Bishops" (ANF 5:355–356; CSEL 3.2:700).

1755 Cyprian of Carthage, *Epistles* 11-7.7, "To the Clergy" (ANF 5:287; CSEL 3.2:501).

1756 Cyprian of Carthage, *Epistles* 43-39.5, "To the People" (ANF 5:318; CSEL 3.2:594).

1757 Cyprian of Carthage, *Treatises* 1.26, "On the Unity of the Church" (ANF 5:429; CSEL 3.2:232).

1758 Cyprian of Carthage, *Epistles* 7-35, "To the Clergy" (ANF 5:314; CSEL 3.2:485).

1759 Cyprian of Carthage, *Epistles* 41-37, "To Caldonius" (ANF 5:315–316; CSEL 3.2:587).

1760 Cyprian of Carthage, *Epistles* 62-59, "To the Numidian Bishops" (ANF 5:355–356; CSEL 3.2:698 sqq.).

nity naturally united them together most effectually.[1761] But alms-giving was not confined to the individual Church: it extended to the entire ecumenical Church. About the time when St. Cyprian lived, the charitable work of the Roman Church, for example, extended to regions of Syria and Arabia, as Dionysius of Alexandria attests.[1762] Even in the middle of the fourth century the aid of the Roman Church was recalled with gratitude in Cappadocia.[1763] St. Cyprian likewise relates similar instances of Church-wide charitable work, and it is remarkable that **he closely links the existence of this charitable work with the dogmatic doctrine of the unity of the Church.** In this respect, particularly deserving of attention is Cyprian's epistle to the Numidian bishops: Januarius, Maximus, Proculus, Victor, Modianus, Nemesianus, Nampulus, and Honoratus. The Numidian bishops had informed the Church of Carthage of the imprisonment of several brethren and sisters. The Christians of Carthage collected a hundred thousand sesterces ("by the contributions of the clergy and people"), which Cyprian then sent along with his epistle. In the epistle Cyprian thanks the Numidian Christians for desiring to make his flock a participant in a good and necessary work, and he sends a list of contributors and requests prayers for them. Here Cyprian writes: "Who would not consider his brother's grief his own?" Having cited the words of the apostle (see 1 Cor. 12:26; 2 Cor. 11:29), Cyprian continues: "Wherefore now also the captivity of our brethren must be reckoned as our captivity, and the grief of those who are endangered is to be esteemed as our grief, since indeed there is one body of our union (*adunationis nostrae corpus unum*); and not love only, but also religion (*religio*), ought to instigate and strengthen us to redeem the members of the breth-

---

1761 Harnack provides a detailed discussion of charitable work in the early Christian Church. See *Die Mission und Ausbreitung des Christentums*[2], 4-tes. Kap.: «Das Evangelium der Liebe und Hilfleistung», 127 ff.

1762 "And all Syria, and Arabia to which you send help when needed ... all everywhere are rejoicing ... for the unanimity and brotherly love." So wrote Dionysius to Stephen, bishop of Rome. (Eusebius, *Church History* 7.5.2 [NPNF[2] 1:294; GrchSch. 9.2:638, 640]).

1763 See Basil the Great, *Letters* 70 (NPNF[2] 8:166–167).

ren."[1764] Thus, according to St. Cyprian, charitable work is the living expression of the dogmatic doctrine of the unity of the Church. From the epistles of the apostle Paul we also learn of far-reaching charitable efforts among different Churches, but the surviving manuscripts of church literature do not inseparably link charitable work and fellowship among the Churches in general with the dogmatic doctrine of the unity of the Church. St. Cyprian emphasizes the dogmatic aspect of the matter for the first time, and thereby in part supplements the early church's idea of the unity of the Church.

But St. Cyprian also speaks of a more effectual outward unification of the individual Churches. When the apostolic Traditions were yet alive, truth was established through intercourse with the Churches founded by the apostles. Each bishop did not think of himself as a wholly isolated head of a separate community: he was not only the center of the unity of the community within itself, but also the organ of the community's outward unification with others. **In St. Cyprian we first encounter a developed theory of the outward unity of the whole Church in the person of its bishops. It is the episcopacy that is the organ of outward unification of the ecumenical Church.** "The Church, which is Catholic and one, is ... connected and bound together by the cement of priests who cohere with one another (*cohaerentium sibi invicem sacerdotum glutino copulata*)."[1765] The episcopacy is one and indivisible, and each takes part in it by common agreement.[1766] Presented here

---

1764 Cyprian of Carthage, *Epistles* 62-59.1, "To the Numidian Bishops" (ANF 5:355; CSEL 3.2:698 sqq.). Concerning the moral unity of Christians see also *Epistles* 37-15.1, "To Moyses and Maximus." To the confessors St. Cyprian writes: "In a certain manner I am also there with you in prison. I think that I who am thus bound to your hearts, enjoy with you the delights of the divine approval. Your individual love associates me with your honour; the Spirit does not allow our love to be separated" (ANF 5:295; CSEL 3.2:576).

1765 Cyprian of Carthage, Epistles 66-68.8, "To Florentius Pupianus" (ANF 5:375; CSEL 3.2:733).

1766 Cyprian of Carthage, *Treatises* 1.5, "On the Unity of the Church" (ANF 5:423; CSEL 3.2:214). The Latin text of this passage is as follows: "Episcopatus unus est, cuius a singulis in solidum pars tenetur." This text is translated and interpreted variously. The various German translations are compiled by Poschmann

is the idea that even the bishop only possesses episcopal authority while he is in agreement with the other bishops.[1767] The episcopacy is one,[1768] "diffused through a harmonious multitude of many bishops,"[1769] and each individual bishop is a bearer specifically of this ecumenical priesthood. Although there are many shepherds, they feed one flock, and they must gather and guard all the sheep which the Lord acquired by His blood.[1770] If the bishop should fall away from the union of his fellow bishops and the unity of the Church, he cannot retain his episcopacy. "The apostle admonishes that we should mutually sustain one another, and not withdraw from the unity which God has appointed, and says, 'Bearing with one another in love, endeavouring to keep the unity of the Spirit in the bond of peace' [Eph. 4:2–3]. He then who neither maintains the unity of the Spirit nor the bond of peace, and separates himself from the band of the Church, and from the assembly of priests, can neither have the power nor the honour of a bishop, since he has refused to maintain either the unity or the peace of the episcopate."[1771] Consequently, the bishops must keep peace among themselves and not enter into strife with their companions and fellow bishops. "Charity

---

in *Die Sichtbarkeit der Kirche*, 8–9, Anm. Cf. Koch, *Cyprian und der römische Primat*, 27–28, Anm. 2. The Russian translation—"wholly takes part in it"—is ambiguous. Our translation considers the context. [In the Russian source, "The episcopacy is one and indivisible, and each takes part in it in common agreement." –*Trans.*]

1767 Koch finds it possible to also apply to the bishop the subsequent analogies of the ray of sun, the tree, and the stream. See *Cyprian und der römische Primat*, 25, 28, 29. Cf. 138–139.

1768 Cyprian of Carthage, *Epistles* 43-39.5, "To the People" (ANF 5:318; CSEL 3.2:594).

1769 Cyprian of Carthage, *Epistles* 55-51.24, "To Antonianus": "Episcopatus unus episcoporum multorum concordi numerositate diffusus" (ANF 5:333; CSEL 3.2:642).

1770 Cyprian of Carthage, *Epistles* 68-66.4, "To Father Stephenus" (ANF 5:369; CSEL 3.2:747).

1771 Cyprian of Carthage, *Epistles* 55-51.24, "To Antonianus": "Episcopatus unus episcoporum multorum concordi numerositate diffusus" (ANF 5:334; CSEL 3.2:643). To abandon union with the bishops means to break ties with the Church and to be together with the heretics and schismatics—*Epistles* 52-48.4, "To Cornelius" (ANF 5:326; CSEL 3.2:620).

of spirit, the honour of our college, the bond of faith, and priestly concord, are maintained by us with patience and gentleness,"[1772] writes St. Cyprian. Agreement with the episcopacy guards each individual bishop against error, and the Church from divisions. "For that reason ... the body of priests is abundantly large, joined together by the bond of mutual concord, and the link of unity; so that if any one of our college should try to originate heresy, and to lacerate and lay waste Christ's flock, others may help, and as it were, as useful and merciful shepherds, gather together the Lord's sheep into the flock."[1773] The idea of the unity and unanimity of the episcopacy in the writings of St. Cyprian and his contemporaries is also expressed in their frequent use of the terms "fellow bishop" and "fellow priest."[1774]

Thus, **a united and unanimous episcopacy likewise unites all the individual Churches into one ecumenical Church.**[1775] The bishops unite together at the Councils. St. Cyprian teaches that it is **the Council of bishops that is the chief organ of the outward unity of the Church.** Naturally, the Councils of the bishops were not the product of this dogmatic doctrine; on the contrary, this very teaching of St. Cyprian concerning

1772 Cyprian of Carthage, Epistles 73-72.26, "To Jubaianus" (ANF 5:386; CSEL 3.2:798). *Epistles* 55-51.24, "To Antonianus": "... fellow-bishops, the whole number of whom has agreed with an absolute unanimity throughout the whole world" (ANF 5:329; CSEL 3.2:629).

1773 Cyprian of Carthage, *Epistles* 68-66.3, "To Father Stephenus" (ANF 5:368; CSEL 3.2:746).

1774 See *Epistles* 17-11.3 "To the People" (CSEL 3.2:523.4); *Epistles* 55-51.1, "To Cornelius" (CSEL 3.2:598.1); *Epistles* 48-44.2 "To Cornelius" (CSEL 3.2:606.18, 608.2); *Epistles* 59-54.5, "To Cornelius" (CSEL 3.2:672); *Epistles* 55-51.1 "To Antonianus" (CSEL 3.2:624.9–10, 15; 628.6, 21; 629.4; 639.1; 642.11); *Epistles* 68-66.1 "To Father Stephenus" (CSEL 3.2:744.5); *Epistles* 72-71.1, "To Stephen" (CSEL 3.2:776.12); *Epistles* 67-67.1 (CSEL 3.2:735.13); *Epistles* 71-70.1, 4, "To Quintus" (CSEL 3.2:771.6, 774.13); *Epistles* 73-72.26, "To Jubaianus" (CSEL 3.2:798). Cf. *The Seventh Council of Carthage under Cyprian* (CSEL 3.2:435.12, 8, 26); *Epistles* 49-45.1, "Cornelius to Cyprian" (CSEL 3.2:610.12).

1775 Cf. Batiffol, *L'eglise naissante et le catholicisme*, 418. Cf. Ibid., 437—an excerpt from the article by I. Delarochelle, "L'idée de l'église dans saint Cyprien," *Revue d'hist. et de litt. relig.*, t. 1 (1896): 531.

the Council had previously been recognized by the very existence of the Councils. Precise information on the Councils is available from as early as the second century. For example, back when Montanism appeared in Asia, an anonymous source in Eusebius reports that "the faithful in Asia met often in many places throughout Asia."[1776] When in the late second century a dispute arose concerning the time of the celebration of Pascha, "synods and assemblies of bishops were held on this account, and all, with one consent, through mutual correspondence drew up an ecclesiastical decree."[1777] The Councils may be considered an original phenomenon in the life of the Christian Church.[1778] Even without thoroughly developed dogmatic theories, the existence of the Councils clearly attests that in the Church there always lived an awareness not only of its unity, but specifically of conciliarity as the supreme manifestation of that unity.[1779] By the middle of the third century the conciliar principle had become firmly established in church practice, and St. Cyprian created a dogmatic theory, grounded in that practice, which corresponded to existing church life and had previously been espoused by church figures, albeit not yet in entirely definite form. In the ecclesiological system of St. Cyprian, the Council comprises the apex of church unity.

The period during which St. Cyprian lived and worked was one rich in Councils. When persecutions prevented the bishops from assembling, Cyprian postponed the resolution of critical ecclesiastical matters until such time as persecutions would cease and the bishops

---

1776 Eusebius, *Church History* 5.16.10 (NPNF² 1:232). In *Church History* 5.19.4 Eusebius likewise reports that the epistle of Serapion of Antioch to Caricus and Pontius bore the signatures of many bishops. It may be supposed that this epistle was from an entire council of bishops (NPNF² 1:237; GrchSch. 9.1:480).

1777 Eusebius, *Church History* 5.23.2; 24.8 (NPNF² 1:241; GrchSch. 9.1:488, 492). Likewise concerning the council: *Church History* 5.25 (NPNF² 1:244; GrchSch. 9.1:496).

1778 For a list of Councils see Archimandrite Sylvester, *The Doctrine Concerning the Church*, 295–300.

1779 An exposition of "the concept of the Church based on the very essence of the phenomenon of the Councils which continually arose within her" is given by Archimandrite Sylvester. See *The Doctrine Concerning the Church*, 301–318.

could convene a Council. In all the epistles of St. Cyprian which he wrote while hiding from persecution, we find exhortations to await the conciliar decisions. "Let them look for my return," he writes concerning the confessors, "that when by God's mercy I come to you, I, with many of my co-bishops, being called together according to the Lord's discipline, and in the presence of the confessors, and with your opinion also, may be able to examine the letters and the wishes of the blessed martyrs."[1780] Concerning those who were anxious to receive peace, St. Cyprian writes to the clergy of Carthage: "(Since this is the cause not of a few, nor of one church, nor of one province, but of the whole world), [they] must wait, in dependence on the protection of the Lord, for the public peace of the Church itself. For this is suitable to the modesty and the discipline, and even the life of all of us, that the chief officers meeting together with the clergy in the presence also of the people who stand fast, to whom themselves, moreover, honour is to be shown for their faith and fear, we may be able to order all things with the religiousness of a common consultation (*consilii communis religione*)."[1781] St. Cyprian wrote the same to the presbyters and deacons of Rome.[1782] The church Council, as it appears before us in the works of St. Cyprian, was specifically the organ that united the Church, primarily in the

----

1780 Cyprian of Carthage, *Epistles* 17-11.3 "To the People" (ANF 5:292; CSEL 3.2:523). *Epistles* 26-17, "To the Presbyters and Deacons": "[This] matter, as it waits for the counsel and judgment of all of us, I do not dare to prejudge, and so to assume a common cause for my own decision. ... Peace being granted to us by the Lord, we shall be able to assemble together into one place, and to examine into the cases of individuals" (ANF 5:296–297; CSEL 3.2:539). Cf. *Epistles* 35-29, "The Presbyters and Deacons Abiding in Rome, to Cyprian" (CSEL 3.2:570).

1781 Cyprian of Carthage, *Epistles* 19-13.2, "To the Clergy" (ANF 5:293–294; CSEL 3.2:526). Cf. *Epistles* 35-29, "The Presbyters and Deacons Abiding in Rome, to Cyprian" (ANF 5:308; CSEL 3.2:570).

1782 Cyprian of Carthage, *Epistles* 20-14.3, "To the Presbyters and Deacons Assembled at Rome": "The cases ... I ordered altogether to be put off, and to be reserved till I should be present, that so, when the Lord has given to us peace, and several bishops (*praepositi*) shall have begun to assemble into one place, we may be able to arrange and reform everything, having the advantage also of your counsel" (ANF 5:295; CSEL 3.2:529).

person of its primates—the bishops. The church Council was not a
disorderly assembly of all the people or of certain elected representatives: it was a Council of bishops, who alone issued the decrees.
For example, the epistle to the clergy and people of Spain concerning Basilides and Martial was written on behalf of the Council, and
its heading lists only bishops.[1783] The heading of the epistle to Januarius and the other Numidian bishops likewise lists the bishops who
took part in the Council, who were 31 in number.[1784] Concerning
the resolution of a matter at the Council Cyprian writes: "When
we had met together, bishops as well of the province of Africa as of
Numidia, to the number of seventy-one, we established...."[1785] At
the council of 256, St. Cyprian's words are addressed to the bishops, and the bishops alone voiced an opinion.[1786] The bishops condemned heretics at the Councils, as Privatus, for example, was condemned in the colony of Lambesa by the common voice of ninety
bishops.[1787] To be sure, presbyters, deacons, and laity were present
with the bishops, but they were merely in attendance. The Councils
were Councils of bishops, but they took place in the presence of the
clergy and the people,[1788] as may be seen from the testimonies of

---

1783 Cyprian of Carthage, *Epistles* 67-67 (ANF 5:369; CSEL 3.2:735).

1784 *Epistles* 70-69 (ANF 5:375; CSEL 3.2:766). Cf. *Epistles* 57-53, "To Cornelius" (CSEL 3.2:650).

1785 Cyprian of Carthage, *Epistles* 73-72.1, "To Jubaianus" (ANF 5:379;
CSEL 3.2:779). Cf. *Epistle* 72-71.1, "To Stephen": "We have thought it necessary
for the arranging of certain matters, dearest brother, and for their investigation
by the examination of a common council, to gather together and to hold a council, at which many priests were assembled at once; at which, moreover, many
things were brought forward and transacted" (ANF 5:378; CSEL 3.2:776.12).

1786 *The Seventh Council of Carthage under Cyprian: Concerning the Baptism of Heretics*
(CSEL 3.2:435 sqq.).

1787 Cyprian of Carthage, *Epistles* 59-54.10, "To Cornelius" (CSEL 3.2:677).
Cf. *Eusebius*, op. cit. 6.43.2 (GrchSch. 9.2:612).

1788 Here, for example, is how the Council of 256 is described: "Cum in
unum Carthaginem convenissent kalendis Septembribus episcopi plurimi ex provincia Africa Numidia Mauritania cum presbyteris et diaconibus, praesentibus
etiam plebis maxima parte [When, in the kalends of September, a great many
bishops from the provinces of Africa, Numidia, and Mauritania, had met together at Carthage, together with the presbyters and deacons, and a considerable part

St. Cyprian concerning the Councils cited above. In an epistle to the presbyters and deacons of Rome, St. Clement says: "When ... several bishops shall have begun to assemble into one place, we may be able to arrange and reform everything, **having the advantage also of your counsel** (*communicato etiam vobiscum consilio*)."[1789] Consequently, the presbyters were invited to the Councils for counsel, but the decision came from the bishops. Sometimes the decision of the Council of bishops was made in accordance with requests from the laity present, as attested by an excerpt from the epistle of Cornelius to Fabius of Antioch, recorded by Eusebius.[1790]

Catholic scholars make every attempt to prove that St. Cyprian considered it essential to the outward unity of the Church to have one person who would unite all the bishops, and that for him this person was allegedly the bishop of Rome.[1791] But in the writings of St. Cyprian, on the contrary, passages may be rather be cited in which he denies that anyone at all has primacy in the Church, and speaks of all the bishops as being equal among themselves.[1792] For example, St. Cyprian sharply condemns those schismatics who "dare ... to set sail ... to the throne of Peter, and to the chief church whence priestly unity takes its source. ... For, as it has been decreed by all of us—and is equally fair and just—that the case of every one should be heard there where the crime has been committed; and a portion of the flock has been assigned to each individual pastor,

---

of the congregation {*or* the people} who were also present] etc." (CSEL 3.2:435).

1789 Cyprian of Carthage, *Epistles* 20-14.3 (ANF 5:295; CSEL 3.2:529). In *Epistles* 59-54.15, "To Cornelius," St. Cyprian likewise separates the presbyters and deacons from the bishops in significance: "If the number of those who judged concerning them last year be reckoned with the presbyters and deacons..." (ANF 5:344; CSEL 3.2:684).

1790 Eusebius, op. cit. 6.43.10: "ᾧ καὶ ἐκοινωνήσαμεν λαϊκῷ, ὑπὲρ αὐτοῦ δεηθέντος παντὸς τοῦ παρόντος λαοῦ [And we communed with him as with a layman, all the people present interceding for him]" (GrchSch. 9.2:618.10–11).

1791 See for example Poschmann, *Die Sichtbarkeit der Kirche*, 11–12, 26; Seitz, *Cyprian und der römische Primat*, 75–80. The most extensive rebuttal of the Catholic references to Cyprian is given by Koch (see *Cyprian und der römische Primat*).

1792 It may be noted that Cyprian makes no division of episcopal sees into apostolic and non-apostolic. Cf. Harnack, *Dogmengeschichte* 1, 420, Anm. 1.

which he is to rule and govern, having to give account of his doing to the Lord; it certainly behoves those over whom we are placed not to run about nor to break up the harmonious agreement of the bishops with their crafty and deceitful rashness, but there to plead their cause, where they may be able to have both accusers and witnesses of their crime; unless perchance the authority of the bishops constituted in Africa seems to a few desperate and abandoned men to be too little, who have already judged concerning them."[1793] And this he writes to the bishop of Rome! To the mind of Cyprian, quite clearly the bishop of Rome has no authority over the other[1794] bishops, who are equal among themselves.[1795] Nor does St. Cyprian speak of agreement with the bishop of Rome as essential: "We," he writes, "ought by all means to maintain the unity of the Catholic Church." In the debate over the baptism of heretics St. Cyprian says much that is completely at odds with the theory of papal primacy. The very occurrence of this debate shows that Cyprian did not conceive truth to be inseparably linked to the bishop of Rome. "Neither must we prescribe this from custom, but overcome opposite custom by reason. For neither did Peter, whom first the Lord chose, and upon whom He built His Church, when Paul disputed with him afterwards about circumcision, claim anything to himself

1793 Cyprian of Carthage, *Epistles* 59-54.14, "To Cornelius" (ANF 5:344; CSEL 3.2:683–684). Cf. the observation of Koch, *Cyprian und der römische Primat,* 92–100.

1794 Cf. the observation of Iordan in *Theologischer Literaturbericht* № 11 (1911): 339: "In the writings of Cyprian, any juridical primacy of Rome is of course out of the question."

1795 Sometimes Catholics see the appeals of schismatics as evidence of the real significance of the bishop of Rome at that time. See for example *Bollandistarum animadversiones,* Migne (PL 3:1078c). But of this evidence even Catholics say that "es ist ein vergebliches Bemühen" (Poschmann, *Die Sichtbarkeit der Kirche,* 31, Anm. 1). Poschmann himself acknowledges that Cyprian explicitly denies that the see of Rome functions as the highest court of appeal (30–31). But Poschmann then goes on to assert that St. Cyprian allegedly considered union with Rome *conditio sine qua non* for the episcopacy. As we have already said, however, in Cyprian's view a bishop is only a bishop when he is in unity with the episcopacy, and Poschmann is quite groundless in substituting the bishop of Rome for the concept of the episcopacy.

insolently, nor arrogantly assume anything; so as to say that he held the primacy, and that he ought rather to be obeyed by novices and those lately come (*nec Petrus … vindicavit sibi aliquid insolenter aut adroganter assumpsit, ut diceret se primatum tenere et obtemperari a novellis et posteris sibi potius oportere*). Nor did he despise Paul … but admitted the counsel of truth, and easily yielded to the lawful reason which Paul asserted, furnishing thus an illustration to us both of concord and of patience, that we should not obstinately love our own opinions (*ut non pertinaciter nostra amemus*), but should rather adopt as our own those which at any time are usefully and wholesomely suggested by our brethren and colleagues, if they be true and lawful."[1796] Even if this did not refer explicitly to the bishop of Rome,[1797] in it St. Cyprian's idea is expressed quite clearly. Every bishop must agree with his brethren and colleagues, as long as their opinion is true and lawful. Consequently, the highest authority is the Council of brother bishops, and not any one person. In this view, the bishop of Rome also, being equal with the rest, must adhere to the conciliar voice of the bishops.[1798]

1796 Cyprian of Carthage, *Epistles* 71-70.2, "To Quintus" (ANF 5:377–378; CSEL 3.2:773). Cf. Koch, *Cyprian und der römische Primat*, 47: "Cyprian erklärt, dass aus der zeitlichen Priorität keinerlei Superiorität gefolgert werden dürfe" (Vgl. 45–47).

1797 In recent times, Catholic scholars have attempted to prove that the epistle to Quintus refers not to Stephen, bishop of Rome, but to certain Maurtanian bishops. This view is expressed and argued by Dr. Johann Ernst (*Papst Stephan I und der Ketzertaufstreit. Forschungen zur christlichen Literatur und Dogmengeschichte*, herausgeg. von Dr. A. Ehrhard und Dr. I. P. Kirsch, V. Band, 4 Heft. [Mainz: 1905], 5–9). Ernst refutes the view of Leo Nelke, expressed in his work *Die Chronologie des Korrespondenz Cyprians* (Thorn: 1902). Ernst's view is wholly shared by Poschmann (*Die Sichtbarkeit der Kirche*, 28–29). We consider it superfluous to undertake a detailed analysis of this opinion (see Koch, *Cyprian und der römische Primat*, 47–49), since for an outline of St. Cyprian's dogmatic teaching on the Church it matters little against whom his epistle was directed. In our opinion, Ernst and Poschmann are groundless in pinning their hopes on a controversial change of the person against whom this epistle to Quintus was written. It is clear that this epistle wholly denies any claims to primacy, whoever the claimant may be. Cf. Koch, *Cyprian und der römische Primat*, 48–49. Vgl. 121.

1798 Cf. Koch, *Cyprian und der römische Primat*, 58, 71. Regarding *Epistles* 71-70.3, Poschmann (op. cit., 28–29) reasons: "Petrus in seinem Verhältnis zu Paulus

St. Cyprian also speaks of the complete equality of all the bishops when deciding matters in council in his opening speech at the Council of 256. After all the various documents pertaining to the case had been named, St. Cyprian said: "It remains, that upon this same matter each of us should bring forward what we think, judging no man, nor rejecting any one from the right of communion, if he should think differently from us. For neither does any of us set himself up as a bishop of bishops, nor by tyrannical terror does any compel his colleague to the necessity of obedience; since every bishop, according to the allowance of his liberty and power, has his own proper right of judgment, and can no more be judged by another than he himself can judge another."[1799] This passage requires several comments. The Bollandists have observed that this passage cannot be left uninterpreted since it contradicts the dignity of the bishop of Rome. The Bollandists proposed the following interpretation: Cyprian is exhorting each of the assembled bishops to freely express his opinion. This is why he says that they are all equal (*sese omnes collegas esse*). And although he presides in Africa, he considers

---

erscheint nun nicht mehr als das Gegenbild des auf seine Primatialstellung pochenden Papstes gegenüber den Bischöfen, sondern als Gegenbild der starrköpfigen Bischöfe, welche auf keine Gründe eingehen wollen vielmehr sich hartnäckig auf unberechtigte Gewohnheiten steifen." But if the bishop of Rome himself is "starrköpflig" and "sich hartnäckig auf unberechtigte Gewohnheiten steifen," as was the case with Stephan, clearly Cyprian's condemnation and the example of the apostle Peter will apply to him also.

1799 *The Seventh Council of Carthage under Cyprian*: "Superest ut de hac ipsa re singuli quid sentiamus proferamus neminem judicantes aut a jure communicationis aliquem si diversum senserit amoventes, neque enim quisquam nostrum episcopum se episcoporum constituit aut tyrannico terrore ad obsequendi necessitatem collegas suos adigit, quando habeat omnis episcopus pro licentia libertatis et potestatis suae arbitrium proprium tamque judicari ab alio non posit, quam nec ipse posit alterum judicare [It remains, that upon this same matter each of us should bring forward what we think, judging no man, nor rejecting any one from the right of communion, if he should think differently from us. For neither does any of us set himself up as a bishop of bishops, nor by tyrannical terror does any compel his colleague to the necessity of obedience; since every bishop, according to the allowance of his liberty and power, has his own proper right of judgment, and can no more be judged by another than he himself can judge another]" (ANF 5:565; CSEL 3.2:435–436).

neither himself nor any of those present to be the bishop of bishops, and does not assume the power to tyrannically give orders to others.[1800] But to this day the majority of scholars[1801] consider the Council of Carthage of 256 to be a Council of opposition to Stephen, bishop of Rome, who forbade the rebaptism of heretics and broke unity with the bishops of both the East and the South, who declared that heretics must be rebaptized. In this case, Cyprian's words cited may be seen as alluding to Stephan. This view is so widespread that Ernst calls it *sententia communis*.[1802] But certain Catholic scholars, such as I. Peters, Griesar,[1803] and especially Ernst who supplements him, based on the fact that nowhere do the decrees of the Council mention any edict of Stephan, deny the supposition that it was this edict that caused the Council to be convened.[1804] For this reason Ernst asserts that Cyprian's words do not pertain to Stephan. Citing the words *liber de rebaptismate*, Ernst opines the following: Cyprian's intensified propaganda of the necessity to rebaptize heretics stirred up discontent among the African bishops, and he was reproached for pride and a desire to promote only his own ideas everywhere. It is against these accusations that St. Cyprian is defending himself in his opening remarks at the Council of 256.[1805] Poschmann shares this view of Ernst entirely.[1806]

1800 See *Animadversiones*, Migne (PL 3:1077c).

1801 These are all listed in various places in the study by Ernst, and also by Poschmann, op. cit., 29, Anm. 3. Ernst (40) lists those scholars who have hesitated to voice a definite opinion. Cf. Batiffol, *L'eglise naissante et le catholicisme*³, 769.

1802 Ernst, *Papst Stephan I*, 40. Vgl. Harnack, *Chronologie* 2, 358–359.

1803 *Zeitschrift für katholische Théologie* (1881), 193 ff.

1804 Ernst devotes a considerable section of his study to this question (39–63). From the same study we may become acquainted with opposing views, since it is conducted purely polemically, primarily against Leo Nelke. See Ernst's own *nhel,* "Neue Untersuchungen über Cyprian und den Ketzer taufstreit (Kritische Glossen zu d'Alès, von Soden u. a.)," *Theologische Quartalschrift* (1911): 260–270.

1805 Ernst, *Papst Stephan I*, 57–59. Vgl. Peters, *Der heilige Cyprian von Karthago*, 515–516.

1806 Poschmann, *Die Sichtbarkeit der Kirche*, 28–30.

But whether we adopt one view or the other, the dogmatic idea
upon which St. Cyprian's entire system is based remains completely
unchanged: neither he himself nor any other bishop can be called
the bishop of bishops, nor can they assume any special authority.[1807]
The bishop of Rome is no exception: all bishops are equal.[1808] The
bishop of Rome in Cyprian's time, however, laid claim to a special
authority, specifically in the dispute over the rebaptism of heretics.
To Stephan's successor, Sixtus, Dionysius of Alexandria wrote: "He
… had written previously concerning Helenus and Firmilianus,
and all those in Cilicia and Cappadocia and Galatia and the neighboring nations, saying that he would not commune with them (ὡς
οὐδὲ ἐκείνοις κοινωνήσων) for this same cause; namely, that they
re-baptized heretics."[1809] St. Cyprian notified Stephan of the conciliar decrees of the African Churches.[1810] Stephan responded to
Cyprian no less bluntly than he had written to the bishops of Asia
Minor. Although the actual letter of Stephan has been lost, we have
significant knowledge of it. Cyprian himself says that Stephan is
in error, that he persists in defending the cause of heretics against
Christians and the Church of God, and that his epistle contains
much that is haughty, unskillful, and rashly written.[1811] Cyprian
mocks Stephan's epistle, considering it degrading to the Church of
God;[1812] he says that Stephan defends what is evil and false, and that

---

1807 Some presume that *episcopus episcoporum* [bishop of bishops] was the
standing title of the bishop of Rome at the time (cf. Tertullian, *On Modesty* 1). But
in not acknowledging that St. Cyprian's words refer to Stephan, Ernst demonstrates that the expression *episcopus episcoporum* was used without any application
to the bishop of Rome (60. Cf. the note on *The Seventh Council in Carthage under Cyprian* in Migne (PL 3:1053d–1054b). See also [the work by] Peters, *Der hl. Cyprian*,
516. It is noteworthy that Catholic scholars alternately see *episcopus episcoporum* as
indicating the primacy of the bishop of Rome or—depending on the circumstances—ascribe it no significance whatsoever.

1808 Vgl. Koch, *Cyprian und der römische Primat*, 51.

1809 Eusebius, *Church History* 7.5.4 (NPNF² 1:295; GrchSch. 9.2:640).

1810 Cyprian of Carthage, *Epistles* 72-71 (CSEL 3.2:775).

1811 Cyprian of Carthage, *Epistles* 74-73.1 "To Pompey" (ANF 5:386; CSEL
3.2:799).

1812 Ibid. 4 (ANF 5:387; CSEL 3.2:802).

this proceeds from a love of presumption and of obstinacy;[1813] he calls Stephan a friend of heretics and an enemy of Christians, because he holds it necessary to remove himself (*abstinendos putat*) from "the priests of God, who support the truth of Christ and the unity of the Church."[1814] Concerning the disagreements with Stephan Cyprian wrote to Firmilian, bishop of Caesarea in Cappadocia, who sent an excellent letter in response. This letter shows quite well, first and foremost, that there was a definite awareness of episcopal unity even at so great a distance. "We have received ... the letter ... and we gave the greatest thanks to the Lord, because it has happened that we who are separated from one another in body are thus united in spirit, as if we were not only occupying one country, but inhabiting together one and the self-same house. Which also it is becoming for us to say, because, indeed, the spiritual house of God is one. ... For the grace of God is mighty to associate and join together in the bond of charity and unity even those things which seem to be divided by a considerable space of earth."[1815] Firmilian attacks Stephan with the severest censure, which precludes any idea of the primacy of the bishop of Rome.[1816] Firmilian even compares Stephan to Judas, and leaves all mention of him until the end of the epistle, "lest, while we remember his audacity and pride (*audaciae et insolentiae*), we bring a more lasting sadness on ourselves from the things that he has wickedly done (*de rebus ab eo improbe gestis*)."[1817] But in the second part Firmilian begins to speak of Stephan, and he does so very sharply indeed. "In this respect I am justly indignant

---

1813 Ibid. 10 (ANF 5:389; CSEL 3.2:807).

1814 Ibid. 8 (ANF 5:389; CSEL 3.2:805).

1815 Cyprian of Carthage, *Epistles* 75-74.1, 3 (ANF 5:390; CSEL 3.2:810, 811). Cf. the observation of Batiffol, *L'eglise naissante et le catholicisme*³, 482.

1816 With good reason many Catholic scholars have made attempts to declare Firmilian's letter spurious. See the note of Balusius in Migne (PL 3:1153–1154), and also an entire dissertation by the French scholar F. Marcellini Molkenbuhr, *De Firmiliani ad S. Cyprianum epistola aliisque ejus operibus*, in Migne (PL 3:1361–1410). Cf. Harnack, *Chronologie* 2, 359–360.

1817 Cyprian of Carthage, *Epistles* 75-74.3 "Firmilian" (ANF 5:390; CSEL 3.2:811).

at this so open and manifest folly (*stultitiam*) of Stephen, that he who so boasts of the place of his episcopate, and contends that he holds the succession (*successionem*) from Peter, on whom the foundations of the Church were laid, should introduce many other rocks. ... Nor does he understand that the truth of the Christian Rock is overshadowed, and in some measure abolished, by him when he thus betrays and deserts unity."[1818] Clearly, the bishop of Rome had been justifying his claims to an exclusive position based on the privileges of his see;[1819] but not only does Firmilian not make the unity of the episcopacy dependent upon each individual bishop being in agreement with the bishop of Rome, he even considers it essential that the bishop of Rome be in agreement and unity with the episcopacy. Consequently, the same evaluation that Cyprian imposed upon every bishop in *On the Unity of the Church* is applied to the bishop of Rome. At the end of Firmilian's epistle we read: "When you communicate with the baptism of heretics, what else do you do than drink from their slough and mud; and while you yourself are purged with the Church's sanctification, you become befouled with the contact of the filth of others? ... But indeed you are worse than all heretics (*tu haereticis omnibus pejor es*). For when many, as soon as their error is known, come over to you from them that they may receive the true light of the Church ... you heap up the darkness of the heretical night. ... What strifes and dissensions have you stirred up throughout the churches of the whole world! Moreover, how great sin have you heaped up for yourself, when you cut yourself off from so many flocks! For it is yourself that you have cut off. Do not deceive yourself, since he is really the schismatic (*schismaticus*) who has made himself an apostate from the communion of ecclesiastical unity (*qui se a communione unitatis apostatum fecerit*). For while you think that all may be excommunicated by you, you have excommunicated yourself alone from all."[1820] It is quite clear that, in the idea of

---

1818 Cyprian of Carthage, *Epistles* 75-74.17 "Firmilian" (ANF 5:394; CSEL 3.2:821). Cf. Harnack's observation in *Dogmengeschichte*[4] 1, 421, Anm.

1819 Böhringer says that Stephan anticipated the future papacy—*Die alte Kirche* 4, 1003. Cf. Batiffol, *L'eglise naissante et le catholicisme*[3], 469.

1820 Cyprian of Carthage, *Epistles* 75-74.23, 24 "Firmilian" (ANF 5:396;

Firmilian and Cyprian, the bishop of Rome must be in a union of peace with the whole episcopacy.[1821] Catholic scholars frequently express and defend this thesis: Stephan excommunicated neither Cyprian nor the Eastern bishops, but merely threatened them with excommunication.[1822] The sources indeed say nothing definite about Stephan excommunicating his opponents,[1823] and even the decisive testimony of Firmilian just cited employs ambiguous terms— *rumpens pacem, a te abstineri, ab omnibus abstinuisti*.[1824] But the majority of scholars[1825] acknowledge that the excommunication actually

---

CSEL 3.2:824, 825). See the observation of Batiffol, *L'eglise naissante et le catholicisme³*, 474–475. Cyprian naturally fully supported all that Firmilian said. It is probable that Cyprian himself translated Firmilian's epistle into Latin. See Fechtrup, *Der hl. Cyprian*, 241; Th. Rettberg, *C. Cyprianus*, 188; Ernst, *Zeitschrift für katholische Théologie* (1894): 238 ff.; *Theologische Quartalschrift* (1911): 393–395. Opposition to this conjecture is expressed by Hans von Soden (*Das lateinische Neue Testament in Africa zur Zeit Cyprians nach Bibelhandschriften und Väterzeugnissen* [Leipzig: 1909]. Texte und Untersuchungen zur Geschichte der altchristlichen Literatur, herausgeg. von Adolf Harnack und Carl Schmidt, Bd. 33, 104); *Streit zwischen Rom und Karthago über die Ketzertaufe* [Rom: 1909], 22).

1821 Vgl. Koch, *Cyprian und der römische Primat*, 140–141.

1822 So [holds] Ernst: the first [we find] in the article "War der hl. Cyprian exkommunizirt?" *Zeitschrift für katholische Théologie* (1894): 473–499; the second— in the above cited study *Papst Stephan I*, §5: "Papst Stephan und die kleinasiatischen Anabaptisten," 80–93. Cf. *Theologische Quartalschrift* (1911): 388–392.

1823 See for example *Epistles* 75-74.6, "Firmilian": "Stephanus nunc ausus est facere rumpens adversus vos pacem, quam semper antecessores ejus vobiscum amore et honore mutuo custodierunt [...Stephen has now dared to make; breaking the peace against you, which his predecessors have always kept with you in mutual love and honour]" (CSEL 3.2:813.28–30). 75-74.25: "Cum tot episcopis dissensisse, pacem cum singulis vario discordiae genere rumpentem, modo cum orientalibus, quod nec vos latere confidimus, modo vobiscum, qui in meridie estis [to have disagreed with so many bishops... breaking peace with each one of them in various kinds of discord: at one time with the eastern churches, as we are sure you know; at another time with you who are in the south]" (CSEL 3.2:826). Cf. *Works*, part 1, 387 [Rus. ed.]. Cf. *Epistles* 74-73.8 "To Pompey" (CSEL 3.2:805).

1824 Concerning this see Ernst, *Papst Stephan I*, 82–83.

1825 See Th. F.W. Rettberg, *C. Cyprianus, Bischof von Carthago*, 181, 183–186; B. Fechtrup, *Der hl. Cyprian*, 234, 237–238; H.V. Soden, *Der Streit Swischen Rom und Karthago über die Ketzertaufe*, 33–34; Koch, *Cyprian und der römische Primat*, 67–68, 148–149; Bolotov, *Lectures on the History of the Early Church*, 2nd ed., 386 ("it

took place.[1826] From the testimonies we have cited it may be seen that even the view expressed by modern Catholic researchers such as Ernst and Poschmann, regarding the significance of the bishop of Rome in the third century, has not the slightest basis. Suppose, even, that Stephan only threatened excommunication. Poschmann holds that union with the bishop of Rome was an essential condition for episcopal authority.[1827] Why is it then that Stephan's threat had not the slightest effect, and he was unanimously condemned in both the East and the South? Does not Firmilian call Stephan himself a schismatic, and even—albeit indirectly—a false Christ and a false apostle[1828] for his break with the episcopacy?[1829] In general, if we compare the epistles which Cyprian wrote to the bishop of Rome at various times with his epistles to other bishops, we cannot help but notice that he writes to the bishop of Rome as he does to any other. In Cyprian's epistles to the bishop of Rome there is no hint of any particular reverence, as we would rightfully expect if Cyprian acknowledged the primacy of the bishop of Rome. For Cyprian the bishop of Rome is his *collega*, his *frater*, and he speaks of his ecclesiastical position exactly as of his own or of the position of any other bishop.[1830] Would it not be better therefore to conclude that, in the mind of the Church, it was not a bishop's agreement with the bishop of Rome that was the condition of his authori-

---

seems"). Cf. Batiffol, *L'eglise naissante et le catholicisme*[3], 471n3.

1826 Incidentally, Seitz points out that Stephan did not even show hospitality to the emissaries of Cyprian (*Epistles* 75-74.25 [CSEL 3.2:826]), apparently as being schismatics. Firmilian reproaches him for this, because in the East, according to the *Apostolic Constitutions* (7.28.4), hospitality was shown even to heretics. See *Die Heilsnotwendigkeit der Kirche*, 201.

1827 Poschmann, *Die Sichtbarkeit der Kirche*, 32: "So ist das Festhalten an der Gemeinschaft mit ihm die notwendige Bedingung der bischöflichen Autorität."

1828 Cyprian of Carthage, *Epistles* 75-74.25, "Firmilian": "Stephen is not ashamed ... to call Cyprian 'a false Christ and a false apostle, and a deceitful worker.' And he, conscious that all these characters are in himself, has been in advance of you, by falsely objecting to another those things which he himself ought deservedly to hear" (ANF 5:397; CSEL 3.2:827).

1829 Vgl. Koch, *Cyprian und der römische Primat*, 71–72.

1830 For more detail see Koch, *Cyprian und der römische Primat*, 121–127.

ty, but the reverse—the essential condition of the authority of the bishop of Rome was his agreement with the entire episcopacy of the Church?[1831] Thus, **neither St. Cyprian's works nor the manuscripts from his time contain the idea that the unity of the episcopacy allegedly has its visible center in the bishop of Rome.** St. Cyprian considered the conciliar union and unanimity of the bishops alone to be this center.[1832] Indeed, the entire ecclesiology of St. Cyprian demands this alone.

But in St. Cyprian's writings even the significance of the Council of bishops for the unity of the Church is not a juridical significance. It is noteworthy that the holy father says nothing whatsoever about the necessity of unconditional submission of the bishop to all

---

1831 Protestant scholars likewise sometimes express the opinion that Cyprian contradicted himself. Amid the grave crisis which his own community was undergoing, he cited the Church of Rome and the bishop of Rome as though communion with this Church in and of itself was the surety of the truth. But in disputing with Stephan, bishop of Rome, concerning the baptism of heretics he explicitly denied that bishop's claims to special rights in the Church that would necessarily proceed from being the successor of the apostle Peter (see Harnack, *Dogmengeschichte*[4] 1, 420, 421, Anm. 494). But Cyprian had spoken earlier of the equality and mutual independence of the bishops (Vgl. Koch, *Cyprian und der römische Primat*, 72–73, 85–86, 100, 141–143), as is inferred from his entire system (Koch, 127–128).

1832 Harnack writes: "The great confederation of Churches that Cyprian presumes and which he designates as the Church had not yet been wholly accomplished in reality; for it cannot be proven either that it extended throughout all regions of the Roman state, or that it encompassed all right-believing and episcopally structured communities within the Roman Empire. Even afterward, at least prior to the fourth century, the conditions were never definitively formulated for a confederation which only became empirical in the full sense from the time of Constantine. Consequently, the idea of one Church, resting upon the bishops and encompassing all Christians, was only ever an idea; and since, in the idea of Cyprian, it is not the idea but only its implementation that has significance, his dogmatic system is refuted by the actual relations that existed" (*Dogmengeschichte* 1, 422). All this however can hardly be so convincingly proven as to justify such decisive conclusions concerning the system of St. Cyprian. The information to be had from Eusebius (*Church History* 7.5.6, 7; 5.19) and Firmilian convincingly show just how lively was the intercourse of bishops among themselves, and what broad circles they encompassed. Cf. Batiffol, *L'eglise naissante et le catholicisme*, 478–482.

conciliar decrees.[1833] We have already cited St. Cyprian's opening
remarks at the Council of Carthage in 256, from which we see that
the Council of bishops must not excommunicate anyone, even if he
should be divergent in his thinking (*neminem ... a jure communicationis,
si diversum senserit amoventes*).[1834] This idea occurs repeatedly in the
various epistles of St. Cyprian.[1835] Even the question of whether
to baptize heretics or to recognize the validity of their baptism—a
question inseparably linked with dogmatic doctrine, as Cyprian
himself constantly argued—is not one that he considers resolved at
the Councils in a manner compulsory for every bishop. In commu-
nicating the decree of the Council of Carthage to Stephan, bishop
of Rome, St. Cyprian writes: "We know that some will not lay aside
what they have once imbibed, and do not easily change their purpose (*propositum*); but, keeping fast the bond of peace and concord
among their colleagues, retain certain things peculiar to themselves
(*usurpata*),[1836] which have once been adopted among them. In which
behalf we neither do violence to, nor impose a law upon, any one,
since each prelate has in the administration of the Church the exercise of his will free, as he shall give an account of his conduct
to the Lord."[1837] In questions of an administrative nature (*in ecclesiae administratione*), even the Council of bishops sets no law. What is

---

1833 See Koch, *Cyprian und der römische Primat*, 54–61; Poschmann, *Die Sichtbarkeit der Kirche*, 30–32.

1834 *The Seventh Council of Carthage under Cyprian* (CSEL 3.2:436).

1835 "For the bishop of Carthage, the chief thesis concerning the self-suf-
ficiency and independence of the bishops that he expressed at the September
council so thoroughly became flesh and blood that he repeats it constantly. For
him, this chief thesis is on a level with the unity of the Church as the chief point
in the *magna charta* of church structure" (Koch, *Cyprian und der römische Primat*, 54).

1836 In the Russian source, "abuses." –*Trans.*

1837 Cyprian of Carthage, *Epistles* 72-71.3, "To Stephen": "Habeat in ecclesiae administratione voluntatis suae arbitrium liberum unusquisque praepositus" (ANF 5:379; CSEL 3.2:778). Cyprian repeats the same in *Epistles* 55-51.21,
"To Antonianus" (ANF 5:332; CSEL 3.2:639); *Epistles* 73-72.26, "To Jubaianus"
(CSEL 3.2:798); *Epistles* 69-75.17, "To Magnus" (CSEL 3.2:765–766); *Epistles*
59-54.14, "To Cornelius" (ANF 5:344; CSEL 3.2:683); and *Epistles* 57-53.5, "To
Cornelius" (CSEL 3.2:655).

most necessary for the unity of the episcopacy is not uniformity of church discipline, but unanimity, peace, and love among the bishops. When these conditions are met, *salvo inter collegas pacis et concordiae vinculo*, as St. Cyprian wrote to Stephan, church practice can vary even in the most essential points.[1838] In governing his Church, each bishop may turn to the Lord's principle of the Tradition of the Gospel and of the apostles.[1839] It is to God that he will answer for his errors.[1840] Cyprian distinguishes between the concepts of *veritas* [truth] and *consuetudo* [custom]. *Veritas*—also called *lex evangelii, praecepta dominica, regula* [law of the gospel, precepts of the Lord, rule]— is an obligatory standard, and every bishop must strive to reconcile the *consuetudo* of his Church with *veritas*.[1841] Agreement with *veritas* is sufficient for peace within the Church and communion among the bishops. "We, as far as in us lies, do not contend on behalf of heretics with our colleagues and fellow-bishops, with whom we maintain a divine concord and the peace of the Lord; especially since the apostle says, 'If any man, however, is thought to be contentious, we have no such custom, neither the Church of God' [1 Cor. 11:16]. Charity of spirit, the honour of our college, the bond of faith, and priestly concord, are maintained by us with patience and gentleness."[1842] Nevertheless, in Cyprian's view the unification

---

1838   This idea is most strikingly expressed in *Epistles* 55-51.21, "To Antonianus": "While the bond of concord remains, and the undivided sacrament of the Catholic Church endures (*perseverante catholicae ecclesiae individuo sacramento*), every bishop disposes and directs his own acts, and will have to give an account of his purposes to the Lord" (ANF 5:332; CSEL 3.2:639).

1839   Cyprian of Carthage, *Epistles* 74-73.10, "To Pompey" (ANF 5:389; CSEL 3.2:808).

1840   Cyprian of Carthage, *Epistles* 57-53.5, "To Cornelius": "If there be any (one) of our colleagues who, now that the contest is urgent, thinks that peace should not be granted to our brethren and sisters, he shall give an account to the Lord in the day of judgment, either of his grievous rigour or of his inhuman hardness" (ANF 5:338; CSEL 3.2:655).

1841   Cyprian of Carthage, *Epistles* 74-73.2, "To Pompey" (ANF 5:380; CSEL 3.2:800). See Harnack's observation in *Dogmengeschichte*[4] 1, 419–420, Anm. 2.

1842   Cyprian of Carthage, *Epistles* 73-72.26, "To Jubaianus" (ANF 5:386; CSEL 3.2:798). Firmilian fully shared Cyprian's idea of the possibility of una-

of the bishops, especially at the Councils, is also significant for the perfection of discipline, for reconciling *consuetudo* with *veritas*. "Many things are revealed to individuals for the better, and that each one ought not obstinately to contend for that which he had once imbibed and held; but if anything has appeared better and more useful, he should gladly embrace it. For we are not overcome when better things are presented to us, but we are instructed, especially in those matters which pertain to the unity of the Church and the truth of our hope and faith."[1843]

The unity of the episcopacy is expressed not only in common agreement, but also in the conciliar appointment and consecration of each new bishop. "For the proper celebration of ordinations all the neighbouring bishops of the same province should assemble with that people for which a prelate is ordained. And the bishop should be chosen in the presence of the people, who have most fully known the life of each one, and have looked into the doings of each one as respects his habitual conduct."[1844] The elected bishop was then consecrated by the laying on of hands. This is precisely how St. Cyprian describes the consecration of Sabinus, bishop of Spain,[1845] and Novatian was likewise consecrated by the laying on

---

nimity and peace among the bishops even given significant differences in church practice. In *Epistles* 75-74.6 he writes: "In very many other provinces also many things are varied because of the difference of the places and names (*hominum*, alternately read *nominum*). And yet on this account there is no departure at all from the peace and unity of the Catholic Church" (ANF 5:391; CSEL 3.2:377).

1843 Cyprian of Carthage, *Epistles* 71-70.3, "To Quintus" (ANF 5:378; CSEL 3.2:774).

1844 Cyprian of Carthage, *Epistles* 67-67, "To the Clergy and People Abiding in Spain" (ANF 5:371; CSEL 3.2:739). Concerning Cornelius Cyprian writes (*Epistles* 55-51.8, "To Antonianus"): "He was made bishop by very many of our colleagues who were then present in the city of Rome, who sent to us letters concerning his ordination, honourable and laudatory, and remarkable for their testimony in announcement of him" (ANF 5:329; CSEL 3.2:629). For more detail on St. Cyprian's teaching concerning the election and appointment of a bishop, see Molchanov, *St. Cyprian of Carthage*, 219–227.

1845 Cyprian of Carthage, *Epistles* 67-67.5 (ANF 5:371; CSEL 3.2:739).

of hands.[1846] Protestant scholarship frequently claims that St. Cyprian sees the laying of hands upon a bishop at his consecration as a mere ritual, one that has no sacramental value.[1847] We have already expounded the teaching of St. Cyprian concerning the divine institution of the hierarchy. Here we may merely note his teaching concerning consecration specifically as a sacrament. St. Cyprian says that God deigns to elect and appoint priests for Himself in his Church.[1848] The Lord God makes one a bishop.[1849] This appointment of the bishop by God lies specifically in the imparting to him of particular power from God: "We who have received the Spirit of God (*spiritum Dei accepimus*)," says St. Cyprian, "ought to have a jealousy for the divine faith."[1850] The grace of the Holy Spirit is only bestowed for the work of serving the one Church. If a bishop severs ties with the Church and falls into grave sins, he is deprived of the Holy Spirit.[1851] But it is St. Cyprian's like-minded contemporaries who most definitively express the view of chirotony as a sacramental act. For example, at the Council of 256, Bishop Nemesianus spoke unequivocally of the communication of the Holy Spirit through the laying on of hands.[1852] Firmilian, bishop of Caesarea, writes to Cyprian: "In the Church ... the elders preside, who possess the power both of baptizing, and of imposition of hands (forgiveness

---

1846 Cyprian of Carthage, *Epistles* 49-45.1, "Cornelius to Cyprian": the confessors from Rome repented that "through being misled they had ... committed schismatical acts, and been the authors of heresy, so that they suffered hands to be imposed on [Novatian] as if upon a bishop" (ANF 5:323; CSEL 3.2:610). Cf. Eusebius, *Church History* 6.43.9 (GrchSch. 9.2:618).

1847 These views are expounded and refuted by Poschmann in *Die Sichtbarkeit der Kirche*, 171 ff.

1848 Cyprian of Carthage, *Epistles* 48-44.4 "To Cornelius" (CSEL 3.2:608).

1849 Cyprian of Carthage, *Epistles* 55-51.8, "To Antonianus" (ANF 5:329; CSEL 3.2:629); *Epistles* 59-54.6, "To Cornelius" (CSEL 3.2:673); *Epistles* 66-68.9, "To Florentius Pupianus" (ANF 5:375; CSEL 3.2:733); *Epistles* 70-69, "To Januarius" (ANF 5:376; CSEL 3.2:770).

1850 Cyprian of Carthage, *Epistles* 73-72.10, "To Jubaianus" (ANF 5:381; CSEL 3.2:785).

1851 65-61.5, "To Epictetus" (ANF 5:364; CSEL 3.2:724–725)

1852 *The Seventh Council of Carthage under Cyprian* (ANF 5:566; CSEL 3.2:436).

of sins),[1853] and of ordaining. For as a heretic may not lawfully ordain nor lay on hands, so neither may he baptize."[1854] Here we see
that chirotony is numbered among such indubitable sacraments as
Baptism. Thus, the episcopacy as a whole possesses a special grace,
which it vouchsafes to each new bishop; consequently, the episcopacy is an unbroken unity that preserves a special grace from God
in the Church.

The unity of the episcopacy manifested at the consecration of
a new bishop, as we see from the works of St. Cyprian, was not
limited solely to the bishops present, but encompassed a far broader
circle. In taking the throne, the bishop would send special epistles
notifying even many individual bishops, who would acknowledge
him in answering epistles and thereby enter into communion with
him.[1855] When two bishops—Cornelius and Novatian—were appointed in Rome simultaneously, both hastened to receive the recognition of the other bishops.[1856] When this difficulty arose, Cyprian sent specially appointed persons to inquire into events in Rome,
so as to have a firm basis for recognizing Cornelius and rejecting
Novatian.[1857] Cyprian's mind was not easy until those sent returned

---

1853 The parenthetical phrase is from the Russian source. −*Trans.*

1854 Cyprian of Carthage, *Epistles* 75-74.7, "Firmilian to Cyprian": "In ecclesia ubi praesident majores natu qui et baptizandi et manum imponendi et ordi-
nandi possident potestatem haereticum enim sicut ordinare non licet nec manum
imponere, ita nec baptizare" (ANF 5:392; CSEL 3.2:814–815). Unfortunately,
the Russian translation (*Works*, part 1, 378 [Rus. ed.]) of this important passage
is highly imprecise in general. In particular, it renders *potestas baptizandi* as власть
распорядиться ("the power of disposing"), completely omitting the idea in the
original that is of most importance to us.

1855 Cyprian of Carthage, *Epistles* 45-41.1, 2, "To Cornelius" (ANF 320;
CSEL 3.2:599–600). *Epistles* 48-44.3: "We decided … that letters should be sent
you—that is, to Cornelius—[so as to] maintain both you and your communion,
that is as well to the unity of the Catholic Church as to its charity" (ANF 5:322;
CSEL 3.2:607). *Epistles* 67-67, "To the Clergy and People Abiding in Spain"
(ANF 5:371; CSEL 3.2:739).

1856 Cyprian of Carthage, *Epistles* 44-40.1, "To Cornelius" (ANF 5:319;
CSEL 3.2:597–498); *Epistles* 55-51.3, "To Antonianus" (CSEL 3.2:625); *Epistles*
59-54.9, "To Cornelius" (CSEL 3.2:676–677).

1857 Cyprian of Carthage, *Epistles* 44-40.1, "To Cornelius" (ANF 5:319;

and delivered to him letters of approval concerning Cornelius from the bishops who had ordained him.[1858] It may be supposed that in other instances, when no such conflicts were in evidence, other bishops entered into communion with the new bishop out of trust in their brother bishops who had appointed him.[1859]

We have expounded how St. Cyprian of Carthage accomplished the first half of the great task that fell to his lot—that of elucidating the doctrine concerning the Church in detail. All the earliest elements of the doctrine concerning the Church as the custodian of the truth of Christ were partly assimilated and partly supplemented by St. Cyprian. He assimilated the doctrine, known since the time of St. Ignatius the God-bearer, of the bishop as the focal point of each individual Church. The previously extensively developed doctrine of episcopal succession was likewise included in his system of ecclesiology. So greatly was this idea assimilated by church consciousness that St. Cyprian makes no attempt to speak of episcopal succession in detail: he does not list a series of bishops stretching back to the apostles, as we saw in the writings of St. Irenaeus of lyons. But St. Cyprian developed in particular detail the doctrine of the unity of the catholic Church and of the episcopacy as the organ of the outward unity of the Church. For St. Cyprian, the bishop is not merely the focal point of the individual Church, but primarily an individual bearer of catholic episcopacy, in which lies the unity of the entire ecumenical Church. Through the bishop each separate Church is inseparably **outwardly** linked with the entire ecumenical Church. The unification of the episcopacy is accomplished

---

CSEL 3.2:597); *Epistles* 45-41.1, "To Cornelius"(ANF 5:320; CSEL 3.2:599–600). *Epistles* 48-44.2, 3: It was determined that all things should be suspended as they were until the truth of the matter should be discovered (ANF 5:322; CSEL 3.2:606–607).

1858 It was to his fellow bishops who were present at the consecration of Cornelius that Cyprian sent Caldonius and Fortunatus. See *Epistles* 44-40.2, "To Cornelius" (ANF 5:319; CSEL 3.2:592); *Epistles* 45-41.1, (ANF 5:320; CSEL 3.2:600); *Epistles* 48-44.4 (CSEL 3.2:608). Cornelius presents the information received from Rome in his epistle to Antonianus (55-51.8), in defense of Cornelius (CSEL 3.2:629–630).

1859 See Molchanov, *St. Cyprian of Carthage*, 226.

at the Council. In Cyprian's doctrine concerning the Church, the dogma concerning the Church was first fully expressed: to what Cyprian said about the unity of the Church, about the episcopacy, or about the hierarchy in general as the organ of that unity, hardly anything **essentially** new was later added. During the third century the conciliar unity of the episcopacy and the conciliar governance of the Church became more and more firmly established, until in the fourth century the all-encompassing phenomenon of the Ecumenical Councils became a part of the life of the Christian Church. In the Ecumenical Council the ecclesiological system of St. Cyprian first received the outward expression that most closely corresponds to it.

But the doctrine of St. Cyprian on the unity of the Church and on the episcopacy was, in a manner of speaking, derivative. The whole of his ecclesiastical activity took place amid intense conflict over other matters: the chief question, of the most vital interest in St. Cyprian's time, was **the question of the sanctity of the Church.** How St. Cyprian resolved the second, most important part of his task we will now undertake to describe.

In disciplinary practice, Callistus, bishop of Rome, had by his edict established that those who had fallen into the sin of adultery were to be restored to communion with the Church. In the period from 220 to 250 this practice became increasingly widespread. The Montanist protest proved unsuccessful in the society of the Church. Concerning this St. Cyprian writes: "Among our predecessors, some of the bishops here in our province thought that peace was not to be granted to adulterers, and wholly closed the gate of repentance against adultery. Still," St. Cyprian continues, "they did not withdraw from the assembly of their co-bishops, nor break the unity of the Catholic Church by the persistency of their severity or censure; so that, because by some peace was granted to adulterers, he who did not grant it should be separated from the Church."[1860] But the inconsistency of church discipline observed by

---

1860 Cyprian of Carthage, *Epistles* 55-51.21, "To Antonianus" (ANF 5:332; CSEL 3.2:638–639). Harnack conjectures that in Rome too, after Callistus, discipline was made more strict. But Harnack likewise notes that thereafter the re-

Tertullian[1861] still remained: apostates were not equated with adulterers, and no practice with regard to them was instituted. Nor was the question one of any particularly vital acuteness in this particular period: at the time persecution was almost nonexistent. But the question arose all the more acutely when the persecution of Decius began. The Decian persecution was rather unique. Christians were not executed for their faith, but were admonished to renounce the Christian faith and return to the pagan faith fostered by the Roman state. Christians were compelled to offer sacrifice to the gods, and whoever refused would be subjected to torture (but not executed). Consequently, during the Decian persecution there were hardly any martyrs—only confessors. But many of the Christians, who were no longer accustomed to persecution and feared the tortures, hastened to offer sacrifice and obtain a certificate of the fact from the authorities. These certificates (*libelli*) were mass produced,[1862] and state officials could not keep up with the demand from the crowds of apostates, as St. Cyprian bitterly recounts.[1863] The lapsed—as those who had sacrificed to idols came to be called—were not idolaters in the proper sense. Their guilt lay solely in that they, fearing torture, had merely received certificates of having fulfilled the decree of the state, although in actuality they had offered no sacrifices and burned no incense to idols. They had never ceased to be Christians

---

ception of those guilty of fleshly sins aroused no controversy (*Novatian*, RE 3, Bd. XIV, 230).

1861 Tertullian, *On Modesty* 9.22. See Harnack, *Lapsi*, RE 3, Bd. XI, 286–287; *Dogmengeschichte*[4] 1, 443–444.

1862 Recently specimens of authentic certificates have been discovered, from which it is clear that they were prepared in advance—the names of the recipient of the certificates are entered in different handwriting.

1863 Cyprian of Carthage, *Treatises* 3, "On the Lapsed": "They indeed did not wait to be apprehended ere they ascended, or to be interrogated ere they denied. Many were conquered before the battle, prostrated before the attack. Nor did they even leave it to be said for them, that they seemed to sacrifice to idols unwillingly. They ran to the market-place of their own accord; freely they hastened to death, as if they had formerly wished it, as if they would embrace an opportunity now given which they had always desired. How many were put off by the magistrates at that time, when evening was coming on; how many even asked that their destruction might not be delayed!" (ANF 5:439; CSEL 3.2:242).

at heart. Naturally, the Church had to determine its stance on this new turn of events. To restore an adulterer to communion after repentance while completely refusing that communion to the *libellatici* would have been most unjust. Comparing the sins of each, St. Cyprian considered the adulterer to have the greater guilt, since he sins voluntarily.[1864] Indeed, in Carthage certain presbyters who had governed the Church in the absence of St. Cyprian took a very lenient view of the lapsed: they received them without the mediation of the martyrs, without any penitential labors, and even without the permission of a bishop. St. Cyprian, however, decreed that those who had fallen undergo penitence (*exomologesis*), and that they not rush to be restored to communion, but that they await the end of the persecutions, when the question of their restoration to communion would be resolved in council.[1865] Only in cases of mortal illness did Saint Cyprian permit those who had certificates from the martyrs to be received—a decree which St. Cyprian made in light of the approaching summer, "a season that is disturbed with continual and heavy sicknesses."[1866] From the very outset Cyprian did not deny the possibility of restoring the lapsed to communion: he was merely combating a tendency among certain of the lapsed, who denied that they had any need of repentance.[1867] Consequent-

---

1864 Cyprian of Carthage, *Epistles* 55-51.26: "The case of an adulterer is by far both graver and worse than that of one who has taken a certificate (*libellatici*), because the latter has sinned by necessity, the former by free will: the latter, thinking that it is sufficient for him that he has not sacrificed, has been deceived by an error; the former, a violator of the matrimonial tie of another, or entering a brothel, into the sink and filthy gulf of the common people, has befouled by detestable impurity a sanctified body and God's temple" (ANF 5:334; CSEL 3.2:644). Cf. the reasoning of Tertullian in *On Modesty* 22: "Nemo volens vegare compellitur, nemo volens fornicatur [No one is compelled with his will to apostatize; no one against his will commits fornication]" (CSEL 20.1:273.10–11).

1865 Concerning this see *Epistles* 16-9, "To the Clergy" (CSEL 3.2:517 sqq.); *Treatises* 11, "Exhortation to Martyrdom" 15–10 (CSEL 3.2:513 sqq.); "To the People" 17–11 (CSEL 3.2:521 sqq.); *Epistles* 55-51.4, "To Antonianus" (CSEL 3.2:625–626).

1866 Cyprian of Carthage, *Epistles* 18-12, "To the Clergy" (ANF 5:293; CSEL 3.2:523 sqq.). The same was also decreed in Rome: *Epistles* 20-14 (CSEL 3.2:527).

1867 Cyprian of Carthage, *Epistles* 35-28, "To the Presbyters and Deacons

ly, this permission to restore those who had sinned to communion cannot be viewed as a relaxation of the formerly strict rigoristic discipline:[1868] in the event of illness the period of repentance was reduced. In the meantime, a lively exchange of opinions arose among various Churches concerning the lapsed. The general opinion was just this—that after appropriate repentance the lapsed could be received, but that the end of the persecutions must be awaited.[1869] Cyprian speaks specifically of the need for unanimous and concordant wholesome counsel to soothe and heal the wounds of the lapsed (*ad fovenda et sananda lapsorum vulnera*).[1870]

When the persecution ended, the Council until which Cyprian had postponed deciding the question of the lapsed was convened in May of the year 251. This Council divided the lapsed into several classes, depending on the gravity of their fall.[1871] Various periods of repentance were set, so as not to weaken the strictness of the eccle-

Abiding in Rome" (ANF 5:306–307; CSEL 3.2:571). See *Epistles* 16-9.2 (CSEL 3.2:518–519); *Treatises* 3.15, "On the Lapsed" (CSEL 3.2:247–248). Given the prevailing rigoristic discipline of the time, these claims are completely inexplicable.

1868 Frequently it is conjectured that Cyprian himself also gradually altered his views, and that initially he did not think it possible to restore those who had sinned mortally to communion with the Church. See Th.C. Rettberg, *Cyprianus*, 75–76, 117. An analysis of this view and an argument for the opposing view are given by Huther, *Cyprians Lehre von der Kirche*, 173–179; Molchanov, *St. Cyprian of Carthage*, 330–335; Kasitsyn, *Schisms of the First Three Centuries of Christianity*, 198–201 (=Addendae, part 44 [1889], 400–403).

1869 Cyprian of Carthage, *Epistles* 20-14.3 (CSEL 3.2:528); *Epistles* 25-19 (CSEL 3.2:538); *Epistles* 26-17 (CSEL 3.2:539); *Epistles* 34-27.2, 5 (CSEL 3.2:569–570); *Epistles* 32-31 (CSEL 3.2:565); *Epistles* 24-18, "Caldonius to Cyprian" (CSEL 3.2:536–537).

1870 Cyprian of Carthage, *Epistles* 34-27.3, "To the Presbyters and Deacons" (CSEL 3.2:570). The history of the Decian persecution is presented in detail by Molchanov in *St. Cyprian of Carthage*, 54–100. Here also [we find] a detailed history of the interactions between Cyprian and the other Churches on the question of receiving the lapsed.

1871 Concerning the classes of the lapsed, see Harnack, *Lapsi*, RE 3, Bd. 11, 285. [This is described] in more detail by Molchanov, op. cit., 57–61. The decrees of the Council of Carthage are presented in Cyprian's epistle to Antonianus (*Epistles* 55-51 [CSEL 3.2:624]).

siastical court, nor to deprive the lapsed of hope for forgiveness.[1872]
At the same council Novatian and Felicissimus, who demanded
more lenient treatment of the lapsed, were definitively excommunicated. In 252, in light of a new persecution, another Council
of Carthage decreed that all who had lapsed during the previous
persecution be received.[1873] In Rome, the question of receiving
the lapsed resolved differently: there the matter ended in schism.
For over a year the Church of Rome was vacant: it was governed
by presbyters, of whom one of the most conspicuous was Novatian—a man highly educated, eloquent, and a strict ascetic.[1874] The
epistles of the Roman clergy to Cyprian, however, show that even
in Rome the clergy espoused no rigoristic movement that treated
the lapsed more strictly than St. Cyprian.[1875] Very frequently in his
epistles St. Cyprian speaks of his agreement with the Church of
Rome.[1876] Novatian likewise was not a rigorist,[1877] as Pacianus emphasizes in his letter to Simpronianus,[1878] based on Epistle 55-51 of
Cyprian. But when Cornelius was elected to the episcopal throne,

1872 Cyprian of Carthage, *Epistles* 55-51.6, "To Antonianus" (CSEL 3.2:627).

1873 For the decrees of this Council, see *Epistles* 57-53, "To Cornelius" (CSEL 3.2:650 sqq.).

1874 His name varies among different writers. Concerning this, as well as de-tails on the life of Novatian, see Harnack, *Novatian*, RE 3, Bd. XIV, 229, 230–231.

1875 Vgl. Frank, *Die Bussdisciplin der Kirche*, 551.

1876 Cyprian of Carthage, *Epistles* 20-14.3 (CSEL 3.2:528–529); *Epistles* 27-22.4 (CSEL 3.2:544); *Epistles* 32-31 (CSEL 3.2:565); *Epistles* 55-51.6, "To An-tonianus" (CSEL 3.2:628). See A. Harnack, "Die Briefe des römischen Klerus aus der Zeit des Sedisvacanz im Jahre 250," in *Theologische Abhandlungen Carl von Weizsäcker zu seinem siebzigsten Geburtstage 11 December 1892 gewidmet* (Freiburg i. B.: 1892), 32–33, 34, 35.

1877 St. Cyprian (*Epistles* 55-51.6, "To Antonianus") relates that Novatian was the author of the epistle he received from the Roman clergy, which among other things mentions the need to grant peace to those of the lapsed who were weak and close to death (CSEL 3.2:627). This epistle protests only against being overly hasty in restoring communion with the lapsed. See also *Epistles* 30-30.3, 8 (CSEL 3.2:551, 556). Vgl. Döllinger, *Hippolytus und Kallistus*, 129; Ioh. Stufler, *Zeitschrift für katholische Theologie* (1907), 594, 601–602. Vgl. Huther, *Cyprians Lehre von der Kirche*, 175–176. See also Harnack, *Die Briefe des römischen Klerus*, 14–17, 32–36.

1878 *Epistles* 3.5 (PL 13:1067a–b).

Novatian and several presbyters separated, found three "rustic and very simple" (ἀγροίκους καὶ ἀπλουστάτους) bishops and compelled them "to confer on him the episcopate through a counterfeit and vain imposition of hands (εἰκονικῇ τινι καὶ ματαίᾳ χειρεπιθεσίᾳ)."[1879] Novatian announced his elevation to the episcopacy in letters to the bishops of various regions, and so began Novatianism. One cannot help but notice the fact that the letters of Cyprian and Cornelius do not mention what dogmatic differences of opinion existed between the Church of Rome under Cornelius and the followers of Novatian. Novatianism is viewed only as an ecclesiastical revolt—not as a heresy in a dogmatic respect. Even Novatian himself in his letters only tries to defame Cornelius personally, and Cornelius and Cyprian defend the bishop of Rome appointed by the majority only with respect to his personal qualities.[1880] Consequently, the schism occurred on personal grounds, not dogmatic.[1881] Perhaps Novatian was not even the chief leader of the schism: in a letter to Dionysius of Alexandria he himself wrote that he was brought to the point of schism against his will;[1882] while St. Cyprian says that he himself appointed the bishop in Rome—that is, Novatian.[1883] The blessed Jerome directly calls Novatian the author (*auctor*) of

1879   Epistle of Cornelius to Fabius of Antioch—Eusebius, *Church History* 6.43.8, 9 (NPNF² 1:288; GrchSch. 9.2:616, 618).

1880   Eusebius, op. cit., 6.43; Cyprian of Carthage, *Epistles* 55-51, "To Antonianus."

1881   This is quite substantially demonstrated by Tillemont. See *Memoires*, vol. 3, 440–442. See also Harnack, *Novatian*, RE 3, XIV, 232–235. Cf. *The Works of St. Hippolytus, Bishop of Rome* ["Творения св. Ипполита, епископа Римского"], 1st ed., XXVII; Priest A. Druzhinin, *The Life and Works of St. Dionysius the Great, Bishop of Alexandria* ["Жизнь и труды св. Дионисия Великого, епископа Александрийского"] (Kazan: 1900), 172–175; Louis Duchesne, *Early History of the Christian Church* ["История древней Церкви"], 275–276 [Rus. ed.].

1882   Eusebius, op. cit., 6.45. Cf. *The Works of St. Dionysius the Great* [Rus. ed.], 48.

1883   Cyprian of Carthage, *Epistles* 52-48.2, "To Cornelius" (CSEL 3.2:618). Novatian was truly a dark personality, who in Rome aligned himself with a party that held opposing views. Cf. Peters, *Der heilige Cyprian von Karthago*, 237 ff. See Pacianus, *Epistles* 3.6 (PL 13:1067c–d).

Novatianism.[1884] Only later did Novatianism take on an aspect of
dogmatic dissidence, specifically regarding the question of the sanctity of the Church. Novatian hastens to establish communion with
various Churches, informing them of his consecration. Clearly, he
had no intent to separate from the Church based on claims that it
was in error, nor did he consider only his own followers to be the
true Church.[1885] Soon after his election to the rank of bishop, at a
large council of 60 bishops Cornelius established a lenient practice with regard to the lapsed: the brethren who through misfortune
had lapsed were to be healed and the medicines of repentance administered to them.[1886] This determination necessarily arose from
the concept of the sanctity of the Church which we noted already
in the early third century. Many were dissatisfied with this decree,
and for a long time no precise practice regarding the lapsed was
established, but no division resulted.[1887] For Novatianism, however,
the practice established regarding the lapsed occasioned their still
greater deviation from the Church.[1888] Little by little, the discord on

---

1884 Jerome, *On Illustrious Men* 70 (PL 23:681b). Cf. Tillemont, *Memoires*, vol.
3, 433, 435.

1885 Vgl. Peters, *Der heilige Cyprian von Karthago*, 248.

1886 Eusebius, op. cit., 6.43.2 (NPNF² 1:286; GrchSch. 9.2:614).

1887 Concerning this see Funk, *Kirchengeschichtliche Abhandlungen und Untersuchungen* 1, 162.

1888 In Rome the schism of Hippolytus seemed to repeat itself. It is note-
worthy that in church literature the schism of Hippolytus was assimilated with
Novatianism. For example, in the hymn of Bishop Damasus (366–384) we read:
   Hippolytus, fertur, premerent cum jussa tyranni,
   Presbyter in schisma semper mansisse
   Novati.
   [Hippolytus, a presbyter, is said to have remained forever in the schism of
Novatus, when the orders of the tyrant were pressing hard.]

   Similarly, the Spanish poet Prudentius likewise says:
   Invenio Hippolytum, qui quondam schisma Novati
   Presbyter attigerat…
   [I find Hippolytus, who once as presbyter had come into contact with the
schism of Novatus]
   (Achelis, *Hippolytstudien*, TU 16.4, 42–44).

personal grounds shifted to a fundamental conflict. In the Novatian society, as it appears before us in the early days of its existence, we see no doctrine on the sanctity of the Church that is in the least consistent. The Novatianists refused to receive the lapsed, because in their view this contradicted the sanctity of the Church; but, as Cyprian attests, they granted forgiveness to adulterers:[1889] the dispute concern the lapsed exclusively. This was naturally inconsistent

---

There is an opinion that Hippolytus also took part in the Novatianist disputes. Eusebius (*Church History* 6.46.5) observes the following: "There is extant also a certain other diaconal epistle of Dionysius, sent to those in Rome through Hippolytus" (NPNF[2] 1:291). Based on this observation of Eusebius, and recollecting the words of Prudentius, in his article "Über Hippolytus, die ersten Monarchianer und die römische Kirche in der ersten Hälfte des dritten Jahrhunderts" (*Theologische Studien und Kritiken* [1853] 4 Heft, 759–787), Gieseler develops the hypothesis that supposedly about the year 251 Hippolytus belonged to the party of Novatian and was a Novatianist bishop near Rome. He was also the envoy sent with the letter which Eusebius mentions. For an analysis of this hypothesis, see Döllinger, *Hippolytus und Kallistus*, 275 ff. Döllinger calls Gieseler's hypothesis a fable built upon a rotten foundation (276). Archpriest Ivantsov-Platonov defended Dieseler's hypothesis—see [his work] *Heresies and Schisms*, from 120 on. This hypothesis was also adopted in an essay on the life and literary activity of St. Hippolytus included with his works in the Russian translation (1st ed., XXVII–XXX), where great significance is ascribed to the supposed fact that Hippolytus served as envoy. Cf. Druzhinin, *The Life and works of St. Dionysius the Great, Bishop of Alexandria*, 190n. But this hypothesis naturally remains a hypothesis. Regarding Eusebius's words, Achelis says: "There can be no question of equating this messenger of Dionysius of Alexandria (247–285) with Hippolytus of Rome. This was an entirely unknown Alexandrian whose name Eusebius read in the address of the letter of Dionysius" (*Hippolytstudien*, TU 16.4, 32, Anm. 1). But it is certain that there was a certain ideological commonality between the protests of Novatian and Hippolytus, although the schism of Novatian was not a direct continuation of the schism of Hippolytus (see Harnack, *Dogmengeschichte*[4] 1, 426)—the more so since between Hippolytus and Callistus there was not the dogmatic dissidence that existed between Novatianism and the Church.

1889 Cyprian of Carthage, *Epistles* 55-51.26, "To Antonianus": "Let him separate the fraudulent and adulterers from his side and from his company" (ANF 5:334; CSEL 3.2:644). *Epistles* 55-51.27: "Neither let the new heretics flatter themselves in this, that they say that they do not communicate with idolaters; although among them there are both adulterers and fraudulent persons, who are held guilty of the crime of idolatry, according to the saying of the apostle" (ANF 5:334; CSEL 3.2:644–645).

of the Novatianists. Later historical accounts relate that the Novatianists ceased restoring to communion anyone who had sinned
mortally, thereby resuming the practice of the Montanists.[1890] Novatian himself was also inclined to this practice,[1891] possibly because
with the end of the persecutions the question of the lapsed lost its
former urgency.[1892]

Nowhere do we find a detailed dogmatic doctrine of the Novatianists regarding the sanctity of the Church, but based on the limited surviving data it may be seen that almost from the outset the No-

---

1890 In the second half of the fourth century Pacianus, bishop of Barcelona,
formulated the doctrine of the Novatians as follows: "Post baptismum poenitere
non liceat, quod mortale peccatum Ecclesia donare non possit, immo quod ipsa
pereat recipiendo peccantes [After baptism let it not be allowed to repent, because the Church cannot forgive a mortal sin; nay rather she herself would be lost
by receiving sinners" (*Epistles* 3.1, *Contra tractatus Novatianarum* [PL 13:1063c–d]).
The historian Socrates cites the following words of the Novatian bishop Ace-
sius: "Οὐ χρὴ τοὺς μετὰ τὸ βάπτισμα ἡμαρτηκότας ἁμαρτίαν, ἣν πρὸς θάνατον
καλοῦσιν αἱ θεῖαι γραφαί, τῆς κοινωνίας τῶν θείων μυστηρίων ἀξιοῦσθαι, ἀλλ'
ἐπὶ μετάνοιαν μὲν αὐτοὺς προτρέπειν, ἐλπίδα δὲ τῆς ἀφέσεως μὴ παρὰ τῶν
ἱερέων, ἀλλὰ παρὰ τοῦ Θεοῦ ἐκδέχεσθαι, τοῦ δυναμένου καὶ ἐξουσίαν ἔχοντος
συγχωρεῖν ἁμαρτήματα [it is not right persons who after baptism have committed a sin, which the sacred Scriptures denominate 'a sin unto death' John 5:16 to
be considered worthy of participation in the sacraments: that they should indeed
be exhorted to repentance, but were not to expect remission from the priest, but
from God, who is able and has authority to forgive sins]" (*Church History* 1.10,
William Bright, ed. (Oxford: 1893), 29. Socrates cites similar words of the bishop
Asclepiades (*Church History* 7.25, 309). The blessed Augustine says of the Cathars in general that they "poenitentiam denegant [deny repentance]"—Haer. 38
(PL 42:32). Cf. Pseudo-Augustine, *Quaest*, 102: "Recte explosa est non ex modica
parte Novatiani assertio, qua duo crimina gravia concessa poenitentiae videntur.
Quia si fornicationi ignosci non debet, sicut Novatiano videntur, quanto magis
homicidio, aut adulterio" (PL 35:2305). "Novatianus, Majora, iniquit, crimina
nominatim remitti probentur, id est, idololatria et fornicatio post lavacrum [No-
vatianus said that it is expressly forbidden to forgive the greater offenses, that is,
idolatry and fornication, after baptism"—ibid. (PL 35:2308; cf. 2307). Cf. Tillemont, *Memoires*, vol. 3, 472–474; Harnack, *Dogmengeschichte* 1, 450, Anm. 453.

1891 See Pseudo-Augustine, *Quaest*, 50 (pars 2) (PL 35:2405).

1892 See Harnack, *Der pseudoaugustinische Traktat Contra Novatianum. Abhandlungen Alexander von Oettingen zum siebzigsten Geburtstag gewidmet von Freunden und Schülern*
(München: 1898), 83–84.

vatianist concept of the Church was somewhat different from that of St. Cyprian and other figures of the Church. Cyprian writes: "They say that one is polluted by another's sin, and ... they contend ... that the idolatry of the delinquent passes over to one who is not guilty."[1893] If the Novatians thought thus, clearly in their opinion receiving one who had lapsed specifically contradicted the sanctity of the Church. On the other hand, they taught that excluding one who had lapsed did not yet mean that all hope of his salvation was lost. For example, if a person had lapsed in one persecution, but then suffered during another, "peace is not necessary to him from the bishop, since he is about to have the peace of his own glory, and about to receive a greater reward from the condescension of the Lord."[1894] Consequently, salvation is possible even outside the Church: the power of the bishop "to loose" does not extend to all sins; and mortal sins may be forgiven by God Himself.[1895] Thus, in Novatianism we see both of the attributes that characterized the Montanist concept of the Church: the Church is a society of saints, and the episcopal "power of the keys" is limited.[1896] But nevertheless this dogmatic dissent was hardly something of which there was ever any clear awareness. Concerning the Novatians St. Epiphanius of Cyprus relates: "They say that they have the same faith as

---

1893   Cyprian of Carthage, *Epistles* 55-51.27, "To Antonianus" (ANF 5:334; CSEL 3.2:645).

1894   Cyprian of Carthage, *Epistles* 57-53.4, "To Cornelius" (ANF 5:337; CSEL 3.2:653).

1895   See Pseudo-Augustine, *Quaest,* 102: "Nec ego renuo agendam poenitentiam admissae idololatriae, sed ego remittere non audeo: quia crimen hoc ab eo remittendum est, in quem admissum est. Hujus rei effectum aut denegas, aut scire se minime profiteris? [I do not reject the repentance that must be done for idolatry committed, but I do not dare remit it, since this offense must be remitted by Him against whom it was committed. The effect of this matter you either deny or profess to know not at all {translated by the editor}]" (PL 35:2310).

1896   Harnack provides a brief but precise outline of the Novatianist doctrine concerning the Church. See *Novatian,* RE 3, XIV, 237–238; *Dogmengeschichte*[4] 1, 450–452. But Harnack naturally repeats the generally accepted Protestant opinion that Novatianism is specifically a revival of the authentic early Christian Church: "Die novatianischen Gemeinden haben unstreitig einen wertvollen Rest der alten Überlieferung bewahrt"—RE 3, XIV, 239; *Dogmengeschichte*[4] 1, 452.

we."[1897] The very name *Cathars* ("The Pure") that Novatian himself gave to his community[1898] points rather to church practice than to dogma. But while assuming for themselves this haughty title the Cathars hardly lived up to the name, as Epiphanius[1899] attests when he humorously calls them the "impure Cathars."[1900]

Previously we established that Novatianism itself did not produce any completely new dogmatic formulae for the doctrine of the sanctity of the Church. Such precise formulae were hardly possible, from the standpoint of the Montanists and the Novatianists, since there is simply no way to precisely delimit which sins do and do not contradict the sanctity of the Church. But this circumstance explains why St. Cyprian likewise says hardly anything in particular concerning the sanctity of the Church: in the conflict with the Novatianists likewise he primarily expounded the doctrine of the unity of the Church and of the church hierarchy, clearly viewing them more as ecclesiastical rebels, regardless of their dogmatic doctrine. This results in a certain incompleteness in St. Cyprian's own teaching on the sanctity of the Church. In his various scattered comments, however, we have nearly sufficient material to trace an outline of his teaching on the sanctity of the Church.

St. Cyprian calls the Church "Holy" (*sponsa Christi incorrupta sancta pudica* [the bride of Christ is pure, holy, chaste).[1901] A person may sin, and it is necessary that he be separated from the Church. But absolute separation with no hope of return must happen only when

---

1897 Haer. 59.3 (PG 41:1021a; *Works* 3:29 [Rus. ed.]).

1898 See Harnack, *Novatian*, RE 3, Bd XIV, 229. Does not Cyprian also point to this when he says that the rebels invent for themselves corrupted names (*nomina adulterata fingentes*)? See *Epistles* 69-75.1, "To Magnus" (ANF 5:397; CSEL 3.2:750).

1899 Haer. 59.7 (PG 41:1028d–1029a; *Works* 3:36 [Rus. ed.]).

1900 Haer. 59.13: "περὶ τούτων τῶν δὴ Καθαρῶν λεγομένων, Ἀκαθάρτων δέ, εἰ δεῖ τἀληθῆ λέγειν [concerning these who are called Cathars {pure} but are Acathars {impure}, if truth be told]" (PG 41:1037a; *Works* 3:44 [Rus. ed.]). Cf. Harnack, *Dogmengeschichte*[4] 1, 453.

1901 Cyprian of Carthage, *Epistles* 59-54.1, "To Cornelius" (CSEL 3.2:667). *Treatises* 1.6, "On the Unity of the Church": "Incorrupta est et pudica" (CSEL 3.2:214).

he persists in his sin. Only those who persist in their obstinacy and madness and refuse to return should be left outside the Church.[1902] "With this their immodest obstinacy, they can never be admitted by us into the Church, lest they should begin to set an example to others to go to ruin by their crimes."[1903] When a sinner sins obstinately and does not submit to the Church, it is clear that he has perished, and that excommunication is merely the consequence of this state of obstinacy.[1904] He has no need of the Church, and can only serve to harm it. "We are to be congratulated when such as these are separated from the Church, lest they should lay waste the doves and sheep of Christ with their cruel and envenomed contagion."[1905] Already from the above we may conjecture how St. Cyprian would view absolute exclusion from the Church. We have seen that he called the Church "one" and "only"; outside the Church there can be no Christian; anyone who is outside the Church is a heathen. But until Christ leads us to God the Father, we will have all the infirmities of the flesh (*carnis incommoda*) in common with the whole race of men.[1906] A person sins continually. "Lest any one should flatter himself that he is innocent, and by exalting himself should more deeply perish, he is instructed and taught that he sins daily, in that he is bidden to entreat daily for his sins."[1907] And so St. Cyprian most decisively expresses the idea that the Church must not cut off sinners from its fellowship, but must heal them. One who has sinned

---

1902   Cyprian of Carthage, *Epistles* 45-41.3 "To Cornelius" (ANF 5:321; CSEL 3.2:602–603).

1903   Cyprian of Carthage, *Epistles* 4-61.4, "To Pomponius" (ANF 5:359; CSEL 3.2:476).

1904 Concerning this see Seitz, *Die Heilsnotwendigkeit der Kirche*, 135; Poschmann, *Die Sichtbarkeit der Kirche*, 52–54; Kasitsyn, *Schisms of the First Centuries of Christianity*, 170–191 (*Addendae to the Works of the Holy Fathers* [1889], part 44, 373–394).

1905   Cyprian of Carthage, *Treatises* 1.9, "On the Unity of the Church" (ANF 5:424; CSEL 3.2:218).

1906   Cyprian of Carthage, *Treatises* 7.8, "On the Mortality" (ANF 5:471; CSEL 3.2:301).

1907   Cyprian of Carthage, *Treatises* 4.22, "On the Lord's Prayer" (ANF 5:453; CSEL 3.2:283).

is specifically infirm.[1908] "We know, according to the faith of the divine Scriptures, God Himself being their author, and exhorting in them, both that sinners are brought back to repentance, and that pardon and mercy are not denied to penitents."[1909] "The highest degree of happiness is, not to sin; the second, to acknowledge our sins. In the former, innocence flows pure and unstained to preserve us; in the latter, there comes a medicine to heal us."[1910] "It behoves the Lord's priest not to mislead by deceiving concessions, but to provide with salutary remedies. He is an unskilful physician who handles the swelling edges of wounds with a tender hand, and, by retaining the poison shut up in the deep recesses of the body, increases it. The wound must be opened, and cut, and healed by the stronger remedy of cutting out the corrupting parts. The sick man may cry out, may vociferate, and may complain, in impatience of the pain; but he will afterwards give thanks when he has felt that he is cured."[1911] To receive the lapsed without penitential labors was incompatible with this treatment, and St. Cyprian, as we have seen, firmly insisted on the necessity of that repentance.[1912] But no less incompatible with

<hr>

1908 Cyprian of Carthage, *Epistles* 55-51.16, "To Antonianus": "Neither let us think them dead, but rather let us regard them as lying half alive, whom we see to have been wounded in the fatal persecution, and who, if they had been altogether dead, would never from the same men become afterwards both confessors and martyrs. But ... in them there is that, which, by subsequent repentance, may be strengthened into faith; and by repentance strength is armed to virtue" (ANF 5:331; CSEL 3.2:635).

1909 Cyprian of Carthage, *Epistles* 55-51.27, "To Antonianus" (ANF 5:335; CSEL 3.2:646).

1910 Cyprian of Carthage, *Epistles* 59-54.13, "To Cornelius" (ANF 5:343; CSEL 3.2:681).

1911 Cyprian of Carthage, *Treatises* 3.14, "On the Lapsed" (ANF 5:441; CSEL 3.2:247).

1912 Cyprian of Carthage, *Epistles* 59-54.13, "To Cornelius": "A full council being held, we decreed, not only with our consent, but also with our threatening, that the brethren should repent, and that none should rashly grant peace to those who did not repent" (ANF 5:343; CSEL 3.2:680). See *Epistles* 55-51.23, "To Antonianus" (CSEL 3.2:641). Vgl. Ioh. Stufler, *Zeitschrift für katholische Theologie* (1907), 592. In particular Stufler notes that Cyprian's exhortations do not even remotely hint that the early Church granted no forgiveness and communion

facilitating salvation was the unconditional rejection of one who had sinned. "It was not right, neither did the love of the Father nor divine mercy allow, that the Church should be closed to those that knock, or the help of the hope of salvation be denied to those who mourn and entreat."[1913] "If we reject the repentance of those who have some confidence in a conscience that may be tolerated; at once with their wife, with their children, whom they had kept safe, they are hurried by the devil's invitation into heresy or schism; and it will be attributed to us in the day of judgment, that we have not cared for the wounded sheep, and that on account of a single wounded one we have lost many sound ones."[1914] What is needed is specifically treatment. It is this treatment that comprises the object and the task of **church discipline.** "Discipline, the safeguard of hope, the bond of faith, the guide of the way of salvation, the stimulus and nourishment of good dispositions, the teacher of virtue, causes us to abide always in Christ, and to live continually for God, and to attain to the heavenly promises and to the divine rewards. To follow her is wholesome, and to turn away from her and neglect her is deadly."[1915] The task of discipline is not to safeguard the sanctity of the Church by cutting off those who have sinned, but to raise up sinners to sanctity. Those who have sinned remain in the Church, and in the Church tares appear.[1916] Even those who have gravely sinned

---

whatsoever to those who had sinned mortally. This, Stufler opines, is proof that rigorism was absent in the Church even prior to 250.

1913 Cyprian of Carthage, *Epistles* 57-53.1, "To Cornelius" (ANF 5:336; CSEL 3.2:650–651).

1914 Cyprian of Carthage, *Epistles* 55-51.15, "To Antonianus" (ANF 5:331; CSEL 3.2:634). Cf. 55-51.16 (CSEL 3.2:635).

1915 Cyprian of Carthage, *Treatises* 2.1, "On the Dress of Virgins" (ANF 5:430; CSEL 3.2:187).

1916 Cyprian of Carthage, *Epistles* 54-50.3, "To the Confessors": "Although there seem to be tares in the Church, yet neither our faith nor our charity ought to be hindered, so that because we see that there are tares in the Church we ourselves should withdraw from the Church: we ought only to labour that we may be wheat, that when the wheat shall begin to be gathered into the Lord's barns, we may receive fruit for our labour and work. ... Let us strive, dearest brethren, and labour as much as we possibly can, that we may be vessels of gold or silver" (ANF

are not left outside the Church. "Let the lapsed, however, who acknowledge the greatness of their sin, not depart from entreating the Lord, nor forsake the Catholic Church, which has been appointed (*constituta*) one and alone by the Lord; but, continuing in their atonements and entreating the Lord's mercy, let them knock at the door of the Church, that they may be received there where once they were, and may return to Christ from whom they have departed."[1917] The presence of those who have sinned does not destroy the sanctity of the Church; the tares do not prevent the wheat from growing. The Novatians taught that the presence of one who had lapsed infects all of society, as it were, and it is then no longer holy. "But with us," writes St. Cyprian, "according to our faith and the given rule of divine preaching, agrees the principle of truth, that every one is himself held fast in his own sin; nor can one become guilty for another, since the Lord forewarns us, saying, 'The righteousness of the righteous shall be upon him, and the wickedness of the wicked shall be upon him' [Ezek. 18:20]. And again: 'The fathers shall not die for the children, and the children shall not die for the fathers. Every one shall die in his own sin' [2 Kgs. 14:6]."[1918] "And do not think, dearest brother," writes Cyprian to Antonianus, "that either the courage of the brethren will be lessened, or that martyrdoms will fail for this cause, that repentance is relaxed to the lapsed, and that the hope of peace is offered to the penitent. The strength of the truly believing remains unshaken; and with those who fear and love God with their whole heart, their integrity continues steady and strong. For to adulterers even a time of repentance is granted by us, and peace is given. Yet virginity is not therefore deficient in the Church, nor does the glorious design of continence languish through the sins of others. The Church, crowned with so many virgins, flourishes; and chastity and modesty preserve the tenor of

---

5:327; CSEL 3.2:622, 623).

   1917 Cyprian of Carthage, *Epistles* 65-61.5, "To Epictetus" (ANF 5:364; CSEL 3.2:725).

   1918 Cyprian of Carthage, *Epistles* 55-51.27, "To Antonianus" (ANF 5:332; CSEL 3.2:638). Cf. *Epistles* 8

their glory. Nor is the vigour of continence broken down because repentance and pardon are facilitated to the adulterer."[1919]

The Montanists and the Novatianists considered salvation possible even outside the visible fellowship of the Church. For them, the Church did not encompass all Christians: the Church was comprised solely of perfected saints. Between the Church and heathenism there are, as it were, several intermediate degrees. One who is outside the Church can only be pardoned and absolved of his sins by God Himself. St. Cyprian however, as we have seen, understood the Church as standing in contrast to the world.[1920] It is therefore logical that St. Cyprian was the first to briefly and decisively formulate this thesis: there is no salvation outside the Church (*salus extra ecclesiam non est*).[1921] As all perished who were outside the house of Rahab in Jericho, so also all who are outside the Church will perish.[1922] "If any one could escape (*evadere*) who was outside the ark of Noah, then he also may escape who shall be outside of the Church."[1923] In the view of the Novatians, to receive one of the lapsed into the Church is to usurp the judgment of God, since whoever is in the Church is saved. But Cyprian teaches that, on the contrary, to excommunicate from the Church would be to usurp the right of God, for one who is cut off from the Church cannot be saved. Consequently, the question concerns the religious significance of the Church.[1924] On several occasions Cyprian quite explicitly expresses his thought that there is no repentance in hell

1919 Cyprian of Carthage, *Epistles* 55-51.27, "To Antonianus" (ANF 5:335; CSEL 3.2:645–646). Cf. *Epistles* 8-2.2: "The Church stands in faith, notwithstanding that some have been driven to fall" (ANF 5:281; CSEL 3.2:487).

1920 For more detail, see Molchanov, *St. Cyprian of Carthage*, 285–313.

1921 Cyprian of Carthage, *Epistles* 73-72.21, "To Jubaianus" (ANF 5:384; CSEL 3.2:795).

1922 Cyprian of Carthage, *Epistles* 69-75.4, "To Magnus" (ANF 5:398; CSEL 3.2:753).

1923 Cyprian of Carthage, *Treatises* 1.6, "On the Unity of the Church" (ANF 5:423; CSEL 3.2:214).

1924 Cf. Harnack, *Novatian*, RE 3, XIV, 237.

(*apud inferos confessio non est nec exomologesis illic fieri potest*).[1925] Hence, whoever wholeheartedly repents and entreats must be received into the Church, and preserved therein for the Lord, Who when He comes to His Church will judge those whom He finds within her.[1926] "To the Lord alone it is granted to break the vessels of earth, to whom also is given the rod of iron [see Rev. 2:27]. The servant cannot be greater than his lord, nor may any one claim to himself what the Father has given to the Son alone, so as to think that he can take the fan for winnowing and purging the threshing-floor, or can separate by human judgment all the tares from the wheat. That is a proud obstinacy and a sacrilegious presumption which a depraved madness assumes to itself. And while some are always assuming to themselves more dominion than meek justice demands, they perish from the Church; and while they insolently extol themselves, blinded by their own swelling, they lose the light of truth."[1927] It must of course be noted that for the Novatians these words of St. Cyprian could not have been particularly convincing: according to their teaching, to cut off someone from the Church entirely did not yet mean to strip them of all hope of salvation, as salvation was possible even outside the Church. Cyprian's entire argumentation only makes sense within his own ecclesiological system. Reasoning thus, both sides were right in their own way, and this is specifically because the dispute primarily centered on questions of practice, while the dogmatic doctrine of the sanctity of the Church was not subjected to any particular examination.

In the context of his overall teaching concerning the Church, St. Cyprian speaks only of temporary excommunication, nor can this even be called excommunication in the proper sense.[1928] We have

---

1925 Cyprian of Carthage, *Epistles* 55-51.29, "To Antonianus" (ANF 5:335; CSEL 3.2:647). Cf. 55-51.17: "Exomologesis apud inferos non est" (ANF 5:331; CSEL 3.2:636).

1926 Cyprian of Carthage, *Epistles* 55-51.29, "To Antonianus" (ANF 5:335; CSEL 3.2:647).

1927 Cyprian of Carthage, *Epistles* 54-50.3, "To the Confessors" (ANF 5:327; CSEL 3.2:623).

1928 Poschmann, *Die Sichtbarkeit der Kirche*, 54–56.

already pointed out St. Cyprian's idea that, until their complete re-unification with the Church, the lapsed still belong to the Church: they are members of the Church, only not fully entitled; they are tares, but they grow together with the wheat; they are deprived for a time of communing in prayer and in the Eucharist.[1929] But the Church did not abandon them entirely: on the contrary, it guided and governed them.[1930] "For what is a greater or a more worthy care of overseers," asks St. Cyprian, "than to provide by diligent solic-itude and wholesome medicine for cherishing and preserving the sheep?"[1931] In the works of St. Cyprian we find testimonies to the fact that the Church undertakes to care for those who repent. The repentance of those who have sinned is one aspect of church life.[1932] In the ecclesiological system of the Novatians, repentance was an individual affair; the Church could have no close involvement in repentance. Before God the sinner repented, and from Him he re-ceived forgiveness, which was not accompanied by visible reunifi-cation with the Church. But in the system of St. Cyprian the affair

---

1929 St. Cyprian specifically spoke out against the fact that certain presbyters were intoning the names of penitents in the prayers and imparting the Eucharist to them. *Epistles* 16-9.2, "To the Clergy" (ANF 5:290; CSEL 3.2:518–519); *Epistles* 17-11.2 "To the People" (ANF 5:292; CSEL 3.2:522); *Epistles* 15-10.1, "To the Martyrs and Confessors" (ANF 5:291; CSEL 3.2:514); *Treatises* 3.16, "On the Lapsed" (ANF 5:441–442; CSEL 3.2:248).

1930 This is already described in the epistle of the Roman clergy to [Cyprian] of Carthage (*Epistles* 8-2.2): "These we did not abandon, although they were separated from us, but exhorted them, and do exhort them, to repent, if in any way they may receive pardon from Him who is able to grant it; lest, haply, if they should be deserted by us, they should become worse" (ANF 5:281; CSEL 3.2:487).

1931 Cyprian of Carthage, *Epistles* 68-66.4 "To Father Stephanus" (ANF 5:369; CSEL 3.2:746–747).

1932 Even previously it had been customary in the Church for sinners to un-dergo public repentance not only for grave sins, but also for lighter offenses. To this Cyprian also attests (*Epistles* 16-9.2, "To the Clergy"): "In smaller sins sinners may do penance for a set time, and according to the rules of discipline come to public confession (*exomologesis*), and by imposition of the hand of the bishop and clergy receive the right of communion" (ANF 5:290; CSEL 3.2:518–519). Concerning repentance according to Cyprian, see Poschmann, *Die Sichtbarkeit der Kirche*, 143–146.

of the penitent is the affair of the Church: if one of her members is afflicted, all the others suffer together with him. The sinner must undergo a period of repentance under the guidance of the Church, primarily the hierarchy. "He repents, who, remembering the divine precept, with meekness and patience, and obeying the priests of God, deserves well of the Lord by his obedience and his righteous works."[1933]

This repentance St. Cyprian calls by the term *exomologesis*, which we have already encountered, and he describes it just as did Tertullian. During St. Cyprian's life the groundwork was laid for developing a complex disciplinary institution of repentance, and this groundwork varied in each individual Church. There is no need for us to enter into a historical study of the forms of penitential discipline.[1934] We may note that amid all this variety of penitential rules, one tendency predominates: that the one stricken by sin be treated in accordance with his infirmity. Such was the approach already at the Council of Carthage, where the qualities of the lapsed were taken into consideration.

Penitence must culminate in **restoration to full communion with the Church.** Every penitent must be absolved of his sin; he must not be permitted to die without his sin having been absolved. "The repentance of the mourners was reasonably prolonged for a more protracted time, help only being afforded to the sick in their departure."[1935] But "it was not right ... that when they

1933 Cyprian of Carthage, *Epistles* 19-13.1, "To the Clergy" (ANF 5:293; CSEL 3.2:525).

1934 Concerning this the following have written: Harnack, *Lapsi*, RE 3, XI, 287; Funk, *Die Bussstationen im christlichen Altertum. Kirchengeschichtliche Abhandlungen und Untersuchungen* 1, 182–209; Smirnov, *The Spiritual Father*, 245–247, 249–251; Frank, *Die Bussdisciplin der Kirche*, 555 ff. Frank observes that initially Cyprian knew of no degrees of repentance (547, 549), although he is familiar with public repentance as a firmly established institution (548). The Novatian schism, according to Frank, did not occasion the establishment of various forms of repentance, since the institution of repentance developed in the East, where Novatianism had no influence whatsoever (555–559).

1935 Cyprian of Carthage, *Epistles* 57-53.2, "To Cornelius" (ANF 5:337; CSEL 3.2:651).

pass from this world, they should be dismissed to their Lord without communion and peace; since He Himself who gave the law, that things which were bound on earth should also be bound in heaven, allowed, moreover, that things might be loosed there which were here first loosed in the Church [see Mt 18:18]."[1936] It was out of these dogmatic considerations that all the lapsed were absolved when a new persecution arose, to prevent the possibility of their dying without the absolution of the Church. It is worth noting that in the text cited above St. Cyprian particularly emphasizes the second half. In the teaching of the Montanists and the Novatians, what was bound on earth could be loosed in the heavens; conversely, St. Cyprian asserts that only that which has been loosed on earth can be loosed in the heavens.

Salvation is possible only within the Church. This was the common conviction of the men of the Church at that time. In his letter to Fabius of Antioch, Dionysius of Alexandria cites the following account of a certain elderly man named Serapion. This Serapion had lapsed during the persecutions, and no one would restore him to communion with the Church. Falling ill, he asked to be given absolution. To the boy who had brought the message the presbyter gave a small particle of the Eucharist, and instructed him to soak it and place into the mouth of the old man. The boy returned, and before he had even entered the room Serapion became more lively and said, "Have you come, my child?" The boy soaked the particle and poured the Eucharist into his mouth. No sooner had the old man swallowed it than he gave up the ghost. "Is it not evident," Dionysius concludes his story, "that he was preserved and his life continued till he was absolved, and, his sin having been blotted out, he could be acknowledged for the many good deeds which he had

---

1936 Cyprian of Carthage, *Epistles* 57-53.1, "To Cornelius" (ANF 5:336–337; CSEL 3.2:651). Cf. *Epistles* 72-71.2, "To Stephen": "[Those] forestalled by death without, have perished outside the Church without communion and peace" (ANF 5:379; CSEL 3.2:777).

done?"[1937] [1938] This account specifically presents the idea that salvation is not possible without communion with the Church, even for one who has completely blotted out his sin. The Lord even keeps a righteous man on earth until he has been restored to communion with the Church. From the Novatian point of view, communion with the Church is not essential. Serapion could have died in the hope that God Himself would absolve him of his sin.

However, St. Cyprian himself did not wholly equate the judgment of the Church with that of God. "We do not prejudge when the Lord is to be the judge; save that if He shall find the repentance of the sinners full and sound, He will then ratify (*ratum faciat*) what shall have been here determined (*statutum*) by us. If, however, any one should delude us with the pretence of repentance, God, who is not mocked [Gal. 6:7], and who looks into man's heart, will judge of those things which we have imperfectly looked into, and the Lord will amend the sentence (*sententiam*) of His servants."[1939] Consequently, only what has been loosed on earth will be loosed in heaven, but not all that has been loosed here will be loosed there. Visible membership in the Church does not necessarily incur certain salvation in heaven. A sinner may deceive the Church by feigning penitence, and in this case belonging to the Church will avail him nothing.

But if St. Cyprian allows that at times the Lord may amend the judgment of His servants, of what value is restoration to communion with the Church, in his view? Quite frequently it is conjectured that this communion was by no means linked to absolution of the sin. The sin remained until the judgment of God. The earthly Church did not forgive mortal sins.[1940] But the works of Cyprian

---

1937 In the source, "till his sin was absolved and the many good deeds he had done restored him to Christ?" – *Trans.*

1938 Eusebius, *Church History* 6.44; *Works of St. Dionysius the Great* (in the Russian translation), 55–56.

1939 Cyprian of Carthage, *Epistles* 55-51.18, "To Antonianus" (ANF 5:331; CSEL 3.2:636).

1940 This view is expressed primarily by Protestant scholars. For a description and detailed analysis of these views, see Poschmann, *Die Sichtbarkeit der Kirche,*

repeatedly state that restoration to communion with the Church is linked to peace in heaven likewise. For example, at the very outset of the persecutions the Roman clergy wrote to St. Cyprian: "[Certain of] the lapsed brethren ... [do] not so much ask for, as claim, peace for themselves; nay, [they] say that they already have it in heaven. If they have it, why do they ask for what they possess? But if, by the very fact that they are asking for it, it is proved that they have it not, wherefore do they not accept the judgment of those from whom they have thought fit to ask for the peace, which they certainly have not got?"[1941] The confessor Lucian, who caused the bishop of Carthage such grief, ordered specifically that they be granted peace and absolved of their sins.[1942] St. Cyprian himself says that the bestowal of peace contains the pledge of life (*pignus vitae in data pace*).[1943] "I wonder," he wrote, "that some ... think that repentance is not to be granted to the lapsed, or to suppose that pardon (*veniam*) is to be denied to the penitent."[1944] "The Lord would not exhort to repentance, if it were not that He promises mercy to them that repent."[1945] Those who sorrow must not be denied the fruit of repentance (*poenitentiae fructus dolentibus non negandus*).[1946] That St. Cyprian taught that restoration to communion with the Church was linked with absolution of the sin is already shown by the fact that St. Cyprian, citing the words of the apostle Paul (see 1

147–161. Cf. [this with] the brief observations of Schanz, "Die Absolutionsgewalt in der alten Kirche," *Theologische Quartalschrift* (1897): 67–69. Poschmann (147, Anm. 4) also lists Catholic literature.

1941 Cyprian of Carthage, *Epistles* 36-29.1 (ANF 5:307; CSEL 3.2:573).

1942 Cyprian of Carthage, *Epistles* 27-22.3, "To the Presbyters and Deacons" (ANF 5:300–301; CSEL 3.2:543).

1943 Cyprian of Carthage, *Epistles* 55-51.13, "To Antonianus" (ANF 5:330; CSEL 3.2:632).

1944 Cyprian of Carthage, *Epistles* 55-51.18, "To Antonianus" (ANF 5:332; CSEL 3.2:639).

1945 Cyprian of Carthage, *Epistles* 55-51.18, "To Antonianus" (ANF 5:333; CSEL 3.2:640).

1946 Cyprian of Carthage, *Epistles* 55-51.29, "To Antonianus" (ANF 5:335; CSEL 3.2:647).

Cor. 11:27), considered it a mockery of the Holy Body of the Lord when the lapsed were admitted to the Eucharist before the bishop and the clergy had laid hands on them as a sign of repentance.[1947] Furthermore, while the persecution lasted St. Cyprian forbade restoring the lapsed to communion because they had an opportunity to receive not only forgiveness, but also a crown.[1948] Here too St. Cyprian equates forgiveness with communion with the Church. St. Cyprian's entire line of reasoning in favor of a lenient approach bespeaks the same: in his epistle to Antonianus St. Cyprian gives a detailed Scripture-based argument for why those who repent should be grated forgiveness.[1949]

Consequently, when St. Cyprian says that the Lord God can amend the errors of His servants, this means only that the priest may be deceived by feigned penitence. Forgiveness can only be granted when the sinner sincerely repents of his transgression. When there is sincere repentance, already here on earth he is granted not only visible communion with the Church, but also true forgiveness of his sin. To the bishop, as the representative of the Church, in full accordance with his entire doctrinal system regarding the Church St. Cyprian ascribes the full extent of "the power of the keys."[1950]

1947 Cyprian of Carthage, *Epistles* 15-10.1, "To the Martyrs and Confessors" (ANF 5:291; CSEL 3.2:514). See *Epistles* 16-9.2, "To the Clergy" (ANF 5:290; CSEL 3.2:518–519); *Treatises* 3.16, "On the Lapsed" (ANF 5:441–442; CSEL 3.2248–249). Poschmann holds that this argument alone sufficiently proves that reunification with the Church was simultaneously a forgiveness of sins (*Die Sichtbarkeit der Kirche*, 151).

1948 Cyprian of Carthage, *Epistles* 55-51.7, "To Antonianus" (ANF 5:329; CSEL 3.2:628).

1949 Cyprian of Carthage, *Epistles* 55-51.21–23, "To Antonianus" (ANF 5:332–333; CSEL 3.2:628 sqq.). Cf. Peters, *Der heilige Cyprian von Karthago*, 228–229. Batiffol opines that although in Rome the lapsed were received into the communion of the Church, this was not linked to the conviction that their sin was forgiven (*Études d'histoire et de théologie positive²*, 122–124). He does not, however, offer any even slightly convincing evidence in support of this highly original opinion. Cf. the observations of Ioh. Stufler, "Die Behandlung der Gefallenen zur Zeit der decischen Verfolgung," *Zeitschrift für katholische Theologie* (1907): 584–587.

1950 Huther, *Cyprians Lehre von der Kirche*, 180–182; Peters, *Der heilige Cyprian von Karthago*, 226–227.

"The power of the keys" also extends to the sin of temporary apostasy in time of persecution. The lapsed must confess their sins and receive forgiveness from the bishop (*remissio facta per sacerdotes*).[1951] St. Cyprian does not even speak particularly of the bishop possessing "the power of the keys," offering no substantiation for this power. The idea of "the power of the keys" in the Church belonging to the bishop is the basis of his reasoning on reception of the lapsed back into the Church, and being generally recognized it required no proof.[1952] The bishops possess this power as successors of the apostles, to whom the Lord gave the right to bind and to loose.[1953] St. Cyprian particularly defended this right of the bishop to bind and to loose when, at the outset of the Decian persecution, the confessors intervened in the matter of receiving the lapsed.

Quite frequently the opinion is advanced that supposedly St. Cyprian's time marked the end of the struggle between the episcopacy and representatives of the former charismatic organization of the Church. It was only in Cyprian's time that the episcopacy completely seized "the power of the keys," excluding from it the confessors, who were the lawful heirs of the fullness of the ecclesiastical rights of the charismatics of old. The final step was taken in

---

1951 Cyprian of Carthage, *Treatises* 3.29, "On the Lapsed" (ANF 5:445; CSEL 3.258). Cf. 3.36 (ANF 5:447; CSEL 3.2:263).

1952 Poschmann, *Die Sichtbakeit der Kirche*, 135.

1953 St. Cyprian repeatedly cites the Lord's words (Mt. 18:18, Jn. 20:23) in *Treatises* 1.4, "On the Unity of the Church" (ANF 5:422; CSEL 3.2:212); *Epistles* 33-26.1, "To the Lapsed": "Our Lord, whose precepts and admonitions we ought to observe, describing the honour of a bishop and the order of His Church (*episcopi honorem et ecclesiae suae rationem disponens*), speaks in the Gospel... [see Mt. 16:18–19]" (ANF 5:305; CSEL 3.2:566); *Epistles* 73-72.7, "To Jubaianus" (ANF 5:381; CSEL 3.2:783); *Epistles* 69-75.7, "To Magnus" (ANF 5:400; CSEL 3.2:759). Cf. *Epistles* 75-74.16, "Firmilian to Cyprian" (ANF 5:394; CSEL 3.2:820–821). Admittedly, for the most part St. Cyprian applies the Lord's words to forgiveness of sins in baptism, but at times he cites them with regard to repentance. That Cyprian is no stranger to applying Mt. 18:18 to forgiveness of sins in repentance is already seen in *Epistles* 57-53.1, "To Cornelius" (ANF 5:336–337; CSEL 3.2:651). See Heinrich Bruders, "Mt. 16, 19; 18, 18 und Jn 20, 22, 23 in frühchristlicher Auslegung," *Zeitschrift für katholische Theologie* (1911): 93–111. Concerning this see Poschmann (163, Anm.).

forming the hierarchical, episcopal organization of the Church.[1954]
We have already demonstrated in detail that there are no indisputable grounds for this particular perception of the history of the
early Church. Specifically, the works of Cyprian show that from
the outset of his ecclesiastical activity "the power of the keys" indisputably belonged to the bishop. There is not one testimony that
explicitly speaks of "the power of the keys" belonging to the martyrs. In Cyprian's time, no one spoke out in defense of this power.
Regarding the time that preceded him, St. Cyprian attests that the
martyrs were then subject to the governance of the clergy.[1955] Cyprian himself treats the martyrs with great respect.[1956] When several of the presbyters restored the lapsed to communion without his
consent, he saw this as a violation of the rights of the bishop, and
also as an affront to the honor of the blessed martyrs.[1957] But the
martyrs themselves were originally far from claiming "the power
of the keys" for themselves. It is worthy of note that in Cyprian's
absence it is first and foremost the presbyters who receive people
back into communion with the Church, and St. Cyprian sees this
as a violation of his episcopal rights. As for the martyrs, from the
very outset they only send a letter asking Cyprian to consider their

---

1954 The complete implementation of an episcopal church structure coincided with the introduction of the unlimited authority to forgive sins. See Harnack,
Dogmengeschichte[4] 1, 444; *Novatian*, RE 3, XIV, 236–237. "The bearer of ecclesiastical office—the bishop—overcame the bearer of the Spirit—the martyr."
Smirnov, *The Spiritual Father*, 240. In the opinion of Karl Holl, in monasticism
there occurred a renaissance of the enthusiasm which the hierarchically structured Church had suppressed in the person of the Montanists and the confessors
(*Enthusiasmus und Bussgewalt*, 153).

1955 Cyprian of Carthage, *Epistles* 15-10.1, "To the Martyrs and Confessors":
"I had indeed believed that the presbyters and deacons who are there present
with you would admonish and instruct you more fully (*plenissime*) concerning the
law of the Gospel, as was the case always in time past under my predecessors;
so that the deacons passing in and out of the prison controlled (*gubernarent*) the
wishes of the martyrs by their counsels, and by the Scripture precepts" (ANF
5:291; CSEL 3.2:513).

1956 See *Treatises* 3.1–2, "On the Lapsed" (ANF 5:437; CSEL 3.2:237–238, 252).

1957 Cyprian of Carthage, *Epistles* 16-9.3, "To the Clergy" (ANF 5:290;
CSEL 3.2:519).

wishes and grant peace to the lapsed once peace has been granted to the Church itself.[1958] Clearly, the martyrs themselves never
considered themselves possessors of "the power of the keys": they
only interceded for the lapsed,[1959] promising to mediate for them
before God.[1960] Over the course of time, this gave rise to numerous
abuses. The martyrs not only mediated, but **demanded** that their
wishes be granted, presenting the matter as though their appeal-
ing to the bishop were a mere formality. To Cyprian the confessors
write: "Know that, to all, concerning whom the account of what
they have done since the commission of their sin has been, in your
estimation, satisfactory, we have granted (*dedisse*) peace; and we have
desired that this rescript (*hanc formam*) should be made known by you
to the other bishops also."[1961] We see however that in his letter to
the clergy St. Cyprian leaves the request of the martyrs unfulfilled,
because he holds the question of restoration to communion with
the Church to be within the competency of the Council of bishops.[1962] In an epistle to the lapsed, citing the Lord's words to the
apostle Peter (see Mt. 16:18–19), he demonstrates that "the Church
is founded upon the bishops, and every act of the Church (*omnis*

1958 Cyprian of Carthage, *Epistles* 16-9.3, "To the Clergy" (ANF 5:290;
CSEL 3.2:519–520). Cf. Poschmann, op. cit., 137–138.

1959 Cyprian of Carthage, *Epistles* 17-11.1 "To the People" (ANF 5:292;
CSEL 3.2:521). Lucian likewise writes to Celerinus concerning two women (*Epistles* 22-21.2): "Since the Lord has begun to give peace to the Church itself, according to the precept of Paulus, and our tractate, the case being set forth before the
bishop, and confession being made (*facta exomologesi*), I ask that ... these may have
peace" (ANF 5:299–300; CSEL 3.2:535).

1960 Concerning this see Stufler, "Die Behandlung der Gefallenen zur Zeit
der decischen Verfolgung," *Zeitschrift für katholische Theologie* (1907): 581–582; Poschmann, *Die Sichtbarkeit der Kirche*, 138. In St. Cyprian's writings we even find an
indication that the *libelli pacis* became valid after the death of the confessor who
had issued them.

1961 Cyprian of Carthage, *Epistles* 23-26, "The Confessors to Cyprian" (ANF
5:296; CSEL 3.2:536).

1962 Cyprian of Carthage, *Epistles* 26-17, "To the Presbyters and Deacons"
(ANF 5:296–297; CSEL 3.2:539).

actus ecclesiae) is controlled by these same rulers."[1963] In an epistle to
the Roman clergy, St. Cyprian speaks of the epistle of the confessors as dissolving "well nigh every bond of faith, and fear of God,
and the Lord's command, and the sacredness and sincerity of the
Gospel." Among the lapsed there were those who overestimated the
role of the martyrs in the matter of their restoration to communion
with the Church. When Cyprian began "to hear the cases of each
one and to examine them," it seemed to many that they were being
denied what they had already received from the martyrs and confessors. The multitude made an attack upon the primates, demand-
ing "that peace be given to them immediately which they all cried
out had been once given to them by the martyrs and confessors."[1964]
But a better interpretation of these facts is provided by members
of the Roman clergy in their answering epistle. The lapsed say that
they already have peace in heaven. "If they have it, why do they ask
for what they possess? But if, by the very fact that they are asking for
it, it is proved that they have it not, wherefore do they not accept the
judgment of those from whom they have thought fit to ask for the
peace, which they certainly have not got? … If the martyrs thought
that peace was to be granted to them, why did not they themselves
grant it? Why did they think that, as they themselves say, they were
to be referred to the bishops? For he who orders a thing to be done,
can assuredly do that which he orders to be done."[1965] Cyprian himself demonstrates in detail that "those cannot be the authority for
the bishops doing anything against God's command (*contra manda-*

1963 Cyprian of Carthage, *Epistles* 33-26.1, "To the Lapsed" (ANF 5:305;
CSEL 3.2:566).

1964 Cyprian of Carthage, *Epistles* 27-22.2, 3 (ANF 5:300–301; CSEL
3.2:542–543). Cf. *Epistles* 35-28: "Certain of the lapsed, who refuse to repent and
to make satisfaction to God, wrote to me, not asking that peace might be given
to them, but claiming it as already given; because they say that Paulus has given
peace to all" (ANF 5:307; CSEL 3.2:571–572).

1965 Cyprian of Carthage, *Epistles* 36-29.1, 2 (ANF 5:307–308; CSEL
3.2:573–574). Furthermore, in this same place the Roman clergy consider it contrary to the law of the Gospel to demand peace on the grounds that the martyrs
have already granted it.

tum Dei), who themselves have done God's command."[1966] [1967] "The martyrs order something to be done; but only if this thing be just and lawful, if it can be done without opposing the Lord Himself by God's priest."[1968] [1969] Without the permission of the bishop, communion cannot be considered valid. "They think that that is peace which some with deceiving words are blazoning forth: that is not peace, but war. ... Why do they call impiety by the name of piety? ... Such a facility does not grant peace, but takes it away; nor does it give communion, but it hinders from salvation."[1970]

From the information here presented it may be seen that both prior to St. Cyprian and at the outset of his labors, church doctrine held that "the power of the keys" in the Church belonged to the bishop: the confessors only mediated before the bishop,[1971] thereby clearly attesting that this "power of the keys" was one they themselves did not possess. If the martyrs did occasionally overstep their bounds, these instances were simply abuses, which St. Cyprian considered it his duty to combat.[1972]

St. Dionysius provides similar testimony concerning the Church of Alexandria. In relating that certain of the martyrs were receiving certain lapsed brethren, leading them into and presenting them in the church, making them communicants in the prayers and meals, St. Dionysius asks: "What counsel then, brethren, do you give us

---

1966 In the Russian source, literally: "Those who themselves have done God's command cannot demand anything of the bishops against God's command." *–Trans.*

1967 Cyprian of Carthage, *Treatises* 3.20, "On the Lapsed" (ANF 5:443; CSEL 3.2:252).

1968 In the Russian source, literally: "Do the martyrs order something to be done? If this thing be just and lawful, if it does not oppose the Lord Himself, the priest of God must do it." *–Trans.*

1969 Ibid. 3.18 (ANF 5:442; CSEL 3.2:250).

1970 Ibid. 3.16 (ANF 5:441; CSEL 3.2:248–249).

1971 Cf. Batiffol, *Études d'histoire et de théologie positive*[2], 116–120.

1972 Vgl. Schanz, *Theologische Quartalschrift* (1897): 62, 64–67; Stufler, "Die Behandlung der Gefallenen zur Zeit der decischen Verfolgung," *Zetschr. Für katholische Theologie* (1907): 581.

concerning such persons? What should we do? Shall we have the same judgment and rule as theirs, and observe their decision and charity, and show mercy to those whom they pitied? Or, shall we declare their decision unrighteous, and set ourselves as judges of their opinion, and grieve mercy and overturn order?"[1973] Here we encounter the same situation that arose in the life of St. Cyprian, where the martyrs are receiving people back into communion with the Church. This instance however is exceptional, and the bishop, while considering it his right not only to ratify but also to overturn the directive of the martyrs, merely asks council as to how he ought to proceed in order to avoid conflict and preserve peace in the Church. St. Cyprian, as we have seen, remained adamant, while St. Dionysius was inclined to make a concession, though he too considers "the power of the keys" his own.[1974]

Finally, at the Council of Carthage in 251 the confessors, together with all the laity who were firm in the faith, were invited to offer consultation; here the confessors were listed after the deacons.[1975] The Council of bishops reached a similar determination, dividing the lapsed into classes; the conciliar decrees say nothing of the martyrs' involvement in the repentance of the lapsed.[1976] The martyrs are also not mentioned in the documents of the Council, which determined that all those who had lapsed before the persecu-

---

1973 Eusebius, *Church History* 6.42.5–6 (NPNF² 1:285–286). We find it impossible to accept the interpretation given this testimony by Smirnov, who sees in this an indication that the martyrs "were in every place the highest court of appeal in matters of church discipline," that "there was no authority higher than they that would have verified and ratified their decision" (*The Spiritual Father*, 231, 232), and that "in Alexandria the role of the martyrs in the matter of receiving the lapsed was of incomparably greater importance than that of the bishop" (ibid., 239n2).

1974 Vgl. Schunz, *Theologische Quartalschrift* (1897): 64.

1975 See Cyprian of Carthage, *Epistles* 30-30.5, "The Roman Clergy to Cyprian" (ANF 5:310). Here also we read: "[We have] no bishop appointed as yet ... who can arrange all things of this kind, and who can take account of those who are lapsed, with authority and wisdom."

1976 Cyprian of Carthage, *Epistles* 55-51.6, "To Antonianus" (ANF 5:328–329; CSEL 3.2:627–628). Vgl. Poschmann, *Die Sichtbarkeit der Kirche*, 139–140; Batiffol, *Études d'histoire et de théologie positive*, 127–128.

tion began were to be restored to communion with the Church.[1977] Events analogous to the Council of Carthage in 251 likewise occurred in the East. In Alexandria also there were great numbers of the lapsed.[1978] Dionysius, the bishop of Alexandria, permitted the lapsed to be restored to communion with the Church, and commanded "that persons at the point of death, if they requested it, and especially if they had asked for it previously, should receive remission, that they might depart with a good hope."[1979] In an epistle (which has been lost) to the brethren in Egypt, Dionysius expounded his opinion regarding the lapsed, determining the degrees of their fall.[1980] Clearly, St. Dionysius and the Church of Alexandria in general resolved the question of the lapsed just as it had been resolved in Rome and in Carthage.[1981] St. Dionysius wholly joined himself to Cyprian and Cornelius in order to suppress the Novatianist movement. He wrote an epistle to Novatian himself,[1982] as well as a series of epistles on repentance and peace within the Church not only to Rome, but also to the brethren in Armenia. He wrote in particular to the Roman confessors, who hitherto had been favorably inclined toward the opinion of Novatian.[1983] The Novatianist schism was somewhat reflected in the East also, where it met with partial sympathy from Fabius, bishop of Antioch.[1984] To this Fabius Dionysius wrote an extensive epistle, opening his eyes to Novatian's person and to his movement.[1985] But some in Antioch wanted to support the schism of Novatian, and in this regard a Council was convened

---

1977 Cyprian of Carthage, *Epistles* 57-53, "To Cornelius" (ANF 5:336–338; CSEL 3.2:650 sqq.).

1978 Eusebius, op. cit. 6.41.11–13 (NPNF[2] 1:284; GrchSch. 9.2:604).

1979 Ibid., 6.44.4 (NPNF[2] 1:290; GrchSch. 9.2:624).

1980 Ibid. 6.46.1.

1981 Cf. Batiffol, *Études d'histoire et de théologie positive*[2], 136; Druzhinin, *The Life and Works of St. Dionysius the Great*, 184.

1982 Eusebius, op. cit. 6.45 (NPNF[2] 1:290–291).

1983 Ibid. 6.46.2. These epistles have been lost.

1984 Ibid. 6.44.1.

1985 Ibid. 6.43.5–22 (NPNF[2] 1:287–290).

in Antioch under Fabius' successor, Demetrianus, at which Council Novatianism was conclusively condemned.[1986] Complete unanimity was soon established in the East regarding the questions stirred up by the Novatianists, as Dionysius informed Stephen, bishop of Rome (A.D. 255–257).[1987] The surviving documents enable us to define only the outward historical aspect of the affair of the lapsed in the East and the controversies over Novatianism,[1988] but we know nothing of whether these controversies touched on the dogmatic aspects of the sanctity of the Church. The fact that the Eastern Churches so swiftly reached an agreement among themselves—the very same that was decided in Rome and in Carthage—shows that the Eastern bishops likewise were no strangers to the dogmatic doctrine of the sanctity of the Church, elucidated by St. Cyprian and espoused by the representatives of the Church of Rome. The Novatian movement compelled the Eastern Churches likewise to turn their attention to the question of the sanctity of the Church, and in them this question received the same answer as in the West.

1986 Ibid. 6.46.3. This Council [is described] in greater detail by Druzhinin, *The Life and Works of St. Dionysius the Great*, 190–192.

1987 Harnack, *Chronologie* 2, 62; Eusebius, op. cit. 7.4–5.2: "Dionysius, therefore, having communicated with him extensively on this question by letter, finally showed him that since the persecution had abated, the churches everywhere had rejected the novelty of Novatus, and were at peace among themselves. He writes as follows: 'But know now, my brethren, that all the churches throughout the East and beyond, which formerly were divided, have become united. And all the bishops everywhere are of one mind, and rejoice greatly in the peace which has come beyond expectation. Thus Demetrianus in Antioch, Theoctistus in Cæsarea, Mazabanes in Ælia, Marinus in Tyre (Alexander having fallen asleep), Heliodorus in Laodicea (Thelymidres being dead), Helenus in Tarsus, and all the churches of Cilicia, Firmilianus, and all Cappadocia. I have named only the more illustrious bishops, that I may not make my epistle too long and my words too burdensome. And all Syria, and Arabia to which you send help when needed, and whither you have just written, Mesopotamia, Pontus, Bithynia, and in short all everywhere are rejoicing and glorifying God for the unanimity and brotherly love'" (NPNF[2] 1:294–295; GrchSch. 9.2:638–640).

1988 For a detailed exposition of the history of the question of the lapsed and of how Novatianism was regarded in the East, see Druzhinin, *The Life and Works of St. Dionysius the Great*, 170–194.

The Council of Carthage in 251 and others like it in the history of penitential discipline are rightly ascribed great significance,[1989] but this significance was **exclusively practical.** Dogmatically speaking, in decreeing that the lapsed were to be restored to communion with the Church and recognizing the power of the bishop, the Council **introduced nothing new.** The question of the rights of the martyrs to loose sins was not even raised: clearly, no one even disputed the bishop's "power of the keys." Consequently, in these decrees of the Council we cannot see a tendency "to shake the trust in the power of the martyrs to loose sins."[1990]

We consider unacceptable the view of the significance of the Council of 251 that the majority of Protestant scholars[1991] defend, together with certain of their Catholic[1992] and Orthodox[1993] colleagues, according to which the Council of 251 seemingly repeated the innovation of Callistus, propagating a lenient approach even to the sin of apostasy that was hitherto unknown to the Church, and thereby grounding Novatianism in the tradition of the early Church. In actuality, we see that it is not the Novatianists, but representatives of the Church who boldly declare that they are grounded in church tradition, from which Novatian is deviating by introducing a new doctrine. Dionysius of Alexandria, for example, wrote that Novatian "has ... drawn some of the brethren into impiety and blasphemy, and has introduced impious teaching concerning God, and has calumniated our most compassionate (χρηστότατον) Lord Jesus Christ as unmerciful (ὡς ἀνηλεῆ)."[1994] The treatise *Ad Novatianum haereticum*[1995] says of Novatian that he deprives of the hope of salvation, denies the mercy of the Father, rejects the penitence

---

1989 Smirnov, *The Spiritual Father*, 239.

1990 Ibid., n2.

1991 See Harnack, *Novation*, RE 3, Bd. XIV, 229 ff.

1992 Funk, *Kirchengeschichteliche Abhandlungen und Untersuchungen* 1, 158 ff.

1993 Smirnov, *The Spiritual Father*, 227–228.

1994 Eusebius, *Church History* 7.8 (NPNF² 1:296).

1995 Harnack considers this the composition of Sixtus II, bishop of Rome, and dates it to A.D. 257–258. See *Chronologie* 2, 287–390.

of his brother, and thereby kills those grievously wounded with an ingenious and new cruelty (*ingeniosa ac nova crudelitate*).[1996] The author of the treatise then directly reproaches Novatian because, although he acknowledged the possibility of repentance for the lapsed until he became an apostate from the Church, he now thinks differently, denying the need to treat the wounds of the lapsed.[1997] Cyprian likewise, as we have noted, hinted at this same alteration in Novatian's views.[1998] In his letter to Simpronianus, having expounded the doctrine of the Novatians, Pacianus says explicitly that neither Moses, nor Paul, nor Christ, Who suffered for sinners, taught these things. These things were taught by Novatian, after the reign of Decius— that is, nearly three hundred years after the suffering of the Lord. Could it be that he followed the prophets, like the Cataphrygians? Or did he himself possess the authority of a prophet? But he had no such gifts as to introduce a new gospel (*evangelium novi juris*). Could it really be that from Christ until Decius no one understood the teaching of Christ? And could it really be that, after Decius, all those who have communion with sinners are in error (*se miscere perditis mallent*)?[1999] Pacianus also brings to bear against his correspondent the testimony of Cyprian that, prior to his apostasy, Novatian himself had

---

1996 1 (CSEL 3.3:52).

1997 14: "O te impium scelestumque, haeretice Novatiane, qui post tot et tanta in Ecclesia, a quibusdam retro voluntarie commissa crimina, quae et tu ipse in domo Dei priusquam apostata esse cognoveras; et haec posse aboleri de memoria, succedente bono, utique docueras, secundum fidem Scripturae dicentis…" (Ezech. XVIII, 2). "Tu hodie retractas, an debeant lapsorum curari vulnera, qui nudati a diabolo ceciderunt [O impious and wicked as you are, you heretic Novatian! Who after so many and great crimes which in past times you had known to be voluntarily committed in the Church, and before you yourself were an apostate in the family of God, had certainly taught that these might be abolished from memory if well-doing followed; according to the faith of the Scripture which says, "But if the wicked will turn from all his sins which he has committed, and will do righteousness, he shall live in eternal life, and shall not die in his wickedness…" (Ezekiel 18:21). Reconsider now, whether the wounds of the lapsed who have fallen, stripped bare by the devil, ought to be cured]" (CSEL 3.3:64).

1998 See Cyprian of Carthage, *Epistles* 55-51.5, "To Antonianus" (ANF 5:328; CSEL 3.2:627).

1999 Pacianus, *Epistles* 3.1 (PL 13:1063d–1064b).

maintained that repentance for the lapsed was possible.[2000] In his epistle Pacianus examines all the arguments[2001] that Simpronianus had so diligently compiled;[2002] but there is absolutely no indication that the latter had any argument from Tradition. As for Cyprian, Pacianus calls him the defender of the ecumenical practice (*catholica jura retinentem*), which Tertullian had likewise defended until his apostasy into Montanism: the Church, in Tertullian's opinion, is able to forgive sins (*posse Ecclesiam peccata dimittere*).[2003] Bearing in mind the discipline of the early Church as we have outlined it above, with regard to the Council of 251 and all decrees whatsoever pertaining to the lapsed during the Decian persecution we can assert that they introduced nothing new, either into ecclesiastical discipline or into the dogmatic doctrine concerning the Church: both in Rome and in Carthage the fate of the lapsed was determined based on the practice of the early Church.[2004]

And while it is in the writings of St. Cyprian that we first encounter a clearly expressed doctrine of "the power of the keys" as the right of the bishop or of the hierarchy in general, he himself cannot be considered the author of this doctrine. We find this doctrine in even more definite form in third-century Eastern historical manuscripts. In the second book, where the ancient manuscript known as the Syriac Didascalia is conveyed, the *Apostolic Constitutions* speak of "the power of the keys" as the right of the bishop alone.

2000 Ibid. 3.5 (PL 13:1067a1–b).

2001 Ibid. 3.27 (PL 13:1082a).

2002 Ibid. 3.2 (PL 13:1064b).

2003 Ibid. 3.24 (PL 13:1079c–d).

2004 These theses are thoroughly substantiated by Johann Stufler in his article "Die Behandlung der Gefallenen zur Zeit der decischen Verfolgung," *Zetschr. Für katholische Theologie* (1907): 579–618. Cf. several observations of Molchanov, *St. Cyprian of Carthage*, 330–335. See also Kasitsyn, *Schisms of the First Centuries of Christianity*, 197–200 (=*Addendae to the Works of the Holy Fathers* [1889], part 44, 400–403). Döllinger likewise acknowledges that the lenient practice with regard to the lapsed was known in the Church even before St. Cyprian; this practice, in his opinion, was established by Callistus, who expanded the edict mentioned by Tertullian (*On Modesty* 1), and which in Döllinger's opinion was issued by Zephyrinus (*Hippolytus und Kallistus*, 126–130).

"So sit in the Church when thou speakest, as having authority to judge offenders. For to you, O bishops, it is said: 'Whatsoever ye shall bind on earth shall be bound in heaven; and whatsoever ye shall loose on earth shall be loosed in heaven' [Mt. 16:19]."[2005] "Be sensible, therefore, O bishop, of the dignity of thy place, that as thou hast received the power of binding, so hast thou also that of loosing."[2006] "By thee does our Saviour say to him who is discouraged under the sense of his sins, 'Thy sins are forgiven thee: thy faith hath saved thee; go in peace' [Mt. 9:2; Mk. 5:34]. But this peace and haven of tranquillity is the Church of Christ, into which do thou, when thou hast loosed them from their sins, restore them (ἀποκαθίστα), as being now sound and unblameable."[2007]

Thus, in the mid-third century church literature contained the doctrine of the bishop's "power of the keys," clearly developed and consistently implemented in church practice. **Consequently, the sanctity of the Church naturally does not lie in the perpetually relative sanctity of its members. In the Church people only strive for sanctity: it governs their penitential labors when they fall, and when the bishop judges it proper it likewise cleanses them of their sins by the power that the Lord gave to the holy apostles, which after them is successively preserved in the hierarchy.** But the Church does not only cleanse its members of their sins: **it is she**

2005 *Constitutions of the Holy Apostles* 2.3.11 (ANF 7:399; Ed. Funk, 47.26–30). Vgl. Achelis und Flemming, *Die Syrische Didascalia*, TU 25.2, 80–81, 299–307.

2006 *Constitutions of the Holy Apostles* 2.18.3 (ANF 7:403; Ed. Funk, 65.24–26). Cf. the composition attributed to Cyprian, *De Aleatoribus* 1: "Quoniam in nobis divina et paterna pietas apostolatus ducatum contulit et vicariam Domini sedem caelesti dignatione ordinavit et originem authentici apostolatus super quem Christus fundavit ecclesiam in superiore nostro portamus, accepta simul potestate solvendi ac ligandi et curatione peccata dimittendi [Since then among us the divine and paternal piety brought along the authority of apostleship and ordained the vicarious seat of the Lord by heavenly honor and we bear in our superior the origin of the authentic apostleship, on which Christ founded His Church, while at the same time having received the power of loosing and binding and of forgiving sins by healing]" (CSEL 3.3:93.1–6). Concerning when and by whom this composition was authored, see Harnack, *Chronologie* 2, 370–381.

2007 *Constitutions of the Holy Apostles* 2.20.9–10 (ANF 7:405; Ed. Funk, 75.26–77).

alone that bestows the power to progress in moral perfection. For salvation, St. Cyprian teaches, human effort alone is insufficient: divine aid is required, which St. Cyprian calls grace. When grace is given to a person, he becomes new, and for him a life in the Holy Spirit begins: what before had seemed difficult is made easy, and the impossible becomes possible. "All our power is of God."[2008] The question of how God's grace acts in a man is the subject of St. Cyprian's early epistle to Donatus.[2009] In order to set out on and walk the path of perfection one must receive divine grace, which is bestowed in baptism. Consequently, only one who has been baptized and reborn can achieve the kingdom of God.[2010] Only through rebirth by baptism do men become children of God. Through baptism the Holy Spirit is received; the water of baptism is the water of life eternal.[2011] A man reborn in baptism receives the Holy Spirit through the laying on of hands.[2012] Those baptized are presented to the prelates of the Church, and through their prayers and the laying on of hands they receive the Holy Spirit and are sealed with the Lord's seal.[2013] Only when they have been reborn through both Sacraments can men become fully sanctified and be made children of God, as Scripture says: "Except a man be born of

2008 Cyprian of Carthage, *Epistles* 1.4, "To Donatus" (ANF 5:276 [n1: "In the Oxford edition this epistle is given among the treatises"]; CSEL 3.2:6).

2009 The doctrine of St. Cyprian concerning grace is briefly but completely presented in the study by A. Katansky, *The Doctrine of the Grace of God in the Works of the Early Holy Fathers and Teachers of the Church Prior to the Blessed Augustine* ["Учение о благодати Божией в творениях древних св. отцов и учителей Церкви до блж. Августина"] (Saint Petersburg: 1902), 91–103.

2010 Cyprian of Carthage, *Testimonies Against the Jews* 3.25 (ANF 5:542; CSEL 3.2:140).

2011 Cyprian of Carthage, *Epistles* 63-62.8, 9, "To Caecilius" (ANF 5:360–361; CSEL 3.2:706, 707). For more detail on St. Cyprian's teaching on baptism, see Poschmann, *Die Sichtbarkeit der Kirche*, 106 ff.

2012 Cyprian of Carthage, *Epistles* 74-73.7, "To Pompey" (ANF 5:388; CSEL 3.2:804). Cf. *Epistles* 69-69.15, "To Magnus" (ANF 5:402; CSEL 3.2:765).

2013 Cyprian of Carthage, *Epistles* 73-72.9, "To Jubaianus" (ANF 5:381; CSEL 3.2:785). Cf. 73-72.6 (ANF 5:381; CSEL 3.2:783).

water and of the Spirit, he cannot enter into the kingdom of God"
(Jn. 3:5).[2014]

But where then can a man receive divine grace in baptism?
Who can bring down upon him the gifts of the Holy Spirit?[2015] To
these questions St. Cyprian replies: a man can receive grace in the
Church. "When we say, 'Dost thou believe in eternal life and remission of sins through the holy Church?' we mean that remission
of sins is not granted except in the Church. ... It is also necessary
that he should be anointed who is baptized; so that, having received
the chrism, that is, the anointing, he may be anointed of God, and
have in him the grace of Christ. Further, it is the Eucharist whence
the baptized are anointed with the oil sanctified on the altar. But he
cannot sanctify the creature of oil,[2016] who has neither an altar nor
a church."[2017] "It is manifest where and by whom remission of sins
can be given; to wit, that which is given in baptism. For first of all
the Lord gave that power to Peter, upon whom He built the Church,
and whence He appointed and showed the source of unity—the
power, namely, that whatsoever he loosed on earth should be loosed
in heaven [see Mt. 16:19]. And after the resurrection, also, He
speaks to the apostles, saying, 'As the Father hath sent me, even so
I send you. And when He had said this, He breathed on them, and
saith, unto them, Receive ye the Holy Ghost: whosoever sins ye
remit, they are remitted unto them; and whosoever sins ye retain,
they are retained' [Jn. 20:21–23]. Whence we perceive that only
they who are set over the Church and established in the Gospel law,
and in the ordinance of the Lord, are allowed to baptize and to

---

2014 Cyprian of Carthage, *Epistles* 72-71.1 (ANF 5:378; CSEL 3.2:775). For
more detail on the imparting of the gifts of the Holy Spirit in the laying on of
hands, see Poschmann, 115–121. At the same time, Poschmann is tendential in
this arena, and justifies the Catholic doctrine concerning confirmation.

2015 In the writings of St. Cyprian, the sanctifying action of the Holy Spirit
is introduced into the general concept of grace, albeit in the broad sense of that
concept (Katanksy, *The Doctrine of the Grace of God* ["Учение о благодати Божией"], 103).

2016 In the Russian source, "the substance of oil." −*Trans.*

2017 Cyprian of Carthage, *Epistles* 70-69.2, "To Januarius" (ANF 5:376;
CSEL 3.2:768).

give remission of sins (*evangelica lege ac dominica ordinatione fundatis*)"[2018] "The Church, setting forth the likeness of paradise, includes within her walls fruit-bearing trees. ... These trees she waters with four rivers, that is, with the four Gospels, wherewith, by a celestial inundation, she bestows the grace of saving baptism. ... It is she who holds and possesses alone all the power of her spouse and Lord. In her we preside; for her honour and unity we fight; her grace, as well as her glory, we defend with faithful devotedness. We by the divine permission water the thirsting people of God; we guard the boundaries of the living fountains."[2019]

St. Cyprian also expresses these very same ideas in his epistles to Pompey and Magnus.[2020] In these epistles St. Cyprian likens the Church to the ark of Noah. "As, in that baptism of the world in which its ancient iniquity was purged away, he who was not in the

---

2018 Cyprian of Carthage, *Epistles* 73-72.7, "To Jubaianus" (ANF 5:381; CSEL 3.2:783). Cf. 73-72.9, 10: "Within, in the Church which is one, and to which alone it is granted to bestow the grace of baptism and to remit sins ... that baptism ... is only granted to the one and only Church" (ANF 5:381–382; CSEL 3.2:784, 785). *The Seventh Council of Carthage under Cyprian* 79: "Clari a Mascula: 'Quibus (apostolis) nos successimus eadem potestate ecclesiam Domini gubernantes et credentium fidem baptizantes [Clarus of Mascula said: ... and to them {the apostles} we have succeeded, governing the Lord's Church with the same power, and baptizing the faith of believers]'" (ANF 5:572; CSEL 3.2:459). Cf. ibid. 1: "Caecilius a Bilta: 'Unum baptismum quod soli ecclesiae a Domino concessum est [Caecilius of Bilta said: ... one baptism, which is granted by the Lord to the Church alone]'" (ANF 5:565; CSEL 3.2:437). Cf. ibid. 2: Primi a Misgirpa; 14: Theogenis ab Hippone; 20: Privati a Sufibus; 21: Hortensiani a Laribus (ANF 5:566–568; CSEL 3.2:437, 443, 444, 445).

2019 Cyprian of Carthage, *Epistles* 73-72.10–11, "To Jubaianus" (ANF 5:382; CSEL 3.2:785, 786). Cf. *The Seventh Council of Carthage under Cyprian* 17: "Fortunati a Tuccabori, 'Potestatem baptizandi episcopis dedit, non haereticis [Fortunatus from Tuccaboris said: ... {Christ} gave the power of baptizing to bishops, not to heretics]'" (ANF 5:567; CSEL 3.2:444).

2020 Cyprian of Carthage, *Epistles* 74-73.6, "To Pompey": "It is the Church alone which, conjoined and united with Christ, spiritually bears sons" (ANF 5:388; CSEL 3.2:804). 74-73.7: "The generation and sanctification of baptism are with the spouse of Christ alone, who is able spiritually to conceive and to bear sons to God" (ANF 5:388; CSEL 3.2:804). Cf. *Epistles* 69-69.15, "To Magnus" (ANF 5:402; CSEL 3.2:765).

ark of Noah could not be saved by water, so neither can he appear
to be saved by baptism who has not been baptized in the Church
which is established in the unity of the Lord according to the sacrament of the one ark."[2021]

Thus, the grace of God that is necessary to progress in moral
perfection may only be received in the Church.[2022] **Cyprian does
not separate the grace of the Holy Spirit from the Church.**
At times he even calls grace "ecclesiastical"[2023] in speaking of the
gifts of the Church. "The Lord is able by His mercy to give indulgence, and not to separate from the gifts of His Church those who
by simplicity[2024] were admitted into the Church, and in the Church
have fallen asleep (*ab ecclesiae suae muneribus non separare*)."[2025] "They
… hasten to us, and implore the gifts and benefits of the Church
our Mother (*munera ac dona ecclesiae matris implorant*), assured that they
can in no wise attain to the true promise of divine grace unless they
first come to the truth of the Church."[2026] The life of grace is wholly enclosed solely within the bounds of the one Church of Christ.
"They who are not in the Church of Christ are reckoned among
the dead … since there is one Church which, having attained (*con-*

2021 Cyprian of Carthage, *Epistles* 74-73.11, "To Pompey" (ANF 5:389;
CSEL 3.2:809). Cf. *Epistles* 69-75.2, "To Magnus": "Only they who are in the
Church can be baptized" (ANF 5:398; CSEL 3.2:751).

2022 Cyprian of Carthage, *Epistles* 69-75.4: "If any one, although he may
have obtained grace in the Church, shall depart and go out of the Church … his
blood shall be upon him; that is … he himself must charge it upon himself that
he perishes" (ANF 5:398; CSEL 3.2:753).

2023 Cyprian of Carthage, *Epistles* 73-72.15, "To Jubaianus": "Nihil eis ad
gratiam ecclesiasticam et salutarem licere [they may do nothing towards conferring the ecclesiastical and saving grace]" (ANF 5:383; CSEL 3.2:789.18). Cf.
73-72.11: "Hujus (ecclesiae) et gratiam pariter et gloriam fideli devotione defen-
dimus [her {the Church's} grace, as well as her glory, we defend with faithful
devotedness]" (ANF 5:382; CSEL 3.2:786).

2024 The words "by simplicity" are absent in the Russian source. –*Trans.*

2025 Cyprian of Carthage, *Epistles* 73-72.23, "To Jubaianus" (ANF 5:385;
CSEL 3.2:796).

2026 Cyprian of Carthage, *Epistles* 73-72.24, "To Jubaianus" (ANF 5:385;
CSEL 3.2:797).

secuta) the grace of eternal life, both lives for ever and quickens the people of God."[2027] "Whatever has proceeded from the womb (*a matrice*) cannot live and breathe in its detached condition, but loses the substance of health (*substantiam salutis*)."[2028]

In the same way, Firmilian, bishop of Caesarea in Cappadocia, writes in his epistle to Cyprian that all power and grace are established in the Church,[2029] and that to the Church alone Christ conceded the power of heavenly grace.[2030] Firmilian likewise speaks of the great celestial gifts of the Church (*magna et caelestia ecclesiae munera*).[2031] It should also be noted that by the grace of the Church both St. Cyprian and Firmilian mean the fullness of grace—both of Christ and of the Holy Spirit.[2032]

Consequently, mid-third century church literature expressed **the doctrine concerning the Church as the treasury of the grace of God: only by means of the Church can a man receive the divine grace-filled assistance necessary for his moral perfection. In the Church, by virtue of its apostolic succession, it is the hierarchy that serves as the organ of divine grace.**[2033]

2027 Cyprian of Carthage, *Epistles* 71-70.1, "To Quintus" (ANF 5:377; CSEL 3.2:772).

2028 Cyprian of Carthage, *Treatises* 1.23, "On the Unity of the Church" (ANF 5:429; CSEL 3.2:231).

2029 Cyprian of Carthage, *Epistles* 75-74.7, "Firmilian to Cyprian": "Omnis potestas et gratia in ecclesia constituta est" (ANF 5:392; CSEL 3.2:814.29–30)

2030 Cyprian of Carthage, *Epistles* 75-74.18, "Firmilian to Cyprian": "Non nisi in ecclesia sola valere posse Christi nomen, cui uni concesserit Christus caelestis gratiae potestatem [the name of Christ could be of no avail except in the Church alone, to which alone Christ has conceded the power of heavenly grace]" (ANF 5:395; CSEL 3.2:822).

2031 Ibid. 75-74.17 (ANF 5:395; CSEL 3.2:884).

2032 Concerning this, see Katansky, *The Doctrine of the Grace of God*, 96.

2033 This latter thought is particularly clearly expressed in *Epistles* 75-74.16, "To Firmilian": "Christ said to Peter alone, 'Whatsoever thou shalt bind on earth shall be bound in heaven, and whatsoever thou shalt loose on earth shall be loosed in heaven' [Mt. 16:19]. And again, in the Gospel, when Christ breathed on the apostles alone (*in solos apostolos insufflavit*), saying, 'Receive ye the Holy Ghost:

From a negative standpoint, these same ideas were developed in greater detail in the well-known **controversy over the baptism of heretics**,[2034] the dogmatic aspect of which we shall now examine.

Once again, it was the Novatian schism that raised **the question of the baptism of heretics**. Should converts from Novatianism, who had been baptized outside the Church, be baptized upon their reception into the Church? This question arose in Africa, but the controversy itself began when Stephen, bishop of Rome, advanced his opinion. Stephen held that heretics must not be baptized, citing the custom in the West, and held that nothing that had not been handed down could be innovated.[2035] Stephen advanced no particular concept concerning the Church, but rather declared the baptism of heretics valid based solely on custom, regardless of Church dogma.[2036] By way of dogmatic substantiation of his custom Stephen cited the fact that the Novatians likewise performed baptisms exactly as in the Church: they likewise baptized in the name of Christ. "The name of Christ is of great advantage to faith and the sanctification of baptism; so that whosoever is anywhere so-ever baptized in the name of Christ, immediately obtains the grace of Christ."[2037] Consequently, to baptize heretics means to al-

---

whose soever sins ye remit they are remitted unto them, and whose soever sins ye retain they are retained' [Jn. 20:23]. Therefore the power of remitting sins was given to the apostles, and to the churches which they, sent by Christ, established, and to the bishops who succeeded (*successerunt*) to them by vicarious ordination (*ordinatione vicaria*)" (ANF 5:394; CSEL 3.2:820–821).

2034 The scholarly literature on this controversy is listed by H. v. Soden, in *Der Streit zwischen Rom und Karthago über die Ketzertaufe*, 1–2.

2035 Cyprian of Carthage, *Epistles* 74-73.1, "To Pompey" (ANF 5:386; CSEL 3.2:799).

2036 Vgl. Böhringer, *Die alte Kirche* 4, 1013; Soden, *Streit zwischen Rom und Karthago*, 35.

2037 Cyprian of Carthage, *Epistles* 75-74.18, "Firmilian to Cyprian": "Omnis potestas et gratia in ecclesia constituta est [all power and grace are established in the Church]" (ANF 5:395; CSEL 3.2:822); *Epistles* 69-75.7, "To Magnus" (ANF 5:400; CSEL 3.2:756); *Epistles* 74-73.5, "To Pompey": "They attribute the effect of baptism to the majesty of the name, so that they who are baptized anywhere

low for a second baptism.[2038] These required only that hands be laid upon them for the imparting of the gifts of the Holy Spirit.

Even before this, however, in Africa and Asia Minor it had been determined that the baptism of the Gnostics and the Montanists was not to be considered valid.[2039] Firmilian writes: "To the Romans' custom we oppose custom, but the custom of truth; holding from the beginning that which was delivered by Christ and the apostles."[2040] Consequently, the practice of rebaptism was also extended to the Novatians. St. Cyprian immediately moves the question of the baptism of heretics into the arena of dogma, of the doctrine concerning the Church. There is one baptism, but only in the one Church.[2041] "He who says that any one can be baptized and sanctified by Novatian must first show and teach that Novatian is in the Church or presides over the Church."[2042] "If heretics are devot-

---

and anyhow, in the name of Jesus Christ, are judged to be renewed and sanctified" (ANF 5:387; CSEL 3.2:802–803).

2038 Some of the African bishops doubted whether heretics ought to be baptized, on the grounds that there is only one baptism. See *Epistles* 71-70.1, "To Quintus" (ANF 5:377; CSEL 3.2:771).

2039 See Tertullian, *On Baptism* 15 (CSEL 20.1:214). Cf. the observation of Adhémar d'Alès in *La Théologie De Tertullien*, 335. The African Council under Agrippinus decreed that heretics were to be rebaptized. See *Epistles* 71-70.4, "To Quintus" (ANF 5:378; CSEL 3.2:774); *Epistles* 73-72.3, "To Jubaianus" (ANF 5:380; CSEL 3.2:780). In Asia Minor, after thoroughly examining the matter, at the Council of Iconium it was decreed that any baptism whatsoever performed outside the Church was to be rejected. See *Epistles* 75-74.19, "Firmilian to Cyprian" (ANF 5:395; CSEL 3.2:823). Similar Councils were held in Synnada and other cities (Eusebius, *Church History* 7.7.5). Cf. Clement of Alexandria, *Stromata* 1.19.96.3: "Τὸ βάπτισμα τὸ αἱρετικὸν οὐκ οἰκεῖον καὶ γνήσιον ὕδωρ λογιζομένη [reckoning heretical baptism not proper and true water]" (GrchSch. 15:62.3–4). In practice these decrees rarely had to be applied, and consequently no controversies arose. Cf. Fechtrup, *Der hl. Cyprian*, 198.

2040 Cyprian of Carthage, *Epistles* 75-74.19, "Firmilian to Cyprian" (ANF 5:395; CSEL 3.2:822); *Epistles* 71-70.4, "To Quintus" (ANF 5:378; CSEL 3.2:774).

2041 Cyprian of Carthage, *Epistles* 71-70.1, "To Quintus" (ANF 5:377; CSEL 3.2:771).

2042 Cyprian of Carthage, *Epistles* 69-75.1, "To Magnus" (ANF 5:397; CSEL 3.2:752).

ed to the Church and established in the Church, they may use both
her baptism and her other saving benefits. But if they are not in the
Church, nay more, if they act against the Church, how can they
baptize with the Church's baptism?"[2043] "When [the apostles] say
that 'they are not of God, but are of the spirit of Antichrist,' how
can they transact spiritual and divine matters, who are the enemies
of God, and whose hearts the spirit of Antichrist has possessed?"[2044]

"No heretics and schismatics at all have any power or right. For
which reason Novatian neither ought to be nor can be expected, inasmuch as he also is without the Church and acting in opposition to
the peace and love of Christ, from being counted among adversaries
and antichrists."[2045] Stephen, bishop of Rome, even recognized the
baptism of the Marcionites as valid.[2046] St. Cyprian on the contrary
made no distinction between all opponents of the Church. "The
blessed Apostle John himself distinguished no heresy or schism, neither did he set down any as specially (*speciatim posuit*) separated; but
he called all who had gone out from the Church, and who acted
in opposition to the Church, antichrists."[2047] St. Cyprian makes no
distinction between the schismatic and the heretic. In sending the

2043　Cyprian of Carthage, *Epistles* 73-72.11, "To Jubaianus" (ANF 5:382;
CSEL 3.2:786). Cf. *The Seventh Council of Carthage under Cyprian* 44: "Pelagiani a
Luperciana" (ANF 5:570; CSEL 3.2:452).

2044　Cyprian of Carthage, *Epistles* 73-72.15, "To Jubaianus" (ANF 5:383;
CSEL 3.2:789). Cf. *The Seventh Council of Carthage under Cyprian* 24: "Secundinus
a Carpos dixit: Haeretici christiani sunt an non? Si christiani sunt, cur in ecclesia Dei non sunt? Si christiani non sunt, fiant (*alt. reading:* 'quomodo christianos
faciunt') [Secundinus of Carpi said: Are heretics Christians or not? If they are
Christians, why are they not in the Church of God? If they are not Christians,
let them become {*alt. reading:* how come they to make Christians?}]" (ANF 5:568;
CSEL 3.2:445). Cf. *The Seventh Council of Carthage under Cyprian* 51, Saturnini a
Victoriana (ANF 5:570; CSEL 3.2:453).

2045　69-75.1, "To Magnus" (ANF 5:397; CSEL 3.2:749).

2046　Cyprian of Carthage, *Epistles* 73-72.4, "To Jubaianus" (ANF 5:380;
CSEL 3.2:781); *Epistles* 74-73.7, "To Pompey" (ANF 5:388; CSEL 3.2:805). Cf.
The Seventh Council of Carthage under Cyprian 52: "Saturnini a Tucca" (ANF 5:570;
CSEL 3.2:454).

2047　Cyprian of Carthage, *Epistles* 69-75.7, "To Magnus" (ANF 5:397; CSEL
3.2:750).

apostles to the Jews first, Christ "commands the Gentiles as yet to be passed over; but by adding that even the city of the Samaritans was to be omitted, where there were schismatics (*schismatici*), He shows that schismatics were to be put on the same level as Gentiles."[2048] And since Novatian is outside the Church, there can be no baptism among the Novatians. "When they say, 'Dost thou believe the remission of sins and life eternal through the holy Church?' they lie in their interrogatory, since they have not the Church."[2049] "If the Church is not with heretics, therefore, because it is one, and cannot be divided; and if thus the Holy Spirit is not there, because He is one, and cannot be among profane persons, and those who are without; certainly also baptism, which consists in the same unity, cannot be among heretics, because it can neither be separated from the Church nor from the Holy Spirit."[2050] Since heretics "have separated themselves from the Church of God, [they] can have nothing of power or of grace (*nihil habere potestatis aut gratiae posseunt*). ... As a heretic may not lawfully ordain nor lay on hands, so neither may he baptize, nor do any thing holily or spiritually, since he is an alien from spiritual and deifying (*deifica*) sanctity."[2051] Consequently, the baptism of heretics is invalid, since they have not the Church, and outside the Church there is no Holy Spirit. In all his arguments Cyprian proceeded from the idea that the Church is one.[2052]

2048 Cyprian of Carthage, *Epistles* 76-75.6, "To Magnus": "Ostendit schismaticos gentilibus adaequari [He shows that schismatics were to be put on the same level as Gentiles]" (ANF 5:399; CSEL 3.2:756).

2049 Cyprian of Carthage, *Epistles* 76-75.7, "To Magnus" (ANF 5:399; CSEL 3.2:756). Cf. *Epistles* 70-69.2, "To Januarius": "Among heretics, where there is no Church, sins cannot be put away. Therefore they who assert that heretics can baptize, must either change the interrogation or maintain the truth; unless indeed they attribute a church also to those who, they contend, have baptism" (ANF 5:376; CSEL 3.2:768).

2050 Cyprian of Carthage, *Epistles* 74-73.4, "To Pompey" (ANF 5:387; CSEL 3.2:802). Cf. *Epistles* 74-73.7: "No heresy at all, and equally no schism, being without, can have the sanctification of saving baptism" (ANF 5:388; CSEL 3.2:805).

2051 Cyprian of Carthage, *Epistles* 75-74.7, "Firmilian to Cyprian" (ANF 5:392; CSEL 3.2:814–815).

2052 Vgl. Fechtrup, *Der hl. Cyprian*, 199–200; Schwane, *Dogmengeschichte der*

But the heretics also have no lawful hierarchy that proceeds successively from the apostles. "Novatian is not in the Church; nor can he be reckoned as a bishop, who, succeeding to no one, and despising the evangelical and apostolic tradition, sprang from himself."[2053] Among the heretics, "he who baptizes has not the power of baptizing."[2054] Only one who has the Holy Spirit can baptize and grant absolution of sins; but heretics have not the Holy Spirit.[2055]

On this latter point—that heretics do not have the Holy Spirit—even the supporters of Stephen of Rome concurred. St. Cyprian says of them that, although otherwise obstinate and unteachable, they at least confess that all heretics and schismatics do not have the Holy Spirit, and therefore although they can baptize, they cannot impart the Holy Spirit.[2056] But the grace of the Holy Spirit is already imparted in the laying on of hands, and Stephen, while recognizing heretical baptism as valid, nevertheless did not recognize the validity of their laying on of hands.[2057] Consequently,

---

vornic. Zeit², 529.

2053 Cyprian of Carthage, *Epistles* 69-75.3, "To Magnus" (ANF 5:398; CSEL 3.2:752). Cf. *Epistles* 69-75.4 (ANF 5:398; CSEL 3.2:753).

2054 Cyprian of Carthage, *Epistles* 76-75.8, "To Magnus" (ANF 5:400; CSEL 3.2:757).

2055 Ibid. 69-75.11, "To Magnus" (ANF 5:400; CSEL 3.2:759–760). Cf. *Epistles* 70-69.2, "To Januarius": "Who, moreover, can give what he himself has not? or how can he discharge spiritual functions who himself has lost the Holy Spirit?" (ANF 5:376; CSEL 3.2:769).

2056 Cyprian of Carthage, *Epistles* 76-75.10, "To Magnus" (ANF 5:400; CSEL 3.2:759).

2057 Scholarly opinion diverges on this point. Some allow for the idea that Stephen did not require that the laying on of hands be repeated, and that Cyprian and Firmilian merely attributed this to him for polemical purposes. Concerning this see Poschmann, *Die Sichtbarkeit der Kirche*, 118–121; Schwane, *Dogmengeschichte der vornicäischen Zeit²*, 536. To be sure, the surviving part of Stephen's edict on recognizing the baptism of heretics (*Epistles* 74-73, "To Pompey") says nothing of laying on hands anew; but it is quite inexplicable how Cyprian and Firmilian could have refuted that which Stephen never wrote, as they spend a considerable portion of their time doing. See *Epistles* 69-75.10, "To Magnus": "In hoc ipso a nobis tenentur" (ANF 5:400). Poschmann likewise acknowledges that Stephen considered the heretics' laying on of hands invalid, and that this

Stephen and those of like mind with him separated the spiritual gifts of grace into two parts: the grace of Christ and the gifts of the Holy Spirit. The Church alone possesses the gifts of the Holy Spirit and imparts them in the laying on of hands. The grace of Christ, however, exists and is conferred in baptism even in heretical communities that are outside the Church.[2058] Consequently, heretics cannot be compared to the pagans: they have left the Church, but they have also renounced paganism, and they too have a portion of grace. Heretics are as though between the Church and the pagan world.[2059] Consequently, the boundaries of the Church do not coincide with those of Christianity in general: it can be envisioned as a smaller concentric circle within a larger one. The Church possesses the fullness of grace, but a part of that grace—namely, the grace of Christ—extends beyond the bounds of the Church.[2060]

---

laying on of hands can only be understood to mean confirmation (*Firmung*) (121). In the opinion of Schwane, Stephen understood the laying on of hands to mean only the ritual at the reunification of penitents to the Church. See *Dogmengeschichte der vornic. Zeit²*, 536. Fechtrup allows for the possibility that Cyprian ascribed to Stephen the opinion of the author of *A Treatise on Re-Baptism*, when in actuality Stephen did not require that the laying on of hands which followed baptism be repeated. See *Der hl. Cyprian*, 224–228. See also Peters, *Der heilige Cyprian von Karthago*, 526–527, 533–535.

2058 Cyprian of Carthage, *Epistles*" 75-74.18, "Firmilian to Cyprian": "Whosoever is anywhere so-ever baptized in the name of Christ, immediately obtains the grace of Christ" (ANF 5:395; CSEL 3.2:822). Cf. *Epistles* 75-74.12: "Illud etiam quale est quod vult Stephanus, his qui apud haereticos baptizantur adesse praesentiam et sanctimonia Christi? [Moreover, what is the meaning of that which Stephen would assert, that the presence and holiness of Christ is with those who are baptized among heretics?]" (ANF 5:393; CSEL 3.2:818). The Russian translation (381 [Rus. ed.]) is not precise.

2059 Concerning this, see Katansky, *The Doctrine of the Grace of God*, 92–95. Cf. H. v. Soden, *Streit zwischen Rom und Karthago*, 38.

2060 During the controversy over the baptism of heretics, an unknown opponent of St. Cyprian published a special composition in defense of baptism outside the Church: *Liber de rebaptismate* (see Harnack, *Chronologie* 2, 393–396). The views on baptism expressed in this composition, despite a certain similarity to the views of the bishop of Rome and his supporters, are distinguished by still greater originality and singular tendencies toward degrading baptism itself. Baptism is not linked to the bestowal of the gifts of the Holy Spirit. The Holy Spirit

But the opponents of the bishop Stephen, led by St. Cyprian, did not hold it possible for grace to be divided, and for the grace of Christ to be distinguished from the gifts of the Holy Spirit. Grace is one and inseparable, and it belongs to the Church alone.[2061] The general idea of all the opponents of Stephen is most concisely expressed by one of the bishops present at the Council of 256: "Heretics can either do nothing, or they can do all."[2062] It is from this standpoint that St. Cyprian and Firmilian treat the baptism of heretics. One cannot put on Christ without the Spirit, and the Spirit cannot be separated from Christ.[2063] This gives rise to the chief argument of St. Cyprian: it is inconsistent to recognize the baptism of heretics while denying their laying on of hands. "Those who patronize heretics or schismatics must answer us whether they have

---

is imparted without the water of baptism (5, CSEL 3.3:75.22 sqq.). Baptism is performed with the invocation of the name of Jesus, and there is a kind of principle of the Lord's sacrament that is common for all members of the Church and for all others (*commune nobis et ceteris omnibus*). This must afterward be supplemented, for without this it would remain of no avail in the day of Judgment (7, CSEL 3.3:78.20 sqq.; cf. 12, CSEL 3.3:84). It should however be noted that the teaching of *Liber de rebaptismate* on baptism is interpreted variously by scholars, regarding which see Dr. Johann Ernst, "Die Tauflehre des 'Liber de rebaptismate,'" *Zeitschrift für katholische Theologie* (1907): 648–699. Cf. Harnack, *Dogmengeschichte* 1, 474–475. A comparison of the teaching of *Liber de rebaptismate* and of Cyprian is given by Peters (*Der Heilige Cyprian von Karthago*, 516–530).

2061 At the end of his epistle to Magnus (69-75.14), touching on the question of clinical baptism, St. Cyprian specifically asserts that "the Holy Spirit is not given by measure (*non de mensura*), but is poured out altogether (*totus*) on the believer," and that "the same spiritual grace which is equally (*aequaliter*) received in baptism by believers, is subsequently either increased or diminished in our conversation and conduct" (ANF 5:401; CSEL 3.2:763).

2062 Cyprian of Carthage, *The Seventh Council of Carthage under Cyprian* 16: "Successus a Abbir Germaniciana dixit: Haereticis aut nihil aut totum licet" (ANF 5:567; CSEL 3.2:443).

2063 Cyprian of Carthage, *Epistles* 74-73.5, "To Pompey" (ANF 5:387; CSEL 3.2:803). Cf. *Epistles* 75-74.12, "Firmilian to Cyprian": "Nisi si a Christo spiritum dividunt ut apud haereticos sit quidem Christus, non sit autem illic spiritus sanctus [unless, perhaps, they divide the Spirit from Christ, so that Christ indeed may be with heretics, but the Holy Spirit not be with them.]" (ANF 5:393; CSEL 3.2:818).

or have not the Holy Ghost. If they have, why are hands imposed on those who are baptized among them when they come to us, that they may receive the Holy Ghost, since He must surely have been received there, where if He was He could be given? But if heretics and schismatics baptized without have not the Holy Spirit, and therefore hands are imposed on them among us, that here may be received what there neither is nor can be given; it is plain, also, that remission of sins cannot be given by those who, it is certain, have not the Holy Spirit."[2064] Stephen linked the grace of Christ with that name which heretics also pronounced at baptism.[2065] St. Cy-

---

2064 Cyprian of Carthage, *Epistles* 69-75.11, "To Magnus" (ANF 5:400; CSEL 3.2:759–760). Cf. *Epistles* 75-74.12, "Firmilian to Cyprian": "Si induit Christum, accipere potuit et spiritum sanctum, qui a Christo missus est, et frustra illi venienti ad accipiendum spiritum manus imponitur [if he has put on Christ, he might also receive the Holy Ghost, who was sent by Christ, and hands are vainly laid upon him who comes to us for the reception of the Spirit;]" (ANF 5:393; CSEL 3.2:818). In the Russian translation (381 [Rus. ed.]) the latter phrase is absent. Cf. *The Seventh Council of Carthage under Cyprian* 70: "Veruli a Russicade: 'Homo haereticus dare non potest quod non habet: multo magis schismaticus quod habuit amisit [Verulus of Rusiccada said: A man who is a heretic cannot give what he has not; much more a schismatic, who has lost what he once had.]' (ANF 5:571; CSEL 3.2:457). See also ibid. 10: "Mannuli a Girba" (ANF 5:567; CSEL 3.2:442).

2065 St. Cyprian sometimes calls the name pronounced at baptism "the name of Christ." *Epistles* 73-72.16, "To Jubaianus": "All who are baptized everywhere, and in any manner, in the name of Jesus Christ, have obtained the grace of baptism" (opinion of Stephen) (ANF 5:383; CSEL 3.2:789–790); cf. *Epistles* 78-72.18 (ANF 5:383–384; CSEL 3.2:791). But it can hardly be supposed that Stephen really considered even a baptism not performed in the name of the Holy Trinity to be valid. Firmilian is aware of the words of Stephen (*Epistles* 75-74.18 [ANF 5:395; CSEL 3.2:822), but he himself writes: "That, moreover, is absurd, that they do not think it is to be inquired who was the person that baptized, for the reason that he who has been baptized may have obtained grace by the invocation of the Trinity, of the names of the Father, and of the Son, and of the Holy Ghost" (ibid. 9 [ANF 5:392; CSEL 3.2:815). By the name of Christ, St. Cyprian means the baptismal formula using the name of the Holy Trinity. He only insists that some heretics have an incorrect understanding of the Holy Trinity, although the formula is spoken accurately (see *Epistles* 73-72.5, 18, "To Jubaianus" [ANF 5:380–381, 383–384; CSEL 3.2:782, 792); *Epistles* 74-73.7, "To Pompey" (ANF 5:388; CSEL 3.2:805). For more details, see Johann Ernst, "Die Ketzertaufange-legenheit in der altchristlichen Kirche nach Cyprian," *Forschungen zur christlichen Literatur und Dogmengeschichte, herausg. von Dr. A. Ehrhard und Dr. I. P. Kirsch*, Bd. 2,

prian refutes this argument, demonstrating that without the Holy Spirit no grace can be imparted. "If they attribute the effect of baptism to the majesty of the name ... **wherefore, in the name of the same Christ, are not hands laid upon the baptized persons among them, for the reception of the Holy Spirit?** Why does not the same majesty of the same name **avail in the imposition of hands, which, they contend, availed in the sanctification of baptism?**[2066] For if any one born out of the Church can become God's temple, why cannot the Holy Spirit also be poured out upon the temple? ... He who, having been baptized among the heretics, is able to put on Christ, may much more receive the Holy Spirit whom Christ sent. ... Moreover, it is silly to say, that ... one may be born spiritually among the heretics, where they say that the Spirit is not. For water alone is not able to cleanse away sins, and to sanctify a man, unless he have also the Holy Spirit. Wherefore it is necessary that they should grant the Holy Spirit to be there, where they say that baptism is; or else there is no baptism where the Holy Spirit is not, because there cannot be baptism with-

Heft 4 (Mainz: 1901), 13–18; *Papst Stephan* 1, 93 ff. See the observations of H. v. Soden, *Streit swischen Rom und Karthago*, 37, Anm. 1; Batiffol, *L'eglise naissante et le catholicisme*[3], 465n3; Tillemont, *Memoires*, vol. 4, 625–629; Fechtrup, *Der hl. Cyprian*, 210, 220–224; Ios. Schwane, *Dogmengeschichte der vornic. Zeit*, 533–534.

2066 The highlighted words clearly show that Cyprian is specifically referring to the fact that Stephen did not recognize the validity of the heretics' laying on of hands at the time of baptism.

out the Spirit."[2067] This latter idea is clearly and decisively expressed by Firmilian[2068] and the bishop Nemesianus.[2069]

Thus, the baptism of heretics is decisively rejected; it is declared to be utterly invalid. A heretic or schismatic who converts to the Church is viewed as an unbaptized heathen. The defenders of heretical baptism thought that heretics must not be baptized because there is one baptism. From St. Cyprian's perspective, this is incorrect. There is one baptism because the Church is one, and baptism is impossible outside the Church. "We say that those who come thence are not re-baptized among us, but are baptized (*non rebaptizari apud nos sed baptizari*).[2070] For indeed they do not receive anything there, where there is nothing."[2071] The baptism of heretics is not baptism, but rather a "sordid and profane washing (*sordida et profana tinctio*)."[2072] A heretic, "stained with the contagion of adulterous water" in "a hiding-place and a cave of robbers ... has not only not put off his old sins, but rather heaped up still newer and

---

2067 Cyprian of Carthage, *Epistles* 74-73.5, "To Pompey" (ANF 5:387; CSEL 3.2:802–803). Cf. *Epistles* 70-69.3, "To Januarius": "If one could baptize, he could also give the Holy Spirit. But if he cannot give the Holy Spirit, because he that is appointed without is not endowed with the Holy Spirit (*foris constitutus cum sancto spiritu non est*), he cannot baptize those who come; since both baptism is one and the Holy Spirit is one, and the Church ... is one also" (ANF 5:376; CSEL 3.2:769).

2068 Cyprian of Carthage, *Epistles* 75-74.9: baptism is valid "when both he who baptizes has the Holy Spirit, and the baptism itself also is not ordained without the Spirit" (ANF 5:392; CSEL 3.2:816). Cf. 75-74.8: "Spiritual birth cannot be without the Spirit" (ANF 5:392; CSEL 3.2:815).

2069 *The Seventh Council of Carthage under Cyprian* 5: "Neque Spiritus sine aqua separatim operari potest nec aqua sine Spiritu [neither can the Spirit operate without the water, nor the water without the Spirit]" (ANF 5:566; CSEL 3.2:439.5–6).

2070 The Russian source is less ambiguous, reading literally: "We assert that we do not re-baptize those who come thence, but rather we baptize them." –*Trans.*

2071 Cyprian of Carthage, *Epistles* 71-70.1, "To Quintus" (ANF 5:377; CSEL 3.2:771).

2072 Ibid. 71-70.1, "To Quintus" (ANF 5:377; CSEL 3.2:772.7–8); *Epistles* 74-73.2, "To Pompey": "Mendacia et contagia profanae tinctionis [the lies and the contagions of a profane washing]" (ANF 5:380; CSEL 3.2:800.6–7).

greater ones."[2073] Firmilian likewise calls the baptism of heretics an "unhallowed and profane dipping."[2074] The water in which heretics are baptized serves only as "a carnal washing, and not a Sacrament of Baptism."[2075] Among the unanimous opinions of the bishops of the Council of 256 regarding the invalidity of heretical baptism (where incidentally we encounter all those same ideas found in St. Cyprian), there is the following phrase: "The Church does not re-baptize heretics, but baptizes them."[2076] And in his closing speech at the Council St. Cyprian says: "Heretics, who are called adversaries of Christ and Antichrists, when they come to the Church, must be baptized with the one baptism of the Church, that they may be made of adversaries, friends, and of Antichrists, Christians."[2077] It should also be noted that St. Cyprian held that the decree that heretical baptism is invalid would be beneficial for converting heretics to the Church; conversely, he held that it would be detrimental to

---

2073 Cyprian of Carthage, *Epistles* 73-72.21, "To Jubaianus" (ANF 5:384; CSEL 3.2:795); *Treatises* 1.11, "On the Unity of the Church": "Men are not washed among them, but rather are made foul; nor are sins purged away, but are even accumulated. Such a nativity does not generate sons to God, but to the devil" (ANF 5:425; CSEL 3.2:219).

2074 Cyprian of Carthage, 75-74.8: "Nec eos qui ab haeresi ad ecclesiam veniunt post inlicitam et profanam eorum tinetionem baptizare dubitemus [nor are we hesitating to baptize those who come to the Church from heresy after their unhallowed and profane dipping]" (ANF 5:392; CSEL 3.2:815.18-20).

2075 Ibid. 75-74.13: "Ac per hoc aqua qua tinguntur lavacrum est illis carnale tantum, non baptismi sacramentum [And thus the water wherewith they are washed is to them only a carnal washing, not a sacrament of baptism]" (ANF 5:392; CSEL 3.2:819.9-10).

2076 *The Seventh Council of Carthage under Cyprian* 35: "Adelphius a Thasvalthe dixit: Sine causa quidam falso et individioso verbo impugnant veritatem ut rebaptizare nos dicant, quando ecclesia haereticos non rebaptizet, sed baptizet [Adelphius of Thasvalte said: Certain persons without reason impugn the truth by false and envious words, in saying that we rebaptize, when the Church does not rebaptize heretics, but baptizes them.]" (ANF 5:569; CSEL 3.2:449). In general, *The Seventh Council of Carthage under Cyprian* constantly echoes the ideas and arguments of St. Cyprian. See H. v. Soden, *Streit swischen Rom und Karthago*, 39–40; Batiffol, *L'eglise naissante et le catholicisme*, 471.

2077 Ibid. 87 (ANF 5:572; CSEL 3.2:461).

recognize the validity of heretical baptism. "If they shall see that it is determined and decreed by our judgment and sentence, that the baptism wherewith they are there baptized is considered just and legitimate, they will think that they are justly and legitimately in possession of the Church also, and the other gifts of the Church (*ecclesiae munera*); nor will there be any reason for their coming to us, when, as they have baptism, they seem also to have the rest. But further, when they know that there is no baptism without, and that no remission of sins can be given outside the Church, they more eagerly and readily hasten to us, and implore the gifts and benefits (*munera ac dona*) of the Church our Mother, assured that they can in no wise attain to the true promise of divine grace unless they first come to the truth of the Church."[2078]

We have already noted that St. Cyprian cited the illegitimacy of the heretical hierarchy. Along with the question of heretical baptism, the following decree was issued regarding members of the hierarchy: "If, again, any presbyters or deacons, who either have been before ordained (*ordinati*) in the Catholic Church, and have subsequently stood forth as traitors and rebels against the Church, or who have been promoted among the heretics by a profane ordination by the hands of false bishops and antichrists contrary to the appointment of Christ (*a pseudoepiscopis et antichristis contra Christi dispositionem profana ordinatione promoti sint*), and have attempted to offer, in opposition to the one and divine altar, false and sacrilegious sacrifices without, that these also be received when they return, on this condition, that they communicate as laymen (*ut communicent laici*)."[2079]

2078 Cyprian of Carthage, *Epistles* 73-72.24, "To Jubaianus" (ANF 5:385; CSEL 3.2:797).

2079 Cyprian of Carthage, *Epistles* 72-71.2, "To Stephen" (ANF 5:379; CSEL 3.2:776). Cf. *The Seventh Council of Carthage under Cyprian*: "Caecilii a Bilta: 'Sacerdotium administrat profanus, ponit altare sacrilegus [the profane person administers the office of the priesthood; the sacrilegious person establishes an altar]'" (ANF 5:567; CSEL 3.2:437).

In the controversies described[2080] concerning the baptism of

---

2080   The renowned contemporary of the Western disputes over baptism, Dionysius, bishop of Alexandria, likewise wrote extensively on the question of the baptism of heretics. In his various epistles, as Eusebius relates, he "treated the question thoroughly" (cf. *Church History* 7.7.5 [NPNF[2] 1:296]), said much about heretics (*Church History* 7.9.1), and "considered the question … with extended argument" (*Church History* 7.9.6 [NPNF[2] 1:298]). But Eusebius has preserved only small excerpts from all these epistles, which are not sufficient to provide an outline of the dogmatic views of their author. From the blessed pope Heraclas St. Dionysius received this rule: "Those that came over from the heretics, although they had apostatized from the Church … he admitted … without requiring them to be re-baptized: for they had received that holy gift already" from him; that is, when they belonged to the Church (*St. Dionysius of Alexandria: Letters and Treatises*, Charles Lett Feltoe, trans. [London: Society for Promoting Christian Knowledge, and New York: The Macmillan Company, 1918], "To Philemon," 57–58). But in the Syrian tongue there survives an excerpt from an epistle to Dionysius and Stephanus, prelates of the Church of Rome, where St. Dionysius writes: "Those who were baptized in the name of the three Persons—the Father, the Son, and the Holy Spirit—though they were baptized by heretics who confess the three Persons, shall not be re-baptized. But those who are converted from other heresies shall be perfected by the baptism of the Holy Church" (ibid., "To Stephanus, Bishop of Rome," 54; *Pitra. Analecta sacra*, vol. 4 [Parisiis: 1883], 170.413–414). Consequently, Dionysius considered heretical baptism invalid, and hence the blessed Jerome says that Dionysius consented to the doctrine of Cyprian and the African Councils on the matter of the baptism of heretics (*Lives of Illustrious Men* 69 [NPNF[2] 3:376; PL 23:677c, 679a]), but that this consent was incomplete, since St. Dionysius held that the baptism of schismatics was valid. St. Dionysius is aware of the decrees of the Councils of Africa and Asia Minor. Dionyisus has complete regard for these Councils, calling them "most significant" (μεγίσται). But Dionysius does not wish to rouse anyone to strife and contention, remembering the words of Scripture: "Thou shalt not remove thy neighbour's landmark, which they of old time have set in thine inheritance" (Deut. 19:14) (Eusebius, *Church History* 7.5.5, 7.5 [NFNF[2] 1:295, 296]), and he expresses the same idea on which St. Cyprian likewise insists. "In regard to causes and affairs about matters which concern individual men—how it is right to receive him who approaches from without and how him who comes from within—we counsel to obey those who stand at the head of every place who by Divine election are put into this ministration—leaving to our Lord the judgment of all things which they do" (*St. Dionysius of Alexandria: Letters and Treatises*, "To Stephanus, Bishop of Rome," 53–54; *Pitra. Analecta sacra*, vol. 4 [Parisiis: 1883], 171.414). Consequently, St. Dionysius constantly exhorted the Roman bishops not to break peace with those who dissented on the baptism of heretics. In the words of Louis Duchesne (*Early History of the Christian Church*, vol. 1, 288 [Rus. ed.]), Dionysius was the Irenaeus

heretics, St. Cyprian and those of like mind with him also seem to emphasize this dogmatic truth from a negative aspect: **there is no salvation outside the Church.** Particular energies of grace are necessary for salvation, and these can only be obtained in the Church. The Church is like an oasis of grace, surrounded by a completely barren dessert. To be without the Church is to be without grace, without the Holy Spirit, and this pertains to the pagan, the heretic, and the schismatic alike. All of them alike are without grace, because they are outside the Church, and all of them alike must be baptized if they wish to enter the Church. **The Church, which exclusively possesses the fullness of the grace necessary for men, imparts it to the faithful through the hierarchy, who by succession from the apostles preserve both the power and the rights that the Lord gave to His disciples.** In accordance with this view, St. Cyprian's own writings and manuscripts from his time refer to members of the hierarchy as priests with particular frequency. It is they who impart the gifts of grace to people in the various sacraments.[2081] To be saved one must not

---

for a new Victor. Cf. Batiffol, *L'eglise naissante et le catholicisme,* 476. For more details on St. Dionysius's involvement in the controversies over the validity of heretical baptism, see Druzhinin, *The Life and Works of St. Dionysius the Great,* 209–237. It should be noted that all excerpts from the epistles of St. Dionysius leave us wholly unenlightened as to the dogmatic considerations by which he justified his recognition of baptisms performed outside the Church. It is clear, however, that in distinguishing between heresies St. Dionysius proceeded not from the idea of the unity of the Church, as did St. Cyprian; rather, he connected baptism with the faith confessed at baptism. In recognizing the validity of schismatic baptism, Dionysius thereby answers the question of whether God's grace is effectual outside the Church in the affirmative. But in all that we have from St. Dionysius, the question of the validity of heretical baptism is in no way connected with the idea of the Church.

2081   As we have seen, St. Cyprian developed the doctrine of baptism and (as we now call it) chrismation in particular detail. But in his writings ordination (*ordo*), repentance, and the Eucharist are also considered sacraments. For more detail, see Poschmann, *Die Sichtbarkeit der Kirche,* 121–181. See also Molchanov, *St. Cyprian of Carthage,* 263–281. St. Cyprian merely does not present them in the same connection with the dogmatic doctrine concerning the Church as he does baptism and the laying on of hands (chrismation). See Harnack, *Dogmengeschichte*[4] 1, 459–462, 469–479.

only believe in Christ, but also visibly belong to His Church and receive divine grace through the organs which God has established therein—that is, through the hierarchy. God saves men through His Church and through her hierarchy.[2082]

Here we encounter **the question of how the work of imparting grace correlates to the person of the member of the hierarchy.** In the teaching of St. Cyprian, is the right to impart grace linked to the person, or to the ecclesiastical office? All that has been said above suggests the answer that the right to impart grace is linked to the ecclesiastical office.[2083] But if we turn to the works of St. Cyprian for a resolution of this question, first of all we will see that he is not indifferent to the moral state of the member of the hierarchy. During the Decian persecutions, which were directed primarily against members of the hierarchy, there were several cases when bishops apostatized. St. Cyprian holds that lapsed bishops are stripped of the Holy Spirit. For example, concerning Fortunatianus St. Cyprian writes to Epictetus and the congregation of the Assuritans: "I was gravely and grievously disturbed, dearest brethren, at learning that Fortunatianus, formerly bishop among you, after the sad lapse of his fall, was now wishing to act as if he were sound, and beginning to claim for himself the episcopate. ... How does he think that he can act as a priest of God who has obeyed and served the priests of the devil? ... In the sacred Scriptures God forbids the priests to approach to sacrifice even if they have been in lighter guilt." (Here there follow quotes from Lev. 21:17–18 and Ex. 19:22, 28:43.) "Those, therefore, who have brought grievous sins upon themselves, that is, who, by sacrificing to idols, have offered sacrilegious sacrifices, cannot claim to themselves the priesthood of God, nor make any prayer for their brethren in His sight. ... Whence also we perceive and believe that this rebuke has come from God's searching out, that they might not continue to stand at the altar; and any further, as unchaste persons,[2084] to have to do with modesty; as perfidious, to have to do with faith; as profane, with

---

2082 Vgl. Seeberg, *Studien zur Geschichte des Begriffs der Kirche*, 36.

2083 Vgl. Huther, *Cyprians Lehre von der Kirche*, 67. Vgl. 60–66.

2084 In the Russian source, "incestuous persons." – *Trans.*

religion; as earthly, with things divine; as sacrilegious, with things sacred. ... The oblation [cannot] be consecrated where the Holy Spirit is not; nor can the Lord avail to any one by the prayers and supplications of one who himself has done despite to the Lord."[2085]

When an analogous incident occurred in Spain, where the bishops Basilides and Martial lapsed, the entire Council of thirty-seven African bishops agreed that they "ought not to hold the episcopate and administer the priesthood of God." Further on in the epistle from this Council we read: "The divine reproof ... manifestly [teaches] and [shows] that all are absolutely bound to the sin who have been contaminated by the sacrifice of a profane and unrighteous priest. ... A people obedient to the Lord's precepts, and fearing God, ought to separate themselves from a sinful prelate, and not to associate themselves with the sacrifices of a sacrilegious priest."[2086] Consequently, bishops and presbyters who had lapsed in times of persecution were customarily restored to communion with the Church as simple laymen. Thus was Trophimus the presbyter received, whom St. Cyprian mentions.[2087] Cyprian himself was accused of grave sins, and he writes the following to Florentius Pupianus: "Unless I may be declared clear in your sight and absolved by your judgment, behold now for six years the brotherhood has neither had a bishop, nor the people a prelate, nor the flock a pastor, nor the Church a governor, nor Christ a representative (*antistitem*), nor God a priest! Pupianus must come to the rescue, and give judgment, and declare the decision of God and Christ accepted, that so great a number of the faithful who have been summoned away, under my rule, may not appear to have departed without hope of

---

2085 Cyprian, *Epistles* 65-63.1, 2, 3, 4, "To Epictetus and to the Congregation of Assurae" (ANF 5:364–365; CSEL 3.2:721, 723, 724, 725).

2086 Cyprian of Carthage, *Epistles* 67-67.1, "To the Clergy and People Abiding in Spain" (ANF 5:370, 371; CSEL 3.2:735, 737–738).

2087 Cyprian of Carthage, *Epistles* 55-51.11, "To Antonianus" (ANF 5:330; CSEL 3.2:631–632). Cf. *Epistles* 67-67.6 (ANF 5:371; CSEL 3.2:739–740). Here we may include the decree that presbyters and deacons who were ordained in the catholic Church, but then turned traitors and rebels against the Church, should be received as laymen. See *Epistles* 72-71.2, "To Stephen" (ANF 5:379; CSEL 3.2:776).

salvation and of peace; that the new crowd of believers may not be considered **to have failed of attaining any grace of baptism and the Holy Spirit by my ministry**; that the peace conferred upon so many lapsed and penitent persons, and the communion vouchsafed by my examination, may not be abrogated by the authority of your judgment."[2088]

The information we have cited from the works of St. Cyprian is subjected to tendential interpretations in Protestant scholarly literature. Some wish to see in it a certain archaistic remnant of the presumed charismatic organization of the early days of Christianity and of the ancient concept of the Church as a society of saints. In requiring greater moral perfection of the bishop, Cyprian thereby shows that he is absolutely no stranger to the view of the bishop as a charismatic, whose personal qualities render him capable of actualizing the divine principles in the life of the Church. The Novatians excluded all who had sinned mortally in the name of the sanctity of the Church, while Cyprian limited the concept of the Holy Church as a society of saints to the clergy, requiring that lapsed members thereof be defrocked. The clergy are "the Holy Church" within the Church, which, in including sinners within itself, is a *corpus permixtum*.[2089]

2088 Cyprian of Carthage, *Epistles* 66-68.5, "To Florentius Pupianus" (ANF 5:373–374; CSEL 3.2:730). Here Cyprian is apparently expressing even the extreme idea that grace is not imparted through a bishop who has sinned from the very moment of his fall into sin.

2089 Here we have presented the thinking of Harnack, *Dogmengeschichte*[4] 1, 447–449). Cf. *Novatian*, RE 3, Bd. XIV, 238–240. Loofs likewise speaks of the "Nachwirkung des alten Kirchenbegriffs" in the writings of Cyprian. See *Leitfaden der Dogmengeschichte* §29.4, 209. Poschmann makes several observations in *Die Sichtbarkeit der Kirche*, 185–189. In Poschmann one may observe the opposite, Catholic tendencies. A somewhat different but nonetheless similar opinion was previously put forward in Protestant literature by Ritschl. Ritschl calls attention to several passages from the epistles of St. Cyprian where he and other bishops cite visions and special revelations—*Epistles* 57-53.5, "To Cornelius": "This is frequently shown to us from above (*divinitus ostendi*)" (ANF 5:338; CSEL 3.2:655). *Epistles* 66-68.10, "To Florentius Pupianus": "Among other things which He condescended to show and to reveal (*ostendere et revelare*)..." (he then goes on to describe visions during sleep—ANF 5:373–375; CSEL 3.2:734)—and he expresses

It is necessary that we determine our stance on this point in the teaching of St. Cyprian. The question of the correlation between the grace of the priesthood and the person of the member of the hierarchy is one that had arisen prior to St. Cyprian. In his pastoral epistles even the holy apostle Paul lists various requirements of members of the priestly order; consequently, certain special qualities had to be required of members of the hierarchy. This is apparent even from a psychological standpoint. No one can ever judge the failings of members of the priestly order in the same way as those of a layman. But in the early third century Montanism advanced the doctrine of universal priesthood.[2090] This doctrine threatened considerable complications for the Church. The hierarchical structure of the Church initially established could have been replaced— as it was in Montanist communities—with a disorderly and therefore short-lived and even unfeasible structure without a hierarchy or with one of almost no significance. At the same time, however, the

---

the thought that supposedly in his actions he [Cyprian—*Trans.*] relied on particular revelations each time: "für jeden einzelnen Moment berechnete Inspiration" (*Die Entstehung der altkatholischen Kirche*, 565). All testimonies from the compositions of Cyprian regarding various revelations are collected by Harnack in a special article, "Cyprian als Enthusiast," in *Zeitschrift für die neutestamentliche Wissenschaft and die Kunde des Urchristentums, herausgeg. von Erwin Preuschen* (1902), 177–191. In Harnack's opinion, all these testimonies "eit Stück urchristlichen Altertums," and in them St. Cyprian is revealed to be "als ein Epigone der tertullianischen, ja einer noch früheren Epoche" (177), so that despite all his clericalism he was "ein Christ alten Schlages" (182). At the same time, Harnack himself acknowledges that St. Cyprian does not connect all his accounts of direct revelations with any definite theory (*Dogmengeschichte*[4] 1, 419, Anm. 1). Furthermore, it may also be noted that all these accounts do not exclude the particular grace of the priesthood, which the bishop possesses by virtue of his office, since Cyprian is also aware of the sacramental work of the bishop. Cf. the observation of Poschmann, *Die Sichtbarkeit der Kirche*, 182, Anm. 2. Thomasius considers the especial aid of the Holy Spirit in particular instances of [the bishop's] work one of the prerogatives of the episcopal office, along with various other prerogatives (*Die Dogmengeschichte der alten Kirche* 1, 585.

2090 This doctrine is examined in detail by Karl Adam. See *Der Kirchebegriff Tertullians*, 190–229. Cf. 88–108, where Tretullian's views in his pre-Montanist period are presented.

Roman bishop Callistus, possibly to counter Montanism,[2091] issued a directive (ἐδογμάτισεν) that if the bishop sinned, even mortally, he should not be deposed. Saint Hippolytus berates Callistus for this, from which we learn of his decree.[2092] Many ascribe great significance to this decree of Callistus, understanding it in an infinitely broad sense,[2093] but the brief observation by Hippolytus hardly provides sufficient grounds for this—the more so given the difficulty in determining which sins Hippolytus is calling "mortal" in this instance and whether the directive of Callistus extended to all mortal sins.[2094] One thing only is clear: the question was not resolved on a Church-wide basis. Concerning the Roman bishop Cornelius, Cyprian relates that he together with all the bishops appointed by him in every place (*in toto mundo constitutis*) determined that lapsed bishops and presbyters be permitted to offer repentance, but that these be prohibited from joining the clergy and holding sacred office.[2095] Although it is known that Stephen of Rome received Basilides and Martial as bishops, St. Cyprian positively asserts that Basilides deceived (*fefellit*) Stephen, who due to distance did not know the details of the events that had transpired.[2096] In any case, there is no definite

---

2091 So asserts Adam. See *Der Kirchebegriff Tertullians*, 206–207.

2092 Hippolytus of Rome, *The Refutation of All Heresies* 9.12: "Οὗτος ἐδογμάτισεν ὅπως εἰ ἐπίσκοπος ἁμάρτοι τι, εἰ καὶ πρὸς θάνατον, μὴ δεῖν κατατίθεσθαι [This one propounded the opinion, that, if a bishop was guilty of any sin, if even a sin unto death, he ought not to be deposed]" (PG 16:3386b). It is hardly likely that Döllinger is accurate in translating ἐδογμάτισεν as *lehrte* (*Hippolytus und Kallistus*, 134). But then, on the very next page in paraphrasing he employs *hingestellt hat*.

2093 Adam, *Der Kirchenbegriff Tertullians*, 228–229; Loofs, *Leitfaden der Dogmengeschichte* §29.4, 209; Harnack, *Dogmengeschichte* 1, 421–422, 447, 494, Anm. 1.

2094 Was Callistus referring to instances of apostasy among the bishops? And were such instances known at that time? By "εἰ καὶ πρὸς θάνατον [if even unto death]," does not Hippolytus mean sins against chastity (προς τὰς ἡδονάς) in his evaluation of which he is known to have differed with Callistus? Vgl. E. Rolffs, *Das Indulgenz-Edict*, TU 11.3, 137, Anm. 1. Döllinger likewise denies that Callistus issued a directive in a boundlessly general sense (*Hippolytus und Kallistus*, 135–139).

2095 Clement of Carthage, *Epistles* 67-67.6 (ANF 5:371; CSEL 3.2:741). Does this not serve to confirm our understanding of the order of Callistus?

2096 Ibid. 67-67.5 (ANF 5:371; CSEL 3.2:739).

information from which we may judge the thinking of Stephen.[2097]
If we now turn our attention to the excerpts cited from the epistles
of St. Cyprian, we shall see that their content is quite insufficient to
provide a precise outline of the views of the holy father. First and
foremost, it is unclear whether St. Cyprian had in mind the **inca-
pacity** or **unworthiness** of *libellatici* bishops to be conductors of
divine grace in the Church. In his epistle to the clergy and people
of Spain he finds fault with them for permitting a sinful bishop
to perform his ministry, since the people have the power to elect
priests who are worthy and depose those who are not. "We observe
to come from divine authority, that the priest should be chosen in
the presence of the people under the eyes of all, and should be
approved worthy and suitable (*dignus atque idoneus*) by public judgment and testimony ... that in the presence of the people either the
crimes of the wicked may be disclosed, or the merits of the good
may be declared, and the ordination, which shall have been examined by the suffrage and judgment of all, may be just and legitimate
(*ordinatio justa et ligitima*).[2098] In the same place St. Cyprian writes:
"Unworthy persons are sometimes ordained, not according to the
will of God, but according to human presumption, and ... those
things which do not come of a legitimate and righteous ordination
are displeasing to God."[2099] But there is not a word about whether
or not an unworthy person can be an organ of grace. To all ap-
pearances, this refers solely to the worthiness of a person elected to
ecclesiastical office. Only so flagrant a crime as apostasy from the

---

2097 Cf. Poschmann's reasoning concerning Stephen in *Die Sichtbarkeit der Kirche*, 186. In *Die Entstehung der altkath. Kirche* (567–569), Ritschl posits that Stephen
knew and recognized the order of Callistus, and that he received Basilides quite
deliberately.

2098 Cyprian of Carthage, *Epistles* 67-67.4 (ANF 5:370–371; CSEL 3.2:738).
St. Cyprian then goes on to describe the procedure for electing a bishop, citing
the example of the election of an apostle to replace Judas (Acts 1:16).

2099 Ibid. 67-67.4 (ANF 5:370–371; CSEL 3.2:739). Cf. 67-76.2: "We ought
in the ordinations of priests to choose none but unstained and upright (*immacula-
tos et integros*) ministers, who, holily and worthily offering sacrifices to God, may be
heard in the prayers which they make for the safety of the Lord's people" (ANF
5:370; CSEL 3.2:736).

faith strips a member of the hierarchy of the ability to retain his
former rank. In other passages St. Cyprian expresses himself more
decisively, as we have seen, asserting that a lapsed bishop is stripped
of the Holy Spirit, and even seemingly positing that a bishop guilty
of a grave sin no longer imparts any grace of the Holy Spirit in
baptism from the very moment of his fall.[2100] But in the same epistle
St. Cyprian expresses his most decisive idea of all: that the Church
is in the bishop and the bishop is in the Church, and that he does
not allow for an instance where the bishop would prove incapable
of being a conductor of grace.[2101] Without God's will nothing at all
takes place, let alone the appointment of a bishop. "To believe that
they who are ordained are unworthy and unchaste, what else is it
than to believe that his priests are not appointed in the Church by
God, nor through God?"[2102] Clearly, St. Cyprian gives no definite
answer to our question, and from his own views he drew no definitive conclusions one way or the other.

Also worthy of particular note are the arguments of the anonymous author of the composition *A Treatise on Re-Baptism*. The author
says that even the apostles did not have perfect and inviolate faith,
yet they baptized and naturally imparted grace.[2103] As if completing
the thought of St. Cyprian, the author puts to him the question:
what would you say of those who are baptized by erring bishops or
by bishops of poor conduct?[2104] In Cyprian's writings we do not find

2100 Cyprian of Carthage, *Epistles* 66-68.5, "To Florentius Pupianus" (ANF
5:373-374; CSEL 3.2:730). For this reason von Soden considers Cyprian a sort
of pre-Donatism Donatist. See *Streit swischen Rom und Karthago*, 35. Cf. Schwane,
dogmengeschichte der vornic. Zeit, 530.

2101 Here, of course, we see reflected St. Cyprian's certainty of his own right-
ness and of the falseness of Pupianus's accusations. Cf. Huther, *Cyprians Lehre von
der Kirche,* 81-83. Cf. Peters, *Der heilige Cyprian von Karthago,* 270.

2102 Cyprian of Carthage, *Epistles* 66-68.5, "To Florentius Pupianus" (ANF
5:373; CSEL 3.2:727). Cf. 66-68.8 (ANF 5:374-375; CSEL 3.2:733).

2103 *A Treatise on Re-Baptism* 9 (ANF 5:672; CSEL 3.3:81.16 sqq.).

2104 Ibid. 10: "Quid dicturus es de his qui plerumque ab episcopis pessimae
conversationis baptizantur: qui tamen tandem cum Deus voluerit, in sceleribus
suis convicti, etiam ipso aut prorsus etiam communicatione privantur? aut quid
statues de eis qui ab episcopis prave sentientibus aut imperitioribus fuerint bap-

an answer to this question, so bluntly put. Although the author of *A Treatise on Re-Baptism* presupposes St. Cyprian's response—that these should be baptized anew[2105]—it must be thought that St. Cyprian himself came to no such decisive conclusions.[2106] Indeed, these conclusions would have completely disrupted his entire system of doctrine concerning the Church, so painstakingly created and tirelessly defended in word and deed throughout the course of his life. In the overall system of St. Cyprian this is of course a contradiction,[2107] or at least an inconsistency, but to explain this inconsistency one hardly need resort to citing a remnant of the supposed charismatic organization of the original Church.[2108] Cyprian teaches with

---

tizati? [What will you say of those who are in many cases baptized by bishops of very bad character, who yet at length, when God so wills it, convicted of their crimes, are even deprived of their office itself, or absolutely of communion? Or what will you decide of those who may have been baptized by bishops, whose opinions are unsound, or who are very ignorant]" (ANF 5:672–673; CSEL 3.3:81.20 sqq.).

2105 Ibid. 10: "Dicturus es enim utique pro tua singulari diligentia hos quoque denuo baptizandos esse, cum maxime eis res desit aut obstet quo minus inviolabile illud divinum mysterium fidei intemeratum possint accipere [You will assuredly say, with that marvellous carefulness of yours, that these too should be baptized again, since this is especially the thing which is wanting to them, or hinders their being able to receive, uncorrupted, that divine and inviolable mystery of the faith]" (ANF 5:673; CSEL 3.3:81.30–82.1).

2106 Vgl. van Soden, *Streit zwischen Rom und Karthago*, 85.

2107 This contradiction is noted by all scholars who have researched the matter. See Huther, *Cyprians Lehre von der Kirche*, 81, 83. See Ritschl, *Die Enstehung der altkatholischen Kirche*, 569; cf. 566–567; Adam, *Der Kirchenbegriff Tertullians*, 207; Poschmann, *Die Sichtbarkeit der Kirche*, 186–188. Harnack writes that it is quite remarkable to find traces of an earlier era in the writings of one who made the episcopacy not only the core of Christianity, but the foundation of the Church, and who in dozens of passages writes like a medieval pope ("Cyprian als Enthusiast," in *Zeitschr. für neuetestamentliche Wissenschaft* (1902): 177. Vgl. *Dogmengeschichte*[4] 1, 447; von Soden, *Streit zwischen Rom und Karthago*, 36, 38). Bolotov likewise acknowledges that in his views Cyprian is already starting down the slippery slope of subjectivism, even though his subjectivisim is based on firmly objective grounds. The grounds Cyprian cites for the invalidity of baptism performed by heretics strike beyond his present target (*Lectures on the History of the Early Church*, 2nd ed., 394).

2108 Poschmann, *Die Sichtbarkeit der Kirche*, 187.

perfect clarity that men are made bishops not solely by virtue of their personal qualities, but by election of the people and following sacramental consecration by the bishops. The Lord Who provides for His Church does not permit the appointment of an unworthy bishop; and in extraordinary instances where a bishop sins mortally, such as by apostatizing from the faith in time of persecution, it is by the Church's judgment that he is stripped of his rank and made a layman. **The bishop possesses the grace of the Holy Spirit by virtue of his ecclesiastical office, but he himself must live up to his office.**[2109] Nevertheless, several of St. Cyprian's expressions create the impression of an apparent contradiction. All these contradictions were to be resolved later, when the schism of the Donatists drew the attention of church writers to this very point that St. Cyprian had not elucidated with sufficiently clarity.

2109 In the opinion of Huther, in answer to the question of what makes a bishop capable of imparting the Holy Spirit—his office or his personal worthiness—Cyprian replied: neither the one nor the other, but both together (*Cyprians Lehre von der Kirche*, 67, 68).

SIXTH ESSAY

The Question of the Church in Dogmatic Polemics with Donatism

The concept of the Church that was first clearly and definitively expressed in the time of St. Cyprian—namely, that the Church is a divine institution for man's increase in moral perfection, and that she alone possesses the grace-filled means essential for this—had been conclusively assimilated and preserved forever in church consciousness.[2110] In this regard the history of this dogma in the proper sense had ceased. St. Cyprian had firmly integrated this particular concept of the Church into church practice, and it may be said that what followed after St. Cyprian is primarily the history of church discipline. Forms of penitential discipline were constantly changing, but behind these changing forms there is always a sense of the invariable fundamental concept of the Church as a hospital for the infirm conscience and in general as the nurturer of the human race. The forms of discipline change in order to best suit this particular purpose of the Church.

2110   It should be noted that for an entire century after his death St. Cyprian enjoyed tremendous respect and had considerable influence on the entire Western Church, his authority ranking very highly indeed. Concerning this see Tillemont, *Memoires*, vol. 4, 185–187; P. Monceaux, *Histoire littéraire de l'afrique chrétienne*, vol. 2, 358–368; Harnack, *Lehrbuch der Dogmengeschichte*, 4-te Aufl. 3 (Tübingen: 1910), 23 and Anm. 2.

By the late third century, in the writings of Eastern Church figures we encounter certain speculations that convey the same dogmatic doctrine concerning the Church that we have seen expressed in particular detail in the works of Western writers, only in different form. Of these speculations we will single out the teaching of **Methodius of Patara** as being the most characteristic of Eastern theology.

In his teaching concerning the Church, St. Methodius proceeds from an allegorical interpretation of the creation of Eve. For him, Adam and Eve are real types of Christ and the Church.[2111] As Eve was created from a rib of Adam as he slept, so also from Jesus Christ, as He lay in the sleep of death, the Holy Spirit proceeded, from Whom the Church was formed. The Church may also be said to be bone of Christ's bone, and flesh of His flesh. For the sake of the Church "the Word, leaving His Father in heaven, came down to be 'joined (προσκολληθησόμενος) to His wife;' and slept in the trance of His passion (ὕπνωσε τὴν ἔκστασιν τοῦ πάθους), and willingly suffered death for her, that He might present the Church to Himself glorious and blameless, having cleansed her by the laver, for the receiving of the spiritual and blessed (τοῦ νοητοῦ καὶ μακαρίου) seed, which is sown by Him who with whispers implants (σπείρει) it in the depths of the mind; and is conceived and formed by the Church, as by a woman, so as to give birth and nourishment to virtue.[2112] For in this way, too, the command, 'Increase and multiply' [see Gen. 1:28] is duly fulfilled, the Church increasing daily in greatness and beauty and multitude (εἰς μέγεθος καὶ κάλλος καὶ πλῆθος), by the union (διὰ σύνερξιν) and communion of the Word."[2113] He likewise descends into each individual person and manifests Himself in moral life. In each person Christ dies again, as it were, and unites him with the whole Church, that in her he might receive certain powers of

---

2111 See Harnack, *Dogmengeschichte* 1, 785, 788. See [the composition] by Methodius, *The Banquet of the Ten Virgins* 3.4, 8 (ANF 6:319; PG 18:72c).

2112 "Ὑποδέχεται δὲ καὶ μορφοῖ δίκην γυναικὸς ἡ Ἐκκλησία εἰς τὸ γεννᾶν τὴν ἀρετὴν καὶ ἐκτρέφειν"

2113 Methodius of Patara, *The Banquet of the Ten Virgins* 3.8 (ANF 6:319; PG 18:73).

grace. Thus all men receive restoration. But that which occurs with each person Christ first accomplished with regard to the Church, and only by becoming a communicant with the Church can each individual person grow spiritually. "Those who are still imperfect and beginning their lessons, are born to salvation, and shaped, as by mothers,[2114] by those who are more perfect, until they are brought forth and regenerated unto the greatness and beauty of virtue; and so these, in their turn making progress, having become a church, assist in labouring for the birth and nurture of other children, accomplishing in the receptacle of the soul, as in a womb, the blameless will of the Word."[2115] It is for this reason that St. Methodius calls the Church a **mother**. The woman of the Apocalypse, who conceived in her womb and cried out from the pangs and torments of childbirth, St. Methodius understands to mean the Church. "The enlightened receive the features, and the image, and the manliness (τοὺς χαρακτῆρας καὶ τὴν ἐκτύπωσιν καὶ τὴν ἀρρενωπίαν) of Christ, the likeness of the form of the Word being stamped upon them, and begotten in them by a true knowledge and faith, so that in each one Christ is spiritually (νοητῶς) born. And, therefore, the Church swells and travails in birth until Christ is formed (μορφωθῇ) in us, so that each of the saints, by partaking of Christ, has been born a christ (χριστός). … Those who were baptized into Christ had been made Christs by communication of the Spirit, the Church contributing here their clearness and transformation into the image of the Word."[2116] For St. Methodius, the Church is the whole assembly of the faithful, but at the same time it possesses special powers that give rebirth to men, and consequently she is properly called the mother of all the faithful.[2117]

2114 In the Russian source, "as in the maternal womb." –*Trans.*

2115 Ibid. 3.8 (ANF 6:320; PG 18:76).

2116 Ibid. 8.8: "Συμβαλλούσης ἐνταῦθα τὴν ἐν τῷ Λόγῳ τράνωσιν αυτῶν καὶ μεταμόρφωσιν τῆς Ἐκκλησίας" (ANF 6:337; PG 18:149b–c). Cf. 8.7: "The Church labours and gives birth to those who are baptized" (ANF 6:337).

2117 Ibid. 3.8: "It is frequently the case that the Scriptures thus call the assembly and mass (το ἄθροισμα καὶ το στῖφος) of believers by the name of the Church, the more perfect in their progress (κατὰ προκοπὴν) being led up to be

In the teaching of St. Methodius we may see the same ideas that had already been developed in the West, except that these ideas receive mystical underpinnings. Only one particularity may be noted: St. Methodius ascribes particular importance to the individual, as is customary in the mystical interpretation of the entire historical mission of the Church.[2118] Given the more external, juridical nature of the questions regarding the Church debated in the West, the individual was naturally passed over, so to speak, and was not a topic of discussion.[2119]

In the fourth century many aspects of church life in the East and West were determined specifically in close connection with the concept of the Church as the nurturer of the human race, who spiritually bears children unto God. The teaching of the great fathers of the East—Sts. Gregory the Theologian and John Chrysostom—on pastoral ministry may be briefly expressed exactly so: pastoral ministry is a the ministry by means of which the Church gives rebirth to sinful men. Here in particular we take note of one of the most important aspects of the overall nurturing work of the Church: **penitential discipline.** This discipline, according to fourth-century

---

the one person and body of the Church" (ANF 6:320; PG 18:73d). Ibid. 8.5: The Church "is certainly, according to the accurate interpretation, our mother ... being a power by herself distinct from her children (ἑτέρα τῶν τέκνων). ... She is the power which is desired to give light (παρωρμημένη φωτίζεσθαι). ... It is the Church whose children shall come to her with all speed after the resurrection, running to her from all quarters" (ANF 6:336; PG 18:145b–c).

2118 Already in St. Methodius Harnack sees the germ of the subjectivisim of the monastic mystic and in general of the contemplative realistic theology of the East (*Dogmengeschichte*[4] 1, 788, 789, 790, and Anm. 1. Cf. Loofs, *Leitfaden der Dogmengeschichte* §30.6d, 229).

2119 Incidentally, already in the very earliest period a doctrine of a mystical relationship between the individual and Christ is encountered even in the works of Western writers, but this doctrine is not linked with the doctrine concerning the Church, as it is in St. Methodius. Concerning this, see Harnack, *Dogmengeschichte*[4] 1, 615, Anm. Cf. 788, Anm. 2. In the works of Origen likewise a person's soul is quite often called the bride of Christ. See *On Prayer* 17 (GrchSch. 3:330; PG 11:472b). Cf. *On Matthew* 17.21: "Νύμφης ψυχῆς γαμουμένης Λόγῳ [a bride, the soul, being wedded to the Word]" (PG 13:1540c); *On the Song of Songs* 4.15 (PG 13:193b).

church doctrine, is specifically intended to **heal** the sinner, not to punish him or to guard the sanctity of the Church. It is this view that is expressed in the most important penitential works of that century—in the epistles of **St. Basil the Great** to Amphilochius, bishop of Iconium, and in the epistle of **St. Gregory of Nyssa** to Letoïus, bishop of Melitene. These epistles, made canonical by the second canon of the Sixth Ecumenical Council, retain their undisputed authority in the Orthodox Church to this day and are included in the Book of Canons. Basil the Great is constantly cited in later penitential literature.[2120]

For the entire penitential discipline of St. Basil the Great, only a single goal is indicated: "to have them rescued from the snare of the Evil One"[2121] and "to annul and destroy sin in all kinds of ways."[2122] St. Basil the Great calls excommunication from the Church by hardly any other name than a "cure."[2123] The letter of Gregory of Nyssa is nothing less than an excellent treatise on pastoral theology. Here St. Gregory calls sin an **illness** and constantly speaks of **curing** sin. "As in the case of bodily treatment the purpose of the art of the physician is to heal the one who is ill, though the kind of care given differs (for the curative method available for each of the diseases has to be suitably chosen with respect to the variety of the ailments); so too, since there is a great variety of affections in the

---

2120   It may be supposed that the penitential nomocanon of the Eastern Church traces its origin back to Basil the Great. Concerning this see Prof. N.A. Zaozersky, *The Nomocanon of John the Faster in its Georgian, Greek, and Slavonic Editions* ("Номоканон Иоанна Постника в его редакциях грузинской, греческой и славянской") (Moscow: 1902), foreword, 64. Prof. A.I. Almazov considers this opinion exaggerated, but he himself nevertheless acknowledges that the compilers of later penitential nomocanons employed the views of Basil the Great. See *The Canonarium of the Monk John: Notes of the Imperial University of Novorossiya* ["Канонарий монаха Иоанна. Записки Императорского Новороссийского университета"] (1907), vol. 109, 143.

2121   Canon 85 of St. Basil the Great, in *The Rudder (Pedalion) of the Metaphorical Ship of the One Holy Catholic and Apostolic Church of the Orthodox Christians,* D. Cummings, trans. (Chicago: Orthodox Christian Educational Society, 1957), 840.

2122   Canon 29 of St. Basil the Great, ibid., 815.

2123   Canon 2 of St. Basil the Great, ibid., 789.

case of a disease of the soul, the curative care will necessarily be of many kinds, and adapted to the disease it is intended to cure."[2124] St. Gregory speaks not only of the curative value of temporary excommunication from the Church, but also of imposing particular acts of penance. "He shall treat the ailment by concentrating his attention upon what is opposed to the disease. I mean that by giving what he has to the indigent, in order that by disposing of what he visibly owns he may cleanse himself of the disease of greediness. But if he possesses nothing, and has only his body, the Apostle bids him to cure such a disease by bodily toil."[2125] Such is the general doctrine on repentance and the significance of penance.[2126]

The system of public repentance was later replaced with the institution of the **Sacrament of Confession,** which gave rise to a whole series of nomocanons connected one way or another with the name of **John the Faster,** patriarch of Constantinople.[2127] These nomocanons are highly characteristic for clarifying the concepts of the Church that had become permanently established in church consciousness. All later nomocanons differ from the canons of St. Basil the Great only in that they are best adapted to curing moral diseases of the individual. The canons of Basil the Great primarily speak of lengthy periods of excommunication from the

---

2124 Canon 1 of St. Gregory of Nyssa, ibid., 866. Cf. canons 4, 6, 8.

2125 Canon 6 of St. Gregory of Nyssa, ibid., 877.

2126 Cf. the teaching on repentance of St. John Chrysostom in his homilies on repentance, on the priesthood, and on the epistle to the Corinthians. In particular see *Works*, vol. 2, 312, 313, 314, 315, 317, 323, 324, 359, 363 [Rus. ed.]. The same is found in the ancient monastic charters, such as the charter of the Tabenna monastic community. See Bishop Theophan, *Ancient Monastic Charters* ["Древние иноческие уставы"] (Moscow: 1882), from 146 on. John of the Ladder depicts repentance entirely as the treatment of one who is gravely ill. Concerning penances, see Smirnov, *The Spiritual Father*, 134–148, particularly 141.

2127 Concerning this nomocanon, see Zaozersky in the foreword to his publication. See also Almazov, *Secret Confession in the Orthodox Eastern Church* ["Тайная исповедь в Православной Восточной Церкви"], vol. 1 (Odessa: 1894); A.S. Pavlov, *The Nomocanon to the Great Book of Needs* ["Номоканон при Большом Требнике"], 2nd ed. (Moscow: 1897), 32–40, 455–491.

Church.[2128] Later nomocanons significantly reduce the periods for which penitents were barred from communion with the Church, but these impose special fasts, prostrations, prayers, and other pious labors on the penitent.[2129] Evaluating this fact from the standpoint of fundamentals, it should be said that church penitential discipline best conformed to that doctrine concerning the Church that had already been clearly expressed in the third century: **the sanctity of the Church lies not in that she does not suffer those who have sinned mortally to remain in her and cuts them off from herself entirely, but in that even those who have fallen into grievous diseases she cures by repentance, imparting to them the grace-filled power of the Holy Spirit for their increase in moral perfection.**

We have briefly indicated how church discipline changed, adapting more and more to the dogmatic doctrine of the sanctity of the Church. Church writers of the time put the question more explicitly, and the answer to it, which had been given since the early third century, receives detailed and extensive argumentation. Here no development of the dogmatic doctrine itself is in evidence. After the time of St. Cyprian, the particular history of the dogma concerning the Church was concentrated in the Western Church and concerned those points that that had barely been touched during the life and work of St. Cyprian and were not fully elucidated at that time: church thought was focused on clarifying **the nature and validity of the grace-filled means of sanctification in the Church.** This question was particularly brought to the fore-

---

2128 It should not however be forgotten that, since the earliest times, temporary excommunication from the Church was always linked in the Church with the performance of certain penitential labors. One need only recall *exomologesis* or *interitus carnis* as understood by Origen.

2129 In the imposition of all these labors the general leniency of the nomocanons is quite marked. After setting forth the rules regarding food the compiler of one early edition of the nomocanon reasons as follows: "I know that for these greatly lenient determinations I will be judged by God, our common Judge, but better for me to be condemned for this than to gain renown for having been unmerciful." (*The Nomocanon*, edition of N.A. Zaozersky and Khakhanov, 69. Cf. the Georgian text, 72.)

front by the schism of the **Donatists** and found its resolution over the course of the conflict with them. The description of this conflict and its dogmatic ramifications is the subject which we now undertake.

The Decian persecution that erupted in St. Cyprian's time quickly passed. But the question of the lapsed arose no less acutely in the last and cruelist persecution of Diocletian in the early fourth century, when even certain of the bishops proved to be among the lapsed. Consequently, in Africa the question arose of whether those guilty of surrendering the sacred books and of apostasy in general could perform the sacraments. At one of the Councils of Carthage, part of the bishops answered this question in the negative, when the ordination of Caecilianus was declared invalid on the grounds that the bishop who had ordained him was suspected of betrayal.[2130] Caecilianus was deposed, and Maiorinus was elected in his place, but the bishops of other provinces were divided, some siding with Caecilianus, others with Maiorinus. A schism resulted, which later came to be called Donatism.[2131] The question that had arisen in the middle of the third century,[2132] as we saw at the end of the preceding essay, now demanded resolution in the beginning of the fourth.

The external history of Donatism is highly tempestuous and complex, but it is of no significance for the history of the dogma

---

2130 This decree is recorded in the anonymous work *Contra Fulgentium Donatistam* 26: "Thurificati, traditores, et qui in schismate a traditoribus ordinantur, manere in Ecclesia Dei non possunt, nisi cognito ululatu suo per poenitentiam reconcilientur. Unde Caeciliano in schismate a traditoribus ordinato non communicare oportet [Those that offered incense, the traitors {i.e. those who handed over the sacred books}, and those that are ordained in schism by traitors cannot remain in the Church of God, unless they be reconciled through repentance, once their lamentation has been approved. Therefore, since Caecilian was ordained in schism by traitors, it behoves not to commune with him {transl. — ED.}]" (PL 43:774).

2131 Donatism is examined from a historical standpoint in the work by N. Kutepov, *The Donatist Schism* ["Раскол донатистов"] (Kazan: 1884), "The Origin of Donatism," 6–16.

2132 A. Harnack, *Der pseudoaugustinische Traktat "Contra Novatianum." Abhandlungen Alexander von Oettingen zum siebzigsten Geburtstag gewidmet von Freunden und Schülern* (München: 1898), 85 ff.

concerning the Church. Significant for this history are the polemical works of church writers directed against the Donatists. We will now undertake to expound the dogmatic doctrine concerning the Church that unfolds in these works.

The writings of the Donatists themselves have been lost, and we can only judge their views from the works of church writers.

In their dogmatic ideas of the Church the Donatists proceeded from a strict concept of the sanctity of the Church and its oneness. By receiving traditors into communion, the Church could not be holy. Traditor bishops could impart no grace; consequently, a Church that had traditor bishops had no sacraments. The personal unworthiness of the bishop deprived the entire Church of grace. Baptism likewise was of no value in the Church, and so one who wished to leave the Church and join the community of the Donatists, which was the one true and holy Church, had to be baptized. It may be noted that the Donatists assimilated several of St. Cyprian's ideas and turned them against the Church.[2133] In their views the Donatists closely resembled the Novatians, who did not recognized the validity of church baptism,[2134] but they differed from other heretics who did not baptize those who converted to them from other heresies, but only received them to communion.[2135] As we know, St. Cyprian wholly equated heretics with schismatics, holding the baptism of both to be invalid. But this view is rather a unique feature of the ecclesiology of St. Cyprian. The Church has always differentiated between heresy and schism, as may be seen for example in the works of St. Irenaeus of Lyons. And by the very terminology that he employs St. Cyprian himself shows that he was aware of the distinction between heresy and schism: the two terms *heresy* and *schism* are often found side by side in his works, and he felt the need to demonstrate what was heretical about the schismatics.[2136] This was the first time the mind of the Church had encoun-

---

2133 Idem, *Dogmengeschichte* 3, 39–41.

2134 Cyprian of Carthage, *Epistles* 73-72.2, "To Jubaianus" (ANF 5:380; CSEL 3.2:779).

2135 Ibid, 74-73.4, "To Pompey" (ANF 5:387; CSEL 3.2: 802).

2136 Concerning this see Harnack, *Dogmengeschichte*⁴ 1, 423–425.

tered a schism like Novatianism, and so the reaction to it was understandably extreme: Novatian baptism was declared invalid. But even Cyprian himself did not firmly treat the question of Novatian baptism on a dogmatic basis, allowing for freedom of local practice. The Donatists however advanced their own dogmatic grounds for this practice: an unworthy person could not impart the sacraments.

At the very outset of Donatism we see conciliar decrees that standardize the treatment of schismatics. The eighth canon of the Council of Arles (314) established that only those heretics who do not confess the Trinity were to be baptized: the African custom of baptizing all who converted to the Church was declared an individual practice that did not merit approval.[2137]

In general, throughout the fourth century we encounter a whole series of conciliar decrees where sacraments performed in schismatic communities are recognized as valid. For example, the First Ecumenical Council issued a decree regarding the Novatians under which their clergy were to be received into the Church with the retention of their rank. "It is fitting for them to confess to this in writing, to wit, that they will agree to and will adhere to the dogmas of the catholic and apostolic Church. That is, that they will hold communion with persons married a second time, and with those who in time of persecution have lapsed from the faith; re-

---

2137 "De Afris autem, quod propria lege sua utantur, ut rebaptizent, placuit ut ad Ecclesiam si aliquis haereticus venerit, interrogent eum Symbolum; et si perviderint eum in Patre et Filio et Spiritu sancto esse baptizatum, manus tantum ei imponatur: quod si interrogatus Symbolum, non responderit Trinitatem, tunc merito baptizetur [But concerning the Africans, as respects that they employ their own proper law to rebaptize, it has been decided that, should any heretic come to the Church, they ask of him the Symbol, and if they see that he was baptized in the Father and the Son and the Holy Spirit, only the hand be laid on him; but if, when asked of the Symbol, he give not the Trinity as his reply, then he is to be deservedly baptized]" (PL 43:787). Here, clearly, those who converted to the Church were required not only to have been baptized in the name of the Trinity, but also to correctly confess the faith in the Trinity in the Symbol of Faith. Only in this latter case were they received without being baptized anew. Cf. Ioh. Ernst, *Dir Ketzertaufangelegenheit in der altchristlichen Kirche nach Cyprian. Forschungen zur christlichen Litteratur und Dogmengeschichte*, herausgeg. von Dr. A. Ehrhard und Dr. I. P. Kirsch. II Band. 4. Heft. (Mainz: 1901), 52–58.

garding whom a length of time has been fixed, and a due season has been set, for their penance. ... Wherever they are the only ones found to have been ordained,[2138] whether in villages or in cities, they shall remain in the same habit (or order)."[2139] Conversely, the baptism and ordination of the followers of Paul of Samosata and the other anti-trinitarians was rejected, even though at baptism they pronounced the baptismal formula invoking the name of the Holy Trinity.[2140] The decree of the Council of Arles was repeated at the Council of Carthage in 348.[2141] At the same council the decree of the First Ecumenical Council on receiving members of a schismatic hierarchy with the retention of their rank was also extended to the Donatists.[2142] The practical aspect of the question of the baptism of heretics is extensively examined by Basil the Great in his letter to Amphilochius, bishop of Iconium. "The older authorities had judged that baptism acceptable which disregarded no point of the faith. Hence they have called some of them heresies, and others schisms, and others again parasynagogues (i.e., conventicles). Heresies is the name applied to those who have broken entirely and have become alienated from the faith itself. Schisms is the name applied to those who on account of ecclesiastical causes and remediable questions have developed a quarrel amongst themselves. ... It therefore seemed best to those who dealt with the subject in the beginning to rule that the attitude of heretics should be set aside entirely; but as for those who have merely split apart as a schism,

---

2138 In the Russian source, "Wherever ... all those found among the clergy prove to have been ordained from them alone..." – *Trans.*

2139 Canon 8 of the First Ecumenical Council, in *The Rudder (Pedalion)*, 176.

2140 Canon 19, ibid. See the commentary on this canon of Ioh. Ernst, *Die Kitzertaufangelegenheit in der altchr. Kirche*, 58–62.

2141 See *Historia Donatistarum:* "Sancitum est illicitas esse rebaptizationes eorum, qui interrogati in Trinitate secundum Evangelii fidem et Apostolorum doctrinam confessi erant ac deinde aqua tincti [It was decreed that unlawful were the rebaptisms of those who, when they had been asked of the faith in the Trinity according to the Gospel and had confessed the doctrine of the Apostles, were again washed in water {transl. —ED.}]" (PL 11:803b).

2142 See "Excerpta ad donatistarum historiam pertinentia. Si hoc paci christianae prodesse visum fuerit, in suis honoribus suscipiantur" (PL 43:809 ad fin.).

they were to be considered as still belonging to the Church (ἔτι ἐκ τῆς Ἐκκλησίας ὄντων)."[2143] St. Basil goes on to say that the question should only arise regarding whom to consider a heretic and whom a schismatic. He knows that St. Cyprian and Firmilian of Caesarea considered even the Cathars heretics, but he himself believes that the Cathars are numbered with the schismatics and that their baptism should be accepted.[2144] At the same time, St. Basil allows for freedom of established variations in practice. The Second Ecumenical Council decreed which erring persons currently reuniting to Orthodoxy and to the portion of the saved were to be accepted through anointing with holy chrism, and whom to receive as the pagans, that is, through baptism.[2145] The decree of the Second Ecumenical Council was later repeated and expanded by the Sixth Ecumenical Council.[2146] This practice is apparently based on a somewhat different dogmatic doctrine concerning the Church's stance on the sacraments than that of St. Cyprian, according to which the Church is the exclusive possessor of grace. As we see from the words of St. Basil the Great, the established practice was based on the idea that schismatics are not entirely estranged from the Church. Only heretics who distorted the very concept of the Triune Godhead are numbered with the pagans.

A scholarly theological elucidation and substantiation of church doctrine on **the correlation between the sacraments and the Church** had to be given. This task was undertaken by those church writers who were destined to conduct the polemics with Donatism. It was these polemics which elucidated the dogmatic bases for the Orthodox practice of the fourth century, and which simultaneously gave definitive expression to certain points of the dogmatic doctrine

---

2143 The Russian source differs markedly, and speaks expressly of baptism. It reads literally: "It therefore seemed best to the fathers who were from the beginning to set aside the baptism of heretics entirely, but to accept the baptism of schismatics, as being not yet estranged from the Church." –*Trans.*

2144 Canon 1 of St. Basil the Great, in *The Rudder (Pedalion)*, 773–774.

2145 Canon 7 of the Second Ecumenical Council, in *The Rudder (Pedalion)*, 217.

2146 Canon 95 of the Second Ecumenical Council, in *The Rudder (Pedalion)*, 400–401.

concerning the Church in general. First and foremost our attention is drawn to the teaching concerning the Church of **Optatus of Milevis.** He presented nearly all the points of the Orthodox doctrine concerning the Church which were later advanced in polemics with the Donatists. Optatus wrote a fairly comprehensive composition in seven books, known by the title of *De schismate donatistarum* (*Against the Donatists*), where he polemicizes with the Donatist bishop Parmenianus, the successor of Donatus.[2147]

In demonstrating the truth of the Church in his polemics against the Donatists, for the first time Optatus clearly and definitively introduces as his chief argument the idea that the true Church must be **ecumenical** in the sense of its outward dispersion. The Church cannot be with heretics and schismatics, because then it would not be ecumenical. If the Church were with the Donatists, it would be limited only to part of Africa, enclosed in one small corner (*in angulo parvae regionis*). The Church would not exist wherever there were no Donatists. The Church would not exist in Spain, in Gaul, in Italy, in Pannonia and Dacia, in Moesia, Thrace, Achaia, Macedonia, and in all of Greece; it would not exist in Pontus, in Galatia, in Cappadocia, in Pamphylia, in Phrygia, in Cilicia, and in the Syrian region; it would not exist in Armenia, in all Egypt and Mesopotamia, and in the innumerable islands and provinces that can hardly be numbered.[2148] This contradicts the concept of the catholicity of the Church.[2149] This limitation of the ecumenical Church is contrary

---

2147 The writing of this work is discussed by Harnack in *Optatus*, Herzog's RE 3, Bd. XIV, 413–414. A detailed description of the polemics between Optatus and Parmenianus is given by Ferdinand Ribbeck in *Donatus und Augustinus oder der erste entscheidende Kampf zwischen Separatismus und Kirche* (Elberfeld: 1857), 160–191.

2148 Optatus of Milevis, *Against the Donatists*, 2.1, in *The Work of St. Optatus, Bishop of Milevis, Against the Donatists*, O.R. Vassall-Phillips, trans. (Longman's, Green, and Co: London, New York, Bombay, Calcutta, and Madras, 1917), book 2, 58–59 (CSEL 26:32–33).

2149 Ibid. 2.1: "Ubi ergo erit proprietas catholici nominis, cum inde dicta sit catholica, quod sit rationabilis et ubique diffusa? [Where in that case will be the application of the Catholic Name, since on this very account was the Church called Catholic, because she is in accordance with reason, and is scattered all over the world?]" (CSEL 26:33.12–14).

to the will of God. Jesus Christ received all nations for His inheritance and all the uttermost parts of the earth for His possession (see Ps. 2:7). All the earth together with all the nations are promised to Christ. This promise is destroyed by the Donatists when they enclose the whole breadth of [these] kingdoms as though in a sort of prison.[2150] "Permit the Son to possess that which has been granted to Him," Optatus exclaims; "permit the Father to fulfill that which He has promised. Why do you put bounds, why set limits?"[2151] In other places likewise Holy Scripture states that the true Church must be expanded to all the ends of the earth. Concerning the Savior Himself it is written: "He shall have dominion from sea to sea, and from the rivers even unto the ends of the inhabited earth" (Ps. 71:8). God gives all lands to Christ without exception, while the Donatists unjustly reduce what was bestowed by the Father, yielding to Christ only a part of Africa and denying Him the whole universe that the Father bestowed upon Him.[2152] Psalm 95 says: "O sing unto the Lord a new song." In order to show that this does not pertain to the Donatists, but to the Church, which is everywhere, the following is added: "sing unto the Lord all the earth. ... Declare among the nations His glory, and among all peoples His wonders" (Ps. 95:1, 3). "Declare among the nations," it is said; and not, "Declare in a small part of Africa, where the Donatists are." "Among all peoples," it is said, excluding no one. But the Donatists alone wish to be the

---

2150 Ibid. 2.1: "Ut quid tale infringitis promissum, ut a vobis mittatur quasi in quemdam carcerem latitudo regnorum? [To what purpose do you break so mighty a promise, so that the breadth of all the kingdoms is compressed by you into a sort of narrow prison?]" (CSEL 26:33.19–21).

2151 Ibid. 2.1 (*Against the Donatists*, 60; CSEL 33.22–24).

2152 Ibid. 2.1: "O vestra ingrata et stulta praesumptio! Christus vos cum ceteris in societatem regni caelestis invitat et coheredes sitis hortatur, et vos cum in hereditate sibi a patre concessa fraudare laboratis, dum Africae partem conceditis et totum terrarum orbem, qui ei a patre donatus est, denegatis [What ingratitude! What folly! What presumption is yours! Christ invites you, with all others, into the company of the Heavenly Kingdom and exhorts you to be coheirs with Him; and you strive to rob Him of the inheritance given Him by the Father, allowing Him a part of Africa and refusing Him the whole world, which the Father has bestowed upon Him]" (*Against the Donatists*, 61; CSEL 34.12–16).

whole, though they have not spread throughout the world. If the
Donatists alone comprise the Church, all the earth must fall silent.
The Donatists must praise the name of the Lord together with the
rest; and if they do not wish to be with the rest, let them alone fall silent.[2153] Thus, Optatus demonstrates that the catholic Church is the
one that is spread throughout the world.[2154] Optatus frequently applies this standard to the community of the Donatists. Parmenianus
called the Church paradise. This is true, Optatus, replies, but "[the
Lord's] garden must be spread far and wide," whereas the Donatists
"deny to Him the Christian peoples of East and North, also those
of all the provinces of the West and of innumerable islands—with
whom [they] share no fellowship of communion—against whom
[they]—few in number and rebels—are ranged, in isolation.[2155] ...
If we are displeasing to you, what wrong has the City of Antioch
done you, or the Province of Arabia?"[2156] The Donatists contradict
themselves when they offer prayers for the one catholic Church:
their Church is not catholic.[2157] Thus, the true Church is the one
"which is contained throughout the entire world" (*quae continetur toto
orbe terrarum*).[2158]

To this argument Optatus adds yet another, one with which we
have long been familiar, which may be called a reference to **the
apostolic origin of the Church.** In it we once again encounter
a list of the bishops of Rome up to and including his contemporary, Siricius, with whom both the Africans and all the world are
in agreement (*cum quo nobiscum totus orbis commercio formatarum, in una*

2153 Ibid. 2.1: "Etiam vos ipsi laudate cum omnibus aut, quia noluistis esse
cum omnibus, soli conticescite [then should you also praise Him, together with
all, or, (since you have refused to be with all,) in your isolation, hold your tongues]"
(*Against the Donatists*, 62–64; CSEL 33.35–36).

2154 Ibid. 2.2: "Eam esse ecclesiam catholicam, quae est intoto terrarum orbe
diffusa" (CSEL 36.4–5). Cf. *Historia Carthaginensis collationis*, Migne (PL 11:1480a).

2155 Ibid. 2.11 (*Against the Donatists*, 90; CSEL 47).

2156 Ibid. 2.12 (*Against the Donatists*, 91; CESL 47.18–19).

2157 Ibid. 2.12: "Unicuique vestrum dicat deus: quid offers pro tota, qui non
es in tota?" (CSEL 47).

2158 Ibid. 2.13 (*Against the Donatists*, 91; CSEL 47.22–23).

communionis societate concordat). And just exactly as did Irenaeus and Tertullian, Optatus exclaims: "Now do you show the origin (*originem reddite*) of your Cathedra, you who wish to claim the Holy Church for yourselves!"[2159]

But the Donatists considered the Church false because it did not meet the requirement of sanctity, since it had fellowship with traditors. Optatus therefore shifts his focus to elucidating the doctrine of the **sanctity** of the Church. First of all he speaks of how man's sanctity in general is relative, citing the words of the apostle John: "If we say that we have no sin, we deceive ourselves, and the truth is not in us" (1 Jn. 1:8). It is inherent in the Christian man to desire what is good, and to strive for that good. But it is not given to man to be perfect, and so there always remains room for God's aid (*restet aliquid Deo, ubi deficienti succurrat*); for Christ the Son of God alone is perfect. All men are half-perfect (*semiperfecti*). Nor did Christ the Savior grant perfection, but only promised it. The Donatists cannot demand perfect sanctity; they themselves are not without sin, and their doctrine is not the truth, but a deception. Why do the Donatists ask for forgiveness of sins in the Lord's prayer, if they are holy? Optatus cites the Lord's parable of the publican and the Pharisee, which was told of those who were confident of themselves that they were righteous and degraded others (see Lk. 18:19–14). The Donatists are like the Pharisee (*quales et vos videmus*); he is their teacher. On top of all this, the Donatists have no lack of grave sins.[2160] In general, throughout his entire work Optatus quite frequently speaks of the faults and the various exceedingly dark sides of the moral life of the Donatists. In the seventh book of his work, written somewhat later, to depict the earthly state of the Church Optatus makes use of a parable long employed in church literature for the

---

2159 Ibid. 2.2–3 (*Against the Donatists*, 65–69; CSEL 36–37). Cf. *Historia Carthaginensis collationis*, Migne (PL 11:1481c–d). Cf. Praef. Balduini (PL 11:1120b–c).

2160 Ibid. 2.20 (*Against the Donatists*, 102–105; CSEL 55–57). Further on (2.21) Optatus lists the crimes of the Donatists, which are so grave that "in comparatione operis vestri latronum levior videtur immanitas [The savagery of highway robbers is seen to be a thing of less account, when compared with the deeds that you have done]" (CSEL 58:13–14). 2.20 is paralleled by 7.2, where the same ideas are repeated (CSEL 168–170).

purpose—the Lord's parable of the field in which there grew both wheat and tares, as they would continue to grow until the day of the Last Judgment. The Lord did not permit the apostles to uproot the tares; consequently the Donatists likewise have no right to do so.[2161] The sin of apostasy or of surrendering the sacred books is not so very great as to completely destroy the sanctity of the Church; the presence of traditors in the Church cannot be considered sufficient grounds to deny her sanctity and to separate from her. Even the apostle Peter denied Christ, yet the other apostles did not expel him from their midst. In persecutions Christians had denied the Lord Whom they had not seen. Peter denied even thrice, but to him the Savior entrusted the keys. The other apostles, themselves being guiltless, could have shut the doors of repentance to him who had lapsed.[2162] Optatus repeats Cyprian's argument that apostasy, being a sin under duress, is not so grave as voluntary sins such as murder or fornication. This must especially be said of the surrendering of sacred books. Even Moses broke the tablets of the law, yet the Lord did not become unmerciful toward Moses. In the Old Testament there is an example of surrendering a sacred book: Baruch gave up the book of the prophet Jeremiah, written at the inspiration of God (see Jer. 36:27), yet God was not moved to anger, and Baruch was not punished. The surrendering of sacred books inflicted no harm upon the Church, since Holy Scripture remained nonetheless. Were it really better that a man be killed than the books surrendered? But here both the people survived and there was no lack of books. The books of the law and God are not the same thing. One may die for God, for He has power both to raise the dead and to grant rewards; but a book not surrendered is capable of neither.[2163]

The Donatists however ascribed such importance to the sin of apostasy that in their opinion a bishop who had stained himself by

---

2161 Ibid. 7.2 (*Against the Donatists,* 279–283; CSEL 169–170).

2162 Ibid. 7.3 (*Against the Donatists,* 283–289; CSEL 171–173). Cf. 4.4 (CSEL 106.16 sqq.).

2163 (PL 11:1098, 1099, 1100, 1101, 1102 passim). At the same time, it should be noted that the publishers do not consider the latter arguments to belong to Optatus (see 1097c–1098a). In his edition Carolus Ziwsa omits them entirely.

this sin could not impart any grace, and the sacraments performed by him were invalid. Consequently, the Donatists baptised catholics who came to them. Outside the Donatist community there was no grace and there were no sacraments; in this heretics and schismatics were perfectly equal. To be sure, St. Cyprian likewise defended this position, as we have seen, but there is also a dogmatic distinction. St. Cyprian based his claim that those outside the Church had no grace specifically on their contradiction of and enmity with the Church. The Donatists denied grace in the Church because she had traditors even among her hierarchy, and consequently she was not holy.[2164]

In the process of thoroughly refuting all these points of the Donatist doctrine, Optatus expounds his own concept of the sanctity of the Church, to which the presence of those who had sinned gravely even among the hierarchy would be no contradiction. The Donatists deny baptism performed by traditors, and they inseparably link the validity of the sacrament with the person of its performer. But this criterion for sacramental validity cannot be accepted. Using the historical method, Optatus establishes that at the outset of Donatism it too had traditor bishops.[2165] Consequently, the validity of all baptism must be denied. If a traditor cannot baptize, the Donatists also cannot baptize, since it has been proven that traditors were among the founders of Donatism. In general, if baptism performed by a sinner is invalid, no baptism exists whatsoever, since the Word of God attests that all men are sinners;[2166] and the Donatists, who are guilty of many grave transgressions, are no exception.[2167]

In proof of their position that the sacrament is invalid unless the person who performs it is holy, the Donatists cited several passages from Holy Scripture, such as: "As for the oil of the sinner, let it not

---

2164 Ibid. 2.9: "Dixisti enim, quod, si sacerdos in peccato sit, solae possint dotes operari [for you have maintained that, if the priest be in sin, the Endowments are able to work alone]" (CSEL 26:45).

2165 Ibid. 1.13 (CSEL 15–16). Cf. 1.28 (CSEL 30–31).

2166 Ibid. 1.5 (CSEL 8:11 sqq.).

2167 This is demonstrated in detail in *Against the Donatists* 4.5–8 (CSEL 104–114).

anoint my head" (Ps. 140:6). To the church hierarchy they applied
the words of the prophet Jeremiah concerning waterless cisterns
(see Jer. 2:13). Optatus analyzes these passages of Holy Scripture
in detail, showing that they could not have the meaning attributed
to them by the Donatists.[2168] On the contrary, these words speak
against the Donatists themselves.[2169] In contrast to the Donatists,
Optatus advances and substantiates his teaching that the sanctifying
power of the sacraments is independent of the moral qualities of
those who perform them. The validity of baptism depends not on
a place or a person, but on the Trinity—such is Optatus's general thesis.[2170] According to the Donatist's teaching, the name of the
Holy Trinity is of no significance where there is no worthy minister
of the sacrament.[2171] But Optatus teaches otherwise. God acts with
the Son and the Holy Spirit even where the human person is absent. In the book of Genesis we read that the waters brought forth
every living creature, and this was of course through the action of
the Holy Trinity. There was no fourth party, nor were there any
Donatists. "If then it be not allowed to the Trinity to do anything
without you," Optatus says with irony, "call back the fishes to their
first beginning (*in originem*); if in your absence the Trinity may not
effect anything, drown in the waters the birds as they fly."[2172] "Christ
[said]: 'He who has once been washed, has no need of being washed
again, for he is altogether clean' [see Jn. 13:10]. And thus did He
make His declaration concerning that washing which he had commanded to be done through the Trinity—not concerning that of
Jews or heretics, who, whilst they wash, defile, but concerning the

---

2168 *Against the Donatists* 4.7, 9 (CSEL 112–116).

2169 Ibid. 4.9 (CSEL 117).

2170 Ibid. 5.1: "Aqua sola et vera ilia est, quae non de loco, non de persona
sed de trinitate condita est [That water alone is true which has been sanctified
not from any place, nor by any {human} person, but by the Trinity]" (CSEL
120.20–22).

2171 Ibid. 5.2: "Dicilis enim trinitatem pro nihilo haberi, ubi non interfuerit
vestra praesentia [You say that the Trinity counts for nothing, unless you be pres-
ent]" (CSEL 122.3–4).

2172 Ibid. 5.2 (CSEL 122).

holy water which flows from the fountains of the Three Names. For thus the Lord Himself commanded, when He said: 'Go, baptise all nations in the Name of the Father and of the Son and of the Holy Ghost' [see Mt. 28:19]. This was the washing of which He said: 'He that has been washed once has no need of being washed a second time.'[2173] In saying *once* He forbade it to be done again, and spoke of the thing, not of the person. For if there had been a difference [to be considered between persons], He would have said: 'He that has been rightly washed once,' but by not adding the word *rightly*, He points out that whatever has been done in the [Name of the] Trinity is done rightly."[2174] Thoroughly analyzing the Sacrament of Baptism, Optatus reasons as follows. "In the celebration of this Sacrament of Baptism there are three elements. ... The first is in the Trinity, the second in the believer [who is baptized], the third in him who operates. But they must not all be weighed by the same measure. For I perceive that two are necessary, and that one is quasi-necessary (*quasi necessariam*). The Trinity holds the chief place, without whom the work itself cannot be done. The faith of the believer follows next." But the person of the minister of the baptism is something external (*vicina*), and is not of equal authority. The Holy Trinity and the faith "remain always unchangeable and ... always preserve their own efficacy." Consequently, "the office of the minister cannot be equal to the other two elements ... because it alone is liable to change." By judging themselves holy, the Donatists "do not hesitate to place [their] pride higher than the Trinity, although the person of the 'Minister' can be changed, but the Trinity cannot be changed." Different people baptize from one day to the next; the sacrament cannot be dependent on the person of its minister, because it cannot be changeable (*sacramenta mutari non possunt*). Consequently, all who baptize are merely the laborers, not the stewards or lords (*operarios esse, non dominos*).[2175] Optatus then firmly declares

---

2173 This sentence is omitted in the Russian source, apparently inadvertently. *—Trans.*

2174 Ibid. 5.3 (*Against the Donatists* 213–214; CSEL 124.12–125.5).

2175 Ibid. 5.4 (*Against the Donatists* 217–219; CSEL 126–127). Cf. 5.7 (CSEL 133 sqq.); 5.3: "Nos docuimus caeleste munus unicuique credenti a trinitate con-

his chief thesis: "The Sacraments are holy through themselves, not through men."[2176]

In linking the efficacy of the sacrament to the person of its minister, the Donatists were refuting the opinion of the catholics and demonstrating the invalidity of baptisms performed by their hierarchy: "How can he give, who has not anything to give?" This argument, which we have also encountered from St. Cyprian, Optatus thoroughly analyzes and refutes. "It is the Lord who is the giver ... it is God who cleanses each man, whoever he may be; for no one can wash away the defilement and stains of the mind (*mentis*), but God alone, who is also the Maker of the mind. Or, if you think," he says to the Donatists, "that it is your washing [that cleanses], tell us what is the nature of this mind, which is washed through the body, or what 'form' it has, or in what part of a man it dwells. To know this has not been granted to any. How, then, do you think that it is you who cleanse, when you do not know the nature of that which you cleanse? It belongs not to man, but to God to cleanse. ... Through the Prophet Isaiah ... He said: 'Even though your sins are like scarlet, I will make you white as snow' [Is. 1:18]. ... If this has been promised by God, why do you wish to give that which it is not permitted to you either to promise, or to give, or to have? ... God has promised Himself to wash those stained by sin, not through a man."[2177] If the Donatists claim that with them it is the minister who bestows all the gifts in the sacrament, this means that with them those baptized are immersed in the name of the minister. But this is not what the apostle Paul says (see 1 Cor. 1:13).[2178] The Donatists asserted that the gift of baptism belongs to the giver, not to the receiver. This is correct if by this they mean God, but a man cannot be considered the giver. Optatus cites the following example. Suppose

---

ferri, non ab homine [we have taught that the heavenly gift is bestowed upon every believer by the Trinity, not by man]" (CSEL 122.22–23).

2176 Ibid. 5.4: "Sacramenta per se esse sancta, non per homines [the Sacraments are holy through themselves, not through men]" (*Against the Donatists* 220; CSEL 127.16).

2177 Ibid. 5.4 (*Against the Donatists* 221–223; CSEL 128.8–129.1).

2178 Ibid. 5.6 (*Against the Donatists* 229; CSEL 132–133).

the Donatists, who consider themselves holy, baptize a non-believer, and the catholics, whom the Donatists call sinners, baptize a believer. The question is, which of the two baptized receives the grace of God? Naturally, it is the one who believes. As a dyer of cloth (*artifex purpurae*) cannot say that he dyes without the aid of valuable dyes, by the touch of his hands alone, so also the minister of the baptism cannot impart anything without the Holy Trinity. Everyone who baptizes in the name of the Father, the Son, and the Holy Spirit performs the work of the apostles. For to the apostles it was commanded that the performance of the sacrament (*opus*) would be [from them], but the sanctification would be from the Trinity; and they did not immerse in their own name, but in the name of the Father, and of the Son, and of the Holy Spirit. Consequently, it is the name that sanctifies, and not the performance of the sacrament. If the Church is a vineyard, men are the vines,[2179] and those duly appointed are the vinedressers. And indeed the apostle Paul ascribes all things to God, not to men (see 1 Cor. 3:7). The minister of the sacrament must not ascribe to himself what belongs to God; this would be wrong. The significance of the minister is very limited: he is but a servant. "Thanks must be rendered, not to those who serve,[2180] but to Him who provides the repast." In his humility, the apostle calls others servants together with himself. That none might think that he ought to place his hope in apostles or bishops alone, Paul said, "For what is Paul, or what Apollos? Surely the ministers of Him, in whom ye have believed?" (1 Cor. 3:5).[2181] All members of the hierarchy have not dominion, but service (*non dominium, sed ministerium*).[2182] Grace is bestowed by God Himself, according to the

---

2179 In the Russian source, "vinedressers." —*Trans.*

2180 That is, at a banquet. —*Trans.*

2181 Optatus alone understands this verse in this way: "Ministri ejus, in quem credidistis." Some Latin codices read, "Ministri ejus cui" (Tischendorf, *Novum Testamentum graece*[8] 2, 471). The Greek text has a somewhat different meaning: "Διάκονοι, δι᾽ ὧν ἐπιστεύσατε [ministers by whom ye believed]."

2182 Ibid. 5.7 (*Against the Donatists* 231–236; CSEL 133–137 passim). And the conclusion: "Vides ergo iam, frater Parmeniane, ex tribus speciebus supra memoratis illam primo tripartitam esse inmotam, invictam et inmutabilem, operantis vero temporariam esse personam [Now, therefore, my brother Parmenian, you

faith of the receiver. Optatus expounds on the significance of faith, and on how one must have it to receive grace, in his interpretation of Christ's miraculous healing of the woman with an issue of blood (see Mt. 9:20–22, Lk. 8:43–48) and the servant of the centurion in Capernaum (see Mt. 8:5–13).[2183]

Thus, at baptism, when the Most Holy Trinity is "met by faith ... he who had once been born to the world may ... be spiritually new-born to God." The Father of men is God, their mother is the holy Church, and the minister (*operarius*) of the sacrament, being a man, claims nothing for himself, as do the Donatists.[2184] The Church possesses the sanctifying gifts of the Spirit, regardless of the worthiness of the members of the hierarchy, and these members are only ministers of the Church at the distribution of her gifts of grace.[2185] The Church possesses all these gifts together, because they are inseparable from one another.[2186] Here Optatus arrives at his definition of the sanctity of the Church. In their pride the Donatists ascribe to themselves a special sanctity (*speciales sanotitatem*), and they set this sanctity as the basis of the sanctity of the Church itself.[2187] The church writers, as Optatus has already shown, did not share this rather unstable principle of the Donatists. The sacraments are

---

see that of the three elements which I have mentioned above, the one which is threefold comes first, is immovable, is supreme and unchangeable, but that the person of any individual minister remains only for a time]" (CSEL 137.4–7).

2183 Ibid. 5.6 (*Against the Donatists* 237–240; CSEL 132–133).

2184 Ibid. 2.10 (*Against the Donatists* 88–89; CSEL 46.5–10).

2185 Ibid. 2.9: "Hujus sanctae ecclesiae est constituta persona et hanc esse catholicam, quae sit in toto orbe terrarum diffusa, cujus membra et nos inter alios sumus, cujus dotes apud illam ubique sunt [of this Holy Church there has been constituted a person {or representative}, and that the Catholic Church is the Church which is scattered over the whole world (of which we amongst others are members), and that her Endowments are with her everywhere]" (CSEL 45.17–20).

2186 Ibid. 2.5: "Quos constat ita sibi connexas et individuas esse, ut intellegatur unam ab altera separari non posse [{these Endowments} are connected one with another, and are distinct, but in such a way, that it may be understood that one cannot be separated from another]" (CSEL 42.11–12).

2187 Ibid. 2.1 (CSEL 32–33).

not dependent on the person of the priest: **they are holy in their own right.** Likewise, the sanctity of the Church is not dependent on the sanctity of its members: on the contrary, the members of the Church themselves receive sanctity from the Church. **The Church is one, and her sanctity lies in the sacraments**, and not in the pride of individual persons.[2188] These last brief words decisively express a formula for the sanctity of the Church, the absence of which had engendered numerous misunderstandings and errors in the Church in the early centuries. The question always remained: how was the sanctity of the Church to be reconciled with the inevitable moral defects of its members? The requirement of a holy life could only ever be relative. And when the very sanctity of the Church was made conditional on this requirement alone, the untenability of this resolution to the matter became obvious. From the beginning the Church had received into communion even those who had gravely sinned, aware of her mission to nurture mankind. A whole series of rigorists accused her of violating sanctity, until finally in the fourth century the ecclesiastical doctrine of the sanctity of the Church was formed, according to which the sinfulness of members of the Church has absolutely nothing to do with the sanctity of the Church itself. It is this doctrine that is the dogmatic product of the conflict with Donatism.[2189]

By especially closely linking the validity of baptism with the confession of the Most Holy Trinity, Optatus was thereby compelled to recognize the validity of schismatic baptism as well, which was in full accord with established church practice. Optatus is in full agreement with his opponent on the fact that the Church is

---

2188 Ibid. 2.1: "Ecclesia una est, cujus sanctitas de sacramentis colligitur, non de superbia personarum ponderatur: ergo hanc unam columbam et dilectam sponsam suam Christus appellat [The Church, then, is One, and her holiness is not measured by the pride of individuals, but is derived from the Sacraments. It is for this reason that she alone is called by Christ His Dove and His own beloved Bride]" (CSEL 32.9–10). Cf. the observations of Harnack, *Optatus*, RE 3, Bd. 14, 415; *Dogmengeschichte*[4] 3, 45.

2189 Vgl. Harnack, *Dogmengeschichte*[4] 3, 41.

one,[2190] the bride of the one Christ,[2191] but he emphatically protests against confusing heretics and schismatics: between the two there is a great difference.[2192] Heretics have rejected the truth and distorted the very symbol of faith (*falsaverunt symbolum*): some say there are two Gods, others wish to see the Father in the person of the Son,[2193] and so on. Consequently, heretics are strangers to the sacraments of the Church;[2194] they have neither the sacraments nor the other gifts of the Church;[2195] their baptism is false; he who is not clean cannot make clean.[2196]

Not at all so the schismatics. They have much in common with the Church; chiefly, they are of one faith with the Church. They have preserved much, because they came out of the Church.[2197]

2190 *Against the Donatists* 1.5, 6, 7 (CSEL 7.15; 9.2, 10–11).

2191 Ibid. 1.10, 2.1 (CSEL 11.21; 32.10).

2192 Ibid. 1.10: "Paeniteat te talibus hominibus (sc. haereticis) etiam schismaticos adjunxisse ... et non attendisti. inter schismaticos et haereticos quam sit magna distantia [Wherefore you should regret that you have coupled schismatics with such men as these {heretics} and... you failed to observe how wide is the gulf between schismatics and heretics]" (CSEL 13, 14 sqq.).

2193 Ibid. 1.10 (CSEL 13.9 sqq.). Cf. 2.8: "Soli sigillum integrum? Id est symbolum catholicum, non habentes [as they alone do not possess the seal, that is to say the Catholic Creed, in its integrity]" (CSEL 44.14–15). 4.8: "Ubi in exterminium fidei corrupta sunt semina [where the very seeds have been corrupted to the destruction of the Faith]" (CSEL 114.10–11). 5.1 (CSEL 121); 1.12: "Haeretici ... veritatis exules, sani et verissimi symboli desertores, de sinu sanctae ecclesiae impiis sensibus depravati [But heretics, exiles from the truth, deserters of the sound and most true Creed, corrupted by their wicked opinions and led astray from the bosom of Holy Church]" (CSEL 14.8–10).

2194 *Against the Donatists* 1.5: "Extraneos esse catholicis sacramentis [strangers to Catholic Sacraments]" (CSEL 7.13); cf. 1.10 (CSEL 11.17–20).

2195 Ibid. 1.10: "Scimus enim haereticorum ecclesias singulorum prostitutas nullis legalibus sacramentis et in se jure honesti matrimonii esse [for we know that the churches of each of the heretics have no lawful Sacraments, since they are adulteresses, without the rights of honest wedlock]" (CSEL 11.18–20).

2196 Ibid. 1.12: "Haereticos ... solos habere varia [alternate reading; *vana*] et falsa baptismata etc. [heretics only... possess various kinds of false {*alternate reading:* vain and false} Baptisms]" (CSEL 14.15 sqq.).

2197 Ibid. 3.9: "Nobis et vobis ecclesiastica una est conversatio, et si hominum

Consequently, schismatic sacraments cannot be denied, even though the schismatics are outside the one ecumenical Church.[2198] The conditions for full unity with the Church are oneness of faith, one true Symbol of Faith, and oneness of mind.[2199] Schismatics lack the latter. "Schism, after the bond of peace has been broken, is brought into existence through passion,[2200] is nourished by hatred, is strengthened by envy and dissensions, so that the Catholic Mother is abandoned, whilst her unfilial (*impii*) children go forth outside and separate themselves … from the root of Mother Church—cut off by the shears of their hatred—and wickedly depart in rebellion. They are not able, however, to do anything new, or different from

---

litigant mentes, non litigant sacramenta … pares credimus et uno sigillo signati sumus necaliter baptizati quam vos, testamentum divinum pariter legimus, unum deum pariter rogamus, oratio dominica apud nos et apud vos una est [you and we have one ecclesiastical discipline, and if men's minds are at war, the Sacraments are not at war… Together we believe the same truths, and have been sealed with one Seal, nor have we been baptised otherwise than you; in like manner we read the divine Testament; in like manner together we worship one God; the Prayer of the Lord is one with you and with us]" (CSEL 93.20–94.3). Cf. 5.1: "Pro utrisque illud est, quod et nobis et vobis commune est, ideo et vobis, quia ex nobis existis, denique et apud vos et apud nos una est ecclesiastica conversatio, communes lectiones, eadem fides, ipsa fidei sacramenta, eadem mysteria [Whatever we share with you is in favour of both. For this reason does it favour you, because from us you went out. Thus, for example, you and we have one ecclesiastical discipline, we read from the same Scriptures, we possess the same Faith, the same Sacraments of Faith, the same Mysteries]" (CSEL 121.13–17).

2198 Ibid. 1.12: "Vobis vero schismaticis, quamvis in catholica non sitis, haec negari non possunt, quia nobiscum vera et communia sacramenta traxistis [But to you schismatics, although you are not in the Catholic Church, these things cannot be denied, since you have shared true Sacraments with us.]" (CSEL 14.22–15.1). For more detail on Optatus's views on baptism outside the Church in relation to baptism in general, see Ernst, *Die Ketzertaufangelegenheit in der altchr. Kirche*, 43–52.

2199 Ibid. 1.11: "Catholicam facit simplex et verus intellectus intellegere, singulare ac verissimum sacramentum et unitas animorum [The Catholic {Church} is constituted by a simple and true understanding <in the law>, by an unique and most true mystery, and by unity of minds]" (CSEL 13.20–21; cf. PL 11:905d1–906b–c, n15–17).

2200 In the Russian source, "through difference of opinion." –*Trans.*

that which long ago they learned from their Mother."[2201] Optatus
viewed the Donatists with considerable leniency. From the very
beginning of his work he calls Parmenianus his brother and justifies his behavior. Citing Is. 66:5, he says that one cannot refuse to
call brethren those who cannot be brethren. They are brethren,
though not good brethren. For even Ham, although he mocked his
father's nakedness, was nevertheless brother to the innocent Shem
and Japheth.[2202] Schismatics likewise, if they are of one confession
with the Church, are brethren to the members of the latter.[2203] The
Donatists' separation from the Church is not an absolute falling
away from her.[2204] They even comprise a Church of sorts, but not
the catholic Church.[2205] At the same time, however, Optatus says
quite decisively that they do not belong to the Church, that they
are outside of her,[2206] that they are merely usurping the name of
the Church.[2207] Optatus asserts that schism is a great and grievous
sin akin to treachery, and even *summum malum* [the highest evil].[2208]
Schism is abhorrent to God;[2209] it causes Him inconsolable tears.[2210]
He who was unwilling to remain with his brethren in the Church
has followed the heretics, and gone forth as an antichrist.[2211] Optatus is inclined to deny that the Donatists have a valid life of grace:

2201 Ibid. 1.11 (*Against the Donatists* 23; CSEL 14.1–7).

2202 Ibid. 1.3 (CSEL 4–5).

2203 Ibid. 1.2 (CSEL 4). Cf. 4.2 (CSEL 102–103).

2204 Ibid. 3.9: "In parte vestis adhuc unum sumus, sed, in diversa pendemus,
quod enim scissum est, ex parte divisum est, non ex toto [In part of the garment
we are still one, but we hang on different sides. For that which has been rent has
been partly divided, not totally]" (CSEL 93.17–19).

2205 Ibid. 3.10: "pars vestra quasi ecclesia est, sed catholica non est [So your
party is a quasi-church, but is not the Catholic Church]" (CSEL 95.21–22).

2206 Ibid. 1.12 (CSEL 14.14–15, 22–23).

2207 Ibid. 1.21 (CSEL 25.5–7).

2208 Ibid. 1.21 (CSEL 22–23, 23.6). In 7.4 Optatus even calls the guilt of the
Donatists blasphemy against the Holy Spirit (see 176).

2209 Ibid. 1.21, 7.1 (CSEL 24.6, 159.6).

2210 Ibid. 1.2 (CSEL 4.3–4).

2211 Ibid. 1.15 (CSEL 18.9–11).

he compares them to branches broken off from a tree, and to shoots of a grape vine that have been cut off: they are "a river separated from its source."[2212]

In Optatus's arguments one cannot help but note a certain instability and incompleteness. He alternately holds that schismatics have left the Church and are outside the Church, but then says that their separation is not a complete falling away. The question therefore very appropriately arises: if the sacraments are valid even in schismatic communities, is not salvation possible outside the Church and even while at enmity with her? Or perhaps, even if the sacraments are valid outside the Church, salvation is only in the Church? But then why are the sacraments of no benefit outside the Church, even though they are valid? To all these questions Optatus has no answer. His clear and definite arguments that the sacraments are holy, independently of the person who performs them, were adopted by the blessed Augustine, who also gave answers to all the questions posed.

The new concept of the sanctity of the Church reaches its full development, substantiation, and elucidation in the work of one of the greatest church writers of the West: **the blessed Augustine.**

The blessed Augustine[2213] was the most prominent contender against Donatism: he contended both orally, speaking at public debates, [and] wrote numerous works refuting Donatism. There was hardly a single phenomenon in the history of the relations between the Church and donatism that did not find its reflection in the numerous theological works of Augustine. Not a single work of the Donatist authors, both contemporary and even those already dead,

---

2212 Ibid. 2.9 (CSEL 45.2–4).

2213 Of the immeasurable body of scholarly literature devoted to the blessed Augustine we primarily employ new, specialized works: Dr. Thomas Specht, *Die Lehre von der Kirche nach dem hl. Augustia* (Paderborn: 1892); P. Capistran Romeis, *Das Heil des Christen ausserhalb der wahren Kirche nach der Lehre des hl. Augustin. Forschungen zur Christlichen Literatur und Dogmengeschichte, herausgeg. von Dr. A. Ehrhard und Dr. I. P. Kirsch,* VIII Band, 4. Heft. (Paderborn: 1908); Vladimir Gerye, *The Builders and Laborers of "The Kingdom of God"* ["Зодчие и подвижники «Божьего Царства»"], part 1: "The Blessed Augustine" ["Блаженный Августин"] (Moscow: 1910).

did he leave unrefuted. Augustine personally polemicized against the Donatist bishops, addressing them in letters, receiving refutations of his own writings in response, and responding to these again with entire books. Finally, [he] briefly expounded the chief ideas of his polemics in the vernacular and even in verse to make them easier to assimilate.[2214]

At times the rather expansive writings of the blessed Augustine against the Donatists are filled with dogmatic reasoning about the Church, and are distinguished by an overwhelming abundance of argumentation.[2215] But since the blessed Augustine had occasion to conduct polemics with various persons regarding the same matters, it is quite logical that in his works one encounters constant almost verbatim repetitions of the same ideas, the same arguments. We shall attempt to present the chief points of the blessed Augustine's dogmatic teaching concerning the Church, while passing over the details of his argumentation.[2216]

In refutation of the Donatist opinion that their community alone comprised the true Church, like Optatus the blessed Augustine says that a sure token of the true Church is its ecumenical nature. The

---

2214 We think it unnecessary to describe the external history of the blessed Augustine's polemics with the Donatists, especially since this history is thoroughly presented in the specialized work of N. Kutepov, *The Donatist Schism*, from page 85 on, and also Vladimir Gerye's "The Blessed Augustine," from 482 on.

2215 We cannot fail to note that the polemics with Donatism bore a vivid dogmatic imprint. From this it may be seen that at the heart of Donatism itself there lay religious and dogmatic interests, and Gerye shows himself to be a tendential historian in depicting Donatism ("The Blessed Augustine," from 437 on) as "a standard who gathered around itself the local elements that opposed Rome and its civilization" (477). Concerning this matter see the reasoning of Prof. A.A. Spassky (*Bogoslovsky Vestnik* [1901] 3, 189–194) and N.N. Glubokovsky ("The Blessed Augustine as Depicted by a Russian Secular Historian" ["Блаженный Августин в изображении русского светского историка"], in *Works of the Kiev Theological Academy* ["Труды Киевской духовной академии"] (1911) 1, 133–136.

2216 The polemical writings of the blessed Augustine are presented in greater detail in the book by V.Z. Belolikov, *The Literary Work of the Blessed Augustine in Opposition to the Schism of the Donatists* ["Литературная деятельность блаженного Августина против раскола донатистов"] (Kiev: 1912).

Donatists also called their community the catholic Church. They taught that the catholicity of the Church is not its territorial ubiquity, but fullness of doctrine and fullness of the sacraments.[2217] Augustine accepts this understanding of the term *catholic* also,[2218] but he insists primarily that **the true Church must be ecumenical, and must extend throughout the whole world.** According to Augustine, catholicity in the sense of dissemination throughout the world is a token of the true Church of Christ, in contrast to heresy or schism. The society of the Donatists lacks this ecumenical quality; ergo, it is not the Church. That the true church must be ecumenical is clear from the very fact that she is termed "catholic." The Greek word καθ' ὅλον means "universal."[2219] In his composition *De unitate Ecclesiae* the blessed Augustine devotes the greater part of the text to proofs of the need for the Church to be ecumenical. To this end he cites a series of proofs, primarily from the Old Testament, in which he sees either prefigurations or prophecies of the ecumenical Church of the New Testament. Here Augustine does not omit a single proof that could in any way be applied to the Church and that could demonstrate the need for it to be ecumeni-

---

2217 Augustine, *Breviculus Collationis cum Donatistis* 3.3.3: "Donatistae responderunt, non catholicum nomen ex universitate gentium, sed ex plenitudine Sacramentorum institutum [The Donatists respond that the catholic name was established not from the the the entirety of the nations but from the fullness of the revelation]" (PL 43:624). *Letters* 93.7.23: "Catholicae nomen non ex totius orbis communione interpretaris, sed ex observatione praeceptorum omnium divinorum, atque omnium Sacramentorum [...you affirm the name Catholic to mean universal, not in respect to the communion as embracing the whole world, but in respect to the observance of all Divine precepts and of all the sacraments]" (PL 33:333).

2218 Augustine, *Letters* 93.7.23 (PL 33:333).

2219 Augustine, *De unitate Ecclesiae* 2: "Quae utique una est, quam majores nostri Catholicam nominarunt, ut ex ipso nomine ostenderent, quia per totum est. Secundum totum enim, καθ' ὅλον graece dicitur [At any rate, it is one, which our elders called Catholic, as they show from the name itself, since it is for the whole. For according to the whole, it is called καθ' ὅλον in Greek]" (PL 43:392). Cf. *Contra litteras Petiliani* 2.38.91 (PL 43:292). *Letters* 52.1 (PL 33:194). *Contra Gaudentius* 2.2.2 (PL 43:741).

cal.[2220] For Augustine, nearly every page of Scripture declares that the Church must disperse throughout the world.[2221] Having founded the Church, Christ sent the apostles to preach His name to the ends of the earth.[2222] Augustine applies the Old Testament prophecies to the Church, finding confirmation of his views in the New Testament Scriptures and disputing the interpretation of the Donatists. These prophecies and the Savior's command came to pass when the Church first came into existence. Augustine breaks down the first two chapters of the Acts of the Apostles,[2223] showing how after the Church was established in Jerusalem it began to spread throughout the world. The history of the subsequent spread of Christianity likewise shows how even in apostolic times the Church strove to realize its ecumenical nature. This nature of the Church was particularly revealed to the apostle Peter in the vision in which he beheld a vessel descending from heaven, knitted at the four corners (see Acts 10:11–12). This vessel signified the whole world and its nations. The four cords with which the vessel was knitted signified the four ends of the world.[2224] The apostles founded Churches to the ends of the earth, and all these Churches comprise the one ecumenical

---

2220 In particular the following passages from the Old Testament are cited: Judg. 6:36–40; Gen. 22:16–18, 26:1–5, 28:10–15; Is. 11:9–10, 41:4–5, 42:1–4, 49:4–23, 52:9–10, 53:11–12, 62:1–4, 64:1–5; Ps. 2:7–8, 21:28–29, 18:5, 56:5–6, 71, etc. (PL 43:398 sqq.). Cf. *Contra ep. Parmeniani* 1.2 (PL 43:35–36); *Contra Crescentium* 3.64.72, 65.73 (PL 43:535–538); *Epistulae* 140.17, 43 (PL 33:556); *Epistulae* 208.6 (PL 33:952).

2221 Augustine, *Sermones* 46.14, 33 (PL 38:289); *In psalmus* 147.6 (PL 37:1924–1925).

2222 Lk. 24:46–47; Acts 1:1–8, 9, 15; Rom. 15:16; *De unitate Ecclesiae* 10–11 (PL 43:408 sqq.).

2223 Augustine, *De unitate Ecclesiae* 11.29 (PL 43:411–412). Cf. *In ep. Iohannem tractatus* 2.2–3 (PL 35:1989–1991).

2224 Ibid., *De unitate Ecclesiae* 11.30: "Iam cui non appareat, illo vase significatum orbem terrarum, cum omnibus gentibus? Unde etiam quatuor initias erat alligatum, propter notissimas quatuor partes, Orientem et Occidentem, Austrum et Aquilonem, quas saepissime Scriptura commendat [Now, to whom does it not appear that in that vessel the world is signified with all the nations? It was bound at the four corners because of the known parts of the globe, East and West, South and North, which Scripture mentions so often]" (PL 43:413).

Church, disseminated throughout the inhabited earth. Even if we suppose that the African Churches were guilty of some offense, this does not yet give the Donatists grounds to break off communion with the other Churches: these Churches did not perish through the crime of the Africans (*criminibus Afrorum*). All the Churches to which the apostle Paul wrote his epistles exist to this day. The Donatists have only the epistles of the apostle, while the Church of Africa maintains communion with the Churches themselves. The Churches to which the apostles Peter and John wrote likewise exist. Perhaps the Donatasts do not even know where a given Church is to be found; yet in their blindness (*caecitate*) they condemn Churches that they know not.[2225] But unity with all the Churches is the token of belonging to the true ecumenical Church.[2226] Consequently, Augustine frequently refers to every local Church as "catholic."[2227]

2225 Ibid. 12.31: "Cognoscite ergo etiam quam longe ab Africa remotae sunt, et dicite nobis cur eas omnino vobis incognitas, et in apostolicis Litteris manifestatas, tam sacrilega temeritate accusetis et tanta dementia criminibus Afrorum periisse dicatis? [Understand therefore how far removed they are from Africa and tell us why with sacrilegious boldness you find fault with them which are altogether unknown to you and manifested in apostolic epistles and why you say with such madness that they perished from the crimes of Africans]" (PL 43:414–415). *Epistulae* 87.2 (PL 33:297).

2226 After this Augustine continues with an analysis of the numerous testimonies from Holy Scripture which the Donatists artfully interpreted and cited as proof that although their society is not ecumenical in nature, it is nevertheless the true Church (PL 43:416 sqq.). Cf. *Contra Cresconium* 3.35, 39 (PL 43:517). Concerning the ecumenical nature of the Church in contrast to local heresies and schisms, see Augustine's works: *Epistulae* 49.2 (PL 33:189–190); *Epistulae* 52.1 (PL 33:194); *Epistulae* 53.1, 6 (PL 33:195–196, 198); *Epistulae* 76.1 (PL 33:263–264); *Epistulae* 142.1–3 (PL 33:583–584); *Epistulae* 185.5 (PL 33:794); *Contra litteras Petiliani* 2.8.19–20 (PL 43:264–265), 2.14.33 (PL 43:268), 2.64.144 (PL 43:306); 2.73.164 (PL 43:310); 2.92.210 (PL 43:330); 3.50.62 (PL 43:380); *Contra Cresconium* 4.54, 64 (PL 43:582–583); 4.57.70 (PL 43:587); *Ad Donatistas post collationem* 2 (PL 43:653); *Contra Gaudentius* 1.20, 22 (PL 43:718–719). See also Th. Specht, *Die Lehre von der Kirche*, 254–256, and in general all of §30: "Die Katholicität der Kirche," 251–268.

2227 See for example *Epistulae* 49.3: "Ecclesia catholica est etiam in Africa [The Catholic Church is also in Africa]" (PL 33:190).

Even in the late fourth century the Donatists held fast to their doctrine of the **sanctity** of the Church. This is shown by a schism that occurred in their ranks over the question of the sanctity of the Church. Among the Donatists there arose people who had a more orthodox understanding of the sanctity of the Church. One such was **Tyconius of Africa,** or **the Grammarian.** He presented his teaching on the Church in a book on seven rules for studying and finding the meaning of Holy Scripture.[2228] Here Tyconius speaks of a bipartite Body of the Lord (*de Domini corpore bipartito*):

The bipartite character of Christ's body is indicated in brief: "I am black and beautiful" (Song of Songs 1:5). By no means is the church—"which has no spot or wrinkle" (Ephesians 5:27), which the Lord cleansed by his own blood—black in any part, except in the left-hand part through which "the name of God is blasphemed among the gentiles" (Romans 2:24). Otherwise it is wholly beautiful, as he says: "you are wholly beautiful, my love, and there is no fault in you" (Song of Songs 4:7). And indeed she says why it is that she is both black and beautiful: "like the tent of Kedar, like the tent-curtain of Solomon" (Song of Songs 1:5). She shows that there are two tents, one royal and one servile. Yet both spring from Abraham, for Kedar is Ishmael's son. ... Yet we cannot claim that the tent of Kedar is outside the church. She herself mentions the "tent of Kedar" and "of Solomon"; and that is why she says, "I am black and beautiful." Those who are outside the church do not make it black. It is in virtue of this mystery that, in the Apocalypse, the Lord now calls the seven angels (i.e., the septiform church) holy and keepers of his precepts and now shows the same angels to be guilty of many crimes and in need of repentance [see Revelation 2–3]. And in the gospel he makes it clear that one of the leaders is a body of diverse merits [*diversi meriti manifestat*]. ... The one body

---

2228 "Liber de septem regulis ad investigandam et inveniendam S. Scripturae intelligentiam." Here we employ the version of Tyconius's composition published by F.C. Burkitt M. A., *Tests and Studies: Contributions to Biblical and Patristic Literature*, J. Armitage Robinson, ed., vol. 3, No. 1: "The Rules of Tyconius" (Cambridge: 1894). Concerning Tyconius, see F. Ribbeck, *Donatus und Augustinus*, 198–205.

is both good and evil. ... Thus, in all the scriptures, the Lord gives testimony that the one body of Abraham's line, in every case, both grows and flourishes and goes to ruin.[2229]

The two bodies have been joined as one; and the one body is praised or blamed in common.[2230]

For Tyconius, Esau and Jacob are images of two composite parts of the Church:

... two peoples wrestling in the one womb of their mother, the church. The one, chosen on the basis of foreknowledge, is loved; the other, by the choice of its own will, is evil. Moreover, Jacob and Esau are in one body and come from one line of descent; but the fact that they clearly came to birth as two individuals shows forth the two peoples. Yet, lest anyone think, as a result, that the two peoples would be sharply separated, it was made plain that both would be in one body, in Jacob. ... Thus it was shown that the two separate individuals were going to remain in one body until the time when they are finally distinguished from each other.[2231] ... Jacob, i.e., the church, never comes for blessing without concomitant deceit, i.e., without false brethren. ... Jacob is the receptacle of both.[2232] ... Although the figures of Ishmael[2233] and Esau had been separated from the faithful, the whole emerged afterwards in one people. Now, when the new [covenant] obtains ... there is no lack of children of slavery.[2234]

2229 Tyconius, *Tyconius' Book of Rules* 2.10–11, William S. Babcock, trans. (Atlanta, GA: Scholars Press, 1989), 19–21.

2230 Ibid. 3.26.13–14, 47.

2231 In the Russian source, "Even before they were divided, concerning both who were divided it was shown that they must be in one." −*Trans.*

2232 Bracketed words added to match the Russian source. −*Trans.*

2233 The Russian source erroneously reads "Israel." −*Trans.*

2234 Ibid. 3.28–30, 51–53.

A similar idea permeates all that Tyconius says when he speaks, "with reference to the mysteries of heavenly wisdom in relation to the teaching of the Holy Spirit," of the particular and the general.[2235] In his fourth rule Tyconius takes the prophecies concerning countries and cities and applies them to the Church, because the narrative concerning them is equally suited to both the particular and the general (that is, the Church).[2236] But everywhere Tyconius finds references specifically to the bipartate makeup of the cities, and this state is ascribed to the Church also. "Many … cities [are] figures of the church. Morever, wherever he names Edom, Teman, Bozrah, Seir, he is signifying the evil brethren; they are Esau's possessions."[2237]

Although he expressed his teaching on the earthly state of the Church in this unique form, one similar to the catholic doctrine, Tyconius nevertheless drew no conclusions from this for himself and remained a Donatist. In Donatist circles Tyconius's composition met with displeasure. Parmenian, the leader of the Donatists, and the other bishops protested vigorously.[2238] First Parmenian exhorted Tyconius in writing to renounce his teaching concerning the Church, then Tyconius was condemned by a Donatist council.[2239] Clearly, among the Donatists another concept of the Church prevailed. What this concept was we may learn in detail from the writings of the blessed Augustine.

According to Donatist doctrine, there must be no sinners in the Church. In proof of this thesis they cited numerous passages from

---

2235 Ibid. 4.1, 55.

2236 Ibid. 4.32 sqq.

2237 Ibid. 4.53, 87.

2238 "Parmenianus autem caeterique Donatistae viderunt hoc esse consequens. et maluerunt suscipere obstinantissimum animum adversus apertissimam veritatem quam Tichonius asserebat [Moreover, Parmenian and other Donatists viewed this as being consequent, and they chose to take a most obstinate stance against the plain truth which Tyconius was asserting {trans. —ED.}]," says the blessed Augustine (*Contra epist. Parmeniani* 1.1 [PL 43:35])

2239 Augustine, *Contra epist. Parmeniani* 1.1 (PL 43:35).

Holy Scripture.[2240] The society of the Donatists approved this requirement; among the Donatists there was no one with any kind
of vice.[2241] When the Donatists separated, this was a separation of
the wheat from the tares: the wheat was reduced to the confines
of Africa alone (*ad solam Africam*), while the tares remained in the
catholic Church.[2242] It is even uncertain whether there are any good
Christians among all the peoples beyond the sea.[2243] Parmenian
even positively asserted that Gaul, Spain, Italy, and their compa-
triots (whom, Augustine observes, he wishes to consider the whole
world to be), by having dealings with the traditors of Africa, are like
them in their crimes.[2244]

   Augustine takes a completely different view of the earthly state
of the Church.[2245] For example, in his "Psalm against the party of
the Donatists" he says of the Church that in her there are many
sinners (*abundantia peccatorum*). And so it ought to be, because the
Lord likened the Church to a net containing different fishes. When
the net is brought to shore, then the fish will begin to be sorted: the
good fish will be put into vessels, and the bad will be thrown back
into the sea. The net is the Church; the present age is the sea; the
shore is the end of the age. But while the net remains in the sea,
the fish are together, both good and bad.[2246] One ought not to sev-

   2240 Is. 59:1–8; Prov. 17:15; 2 Tim. 2:19; Eph. 5:11; 1 Cor. 6 (Augustine,
Contra epist. Parmeniani 2.3.6 sqq. [PL 43:53 sqq.]).

   2241 Augustine, *Contra epist. Parmeniani* 2.6.13 (PL 43:58).

   2242 Ibid. 2.2.5 (PL 43:52).

   2243 Ibid. 1.2.4 (PL 43:51).

   2244 Ibid. 1.2.2 (PL 43:35).

   2245 For more detail on the earthly state of the Church according to Augustine, see Specht, *Die Lehre von der Kirche*, 67 ff.

   2246 This psalm is also called the *Abecedarium*, because its strophes begin with the
letters of the alphabet in order. Here we have cited the first strophe. PL 43:24–25:
"Genus autem mixtum piscis, justus est cum peccatore [Moreover, the mixed race
of fish signifies the righteous man along with the sinner]." The net is also called "similitudo apertissima de commixtione malorum et bonorum [a very clear parable
on the mixture of good and evil]" (*De unitate Ecclesiae* 14.35 [PL 43:418]). Cf. *Contra
epist. Parmeniani* 3.3.19 (PL 43:97); *Epistulae* 93.9, 34 (PL 33:338); *De civitate Dei* 18.49
(PL 41:611); *Ad Donatistas post collationem* 8.11 (PL 43:659), 10.14 (PL 43:660).

er fellowship with sinners, but one must naturally withdraw from fellowship in sins.[2247] Sinners in the Church can be of no harm. They should only be excluded in extreme cases, but peace should be preserved (*salva pace*). If this exclusion would break the peace, it were better to exclude them only from one's heart. The prophet Ezekiel (Ezek. 9:4) speaks of people who wept over the sins of their brethren, but did not separate themselves from them. So also we ought not to separate ourselves from our mother, the Church.[2248] In the Hebrew nation also, the seven thousand men faithful to God (see 1 Kgs. 19:18) and other pious people did not separate from the unity of the people due to the idolatry of a few, or even of the majority. They came together with them in the same temple (*uno tempeo miscebantur*), but their hearts were far away (*mixti non erant corde*).[2249]

The ark of Noah is also a symbol of the Church, yet it contained both clean and unclean animals. "Let us learn to understand the ark of Noah, which is a figure of the Church, and let us enter it together, like the clean animals. Let us not stubbornly insist that there be no unclean animals there with us until the end of the flood."[2250]

2247 Augustine, *Abecedarium* G (PL 43:27). Cf. *Epistulae* 105.5.16 (PL 33:403); *Epistulae* 108.3.7 (PL 33:409).

2248 Augustine, *Abecedarium* N (PL 43:28–29). Cf. *Contra epist. Parmeniani* 2.1.3 (PL 43:51); *De unitate Ecclesiae* 14.35: "Nulla ergo malorum commixtio terret bonos, ut propterea velint tanquam retia rumpere, et a congregatione unitatis exire [Therefore, no mingling with the wicked should terrify the good so that they would want to break their nets and go out from the congregation of unity]" (PL 43:418). See also *Epistulae* 98.4.15, 9.34 (PL 33:329, 338); *Epistulae* 87.2 (PL 33:297); *Epistulae* 129.5 (PL 33:492); *Epistuale* 43.8.21: "Ne nomen Christi per horribilia schismata blasphemetur, pro bono unitatis tolerant, quod pro bono aequitatis oderunt [in order to prevent the name of Christ from being reproached by odious schisms, they tolerate in the interest of unity that which in the interest of righteousness they hate]" (PL 33:170); *Epistulae* 44.5.11 (PL 33:19); *Epistuale* 53.3.6 (PL 33:198); *Epistulae* 76.2–3 (PL 33:265).

2249 Augustine, *Abecedarium* P (PL 43:29); *Ad Donatistas post collationem* 20.31 (PL 43:671–672).

2250 Augustine, *Epistulae* 108.7.20 (PL 33:417). Cf. *Breviculus collationis cum Donatistis* 9.16: "When the raven flew out of the ark, unclean animals yet remained within it, but the clean and the unclean remained in it until the end of the flood. So also in the Church there are good and evil, until the end of the age. But as

The parable of the tares describes the same. The Lord Himself
explained that the harvest is the end of the age, and the field where
the tares and the wheat were sown is the world. It is plain that both
must grow in the world until the end of the age.[2251] "The field is the
world—not only Africa; and the harvest is the end of the world—
not the era of Donatus."[2252] Christ said that the harvest is the end of
the age, and that the reapers are the angels; but Donatus says that
the wheat was separated when his schism began, and that before
the harvest he and his companions had done what Christ said the
angels must do during the harvest. You choose whom to believe![2253]
Even if the majority in the Church are sinners, one must not deride
the whole Church, as do the heretics. In the Old Testament there
were instances when few righteous men remained. So it was in the
days of Enoch, Noah, Abraham, Isaac, and Jacob; and the apostles
were only twelve in number. To be sure, two tribes did once separate themselves from the ten, but this was a separation of state,
and not of religion. God never commands one to be in heresy or
schism.[2254] In Holy Scripture the Lord Himself says that there will
be few good people; but of these few it is said that they will be many.
In Revelation it is said that there will be thousands of thousands of
holy children of the Church (see Rev. 5:11). They will only be few
in comparison with the unworthy.[2255]

Noah offered a sacrifice not of the unclean animals, but of the clean, so also it is
not the evil men in the Church who will come to God, but those who are good"
(PL 43:633).

2251 Augustine, *De unitate Ecclesiae* 14.35 (PL 43:418); *Contra litteras Petiliani*
2.45.106 (PL 43:296), 2.47.110 (PL 43:297); 2.78.174 (PL 43:312); *Contra Crescon*
3.65.73, 3.66.75 (PL 43:536, 537); *Epistulae* 10.3.11 (PL 33:411).

2252 Augustine, *Contra litteras Petiliani* 3.2.3 (NPNF¹ 598; PL 43:349).

2253 Augustine, *Contra litteras Petiliani* 2.2.5 (PL 43:52). Cf. *Contra litteras Petiliani*
2.90.199 (PL 43:321–322); *Contra epist. Parmenian* 3.3.19 (PL 43:97).

2254 Augustine, *De unitate Ecclesiae* 13.33 (PL 43:416–417).

2255 Here Augustine also cites Mt. 7:13–14; Gen. 15:5, 22:27; Rom. 9:7; Is.
54.1; Mt. 8:11–12; Tit. 2.14 (*De unitate Ecclesiae* 14.36 [PL 43:418–419]). In addition to the Donatists, the Pelagians also held that the Church consisted exclusively
of saints, based on an incorrect understanding of the words of the apostle John
(1 Jn. 3:9) and the apostle Paul (Eph. 5:25–27). In polemics against the Pelagians

So reasons the blessed Augustine regarding the earthly state of the Church: here the tares grow together with the wheat, and the sanctity of the Church does not require that the wheat be separated out. The sins of one man do not defile the others.[2256] But the blessed Augustine himself says that this concept of the Church in no way implies neglect of church discipline, or that each may do as he pleases, without any attempt to correct him on the part of the Church.[2257] The apostle Paul says, "Warn them that are unruly, comfort the feebleminded, support the weak, be patient toward all men. See that none render evil for evil unto any man" (1 Thess. 5:14–15). Based on these words Augustine defines the essence of church discipline: its purpose is to instruct. It is not the blade of a foe inflicting a wound, but that of a physician incising a wound, as Augustine puts it.[2258] With the Donatists, however, their discipline serves only to divide them not only from the corrupt, but also from the majority of the good.[2259] In the Church, discipline is not applied so irrationally. The Church may likewise excommunicate sinners at times, but this occurs only when a steadfast, diligent, and wise minister (*dispensator*) of Christ sees that there is no rational justification for the sin. There are countless examples of how bishops or persons of other hierarchical ranks were defrocked (*degradati*) or fled out of shame to other lands, joining the Donatists or other her-

---

Augustine demonstrates that, both for the individual and for the Church, the state of sanctity is the fruit of a lengthy process. See Specht, *Die Lehre von der Kirche*, 84–88.

2256 Augustine, *Epistulae* 93.9.36 (PL 33:339). Cf. *Contra litteras Petiliani* 3.37.43 (43:370), *Retractationes* 2.17 (PL 32:637).

2257 Augustine, *Contra litteras Petiliani* 3.4.5: "Neque hoc ideo · dixerim ut neglegatur ecclesiastica disciplina, et permittitur quisque facere quod velit, sine ulla correptione, et quadam medicinali vindicta et terribili lenitate et charitatis severitate [Nor would I say this for that reason, that ecclesiastical discipline be neglected and anybody be permitted to do as he wills, without any reproach, and {without} a certain medicinal staff and a terrible gentleness and a severity of love {trans. —ED.}]" (PL 43:350).

2258 Ibid. 3.4.5: "Neque enim ferrum est inimici vulnerantis, sed medici secantis" (PL 43:350).

2259 Augustine, *Contra litteras Petiliani* 3.4.5 (PL 43:350).

etics. If Petilian had called to mind these numerous examples, he would never have fallen into so clearly false and empty an opinion as that of which he says, "None of you is guiltless, because no guiltless man is ever punished."[2260] Augustine reminds Petilian how he received the deposed deacon Splendonius through rebaptism, ordained him presbyter, and then excommunicated him himself.[2261] Consequently, excommunication can occur in the Church also, but we see clearly what care must be exercised so as not to cast out the wheat along with the tares.[2262] First and foremost, the excommunication itself must be have as its purpose not just eradication, but rather correction (*non ad eradicandum, sed ad corrigendum*). The blessed Augustine speaks of *prohibitio a communione medicinalis* [a medicinal prohibition from communion].[2263] If the sinner does not repent and does not mend his ways through repentance, he himself goes out of the Church and of his own volition he is severed from the unity of the Church. Given this approach to discipline, the wicked separate from the Church without harming peace and unity and without any detriment to the wheat.[2264] With these sinners all fellowship is

---

2260 Ibid. 3.37.43 (PL 43:370).

2261 Ibid. 3.38.44 (PL 43:370–371).

2262 Augustine, *Contra epist. Parmeniani* 2.20.39 (PL 43:80).

2263 Augustine, *Sermones* 351.10 (PL 39:1546).

2264 Augustine, *Contra epist. Parmeniani* 3.2.13: "Non dormiat severitas disciplinae, in qua tanto est efficacior emendatio pravitatis, quando diligentior conservatio charitatis. Tunc autem hoc sine labe pacis et unitatis, et sine laesione frumentorum fieri potest, cum congregationes Ecclesiae multitudo ab eo crimine quod anathematur, aliena est [Let not the severity of discipline slumber, in which the correction of perverseness is so much more effective, as much the preservation of charity is more diligent. Indeed, then this can be done without the destruction of peace and unity, and without hurting the fruit, since the multitude of the Church's congregation is foreign to that crime which is being anathematized {trans. —ED.}]" (PL 43:92). Cf. *Breviculus collationis cum Donatistis* 3.9.16: "Quamvis debeat vigilare ecclesiastica disciplina, ad eos non solum verbis, sed etiam excommunicationibus et degradationibus corripiendos, tamen non solum in ea latentes nesciantur, sed plerumque propter pacem unitatis etiam cogniti tolerentur [Although ecclesiastical discipline ought to be vigilant to take hold of them not only by words but also by excommunications and degradations, nevertheless in her {the Church, evil men} not only exist without being known, escaping no-

severed; and when they see themselves deprived of all fellowship, then they may be cured by shame, for they will have no confederates for sin.[2265] The blessed Augustine explains the passages from the epistles to the Corinthians that describe the excommunication of the incestuous man. In this Augustine specifically sees the idea that excommunication from all the rest has a curative effect for the sinner himself.[2266] But if many sin, these cannot be corrected by separating them from fellowship:[2267] this will no longer be a separation, but a division, which will serve less to correct those who are bad, but strong-willed, than to dismay those who are good, but weak.[2268] Every man must try to correct what he can; as for what he cannot, let him patiently endure and grieve with love, until the sinner himself improves; or else let him wait until the harvest for the tares to be plucked out. If Christians keep company with the desperate, whom they lack the strength to correct, let them cast out evil from their own selves, that they themselves might not have within them that which they dislike in the deeds of others. This kind of separation of good from evil is always possible; as for physical separation, let it take place at the end of the age. "Put away wickedness (*malum*) from among yourselves," says the apostle (see 1 Cor. 5:13); that is, if you cannot remove the wicked from your midst, remove what is most wicked from your own selves. If care must be taken lest the peace of

---

tice, but for the most part even when discovered they are tolerated for the sake of the peace of unity {trans. —ED.}]" (PL 43:632).

2265 Ibid. 3.2.13: "Tunc etiam ille et timore percutitur, et pudore sanatur, cum ab universa Ecclesia se anathematum videns, sociam turbam cum qua in delicto suo gaudeat et bonis insultet non potest invenire [Thereupon he is also both struck with fear and healed by shame when, seeing himself anathematized from the universal Church, he cannot find his allied crowd with which he would rejoice in his own sin and jeer at good men {trans. —ED.}]" (PL 43:92).

2266 Ibid. 3.2.14 (PL 43:92–93).

2267 Ibid. 3.2.14: "Jam propter multitudinem non poterant ita corripi, ut ab eorum conjunctione se caeteri continerent, et eos erubescere facerent [Now, on account of their great numbers, they cannot be corrected in that manner, {namely} that the rest would keep themselves from joining them and {thus} make them be ashamed {trans. —ED.}]" (PL 43:93).

2268 Idem.

the Church be harmed, the wheat must be greatly spared, so as not to uproot it together with the tares. If anyone gives diligent thought to this, he will note strictness of discipline even in the preservation of unity, and will not break the bond of fellowship by his excessive demands.[2269] One must not censure the Church for the mores of those whom she herself condemns and whom she strives daily to correct.[2270]

The Donatists sometimes cited the time of St. Cyprian, saying that in his time the Church was holy. Augustine explains in detail that although St. Cyprian judged sharply concerning corrupt people, he did not sever ecclesiastical fellowship with them, though he naturally remained far from their life and mores.[2271] St. Cyprian partook of the Lord's Bread and drank of the Lord's Cup not only with corrupt laity, but even with unworthy bishops.[2272] The Donatists ought to say that by then the Church had already perished. And if this be so, then there is no point in Donatism itself. A corrupt Church could not have produced one that is holy and blameless.[2273]

2269 Ibid. 3.2.15: "Haec qui diligenter cogitat, nec in conservatione unitatis neglegit disciplinae severitatem, nec immoderatione coercitionis disrumpit vinculum societatis [Whoever thinks on thiese things diligently does neither neglect the severity of discipline in the preservation of unity nor break the chain of society by punishing excessively {trans. —ED.}]" (PL 43:94). *Contra litteras Petiliani* 3.3.4 (PL 43:349); In *Retractationes* 2.17, based on the Greek text, Augustine corrects the explanation given in *Contra epist. Parmeniani* on 1 Cor. 5:13: "Sic potius intelligendum ut homo malus auferatur ex hominibus bonis, quod fit per ecclesiasticam disciplinam [This is better to be understood thus, that a wicked man be taken away from among good men, which should be done by means of ecclesiastical discipline {trans. —ED.}]" (PL 32:637). Concerning Augustine's views on excommunication from the Church, see C. Romeis, *Das Heil des Christen ausserhalb der wahren Kirche*, 40 ff.

2270 Augustine, *De moribus ecclesiae catholicae et de moribus manichaeorum* 1.34.76 (PL 32:1342).

2271 Augustine, *Contra epist. Parmeniani* 3.2.8 (PL 43:88–89). *Epistulae* 93.10.36: "Unitatem orbis terrae atque omnium gentium et diligendo tenuit, et disputando defendit [he maintained with loyalty, and defended in debate, the unity of {the Church in} the world and in all nations]" (PL 33:339).

2272 Ibid. 3.2.9 (PL 43:90).

2273 Ibid. 3.2.11: "Quid eis prodest quod avaros et rapaces, modo se vel non

Augustine says frequently and extensively that in their moral state even the society of the Donatists does not comply with their dogmatic doctrine on the sanctity of the Church: their doctrine on the Holy Church is merely a failed theory that does not apply to reality. The Donatists censured the Church for a wide variety of vices and crimes among its members; in response to this Augustine in turn points out their own faults. With particular frequency polemicists against Donatism would point out the outrageous doings of the Circumcellions, with whom the Donatists nevertheless never broke unity.[2274] The crimes of members of the Church were in the past, but the Circumcellions live and act to this day.[2275] All this mutual censure of each other between the Church and the Donatists is of course more of historical interest, but they also have a certain significance from a dogmatic standpoint. When the Donatists pointed out the sinful members of the Church, this presented no dogmatic

---

habere in congregatione sua, vel incognitos sibi esse mentiuntur; quandoquidem fuerunt tales in illa unitatis Ecclesia, unde se isti exortos esse sic jactant, ut eam in sua sola societate, id est, in communione Donati remansisse persuadere conentur? Si enim dicunt per talium communionem perire Ecclesiam, cur eam non dicunt jam Cypriani perisse temporibus? [For what is to their advantage, insofar as they merely pretend either that they do not have in their congregation greedy and grasping men or that these are unknown to them? seeing that such men have been in this Church of unity, from which they boast that they have arisen, so that they are attempting to persuade{us} that this {Church} has remained only in their company, that is, in the communion of the Donatists. For if they say that the Church perishes from such a communion, why do they not say that She had already perished in Cyprian's days? {trans. —ED.}]" (PL 43:90–91). *De baptismo contra Donatistas* 2.6.8 (PL 43:131), 2.7.11 (PL 43:133); *De unico baptismo* 14.23–24 (PL 43:607–608); *Epistulae* 93.10.37, 42, 46 (PL 33:339, 341, 342).

2274 Concerning the origin and nature of the Circumcellions, see Kutepov, *The Donatist Schism*, from 38 on. Augustine always closely links the Circumcellions with the Donatists. See *Contra litteras Petiliani* 2.83.184 (PL 43:317); *Epistulae* 105.3 (PL 33:397). Addressing the Donatists, Augustine calls the Circumcellions "vestri [yours]" (*Epistulae* 88.1 (PL 33:302).

2275 Augustine, *Abecedarium* L: "Clamatis vos de Macario, et nos de Circumcellione. Illud, nostrum jam transactum: vestri non cessant usque hodie [You cry for Macarius, and we for Circumcellion. The former, ours, is already finished: yours do not cease to this day {trans. —ED.}]" (PL 43:28). Cf. *De Haeresibus* 69 (PL 42:43).

danger for the Church. The doctrine of the sanctity of the Church that the church writers espoused in no way suffered from the presence of sinners in the Church. The blessed Augustine acknowledges the sinfulness of certain members of the Church, but he does not consider this circumstance sufficient proof that the Church is not authentic. The blessed Augustine has a different purpose in pointing out the faults of the Donatists. For their concept of the Church this presented an insurmountable difficulty, since according to their teaching the Church must contain only wheat, yet here among that wheat tares are suddenly found. By simply shifting to their dogmatic point of view, Augustine was able censure the Donatists for their moral shortcomings, and thereby to show the impossibility of their doctrine concerning the Church, since if taken to its logical conclusion it would mean acknowledging that there is no Church at all, and that the Church has already perished. The ecclesiological system of the blessed Augustine himself leaves no room for any such conclusions. Until the Judgment and until the end of the age the Church comprises the field, where wheat and tares grow together. The blessed Augustine says that in the life of the Church two periods should be distinguished (*distinguenda esse tempora Ecclesiae*). At present there are sinners in the Church, but the time will come when it will consist solely of saints.[2276] In Holy Scripture these two periods are symbolically depicted in the two miraculous catches of fish. At the first catch (see Lk. 5:4) the Lord says nothing of the right and left sides, thereby showing that the nets of His Sacraments will not contain only the wicked or only the good, but rather the wicked and the good will be mixed. After His resurrection, however, [He] commanded that the net be cast on the right side (see Jn. 21:6–11), that we might understand that after our resurrection only the good will be in the Church.[2277]

2276 See *Epistulae* 187.7.28 (PL 33:842); *De gestis Pelagii* 12.27 (PL 44:336); *De nuptiis et concupiscentia* 33.38, 34.39 (PL 44:435); *Contra duas epist. Pelagianorum* 4.7.17–18 (PL 44:621–622); *De natura et gratia* 63.75 (PL 44:285); *De perfect. just.* 15.34–35 (44:310); *Epistulae* 185.9.38–39 (PL 33:810).

2277 Augustine, *Breviculus collationis cum Donatistis* 3.9.16 (PL 43:633). Cf. *Ad Donatistas post collationem* 9.12 (43:659).

So says the blessed Augustine concerning the earthly Church. And here he is speaking specifically of the historically known visible Church, which originated in Jerusalem and spread throughout the whole world.[2278] Augustine was aware of allegorical interpretations of the entire initial history of Christianity. Jerusalem, it was claimed, should be understood to mean not this visible city; it was only a figure of speech. The whole Church should be understood spiritually, as the eternal Celestial Church, which in part is sojourning on earth. All this Augustine firmly rejects. If all reference to the Church is to be understood figuratively, the sufferings of Christ should be understood likewise, and this would mean to renounce Christianity. Analyzing the evangelist's account of the Lord's ascension (see Lk. 24:49–52), Augustine particularly draws attention to the fact that after the ascension the apostles returned specifically to the earthly Jerusalem.[2279] The book of Acts (see 1:4 and 8) likewise names specific localities and cities where the Church spread, and this is as though in order to indicate the visibility both of the Church and of Jerusalem, where it was spreading.[2280] It was in this visible Church that the good were mixed with the wicked: they lived together inseparably.

2278 Augustine, *De unitate Ecclesiae* 10.25: "Teneamus Ecclesiam ex ore Domini designatam, unde coeptura, et quousque perventura esset; coeptura scilicet ab Ierusalem, et perventura in omnes gentes [let us hold the Church delineated from the mouth of the Lord from where it would begin and until it would fully arrive; namely begin from Jerusalem and arrive in all the nations]" (PL 43:409).

2279 Ibid. 10.26 (PL 43:409).

2280 Ibid. 11.27: "Nullus omnino dubitare permittatur, nisi qui de sanctarum Scripturarum fide dubitat, illam esse Ierusalem visibilem civitatem, unde coepit Ecclesia post Domini Iesu Christi resurrectionem et ascensionem; nec aliud eum voluisse ostendere, nisi hujus terrae loca, unde illi daret initium, et quomodo eam per cuncta inde diffunderet [Nobody is allowed altogether to doubt unless he doubts in his own faith in Holy Scripture, that it is the visible city of Jerusalem from which the Church began after the resurrection and ascension of our Lord Jesus Christ and that he did not wish to show them anything other than the places of this land where he would give it a beginning and how he would spread it from there through all places]" (PL 43:409–410). Cf. 11.28 and 24.70 (PL 43:441–442).

At the same time, the writings of Augustine also contain the idea that worthy members of the Church share a particular relationship.[2281] Through baptism a man enters the Church, and throughout his life he remains united to her. He may however fall into sins which, according to the apostle, render him incapable of inheriting the kingdom of heaven (see Gal. 5:19–21). Such sinners only appear to have fellowship with the Church. They participate in the sacraments, yet they are not in the Church. There has been no visible excommunication, but there is also no full unification with the Church.[2282] Such people are outside the Church, although they appear to belong to her.[2283] The true Church is comprised only of the good: they are the true members of the Body of Christ, and certain words of Holy Scripture apply only to the Church of the saints.[2284] The Church is in those who build their house upon stone—that is, it is in those who fulfill the teaching of Christ, and not in those who do not fulfill it.[2285] It is from this Church, which has neither spot

2281 Vgl. Harnack, *Dogmengeschichte*[4] 3, 147, Anm. 2; Vladimir Guerrier, *The Blessed Augustine* ["Блаженный Августин"], 610.

2282 Augustine, *De unitate Ecclesiae* 25.74: "Multi tales sunt in Sacramentorum communione cum Ecclesia, et tamen jam non sunt in Ecclesia. Alioquin situnc quisque praeciditur cum visibiliter excommunicatur; consequens erit ut tunc rursus inseratur, cum visibiliter communioni restituitur [There are many such men in the communion of sacraments within the Church and yet they are not now in the Church. Rather if anyone is cut off when he is visibly excommunicated it will follow that he is then sown when he is visibly restored to communion]" (PL 43:444). Cf. *In Ioannos tractatus* 5.7 (PL 35:2016); *In ep. Iohannem tractatus* 7.6 (PL 35:2032).

2283 Augustine, *De baptismo contra Donatistas* 1.10.14; 4.3.4; 5.27.38; 6.14.23 (PL 43:117, 155, 156, 196, 207); *In ep. Iohannem tractatus* 7.13 (PL 35:2028); *In psalmus* 25 en. 2.2 (PL 36:189).

2284 Literally, "the Church of those that are holy." —*Trans.*

2285 Augustine, *De unitate Ecclesiae* 21.60: "Nec regenerati spiritualiter in corpus et membra Christi coaedificientur nisi boni; profecto in bonis est illa Ecclesia, cui dicitur. Sicut lilium in medio spinarum, ita proxima mea in medio filiarum (Can. II, 2). In his est enim qui aedificant super petram, id est, qui audiunt verba Christi, et faciunt. Non est ergo in eis, qui aedificant super arenam, id est, qui audiunt verba Christi, et non faciunt [those reborn spiritually in the body and members of Christ are not built up unless they are good, and certainly that

nor blemish, that the sinner is excommunicated, though he should outwardly be united with the saints.[2286] Nor are the sacraments of any benefit to him.[2287] Sometimes the saints alone are even termed the Church.[2288] One may be visibly in the Church and yet a stranger to that spiritual bond of love that forms the true Church.[2289] One must discern between visible fellowship with the Church and invisible participation in the unity in love that is the inheritance of the good. Love can sometimes even substitute for the sacraments: for example, the martyrs invisibly fulfill what they were unable to do visibly.[2290]

In all the passages cited above it is impossible to find in Augustine the idea that the Church is invisible in its essence. Otherwise the teaching of Augustine would contain an irreconcilable contra-

---

Church is in the good when it is said as a lily among the brambles, so is my love among the maidens (Cant. 2:2). He is among these who build upon the rock, that is, who hear the words of Christ and act... It is not therefore among those who build on sand, that is, those who hear the words of Christ and do not act]" (PL 43:436). Cf. *De baptismo contra Donatistas* 5.27.38 (PL 43:195).

2286 Augustine, *De baptismo contra Donatistas* 1.17.26: "Semper ab illius Ecclesiae quae sine macula et ruga est unitate divisus est, etiam qui congregationi sanctorum in carnali abduratione miscetur [And even that man is always severed from the unity of the Church which is without spot or wrinkle, who associates with the congregation of the saints in carnal obstinacy]" (PL 43:123). Cf. 3.18.23: "Ad illam gloriosam Ecclesiam non pertineant [to that glorious Church they do not belong]" (PL 43:150); 4.18.25 (PL 43:170).

2287 Augustine, *Contra litteras Petiliani* 2.55.126 (PL 43:302).

2288 Augustine, *De baptismo contra Donatistas* 3.18.23: "Orationes sanctorum, id est columbae gemitus [the prayers of the saints, that is, the groans of the dove]" (PL 43:150); *Epistulae* 98.5: "Ecclesia, quae in sanctis est [the Church, which is in the saints]" (PL 33:362); *Epistulae* 187.12.41 (PL 33:848).

2289 Augustine, ibid. 3.19.26: "Cum intus videntur, ab illa invisibili charitatis compage separati sunt [while they seem to be within, they are severed from that invisible bond of love]" (PL 43:152). Cf. *contra litteras Petiliani* 2.108.247 (PL 43:345); *In psalmum* 131.13: "Ille enim ad domum Dei pertinet, qui est in charitate compaginatus lapidibus vivis [For he belongs to the house of God, who is joined together in love with the stones of the living]" (PL 37:1721); *In psalmum* 39.1 (PL 36:433); *In psalmum* 95.2 (PL 37:1228).

2290 Augustine, ibid. 4.22.29 (PL 43:173–174). See also Romeis, *Das Heil des Christen ausserhalb der wahren Kirche*, 28–30.

diction: in the Church there are both righteous and sinners, but the Church consists of the righteous alone. Augustine considers righteous people to be the Church predominantly, but not exclusively. While the Church is on earth, the righteous and the sinners alike comprise it.[2291] The Church of the saints, in the teaching of the blessed Augustine, is not a separate entity: we have already seen how Augustine insisted on the inseparability of the righteous and sinners. The wheat cannot be separated from the tares, nor is there any need of this. The Holy Church is the Church of the age to come.[2292] Conversely, Augustine says that outside ecclesiastical unity it is impossible to preserve Christian love; while without love, faith itself and all the sacraments mean nothing.[2293] Consequently, all holy people likewise belong to the same Church, in which there are also unworthy members. And indeed, this is how all truly good people behave. Their sanctity not only does not prompt them to abandon ecclesiastical unity, but even unites them more closely to the Church.[2294] To separate from the Church on the pretense of

---

2291 Vgl. Seeberg, *Studien zur Geschichte des Begriffs der Kirche*, 41–42; Thomasius, *Dogmengeschichte* 1, 593–596; Guerrier, *The Blessed Augustine*, 606–610.

2292 "Depending on the varying membership of the Church," writes Guerrier, "at various times its nature could comprise the polar opposite." But only the members of the earthly Church will enter the celestial Church; consequently, we cannot speak of any polar opposition between the former Church and the latter. Cf. the remark of Prof. N.N. Glubokovsky, "The Blessed Augustine as Depicted by a Russian Secular Historian," in *Works of the Kiev Theological Academy* (1911), vol. 1, 143–146.

2293 Augustine, *Contra litteras Petiliani* 2.77.172: "Charitas enim christiana nisi in unitate Ecclesiae non potest custodiri. ... Tenemus autem charitatem, si amplectimur unitatam: amplectimur autem unitatem, si eam non per verba nostra in parte confingimus, sed per verba Christi in unitate cognoscimus [for Christian charity cannot be preserved except in the unity of the Church... we hold fast charity if we cling to unity; while we cling to unity, if we do not make a fictitious unity in a party by our own words, but recognize it in a united whole through the words of Christ]" (PL 43:312). Cf. *Contra Cresconium* 2.12.15 (PL 43:476); 2.13.16 (idem).

2294 Augustine, *De baptismo contra Donatistas* 1.17.26: "Spiritales ... non eunt foras: quia et cum aliqua vel perversitate vel necessitate hominum videntur expelli, ibi magis probantur, quam si intus permaneant, cum adversus Ecclesiam nullatenus eriguntur, sed in solida unitatis petra fortissimo charitatis robore radicantur

sanctity, as did the Donatists, is the part of one who is impious, haughty, and proud.[2295] "I adhere to the Church full of wheat and tares," writes Augustine. "If there are traditors that are unknown to me, when you show them I will turn away from them in both body and heart; but by reason of these dead I will not separate from those who remain alive in the holy unity of this same Church. I have no need to separate. If I learn of such in the unity of the Mysteries, by the word and law (*disciplina*) of the Lord I correct whomever I can, and endure whom I am unable to correct. I flee the tares lest I become one myself, but I do not leave the threshing floor, lest I become naught."[2296] Thus, the saints in the Church abide together with the sinners. They never separate themselves, but rather they are always in one part of the Church or another. Righteous men are only the primary executors of the idea of the Holy Church.[2297] Sometimes sin spreads so greatly that it seems as though the wheat of God were no longer there. But in reality this wheat is never lacking: it is predestined beforehand, and everywhere it is sown.[2298]

The teaching of the blessed Augustine on the Church is linked to his teaching on predestination, although certain scholars see these two points as contradicting each other in the system of the blessed Augustine. The blessed Augustine ascribes great impor-

---

[But the spiritual... do not stray without the pale; since even when, by some perversity or necessity among men, they seem to be driven forth, they are more approved than if they had remained within, since they are in no degree roused to contend against the Church, but remain rooted in the strongest foundation of Christian charity on the solid rock of unity]" (PL 43:123–124).

2295 Augustine, *Contra Cresconium* 4.59.71: "Non est enim alius impiae superbiae tumor apud omnes, qui se a Christi unitate discindunt, quam se solos Christianos esse jactare, et damnare caeteros, non solum quibus eorum lis nota est, verum etiam quibus eorum nec nomen auditum est [For there is no other swelling of impious pride among all those who separate themselves from the unity of Christ than to boast that they alone are Christians and to condemn the rest, not only for those whose case is known but also for those of whom not even the name has been heard {trans. —ED.}]" (PL 43:587–588).

2296 Ibid. 3.35.39 (PL 43:517).

2297 For more detail, see Specht, *Die Lehre von der Kirche*, 76–81.

2298 Augustine, *De unitate Ecclesiae* 25.73 (PL 43:443).

tance to predestination in the matter of salvation.[2299] Those predestined for salvation may stray from the path and lead an evil life, but grace can always guide them to the path of salvation. They cannot perish; sooner or later grace will lead them to salvation,[2300] and they will attain to this salvation specifically in the Church.[2301] The determination of a man's fate is only fully disclosed at the end of his life. Only the last moment finally parts for him the mysterious curtain

---

2299 This link between his teaching on predestination and on the sanctity of the Church is especially prominent in *De baptismo contra Donatistas* 5.27.38 (PL 43:195). Cf. Romeis, *Das Heil des Christen ausserhalb der wahren Kirche,* 21–23.

2300 Augustine's teaching on predestination is expounded in detail in the work by L. Pisarev, *The Teaching of the Blessed Augustine, Bishop of Hippo, on Man in his Relation to God* ["Учение блж. Августина, епископа Иппонского, о человеке в его отношении к Богу"] (Kazan: 1894), from 306 on. Concerning the correlation between his teaching concerning the Church and his teaching on grace, see Seeberg, *Studien zur Geschichte dez Begriffs der Kirche,* 41–42, 49–50.

2301 Augustine most decisively expresses the thought that "sancti regno Dei praedestinati dividi ab Ecclesia nullo modo possunt [In no way can the saints, predestined for the kingdom of God, be separated from the Church {*trans.* — *ED.*}]" (*Contra Cresconium* 2.33.42 [PL 43:491]). For more detail about how those pre-appointed are saved not without the Church, see Romeis, *Das Heil des Christen ausserhalb der wahren Kirche.* We must declare baseless the reasoning of Guerrier alleging that "the sphere of the Church in the former sense of a mixed body (*corpus permixtum*) intersects with another sphere of the community of the chosen, which is more narrow, but at the same time in several of its parts protrudes beyond the former church sphere" (*The Blessed Augustine,* 612; cf. Harnack, *Dogmengeschichte*[4] 3, 165). See also the remark of Glubokovsky, "The Blessed Augustine as Depicted by a Russian Secular Historian," in *Works of the Kiev Theological Academy* (1911), vol. 1, 146–147: "Predestination did not occur exclusively through the Church, although the latter is the chief, accessible, and legitimized arena of her saving action." But above, on the same page (147), the author expresses himself more firmly and unambiguously: "For Augustine the Church is the only normal and sanctioned institution of the application to man of the saving predestining will of God that has been revealed to us." In essence, Romeis arrives at the same conclusion in his representation of Augustine's view on the possibility of salvation outside the Church (94–115). Salvation outside the Church is at any rate an extraordinary path, and Augustine does not dwell particularly on this point (114). Cf. Specht, *Die Lehre von der Kirche,* 66–67, 89–94, 307–312. Specht arrives firmly at the conclusion that the teaching on predestination in no way violates the overall ecclesiological system of the blessed Augustine.

of predestination.[2302] Quite logically, this kind of teaching on pre-destination was in complete disagreement with the Donatist view of the Church. One cannot excommunicate every sinner from the Church because, despite his grave sins, he may nevertheless prove predestined for salvation. When Augustine says that we must not hasten to pull up the tares, because we may destroy the wheat also, in these instances his words have a particular meaning: men's fate is hidden from them, and they must not forestall the judgment of God. The task of the Church is not to judge sinners, but to give them the opportunity for correction; and even excommunication from the Church must pursue this same goal. It should also be not-ed that, in speaking of predestination, Augustine is quite far from the supposition that only the predestined comprise the Church. On the contrary, many of the predestined spend almost their whole lives outside the Church, while among the most faithful sons of the Church there are those who are not predestined for salvation.[2303] Not only the predestined belong to the Church, and not all who are predestined belong to the Church.[2304]

The writings of the blessed Augustine in which he polemicizes with Donatism give the impression that he is constantly defending sinners. It is not sinners who defile the Church,[2305] but rather the Church that sanctifies and nurtures sinners, influencing them both by doctrine and by discipline. Consequently, the Church is essential for them, and they ought not to be excommunicated from her. In this way the works of the blessed Augustine give full expression and substantiation to the truth that the earthly Church does not consists solely of saints and the perfect, but rather the purpose of its earthly existence is to nurture and correct sinners.[2306] The Church is mere-

---

2302 Pisarev, op. cit., 308.

2303 Augustine, *De civitate Dei* 1.35 (PL 41:46).

2304 For more detail see Specht, *Die Lehre von der Kirche*, 89–94.

2305 Augustine, *Contra litteras Petiliani* 3.37.43: "Alienis peccatis non maculatur Ecclesia [the sins of other men do not defile the Church]" (PL 43:370); *Epistulae* 93.10.37: "Manifestum est non contaminari justos alienis peccatis [it is manifest that the righteous are not defiled by the sins of other men]" (PL 33:339).

2306 Vgl. Romeis, *Das Heil des Christen ausserhalb der wahren Kirche*, 18.

ly preparing to become glorious, without spot or blemish.[2307] The absolute separation of the righteous from sinners will occur in the age to come.

When the Orthodox and the Donatists were engaged in what was occasionally quite a heated debate over the comparative levels of the moral life of each, as noted above, this debate also had a certain fundamental significance, although ordinarily similar debates are merely the inevitable companions to more substantial dogmatic dissent. Intimately related to the differing dogmatic concepts of the Church was **the question of the moral merit of members of the hierarchy.** It was they, after all, who had in fact caused the schism of the Donatists.[2308] A sacrament performed by a traditor is invalid—this was one of the chief dogmatic theses of Donatism.[2309] Furthermore, in imparting grace to people the Church is wholly dependent on the moral qualities of its hierarchy,[2310] and it cannot endure traitors among its hierarchy without violating its own sanctity.

In all of those writings of the blessed Augustine having to do with Donatism we find a resolute opposition to this view, which for

2307 Augustine, *Retractationes* 2.18 (PL 32:637–638).

2308 It may be thought that the question of the dependence of the sacraments on the personal moral qualities of their ministers had come to a head in Novatian communities, as well, where the tendency was to resolve it in a spirit of Donatism, although independently of the latter. See Pseudo-Augustine, *Quaest.* 102 (PL 35:2311); A. Harnack, *Der pseudoaugustinische Traktat Contra Novatianum. Abhandlungen Alexander von Oettingen gewidmet* (München: 1898), 85–89.

2309 Augustine, *Contra litteras Petiliani* 1.2.3: "Qui fidem a perfido sumpserit, non fidem porcipit, sed reatum [he who receives faith from the faithless receives not faith, but guilt]" (PL 43:247). *Epistulae* 89.5: "De Baptismo solent dicere, tunc esse Baptismum Christi, cum ab homine justo datur [they are accustomed to say regarding baptism, viz. that it is the true baptism of Christ only when it is administered by a righteous man]" (PL 33:311). Cf. *Contra epist. Parmeniani* 2.17.36 (PL 43:77).

2310 Augustine places these words into the mouth of the Donatist (*Sermones* 292.4–6): "Ego baptizo, ego justifico, ego justum facio [*I* baptize, *I* justify, *I* make righteous]" (PL 38:1323–1324). Cf. *Contra epist. Parmeniani* 2.11.23 (PL 43:66). *Contra Cresconium* 4.16.19: "Quam jueti sumus, tam justum Baptismum esse faciamus [As much as we are righteous, so much do we make baptism to be righteous]" (PL 43:559).

him is *res falsissima et absurdissima* [a most deceptive and absurd matter].[2311] Above all, in the writings of the blessed Augustine we find a sort of immanent criticism of the Donatist view. Scripture calls every man a liar who says he is without sin (see 1 Jn. 1:8); consequently, among men there is no one to be found who could truly baptize, if the sacrament depends wholly on the personal qualities of its minister.[2312] One would have to seek an angel in order to be baptized of him.[2313]

The moral qualities of people vary, and if the validity of baptism is dependent upon these qualities, clearly baptism also varies: it is not the same for all.[2314]

The practice of the Donatists themselves does not correspond to their dogmatic doctrine. If the sacraments performed by an unworthy member of the hierarchy are invalid, the Donatists must also rebaptize all those who were baptized by an unworthy person in their own society.[2315] For they cannot possibly deny that in their own society likewise, albeit perhaps unbeknownst to them, there are unworthy hierarchs.[2316] For before these persons were excommunicated they naturally performed sacraments: clearly, these sacraments are invalid, and the people baptized by one who is unworthy do not have true baptism and have not yet entered the Church. Nor do the Donatists baptize those who have separated from them, such as the Maximianists, though they deride them no less than they do

---

2311 Augustine, *De unitate Ecclesiae* 21.59 (PL 43:435).

2312 Augustine, *Contra Cresconium* 2.27.33 (PL 43:487). Cf. 2.16.19 (PL 43:559).

2313 Ibid. 2.28.35 (PL 43:488).

2314 Augustine, *In Ioannos tractatus* 6.8 (PL 35:1428–1429).

2315 Augustine, *Contra epist. Parmeniani* 2.10.21: "Cur mendaces et infideles eorum ministri, non aquam mendacem, sed veracem vel dare vel habere creduntur? Cur ab illorum mortuis qui baptizantur, proficit aliquid lavatio eorum? [Why do the false and faithless ministers of theirs believe that they either give or have not false but true water? Why does their washing accomplish anything of their dead, who are being baptized? {trans. —ED.}]" (PL 43:64).

2316 Augustine, *Contra epist. Parmeniani* 2.10.21: "Fictos bonos, id est occultos malos, apud se esse negare non possunt [They cannot deny that there are feigned good men, that is, hidden evil men, among them {trans. —ED.}]" (PL 43:64–65); *Epistulae* 93.11.49 (PL 33:345).

the Orthodox.[2317] To be consistent, when receiving Maximianists the Donatists would have to rebaptize them. The Donatists themselves reasoned as follows: the sacraments of one who is unworthy are invalid, but only when his unworthiness is known to the Church. If it is unknown, the sacrament remains valid.[2318] In his response to Augustine, Petilian and the Donatists in general made this addendum: a sacrament is invalid if it is received from a known (*sciens*) infidel.[2319] The Donatists did not deny the validity of sacraments performed by hypocrites. But the blessed Augustine naturally found this explanation to be wholly unsatisfactory. A crime is not lessened merely because it is unknown to others. It is known to God. Why is it, then, that only the Church judges validly concerning the sinfulness of any given person, while God does not? God condemns the sin the moment it is committed, though it should long remain unknown to men. The sinner is already dead; he has already lost the Holy Spirit.[2320] If the validity of the sacrament is to be tied to the person of its minister, then assuredly the sacraments performed by a sinful man must be declared invalid from the very moment of his

---

2317 Ibid. 1.13.31 (PL 43:73); 2.15.34 (PL 43:76). Concerning the Maximianists see F. Ribbeck, *Donatus und Augustinus*, 206–236.

2318 Ibid. 2.10.21: "Tunc posse a malo baptizari quemquam, si lateat malitia baptizantis [Then is it possible for anyone to be baptized by a wicked man, if the wickedness of the baptizer escapes notice {trans. —ED.}]" (PL 43:64). Cresconius (*Contra Cresconium* 2.17.21) says that the sanctity of a baptist should be judged "secundum famam, non secundum sinceritatem, quae in illa videri non potest [by reputation, not by honesty, which {sanctity} cannot be seen in that {honesty} {trans. —ED.}]" (PL 43:478).

2319 Augustine, *Contra litteras Petiliani* 3.27.32 (PL 43:363). Cf. *Contra epist. Parmeniani* 2.11.23 (PL 43:67); *Epistulae* 89.5 (PL 33:311).

2320 Augustine, *Contra epist. Parmeniani* 2.10.21 (PL 43:65); 2.13.31: "Nec ullo modo isti expedire se possunt, cum eis proponitur, cur sanctitas sacramenti et haberi et dari possit ab eo, quem intus sceleratum jam Deus damnavit, et tunc incipiat ab eo dari non posse, cum ab hominibus damnatus fuerit, cum tamen nec tunc eam possit amittere [And they cannot in any way disentangle themselves when they are asked why he whom God has already condemned among criminals can both have and give the holiness of the sacrament, and why he ceases to be able to give it when he has been condemned by men—and yet even then he cannot lose it {trans. —ED.}]" (PL 43:73).

sin. From him, as one deprived of the Holy Spirit, it would be impossible to receive sanctification.[2321] If therefore the Donatists wish
to be consistent, all those baptized by one whom they have excommunicated prior to his excommunication must be rebaptized.[2322]
Augustine's demand was, of course, quite justified. The Donatists
lacked consistency in their doctrine concerning the dependence of
the sacraments upon the person performing them. While denying
the validity of Orthodox sacraments on the alleged basis that they
were performed by unworthy ministers, in their own society they
nevertheless recognized the validity of baptism independently of
the personal sanctity of the minister—specifically, when his unworthiness is unknown. The conclusion is that only that which the Donatists wish to consider holy is actually so.[2323] But it is also plain that

---

2321   Ibid. 2.10.21, 24 (PL 43:65–67); *Contra litteras Petiliani* 3.47.57 (PL
43:377–378); 3.52.64 (PL 43:382); 3.30.35 (PL 43:366); *Contra Cresconium* 2.26.31:
"Ita ne quia fictus est mortuus non est? [So, since he is false, is he not dead?
{trans. —ED.}]" (PL43:485).

2322   Ibid. 2.15.34 (PL 43:76); *Contra litteras Petiliani* 1.2.3: "Ecce stat perfidus
baptizaturus, at ille qui baptizandus est, perfidiam ejus ignorat: quid eum accepturum esse arbitraris? utrum fidem, an reatum? Si dixeris fidem: concedes
posse fieri ut a perfido quisque fidem percipiat, non reatum; et falsum erit illud
quod dictum est, Qui fidem a perfido sumpserit, non fidem percipit, sed reatum.
Invenimus enim fieri posse ut etiam a perfido fidem quis percipiat, si perfidiam
dantis ignoret. ... Rebaptizent ergo illos quos ab eis baptizatos esse constiterit,
qui diu apud ipsos conscelerati latuerunt, et postea proditi convictique damnati
sunt [There stands before us one that is faithless ready to baptize, and he who
should be baptized is ignorant of his faithlessness: what think you that he will
receive? Faith, or guilt? If you answer faith, then you will grant that it is possible
that a man should receive not guilt, but faith, from him that is faithless; and the
former saying will be false, that "he who receives faith from the faithless receives
not faith, but guilt." For we find that it is possible that a man should receive faith
even from one that is faithless, if he be not aware of the faithlessness of the giver... then let them rebaptize those who are well known to have been baptized by
men who in their own body have long concealed a life of guilt, but have eventually been detected, convicted, and condemned]" (PL 43:247). *Contra litteras Petiliani*
3.27.32 and thereafter (PL 43:363 sqq.).

2323   Ibid. 2.13.31: "Quid est hoc aliud, quam quod eorum Tichonius de illis
ait, quod volumus sanctum est [What is this other than what their Tyconius says
of them: 'What we wish is holy'? {trans. —ED.}]" (PL 43:73).

the dogmatic view of the Donatists cannot possibly be made the guiding principle of church practice. To declare invalid all sacraments performed by a sinful man from the moment of his sin would mean to destroy the sacraments completely. For a sinful clergyman may conceal his sin until his death, and then all those baptized by him lose their hope of salvation. This latter result means that there is no way of knowing who belongs to the Church and who does not. No one can be certain that he belongs to the Church. There is always room for the question: What if I was baptized by a clandestine sinner?[2324] Once Augustine has pointed out this contradiction in the views of the Donatists, it is plain to see why Augustine is so insistent upon it.[2325]

Finally, Augustine asks: why then consider the baptism of infants invalid? For they do not know that they are baptized by a sinner. The Donatists ought not to rebaptize infants when receiving them into their society, just as they do not baptize anyone who in their society was baptized by a sinner unbeknownst to him.[2326]

Having shown the Donatist view to be inherently contradictory and baseless, the blessed Augustine, generally following Optatus,[2327] expounds in greater detail the view of the Church on the significance of the hierarchy for the sanctifying work of the Church. The Donatists asserted that there were sinful bishops in the Church, and by virtue of this fact alone the people could not be holy. To this Augustine replies that the people may be good even where the bishops are bad. Conversely, the Hebrew people proved wicked although they had Moses as their leader. After all, Christ Himself said of the scribes and Pharisees: do whatsoever they tell you, but do not as they do, "for they say, and do not" (Mt. 23:3). Good may be heard

---

2324 Augustine, *Contra litteras Petiliani* 1.4.5 (PL 43:248). Cf. 3.27.32 (PL 43:364).

2325 Ibid. 3.32.37: "Hinc satago, hoc urgenter interrogo, hoc ut respondeatur vehementissime flagito [This is the point from which I make my effort; this is the question that I press most earnestly; to this I do most urgently demand an answer]" (PL 43:367).

2326 Ibid. 3.26.31 (PL 43:363).

2327 Harnack, *Dogmengeschichte* 3, 154.

even from one who is wicked, and a good work is beneficial regardless of who taught it—a good man or a wicked one. Furthermore, Augustine notes that the Donatists do not apply this criterion to themselves: as an example he cites an instance when among the Donatists the bishop Optatus was found to be corrupt, yet the Donatists did not conclude from this that his whole flock was sinful.[2328] Besides, though he were not a traditor, every bishop may be said to be sinful, like any other man.[2329] We ought not therefore to to make our whole salvation exclusively dependent upon the ever uncertain moral qualities of the persons who perform the sacraments. This is contrary to the teaching of Holy Scripture, which says: "It is better to trust in the Lord than to trust in man" (Ps. 117:8), and, "Cursed be the man that trusteth in man" (Jer. 17:5). All those fall under this curse who make the sacraments dependent not upon God alone, but upon man.[2330] Salvation that is grounded in man is nothing. "Salvation is of the Lord" (Ps. 3:8), and "vain is the salvation of man" (PS. 59:13). Consequently, cursed is he who places his hope in man, though he should know him to be righteous and blameless. For this same reason the apostle Paul likewise censures those who said that they were of Paul, and said, "Was Paul crucified for you? or were ye baptized in the name of Paul?" (1 Cor. 1:13).[2331] One must hope in God the Father, the Son, and the Holy Spirit, and not in Peter or Paul, let alone Donatus or Petilian.[2332] The priest is not an essential mediator between God and man. The apostles John and Paul say that there is one mediator between God and man—Jesus Christ

---

2328 Augustine, *Contra epist. Parmeniani* 2.4.8 (PL 43:55–56). Idem 2.9.18 (PL 43:61). Idem 2.7.12 (PL 43:57–58). *Contra litteras Petiliani* 1.7.8 (PL 43:249); 2.5.11 (PL 43:261).

2329 Augustine, *Contra litteras Petiliani* 2.103.237 (PL 43:340); *Contra epist. Parmeniani* 2.10.20 (PL 43:63).

2330 Concerning the Donatists Augustine says (*In psalmus* 75.7), "Quare computant salutem suam in hominibus esse, non in Deo? [How do they reckon that their salvation is in men, not in God? {trans. —ED.}]" (PL 36:961).

2331 Augustine, *Contra litteras Petiliani* 1.3.4 (PL 43:247–248); 2.5.11 (PL 43:260); 3.28.33 (PL 43:364). Cf. *Epistulae* 89.5 (PL 33:311); *Contra epist. Parmeniani* 2.4.8 (PL 43:55).

2332 Ibid. 2.108.247 (PL 43:346).

(see 1 Jn. 2:1–2), whom the high priest symbolically prefigured in the Old Testament. The apostle Paul says that all, being members of one Body, must pray for each other, and not think themselves to be mediators between God and man.[2333] We cannot even say that a mediator is essential for the conferring of grace at all, because after all there must be a direct conferral of grace to begin with.[2334] Holy Scripture describes instances when the grace of God was poured forth upon people directly. From whom did John the Baptist receive grace? No one laid hands upon the hundred and twenty men upon whom the Holy Spirit descended (see Acts 2:1–4). Even when the Church already existed (*constituto jam ordine Ecclesiae*), before his baptism and before the laying on of hands, Cornelius the centurion was filled with the Holy Spirit together with all those around him, so that even the apostle Peter himself marveled (see Acts 10:44).[2335] It is true none can receive anything without a giver, but the giver is not a man, but God. God Who gives and the person who receives are both present at the sacraments. Either God Himself gives, or He does so through an angel, or through a holy man, through Peter or John, or through an unworthy man, of whom there are many, both secret and obvious.[2336] If the minister is wicked, he performs

---

2333 Augustine, *Contra epist. Parmeniani* 2.8.15–16 (PL 43:59–60).

2334 Ibid. 2.15.33: "Si et ipse a justo homine, et de illo ita quaero, donec ab ipso capite ordinis humani ad aliquem perveniam, qui non ab homine acceperit, atque ita falsum esse doceam, quod non potest homo accipere quidquam, nisi fuerit ei ab homine darum [If {the righteous man} himself also received it from a righteous man, I will then inquire about that {other} one, until from the very head of human succession I arrive at someone who did not receive from man, and so I would show it to be false that man cannot receive something unless it be given him from a man {trans. —ED.}]" (PL 43:75).

2335 Ibid. 2.15.34 (PL 43:76).

2336 Ibid. 2.15.34 (PL 43:76); *De baptismo contra Donatistas* 4.10.16: "In ista quaestione de baptismo non esse cogitandum quis det, sed quid det [in the question of baptism we have to consider, not who gives, but what he gives]" (PL 43:164). 5.21.29: "Sacramentum gratiae dat Deus etiam per malos: ipsam vero gratiam non nisi per se ipsum vel per sanctos suos [Wherefore God gives the sacrament of grace even through the hands of wicked men, but the grace itself only by Himself or through His saints]" (PL 43:191). Cf. *De baptismo contra Donatistas* 3.19.27 (PL 43:152–153); *Contra Crcesconium* 2.21.26 (PL 43:482). Cf. *Epistulae*

only the visible form of the sacrament, while God imparts the invisible grace.[2337] For even the pagans hold that they receive their sham sanctification not from the priests, but from the gods.[2338] Even the Donatists themselves, who consider valid a baptism performed by a clandestine reprobate—do they not acknowledge that in these instances all proceeds from Christ alone, and not from the unworthy minister?[2339] "I believe, not in the minister by whose hands I am baptized," writes Augustine, "but in Him who justifieth the ungodly, that my faith may be counted unto me for righteousness."[2340] Christ alone baptizes, for of Him it is said: "He which baptizeth with the Holy Ghost" (see Jn. 1:33).[2341] Interpreting these words, the blessed Augustine demonstrates in detail that at the Lord's baptism and at the descent of the Holy Spirit in the form of a dove, John the Baptist was convinced specifically of the truth that the power of baptism (*potestas dominici baptismi*) belongs to Christ alone, and does not pass on to any man. Only the ministry passes on to men, and that to both the wicked and the good. The power of baptism, however, the Lord Himself possessed here on earth, as He would possess it

---

89.7: "Sacramenta non humana sunt, sed divina [The sacraments are not human but divine]" (PL 33:312).

2337 Augustine, *Epistulae* 105.3.12: "Semper Dei est illa gratia et Dei Sacramentum, hominis autem solum ministerium; qui si bonus est, adhaeret Deo, et operatur cum Deo; si autem malus est, operatur per illum Deus visibilem Sacramenti formam, ipse autem donat invisibilem gratiam. Hoc sapiamus omnes, et non sint in nobis schismata [That grace is always God's and the sacraments are God's, while only the ministering belongs to man, who, if he is good, cleaves to God and works with God; but if he is wicked, God works through him the visible form of the sacrament, while He Himself bestows the invisible grace. Let us all know this, and let there not be schism among us {trans. —ED.}]" (PL 33:401). *Epistulae* 89.5 (PL 33:311).

2338 Augustine, *Contra litteras Petiliani* 1.9.10 (PL 43:250).

2339 Augustine, *Contra Cresconium* 3.11.13 (PL 43:502).

2340 Augustine, *Contra litteras Petiliani* 1.7.8 (NPNF[1] 4:522; PL 43:249); 2.4.9 (PL 43:260).

2341 Augustine, *Contra epist. Parmeniani* 2.11.23 (PL 43:67); *Contra Cresconium* 2.25.30 (PL 43:484); *De baptismo contra Donatistas* 3.4.6 (PL 43:143).

after ascending bodily into heaven.[2342] Even baptisms performed by Judas were valid.[2343] So also today, a man cannot impart sanctification, whatever he may be, because he is not God.[2344] Only Christ lives eternally; consequently, the sanctification given by Him is always valid.[2345] When sending His apostles forth to preach, Christ breathed upon them and said, "Receive ye the Holy Ghost" (Jn. 20:22). By this He clearly showed that it was not they themselves who would remit sins, but the Holy Spirit through them, just as another passage states: "It is not ye that speak, but the [Holy] Spirit ... which speaketh in you" (Mt. 10:20). Parmenian cited Christ's words: "That which is born of the flesh is flesh; and that which is born of the Spirit is spirit" (Jn. 3:6). But from the Orthodox standpoint of Augustine, these words in no way pertain to baptism by an unworthy minister. The minister does not beget spiritual children himself. It is the Holy Spirit Who begets spiritual children, though the minister were unworthy. The apostle Paul says, "In Christ Jesus I have begotten you through the gospel" (1 Cor. 4:15). Yet Judas too was able to preach the Gospel, and that naturally without detriment for the faithful. Although the Holy Spirit indeed abandons unworthy ministers of the sacraments, sons may be spiritually begotten of God through them.[2346] The presence of corrupt bishops can be of no detriment to laymen, because they have a priest "after the order of Melchisedec," Who sits "on the right hand of God" (Heb. 7:17, 10:12), "who was delivered for our offenses, and was raised again for our justification" (Rom. 4:25).[2347] Naturally, in admitting anyone to the ministry of the sacraments, he ought to "first be proved" (1

2342 Augustine, *In Ioannos tractatus* 5.9.11, 6.7 (PL 35:1419, 1428). Cf. *De consensu evang.* 2.15.32 (PL 35:1093). This interpretation of the blessed Augustine is accorded an important polemical significance: "omnino eorum (donatistarum) ora claudentur [their {the Donatists'} mouths will be altogether shut]" (*In Ioannos tractatus* 4.16 [PL 35:1414]).

2343 Ibid. 5.18 (PL 35:1423–1424).

2344 Augustine, *Contra litteras Petiliani* 2.6.13 (PL 43:261).

2345 Ibid. 2.7.15 (PL 43:262).

2346 Ibid. 2.11.23 (PL 43:66–67); 2.14.32 (PL 43:74).

2347 Augustine, *Contra epist. Parmeniani* 2.5.10 (PL 43:57); 2.8.15 (PL 43:59).

Tim. 3:10), in accordance with the injunction of the apostle Paul; but no proving can fully safeguard against one who is unworthy.[2348] For even among the Donatists themselves unworthy bishops were found.[2349]

By way of arguments such as these Augustine arrives at a clear and definite formulation of his thesis: **the sanctity of a sacrament is not dependent on the sanctity of its minister.**[2350] The Holy Spirit in the Church is united with the celebrant or minister in such a way that if he is not a hypocrite (*fictus*), the Holy Spirit acts through him, supplying an eternal reward to him and rebirth to those initiated or instructed by him. If he should be a hypocrite, he loses his own salvation, but his ministry remains valid and provides salvation to others. For this reason the apostle says: "If I preach voluntarily, I have a reward; if not voluntarily, I am simply discharging the trust committed to me" (1 Cor. 9:17 NIV). That is, the ministry is beneficial for those who avail themselves of it, but not for me, because I am a hypocrite. He did not say that his ministry is of no significance: he deprives only himself of the reward of salvation, and not those to whom the wicked servant distributes the Lord's food.[2351] Truth remains truth, though it were spoken by one who is wicked. For even the demons confessed Christ in the same way as the apostle Peter (see Mt. 16:16, 8:29; Mk. 1:24; Lk. 8:28). So also the sacrament of Christ, whether performed by one who is unworthy or one who is righteous, is none other than the sacrament of Christ. If the minister of the sacrament is corrupt, only his personal unworthiness may be judged from this: the sacrament

---

2348 Augustine, *Contra litteras Petiliani* 3.30.35 (PL 43:365). Cf. *In Ioannos tractatus* 5.15 (PL 35:1422).

2349 Ibid. 3:34.40 (PL 43:368).

2350 See for example *Contra Cresconium* 4.16.19: "Non eorum meritis a quibus ministratur, nec eorum quibus ministratur, constare Baptismum, sed propria sanctitate atque veritate [Baptism does depend upon the value of those by whom it is ministered, nor on the value of those for whom it is ministered, but on its own holiness and truth {trans. —ED.}]" (PL 43:559).

2351 Augustine, *Contra epist. Parmeniani* 2.11.24 (PL 43:67–68). Cf. *Contra litteras Petiliani* 2.30.69 (PL 43:281–282); 3.55.67 (PL 43:384–385).

must not be condemned.[2352] The spiritual action of the sacrament
is like a ray of sunlight, which is not soiled even if it passes through
impure places.[2353] "I do not fear the adulterer, the drunkard, or the
murderer," writes Augustine, "because ... it is said to me, 'This is
He which baptizeth.'"[2354] ... I have ... the baptism of Christ,"[2355]
and it always remains the same.[2356] The sacraments of the ungodly
harm only those who perform them unworthily. The sacrament is
the same by virtue of the name of the Lord invoked, and it is always holy, and for everyone who approaches to receive it, it is such
as to correspond with the state of his heart.[2357] "He that eateth and
drinketh unworthily, eateth and drinketh damnation to himself" (1
Cor. 11:29). It says not "damnation unto all," but damnation "to

---

2352 Augustine, *Contra litteras Petiliani* 3.34.39: "Cum ergo Baptismus Christi, sive per iniquum sive per justum ministratus, nihil aliud sit quam Baptismus
Christi; ab homine cauto et bono fideli iniquitas hominis est vitanda, non Dei
sacramenta damnanda [Seeing, therefore, that the baptism of Christ, whether
administered by an unrighteous or a righteous man, is nothing but the baptism of
Christ, what a cautious man and faithful Christian should do is to avoid the unrighteousness of man, not to condemn the sacraments of God]" (PL 43:368). Cf.
2.47.110 (PL 43:298). See also *De baptismo contra Donatistas* 5.20.27: "Sacramenta
Dei ubique recta sunt, et mali homines, quibus nihil prosunt, ubique perversi sunt
[the sacraments of God are everywhere valid, and evil men whom they profit
not are everywhere perverse]" (PL 43:190). *Contra Cresconium* 2.10.12: "nec curo
per quem fuerint (sacramenta) seminata, sed a quo creata [I do not worry about
through whom {the sacraments} were sown, but by whom they were made to
grow {trans. —ED.}]" (PL 43:474).

2353 Augustine, *In Ioannos tractatus* 5.15 (PL 35:1422).

2354 Ibid. 5.18 (NPNF¹ 7:38; PL 35:1422).

2355 Ibid. 5.13, 18 (NPNF¹ 7:36; PL 35:1421, 1424).

2356 Ibid. 6.8 (NPNF¹ 7:41–42; PL 35:1429).

2357 Augustine, *Contra epist. Parmeniani* 2.6.11: "Nam unum atque idem sacrificium propter nomen Domini quod invocatur, et semper sanctum est et tale
cuique sit, quali corde ad accipiendum accesserit [For the sacrifice is one and the
same, on account of the name of the Lord which is invoked, and it is always holy
and will be for each one, of what sort of heart he approaches to receive {trans.
—ED.}]" (PL43:57). Cf. *Contra litteras Petiliani* 2.108.247 (PL 43:345).

himself."[2358] Thus, the sacrament preserves its sanctity even if the minister is unworthy.[2359]

This point in the teaching of the blessed Augustine is of great importance. The sanctity of the Church is not dependent on the sanctity of the members of the hierarchy. **The Church is holy in her sacraments.** The person performing the sacrament may be unworthy, but this does not cause the sacrament to lose its sanctity. A member of the church hierarchy conveys grace in the sacraments by virtue of his ecclesiastical post, and not by virtue of what are naturally his always relative moral qualities. This conclusion was perfectly natural, because the opposite view of the Donatists was clearly baseless and inconsistent—it necessarily ended in absurdity. It is of great importance that in his polemics with Donatism the blessed Augustine was able to resort to immanent criticism. In the preceding history of the dogma concerning the Church, as we have seen, the doctrine of the sanctity of the Church had not been fully thought out and precisely formulated. Even in the writings of Cyprian there are apparently certain passages that place the sanctity of the Church in a certain dependence on the personal sanctity of members of the hierarchy. The blessed Augustine, like Optatus, gave a definition of the sanctity of the Church that did not contradict the inevitable earthly state of the Church, where no man is without sin.

But acknowledging the sacraments to be fully independent of the person of their minister logically necessitated **the acknowledgment of sacraments outside the Church as well.** The baptism of schismatics must be recognized as valid, because their confession is the same as in the Church.[2360] The blessed Augustine

---

2358 Augustine, *In Ioannos tractatus* 6.15 (PL 35:1432).

2359 See also Specht, *Die Lehre von der Kirche*, 141, 207–214.

2360 This inseparable link between acknowledging the sacrament to be independent of the moral qualities of the person performing it and acknowledging the validity of schismatic baptism is one which Augustine himself insistently emphasizes. In *De baptismo* we constantly encounter arguments such as these: if a sacrament performed by a sinner who has not separated from the Church is valid, then a sacrament performed by a schismatic outside the Church is also valid. For both the one and the other can contribute nothing of their own to

acknowledges the baptism of the Donatists likewise to be fully valid. To this question of baptism he devoted a separate work in seven books written against the Donatists.

The sacraments remain the sacraments, wherever they may be.[2361] They are sacred in and of themselves.[2362] Outside catholic unity baptism can not only be preserved, but can even be imparted.[2363] The blessed Augustine offers a theoretical substantiation of his thesis. One who is baptized in the catholic Church preserves his baptism even when he falls away into schism. But one who received ordination likewise preserves the grace of the priesthood, and that grace includes the right to impart baptism. We must not be unfair in our treatment of any one of the sacraments.[2364] It would be inconsistent to acknowledge that baptism is retained, but to deny schismatics the right to impart it, considering baptism imparted by

---

the validity of the sacrament, which God Himself performs. To acknowledge a sacrament performed by a sinner as valid, while simultaneously rejecting a sacrament performed by a schismatic, is completely inconsistent. See 4.5.7, 4.7.10, 6.26.50, 6.31.60, 6.40.78, 6.43.84, 6.41.80, 7.12.23, 7.15.29, 7.37.73, 7.54.103 (PL 43:158, 160, 215, 217, 221, 222, 230, 231, 236, 244). Cf. *Epistulae* 109.11.48 (PL 43:344).

2361 Augustine, *Contra epist. Parmeniani* 2.13.28: "Quae ubicumque sunt, ipsa sunt" (PL 43:70). *Contra litteras Petiliani* 2.108.247 (PL 43:345–346); *Epist.* 87.9: "Non quaerimus ubi sit, sed ubi prosit [we do not ask where it may be but where it may be useful {trans. —ED.}" (PL 33:301). *Epistulae* 98.5 (PL 33:362).

2362 Augustine, *De baptismo contra Donatistas* 4.10.16 (PL 43:164); 5.4.4: "Baptismus Christi per se ipsum reverendissimum atque sanctissimum esse posse credamus [to believe that... the baptism of Christ is yet in itself most holy, and most highly to be reverenced]" (PL 43:179).

2363 Ibid. 1.1.2 (PL 43:109); 4.1.1, 5.23.33, 6.5.7: "Potest tamen tradere separatus, sicut potest habere separatus [yet he that is separated may confer it, as he that is separated may have it]" (PL 43:155, 193, 200).

2364 Ibid. 1.1.2: "Sicut autem baptizatus, si ab unitate recesserit, sacramentum Baptismi non amittit, sic etiam ordinatus, si ab unitate recesserit Sacramentum dandi Baptismi non amittit. Nulli enim Sacramento injuria facienda est [And as the baptized person, if he depart from the unity of the Church, does not thereby lose the sacrament of baptism, so also he who is ordained, if he depart from the unity of the Church, does not lose the sacrament of conferring baptism. For neither sacrament may be wronged]" (PL 43:109). Cf. *Contra epist. Parmeniani* 2.13.30 (PL 43:72).

schismatics to be invalid. The right to impart baptism is not some kind of new right—it belongs to the sphere of rights of a different sacrament: the priesthood, which schismatics retain just as they do baptism itself.

Furthermore, the blessed Augustine cites several passages from Holy Scripture in defense of schismatic baptism. He recalls and comments on the Gospel account of the man who was casting out devils in the name of Jesus Christ though he was not His disciple. At that time Christ said to His disciples, "He that is not against us is for us" (Lk. 9:50). It should be seen from this that in certain areas those outside the Church are not against the Church: they have something of the grace of the Church, and they have its sacraments likewise.[2365] They have stolen these sacraments from the Church, as it were.[2366] When they convert to the Church, they have no more need to receive that which they do not require, because they had it even before this. They need only correct that in which they have erred. This reasoning is applicable to all schismatics: they are not excommunicated from the Church in every aspect. There are areas in which they are not against the catholic Church; consequently, they are with the Church.[2367] Finally, Augustine confronts the Donatists with the fact that while they rebaptize catholics they do not

---

2365 Augustine, *Epistulae* 87.9: "Sacramenta quae non mutastis, sicut habetis approbantur a nobis [the sacraments which you have not changed are approved by us as you have them]" (PL 33:301). *Epistulae* 93.11.46: "Ex catholica Ecclesia sunt omnia dominica Sacramenta, quae sic habetis et datis, quemadmodum habebantur et dabantur, etiam priusquam inde exiretis [For from the Catholic Church are all the sacraments of the Lord, which you hold and administer in the same way as they were held and administered even before you went forth from her]" (PL 33:343). *Sermo ad plebem Caesariensis ecclesiae* 2: "Ecclesiae habent bona" (PL 43:691).

2366 Augustine, *Contra Cresconium* 2.12.14 (PL 43:474).

2367 Augustine, *De baptismo contra Donatistas* 1.7.9: "Si forte veniret ad Ecclesiam non illud quod habebat ibi acciperet, sed in quo aberraverat emendaret [if it should have so happened that he sought union with the Church, he should not have received what he already possessed, but be made to set right the points wherein he had gone astray]" (PL 43:115; cf. 114). 1.8.10: Augustine cites the example of the centurion Cornelius. Cf. *Epistulae* 109.11.46 (PL 33:343); *Contra Cresconium* 2.12.14 (PL 43:474); *Epistulae* 93.11.46 (PL 33:343).

rebaptize their own schismatics, such as the Maximianists.[2368] The
blessed Augustine even takes a providential view of the schism of
Maximian: it was a divine benefaction, since it convicts the error of
the Donatists most visibly.[2369] These Maximianists are the subject
of the entire fourth book of Augustine's work *Against Cresconius.*[2370]
Additionally, Augustine also wrote a separate brief work that has
since been lost, *Admonitio Donatistarum de Maximianistis,*[2371] followed
by *Librum de Maximianistis contra Donatistas, non brevissimun sicut antea,
sed grandem, multo diligentius.*[2372] This work has likewise been lost.

But the Donatists had another argument in support of schismatic baptism: they cited the teaching of St. Cyprian of Carthage
on this subject, with which we are already familiar, and the decree
of the entire Council of Carthage. The reference to Cyprian was
a favorite and quite commonly employed among the Donatists.[2373]
Apparently, the blessed Augustine himself ascribed particular significance to this argument of the Donatists—almost the whole of
his work *On Baptism* is devoted specifically to elucidating the contradiction between his own teaching and the church practice of his
day, on the one hand, and the teaching of St. Cyprian, on the other. The blessed Augustine acknowledges that St. Cyprian indeed
thought differently regarding the baptism of schismatics. Nevertheless, the Donatists have no right to cite the authority of Cyprian.
Augustine cites the well-known opening remarks of St. Cyprian at

2368 Ibid. 1.1.2, 1.5.7 (PL 43:109–110, 113). Cf. *De haeres.* 69 (PL 42:43–44);
Epistulae 108.2.6 (PL 33:408); *Contra litteras Petiliani* 1.10.11, 1.11.12 (PL 43:251,
253); *Contra Gaudentius* 2.7 (43:745); *Contra Cresconium* 4.5.6 (PL 43:551), 4.16.19
(PL 43:559).

2369 Augustine, *Contra Cresconium* 4.1.1 (PL 43:547).

2370 Augustine, *Retractationes* 2.26 (PL 32:641).

2371 "Admonition of the Donatists Regarding the Maximianists", ibid. 2.29
(PL 32:642).

2372 "Book on the Maximianists Against the Donatists, Not Short Like the
Previous One, but Large, Much More Thorough", ibid. 2.35 (PL 32:645).

2373 Augustine, *De baptismo contra Donatistas* 2.3.4: "Vos certe nobis objicere
soletis Cypriani litteras, Cypriani sententiam, Cypriani concilium [You are wont,
indeed, to bring up against us Cyprian's letters, Cyprian's opinion, Cyprian's
Council]" (PL 43:128).

the Council of Carthage in 256, where he refuses to compel anyone at all to agree with him. Cyprian even allows for the possibility of differences in thinking, and he calls upon his hearers not to sunder church unity over differences of opinion.[2374] He was a particular champion of peace in the Church: he himself did not separate from those who thought differently, and he exhorted others to maintain church unity.[2375] For this reason Augustine puts this question to the Donatists: given that they cite the opinion and decree of Cyprian with such frequency, why do they not follow his example of how one ought to hold fast to peace in the Church?[2376] In this Cyprian reproves the Donatists by his example,[2377] and the blessed Augustine frequently and insistently inquires of the Donatists: *Quare vinculum disrupistis? Quare vos separastis?*[2378] Cyprian thought otherwise: he did not place differences of opinions higher than church unity.[2379] Expounding on Cyprian's epistles to Jubaianus and Quintus in detail, Augustine demonstrates just how far Cyprian is from the Donatists.

Furthermore, in his epistle to Quintus St. Cyprian himself cites the example of the apostle Peter—how after being convinced by Paul he altered his incorrect understanding of the Gospel (*non recte in aliquo ingredi ad veritatem Evangelii*). And Cyprian himself was al-

---

2374 Ibid. 2.2.3 (PL 43:128).

2375 Ibid. 1.18.28 (PL 43:124); 2.8.13 (PL 43:134); 2.5.6 (PL 43:129).

2376 Ibid. 2.3.4 (PL 43:128); 2.7.12: "Tenete nobiscum exemplium Cypriani ad unitatis conservationem [cling with us to the example of Cyprian for the preservation of unity] (PL 43:132).

2377 Ibid. 1.1.1: "Non solum eos non adjurari auctoritate Cypriani, sed per ipsam maxime convinci atque subverti [so far from Cyprian's authority being in their favor, it tends directly to their refutation and discomfiture]" (PL 43:109). *Epistulae* 108.3.9 (PL 33:410); *Epistulae* 93.9.41 (PL 33:341).

2378 "Why have ye broken the bond? Why have ye separated yourselves?", ibid. 2.6.7, 8; 2.7.10 (PL 43:130, 131, 132). In another instance Augustine's question is put still more bluntly: "Ad ista respondete, lupi rapaces, qui pellibus ovinis indui cupientes, beati Cypriani litteras pro vobis esse arbitramini [Answer me this, you ravening wolves, who, seeking to be clad in sheep's clothing, think that the letters of the blessed Cyprian are in your favor]" (ibid. 2.7.11; PL 43:133).

2379 Ibid. 2.5.6 (PL 43:130).

ways prepared not only to teach, but to learn, and was willing to readily accept that which was shown to him to be better.[2380]

The question of schismatic baptism was highly controversial, and it ought to be resolved only amid differences in thinking, amid the reflections of the bishops.[2381] In his own resolution of the question, Cyprian drew on the decision of a previous Council under Aggripinus and on local custom.[2382] At that time no consensus of the whole Church (*totius Ecclesiae consensio*) on the question had been established, and the opinion of the plenary Council (*plenarii concilii*) had not been declared.[2383] For this reason Cyprian did not think it possible to require that all agree with this custom. Afterward, however, amid numerous arguments and investigations from many different aspects, something different was not only established, but decreed by authority of the whole Council, which was held after Cyprian suffered and before we were born. The universal is always rightly preferred over the individual (*universum partibus semper jure optimo praeponitur*).[2384]

If St. Cyprian did not consider his opinion binding, consequently he allowed for the possibility that another opinion might in fact be the true one. But even if the true opinion is that of Cyprian and the Donatists, it must nevertheless be said that the Donatists are not right in separating from the catholics. They separate, naturally, because they consider fellowship with them to mean the destruction of the true Church. And yet St. Cyprian did not separate from those who thought differently; consequently, the Church had already perished in Cyprian's day, and Donatus received both his baptism and his ordination outside the true Church. Conversely, if the Church had not perished in Cyprian's time, the Donatists are wrong in separating from the catholic Church.[2385]

2380 Ibid. 2.1.2, 2.8.13 (PL 43:126–127, 134).

2381 Ibid. 2.4.5 (PL 43:129).

2382 Ibid. 2.7.12, 2.8.13, 2.9.14 (PL 43:133, 134, 135).

2383 Ibid. 1.18.28 (PL 43:124).

2384 Ibid. 2.9.4 (PL 43:135). Here Augustine is probably referring to the Council of Arles of 314. Cf. *Nota* a (PL 43:135–136).

2385 Ibid. 2.6.7–8 (PL 43:130–131).

But most important of all, from a historical and dogmatic standpoint, is the fact that Augustine does not consider St. Cyprian's teaching concerning the Church to be fully complete and consistently developed: in Cyprian also he discovers certain elements of the same teaching which he himself decisively expresses. Augustine calls particular attention to the following words of Cyprian in his epistle to Jubaianus. Cyprian asks, "What, then, shall become of those who in past times, coming from heresy to the Church, were received without baptism?" And he answers: "The Lord is able by His mercy to give indulgence, and not to separate from the gifts of His Church those who by simplicity were admitted into the Church, and in the Church have fallen asleep."[2386] [2387] It is plain that Cyprian considered such people baptized after all. They could not be saved if they were not in the ark—that is, the Church—but how are they in the ark when they have not been reborn in water? For the sake of their unity with the Church, the water of baptism performed outside the Church has served for their salvation. All those who at heart are in the Church, in the unity of the ark, are saved by the same water which for all opponents of unity, who at heart stand without, whether or not they are actually separated from the Church, serves unto their destruction.[2388]

Such is the defense of schismatic baptism which the blessed Augustine offers. But if schismatic baptism is valid, and **if the Church alone does not possess the sacraments, is not salvation possible both outside the Church and without the**

2386 Cyprian of Carthage, *Epistles* 72–60, "To Jubaianus" 23 (ANF 5:385; CSEL 3.2:796).

2387 Here the numbering of the end notes in the source skip a number, going directly from 265 to 267. Consequently, from here on the numbering will be off by one between the source and the translation. – *Trans.*

2388 Augustine, *De baptismo contra Donatistas* 6 [5].28.39: "Omnes qui corde sunt intus, in arcae unitate per eamdem aquam salvi fiunt, per quam omnes qui corde sunt foris, sive etiam corpore foris sint, sive non sint, tanquam unitatis adversarii moriuntur [all who are within in heart are saved in the unity of the ark through the same water, through which all who are in heart without, whether they are also in body without or not, die as enemies of unity]" (PL 43:196, 197–198). Cf. 2.14.19 (PL 43:138–139); *Contra Cresconium* 2.33.41 (PL 43:491).

Church? Does this not allow for the existence of multiple Churches, mutually divided, and even hostile to each other? How is the
validity of baptism outside the Church to be reconciled with the
unity of the Church? These are questions that the blessed Augustine must answer, the more so since the Donatists sometimes raised
the following objection: You acknowledge our baptism, but we do
not acknowledge yours; consequently, our baptism is more reliable,
and every man must prefer our baptism as better able to secure his
salvation.[2389]

How does the blessed Augustine answer these questions put to
him?

The baptism of schismatics, Augustine states, is the same baptism, but it is of no benefit to them; indeed, it is only to their detriment.[2390] It leads not to eternal life, but to eternal punishment.[2391]
Gold is certainly good, and gold it remains even in the hands of
robbers, but it serves ill purposes: one who possesses gold must not
have robbers as his confederates.[2392] Much that is good in general
has a good purpose, but it can only be truly good in the hands of
those who employ it well. Light is an aid (*adjumentum*) to sound eyes,

2389 So reasoned Cresconius, for example—*Contra Cresconium* 1.21.26, 1.26.31
(PL 43:460, 462). Cf. *De baptismo contra Donatistas* 1.3.4 (PL 43:111).

2390 Augustine, *De baptismo contra Donatistas* 1.2.3, 6.40.78 (PL 43:110, 221);
Contra Cresconium 1.22.27 (PL 43:460). Augustine delineates the concepts of "to
have" and "to have to one's benefit" (*utiliter, salubriter*). See *De baptismo contra Donatistas* 4.17.24 [25]: "Aliud est non habere, aliud non utiliter habere [it is one
thing not to have, another to have so as to be of no use]" (PL 43:170). *Contra epist.
Parmeniani* 2.13.28: "Aliud est non habere, aliud perniciose habere, aliud salubriter habere [it is one thing not to have, another to have destructively, another to
have beneficially {trans. —ED.}]" (PL 43:71).

2391 Augustine, *Contra Cresconium* 2.13.16, 4.21.26 (PL 43:476, 563); *De baptismo contra Donatistas* 4.10.16 (PL 43:164), 4.9.13 (PL 43:162); *Epistulae* 108.2.6 (PL
33:408), cf. 6.16 (PL 33:415); *De unico bapt. Contra Petilian* 6.7, 10.17 (PL 43:599,
604); *Contra Faustum* 12.17.20 (PL 42:263, 264, 265). See also *De baptismo contra Donatistas* 1.2.3, 3.10.13, 4.13.20, 4.17.24, 5.4.4, 7.33.65, 7.38.75 (PL 43:110, 144,
167, 170, 179, 235, 236); *Contra litteras Petiliani* 1.23.25, 3.40.46 (PL 43:257, 372);
De unitate Ecclesiae 22.61 (PL 43:437); *Sermo de Rusticiano* 1 (PL 43:756); *Epistulae*
61.1.2 (PL 33:229).

2392 Ibid. 1.22.27 (PL 43:460).

but to infirm eyes it is torment. The same food can nourish some while weakening others; a weapon defends some while only barring the way to others; clothing covers some but trips up others. So also baptism leads some to the Kingdom, but others to damnation,[2393] as the waves of the Red Sea served for the salvation of the Israelites, but for the undoing of pharaoh.[2394] During the flood the water destroyed all those who were outside the ark, and by the same means good members of the Church (*boni catholici*) are saved, while the wicked (*mali catholici*) or heretics perish.[2395] The apostle Paul said concerning the law: "The law is good, if a man use it lawfully" (1 Tim. 1:8). But if anyone uses the law unlawfully, clearly the law remains good, but it serves for the undoing of the wicked.[2396] Even concerning the very Body and Blood of the Lord, that sole Sacrifice for our salvation, the apostle says: "Whosoever shall eat this bread, and drink this cup of the Lord, unworthily, shall be guilty of the body and blood of the Lord" (1 Cor. 11:27).[2397] Why cannot the same be said of baptism? Is everyone who receives baptism really necessarily good? Although baptism is good, it does not benefit everyone who possess it.[2398]

But why is it specifically schismatic baptism that incurs damnation instead of justification? To this Augustine firmly and insistently replies: because **the heretics have no love, as attested by their separation from the Church.** Whoever has love cannot be a heretic or a schismatic.[2399] Whoever has separated from the Church has no love. Whoever does not love the unity of the Church has not the love of God.[2400] If anyone does not hold fast to unity, it

---

2393 Ibid. 1.23.28 (PL 43:460).

2394 Augustine, *In psalmus* 135.9 (PL 37:1760).

2395 Augustine, *De baptismo contra Donatistas* 5.28.39 (PL 43:197–198). Cf. *Contra Faustum* 12.17 (PL 42:263).

2396 Augustine, *Contra Cresconium* 1.24.29 (PL 43:461). The law [is discussed] in more detail with a reference to Rom. 3:10–19, 7:7–13 (ibid. 25.30 [PL 43:461]).

2397 Ibid. 1.25.30 (PL 43:462). Cf. *In Ioannos tractatus* 7.6 (PL 35:2032).

2398 Ibid. 1.26.31–27.32 (PL 43:462).

2399 Ibid. 2.13.16 (PL 43:476).

2400 Augustine, *De baptismo contra Donatistas* 3.16.21 (PL 43:148). Cf. *In Ioannos*

is in vain that he says he has the love of Christ.[2401] There can be no lawful reason for separating from the Church,[2402] and for this reason schism itself is invariably a grave sin,[2403] which strips a person of all the saving grace of the sacraments. Whoever is outside the Church can no longer be good. He is already wicked by virtue of having separated from the Church.[2404] The blessed Augustine cites the exalted words of the apostle Paul, where the latter says, that whatever gifts he may possess, he is nothing if he has not love (see 1 Cor. 13:1–3). Caiaphas prophesied (see Jn. 11:49–52), but was condemned. So also the sacraments cannot save schismatics, for they

---

tractatus 6.14: "Quomodo habeat charitatem, qui dividit unitatem [how can he who divides unity have charity?]" (PL 35:1432).

2401 Augustine, *Epistulae* 61.2 (PL 33:229).

2402 Augustine, *Contra epist. Parmeniani* 2.11.25: "Praecidendae unitatis nulla est justa necessitas [there is no justified necessity for cut off unity {trans. —ED.}]" (PL 43:69).

2403 Ibid. 2.11.25: "Non esse quidquam gravius sacrilegio schismatis [there is nothing more serious than the sacrilege of schism {trans. —ED.}]" (PL 43:69). Cf. *Contra litteras Petiliani* 2.96.221: "Vos omnes nocentes et sceleratos esse ... crimine schismatis, a quo immansissimo sacrilegio nemo vestrum se potest immunem, quamdiu non communicat unitate omnium gentium [you are all guilty and accursed... by the sin of schism; from which most heinous sacrilege no one of you can say that he is free, so long as he refuses to hold communion with the unity of all nations]" (PL 43:333). Cf. *De baptismo contra Donatistas* 1.5.6 (PL 43:113). Concerning Augustine's sharp arguments regarding heresies and schisms, see Romeis, *Das Heil des Christen ausserhalb der wahren Kirche*, 71–73.

2404 Augustine, *Epistulae* 208.6: "Ab ea (Ecclesia) separati, quamdiu contra illam sentiunt, boni esse non possunt; quia et si aliquos eorum bonos videtur ostendere quasi laudabilis conversatio, malos eos tacit [facit] ipsa divisio [those who are separated from the Church, as long as they are opposed to it cannot be good; although an apparently praiseworthy conversation {way of life} seems to prove some of them to be good, their separation from the Church itself renders them bad]" (PL 33:952). Cf. *Contra epist. Parmeniani* 2.3.6 (PL 43:54); *De baptismo contra Donatistas* 1.8.10 (PL 43:115); *Epistulae* 185.9.42: "Nemo potest esse justus, quamdiu fuerit ab unitate hujus corporis separatus [no one can be righteous so long as he is separated from the unity of this body]" (PL 33:811). *Sermones* 312.6: "Nulla esset charitas christiani, a quo non custodiretur unitas Christi [There would not be any love of a Christian by whom the unity of Christ is not guarded {trans. —ED.}]" (PL 38:1422).

have not love.[2405] Without love and unity there is no Holy Spirit, and without the Spirit there is no benefit from the sacraments either,[2406] and true virtue is impossible.[2407] The apostle says that if I "understand all mysteries (*sacramenta*) … and have not charity, I am nothing" (1 Cor. 13:2). What is baptism? A sacrament (*sacramentum*). Clearly, without love it too will be of no benefit. He did not say that without love all the things he has listed are nothing, but that he himself is nothing. All that he is listed is great, and I possess great things; yet I myself am nothing if I have not love. Only love renders all things beneficial for me. I may have all that is great, but without love it will be of no benefit to me.[2408]

Augustine repeats this primary thesis when answering various questions regarding sacraments outside the Church. **Does the baptism of the Donatists beget children unto God**, he was asked? If it does, then Donatism is the true Church. If it does not, they must be rebaptized upon their conversion.[2409] Augustine resolves this conundrum as follows. Schismatics separate from the Church not by their baptism, for their baptism is of the Church, but rather specifically by their isolation. It is not separation from the Church that begets them, but the baptism which they preserve even in their separation from the Church. But they are begotten to

---

2405 Augustine, *De baptismo contra Donatistas* 1.9.12 (PL 43:116); 3.14.19 (PL 43:147); 3.16.21 (PL 43:148); *In Ioannos tractatus* 6.21 (PL 35:1435).

2406 Ibid. 4.1.1; 5.23.33 (PL 43:155, 193); *Sermones* 268.2: "Qui cunque praeter hanc Ecclesiam est, non habet Spiritum sanctum [He who is at any time contrary to this Church does not have the Holy Spirit {trans. —ED.}]" (PL 38:1232). *In ep. Iohannem tractatus* 6.11 (PL 35:2026).

2407 Augustine, *Sermones* 71.19.32: "Virtus pietatis invisibilis et spiritualis ita in eis non potest esse, quemadmodum sensus non sequitur hominis membrum, quando amputatur a corpore [The virtue of piety, invisible and spiritual, thus cannot be in them, just as feeling does not follow a human member when it is cut off from the body {trans. —ED.}]" (PL 38:463).

2408 Augustine, *Sermo ad caesarensis ecclesiae plebem* 3 (PL 43:692–693). The explanation of 1 Cor. 13:1–3 is marked by a particular vividness in this speech. See also *In 1 Ioannos tractatum* 5.6 (PL 35:2015); *In Ioannos tractatum* 32.8 (PL 35:1646); *De baptismo contra Donatistas* 5.23.33 (PL 43:193).

2409 Augustine, *De baptismo contra Donatistas* 1.10.13 (PL 43:116–117).

no effect. One reborn in baptism receives no benefit from this if he fails utterly to preserve love, even if he has not visibly separated from the Church; outside the Church all the sacraments are still more useless. The man without love and the schismatic alike receive no benefit from baptism while they remain in that state. For a sinner who is in the Church, baptism begins to be salvific when he acquires love, and for the schismatic—when he unites himself to the Church. But just as the former is not rebaptized, so also the latter ought not to be. He possesses baptism, but it is of no benefit. But when he unites himself to the Church, that which he already had becomes beneficial. The Church bears children both from her own womb (*per uterum suum*), and from the womb of her handmaidens (*per uteros ancillarum*), bearing them by means of the same sacraments, from the seed of her Husband. With good reason the apostle Paul says that Hagar and Sarah are images (cf. Gal. 4:24). The proud schismatics, not wishing to join themselves to their lawful mother, are like Ishmael, who was not the heir of Abraham (see Gen. 21:10). Schismatics who convert to the Church are like the sons of Jacob who, although born of bondwomen, were his heirs (see Gen. 30:3). Those who are born in the Church but who have neglected grace are like Esau, who was Isaac's son but was rejected (see Gen. 25:24, Mal. 1:2–3).[2410]

2410   Augustine, *De baptismo contra Donatistas* 1.5.7, 1.10.14, 7.6.11, 7.44.87, 7.54.103 (PL 43:113, 117–118, 228, 238, 244). Cf. 1.15.23: "Ecclesia omnes per Baptismum parit, sive apud se, id est, ex utero suo; sive extra se de semine viri sui, sive de se, sive de ancilla [it is the Church that gives birth to all, either within her pale, of her own womb; or beyond it, of the seed of her bridegroom—either of herself, or of her handmaid]" (PL 43:121–122). Cf. *De baptismo contra Donatistas* 4.17.24 [25]: "Qui non habet est baptizandus ut habeat: qui autem non utiliter habet, ut utiliter habeat corrigendus [he who has not must be baptized that he may have; but he who has to no avail must be corrected, that what he has may profit him]" (PL 43:170). *Contra Cresconium* 1.29.34: "Non cum ad nos veneritis alterum (baptismum) accipiatis, sed ut eum qui jam apud vos erat, utiliter habeatis [not so that, when you have come to us, you may receive another {baptism}, but so that what you already had you might have profitably {trans. —ED.}]" (PL 43:463–464). *De baptismo contra Donatistas* 5.28.39: "Illic eis aqua incipit prodesse ad salutem [within the water begins to be profitable to them unto salvation]" (PL 43:196). *Contra Cresconium* 2.12.14, 2.13.16 (PL 43:474, 476); *De baptismo contra*

He was also asked: **Are sins forgiven in baptism among the Donatists?** If so, the Donatists have the Holy Spirit and their society is the Church. If not, their baptism is not true, and they must be rebaptized.[2411] But can sins be forgiven where there is no love? One who is baptized has put on Christ (see Gal. 3:27), "but he that hateth his brother is in darkness" (1 Jn. 2:11): consequently he has not put on Christ, and consequently he is not baptized.[2412]

Augustine responds by asking: what if a man approaches baptism in hypocrisy (*fictus*)? Are his sins forgiven or not? If they are not, he ought to be rebaptized when he ceases to be a hypocrite, but the Donatists themselves do not do this. We should therefore reason as follows. The baptism of Christ renews a man, but his heart, which persists in wickedness or schism (*sacrilegio*), does not allow remission of sins to occur. In societies that have separated from the Church people do receive baptism, but in this instance the grace of baptism, which remits sins if the one being baptized is united to the Church, is as though paralyzed, so that the sins of the one being baptized are retained and cannot be remitted.[2413] If however one who received

---

Donatistas 6.31.60 (PL 43:217); *Epistulae* 108.2.6: "Quando cum illo ad Ecclesiam venerit, quod foris oberat, intus proderit; non cum ipse repetitur Baptismum, sed cum corrigitur baptizatus [When it comes with him to the Church, what was hurtful without will profit him within; not when he himself repeats the baptism, but when he is corrected having been baptized {trans. —ED.}]" (PL 33:408); cf. 6.16 (PL 33:415). *Epistulae* 93.2.46 (PL 33:343); *Contra litteras Petiliani* 3.40.46 (PL 43:372); *Contra Cresconium* 2.28.34: "Tunc ei prodesse incipere, cum transit ad corpus Christi, quod est Ecclesia Dei vivi [then it starts to profit him, when he crosses over to the body of Christ, which is the Church of the living God {trans. —ED.}]" (PL 43:487); cf. 2.28.36 (PL 43:488). *Contra Gaudentius* 1.12.13 (PL 43:711); *De civitate Dei* 21.27.3 (PL 41:748); *In Ioannos tractatum* 6.14, 17, 18 (PL 35:1432, 1433, 1434).

2411 Augustine, *De baptismo contra Donatistas* 1.11.15 (PL 43:118).

2412 Ibid. 1.11.16 (PL 43:118).

2413 Ibid. 1.12.18: "Qui tamen tunc prosit ad remissionem peccatorum, cum quis reconciliatus unitati, sacrilegio dissensionis exuitur, quo ejus peccata tenebantur, et dimitti non sinebantur [it will only then be of avail for the remission of sins, when the recipient, being reconciled to the unity of the Church, is purged from the sacrilege of deceit, by which his sins were retained, and their remission prevented]" (PL 43:119).

baptism in societies that have separated from church unity converts to the true Church, the force witholding forgiveness of sins is removed, and forgiveness of sins ensues without a new baptism: the grace of baptism, formerly held back by hardened obstinacy and a refusal to unite with the Church, comes into effect, so to speak.[2414] While they have no love for unity, baptism serves for schismatics unto perdition.[2415]

The action of baptism among schismatics may also be pictured in this way. The sins of the recipient of baptism are forgiven, but immediately they return to him again. The sacrament is holy in and of itself (*per se ipsum*), and one who receives baptism outside the Church passes through a narrow band of light, as it were, and out again into darkness. For a time, namely, while he is passing through this band of light, he is cleansed of sins, because baptism belongs to the Church. But since immediately after baptism he again enters the darkness of his schism (*ad dissensionis suae tenebras*), his sins promptly return.[2416] The Lord vividly showed that forgiven sins return again if brotherly love is lacking when He told of the servant to whom his master forgave ten thousand talents. When that servant did not take pity upon his fellow servant who owed him a hundred denarii, the master commanded that he repay all that he owed him. Just as that servant received forgiveness of his debt for a time, so also one who is baptized outside the Church is temporarily freed from his sins. But since even after baptism a schismatic has no love for his brethren, remaining outside the Church, all the sins he committed even before baptism are imputed to him once again.[2417] Schismatics are forgiven their sins only when they unite themselves to the Church with

---

2414 Ibid. 1.12.18: "ipsa ei reconciliatione ac pace praeastatur, ut ad remissionem peccatorum ejus in unitate jam prodesse incipiat Sacramentum, quod acceptum in schismate prodesse non poterat [it will only then be of avail for the remission of sins, when the recipient, being reconciled to the unity of the Church, is purged from the sacrilege of deceit, by which his sins were retained, and their remission prevented]" (PL 43:119).

2415 Augustine, *Contra epist. Parmeniani* 2.13.28 (PL 43:71).

2416 Augustine, *De baptismo contra Donatistas* 1.12.19, 7.3.5 (PL 43:119–120, 227).

2417 Ibid. 1.12.20 (PL 43:120).

love.[2418] Then there is no need to rebaptize them: their baptism was the same as that which is in the Church, and they did not differ in this from the members of the Church, but they lacked love. When this lack is supplied, however, that which they already have begins to benefit them. "Charity shall cover a multitude of sins" (1 Pet. 4:8). Schismatics lose their hope of salvation not because their baptism is invalid, but only because they are outside the Church and are at enmity with her. Though Esau was born of the wife, he was separated from the people of God for his strife with his brother. Though Asher was born of a slave, through the authority of the wife he inherited the promised land for his brotherly love. Ishmael was cut off from the people of God not because he was born of a slave, but because he hated his brother: not even the authority of the wife, by whose will he was born of a slave, was of any benefit to him. So also in baptism all are born and—if they have love for their brethren— inherit the promised land, not by being reborn from their mother's womb, but by virtue of their father's seed. If however they are at enmity with their brethren, their lot is the lot of Ishmael.[2419]

In the teaching of the blessed Augustine concerning schismatic baptism here presented we cannot fail to notice a somewhat different evaluation of schismatics than that which we saw in St. Cyprian. In denying baptism outside the Church, St. Cyprian cited the fact that the heretics have a different faith—that is, he spoke of heretics, to whom he also equated schismatics. For St. Cyprian, the boundaries of the one Church coincide with those of Christianity in gen-

---

2418 Ibid. 1.13.21; 6.34.65 (PL 43:121, 219); *Contra Gaudentius* 1.12.13: "Ipsa catholicae unitatis charitate mundari, ut non incipiat eis intus inesse quod et foris inerat, sed incipiat eis prodesse intus quod foris oberat [...They themselves {can} be cleansed by the love of catholic unity, so that what was in them without does not begin to be in them within, but what was harmful without begins to profit them within {trans. —ED.}]" (PL 43:711). *Epistulae* 61.1: "Sanctum Sacramentum quod foris ab Ecclesia habent ad perniciem, in pace Ecclesiae habeant ad salutem [they may have within the peace of the Church that holy sacrament for their salvation, which they meanwhile have beyond the pale of the Church for their destruction]" (PL 33:229). Cf. *Epistulae* 141.13 (PL 33:583); *Epistulae* 89.7 (PL 33:312); *Epistulae* 61.2 (33:229).

2419 Ibid. 1.15.23 (PL 43:121–122).

eral. The blessed Augustine fully allows for the possibility that true faith can be preserved even outside the Church. In proof of this Augustine even cites several passages of Holy Scripture: the words of the apostle Paul in the Areopagus in Athens (see Acts 17:23), and the testimony of the apostle James that "the devils also believe" (Jas. 2:19)—the latter naturally being outside the Church.[2420] Consequently, the Church is a more narrow concept than Christianity, understood in the sense of known theoretical tenets. One may be in agreement with these theoretical tenets, and yet not be in the Church. Union with the Church also requires a consensus of the will (*consensio voluntatum*).[2421] Whoever is outside the Church cannot have love,[2422] that grace of the New Testament.[2423] Only love of unity binds the members of Christ's Body to each other and to Christ, the Head of the Body of the Church,[2424] and only when there is a unity of love does one assimilate the gifts of the Holy Spirit,[2425] Who enlivens only the one Body of the Church.[2426] For this reason

---

2420 Augustine, *Contra Cresconium* 1.29.34 (PL 43:463–464).

2421 Augustine, *De baptismo contra Donatistas* 1.1.2 (PL 43:110).

2422 Augustine, *Contra litteras Petiliani* 2.77.172: "Charitas enim Christiana nisi in unitate Ecclesiae non potest custodire… Tenemus autem charitatem, si amplectimur unitatem [Christian charity cannot be preserved except in the unity of the Church… But we hold fast to charity if we cling to unity]" (PL 43:312); *De baptismo contra Donatistas* 4.17.24 (PL 43:169); *Sermones* 312.6: "Nulla esset charitas christiani, a quo non custodiretur unitas Christi [There would not be any love of a Christian by whom the unity of Christ is not guarded {trans. —ED.}]" (PL 38:1422).

2423 Augustine, *Quaest. in heptat.* 5.15 (PL 34:755).

2424 Augustine, *De unitate Ecclesiae* 2.2 (PL 43:392); *In psalmus 30, sermones* 2.1 (PL 36:239); *In ep. Iohannem tractatus* 2.3 (PL 35:1992).

2425 Augustine, *Contra Cresconium* 2.12.15, 2.13.16 (PL 43:476), 2.14.17: "Nec quemquam accepturum Spiritum sanctum nisi qui ejus (Ecclesiae) unitatem copularetur [no one will receive the Holy Spirit unless he be physically joined to the unity of the Church {trans. —ED.}]" (PL 43:477). Cf. *In Ioannos tractatum* 32.8 (PL 35:1645–1646).

2426 Augustine, *Epistulae* 185.10.46 (PL 33:813). Cf. *Epistulae* 185.9.42: "Quemadmodum enim membrum si praecidatur ab hominis vivi corpore, non potest tenere spiritum vitae, sic homo qui praeciditur de Christi justi; corpore, nullo modo potest spiritum tenere justitiae, etiam si figuram membri teneat, quam

without unity with the Church, mere theoretical agreement with Christian truth is completely useless,[2427] and without the Church there is no salvation either. Outside the catholic Church one may have all things except for salvation. One may have the sacraments, the Gospel, and faith in the Father, the Son, and the Holy Spirit, but nowhere can one acquire salvation except in the catholic Church.[2428] Augustine cites the opinion of St. Cyprian: *Salus extra Ecclesiam non est* ("There is no salvation outside the Church"), and he adds: *Quis negat?* "Who denies this?" [2429] Whoever has separated from the Church, however laudable his life may be, will not have life, simply for the crime of having separated from the unity of Christ; rather, the wrath of God will be upon him.[2430] Whereas St. Cyprian applies a strictly dogmatic standard in his evaluation of schism, the blessed Augustine carries the matter into more practical, moral territory. Quite naturally, St. Cyprian's view of schismatics had more difficulty gaining Church-wide acceptance, since proving that every schismatic has another faith is always fraught with difficulty. Conversely, it is always plain that the schismatic does not have love, as witnessed by his very separation from the Church. In the writings of the blessed Augustine, the schismatic is nearly equated to one who, although in apparent unity with the Church, is a hardened sinner: both alike

---

sumpsit in corpore [in the same manner as if a limb be cut off from the body of a living man, it cannot any longer retain the spirit of life; so the man who is cut off from the body of Christ, who is righteous, can in no wise retain the spirit of righteousness, even if he retain the form of membership which he received when in the body]" (PL 33:811). Cf. *Sermones* 268.2 (PL 38:1232).

2427 Augustine, *Contra litteras Petiliani* 2.77.172: "Non prosit hominibus, quamvis in eis sint vel Sacramenta vel fides, ubi charitas non est... sine illa (charitate) nihil vos esse, et si Baptismum et fidem teneatis... teneamus charitatem, sine qua et cum Sacramentis et cum fide nihil sumus [how profitless it is to man that he should be in possession of faith or of the sacraments, when he has not charity... without it you are nothing, even though you may be in possession of baptism and faith... let us hold fast charity, without which we are nothing even with the sacraments and with faith]" (PL 43:312).

2428 Augustine, *Sermo ad caesareensis ecclesiae plebem* 6 (PL 43:695).

2429 Augustine, *De baptismo contra Donatistas* 4.17.24 (PL 43:170).

2430 Augustine, *Epistulae* 141.5 (PL 33:579).

have the same faith and the same sacraments as the Church, but all this leads to nothing but their own condemnation.

Thus, in the writers of the fourth century we may observe only one particularity in which they differ from St. Cyprian: they are more lenient toward schismatics. According to Optatus, schismatics have separated from the Church *ex parte, non ex toto* [from a part, not from the whole]; for Augustine they *in quibusdam rebus nobiscum sunt* [in certain matters they are with us]; and in the opinion of Basil the Great they ἔτι ἐκ τῆς Ἐκκλησίας. But in the essential points the fourth-century writers are in full agreement both with each other and with St. Cyprian. St. Cyprian wholly rejected the life of grace outside the Church, and St. Basil the Great is in full agreement with him in his canonical response, according to which one who has withdrawn from the Church even through schism (διὰ σχίσματος) has not the grace of the Holy Spirit: their hierarchy are laity (λαϊκοὶ γενόμενοι) who are unable to impart the grace of the Holy Spirit (οὐκέτι δυνάμενοι χάριν Πνεύματος Ἁγίου ἑταίροις παρέχειν ἧς αὐτοὶ ἐκπεπτώκασι). And if at the same time Basil the Great considers it possible to receive schismatics without baptism, while the blessed Augustine demonstrates the validity of baptism outside the Church, this must not be viewed as a contradiction or an allowance for the possibility of an authentic life of grace outside the Church. For, according to Augustine, the grace of baptism begins to act only from the moment of unification with the catholic Church, which is why outside the Church there is no salvation. Correct ministration of baptism outside the Church, according to both Augustine and Basil the Great, is merely the basis on which the Church may receive a schismatic into her bosom even without baptism. Furthermore, the motive for this reception is that it is seen as benefiting the peace of the Church, as [posited by] both St. Basil the Great (οἰκονομίας ἕνεκα τῶν πολλῶν) and the 79th canon of the Council of Carthage (διὰ τὴν τῆς Ἐκκλησίας εἰρήνην καὶ χρησιμότητα ἐὰν τοῦτο συμβάλλεσθαι τῇ Χριστιανῶν εἰρήνῃ φανείῃ). Clearly, allowance for this possibility is made for the sake of peace in the Church and changing practice, since the conditions of this peace may be completely different. In his epistle to Jubaianus, for the good of the Church St. Cyprian did indeed require that the Novatians be rebaptized.[2431] St. Cyprian and Firmilian considered it the task of the bishop to determine what was good for the Church and which practice this merited, thereby allowing for the possibility of different means of receiving heretics and schismatics into the Church at different times and in different Churches. Nor do Basil the Great and Amphilochius of Iconium, to whom St. Basil wrote his canonical epistle, deny this possibility. This is naturally because the fathers considered all those outside the Church to be equally graceless, but depending on the circumstances of place and time they found it possible sometimes not to require baptism for schismatics, if this was declared beneficial for the Church. The blessed Augustine explains that union with the Church, in destroying the mortal sin of schism through repentance, gives the schismatic the grace of baptism which he had lost and did not in the least possess. Union with the Church makes a person a Christian, and without that union he is nothing, though he were baptized. Nevertheless, in the reasoning of Optatus and Augustine concerning schismatic baptism one may observe the germ of the doctrine of *opus operatum*[2432], which is absent in the epistle of Basil the Great.

In the system of the blessed Augustine, the doctrine concerning the sanctity of the Church received its final development, elucidation, and substantiation. As we have seen, the question of the sanctity of the Church quite frequently came up for discussion, primarily in the polemical literary conflict with Montanism, Novatianism, and Donatism. That the sanctity of the Church is not the sanctity of the members who comprise it was already established in the first six decades of the third century. This truth, which had already conclusively become the foundation of church practice, the blessed Augustine merely argues in greater detail using data from Holy Scripture. The sanctity of the Church was understood as the sanctity of

2431 Cyprian of Carthage, *Epistles* 72–60, "To Jubaianus" 24 (ANF 5:385; CSEL 3.2:797).

2432 Lit. "Work done", a phrase used to denote the spiritual effect in the performance of a religious rite which accrues from the virtue inherent in it, or by grace imparted to it, irrespective of the performer. —ED.

the full range of its means for sanctification, which also facilitate the attainment of personal sanctity of each individual member of the Church. The Church is the spiritual union in which alone these means for sanctification are effectual. The basis of this union is not only outward membership in it or acknowledgment of church doctrine, but the moral unity of all members in love: to be without the Church is to be without love, and vice versa. **The Church as a visible institution does not ensure certain salvation, but merely facilitates it. Separation from the Church leads to certain perdition.** This point in the doctrine concerning the Church was clearly indicated in the earliest church literature, but it only reached its full elucidation in the writings of the blessed Augustine (and Optatus), where the **doctrine concerning the sanctity of the Church as the sanctity of its sacraments** is clearly and definitively formulated.

The Donatists however made this sanctity dependent on the personal qualities of members of the hierarchy, and this naturally undermined the sanctity of the Church itself. Church writers had combated this view from the very earliest days. As far back as the third century, predominantly in the conflict with Montanism and Novatianism, "the power of the keys" of the bishop was conclusively established, but the dogmatic bases of the sacramental work of the hierarchy in general were not sufficiently clarified. In the conflict with Donatism a question that demanded theological resolution was put directly: **Is the validity of the sacraments dependent on the personal qualities of their minister? Optatus and the blessed Augustine responded with a definitive "No":** even sacraments performed by schismatics were acknowledged. **The sacrament is the property not of the person, but of the Church**; schismatics can retain the sacraments just as they retain church doctrine. **A member of the hierarchy may impart the sacraments of the Church by virtue of his hierarchical rank or post. The Church possesses the sacraments that sanctify a person independently of the moral qualities of their minister, and in this lies her sanctity.** This is the result at which the theological thought of the Church arrived over the course of the fourth century in elucidating the doctrine of the sanctity of the Church.

SOURCES & REFERENCES

Only the primary sources and references are listed here.
All others are cited in full where referenced.

Sources:

Die apostolischen Väter, herausgegeben von F.X. Funk. 2-te, verbesserte Auflage (Tübingen: 1906).

Corpus apologetarum christianorum saeculi secondi. Edidit Io. Car. Th. Eques de Otto: voll. 1–2. Iustini philosophi et martyris opera. Jenae 1875–1879. Vol. 8. Theophili episcopi Antiocheni ad Autolycum libri tres. Jenae 1861.

Zwei griechische Apologeten, herausgegeben von J. Geffcken (Leipzig und Berlin: 1907).

Des heiligen Irenäus Schrift zum Erweis der apostolischen Verkündigung, in armenischer Version entdeckt, herausgegeben und ins deutsche übersetzt von Lic. Dr. Karapet Ter-Mekerttschian und Lic. Dr. Erwand Ter-Minassianz, mit einem Nachwort und Anmerkungen von Adolf Harnack, TU 31 (Leipzig: 1907).

Didascalia et constitutions apostolorumn Edidit Franciscus Xaverius Funk. Voll. 1–2. (Paderbornae: 1906).

Corpus scriptorium ecclesiasticorum latinorum editum consilio et impensis academiae litterarum caesareae vindobonensis:

Vol. 1. *Minucii Felicis Octavius. Recensuit et commentario critic instruxit C. Halm.*

Vol. 3 in 3 partibus. *Th. C. Cypriani opera omnia.* Recensuit et commentario critic instruxit G. Hartel (Vindobonae: 1868–1871).

Vol. 20 pars 1. *Quinti Septimi Florentis Tertulliani opera* ex recensione Augusti Reifferscheid et Georgii Wissowa (Vindobonae: 1890).

Vol. 26. *S. Optati Milevitani libri VII.* Recensuit Carolus Siwsa (Vindobonae: 1893).

Vol. 47. *Quinti Septimi Florentis Tertulliani opera* ex recensione Aemilii Kroymann (Vindobonae: 1906).

Die Griechischen Christlichern Schriftsteller der ersten drei Jahrhunderten, herausgegeben von der Kirchenväter-Commission der Königlich-Preussischen Akademie der Wissensehaften:

Bd. 3. *Origenes Werke.* 2-er Bd. Herausgegeben von Prof. Dr. Paul Koetschau (Leipzig: 1899).

Bd. 4. *Der Dialog des Adamantius.* Herausgegeben von Dr. W.H. van de Sande Bakhuyzen (Leipzig: 1901).

Bd. 6. *Origenes Werke.* 3-er Bd. Herausgegeben von Dr. Erich Klostermann

(Leipzig: 1901).

Bd. 9.1–2. *Eusebius Werke.* 2-er Bd. Herausgegeben von Prof. Dr. Eduard Schwartz (Leipzig: 1903, 1908).

Bd. 12, 15, 17. *Clemens Alexandrinus.* Herausgegeben von Dr. Otto Stählin (Leipzig: 1-er Bd., 1905; 2-er Bd., 1906; 3-er Bd., 1909).

Migne, *Patrologiae cursus completes.* Series graeca:

Vols. 8–9. *Clemens Alexandrinus.*

Vols. 11–14, 16. *Origenis opera omnia.*

Vol. 18. *S. Methodius episcopus et martyr.*

Vol. 41. *S. Epiphanii Cyprii opera.*

Series Latina:

Vol. 13. *Pacianus, Barcilononsis episcopus.*

Vols. 32–45. *S. Aur. Augustinus, Hipponensis episcopus.*

Texts and Studies: Contributions to Biblical and Patristic Literature, J. Armitage Robinson, ed., vol. 3: *The Rules of Tychonius* (Cambridge: 1894).

Russian translations:

The Writings of the Apostolic Men ["Писания мужей апостольских"]. Archpriest P. Preobrazhensky, trans. (Saint Petersburg: 1895).

The Writings of the Early Christian Apologists ["Сочинения древних христианских апологетов"], Archpriest P. Preobrazhensky, trans. (Saint Petersburg: 1895).

The Writings of Saint Irenaeus, Bishop of Lyons ["Сочинения святого Иринея, епископа Лионского"], Archpriest P. Preobrazhensky, trans. (Saint Petersburg: 1900).

A. Pokrovsky, *Aristides the Philosopher and his Recently Discovered Apology* ["Философ Аристид и его недавно открытая апология"] (Sergiev Posad: 1898).

The Works of the Hieromartyr Cyprian, Bishop of Carthage ["Творения священномученика Киприана, епископа Карфагенского"], parts 1 and 2, 2nd ed. (Kiev: 1891).

The Works of St. Dionysius the Great, Bishop of Alexandria ["Творения св. Дионисия Великого, епископа Александрийского"], Priest A. Druzhinin, trans. (Kazan: 1900).

The Newly Discovered Work by St. Irenaeus of Lyons, "Demonstration of the Apostolic Preaching," N.I. Sagardy, trans. (Khristianskoe Chtenie: 1907), vol. 223, part 2, 664–691, 851–875.

St. Methodius, Bishop, Martyr, and Third-century Father of the Church: Complete Collected Works ["Св. Мефодий, епископ и мученик, отец Церкви III века. Полное собрание его творений"], Prof. Evgraf Lovyagin, trans. (from the Greek), 2nd ed. (Saint Petersburg: 1905).

The Writings of Eusebius Pamphilus, Translated from the Greek under the Auspices of the Saint Petersburg Theological Academy ["Сочинения Евсевия Памфила, переведенные с греческого при Санкт-Петербургской духовной академии"], vol. 1 (Saint Petersburg: 1858).

The Works of St. Epiphanius of Cyprus ["Творения св. Епифания Кипрского"] (Moscow: Saint Petersburg Theological Academy), part 1 (1863), part 2 (1864), and part 3 (1872).

The Apostolic Constitutions (Translated into Russian) ["Постановления апостольские (в русском переводе"] (Kazan: 1864).

The works of St. John Chrysostom [Творения св. Иоанна Златоуста] (Saint Petersburg Theological Academy); the works of St. Ephraim the Syrian, St. Isidore of Pelusium, St. Basil the Great, and the blessed Theodoret [твоериня св. Ефрема Сирина, св. Исидора Пелусиота, св. Василия Великого и блаженного Феодорита] (Moscow Theological Academy); the works of Tertullian and the blessed Jerome [творения Тертуллиана и блаженного Иеронима] (Kiev Theological Academy); the works of Origen and the blessed Theophylact [творения Оригена и Феофилакта] (Kazan Theological Academy).

English translations:

Ante-Nicene Fathers, volumes 1–10, 2nd ed. (Peabody, MA: Hendrickson Publishers, Inc., 1995).

Nicene and Post-Nicene Fathers, series 1, volumes 1–8, 2nd ed. (Peabody, MA: Hendrickson Publishers, Inc., 1995).

Nicene and Post-Nicene Fathers, series 2, volumes 1–14, 2nd ed. (Peabody, MA: Hendrickson Publishers, Inc., 1995).

Tyconius: The Book of Rules, William S. Babcock, trans. (Atlanta, GA: Scholars Press, 1989).

References:

(a) In Russian:

E. Akvilonov, *The Church: Scholarly Definitions of the Church and the Apostolic Doctrine Concerning It as the Body of Christ* ["Церковь. Научные определения Церкви и апостолькое учение о ней как о Теле Христовом"] (Saint Petersburg: 1894).

D.I. Bogdashevky, *The False Teachers Denounced in the First Epistle of the Apostle John* ["Лжеучители, обличаемые в Первом послании апостола Иоанна"] (Kiev: 1900).

D.I. Bogdashevsky, *The Epistle of the Holy Apostle Paul to the Ephesians* ["Послание св. ап. Павла к Ефесянам"] (Kiev: 1904).

V.V. Bolotov, prof., *Lectures on the History of the Early Church* ["Лекции по истории древней Церкви"], part 1 (Saint Petersburg: 1907) and part 2 (Saint Petersburg: 1910).

Vladimir Guerrier, *The Blessed Augustine* ["Блаженный Августин"] (Moscow: 1910).

N. N. Glubokovsky, prof., *The Preaching of Holy Apostle Paul in its Origin and Substance* ["Благовестие святого апостола Павла по его происхождению и существу"], book 2 (Saint Petersburg: 1910).

A.V. Gorsky, *The History of the Gospel and of the Apostolic Church* ["История евангельская и Церкви апостольской"], 2nd ed. (Holy Trinity-Sergius Lavra: 1902).

A. Druzhinin, priest, *The Life and Works of St. Dionysius the Great, Bishop of Alexandria* ["Жизнь и труды св. Дионисия Великого, епископа

Александрийского"] (Kazan: 1900).

Louis Duchesne, *Early History of the Christian Church* ["История древней Церкви"], translated from the French, vol. 1 (Moscow: 1912).

N.A. Zaozersky, prof., "On the Essence of Church Law" ["О сущности церковного права"], in *Bogoslovsky vestnik* (1909), vol. 3.

N.A. Zaozersky, prof., "The Hierarchical Principle in Church Organization" ["Иерархический принцип в церковной организации"], in *Bogoslovsky vestnik* (1911), vol. 1.

Rudolph Sohm (*Church Structure in the First Centuries of Christianity* ["Церковный строй в первые века христианства"], A. Petrovsky and P. Florensky, trans. (Moscow: 1906).

A.M. Ivantsov-Platonov, archpriest, *Heresies and Schisms of the First Three Centuries of Christianity* ["Ереси и расколы первых трех веков христианства"] (Moscow: 1877).

D. Kasitsyn: *Schisms of the Early Centuries of Christianity: Montanism, Novatianism, Donatism, and Their Influence on the Development of the Doctrine Concerning the Church* ("Расколы первых веков христианства. Монтанизм, новацианство, донатизм и влияние их на раскрытие учения о Церкви") (Moscow: 1889) (Addendae to the Works of the Holy Fathers [Прибавления к творениям свв. отцов], parts 43 and 44).

Alexander Klitin, *The Authenticity of the Epistles of the Holy Apostle Paul to Timothy and Titus* ["Подлинность посланий святого апостола Павла к Тимофею и Титу"] (Kiev: 1887)

F.A. Kurganov, "Did St. Irenaeus, Bishop of Lyons, Attest to the Primacy and Infallible Teachership of the Roman Church, and Particularly of its Pontiff?" ["Свидетельствовал ли св. Ириней, епископ Лионский, о приматстве и непогрешимом учительстве Римской Церкви, в частности—ее первосвященникеа?"] (Kazan: 1893).

N. Kutepov, *The Donatist Schism* ["Раскол донатистов"] (Kazan: 1884).

Ivan Mansvetov, *The New Testament Teaching Concerning the Church* ["Новозаветное учение о Церкви"] (Moscow: 1879).

Alexey Molchanov, priest, *St. Cyprian of Carthage and His Teaching on the Church* ["Св. Киприан Карфагенский и его учение о Церкви"] (Kazan: 1888).

M.D. Muretov, prof., *On the Significance of the Term* **katholikos** ["О значении термина **katholikos**"]. Appendix to the book *Ancient Hebrew Prayers Ascribed to the Apostle Peter* ["Древнееврейские молитвы под именем ап. Петра"] (Holy Trinity Sergius Lavra, 1905).

V.N. Myshtsyn, *Organization of the Christian Church in the First Two Centuries* ["Устройство христианской Церкви в первые два века"] (Sergiev Posad: 1909).

Nikanor, archimandrite (archbishop), *An Analysis of the Roman Teaching Concerning Apparent (Papal) Supremacy in the Church* ["Разбор римского учения о видимом (папском) главенстве в Церкви"], 2nd ed. (Kazan: 1871).

Sylvester, archimandrite, *The Doctrine Concerning the Church in the First Three Centuries of Christianity* ["Учение о Церкви в первые три века христианства"]

(Kiev: 1872).

S.I. Smirnov, *The Spiritual Father in the Early Eastern Church* ["Духовный отец в древней Восточной Церкви"], part 1 (Sergiev Posad: 1906).

Nikolai Shternov, *Tertullian, Presbyter of Carthage* ("Тертуллиан, пресвитер Карагенский") (Kursk: 1889).

Theophan, bishop, *Explanation of the Epistle of the Holy Apostle Paul to the Ephesians* ["Толкование Послания св. апостола Павла к Ефесеям"], 2nd ed. (Moscow: 1893).

Mikhail Fiveisky, priest, *Spiritual Gifts in the Initial Christian Church* ("Духовные дарования в первоначальной христианской Церкви") (Moscow: 1907).

(b) In foreign languages:

Hans Achelis, *Hippolytstudien*, TU 16.1 (Leipzig: 1897).

Karl Adam, *Der Kirchenbegriff Tertullians* (Paderborn: 1907).

M.A. Aitken, *Apostolical Succession Considered in the Light of the Facts of the History of the Primitive Church* (London: 1903).

Adhémar d' Alès, *La Théologie de saint Hippolyte* (Paris: 1906)

Adhémar d' Alès, *La Théologie de Tertullien* (Paris: 1905).

Adhémar d' Alès, "Tertullien et Calliste," *Revue d'histoire ecclésiastique* 13 (1912).

O. Bardenhewer, *Patrologie*, 3-te Aufl. (Freiburg im Breisgau: 1910).

Pierre Batiffol, *Etudes d' histoire et de théologie positive*, 2-me éd. (Paris: 1902)

Pierre Batiffol, *L'église naissante et le catholicisme*, 3-me éd. (Paris: 1909).

P. Beuzart, *Essai sur la théologie d'Irénée* (Paris: 1908).

H. Boehmer, "Zu dem Zeugnisse des Irenäus von dem Ansehen der römischen Kirche," *Zeitschrift für die neutestamentliche Wissenschaft und die Kunde des Urchristentums* (1906).

Nathanael Bonwetsch, *Hippolyts Kommentar zum Hohelied auf Grund von N. Marrs Ausgabe des grusinischen Textes herausgegeben*, TU 23.2 (Leipzig: 1902).

Nathanael Bonwetsch, *Drei georgisch erhaltene Schriften von Hippolytus*, TU 26: a (Leipzig: 1904).

Nathanael Bonwetsch, "Der Schriftbeweis für die Kirche aus der Heiden als das wahre Israel bis auf Hippolyt," *Theologische Studien*, Theodor Zahn zum 10. Oktober, 1908 dargebracht (Leipzig: 1908).

Friedrich Böhringer, *Die Alte Kirche*, Th. 1–4, 2-te Ausgabe (Stuttgart: 1873–1874).

Heinrich Bruders, *Die Verfassung der Kirche von den ersten Jahrzehnten der apostolischen Wirksamkeit an bis zum Jahre 175 n. Chr.* (Mainz: 1904).

Heinrich Bruders, "Mt. 16, 19; 18, 18 und In. 20, 22–23 in frühchristlicher Auslegung," in *Zeitschrift für katholische Theologie* (1910, 1911).

Hermann Cremer, *Biblisch-theologisches Wörterbuch der Neutestamentlichen Gräcität*, 9-te Auflage (Gotha: 1902).

Henri Dannreuther, *Du témoingnage d' Hégésippe sur l'église chrétienne aux deux premiers siécles* (Nancy: 1878).

Döllinger, *Hippolytus und Kallistus oder die römische Kirche in der ersten Hälfte des dritten Jahrhunderts* (Regensburg: 1853).

Johann Ernst, *Papst Stephan I und der Ketzertaufstreit* (Mainz: 1905).

Johann Ernst, "Die Ketzertaufangelegenheit in der altchristlichen Kirche nach Cyprian" (Mainz: 1901).

Gerhard Esser, *Die Busschriften Tertullians "De paenitentia" und "De pudicitia" und das Indulgenzedikt des Papstes Kallistus* (Bonn: 1905).

Bernhard Fechtrup, *Der hl. Cyprian. Sein Leben und seine Lehre* (Münster: 1878).

Friedrich Frank, *Die Bussdisciplin der Kirche von den Apostelzeitben bis zum siebenten Jahrhundert* (Mainz: 1867).

F. X. Funk, *Kirchengeschichtliche Abhandlungen und Untersuchungen,* 3-ter Band (Paderborn: 1907).

F.X. Funk, *Die Echtheit der ignatianischen Briefe* (Tubingen: 1883).

F.X. Funk, "Das Indulgenzedikt des Papstes Kallistus," *Theologische Quartalschrift* (1906).

Adolf Harnack, *Lehrbuch der Dogmengeschichte,* 4-te Aufl. 1-er Bd. (Tübingen: 1909), 3-er Bd. (Tübingen: 1910).

Adolf Harnack, *Die Chronologie der altchristlichen Literatur bis Eusebius,* 1-er. Bd. (Leipzig: 1897), 2-er Bd. (1904).

Adolf Harnack, *Die Mission und Ausbreitung des Christentums in den ersten drei Jahrhunderten,* 2-te Aufl. (Leipzig: 1906).

Adolf Harnack, *Die Lehre der zwölf Apostel. Prolegomena,* TU 2.1 (Leipzig: 1884).

Adolf Harnack, *Der erste Klemensbrief. Sitzungsberichte der Königlich-Preussischen Akademie der Wissenschaften* (Berlin: 1909).

Adolf Harnack, "Ueber den sogenannten zweiten Brief des Clemens an die Korinther," in *Zeitschrift für Kirchengeschichte* (1876).

Adolf Harnack, *Die Altercatio Simonis Iudaei et Theophili Christiani nebst Untersuchungen über die antijüdische Polemik in der alten Kirche,* TU 1.3 (Leipzig: 1883).

Adolf Harnack, *Entstehung und Entwickelung der Kirchenverfassung und des Kirchenrechts in den zwei ersten Jahrhunderten* (Leipzig: 1910).

Adolf Harnack, *Ueber den dritten Iohannesbrief,* TU 15.3b (Leipzig: 1897).

Adolf Harnack, *Lapsi,* RE 3, Bd. 11.

Adolf Harnack, *Novatian,* RE 3, Bd. 11.

Paul Heinisch: *Der Einfluss Philos auf die äteste christliche Exegese* (Münster i. W.: 1908).

Gustav Hoenicke, *Das Judenchristentum im ersten und zweiten Jahrhundert* (Berlin: 1908).

Carl Holl, in *Enthusiasmus und Bussgewalt beim griechischen Mônchtum* (Leipzig: 1898).

Johann Eduard Huther, *Cyprians Lehre von der Kirche* (Hamburg und Gotha: 1839).

Rudolf Knopf, *Das Nachapostolische Zeitalter* (Tübingen: 1905).

Hugo Koch, *Cyprian und der römische Primat,* TU 35.1 (Leipzig: 1910).

Hugo Koch, "Sündenvergebung bei Irenaus," *Zeitschrift für die neutestamentliche Wissenschaft und die Kunde des Urchristentums* (1908).

Julius Kustlin, *Das Wesen der Kirche nach Lehre und Geschichte des Neuen Testamentes,* 2-te Aufl. (Gotha: 1872).

P. de Labriolle, "La Polémique antimontaniste centre la prophétie estatique," in *Revue d'histoire et de littéerature religieuses,* vol. 11 (1906).

Johannes Leipoldt, *Geschichte des neutestamentlichen Kanons,* 1-er Th. (Leipzig: 1907).

Rudolf Liechtenhan, *Die Offenbarung im Gnosticismus* (Göttingen: 1901).

Alfred Loisy, *L'Évangile et L'Église.* 4-me éd. (Ceffonds: 1908).

Friedrich Loofs, *Leitfaden zum Studium der Dogmengeschichte,* 4-te Aufl. (Halle: 1906).

J. Meritan, "L'Ecclésiologie de l'épître aux Éphésiens," *Revue biblique internationale* (1898), vol. 7.

E. Michaud, "L' ecclésiologie de St. Cyprien," *Revue internationale de théologie* (1905).

E. Michaud, "L'ecclésiologie de Tertullien," *Revue internationale de théologie* (1905).

Paul Monceaux, *Histoire littéraire de L'Afrique Chrétienne depuis les origines jusqu'a l'invasion arabe,* vol. 1 (Paris: 1901), vol. 2 (Paris: 1902).

Friedrich Nitzsch, *Grundriss der christlichen Dogmengeschichte,* 1-er Th. (Berlin: 1870).

Johannes Peters, *Der heilige Cyprian von Karthago, Bischof. Kirchenvater und Blutzeuge Christi, in seinem Leben und Kirken dargestellt* (Regensburg: 1877).

Bernhard Poschmann, *Die Sichtbarkeit der Kirche nach Lehre des hl. Cyprian* (Paderborn: 1908).

Erwin Preuschen, *Tertullian. De Paenitentia. De Pudicitia. Herausgegeben von Erwin Preuschen* (Freiburg im Breisgau: 1891; 2-te Aufl. Tübingen: 1910).

Erwin Preuschen, "Zur Kirchenpolitik des Bischofs Kallist," in *Zeitschrift für die neutestamentliche Wissenschaft und die Kunde des Urchristentums* (1910).

Joseph Reinkens, *Die Lehre des heiligen Cyprian von der Einheit der Kirche* (Würzburg: 1873).

Friedrich Wilhelm Rettberg, *Thascius Cäcillus Cyprianus, Bischof von Carthago* (Gottingen: 1831).

Ferdinand Ribbeck, *Donatus und Augustinus oder der erste entscheidende Kampf zwischen Separatismus und Kirche* (Elberfeld: 1857).

Albrecht Ritschl, *Die Entstehung der altkatholischen Kirche,* 2-te Auflage (Bonn: 1857).

Ernst Rolffs, *Das Indulgenz Edict des römischen Bischofs Kallist,* TU 11.3 (Leipzip: 1893).

Ernst Rolffs, *Urkunden ausdem antimontanistischen Kampfe des Abendlandes,* TU 12.4 (Leipzig: 1895).

P. Capistran Romeis, *Das Heil des Christen ausserhalb der wahren Kirche nach der Lehre des hl. Augustin* (Paderborn: 1908).

Schanz, "Die Absolutionsgewalt in der alten Kirche," *Theologische Quartalschrift* (1897).

Schanz, "Der Begriff der Kirche," *Theologische Quartalschrift* (1893).

Joseph Schwane, *Dogmengeschichte der vornicäischen Zeit,* 2-te Aufl. (Freiburg im Breisgau: 1892).

Reinhold Seeberg, *Studien zur Geschichte des Begriffs der Kirche* (Erlangen: 1885).

Anton Seitz, *Die Heilsnotwendigkeit der Kirche nach der altchristlichen Literatur bis dzur Zeit des hl. Augustinus* (Freiburg im Breisgau: 1903).

Anton Seitz, *Cyprian und der römische Primat oder Urchristliche Primatsentwicklung und Hugo Kochs modernistisches Kirchenrecht* (Regensburg: 1911).

Hans von Soden, *Der Streit Swischen Rom und Karthago über die Ketzertaufe* (Rome: 1909).

Thomas Specht, *Die Lehre von der Kirche nach dem hl. Augustia* (Paderborn: 1892).

Johann Stufler, "Die Bussdisziplin der abendländischen Kirche bis Kallistus," *Zeitschrift für katholische Theologie* (1907).

Johann Stufler, "Die Sündenvergebung bei Origenes," *Zeitschrift für katholische Theologie* (1907).

Johann Stufler, "Die Behandlung der Gefallenen zur Zeit der decischen

Verfolgung," *Zeitschrift für katholische Theologie* (1907).

Tillemont, *Memoires pour servir a l' histoire ecclesiastique des six premiers siecles,* vols. 3–4 (Paris: 1695–1696).

Thomasius, *Die Dogmengeschichte der Alten Kirche,* 2-te Aufl. (Erlangen: 1886).

Joseph Turmel, *Histoire de la théologie positive depuis l'origine jusqu'au concile de Trente,* 3-me éd. (Paris: 1904).

Turmel, *Tertullien,* 2-me éd. (Paris: 1905).

Heinrich Gisbert Voigt, *Eine verschollene Urkunde des Antimontanistischen Kampfes* (Leipzig: 1891).

F. Volkmar, *Hippolytus und die römischen Zeitgenossen* (Zürich: 1855).

Carl Weizsäcker, *Das apostolische Zeitalter der christlichen Kirche,* 3-te Aufl. (Tübingen und Leipzig: 1902).

Theodor Zahn, *Der Hirt des Hermas* (Gotha: 1868).

Theodor Zahn, *Geschichte des neutestamentlichen Kanons.* Bd. 1–2 (Erlangen und Leipzig: 1888–1892).

Theodor Zahn, *Glaubensregel und Taufbekenntniss in der alten Kirche. Skizzen aus dem Leben der alten Kirche.* 2-te Aufl. (Erlangen und Leipzig: 1898).

Theodor Zahn, *Einleitung in das Neue Testament.* Bd. 2, 3-te Aufl. (Leipzig: 1907).

Franciscus Zorell, *Novi Testamenti lexicon graecum* (Parisiis: 1911).

Abbreviations:

ANF – *Ante-Nicene Fathers*

CAG – *Corpus apologetarum christianorum saeculi secondi,* ed. de Otto.

CSEL – *Corpus scriptorum ecclesiasticorum latinorum.*

GrchSch – *Die Griechschen christlichen Schriftsteller der ersten drei Jahrhunderte.*

NPNF[1] – *Nicene and Post-Nicene Fathers,* series 1.

NPNF[2] – *Nicene and Post-Nicene Fathers,* series 2.

PG – Migne, *Patrologiae cursus completes, series graeca.*

PL – Migne, *Patrologiae cursus completes, series Latina.*

RE 3 – *Realencyklopädie für protestantische Theologie und Kirche,* begründet von J.J. Herzog, im dritten Auflage herausgegeben von Albert Hauck.

TU – *Texte und Untersuchungen zur Geschichte der altchristlichen Literatur,* herausgegeben von Oscar von Gebhardt und Adolf Harnack (oder von Adolf Harnack und Carl Schmidt).

APPENDIX

Excerpt from:
The Unity of the Church and the
World Conference of Christian Communities

A Letter to Mr. Robert Gardiner, secretary of the Commission to
arrange a World Conference of Christian Communities

(Excerpt from pages 28-39)

The truth of ecclesiastical unity does not recognize the grace of
the mysteries administered within extra-ecclesiastical communities.
It is impossible to reconcile Church unity with the validity of extra-ecclesiastical Mysteries. Even the genius of Augustine had been
unable to solve this problem satisfactorily. Augustine's teaching on
the necessity to recognize the mysteries administered outside the
Church has been discussed by me in detail in a book devoted to the
history of dogmas concerning the Church.[1] In Augustine's opinion,
recognition of the complete independence of the mysteries from
the person of the celebrant (in the Church) inevitably entails a recognition of the validity of the mysteries outside the Church. This
idea permeates Augustine's entire treatise "De baptismo." Having
admitted, however, the paradoxical thought as to complete identity

---

1   See chapter six above. The original Russian edition, *Essays on the History of
Church Dogma*, Sergiev Possad, 1912, p. 527.

of a sinful (and who is a saint?) priest of the Church with a hierarch of an extra-ecclesiastical society, Augustine finds himself in a kind of a dead end because for him the only path to salvation lay via the Catholic Church. To recognize as valid the mysteries administered outside the Church means to recognize the operation of grace outside the Church, to recognize the possibility of salvation apart from the Church and in hostility towards her; in a word, this means to recognize that the Church is not obligatory, and to cast away the faith in One, Holy, Catholic and Apostolic Church.

But Augustine also wished to retain the truth of there being no salvation outside the Church.[2] With this purpose in mind, Augustine started to differentiate between the concepts "to have mysteries" and "to have mysteries with profit." "The one," he says, "is not to be had, another it is pernicious (pernitiose) to have, and another still is saving (salubriter)."[3] Schismatics, according to Augustine's teaching, possess the mysteries, yet without any profit towards salvation, only to the detriment of it. Augustine displays here in rudimentary form the subsequent scholastic distinction between the validity of the Mysteries and their efficacy. The mysteries may be valid yet ineffectual. This idea is difficult to assimilate if one is grounded in religious experience instead engaging in scholastic play of words. What kind of grace is this if it brings nothing but harm? While possessing the mysteries, schismatics, in Augustine's opinion, are deprived of their grace-bestowing and saving effect because of their separation from the Church. This separation shows that they have no love. Without love man cannot be virtuous; the Holy Spirit cannot abide in him. Thus the schismatics, who are outside the Church, have not the Holy Spirit.[4]

This objection inevitably rises in the mind: If schismatics do not have the Holy Spirit, how is their baptism effectuated? Augustine makes the strange assumption that presumably at the moment of baptism, and only at that moment, the Holy Spirit operates outside

---

2 De Baptismo IV, 17, 24. PL., t. 43, col. 170. Cf. col. 695.

3 Contra epist. Parmeniani II, 13, 28. PL. t. 43, col 71.

4 De Baptismo IV, 1, 1. V, 23, 33. PL, t.43, col. 155, 193. Serum. 268, 2. PL, t. 38, col. 1232. In ep. Ioan. Tr. 6, 22. PL, t. 35, col. 2026.

the Church as well. The sins of the person being baptized — so goes Augustine's reasoning — are forgiven but return upon him at once. He who is baptized outside the Church passes at it were through a narrow zone of light and again enters darkness. While he passes through the zone of light, he is cleansed of his sins, but since immediately after baptism he returns to the darkness of dissent, his sins return immediately upon him. The Lord spoke in a parable about the servant whose master remitted his debt of a thousand talents. When the servant showed no pity toward his debtor, the master demanded payment of the entire debt. The same happens to a schismatic who received baptism outside the Church. After receiving forgiveness for his debt before God, he again becomes responsible for that debt because he reveals enmity towards his brethren who are in the Church. In order for a schismatic to receive the fruits of grace after his baptism, he must show his love towards his brethren, that is, he must lovingly come into union with the Church. When such union takes place, he no longer needs to be baptized.[5]

It is difficult to recognize such a solution to the problem of the reconciliation of the unity of the Church with the validity of Mysteries outside the Church as satisfactory. You see, schismatic baptism is accomplished outside the Church. Why then is the Church's baptism also to be found among the schismatics, although only at the moment of its accomplishment? For the schismatic is converted not to the Church, but to the schism (for the time of Augustine to Donatism): he is converted perhaps after making a conscious choice and after consciously condemning the Church. He is even at the very moment of baptism at war with the Church. While asking remission of his debt, he declares at the same time that he has no love for the Church. In Augustine the beginnings of the Catholic doctrine of *opus operatum* are noticeable. The Mystery is conceived of as not being dependent on the Church, but only on the pronouncing of a certain formula. The Spirit of God gives life only to the body of the Church, and outside this body He cannot be, whatever words were pronounced there. It is not important who pronounces

---

5 De Baptismo 1, 12, 19.21. VI, 34, 65. VII, 3, 5. PL, t. 43, col. 119-121, 219, 227

these words — a false Christian, a heretic, a schismatic, a heathen, or a Jew — only one thing is important; that these words are pronounced outside the Church. For certainly the essence of Christianity is not in the fact that in it is given a collection of incantations by means of which man can force from the Divinity the supernatural help which he needs. Firmilian, in his day, protested against such an understanding of the baptismal formula, saying that the pronunciation of names is not sufficient for the remission of sins and the sanctification of baptism.[6] The Augustine idea received further development in the works of Latin theologians. We can only thank God that the doctrine of the Eastern Church was formulated outside the sphere of Augustinianism, and we can and must consider this sphere alien to ourselves. In the great Eastern theologians, we do not find even a trace of arguments similar to those cited by the Augustinians. This is the reason why it is indispensible to turn to the doctrine and practice of the ancient Church.

The problems of theology and Church life are astonishingly eternal. In the twentieth century I must write from Russia to America about that which was written from Asia Minor to Carthage and from Alexandria to Rome as long ago as the third century. We have a sufficient quantity of historical material: however, nowhere are there Augustinian arguments. You see, the original ecclesiastical decisions ordered baptism for all being converted from heresy to the Church. Around the year 220, a council of African and Numidian bishops under the presidency of Agrippinus determined that heretics be baptized, "and from that time," testifies St. Cyprian, "until now, so many thousands of heretics in our regions, who were converted to the Church, not only did not disdain or hesitate to receive the grace of the life-giving font and saving baptism, but still more insisted upon it reasonably and willingly."[7] "I learned," writes St. Dionysius of Alexandria, "that such an opinion existed from ancient times among the previous bishops, in the most populous

---

6 Ep. 75, cap. 9.

7 Epist. 73-60 ad Jubajanum. cap. 3. Ep. 71-58 ad Quintum. cap. 4 (the author lists two editions of the letters of St. Cyprian whose numeration differ - note of translator).

churches, and at the councils of brethren in Iconium, in Synades, and in many other countries."[8] In the middle of the fifties of the third century Firmilian, bishop of Caesarea in Cappadocia, recalls in a letter to St. Cyprian: "Already for a long time, since we came down from Gaul, Cilicia, and the other closest regions, to the council at Iconium, which is in Phrygia, we have decreed to hold firmly to such an opinion of heretics and to defend it when any doubt concerning this subject is discovered. Here among certain people doubt has arisen concerning the baptism of those who, although they recognize new prophets, however know, apparently, the same Father and Son as we do. But we, having examined this topic with all thoroughness, resolved at the council at Iconium to reject completely every baptism performed outside the Church."[9]

There is no need to set forth in detail an account of the controversies which in the middle years of the third century flared up around the question of the reception into the Church of converting Novatians, where the Roman bishop, wishing to see the Roman practice everywhere, met with objection from various quarters. I will only direct your attention to certain details of these disputes. First of all, the dogmatic position of the Roman bishop Stephen, who had denied the need of baptism, presents itself as indefinite and rather precarious. One automatically recalls the opinion of St. Cyprian, that in the letters of Stephen there is much which either has no relation at all to the matter at hand, or which is self-contradictory and in general written unskillfully and thoughtlessly. Saint Cyprian imparts to us the genuine words of Stephen: "If one turns to you from whatever heresy, then in this case introduce nothing new, other than what was transmitted to you that is that upon such a person the laying-on of hands alone should be performed as a sign of repentance."[10]

Thus all heresies have the grace of baptism, and one need not baptize any of those being converted to the Church. St. Cyprian

---

8 Euseb. H. E. V. 7, 5.

9 Epist. Firmiliani, cap. 7, 19. CSEL 3 pp 815, 828. Russian translation in the works of Cyprian, Article 1, pp. 378, 384-385.

10 Ep. 74-61 ad Pompejum, cap. 1.

On the Dogma of the Church

testifies that Stephen did not even baptize the Marcionites.[11] Yes, Stephen wishes to stand only on the soil of the tradition of the Roman church; the main thing for him is to preserve *quod traditum est*. But the soil is especially unsteady under Stephen when he demands all the same the laying-on of hands on those being converted and on schismatics, such as were the Novatians. Observe that by the laying-on of hands of which Stephen speaks, even Latin scholars understand chrismation, the mystical transmission of the gifts of the Holy Spirit, Whom, obviously, the schismatics do not have, even according to the opinion of Stephen. How was baptism accomplished among them without the Holy Spirit? It is sufficient to read the letters of Cyprian to Jubaian, Pompeius, and Magnus, and the letter of Firmilian to Cyprian to be convinced how much more sound is the dogmatic position of Stephen's opponents, who affirm the invalidity of every baptism outside the Church.

St. Cyprian points out this very groundlessness of the dogmatic teaching of his opponent. "We will stop those who, although they are in other matters stubborn and slowwitted, nevertheless acknowledge that all heretics and schismatics do not have the Holy Spirit and that therefore, although they can baptize, they cannot however give the Holy Spirit. We will stop them on this point, in order to say that those who do not have the Holy Spirit decidedly cannot even baptize. Only he who has the Holy Spirit can baptize and give remission of sins. Let those who patronize heretics and schismatics answer us: do they have the Holy Spirit or do they not? If they do, then why do we lay our hands on those baptized by them, when they come to us, to bring down upon them the Holy Spirit. The Holy Spirit would, of course, have been received where He was given, if He were there. If those baptized outside the Church, heretics and schismatics, do not have the Holy Spirit, then it is obvious that the remission of sins also cannot be given by them about whom it is known that they do not have the Holy Spirit.[12] Stephen explained the validity of baptism outside the Church and without the Holy

---

11 Ep. 73-60, cap. 4-5.

12 Ep. 69-72 ad Magnum, cap. J 0-11. CSEL 3 p. 759 sq. Russian translation. Part 1, pp. 368-369.

Spirit by the Majesty of the Name of Christ. "The Name of Christ greatly aids faith and the holiness of baptism, so that he who is baptized into Christ at once receives the grace of Christ."[13]

St. Cyprian convincingly refutes the opinion of Stephen. "If they ascribe the validity of baptism to the name, so that they consider as renewed and sanctified everyone baptized in the Name of Jesus Christ, no matter by whom, according to this criterion alone, then why among them, in the Name of the very same Christ, does not the laying-on of hands upon the baptized person for the reception of the Holy Spirit have its effect? Why does not the same Majesty of the one and the same Name not reveal the same power in the laying-on of hands which is attributed to it in the sanctification of baptism? If one who has been reborn outside the Church can make himself a temple of God, then why can he not also make himself a temple of the Holy Spirit? For whoever, having put off his sins in baptism, has been sanctified and spiritually transfigured into a new man has through this already made himself capable of receiving the Holy Spirit. The Apostle says: 'For as many of you as were baptized into Christ have put on Christ' (Gal. 3: 2 7). So if one who has been baptized among the heretics can put on Christ, then he can all the more receive the Holy Spirit, Who was sent by Christ. Otherwise, if one baptized outside the Church could put on Christ but could not receive the Holy Spirit, then He who was sent would be greater than He who sent Him.

However, can one really either put on Christ without the Spirit, or separate the Spirit from Christ? Moreover, the second birth by which we are born in Christ through the laver of regeneration is a spiritual birth: and therefore do they not affirm an obvious absurdity when they say that one can be spiritually born among the heretics, where they themselves do not recognize the existence of the Spirit. For water alone without the Holy Spirit, cannot, of course, cleanse a man of sins and sanctify him. So, there exists one of two alternatives: either to agree that there, where they think there is baptism, the Holy Spirit is also present, or, where the Holy Spirit is not,

---

13 Ep. Firmiliani 75, cap. 18, p. 822. Part l, p. 384. Ep. ad Pompejum cap. 5 pp. 802-803, Article 1, p. 353.

no baptism can be recognized either, for there can be no baptism without the Holy Spirit.[14] St. Cyprian and those of the same mind decisively express the proposition that outside the Church there can be no baptism and no grace-giving acts of the Holy Spirit at all. "If heretics have come over to the Church and are found within the Church, then, of course, they may make use of her baptism and other saving blessings. If, however, they are not within the Church and even act against the Church, then how can they be baptized with the baptism of the Church?"[15]

As it can be seen, in the arguments of St. Cyprian, the train of thought is the opposite of that which is sometimes proposed in our time. The first problem which St. Cyprian solves is the question of whether heretics and schismatics belong to the Church and are in communion with her. If not, then they have fallen away from the body of the one Church and have been deprived of the Holy Spirit. But especially one should note that even Bishop Stephen is not very far from the thoughts of Cyprian. Observe that he, the same as St. Cyprian, acknowledged that heretics and schismatics have fallen away from the Church, that they are outside her, that outside the Church they cannot have the Holy Spirit. Upon the practice of the Roman Church, Stephen laid an unfortunate foundation, which met with just criticism on the part of Cyprian and Firmilian. Not without reason do Latin scholars, wishing to justify the Roman bishop, make the rather strange and completely groundless proposition that Stephen supposedly did not express a thought about the absence of the Holy Spirit among heretics and schismatics, but that St. Cyprian only ascribed it to him, so to speak, in the heat of polemics.

But still more does this fact call attention to itself, that St. Cyprian and all those who took sides with his views, despite the exact certainty of their opinion about the complete lack of grace of all communities outside the Church, considered it possible to allow a varying practice in the different churches, if only the union of peace

---

14 Ep. 74-61 ad Pompejum cap. 5.

15 Ep. 73-60 ad Jubajanum, cap. 11 p. 786. pp. 338-339.

and concord among the bishops was preserved. Every president is free to govern his church according to his will, of which matter he will give an account before the Lord. St. Cyprian repeats this thought many times in his letters (to Stephen, to Magnus, to Jubainan, to Cornelius et al.) St. Dionysius of Alexandria, a contemporary of St. Cyprian, also reasons in complete agreement, recalling the words of the Deuteronomy: "Move not the boundaries of your neighbour, which your fathers established."[16] "In judgments and affairs concerning separate persons," writes St. Dionysius, "how must we act towards those who are outside the Church and how must one treat those who belong to her? In our opinion, one must subordinate oneself to the presidents of the separate churches, who, in the power of Divine consecration stand at the head of the service. And the judgment about these matters we will present to our Lord."[17]

From Stephen's point of view, one must not allow a varying practice; this would mean to deny one baptism in spite of the Symbol of Faith. This is why Stephen demanded uniform practice without fail. But here we see that the opponents of Stephen allow diversity of practice in principle. What does this mean? You know that they looked upon heretics and schismatics as upon unbaptized persons, and of course, for all the churches schismatics were unbaptized persons. I think that the views of Stephen's opponents on the permissibility of diverse practices in relation to the reception of heretics and schismatics can be explained only by the assumption that, for the sake of the peace and the good of the Church, they considered it possible sometimes not to demand a second performance of the correct rite of baptism, believing in the mystical-charismatic significance of union with the Church itself. Before, the rite performed outside the Church was only an external form, which in the Church is filled with grace-giving content. You see, the same St. Cyprian says quite a lot about the "baptism of blood," which is accomplished, of course, without any sort of rite or form.

---

16 Deut. XIX, 14. Euseb. H. E. VII, 7, 5.

17 Pitra. *Analecta Sacra*, t. 4. Parisiis 1883, pp. 171, 414. Works in Russian translation, Kazan 1900, p. 60.

This proposition which I have assented to has grounds in the arguments of the writers of the Church. St. Cyprian was asked the question: "What will happen to those who before this time, having turned from heresy to the Church were received into the Church without baptism?" St. Cyprian answers, "The Lord in His mercy is able to grant them forgiveness, and those who have been received into the Church and have fallen asleep in the Church, He does not deprive of the gifts of His Church."[18] Saint Firmilian is inclined to require baptism of such persons if they are alive; if they have reposed, then he admits that they will receive the fruit of truth and' faith such as they have deserved.[19] It is beyond all doubt that even in the age of Cyprian the question of the good of the Church arose. Cyprian finds that requiring baptism is even useful for a more successful conversion of schismatics to the Church.[20] [...]

Of the two points of view — Cyprian's and Stephen's — I dare say that one can be fully satisfied only with the viewpoint of St. Cyprian. Here the unity of the Church is preserved and a possible condescension and independence of words and formulae is given. Stephen preserves the unity of the Church only in the thought that heretics and schismatics do not have the Holy Spirit and therefore, upon their reception into the Church, it is indispensible to perform the laying-on of hands for the transmission of the gifts of the Holy Spirit. But this thought, which is expressed still more decisively in the *Liber de rebaptismate*, belittles and even makes poorly understood the meaning of baptism. In the *Liber de rebaptismate,* the grace-filled gifts of the Holy Spirit are considered the exclusive property of the Church, but baptism performed in the name of Jesus is common to the Church and to others. Such a baptism washed only the body and, outside the Church, remains without benefit on the Day of Judgment. (Sarr. 7. 12. 18) But what sort of mystery is this? How can a mystery be performed without the grace of the Holy Spirit? If the grace-giving baptism of the Holy Spirit is permitted outside the Church, then it is completely impossible to preserve the unity of the Church.

---

18 Ep. 73-60 ad Jubajanurn. cap. 23, p. 796, p. 347.

19 Ep. 75, cap. 21.

20 Ep. 73-60 ad Jubajanum. cap. 23.

UNCUT MOUNTAIN PRESS TITLES

Books by Archpriest Peter Heers

Fr. Peter Heers, *The Ecclesiological Renovation of Vatican II: An Orthodox Examination of Rome's Ecumenical Theology Regarding Baptism and the Church*, 2015

Fr. Peter Heers, *The Missionary Origins of Modern Ecumenism: Milestones Leading up to 1920*, 2007

The Works of our Father Among the Saints, Nikodemos the Hagiorite

Vol. 1: *Exomologetarion: A Manual of Confession*

Vol. 2: *Concerning Frequent Communion of the Immaculate Mysteries of Christ*

Vol. 3: *Confession of Faith*

Other Available Titles

Elder Cleopa of Romania, *The Truth of our Faith, Vol. I: Discourses from Holy Scripture on the Tenants of Christian Orthodoxy*

Elder Cleopa of Romania, *The Truth of our Faith, Vol. II: Discourses from Holy Scripture on the Holy Mysteries*

Fr. John Romanides, *Patristic Theology: The University Lectures of Fr. John Romanides*

Demetrios Aslanidis and Monk Damascene Grigoriatis, *Apostle to Zaire: The Life and Legacy of Blessed Father Cosmas of Grigoriou*

Protopresbyter Anastasios Gotsopoulos, *On Common Prayer with the Heterodox According to the Canons of the Church*

Robert Spencer, *The Church and the Pope*

G. M. Davis, *Antichrist: The Fulfillment of Globalization*

Athonite Fathers of the 20th Century, Vol. I

St. Gregory Palamas, *Apodictic Treatises on the Procession of the Holy Spirit*

Fr. Alexander Webster and Fr. Peter Heers, Editors, *Let No One Fear Death*

Subdeacon Nektarios Harrison, *Metropolitan Philaret of New York: Zealous Confessor for the Faith*

Elder George of Grigoriou, *Catholicism in the Light of Orthodoxy*

Archimandrite Ephraim Triandaphillopoulos, *Noetic Prayer as the Basis of Mission and the Struggle Against Heresy*

Select Forthcoming Titles

Nicholas Baldimtsis, *Life and Witness of St. Iakovos of Evia*

Georgio, *Errors of the Latins*

Fr. Peter Heers, *Going Deeper in the Spiritual Life*

Abbe Guette, *The Papacy*

Athonite Fathers of the 20th Century, Vol. II

This 1st Edition of

On the Dogma of the Church

AN HISTORICAL OVERVIEW OF THE
SOURCES OF ECCLESIOLOGY

written by St. Hilarion (Troitsky) the Hieromartyr,
translated by Fr. Nathan Williams, with cover design
by George Weis, typeset in Baskerville, printed in this
two thousand and twenty second year of our Lord's
Holy Incarnation is one of the many fine titles available from Uncut Mountain Press, translators and
publishers of Orthodox Christian theological and
spiritual literature. Find the book you are looking for at

uncutmountainpress.com

**GLORY BE TO GOD
FOR ALL THINGS**

AMEN.

Printed in the USA
CPSIA information can be obtained
at www.ICGtesting.com
LVHW050026260823
756256LV00014B/328/J